Studies in Computational Intelligence

Volume 1253

The series "Studies in Computational Intelligence" (SCI) publishes new developments and advances in the various areas of computational intelligence—quickly and with a high quality. The intent is to cover the theory, applications, and design methods of computational intelligence, as embedded in the fields of engineering, computer science, physics and life sciences, as well as the methodologies behind them. The series contains monographs, lecture notes and edited volumes in computational intelligence spanning the areas of neural networks, connectionist systems, genetic algorithms, evolutionary computation, artificial intelligence, cellular automata, self-organizing systems, soft computing, fuzzy systems, and hybrid intelligent systems. Of particular value to both the contributors and the readership are the short publication timeframe and the world-wide distribution, which enable both wide and rapid dissemination of research output.

Indexed by SCOPUS, DBLP, WTI AG (Switzerland), zbMATH, SCImago.

All books published in the series are submitted for consideration in Web of Science.

Fadele Ayotunde Alaba · Ilésanmí Gabriel Ajibola ·
Alvaro Rocha

Learning Beyond the Classroom

Software in Humanities Education

Springer

Fadele Ayotunde Alaba
Federal University of Education
Zaria, Nigeria

Ilésanmí Gabriel Ajibola
Federal University of Education
Zaria, Nigeria

Alvaro Rocha
University of Lisbon
Lisbon, Portugal

ISSN 1860-949X ISSN 1860-9503 (electronic)
Studies in Computational Intelligence
ISBN 978-3-032-14432-4 ISBN 978-3-032-14433-1 (eBook)
https://doi.org/10.1007/978-3-032-14433-1

This Springer imprint is published by the registered company Springer Nature Switzerland AG
The registered company address is: Gewerbestrasse 11, 6330 Cham, Switzerland

Introduction

The integration of software into humanities education is transforming how students engage with knowledge beyond traditional classroom boundaries. As the digital age reshapes learning, there is a growing need to explore how technological tools, platforms, and pedagogical innovations are redefining the landscape of humanities instruction. This book, *Learning Beyond the Classroom*, provides a comprehensive guide to the purposeful use of software in enriching, expanding, and supporting learning across various disciplines in the humanities.

Purpose and Scope of the Book

The primary purpose of this book is to investigate the role and impact of software tools in humanities education. It aims to equip educators, scholars, and institutional leaders with theoretical insights, practical strategies, and evidence-based analysis of digital integration. The book explores how digital tools extend learning beyond the classroom, foster critical thinking, enhance collaboration, and promote autonomous learning among students.

The scope includes:

- Pedagogical theories supporting digital integration
- Practical examples and case studies of software usage
- Examination of digital literacy, ethics, and access
- Frameworks for curriculum design and assessment in technology-enhanced environments

By focusing on the unique needs and contexts of humanities education, the book provides targeted insights that bridge the gap between traditional scholarship and digital innovation.

Structure of the Book

The book is organized into eight comprehensive chapters:

1. **Introduction**—Establishes the rationale, significance, and objectives of software integration in humanities.
2. **Literature Review**—Reviews theoretical, conceptual, and empirical studies on educational software and digital pedagogy.
3. **Theoretical Framework**—Discusses the educational theories (e.g., constructivism, connectivism, TPACK) that underpin this research.
4. **Methodology**—Outlines the research design, tools, sampling techniques, and analytical approaches.
5. **Software Tools and Digital Resources in Humanities**—Profiles specific tools and evaluates their applications in learning environments.
6. **Results and Analysis**—Presents empirical findings from the study, using both qualitative and quantitative methods.
7. **Discussion and Interpretation of Findings**—Connects findings to theoretical perspectives and educational implications.
8. **Conclusion and Recommendations**—Summarizes key insights and offers recommendations for policy, practice, and further research.

Significance of Quantitative Research

Quantitative research plays a crucial role in this study, allowing for objective analysis of the impact of software on student learning outcomes. Through surveys, assessments, and statistical modeling, this method provides measurable evidence on factors such as student engagement, critical thinking development, and academic performance. In a field often dominated by qualitative inquiry, quantitative analysis lends credibility and generalizability to the findings, supporting data-driven decision-making in curriculum design and policy formulation.

The Researcher's Role

The researcher in this study assumes a multifaceted role—as a designer of inquiry, facilitator of learning, and interpreter of educational trends. Guided by a commitment to advancing humanities education through innovation, the researcher bridges theory and practice, engages with both digital tools and human values, and maintains reflexivity throughout the research process. The researcher also plays a critical role in ensuring ethical standards, inclusivity, and academic rigor in the application of software in education.

Conclusion

This introductory chapter has laid the foundation for exploring how software can extend learning beyond traditional classroom settings. By framing the study's purpose, structure, and significance within a strong theoretical and methodological context, the book invites educators, researchers, and policymakers to reimagine the future of humanities education in a digitally connected world.

Contents

Chapter 1
Introduction

1.1 Background to the Study

The educational system is only one area that has been profoundly affected by the technological revolution of the twenty-first century. The use of digital tools and platforms has been on the rise in many academic fields, but it is most noticeable in the humanities, which have long placed an emphasis on human culture, ideas, and expression. Aiming to make learning more interactive, accessible, and data-driven, the incorporation of software into humanities education reflects wider trends in pedagogy and academic practice. This background information lays the groundwork for a thorough examination of the ways and reasons digital tools have become prevalent in an area that was previously dominated by traditional, in-person methods of education centred on text [1].

Interpretative and qualitative approaches have long been the backbone of the humanities. Courses in literature, philosophy, history, and languages often emphasised reading texts critically and developing one's theoretical frameworks. Assessments for students usually took the form of written essays and exams, and most classrooms relied on lecture formats. Although these methods are still necessary, they aren't cutting it in today's information economy or with today's technologically savvy youth. Many people now refer to today's students as "digital natives" because of their comfort level with using various forms of online collaboration, multimedia, and hyperlinked information. Teachers in the arts and social sciences have started to use interactive software that encourages students to think critically and creatively. The rise of Digital Humanities (DH) as a legitimate field of study is indicative of the integration of computer methods with more conventional forms of humanistic inquiry. Innovative content engagement is made possible via the use of software such as text analysis tools, digital archives, mapping and GIS systems, interactive platforms, and research databases. For instance, text mining technologies such as AntConc and Voyant have made it possible for literary researchers to analyse trends, patterns, and word frequencies in massive corpora. By plotting the

F. A. Alaba et al., *Learning Beyond the Classroom*, Studies in Computational Intelligence 1253, https://doi.org/10.1007/978-3-032-14433-1_1

movement of people and ideas throughout time, historians may use mapping tools to bring historical tales to life using geographical data. Apps that recognise spoken language, interactive grammar checkers, and immersive language settings all help students learn a new language more effectively [2].

A further important contextual element is the increasing need for multidisciplinary methods in academic settings. The development of interdisciplinary curriculum is a growing trend in humanities departments, with many partnering with data analytics, media studies, and computer science departments. Students benefit in both their academic and professional careers from a hybrid skill set that includes both technical literacy and critical thinking, which they are able to cultivate via this integration. Graduates with strong analytical, problem-solving, writing, reasoning, and computer literacy skills are in high demand by employers today. Teachers are responding to changing demands in the job market by incorporating software into humanities curricula, which is a pedagogical innovation in and of itself. The use of digital tools is being supported by educational policies and financing mechanisms across the world. Programs to digitise textbooks, provide access to online education, and modernise classroom technology have been initiated by both governments and educational institutions. Blended learning modules, online archives, and digital humanities laboratories have been created by several institutions as a result. Communities of open-source software developers and nonprofits that make educational resources freely available bolster these initiatives. So, changes in legislation and infrastructure, in addition to scholarly tendencies, are bolstering the digital revolution in the humanities [3].

Bringing software into humanities education has both positive and negative aspects in the Nigerian setting, as well as in Sub-Saharan Africa generally. One positive aspect is that technology may help update the curriculum, provide access to resources, and close achievement disparities. However, there are substantial obstacles due to a lack of infrastructure, gaps in digital literacy, and insufficient financing. The National Open University of Nigeria (NOUN) and a number of federal universities have begun to use technological solutions for education, paving the way for other schools to do the same. All things considered, the study's setting is the local and worldwide confluence of education and technology. A number of factors, including changes in pedagogy, innovations in technology, efforts by institutions, and socioeconomic realities, have contributed to software's increased use in humanities education. We want to learn more about these dynamics in our project, which will concentrate on how digital tools might change humanities education outside of the classroom [4].

1.2 Statement of the Problem

1.2.1 Introduction to the Problem

The rapid technological progress in the twenty-first century has greatly altered educational approaches and material distribution across disciplines. While science, technology, engineering, and mathematics (STEM) professions have readily embraced software programs and computational tools, the humanities have generally lagged in technology integration. This gap creates a multidimensional dilemma that weakens the effectiveness and current relevance of humanities education.

1.2.2 Technological Divide in the Humanities

There is still a significant technical gap between the humanities and other fields of study, despite the fact that digital tools and platforms are becoming more widespread. The lack of exposure to and utilisation of instructional software in humanities classes results in an imbalance that is detrimental to both students and teachers. This imbalance impedes the development of digital literacy and technological fluency in subjects that are not related to STEM [5] (Fig. 1.1).

1.2.3 Pedagogical Limitations

Pedagogical approaches that are traditionally used in the humanities, which are mostly centred on lectures, essays, and textual analysis, may not be compatible with the learning styles of students who were born and raised in the digital age. When there are no software-based and interactive learning tools available, students often get disengaged and less motivated, which has a negative impact on their academic achievement as well as their ability to think critically [7].

1.2.4 Accessibility and Inclusivity Concerns

Developing nations with less developed infrastructure and underfunded institutions face the double whammy of unequal access to digital resources. Computers, reliable internet connections, and digital libraries are cornerstones of contemporary learning, yet many teachers and students do not have access to these resources. As a result of this inequality, students from less wealthy backgrounds are forced to rely on antiquated or conventional teaching techniques, whereas students from more affluent backgrounds have access to innovative, technology-driven learning

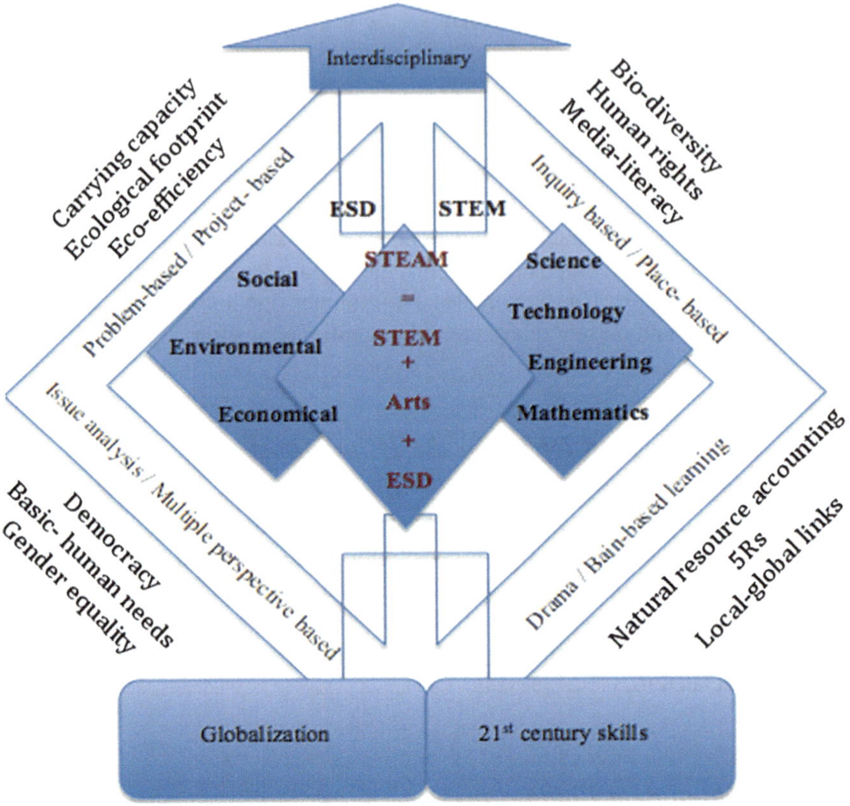

Fig. 1.1 The STEMarts model [6]

experiences. By reducing chances for research, cooperation, and exposure to varied viewpoints that internet platforms may provide, the chasm undermines the general quality of education as well as specific pupils. Beyond being an annoyance, the effects of this digital gap determine how future humanities education will be structured by perpetuating existing disparities. Students in impacted areas miss out on the wider intellectual environment that technology allows since they cannot access online courses, academic conversations, and digital archives. Because of this marginalisation, they are less likely to be able to take part in scholarly discussions on a global scale, to innovate within their own professions, or to get jobs that need technical proficiency. To tackle this issue, we need to make sure that socioeconomic barriers do not limit access to humanities education. This includes investing in digital infrastructure, reforming policies to distribute resources fairly, and working together as educational institutions, governments, and technology providers [8].

Table 1.1 Interdisciplinary cooperation

Institution	Discipline	Software use (%)	Observation
University A	Humanities	15	Minimal integration
University A	STEM	80	Extensive usage
University B	Humanities	22	Occasional use
University B	STEM	75	High integration

1.2.5 Empirical Evidence of Software Underuse

The humanities remain behind the scientific and technological communities when it comes to the use of software, even though technology is becoming more integrated into all areas of education. Despite the obvious benefits of digital tools and software for research, analysis, and collaboration, studies reveal that humanities departments seldom use them. One possible explanation for this discrepancy is the persistence of older approaches that did not necessarily need for specialised software, including discussion-driven learning and text-based analysis. There is a delay in the use of technology resources within these departments due to a lack of institutional support for digital humanities projects and inadequate financing.

Table 1.1 shows how often software is used in humanities departments compared to science and technology departments. The data comes from different universities. There is a clear divide in the use of software among academic fields. Science and technology departments often use tools for data analysis, programming, and simulation, whereas humanities departments depend on word processors and basic research databases. This disparity highlights the need to raise awareness, provide education, and fund digital technologies that might improve humanities research. A more equitable use of software across all fields of study might result from initiatives to promote interdisciplinary cooperation and increase technical proficiency among humanities researchers.

1.2.6 Skill Gap in Graduates

Students majoring in the arts and social sciences often struggle to find work after graduation because they lack the technical skills employers need. Employers are looking for employees with strong digital skills, data literacy, and knowledge of software tools, yet these areas are underrepresented in conventional humanities degree programs.

1.2.7 Institutional Barriers

The matter is made even more complicated by the fact that educational institutions and teachers are reluctant to accept new technology. Software integration in humanities education is hampered by institutional inertia, a lack of expertise, and inadequate financing for digital infrastructure. This perpetuates educational approaches that are no longer relevant (Fig. 1.2).

1.3 Summary of the Problem

The inability to adequately incorporate software into humanities education is a systemic problem that has extensive ramifications for teaching, learning, and the preparation of students for the workforce. In order to effectively address this issue, it is necessary to have a complete knowledge of the factors that brought about the situation, as well as a strategic strategy to bringing about change at both the policy and institutional levels.

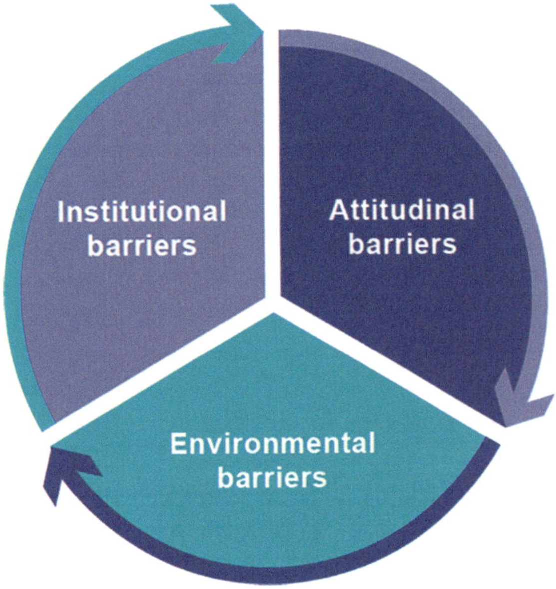

Fig. 1.2 Institutional barriers [9]

1.4 Objectives of the Study

1.4.1 Introduction to Study Objectives

The research study's goals are the bedrock upon which the whole investigation rests. They play a crucial role in deciding the methodology, data gathering, and analytic procedures, and in outlining the research's scope, emphasis, and intended results. Goals must be defined in a way that is both thorough and practical if this research on software integration in humanities education is to be successful. These goals not only guide the study's trajectory but also guarantee that its results will have a significant impact on scholarly discussions and the creation of educational policies.

1.4.2 General Objective

The overarching goal of this research is to look at how software tools are being used in humanities classes, and how they are improving learning outcomes, getting students more involved, and overcoming the limits of conventional teaching methods. This research seeks to provide practical answers for software implementation in the humanities classroom by exploring the connection between digital technology and humanistic inquiry. It intends to identify best practices, expose current gaps, and provide practical solutions.

1.4.3 Specific Objectives

The project aims to investigate many aspects of software usage in humanities education via a number of particular goals. Some of these tasks include finding out how integrated software is now, what the biggest obstacles are to adoption, and how digital tools affect students' involvement and performance. In addition, the research aims to investigate how institutional rules promote or impede the use of technology, as well as teachers' attitudes and readiness to use such tools.

1.4.4 Objective 1: Assessing Current Use of Software in Humanities

To achieve this objective, we will analyse the software tools used by humanities departments at different universities. The goal is to create a map of the most popular software kinds, how often they are used, and where they are most useful. Multimedia educational apps, collaborative platforms, textual analysis tools, and digital archiving systems are all part of this category.

1.4.5 Objective 2: Identifying Challenges in Software Integration

Integration of software into humanities education is riddled with difficulties, despite the fact that it may have some potential advantages. Problems ranging from educational considerations, such as opposition to change among faculty members, to technical restrictions, such as insufficient infrastructure, are included in this category. The purpose of this objective is to methodically identify these obstacles and assess the degree to which they are inhibiting progress, with the end goal of recommending specific tactics for overcoming them.

1.4.6 Objective 3: Measuring Impact on Student Learning Outcomes

A key objective of the study is to assess whether and how the use of software tools contributes to improved student learning outcomes. This includes evaluating comprehension, analytical thinking, digital literacy, and engagement levels. By collecting both qualitative and quantitative data, the study aims to present a nuanced view of the academic and cognitive benefits of digital integration.

1.4.7 Objective 4: Understanding Educator Preparedness and Attitudes

One of the most important factors in the implementation and effectiveness of educational technology is the role that teachers and lecturers play. The purpose of this aim is to have a better understanding of their willingness to utilise software in the classroom, their need for training and assistance, and their perspectives on the evolution of electronic technology. Following the completion of surveys and interviews, the data collected will be analysed in order to construct educator profiles and establish relationships between readiness and successful implementation.

1.4.8 Objective 5: Analysing Institutional and Policy Frameworks

In the field of education, the rate of software integration and the degree to which it occurs are both highly impacted by institutional policies and national education plans. The purpose of this goal is to investigate the ways in which policies either encourage or discourage the use of digital technology in the humanities, as well as to investigate the availability of money, administrative assistance, and possibilities for professional development. Case studies of various institutions will be used in order to highlight the many techniques and results that are available.

1.4.9 Objective 6: Developing a Model for Effective Software Integration

An all-encompassing and malleable framework for incorporating software into humanities education is the goal of this project, which builds upon the data that was obtained. The model that is being presented will define strategic suggestions for the development of the curriculum. These recommendations will ensure that digital tools complement conventional pedagogical techniques while simultaneously supporting interdisciplinary learning. This is in recognition of the increasing role that technology plays in academic fields. Furthermore, it will discuss the significance of specialised teacher training programs that make it possible for educators to acquire the skills required to successfully integrate software into their educational strategies. The framework strives to bridge the gap between traditional humanities education and the growing need for digital literacy by placing equal emphasis on theoretical frameworks as well as practical implementations. Furthermore, the research emphasises the many institutional landscapes in which humanities education is carried out. These landscapes range from universities that are well-funded to schools that have minimal resources. As a result, the model will recommend investments in infrastructure that are scalable, which will make the incorporation of technology practicable across a range of resource availability levels. In addition to this, it will offer evaluation procedures that are meant to measure the level of engagement that students have with digital tools. This will ensure that the integration of software improves students' ability to think critically, do research, and express themselves creatively. This framework seeks to develop an inclusive strategy that enables all institutions, regardless of their budgetary limits, to benefit from the improvements in educational technology. This is accomplished by taking into consideration the discrepancies that exist between their respective institutions.

1.5 Summary of Objectives

In summary, this study's aims are broad in scope and grounded in both empirical research and theoretical analysis. They highlight the need for a comprehensive grasp of how to successfully incorporate software into the humanities in order to improve educational results. The effective completion of these goals will not only add to academic knowledge, but will also influence policy, curriculum design, and teaching methods at all levels of education.

1.6 Research Questions

1.6.1 Introduction to Research Questions

Any academic investigation is built around research questions, which guide the direction and scope of the study. In the context of incorporating software into humanities education, the formulation of clear, precise, and researchable questions is critical for defining the study's parameters and goals. These questions provide a structured framework for systematic inquiry, allowing researchers to investigate the effectiveness, challenges, and impact of technological integration in humanities curricula. By defining significant areas of inquiry, such as educational approaches, institutional preparation, and student participation, research questions influence the study's analytical approach and help to narrow the emphasis on relevant issues. Furthermore, well-crafted research questions enable meaningful data collection, ensuring that qualitative and quantitative insights are consistent with the study's objectives. They guide methodological decisions such as choosing appropriate tools for measuring software adoption and evaluating its impact on critical thinking, creativity, and interdisciplinary learning. The clarity and specificity of research questions also contribute to the study's credibility, making it easier to develop evidence-based recommendations for curriculum design, teacher training, and policy formulation. Finally, these questions serve as a link between theoretical research and practical application, assisting institutions in navigating the ever-changing intersection of technology and humanities education.

1.6.2 Primary Research Question

"How does the integration of software influence the teaching and learning of humanities in higher education institutions?" is the major or main research topic that will be investigated in this study. As the basis upon which all of the other subsidiary questions are constructed, this overarching question helps to embody the primary objective of the research.

1.6.3 Secondary Research Questions

The study presents secondary research questions that dive into particular aspects of the subject matter in order to provide a comprehensive analysis of the issue of software integration in humanities education. The purpose of these investigations is to investigate the efficacy of digital tools in improving learning outcomes by evaluating the influence that these technologies have on the retention of information, critical thinking, and cooperation across professional disciplines. Additionally, they investigate usability, with a particular emphasis on the degree to which different software programs are accessible and adaptive for both students and teachers, as well as the technological problems that may be encountered. In addition to the capabilities of the software, educator preparedness is an essential component. This is because teachers absolutely need to be provided with the appropriate training and assistance in order to incorporate technology into their instructional strategies in a smooth manner. The degree to which digital technologies can be effectively adopted is influenced by a number of factors, including finance, infrastructure, and administrative regulations. Institutional support plays a crucial part in this process.

1.6.4 Questioning the Extent of Software Integration

The utilisation of software in humanities departments within tertiary institutions varies greatly depending on the resources available to the school, the experience of the staff, and the particular requirements of the many fields of study under consideration. There is a growing trend in the field of humanities education to include digital technologies, which may be used for a variety of purposes, ranging from providing aid with research to creating interactive learning environments. A number of educational establishments have used web-based and computer-based learning systems in order to improve student results and make academic engagement more effective. It is common practice for some educational institutions to implement integrated tertiary software systems in order to expedite administrative and academic procedures. This helps to ensure that student information and faculty resources are managed effectively. In addition, artificial intelligence is being investigated for its possible applications in educational management. This approach has the potential to provide solutions for the optimisation of data, the creation of research, and the execution of training programs. On the other hand, the amount to which software is used in humanities education is still influenced by obstacles such as accessibility, technical knowledge, and institutional support. Having a solid understanding of these aspects is very necessary in order to devise efficient tactics that will improve digital integration in the field.

1.6.5 Investigating Pedagogical Transformation

Pedagogical techniques have been drastically transformed as a result of the incorporation of software into humanities education, which has resulted in the creation of learning environments that are more dynamic and interactive. The restructuring of the curriculum is one of the most remarkable developments. With the help of digital technologies, educators are able to mix interdisciplinary methodology, data-driven analysis, and computational techniques into conventional topics that are related to the humanities. As a result of this transition, students are able to connect with historical documents, linguistic patterns, and cultural artefacts via the use of digital visualisation, which helps them improve their analytical abilities and widen their views on difficult subjects. As a result of the development of software that enables collaborative research, virtual simulations, and gamified educational experiences, interactive learning designs have also progressed. Students are given the opportunity to participate in hands-on projects via the use of digital platforms. These projects may include working with artificial intelligence to analyse literary themes or coding for applications related to digital humanities. Through the implementation of these advances, active engagement and critical thinking are encouraged, hence surpassing passive learning approaches.

Additionally, multimodal teaching strategies have become increasingly popular. These techniques include the incorporation of text, audio, video, and interactive media in order to provide educational experiences that are more immersive. Methodologies in the field of digital humanities, such as data visualisation and analysis powered by artificial intelligence, provide students the opportunity to investigate patterns within large datasets, therefore rendering abstract ideas more concrete and approachable. Not only does this technique improve students' understanding, but it also allows them to better prepare themselves for the rapidly changing technology environment in the academic world and beyond. In general, the incorporation of software has had a transformative effect on the field of humanities education. This is because it has broadened the scope of educational options, encouraged cooperation across disciplines, and provided students with the digital literacy skills absolutely necessary for modern study.

1.6.6 Evaluating Student Engagement and Performance

Students' involvement and academic performance in humanities education have been profoundly impacted by the incorporation of software, which has resulted in the transformation of conventional learning experiences via the use of digital resources. Through the provision of learning settings that are both interactive and immersive, research reveals that technology encourages greater cognitive participation inside individuals. Humanities disciplines are made more accessible and interesting via the use of digital platforms such as virtual classrooms, educational applications, and online discussion forums. These platforms promote active participation, collaboration, and personalised learning experiences. According to studies, the use of technology improves students' motivation and understanding by providing them with the opportunity to engage with the elements of the course in a dynamic manner. Students are able to improve their analytical abilities and critical thinking by using digital humanities tools, such as those that allow them to analyse historical texts, linguistic patterns, and cultural artefacts using visualisation approaches. In addition, the incorporation of software facilitates self-regulation and participation within the larger academic community, therefore assisting students in the development of digital literacy and research skills that are important for current scholarship.

The digital gap, diversions, and an over dependence on technology are some of the difficulties that need to be taken into consideration while evaluating the influence of technology. Despite the fact that software integration provides a multitude of advantages, its efficacy is contingent upon the support of the institution, the training of the faculty, and the provision of equal access to digital resources. It is possible for educators to maximise the role that technology plays in humanities education by addressing these elements. This will ensure that technology serves to improve student engagement and academic achievement.

1.6.7 Educator Readiness and Professional Development

Digital literacy, availability to training, and institutional support are some of the elements that determine the degree to which educators are prepared to include software into humanities teaching. This level of readiness varies greatly from institution to institution. The capacity of educators to successfully incorporate digital resources into their classrooms is dependent on their familiarity with software applications and the availability of professional development programs, according to studies. This is despite the fact that many educators acknowledge the usefulness of digital tools in enriching humanities education. When it comes to providing teachers with the knowledge and abilities they need to successfully integrate digital technologies into their instructional strategies, training opportunities are of immense importance. A number of educational institutions provide specialised seminars, online courses, and faculty development programs with the objective of enhancing digital literacy among education professionals working in the field of humanities. On the other hand, broad adoption may be hampered by obstacles such as opposition to change, a lack of finance, and restricted access to technology resources.

1.6.8 *Institutional Policies and Infrastructure*

In the realm of humanities education, the degree to which software is included into the curriculum is significantly influenced by the policies and resources of the institution. Policies that encourage faculty members to use technology into their teaching approaches are often implemented by universities that have well defined digital strategies. It is possible that these policies will include budget allocations for the acquisition of software, standards for the training of digital literacy, and incentives for instructors who use novel technology techniques. Additionally, universities that place a high priority on research efficiency and multidisciplinary cooperation are more likely to encourage software integration. This is accomplished by cultivating connections with technology suppliers and investing in digital humanities programs. On the other hand, the broad use of instructional software may be hampered by specific institutional hurdles. It is possible for technological developments in humanities departments to be slowed down by factors such as limited financial resources, bureaucratic restraints, and reluctance to change among faculty members respectively. There are certain institutions that suffer with having an outdated infrastructure, since they do not have the requisite hardware, software licenses, or technical assistance to permit digital integration that is complete and smooth. Furthermore, discrepancies in software accessibility may be caused by differences in institutional policies across various areas and educational systems. These inconsistencies can have a negative impact on students and teachers who are enrolled in institutions that fail to get enough funding.

Several recent conversations have brought to light the significance of policy management software in educational institutions. This software facilitates the streamlining of the process of creating and monitoring institutional policies that are associated with the deployment of technology. Furthermore, research on the influence of institutional policies on research productivity reveals that institutions that have robust administrative structures and support from leadership tend to cultivate an atmosphere that is more favourable to digital transformation. For the purpose of establishing methods that improve software integration while simultaneously addressing institutional obstacles, it is vital to have a solid understanding of these aspects.

1.6.9 *Comparative Effectiveness of Different Software Tools*

A number of programs have been developed with the express purpose of improving humanities education via facilitating research, teamwork, and active learning. Text analysis software, such as AntConc and TXM, gives students and academics the ability to investigate linguistic patterns, carry out corpus analysis, and investigate textual material in ways that are not possible with conventional methodologies. Literary studies, historical research, and language analysis are all areas that may benefit greatly from the use of these techniques, which allow for a more profound interaction with texts. Students have the opportunity to produce digital projects that integrate visual storytelling, documentary production, and interactive presentations via the use of multimedia editors, which include tools for editing both audio and video. These technologies encourage creative thinking and learning across disciplines, which in turn makes studies related to the humanities more interesting and approachable. Moodle and Blackboard are examples of learning management systems that ease the administration of courses, stimulate conversations, and give organised access to educational resources, all of which contribute to an improvement in student performance [10].

1.6.10 Emerging Challenges and Solutions

There are a number of obstacles that must be overcome to successfully include software into humanities education. These obstacles include institutional reluctance, budgetary limits, and training shortages. The unwillingness of educators and administrators to accept digital technologies is one of the key challenges. This hesitation is sometimes caused by worries about upsetting established educational approaches or scepticism over the efficiency of technology in humanities fields. It is necessary to implement focused professional development programs in order to overcome this challenge. These programs should highlight the advantages of software integration while also giving faculty members hands-on training to enhance their confidence and competence. The inability of many institutions to provide adequate finances for the purchase of software licenses, the updating of infrastructure, and the maintenance of technical assistance is another factor that creates barriers to wider adoption. In order to solve this issue, educational institutions have the ability to investigate cost-effective options such as open-source software, collaborative financing methods, and collaborations with technology companies in order to ensure that digital tools are accessible at an inexpensive price [11].

There is a shortage of formal training options for educators, which may lead to uneven implementation and underutilisation of existing technologies. This is another key difficulty that educators face. The incorporation of digital literacy into faculty development programs, the provision of workshops, and the formation of multidisciplinary alliances that stimulate knowledge-sharing among educators are all ways in which educational institutions may ameliorate this issue. Furthermore, the degree to which software may be included in humanities instruction is impacted by the inequities that exist in the resources that are available within institutions. It may be difficult for educational institutions that have a restricted technology infrastructure to offer students and teachers sufficient access to digital application tools. In order to address this issue, deliberate investments in infrastructure that can be scaled up are required. This will ensure that even institutions with limited resources are able to reap the benefits of technological breakthroughs. The findings of this research draw attention to the significance of multidisciplinary education and creative instructional

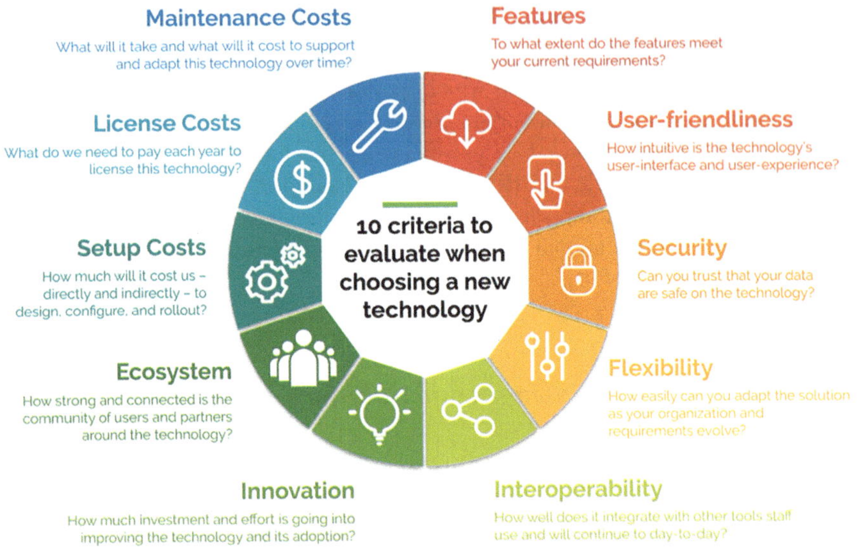

Fig. 1.3 Criteria to evaluate when choosing a new technology [12]

strategies in the process of overcoming these problems. The establishment of a framework for the incorporation of software in humanities education that is more inclusive and efficient may be accomplished by institutions via the promotion of a culture of adaptation, the provision of financial assistance, and the prioritisation of educator training [1] (Fig. 1.3).

1.6.11 Summary Table of Research Questions

Table 1.2 presents key research areas alongside their corresponding research questions, outlining the central themes explored in the study on software integration in humanities education. It first examines the extent of integration, seeking to understand how frequently and effectively software tools are used in humanities departments.

1.6.12 Conclusion on Research Questions

Pedagogical, technical, institutional, and cognitive aspects are all covered by the research topics that have been described above. These questions highlight the complex character of this study. From the beginning of the study process to the end, these questions will act as navigational guides, ensuring that all of the important topics concerning the incorporation of software in humanities education are

Table 1.2 Table of research questions

Research area	Corresponding research question
Extent of integration	What is the current extent of software usage in humanities departments within tertiary institutions?
Pedagogical transformation	In what ways has the use of software transformed pedagogical approaches in humanities education?
Student engagement	How does software integration impact student engagement and academic performance in the humanities?
Educator preparedness	What is the level of educator preparedness for integrating software in humanities education?
Institutional frameworks	What institutional policies and infrastructural resources support or hinder software integration?
Comparative software effectiveness	Which software tools are most effective in facilitating humanities education?
Implementation challenges	What are the major challenges and solutions in software integration for the humanities?

investigated. By addressing them, a rigorous analytical framework will be provided, which will allow for the formulation of relevant findings and the recommendation of methods that may be implemented.

1.7 Research Hypotheses (If Applicable)

1.7.1 Introduction to Research Hypotheses

In the field of research, hypotheses serve as structured predictions that frame investigations and guide data collection and analysis. This is especially true within the empirical and mixed-method domains. In the context of research, a hypobook is a provisional response to a question that may be evaluated by empirical evidence. Historically, research in the humanities has been more inclined towards qualitative analysis and interpretive methodologies. However, the present landscape of educational research is increasingly embracing transdisciplinary and evidence-based approaches. As a result of the incorporation of software into humanities education, which has traditionally been centred on speech, story, and interpretation, it is of the utmost importance to treat this innovation with both philosophical depth and scientific rigour. In light of this, the research involves the incorporation of testable hypotheses to investigate the consequences of software utilisation across pedagogical dimensions in the field of humanities education [13].

1.7.2 The Function of Hypotheses in This Study

In this particular investigation, hypotheses play a significant part in the process of transforming theoretical assumptions into quantifiable variables. This helps to guarantee that the research is founded on the principles of scientific rigour. Through the establishment of certain cause-and-effect links, hypotheses provide a systematic framework that may be used to investigate the influence that the incorporation of software has on the field of humanities education. It is possible to do a systematic analysis of variables such as the utilisation of software, the efficacy of teaching, the level of student involvement, the level of educator readiness, and the support provided by the institution in order to identify correlations and possible causative relationships. The use of this analytical technique makes it possible to conduct an objective evaluation, hence minimising the potential for biases to result from subjective interpretations and anecdotal observations. In order to ensure that the conclusions are backed by evidence rather than guesswork, the research builds a framework for empirical validation via the use of hypobook-driven inquiry [14].

1.7.3 Categories of Hypotheses

In order to conduct a thorough and well-balanced investigation on the incorporation of software in humanities education, this research takes into account both the null hypobook and the alternative hypobook. According to the null hypobook, software tools do not have a substantial influence on pedagogical practices, student engagement, or academic success. This hypobook suggests that conventional teaching techniques continue to be equally effective regardless of the presence of digital intervention. It is the purpose of this study to examine this assumption in order to ascertain if any impacts that have been seen as a result of the use of software in the teaching of humanities are just accidental or statistically inconsequential. On the other hand, the alternative hypobook contends that software tools do, in fact, improve instructional techniques, encourage more profound cognitive engagement, and make a beneficial contribution to academic achievements. The purpose of this study is to investigate whether or not digital technologies can increase accessibility, enable interactive learning, and foster multidisciplinary cooperation in the field of humanities sciences. The purpose of this research is to determine, via the analysis of empirical data, if the incorporation of educational technology results in demonstrable benefits, which would therefore provide support to the use of digital tools in higher education humanities programs. The use of this dual technique makes it possible to conduct an exhaustive evaluation, which guarantees that the results are founded on objective facts rather than on the subjective interpretation of the data. This research employs both null and alternative hypotheses:

1. **Null Hypobook (H_0)**: Proposes that there is no relationship or effect between the studied variables.

2. **Alternative Hypobook (H_1)**: Suggests the presence of a significant relationship or effect.

To validate or disprove presumptions and ascertain the relevance of observable patterns, the study tests these pairings of hypotheses.

1.7.4 Hypobook 1: Impact of Software on Teaching Effectiveness

In the first hypobook of this research project, the question of whether or not digital tools improve instructional practices in the field of humanities education is being investigated. Specifically, it investigates the degree to which digital resources contribute to enhanced teaching techniques, more flexibility in the curriculum, and increased student involvement. By analysing how technology influences the efficacy of teaching, the hypobook investigates if the incorporation of software makes it easier for students to engage in interactive learning, encourages cooperation across disciplines, and gives teachers the ability to communicate difficult topics in the humanities in a manner that is more approachable. Through the use of empirical analysis, the purpose of this research is to determine whether or not digital technologies provide a supplement to conventional instructional methods or if they present new issues that need to be addressed.

Furthermore, the hypobook takes into consideration the impact that educator preparedness and institutional support have in determining the efficacy of software-driven education. When it comes to assessing whether or not technology integration will be successful, factors such as faculty training, the availability of digital tools, and investments in infrastructure come into play as crucial factors. The project will give insights into whether software tools enhance humanities teaching in a quantifiable and sustainable way by evaluating this hypobook via qualitative and quantitative research methodologies. The ultimate goal of the study is to guide best practices for the implementation of digital technology in higher education [15].

- **H_{01}**: The use of software in humanities education does not significantly improve teaching effectiveness.
- **H_{11}**: The use of software in humanities education significantly improves teaching effectiveness.

This hypobook explores whether tools such as digital archives, learning management systems, and data visualization platforms enhance how educators deliver content and interact with students.

1.7.5 Hypobook 2: Influence on Student Engagement

In the second hypobook, the link between software integration and student involvement is investigated. Specifically, the test is designed to determine whether or not digital tools actively foster participation and intellectual curiosity in the field of humanities education. The purpose of this study is to investigate the ways in which interactive learning environments, such as digital platforms, multimedia resources, and collaboration tools, have an impact on the degree to which students are motivated to participate with the educational content. The purpose of this research is to assess whether or whether software encourages greater cognitive engagement, critical thinking, and creative inquiry within the realm of humanities disciplines. This will be accomplished by analysing the levels of participation in classes that have been upgraded with technology. Additionally, the hypobook investigates whether or whether the use of digital tools results in a more inclusive and individualised educational experience. This would enable students to investigate intricate humanities themes in a manner that is congruent with their own learning styles and areas of individual interest. The purpose of this evaluation is to determine whether or not software can promote debates, interactive assignments, and multidisciplinary methods that drive analytical thinking and inspire curiosity. By evaluating quantitative outcomes such as student engagement measures, knowledge retention, and academic achievement, the purpose of this research is to determine whether or not technology significantly improves student participation in humanities education, or whether or not conventional approaches continue to be equally successful. The second hypobook evaluates the extent to which software fosters active participation and intellectual curiosity among students [16].

1. $\mathbf{H_{02}}$: Software integration does not significantly influence student engagement in humanities education.
2. $\mathbf{H_{12}}$: Software integration significantly influences student engagement in humanities education.

Engagement includes dimensions such as frequency of participation, motivation, comprehension, and collaboration. Tools like discussion boards, annotation platforms, and gamified learning environments are critical to this inquiry.

1.7.6 Hypobook 3: Educator Preparedness

The purpose of this hypobook is to investigate the ways in which the accessibility of software in humanities education is influenced by the level of digital literacy and openness to technological change among educators. The purpose of this evaluation is to determine whether or not teachers have the technical expertise required to successfully integrate digital technologies into their instructional strategies, as well as to determine how their readiness to embrace innovation influences the level of engagement in the classroom. The purpose of this research is to evaluate whether or not a solid foundation in digital literacy leads to more successful deployment and utilisation of technology in humanities classroom. This will be accomplished by measuring the ability of faculty members with educational software.

In addition to this, the hypobook investigates the availability of professional development programs that are intended to improve instructors' digital abilities as well as the efficacy of these programs. Specifically, it investigates whether or if a culture of flexibility among faculty members is fostered by the availability of training opportunities, institutional support, and peer cooperation. Additionally, the research explores possible obstacles, such as reluctance to change, a lack of institutional resources, and questions about the value of technology in educational fields related to the humanities. The purpose of this study is to give insights into the link between educator readiness and effective software integration by analysing these characteristics. Additionally, the research intends to provide suggestions for strengthening digital literacy training and support systems in higher education. This hypobook investigates the role of educators' digital literacy and willingness to adapt to new tools.

1. $\mathbf{H_{03}}$: There is no significant relationship between educator preparedness and effective software integration.
2. $\mathbf{H_{13}}$: There is a significant relationship between educator preparedness and effective software integration.

The hypobook assumes that educators with higher technological proficiency and training are more likely to integrate software effectively and meaningfully into their teaching practices.

1.7.7 Hypobook 4: Role of Institutional Support

The purpose of this hypobook is to investigate the degree to which institutional architecture and regulatory frameworks have an impact on the effective incorporation of software into humanities education. In spite of the fact that individual educators play a significant part in the process of adopting and using digital technologies, the efforts of these educators are often influenced by the more comprehensive support systems that are offered by universities and colleges. There are a number of factors that contribute to the success of software adoption. These include budget allocations, access to technology resources, administrative rules, and the culture of the organisation. Institutions that have solid digital strategies and well-defined technology regulations have a tendency to support simpler transitions to software-enhanced pedagogy. On the other hand, institutions that have little infrastructure or unclear rules may encounter major challenges to implementation.

In addition, the hypobook investigates whether or whether educational institutions provide faculty members with organised training programs and technical help. This is done to ensure that educators are able to properly use digital technologies into their teaching approaches. Additionally, the adoption rate of digital tools in humanities disciplines is influenced by institutional regulations concerning software licensing, curriculum creation, and multidisciplinary cooperation. These policies also have an effect on the overall usefulness of digital tools. The purpose of this project is to evaluate if strong institutional support leads to more effective and sustainable software integration, which will eventually shape the future of humanities teaching in higher learning institutions. This will be accomplished by evaluating the role that infrastructure and policy play in the process. Software integration is not solely dependent on individuals but also on institutional infrastructure and policy. This hypobook examines the support systems provided by educational institutions.

1. $\mathbf{H_{04}}$: Institutional support does not significantly affect software adoption in humanities education.
2. $\mathbf{H_{14}}$: Institutional support significantly affects software adoption in humanities education.

Support mechanisms include funding, ICT infrastructure, training programs, and institutional policy on digital innovation.

1.7.8 Hypobook 5: Relationship with Academic Performance

The purpose of this hypobook is to investigate the degree to which software tools improve academic results in humanities education by analysing the influence that these tools have on student performance, the retention of information, and the development of different skills. Text analysis software, multimedia platforms, and interactive learning environments are examples of digital technologies that are rapidly being included in humanities programs. These tools provide students with new methods to engage with difficult subjects. It is possible that software tools might contribute to increased understanding and academic achievement by encouraging deeper analytical thinking, cooperation across disciplines, and personalised learning experiences. The purpose of this study is to establish whether the implementation of these technological interventions results in observable enhancements to the students' levels of proficiency in doing research, conducting critical analysis of texts, and successfully applying theoretical frameworks.

In addition, the hypobook investigates whether the incorporation of software contributes to the development of long-term academic progress by promoting digital literacy and research competences that are necessary for current scholarship. The purpose of this study is to determine whether students who use digital tools exhibit better levels of engagement, motivation, and intellectual curiosity in comparison to those who depend only on conventional means. It is also important to note that the success of software-driven learning is influenced by institutional variables such as the availability of technology, the training of professors, and the process of curriculum development. The purpose of this project is to give evidence-based insights into whether digital technologies serve as important assets in humanities education or whether their influence remains constrained by external restrictions. These insights

Table 1.3 Research hypotheses

Hypobook code	Null hypobook (H_0)	Alternative hypobook (H_1)
H_{01}/H_{11}	Software use does not significantly improve teaching effectiveness	Software use significantly improves teaching effectiveness
H_{02}/H_{12}	Software use does not significantly influence student engagement	Software use significantly influences student engagement
H_{03}/H_{13}	No relationship exists between educator preparedness and software integration	A significant relationship exists between educator preparedness and software integration
H_{04}/H_{14}	Institutional support does not affect software adoption	Institutional support significantly affects software adoption
H_{05}/H_{15}	Software use does not influence student academic performance	Software use influences student academic performance

will be provided by analysing the factors that are being studied. Another critical area of investigation is whether software tools contribute to improved academic outcomes.

1. $\mathbf{H_{05}}$: Software use does not significantly influence student academic performance in humanities subjects.
2. $\mathbf{H_{15}}$: Software use significantly influences student academic performance in humanities subjects.

This hypobook addresses whether software can contribute to better comprehension, analysis, and application of knowledge in assessments, projects, and exams.

1.7.9 Research Hypotheses

Table 1.3 summarises the five primary hypotheses guiding this research.

1.7.10 Analytical Methods for Hypobook Testing

In order to put these assumptions to the test, the research will make use of a variety of statistical methods, which will vary according to the kind of data that is gathered. The data will be summarised using descriptive statistics, while inferential statistics, which include t-tests, correlation analysis, and regression models, will assess the strength of the correlations between variables as well as the direction in which they are moving. For categorical data, chi-square tests might be utilised, and analysis of variance (ANOVA) could be used to examine differences between a number of different groups [17].

1.7.11 Justification for Including Hypotheses in Humanities Research

The use of hypotheses in educational research about the humanities is growing in significance, despite their prevalence in STEM domains. The use of hypotheses helps to bridge the gap in methodology that exists between qualitative investigation and quantitative accuracy. with addition to this, it addresses the increased desire for teaching techniques that are supported by evidence and accountability with respect to educational results. Furthermore, the adoption of software in educational settings carries with it a number of quantifiable factors, including the frequency of use, completion rates, assessment scores, and interaction counts. As a result, the incorporation of hypotheses into the research framework is both a logical and helpful component.

1.7.12 Limitations and Ethical Considerations

Although hypotheses are useful for organising research, it is crucial to recognise that they do not always include the whole complexity of human experience, especially in fields that value subjective analysis and critical thinking. As a result, the research will use qualitative methodologies (such as interviews and focus groups) to give a more comprehensive insight. The study will also be guided by ethical issues, particularly concerning the gathering of data, the protection of privacy, the acquisition of permission, and the prevention of digital marginalisation [18].

1.7.13 Conclusion

The hypotheses that were generated for this study provide a framework that is both explicit and testable, which makes it easier to conduct an impartial investigation of the ways in which software influences education in the humanities. These components serve as a foundation for the empirical aspects of the research and guarantee that the assertions made are backed up by facts. Through the combination of hypobook-driven inquiry and qualitative investigation, the study maintains a sensitivity to the interpretative traditions that are associated with the humanities. The findings of the hypobook testing will not only support or question the assumptions that are now in place, but they will also provide educators, institutions, and policymakers with insights that can be put into practice in order to modernise the education of humanities students via the incorporation of software [19].

1.8 Significance of the Study

1.8.1 The Integration of Software Tools

The integration of software tools in humanities education represents a critical evolution in pedagogical strategy and curriculum design. This study's significance lies in exploring how software applications enrich learning, improve accessibility, and align the humanities with the demands of a digital era.

1.8.2 Educational Innovation

The learning experience is transformed when instructional software is included into humanities subjects. This is accomplished by creating settings that are dynamic and interactive, which in turn fosters engagement. Students are able to actively engage in their own learning via the use of digital tools, which include immersive features such as visualisation, simulations, and collaborative platforms. Traditional teaching techniques often focus on text-based debates and lectures. Learners are able to get a deeper understanding of difficult humanities subjects via the use of software that incorporates elements like as real-time text analysis, multimedia presentations, and virtual excursions. In addition, these advances cater to a variety of learning styles, which makes courses such as literature, history, philosophy, and cultural studies more approachable and engaging [20].

Educational software not only helps students become more engaged, but it also helps them comprehend material better and remember it better. By enabling students to modify data, interact with digital archives, and investigate historical or literary settings in a more hands-on way, interactive technologies foster critical thinking and encourage students to use their critical thinking skills. In addition, students are able to improve their analytical abilities and strengthen their knowledge of the content covered in the course by participating in personalised learning experiences. These experiences include adaptive tutorials and feedback systems powered by artificial intelligence. As the field of humanities education continues to transform, the incorporation of digital technology guarantees that students not only take in information but also use it creatively and critically, therefore preparing them for a technologically advanced academic and professional environment [21].

1.8.3 Enhanced Accessibility and Inclusion

In order to help children from all backgrounds and locations succeed in school, software tools are especially important for those in rural areas or who have physical limitations. The use of assistive technology, such as screen readers and voice-to-text programs, enables educational institutions to guarantee that visually impaired students have equal access to the information included within the curriculum. It is possible for students who are deaf or hard of hearing to participate meaningfully in lectures and multimedia material thanks to captioning services, which further improve accessibility for these students. In addition, multilingual platforms eliminate language barriers, making it possible for students who come from a variety of linguistic backgrounds to take part in academic conversations and access learning materials in the language of their choice. In addition to facilitating accessibility for individuals, these digital technologies contribute to a more comprehensive vision of equitable education by assisting educational institutions in the development of learning environments that are more flexible and welcoming to everyone. By giving access to virtual classrooms, online libraries, and real-time collaboration tools, software-driven education helps students who live in distant places, therefore reducing the impact of geographical limits on their educational experiences. Students are able to advance at their speed thanks to features such as adaptive learning platforms, which cater to a wide range of learning demands while still preserving academic standards throughout the process. It is possible for educators and institutions to encourage a more inclusive approach to humanities education by using technology in this manner. This will ensure that all students, regardless of their location or physical ability, are able to fully interact with educational material [22].

1.8.4 Bridging Traditional and Modern Pedagogies

The incorporation of software into traditional teaching techniques in the humanities does not replace these approaches; rather, it complements them by providing additional dimensions of engagement and participation. The traditional method of teaching, which is based on reading, listening to lectures, and participating in group discussions, offers a solid basis for developing analytical and critical thinking abilities. However, the use of digital resources such as archives, annotation software, and virtual simulations enhances these learning experiences by rendering abstract ideas more physical and accessible to the learner. Students are provided with unparalleled access to historical manuscripts, rare literary works, and cultural artefacts via the use of digital archives. This presents an opportunity for students to do more in-depth study and comparative analysis across a variety of time periods and points of view. By enabling students to interact with texts in real time, share their thoughts, and construct personalised interpretations, annotation tools encourage collaborative engagement and develop a sense of community among students. Not only can these technologies enhance students' comprehension abilities, but they also motivate students to take an active role in the creation of their knowledge [23].

The use of virtual simulations in humanities education provides students with the opportunity to engage in experiential learning by immersing them in historical events, philosophical debates, or creative movements. The use of these tools enables students to visualise and contextualise complicated concepts that may be difficult to understand only via the use of text alone. These technologies simulate settings from various times. They foster interdisciplinary thinking by bridging the links between history, literature, philosophy, and cultural studies in a manner that is not possible with static resources. By using these tools, instructors are able to preserve the depth of traditional humanities teaching while simultaneously improving accessibility, engagement, and understanding. This ensures that students are able to benefit from both traditional and digital learning techniques.

1.8.5 Data-Driven Instruction

Software designed for education makes it easier to gather data and do analytics on student performance. This, in turn, helps teachers to modify their lessons in order to better suit the requirements of their students. This fosters a transition away from generic learning experiences and towards more personalised ones.

1.8.6 Encouraging Digital Literacy

Technology in humanities courses improves subject-specific learning and gives students digital literacy abilities for current academic and professional environments. With the advent of digital resources, students must learn to critically analyse online material, distinguishing reliable sources from falsehoods and comprehending digital publication ethics. By using digital archives, research databases, and analytical tools, students learn to ethically analyse and synbooke material, improving their intellectual rigour in academic conversations. Technology helps students analyse digital communication, recognise biases, and properly engage with online material in addition to research skills. In an age where digital discourse impacts public understanding, legislation, and cultural narratives, these skills are essential. Technological integration provides students with collaborative digital workspaces, improving their capacity to use citation management software, visualisation platforms, and automated transcribing services for transdisciplinary assignments. By incorporating digital literacy into humanities education, institutions equip students to understand their fields and adapt to changing technology in academia, media, and beyond [24].

1.8.7 Professional and Career Relevance

The abilities that are taught using software-supported humanities education, including as analytical thinking, digital communication, and critical investigation, are highly appreciated in today's labour market. These talents enable graduates to be flexible and adaptable in a profession that is continually developing. Students can develop their skills in analysing complicated material, effectively communicating ideas across digital platforms, and performing in-depth study that is supported by evidence when technology is integrated with traditional humanities subjects. In addition to being vital in disciplines such as education, publishing, and cultural heritage, these abilities are also essential in new professions such as data analysis, content production, and user experience design. A growing number of employers are looking for people who are able to combine humanistic understanding with technological expertise. This ensures that graduates of the humanities are well-prepared for a variety of positions. Students are prepared for a wide variety of professional routes, ranging from corporate settings to charitable organisations, as a consequence of this multidisciplinary study, which fosters both intellectual development and job preparedness in a global market that is highly competitive [25].

1.8.8 Contribution to Research and Policy Development

This study offers evidence-based views on how technology reshapes learning settings, contributing vital empirical data and theoretical understanding to the continuing debate on digital transformation in education. Specifically, this research offers insights into how technology creates new learning environments. This research presents actionable results that may drive institutional initiatives, so assisting educational institutions like universities and schools in optimising their technology integration. These findings are derived on an analysis of the usefulness of digital technologies in humanities education. A further contribution of this study is that it provides support for curricular revisions by highlighting essential characteristics that need to be emphasised in contemporary teaching. These qualities include critical thinking and digital literacy. These findings may also be used by policymakers in order to define activities pertaining to education technology, so guaranteeing that fair access and meaningful implementation are achieved. This research, in the end, helps to bridge the gap between theory and practice, so helping educators, administrators, and lawmakers to make choices that are informed and that improve both teaching and learning in the digital era [26] (Table 1.4).

Table 1.4 Summary of key significance areas in software integration for humanities

Significance area	Impact on humanities education	Societal value
Educational innovation	Transforms passive learning into active engagement	Supports lifelong learning
Accessibility and inclusion	Reduces learning barriers	Promotes educational equity
Traditional-modern bridge	Combines classical content with digital tools	Preserves cultural relevance
Data-driven instruction	Personalises learning pathways	Improves academic performance
Digital literacy	Teaches critical digital engagement	Prepares students for the digital world
Career relevance	Develops market-relevant skills	Enhances employability
Policy development	Provides data for informed decisions	Shape effective education policies

1.9 Scope and Delimitation

Scope and delimitation are essential elements that must be included in each academic research project. The scope of the research is what determines its bounds and breadth, while the delimitation is what specifies what is purposefully left out of the investigation. Taking them into consideration as a whole, they provide a practical structure within which the research is carried out. The limitations of the research on the integration of software in humanities education are discussed in this part. These limitations are categorised as thematic, geographical, and methodological.

1.9.1 Thematic Scope

This research investigates the relationship between humanities education and digital technology, specifically how software tools contribute to new teaching approaches and intellectual engagement. Digital platforms provide up new possibilities for interpretation, study, and academic cooperation in fields including literature, history, philosophy, and cultural studies. Educators may provide students with interactive and data-driven methods to explore complicated subjects by using resources such as digital archives, text analysis software, and virtual learning environments. These technologies improve accessibility by enabling students to interact with historical records, philosophical literature, and cultural artefacts in novel ways that go beyond typical classroom procedures.

Furthermore, the research looks at how software promotes critical thinking and analytical reasoning by allowing students to do computational text analysis, visualise historical patterns, and interact with multimedia resources. Digital technologies promote interdisciplinary learning, bridging the gap between humanities and technology and equipping students to do research in more digitised academic settings. The project intends to give insights into how technology might complement and improve humanities education by assessing the efficacy, obstacles, and institutional support associated with software integration, ensuring that digital developments fit with pedagogical best practices.

1.9.2 Geographical Scope

The research is able to investigate how local infrastructural, cultural, and academic variables influence the incorporation of software into humanities curriculum since it focusses on higher education institutions in Nigeria. Through the process of narrowing the geographical scope, the study offers a comprehensive analysis of the technology environment within Nigerian universities. It investigates the ways in which adoption rates are influenced by factors such as access to digital tools, teacher preparation, and institutional regulations. In addition, the efficiency of digital integration is significantly influenced by cultural attitudes towards the use of technology in education, the availability of money, and the differences in infrastructure that exist across regions. This technique, which is tailored to the specifics of Nigerian higher education, guarantees that the results are directly applicable to the issues and possibilities facing the country. Even though this study was conducted in a specific locale, the insights that were gathered from it contribute to larger worldwide conversations on the topic of technology-enhanced humanities education. A significant number of the issues that are encountered are shared by universities all across the globe. These challenges include instructor preparedness, digital literacy, institutional support, and the availability of resources. In order to highlight techniques and best practices that may be relevant in other places undergoing comparable pedagogical revolutions, the research may emphasise the Nigerian context, which allows for the examination of the Nigerian setting. The results provide a comparative viewpoint that contributes to the advancement of worldwide discussions on the role of software tools in enhancing humanities teaching. They also demonstrate how digital innovation may be used to solve educational difficulties that are shared by several countries.

1.9.3 Institutional Scope

This research looks at how the digital revolution affects both public and private institutions, with a particular emphasis on arts and humanities faculties. The study includes important players such as lecturers who incorporate digital tools into pedagogy, administrative personnel who maintain technology infrastructure, and students who use these resources as part of their academic progress. The study's focus on higher education institutions provides a specific investigation of how digitalisation affects teaching techniques, curriculum delivery, and institutional operations at the tertiary level. While elementary and secondary schools are also experiencing digital transformations, they are intentionally ignored to retain a clear focus on the particular difficulties and possibilities found in university settings. This technique provides greater insights into how humanities fields respond to technological changes in higher education.

1.9.4 Methodological Scope

Methods of qualitative research predominate throughout the work. To capture nuanced opinions on the use of software in humanities education, interviews, focus groups, and document analysis are utilised among other methods. In spite of the fact that some quantitative data is provided for triangulation, the primary focus is still on interpretative and descriptive insights that are in line with the epistemological position of the research.

1.9.5 Delimitation of Technology Types

This research focuses on specialised instructional and analytical software designed for humanities education, omitting larger digital tools that lie beyond its scope. The study looks specifically at platforms like Voyant for text analysis, AntConc for corpus linguistics, and Moodle for learning management tools that are deliberately developed or modified to improve humanities scholarship. General-purpose administrative systems, non-educational mobile applications, and proprietary software that were unavailable to the study's participants (including professors, students, and staff from arts and humanities faculties) were purposefully excluded. This selective approach guarantees that the results clearly address how discipline-specific digital tools impact teaching, research, and institutional practices in higher education, giving practical insights for stakeholders interested in the junction of technology and the humanities.

1.9.6 Time Frame of the Study

The research was conducted between twelve months. This period provided sufficient time to observe technological adaptation trends, evaluate pedagogical impacts, and analyse stakeholder feedback. Events outside this timeframe, such as post-pandemic digital shifts, are referenced but not comprehensively studied.

Table 1.5 Scope and delimitation

Category	Included	Excluded
Theme	Humanities software integration	STEM or general-purpose applications
Geography	Universities in Nigeria	International institutions
Institutions	Public and private universities	Primary and secondary schools
Methodology	Qualitative dominant	Experimental or purely quantitative approaches
Technology	Educational and analytical tools	Administrative and unrelated apps
Time Frame	Jan 2023–Mar 2024	Pre-2023 data or future projections

1.10 Summary of Scope and Delimitation

The following table presents a summary of the key areas included and excluded from the study to enhance clarity and transparency (Table 1.5).

1.11 Definitions of Key Terms

1. **Humanities**: One of the academic fields that focusses on the study of human culture, including but not limited to the fields of literature, philosophy, history, art, music, and languages. Specifically, it emphasizes analytical thinking, critical thinking, and the comprehension of human experience and expression.
2. **Educational Software**: Computer programs that have been developed with the express purpose of facilitating the teaching and learning processes. Assessment tools, classroom management tools, simulation tools, and content development tools are all included in this category.
3. **Digital Humanities**: In order to analyse, interpret, and convey human culture, this topic is an example of an interdisciplinary field that combines the conventional disciplines of the humanities with computer methodologies and digital technologies.
4. **E-Learning**: Learning that is carried out via the use of electronic media, most often on the Internet. It comprises a broad variety of modalities, such as online courses, video tutorials, virtual classrooms, and digital resources, among others.
5. **ICT**: An umbrella word that encompasses all technologies that are used for the modification and transfer of information. Computers, software, networks, and several other digital instruments are included in this category when discussing the educational setting.
6. **Blended Learning**: A form of education that blends the conventional techniques of teaching in a classroom setting with the digital material that is available online. Both the instructor and the student must be physically present as well as for the learner to have some degree of control over the time, location, route, or speed of the activity.

7. **Pedagogical Tools**: Educators make use of several resources in order to enhance education and the results for their students. Examples of these include learning management systems, interactive whiteboards, digital simulations, and software designed specifically for instructional purposes.
8. **Digital Literacy**: The capacity to efficiently and critically access, assess, and produce information utilising a variety of digital tools. It encompasses skills like media literacy, internet safety, and effective communication in digital settings [27].

1.12 Justification for Software Integration

In recent years, the incorporation of software into humanities education has become not only useful but crucial. This trend is driven by the rising significance of digital instruments in knowledge generation, distribution, and preservation. The disciplines of the humanities need to adapt to the advances in technology that are occurring in the world. They should make use of software in order to improve educational results and expand their relevance to society.

1. **Enhancing Student Engagement**: Student engagement may be increased via the use of software tools such as interactive learning platforms, simulations, and multimedia information. These technologies enable students to better understand abstract topics. Visualisation tools and annotation software are beneficial to students studying fields such as literature and philosophy because they assist students in better analysing texts and more accurately interpreting their contents.
2. **Improving Accessibility and Inclusivity**: The incorporation of software makes it possible to provide variable learning routes, which in turn make education more accessible. Text-to-speech, closed captioning, and customisable interfaces are some of the elements that guarantee that learning environments are accessible to students who have impairments. Additionally, software promotes distant learning, which enables students to obtain high-quality education even when they are located in somewhat remote regions.
3. **Supporting Collaborative Learning**: In order to facilitate collaborative work, platforms such as Google Workspace and Microsoft Teams, as well as project management tools such as Trello, are available. Students and instructors are able to collaborate in real time, exchange materials, offer feedback, and cultivate a sense of community via the use of these technologies, which is something that is sometimes difficult to do in conventional learning settings.
4. **Enabling Data-Driven Insights**: As a result of its ability to facilitate the collecting and analysis of data on student performance, software plays an essential role in contemporary education. The track of academic progress, the identification of learning gaps, and the establishment of feedback loops that improve student engagement are all achieved with the assistance of LMS. These data-driven insights provide educators the ability to adopt teaching practices that are supported by evidence, guaranteeing that they may better adjust their approaches

to match the specific learning requirements of each individual student. Teachers are able to create more personalised learning experiences for their students, improving student results, and cultivating an educational atmosphere that is more adaptable when they make use of technology. This seamless integration of software in education revolutionises conventional teaching methodologies, making instruction more effective and sensitive to the specific obstacles that students face based on their individual circumstances.

5. **Aligning with Global Educational Trends**: As a whole, educational systems throughout the world are shifting towards curriculums that are increasingly focused on technology. Incorporating software into the study of humanities is in line with this transition and helps students become ready for a job that is more digital. It is now widely acknowledged that digital literacy is a fundamental skill, and students of the humanities need to be educated with the skills necessary to properly engage in this environment.
6. **Empowering Educators**: The method in which educators organise, deliver, and evaluate education has been revolutionised by digital technologies, which enable both efficiency and flexibility in the classroom in terms of instruction. It is possible for professors to devote more of their attention to student participation when they use platforms such as Moodle, Blackboard, and Turnitin since these platforms simplify administrative chores like as grading and content administration. These technologies also improve the delivery of training by allowing interactive learning experiences, making communication easier, and providing support for a variety of instructional approaches. Furthermore, digital solutions encourage creative thinking in the process of course creation by providing educators with the ability to add gamification, adaptive learning strategies, and multimedia components. With the use of technology, educators are able to develop dynamic and personalised learning environments that are able to meet the diverse requirements of their students and enhance the overall educational results.
7. **Promoting Lifelong Learning**: Open-access courses, digital archives, and interactive learning environments are some of the ways that software may help promote learning that continues throughout one's life. Regardless of their age or experience, people have the opportunity to participate in continuous learning via the use of platforms such as Khan Academy, edX, and Coursera (Table 1.6).

Table 1.6 Examples of educational software used in the humanities

Software name	Functionality	Disciplinary application
Voyant tools	Text analysis and visualisation	Literature, Linguistics
TAPoR	Text analysis portal for research	Digital Humanities
Omeka	Exhibit and archive digital collections	History, Museum Studies
Palladio	Visual network analysis	History, Cultural Studies
Scalar	Multimedia online publishing	Media Studies, Cultural Theory
Hypobook	Collaborative web annotation	Literature, Philosophy

1.12.1 The Role of Humanities in Modern Education

The development of analytical skills, cross-cultural understanding, and moral reasoning are all areas that the humanities have traditionally helped students with. As nations continue to struggle with a variety of difficult moral, political, and social concerns, the use of the humanities in contemporary education is becoming more important. In light of the fast advancements in technology and the economy, this section investigates how the humanities continue to wield relevance.

1. **Defining the Humanities**: Humanities encompass academic disciplines that study human culture, including literature, history, philosophy, art, music, language, and religion. These fields emphasize interpretation, contextual analysis, and reflection on the human condition, as opposed to the empirical methodologies prevalent in the sciences.
2. **Promoting Critical Thinking and Analytical Skills**: In today's classrooms, students are encouraged to think critically and solve problems as a means of developing into well-rounded people who can handle difficult situations. Through the study of literature, history, philosophy, art, music, language, and religion, the humanities play a significant role in the development of these skills a function that is particularly important. Students gain the capacity to think critically, assess diverse views, and make judgements based on accurate information when they engage in activities such as analysing texts, analysing historical events, debating philosophical arguments, and understanding creative representations. These qualities are very essential in a world that is always changing and increasingly placing a high value on creativity, flexibility, and intellectual depth. They enable people to make significant contributions to society and the conversation that is taking place on a global scale.
3. **Cultivating Ethical and Civic Awareness**: Students are equipped with the necessary skills to overcome ethical challenges, investigate moral philosophy, and comprehend their civic obligations via the study of humanities courses. When students investigate various conceptions of justice, human rights, and global citizenship, they gain a more profound understanding of the values that society upholds and the role that these values play in the formation of equitable societies. In democratic societies, where well-informed individuals contribute to meaningful conversation and responsible government, this intellectual engagement is of the utmost importance. Additionally, having a global perspective helps people develop empathy, cross-cultural understanding, and ethical leadership, which ensures that individuals are ready to face modern concerns and fight for social justice in a world that is becoming increasingly linked.
4. **Fostering Cultural Literacy and Empathy**: By immersing students in a variety of cultures, belief systems, and historical narratives, education in the humanities increases the breadth of viewpoints that students have. Literature, philosophy, history, and the arts provide pupils with the opportunity to develop a more profound respect for other ways of thinking and living, which in turn helps to

cultivate empathy and cultural literacy. In a world that is more linked, where cooperation and mutual understanding are the foundations for progress towards peace and sustainable development, these characteristics are very necessary. Individuals develop more adaptability and open-mindedness as a result of their engagement with a variety of traditions and points of view. This makes them better suited to negotiate difficult global challenges, form meaningful connections across cultures, and contribute to a society that is more inclusive and peaceful.

5. **The Humanities and Interdisciplinary Learning**: The integration of the humanities with STEM leads to holistic education models. Interdisciplinary approaches encourage students to evaluate the ethical implications of technological advancements and apply humanistic perspectives to real-world challenges.
6. **Humanities in the Digital Age**: With the advent of digital tools, humanities disciplines have transformed through digital archives, computational text analysis, and virtual reconstructions. These innovations have revitalised interest in the humanities and provided new platforms for scholarly engagement.
7. **Relevance to the Job Market**: Communication, critical thinking, and flexibility are just a few of the diverse talents that graduates of humanities programs possess. Humanities graduates are sometimes criticised for what is believed to be a lack of definite professional options. These are becoming more valuable in a variety of disciplines, including the creative industries, the legal system, public service, and education (Table 1.7).

Table 1.7 Core contributions of the humanities to modern education

Area of contribution	Educational benefit	Societal impact
Critical thinking	Sharpens analysis, evaluation, and reasoning	Informs democratic participation and leadership
Ethical awareness	Encourages moral reasoning and debate	Supports justice and responsible citizenship
Cultural literacy	Builds understanding of diverse perspectives	Fosters tolerance and global cooperation
Communication skills	Develops effective writing and speaking	Enhances professional and interpersonal success
Digital humanities	Integrates technology into traditional disciplines	Expands access and research potential
Interdisciplinary insight	Links human values with STEM	Promotes responsible innovation
Creative expression	Encourages imagination and narrative thinking	Strengthens cultural heritage and identity

1.13 Overview of Technological Trends in Education

1.13.1 Introduction to Technological Trends

The rapid advancement of digital technologies has significantly reshaped the educational landscape. Traditional teaching methods are evolving to incorporate new tools and platforms that enhance learning, foster engagement, and democratise access to education. These changes are not just limited to technical or vocational subjects; even fields like the humanities are embracing digital transformation. This section provides an overview of key technological trends currently influencing education and discusses their relevance in modern pedagogy.

1.13.2 E-Learning and Online Education

In the field of education, the proliferation of e-learning platforms has been one of the most significant transformational innovations. Learners are able to access academic information online inside these systems, often in an asynchronous manner, which enables them to study at their speed. LMS such as Moodle, Blackboard, and Canvas, in conjunction with MOOCs offered by platforms such as Coursera, edX, and FutureLearn, have expanded the scope of educational options beyond the confines of conventional classrooms. A more individualised and adaptable educational experience may be achieved via the use of e-learning, which allows for the incorporation of multimedia, interactive quizzes, and discussion forums [28].

1.13.3 Artificial Intelligence in Education

AI is increasingly used to personalize education. Adaptive learning systems analyse student responses and performance data to recommend specific learning paths. AI-powered tools also assist in grading, provide real-time feedback, and offer tutoring through chatbots. For instance, platforms like Century Tech and Carnegie Learning leverage AI to enhance learner engagement and instructional effectiveness. In the humanities, AI tools can be used for text analysis, language translation, and even creative writing assistance [29].

1.13.4 Gamification and Game-Based Learning

Gamification introduces elements of gaming such as points, levels, and rewards into educational contexts to increase student motivation and participation. Platforms like

Kahoot!, Quizizz, and Classcraft utilise gamification strategies to make learning more engaging. Game-based learning can be particularly effective in humanities subjects by promoting narrative exploration, historical reenactments, and language acquisition through immersive storylines and simulations [30].

1.13.5 Virtual Reality (VR) and Augmented Reality (AR)

Learning via experience has been expanded to include new dimensions thanks to the advent of virtual reality and augmented reality. Students are able to visit historical landmarks, investigate creative movements, and perform virtual lab activities while they are immersed in virtual reality surroundings. AR is a technology that superimposes digital material onto the physical environment. This technology may be very helpful in improving printed textbooks or classroom displays. Immersive instructional information is made available by tools such as Google Expeditions and Nearpod VR. This content helps to make topics that are more abstract or remote more palpable [31].

1.13.6 Mobile Learning and BYOD (Bring Your Own Device)

The rising use of mobile devices, such as smartphones and tablets, has led to the rise of mobile learning as a prominent trend. Educational applications are designed to meet a wide range of learning requirements, from English language instruction to test preparation. Bring-your-own-device (BYOD) rules are also being adopted by educational institutions, which enable students to use their devices for academic reasons. Not only does this tendency encourage informal learning alongside formal teaching, but it also facilitates ubiquitous learning, which makes it possible to access educational materials whenever and wherever they are needed [32].

1.13.7 Cloud Computing and Collaborative Tools

Cloud-based platforms such as Google Workspace and Microsoft 365 allow for real-time collaboration, file sharing, and storage. Students can co-edit documents, participate in group projects, and communicate more effectively with peers and instructors. These tools are crucial for facilitating online and hybrid learning models and have become standard in many educational institutions around the world [33].

Table 1.8 Major technological trends in modern education

Technology	Educational application	Impact on learning
E-Learning platforms	Online courses, LMS integration	Increases accessibility and flexibility
Artificial intelligence	Personalized learning, grading automation	Enhances student engagement and outcomes
Gamification	Interactive learning through games	Improves motivation and retention
Virtual & augmented reality	Immersive 3D environments	Facilitates experiential learning
Mobile learning	Learning via smartphones/tablets	Supports anytime, anywhere learning
Cloud computing	Collaborative tools and storage	Enables seamless group work
Learning analytics	Data-driven instruction	Improves learner performance and support

1.13.8 Data Analytics and Learning Insights

Educational institutions are increasingly leveraging data analytics to enhance instructional decision-making. Learning analytics involves collecting and analysing data on student behavior, performance, and engagement to identify trends and predict outcomes. Dashboards provided by LMS platforms allow teachers to intervene early when students are at risk of falling behind. Such insights enable more targeted, efficient, and equitable education [34] (Table 1.8).

It is not a passing fad but rather a long-term development that is reshaping the way in which information is received and processed that the incorporation of technology into educational settings is. The introduction of these technology advancements has the potential to alter conventional educational settings into places that are dynamic, participatory, and welcoming to all persons. These kinds of tendencies, when applied to the field of education in the humanities, provide instruments that supplement interpretive learning, foster creative participation, and democratise access to information. At the same time as these technologies continue to advance, it is imperative that educational institutions, policymakers, and educators continue to be proactive in embracing and modifying them to meet the requirements of all students.

1.13.9 Structure of the Book

The book is organized into eight comprehensive chapters:

1. **Introduction**—Establishes the rationale, significance, and objectives of software integration in humanities.

2. **Literature Review**—Reviews theoretical, conceptual, and empirical studies on educational software and digital pedagogy.
3. **Theoretical Framework**—Discusses the educational theories (e.g., constructivism, connectivism, TPACK) that underpin this research.
4. **Methodology**—Outlines the research design, tools, sampling techniques, and analytical approaches.
5. **Software Tools and Digital Resources in Humanities**—Profiles specific tools and evaluates their applications in learning environments.
6. **Results and Analysis**—Presents empirical findings from the study, using both qualitative and quantitative methods.
7. **Discussion and Interpretation of Findings**—Connects findings to theoretical perspectives and educational implications.
8. **Conclusion and Recommendations**—Summarizes key insights and offers recommendations for policy, practice, and further research.

References

1. K.C. Obi, O. Iwuanyanwu, Innovation in the assessment of primary school mathematics: an approach to revamping Nigeria education. J. Teach. Perspect. **18**(1), 51–66 (2023) [Online]. Available: http://repositorio.unan.edu.ni/2986/1/5624.pdf%0Ahttp://fiskal.kemenkeu.go.id/ejournal%0A10.1016/j.cirp.2016.06.001%0A10.1016/j.powtec.2016.12.055%0A10.1016/j.ijfatigue.2019.02.006%0A10.1
2. J. Kehinde, H.B. Akinlabi, Impact of leadership skill and strategies on banking sector performance: a survey of selected consolidated banks in Nigeria. Int. Trader Acad. Res. Conf. **3**(1), 7–8 (2012)
3. C. Gareau-Brennan, J.Y. Kung, Systematic review of effective library instruction for business students. J. Bus. Financ. Librariansh. **27**(2), 81–103 (2022). https://doi.org/10.1080/08963568.2021.2015849
4. S.D. Keesstra et al., The significance of soils and soil science towards realization of the United Nations sustainable development goals. Soil **2**(2), 111–128 (2016). https://doi.org/10.5194/soil-2-111-2016
5. D.G. Collings, K. Mellahi, Commentary on: 'Talent-innate or acquired? Theoretical considerations and their implications for talent management.' Hum. Resour. Manag. Rev. **23**(4), 322–325 (2013). https://doi.org/10.1016/j.hrmr.2013.08.003
6. K. Gyau Baffour Awuah, C.K. Bijimi, Discovering the core stakeholders in the Nigerian urban water supply system. Sustain. Water Resour. Manag. **10**(1), 1–22 (2024). https://doi.org/10.1007/s40899-023-00986-0
7. E. Hofer, W. Musakwa, S. van Lanen, T. Gumbo, S. Netsch, K. Gugerell, Inclusivity insights: two urban development projects in Johannesburg. J. Hous. Built Environ. **11** (2021). https://doi.org/10.1007/s10901-021-09916-y
8. M. McCampbell, C. Schumann, L. Klerkx, Good intentions in complex realities: challenges for designing responsibly in digital agriculture in low-income countries. Sociol. Ruralis **62**(2), 279–304 (2022). https://doi.org/10.1111/soru.12359
9. D. Kuteyi, H. Winkler, Logistics challenges in Sub-Saharan Africa and opportunities for digitalization. Sustainability **14**(4) (2022). https://doi.org/10.3390/su14042399
10. M. Nichols, A comparison of two online learning systems. J. Open Flex. Distance Educ. **20**(1), 19–32 (2016) [Online]. Available: http://www.jofdl.nz/index.php/JOFDL/article/view/257

11. L. Umek, D. Keržič, N. Tomaževič, A. Aristovnik, Moodle e-learning system and students' performance in higher education: the case of public administration programmes, in *Proceedings of International Conference on e-Learning 2015, E-Learning 2015—Part Multi Conference Computer Science Information Systems* (2015), pp. 97–104
12. G.B. Porsani, K.D.V. de Lersundi, A.S.O. Gutiérrez, C.F. Bandera, Interoperability between building information modelling (BIM) and building energy model (BEM). Appl. Sci. **11**(5), 1–20 (2021). https://doi.org/10.3390/app11052167
13. D. Asamoah, B. Agyei-Owusu, F.K. Andoh-Baidoo, E. Ayaburi, Inter-organizational systems use and supply chain performance: mediating role of supply chain management capabilities. Int. J. Inf. Manage. **58**(23), 12–39 (2021). https://doi.org/10.1016/j.ijinfomgt.2020.102195
14. A. Stojanović, N. Sofranova, S. Arsić, I. Milošević, I. Mihajlović, The effects of CSR activities on business according to employee perception. Eur. Rev. (2021). https://doi.org/10.1017/S1062798721000156
15. R. Said, M.I. Bhatti, A.I. Hunjra, Toward understanding renewable energy and sustainable development in developing and developed economies: a review. Energies **15**(15) (2022). https://doi.org/10.3390/en15155349
16. C.E. Iheame, Assessment of the effectiveness of construction managers on maintaining quality, cost and time on project delivery in Delta State, (Case study of Isoko Community). Assess. Eff. Constr. Manag. **XI**(Ii), 2330–4480 (2022) [Online]. Available: www.pmworldlibrary.net
17. T. Francis, Alarming rate of child poverty in Northern Nigeria: implications for national security. Am. Res. J. Humanit. Soc. Sci. 2019 ARJHSS J. **01**, 1–10 (2019) [Online]. Available: www.arjhss.com
18. A.C. Okoli, F.T. Agada, Kidnapping and national security in Nigeria. Res. Humanit. Soc. Sci. **4**(6), 137–146 (2014)
19. A. Ekwueme, A. Nehemiah, The influence of online marketing of Jumia and Konga on consumer purchasing behaviour among Kogi state residents of Nigeria. Glob. J. Human-Soc. Sci. Arts Humanit. **17**(6), 25–32 (2017)
20. V. Arufe-Giráldez, A. Sanmiguel-Rodríguez, O. Ramos-Álvarez, R. Navarro-Patón, News of the pedagogical models in physical education—a quick review. Int. J. Environ. Res. Public Health **20**(3). https://doi.org/10.3390/ijerph20032586
21. B.I. Nkambule, Organisational learning and knowledge sharing culture in township schools: an exploration of effective and ineffective practices. J. Penelit. dan Pengkaj. Ilmu Pendidik. e-Saintika **7**(1), 60–74 (2023). https://doi.org/10.36312/esaintika.v7i1.1123
22. Z. Shana, E.S. Abulibdeh, Cloud computing issues for higher education: theory of acceptance model. Int. J. Emerg. Technol. Learn. **12**(11), 168–184 (2017). https://doi.org/10.3991/ijet.v12i11.7473
23. S. Assar, Information and communications technology in education. Int. Encycl. Soc. Behav. Sci. Second Ed. **12**, 66–71 (2015). https://doi.org/10.1016/B978-0-08-097086-8.92104-4
24. M. Sharma, S. Luthra, S. Joshi, A. Kumar, Developing a framework for enhancing survivability of sustainable supply chains during and post-COVID-19 pandemic. Int. J. Logist. Res. Appl. **25**(4–5), 433–453 (2022). https://doi.org/10.1080/13675567.2020.1810213
25. M. Ahsan, K.E. Nygard, R. Gomes, M.M. Chowdhury, N. Rifat, J.F. Connolly, Cybersecurity threats and their mitigation approaches using machine learning—a review. J. Cybersecurity Priv. **2**(3), 527–555 (2022). https://doi.org/10.3390/jcp2030027
26. K. Matthews, K. Ong, Is inflation caused by deteriorating inflation expectations or excessive monetary growth? Econ. Aff. **42**(2), 259–274 (2022). https://doi.org/10.1111/ecaf.12518
27. F.A. Alaba, M. Amina, U. Ibrahim, H.A. Sulaimon, A. Zainab Aliyu, Exploring the role of the internet of things (IoT) on economic growth in Nigeria: challenges and opportunities. Eng. Technol. Trends **2**(6) (2024)
28. R.A. Rahman, S. Halid, N. Zamri, *Academic Dishonesty and Financial Reporting Fraud Intention* (2022), pp. 2650–2655
29. J.P.B. Batista, C. Torre, J.M. Sousa Lobo, B. Sepodes, A review of the continuous professional development system for pharmacists. Hum. Resour. Health **20**(1), 1–12 (2022). https://doi.org/10.1186/s12960-021-00700-1

30. C. Purcell et al., A peer-led, school-based social network intervention for young people in the UK, promoting sexual health via social media and conversations with friends: intervention development and optimisation of STASH. BMC Public Health **23**(1), 1–12 (2023). https://doi.org/10.1186/s12889-023-15541-x
31. C. Stone, J. Downing, J. Dyment, *Improving Student Retention and Success Within the Context of Complex Lives and Diverse Circumstances* (2021), pp. 161–178. https://doi.org/10.1007/978-3-030-77673-2_9
32. R. Jahangir, Y.W. Teh, G. Mujtaba, R. Alroobaea, Z.H. Shaikh, I. Ali, Convolutional neural network-based cross-corpus speech emotion recognition with data augmentation and features fusion. Mach. Vis. Appl. **33**(3), 1–16 (2022). https://doi.org/10.1007/s00138-022-01294-x
33. I. Adumbabu, K. Selvakumar, An improved lifetime and energy consumption with enhanced clustering in WSNs. Intell. Autom. Soft Comput. **35**(2), 1939–1956 (2023). https://doi.org/10.32604/iasc.2023.029489
34. R.M. Abdullah, A.Z. Abualkishik, N.M. Isaacc, A.A. Alwan, Y. Gulzar, An investigation study for risk calculation of security vulnerabilities on android applications. Indones. J. Electr. Eng. Comput. Sci. **25**(3), 1736–1748 (2022). https://doi.org/10.11591/ijeecs.v25.i3.pp1736-1748

Chapter 2
Literature Review

2.1 Concept of Humanities Education

The study of human culture, cognition, and expression through critical and analytical perspectives is the focus of education in the humanities, which is a multidisciplinary area of study. Literature, philosophy, history, languages, religious studies, music, art, and cultural studies are some of the areas that are typically included in its scope. The fundamental goal of education in the humanities is to gain an understanding of the human condition and the many ways in which people and communities interpret their experiences over the course of long periods. Due to the fact that it places an emphasis on interpretive analysis, debate, critical thinking, and empathy, this discipline is considered to be an essential component of liberal education all over the world [1].

Education in the humanities is confronted with several difficulties and possibilities in the context of the twenty-first century. These challenges and opportunities are brought about by the digital revolution, globalisation, and evolving educational paradigms. Even though many contend that the humanities have been pushed to the background as a result of the growing emphasis on STEM, there are others who claim that the humanities are more important than they have ever been in terms of addressing the ethical, philosophical, and cultural aspects of modern life [2].

In this part, we will look into the fundamental characteristics of humanities education, including its development, its importance in a contemporary setting, and its incorporation with digital tools and pedagogical advances.

a. Historical Background of Humanities Education

The origins of education in the humanities may be traced back to ancient antiquity, namely in the Greco-Roman culture. During this period, education began to emphasise grammar, rhetoric, and logic, often known as the trivium, as essential disciplines for civic life and moral growth. The humanities were brought back into prominence during the Renaissance period as a component of the studia

F. A. Alaba et al., *Learning Beyond the Classroom*, Studies in Computational Intelligence 1253, https://doi.org/10.1007/978-3-032-14433-1_2

humanitatis, which was a curriculum that aimed to produce people who were both moral and well-informed. This humanist tradition had an impact on education in Europe and, later, in the United States, and is credited with contributing to the establishment of liberal arts institutions that placed an emphasis on learning that was both comprehensive and all-encompassing.

b. Defining the Humanities

It is not only the subject matter that defines the humanities, but also the way in which they undertake inquiry that defines them. In contrast to the scientific sciences, which are highly dependent on actual observation and experimentation, the humanities make use of critical interpretation, contextual analysis, and theoretical frameworks. Texts, artefacts, performances, and historical events are all examined by researchers in the humanities in order to get a better understanding of meaning, value, and the human experience. Because of its interpretative character, it is possible to have a variety of viewpoints, and it helps to cultivate an understanding for ambiguity and complexity.

c. Objectives and Values of Humanities Education

The overarching objectives of humanities education include the development of:

- Critical thinking and analytical skills
- Ethical reasoning and moral reflection
- Communication and argumentation proficiency
- Cultural awareness and intercultural competence
- Creativity and intellectual curiosity

These objectives contribute not only to personal growth but also to the cultivation of active, informed, and empathetic citizens. In democratic societies, humanities education plays a vital role in fostering civic engagement and ethical leadership.

d. Humanities Education in Contemporary Curricula

There are many different methods in which contemporary educational institutions include the humanities into their curriculum, ranging from specialised degree programs to general education requirements. It is becoming more usual to use an interdisciplinary approach, which involves mixing the humanities with the social sciences, technology, or environmental studies. Digital humanities, for example, helps to bridge the gap between conventional humanistic inquiry and computer technologies, which in turn makes it possible for new types of research and education to be developed.

e. Challenges Facing Humanities Education

Despite its importance, humanities education faces several challenges:

- Declining student enrollment in humanities majors
- Reduced funding for humanities departments
- Perception of limited career prospects
- Emphasis on STEM fields and vocational training

These challenges have prompted educators and policymakers to rethink how humanities education is delivered and perceived. Innovative teaching methods, community engagement, and integration with digital tools are some strategies being employed to revitalise interest and relevance.

f. The Role of Technology in Humanities Education

The use of digital technologies has opened up new avenues for humanities education and study. Access and engagement are both improved by the use of software such as platforms for text analysis, digital archives, visualisation tools, and learning management systems. Through the use of these technologies, educators are able to create learning environments that are dynamic and welcoming to all students, while also providing pupils with the digital literacy skills that are necessary in the modern world.

g. Global Perspectives on Humanities Education

The education of the humanities differs depending on the cultural and national setting. It is firmly based in philosophical and theological traditions in certain countries, while in others, it is formed by postcolonial and decolonial discourses. In some locations, it is profoundly entrenched in tradition. A more comprehensive and diverse perspective of human experience is becoming possible as a result of the expansion of international cooperation and comparative humanities programs.

h. Future Directions

It is adaptation and innovation that will determine the future of education in the humanities. The importance of embracing cooperation across disciplines, tackling modern concerns on a global scale, and learning to harness the power of digital media cannot be overstated. The distinctively human qualities that are nurtured by the humanities, such as empathy, ethics, communication, and creativity, will become even more vital as the workforce is reshaped by automation and AI (Table 2.1).

Thus, education in the humanities continues to be an essential component of a comprehensive academic and civic education to be considered. Not only does it educate students for a wide range of occupations, but it also prepares them for meaningful involvement in society. This is accomplished by encouraging intelligent contemplation, nuanced understanding, and ethical engagement. The incorporation of digital technologies and the growth of pedagogical approaches offers the potential to bring about a future that is more dynamic and relevant (Fig. 2.1).

2.2 Evolution of Educational Technology

The development of instructional technology is a dynamic story that spans decades and is characterised by invention, adaptation, and transition. The use of educational technology (EdTech) has continuously transformed the processes of teaching and learning, beginning with the use of simple instruments such as chalk and slates

Table 2.1 Key components of humanities education

Component	Description	Examples
Critical thinking	Ability to analyse, interpret, and evaluate information and arguments	Debating ethical dilemmas; analyzing historical events
Cultural awareness	Understanding and appreciation of diverse cultures and worldviews	Studying world religions; exploring global literatures
Communication skills	Proficiency in written, oral, and visual communication	Writing essays; delivering presentations
Ethical reasoning	Capacity to consider moral and philosophical questions	Discussing social justice; examining ethical theories
Historical context	Understanding the past to inform the present and future	Learning about revolutions; timelines of empires
Aesthetic appreciation	Recognition and critique of artistic and literary works	Analyzing poetry; visiting museums or galleries
Interdisciplinary learning	Integration of knowledge from various disciplines for holistic understanding	Combining history with literature or philosophy
Research skills	Ability to investigate topics, evaluate sources, and present findings	Archival work; citation and referencing
Digital literacy	Competence in using digital tools for exploration, creation, and analysis	Using Voyant for text analysis; creating digital exhibits
Empathy and perspective-taking	Understanding others' experiences and viewpoints through study and dialogue	Role-playing in literature; analysing diaries or narratives

and progressing to the complex digital ecosystems that characterise contemporary classrooms. This development is not only a record of tools; rather, it is a reflection of altering educational philosophies, the requirements of society, and the improvements in technology [3].

a. **Early Foundations: Oral Tradition to Print Revolution**

Oral education was the primary mode of instruction in ancient cultures, with the transfer of information being accomplished mostly by memorisation and recitation. Storytellers, elders, and scholars all played an important part in the process of maintaining and transmitting historical information, cultural practices, and educational lessons. The development of writing systems brought about a revolution in this process, making it possible to chronicle and save knowledge for future generations. The availability of written records ensured that information was no longer limited to those who had great oral recall abilities. Written records gave stability, accuracy, and accessibility. The invention of the printing press by Johannes Gutenberg in the 15th century was another momentous occasion in the

Fig. 2.1 Parts of humanities and social sciences

history of education. This event was significant because it democratised access to knowledge by making books and other educational resources more accessible to the general public. Literacy and intellectual interaction were both fostered as a result of this movement, which turned education from a luxury reserved for the few to a function of society. Education grew into an organised system that created civilisations, stimulated academic debate, and widened chances for knowledge acquisition across all social strata as a result of the proliferation of printed curriculum, libraries, and textbooks as essential components of the educational process [3, 4].

b. **19th and Early 20th Century: Industrialisation and Mechanisation**

Mass education became necessary as a result of the rise of industrialisation. During the 19th century, blackboards, textbooks, and formal teacher training were all introduced to the classroom. At the beginning of the 20th century, educational films, radio broadcasts, and teaching machines came into existence, therefore laying the framework for the development of multimedia instruction. The teaching machine that B.F. Skinner's developed in 1958 is a remarkable example of early efforts to personalise learning via the use of technology. This machine utilised the concepts of behaviourist psychology [5].

c. **The Rise of Audiovisual Aids**

During the middle of the 20th century, educational institutions began to adopt audiovisual aids like as slide projectors, overhead projectors, and audio recordings. These aids improved visual learning and accommodated a variety of learning styles. Additionally, during this period, the concept of programmed teaching emerged, which was inspired by behavioural learning theories and intended to plan classes in a way that allowed for individual learners to pace themselves. Education in the modern era was shaped by the incorporation of psychological principles into instructional design, which resulted in more efficient teaching methods. In the meantime, educational television shows such as Look and Read on the BBC and Sesame Street in the United States have revolutionised early childhood education by combining entertainment and teaching. This has made education more interesting and accessible to young students. Through these developments, the groundwork was set for learning strategies that are based on multimedia [6].

d. **The Computer Age and the Digital Turn**

One of the most significant events in the history of education was the introduction of computers into classrooms in the 1980s. This event paved the way for learning that is driven by technology. Computers were first used to provide computer-assisted instruction (CAI) and fundamental programming training, providing students with the opportunity to get practical experience with digital tools. During the 1990s, the availability of personal computers increased, which led to a considerable expansion of their involvement in the transmission of educational content. By offering knowledge that was both interactive and entertaining, educational software and multimedia CDs brought about a revolution in the learning process. A number of well-known applications, such as Microsoft Encarta, Reader Rabbit, and Oregon Trail, combined educational content with entertaining content, so making the process of acquiring information more immersive. These advancements provide the groundwork for contemporary educational technology, aiding in the development of digital literacy and creating learning environments that encourage interaction [7].

e. **The Internet and Networked Learning**

The 1990s and early 2000s saw the advent of the internet, fundamentally altering educational landscapes. Web-based resources, e-learning platforms, and virtual libraries extended learning beyond the classroom. LMS such as Moodle and Blackboard enabled structured online education. Distance learning and MOOCs gained prominence, offering flexible, scalable education across geographical boundaries [8].

f. **Mobile and Ubiquitous Learning**

With the proliferation of smartphones and tablets, learning has become increasingly mobile. Apps, podcasts, digital textbooks, and cloud storage enabled students to access educational content anytime, anywhere. BYOD policies and mobile learning strategies gained traction in educational institutions. Gamification and adaptive learning software personalised learning experiences and boosted engagement [9].

g. **AI and Smart Learning Environments**

The recent integration of AI has brought about intelligent tutoring systems, predictive analytics, and personalised learning environments. AI-powered platforms assess student performance, recommend learning paths, and provide real-time feedback. Voice assistants and chatbots enhance accessibility, especially for students with disabilities. AR and VR technologies further enrich experiential learning by creating immersive environments [10].

h. **Educational Technology During and After COVID-19**

The COVID-19 pandemic catalyzed rapid EdTech adoption. Schools and universities worldwide shifted to remote learning, highlighting both the potential and challenges of digital education. Video conferencing tools like Zoom, collaborative platforms like Google Classroom, and content-sharing services like YouTube became essential components of education. The post-pandemic era continues to explore hybrid and blended learning models that combine online and in-person instruction [8].

i. **Challenges and Considerations**

Despite its promise, educational technology faces several hurdles:

- Digital divide and inequitable access to devices and connectivity
- Data privacy and cybersecurity concerns
- Teacher training and digital literacy gaps
- Pedagogical alignment with technological tools

These challenges necessitate comprehensive strategies that prioritise inclusion, security, and professional development (Figs. 2.2 and 2.3; Table 2.2).

The evolution of educational technology illustrates a continuous quest to enhance learning outcomes and democratise education. From oral traditions to AI-driven platforms, each stage of development reflects broader societal changes and educational goals. As we move forward, the focus must remain on leveraging technology to support pedagogical innovation, equitable access, and lifelong learning [13].

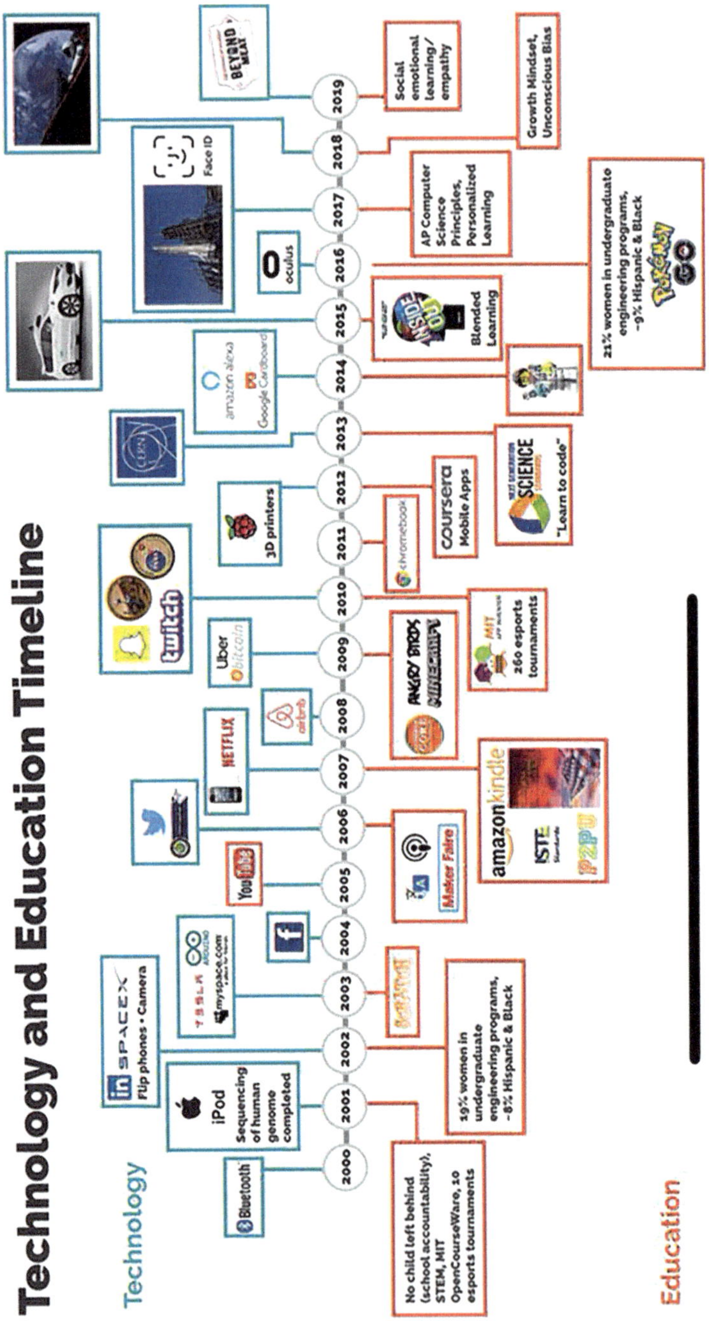

Fig. 2.2 Technology and education timeline [11]

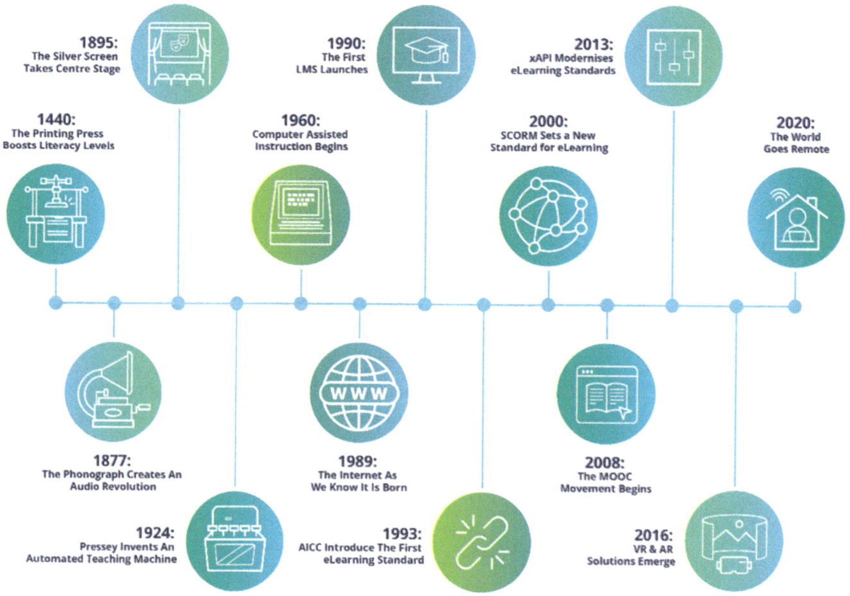

Fig. 2.3 Key dates in learning technology [12]

2.3 Learning Theories Relevant to Digital Learning

Understanding the theoretical underpinnings of learning is essential to effectively integrating digital tools into education. Learning theories provide a framework for designing, implementing, and evaluating digital learning experiences. This section explores key learning theories that have shaped digital learning environments and examines how they are applied in contemporary educational technology.

1. **Behaviourism**

   Behaviourism, championed by psychologists like B.F. Skinner and John Watson, views learning as a change in observable behaviour, influenced by stimuli and reinforced through repetition and feedback. Digital learning environments often reflect behaviourist principles through drill-and-practice programs, gamification, and immediate feedback mechanisms.

   Applications in Digital Learning:

   - Language learning apps (e.g., Duolingo) use repetition and rewards to reinforce vocabulary.
   - Educational games incorporate levels, points, and badges to encourage persistence and task completion.
   - Learning Management Systems (LMS) use quizzes and automatic grading to provide immediate feedback.

Table 2.2 Milestones in the evolution of educational technology

Era / Year	Milestone	Significance	Example/Technology
1920s–1930s	Introduction of radio in education	Enabled mass broadcasting of educational content	Educational radio programs
1950s	Teaching machines and programmed instruction	Early automated learning; paved the way for computer-based instruction	B.F. Skinner's teaching machine
1960s	Computer-Assisted Instruction (CAI)	Computers began to be used for individualised learning	PLATO system at the University of Illinois
1970s	Rise of educational television	Visual learning became widespread in homes and classrooms	Sesame Street, PBS educational content
1980s	Personal computers in schools	Marked the beginning of digital literacy in classrooms	Apple II, BBC Micro
1990s	Internet and online learning platforms	Enabled global access to information and distance education	Blackboard, early MOOCs
Early 2000s	Learning Management Systems (LMS)	Structured digital course delivery became standardised	Moodle, WebCT
2010s	Mobile learning and apps	Allowed learning anytime, anywhere using smartphones and tablets	Duolingo, Khan Academy
2012 onward	Massive Open Online Courses (MOOCs)	Democratised access to quality education on a large scale	Coursera, edX, Udacity
Late 2010s–2020s	AI and adaptive learning	Personalised education through intelligent algorithms	ChatGPT, Smart Sparrow, Knewton
2020 (COVID-19)	Emergency remote teaching	Accelerated global adoption of edtech for continuity of education	Zoom, Google Classroom
2020s onward	Immersive and XR technologies	Enhanced engagement through VR and AR	ClassVR, Google Expeditions

2. **Cognitivism**

Cognitivism emerged as a response to behaviourism, emphasising the internal mental processes involved in learning. It focuses on how information is received, organised, stored, and retrieved. Influenced by theorists such as Jean Piaget and Jerome Bruner, cognitivism highlights the role of memory, perception, and problem-solving.

Applications in Digital Learning:

- Interactive simulations and concept mapping tools support the organization of knowledge.
- E-learning modules with structured content help learners build cognitive schemas.
- Multimedia content is designed to reduce cognitive overload and facilitate retention.

3. **Constructivism**

Constructivism posits that learners actively construct their own understanding based on experiences. It encourages exploration, inquiry, and collaboration. Lev Vygotsky's concept of the Zone of Proximal Development (ZPD) and Piaget's stages of development are central to constructivist thinking.

Applications in Digital Learning:

- Project-based learning platforms promote inquiry and self-directed learning.
- Wikis and blogs facilitate collaborative construction of knowledge.
- VR environments allow learners to immerse themselves in exploratory scenarios.

4. **Social Learning Theory**

Albert Bandura's Social Learning Theory emphasizes learning through observation, imitation, and modelling. It underscores the role of social interaction in knowledge acquisition.

Applications in Digital Learning:

- Discussion forums, peer reviews, and collaborative tools foster social learning.
- Video-based learning (e.g., tutorials, vlogs) allows learners to observe and replicate skills.
- Social media platforms and learning communities encourage peer interaction and shared knowledge.

5. **Connectivism**

Developed by George Siemens and Stephen Downes, connectivism addresses learning in the digital age. It proposes that knowledge is distributed across a network of connections and learning consists of the ability to construct and traverse those networks.

Applications in Digital Learning:

- MOOCs and online learning networks exemplify distributed, non-linear learning.
- RSS feeds, blogs, and forums allow learners to access and connect diverse information sources.
- AI-based recommendation systems help learners navigate vast digital content.

6. **Experiential Learning**

   David Kolb's Experiential Learning Theory emphasises learning through experience, reflection, conceptualisation, and experimentation. It aligns closely with active learning and the use of simulations and role-playing in digital platforms.

   Applications in Digital Learning:

   – Virtual labs and simulation tools offer hands-on learning experiences.
   – Reflection journals and e-portfolios support critical thinking and self-assessment.
   – Interactive case studies and scenarios engage learners in real-world problem-solving.

7. **Situated Learning**

   Situated Learning, proposed by Jean Lave and Etienne Wenger, emphasises learning in context and through participation in communities of practice. It recognises the social and cultural dimensions of learning.

   Applications in Digital Learning:

   – Apprenticeship-based models using online mentoring and expert feedback.
   – Collaborative projects with real-world relevance.
   – Learning environments that replicate authentic professional contexts (Table 2.3).

   To build digital learning experiences that are both effective and efficient, theoretical frameworks act as designing guidelines. Educators are able to create settings that not only facilitate the dissemination of information but also promote student engagement, motivation, and critical thinking by aligning technology tools with suitable learning theories. A more comprehensive knowledge of these ideas makes it possible to integrate technology into humanities teaching in a manner that is both more deliberate and more likely to be pedagogically sound [14].

2.4 Software Tools in Education

The provision of dynamic, interactive, and individualised learning experiences has been made possible by software tools, which have revolutionised educational procedures. Within the context of the educational setting, these technologies make communication, the production of material, evaluation, cooperation, and management easier to do. The use of such software in the field of humanities improves students' critical thinking and creativity, as well as the level of engagement they have with their teachers.

Table 2.3 Learning theories and their applications in digital learning

Learning theory	Key concepts	Application in digital learning	Examples
Behaviorism	Learning is a change in behavior due to reinforcement or punishment	Gamified learning platforms use rewards, scores, and repetition to reinforce learning	Duolingo badges, quiz-based feedback
Cognitivism	Learning involves internal processes like memory, thinking, and problem-solving	Structured modules and scaffolding support cognitive processing in learners	Interactive tutorials; branching scenarios
Constructivism	Learners construct knowledge through experiences and reflection	Learners explore simulations and real-world problems, developing their understanding	Virtual labs, project-based e-learning
Social learning theory	Learning occurs through observation, imitation, and modeling in social contexts	Collaborative tools and peer-to-peer learning environments promote social interaction	Discussion forums, group wikis, peer feedback
Connectivism	Learning occurs through connections within a network of people and information	Emphasizes networking and navigating diverse digital sources to build knowledge	MOOCs, social media learning, knowledge curation
Experiential learning	Knowledge is created through experience and reflection on doing	Encourages hands-on tasks, simulations, and reflections in digital contexts	Scenario-based learning, digital storytelling
Situated learning	Learning is embedded in context and activity	Context-aware apps and immersive environments support learning through doing	AR field trips, job-shadowing simulations
Transformative learning	Learning transforms perspectives through critical reflection	Digital portfolios and reflective journals allow learners to challenge assumptions	E-portfolios, reflective blogs
Self-Directed learning	Learners take initiative in diagnosing needs, formulating goals, and evaluating	LMS platforms allow learners to pace and track their own progress	Khan Academy, Coursera "learn at your pace"

2.4.1 Learning Management Systems (LMS)

Moodle, Canvas, Blackboard, and Google Classroom are examples of LMS platforms that provide instructors with full settings in which they may upload resources, assign assignments, monitor progress, and make communication with students. Syllabi,

Table 2.4 Learning management systems features

Feature	Description
Course Delivery	Modular content upload, scheduling, and announcements
Communication	Forums, messaging, and feedback options
Assessment Tools	Online quizzes, assignments, rubrics, and gradebooks
Analytics	Student progress tracking and engagement statistics

Table 2.5 Authoring tools

Tool	Strengths
Articulate Storyline	Drag-and-drop interface, interactive scenarios, SCORM compatibility
Adobe Captivate	Video demos, responsive design, VR support
H5P	Open-source, embeddable content (quizzes, timelines, presentations)

reading materials, examinations, and discussion forums are all accessible via a centralised location thanks to their provision [15] (Table 2.4).

2.4.2 *Authoring Tools*

Educators leverage powerful authoring tools such as Articulate Storyline, Adobe Captivate, and H5P to create dynamic, interactive, and multimedia-rich educational content without requiring programming skills. These tools enable teachers and instructional designers to develop customized lesson plans tailored to different learning styles, fostering engagement through animations, simulations, quizzes, and interactive assessments. With user-friendly interfaces and drag-and-drop functionalities, these platforms empower educators to design engaging digital courses that enhance comprehension and retention. By integrating multimedia elements, real-world scenarios, and adaptive learning pathways, authoring tools revolutionize instructional delivery, making education more immersive, accessible, and effective in both traditional and online learning environments [16] (Table 2.5).

2.4.3 *Content Management Systems (CMS)*

Educators and educational institutions build robust digital platforms for learning and knowledge dissemination using robust content management systems such as Drupal, Joomla, and WordPress. Access to OER, as well as course materials, research papers, and blogs, may be readily accessible via the use of these technologies, which enable the establishment of educational websites and digital archives. Educators are able to create dynamic places for the purpose of displaying instructional material, promoting

Table 2.6 Content management systems

Use case	Example
Course portfolios	Digital presentation of student work
OER repositories	Hosting openly licensed course materials and e-books
Institutional archives	Digital collections of historical documents and cultural media

Table 2.7 Communication and collaboration tools

Tool	Features
Zoom	Video conferencing, breakout rooms, webinar mode
Teams	Integration with Office apps, threaded conversations, and team channels
Slack	Channel-based communication, integrations with Google Drive, and Trello
Discord	Voice/text chat, custom servers, screen sharing

collaboration, and enabling conversations by using plugins, customisable themes, and interactive features. Furthermore, the digital archives that are kept on these platforms guarantee the long-term preservation of academic resources, which makes them very useful instruments for contemporary education in both formal and informal contexts [17, 18] (Table 2.6).

2.4.4 Communication and Collaboration Tools

Zoom, Microsoft Teams, Slack, and Discord are examples of digital platforms that are essential to the success of remote and hybrid learning since they enable smooth communication and collaboration respectively. These tools make it possible for students and teachers to communicate in real time using technologies like as video conferencing, chat messaging, and phone calls. This ensures that they remain linked regardless of where they are located. Because they allow for the exchange of files, it is simple to share lecture materials, assignments, and resources around the classroom. Furthermore, the incorporation of productivity tools, such as breakout rooms, threaded conversations, and automatic scheduling, contributes to the enhancement of group activities and collaborative efforts. Through the use of these platforms, contemporary education is made more accessible, interactive, and adaptable to a variety of learning situations [19, 20] (Table 2.7).

2.4.5 Assessment and Feedback Tools

The evaluation process has been revolutionised with the introduction of digital assessment technologies such as Google Forms, Kahoot!, Socrative, and Turnitin. These

Table 2.8 Assessment and feedback tools

Tool	Purpose
Google Forms	Surveys, quizzes, automatic grading
Kahoot!	Game-based learning and real-time quiz competitions
Socrative	Formative assessments with real-time analytics
Turnitin	Plagiarism detection, feedback studio, similarity reports

tools have made the evaluation process more efficient and engaging. Educators are able to streamline the process of data gathering and grading by using Google Forms, which allows them to construct customisable quizzes and surveys. Through the use of gamified quizzes, Kahoot! increases engagement, which in turn serves to encourage participation and reinforce learning in a manner that is both enjoyable and competitive. Through the use of interactive polls and quizzes, Socrative makes it possible for instructors to conduct real-time evaluations, which enables them to evaluate students' level of comprehension in an instant. By comparing contributions to a massive database of texts, Turnitin is able to identify instances of plagiarism automatically, so guaranteeing that academic integrity is maintained. These technologies, when combined, provide teachers the ability to offer dynamic assessments, to provide instant feedback, and to maintain educational standards (Table 2.8).

2.4.6 *Simulation and Virtual Reality (VR) Tools*

Through the provision of immersive learning experiences that extend beyond the confines of the conventional classroom, VR and simulation platforms, such as Labster, Google Expeditions, and Oculus, are revolutionising the educational system. Students have the opportunity to investigate scientific topics in a simulated setting with realistic circumstances via the use of Labster, which allows them to perform interactive virtual lab experiments. With the help of Google Expeditions, students may experience the thrill of going on virtual field excursions to historical monuments, museums, and cultural places without ever having to leave the comfort of their classrooms. Students are able to better visualise difficult topics and obtain deeper insights with the assistance of Oculus, which promotes engagement via interactive storytelling and high-definition simulations. Because of these tools, experiential learning is encouraged, which in turn makes education more dynamic, accessible, and effective [21] (Table 2.9).

Table 2.9 Simulation and VR tools

Tool	Educational application
Labster	Virtual science labs with interactive experiments
Google expeditions	Virtual field trips and 360-degree tours
Oculus	Custom humanities-based VR experiences (e.g., ancient civilisations)

2.4.7 Digital Humanities Tools

Textual analysis, linguistic studies, digital archiving, and data visualisation are all areas that may be considerably improved with the use of specialised digital tools. These technologies are very beneficial for studying and teaching in the humanities. A user-friendly platform for analysing text corpora is provided by Voyant Tools. This platform enables academics to investigate word frequencies, trends, and thematic patterns in literary masterpieces, historical records, and academic writings. Scholars are able to study word patterns, collocations, and textual linkages within enormous datasets with the use of the strong concordance tool known as AntConc, which was developed specifically for the field of linguistic studies. Omeka is a platform that assists digital archiving by allowing educational institutions and institutes of higher learning to construct well-organised and interactive archives for academic projects, cultural artefacts, and historical documents. TAPoR, which stands for Text Analysis Portal for Research, is a collection of several text-analysis tools that allows for a more in-depth evaluation of features of language, rhetoric, and style. The combination of these instruments offers academics, teachers, and students new approaches to investigating topics related to the humanities, including the promotion of more profound understandings and the preservation of information in digital forms that are easily accessible [22] (Fig. 2.4 and Table 2.10).

2.4.8 Integration and Interoperability

In current educational contexts, interoperability across digital learning technologies is vital for efficiency and scalability. Standards such as SCORM (Sharable information Object Reference Model), LTI (Learning Tools Interoperability), and xAPI (Experience API) make it possible to integrate seamlessly across a variety of LMS. This ensures that both teachers and students are able to access information without encountering any technological obstacles. E-learning information that is organised may be made portable and reused across a variety of platforms thanks to SCORM, which helps the process. LTI makes it possible for third-party apps to interface with learning management system environments in a seamless manner, which improves immersive learning experiences. xAPI, on the other hand, monitors learner activity outside of the LMS, recording real-world learning interactions across a variety of devices and forms. These standards ensure that user experiences are optimised, that

Fig. 2.4 Digital Technologies [23]

Table 2.10 Digital humanities tools

Tool	Functionality
Voyant tools	Web-based text analysis and word cloud generation
AntConc	Concordance software for corpus linguistics
Omeka	Digital curation and exhibition of historical/cultural artifacts
TAPoR	Access to a wide array of textual analysis tools for humanities

Table 2.11 Integration and interoperability

Standard	Description
SCORM	Enables course content interoperability across LMS platforms
LTI	Allows external tools to launch from within an LMS securely
xAPI	Tracks a wide range of learner activities, including informal learning

data monitoring is improved, and that adaptive learning technologies are supported, all of which contribute to education being more dynamic and accessible [24, 25] (Table 2.11).

2.4.9 Challenges and Considerations

Although software tools have brought about a revolution in education, they also bring significant obstacles that need to be addressed in order to ensure that their deployment is both fair and successful. Due to the fact that many students do not have access to dependable internet or proper equipment, the digital gap continues to be a substantial obstacle, which results in chances for learning that are unequally distributed. Institutions should have strong rules in place to prevent the unauthorised access or abuse of student information, which is another worry about data privacy. In addition, there are challenges associated with training demands, including the fact that both teachers and students need sufficient teaching in order to effectively traverse sophisticated digital technologies. Lastly, maintenance is quite important, since software has to be updated on a regular basis and get professional assistance in order to guarantee the highest possible level of performance and safety. For the purpose of maximising the advantages that technology may bring to education, addressing these problems is essential.

Thus, software tools have revolutionised the way information is presented, accessed, and interacted with in modern education, making them crucial. When it comes to the humanities, technology does more than just make learning easier; it also revolutionises education by offering novel methods to engage with texts, cultures, and intricate concepts. Enhanced comprehension of historical narratives and philosophical discourse may be achieved by the use of digital platforms, which make it possible to conduct more in-depth analyses through the utilisation of textual mining, virtual archives, and multimedia storytelling. Implementing these tools with careful consideration ensures that they are accessible to a wider audience, which in turn enables students from a variety of backgrounds to participate in scholarship. Through the ongoing development of education, software continues to play an essential role in maintaining the fundamental principles of humanistic inquiry while simultaneously adapting them to a world that is becoming more digital and networked [26, 27].

2.5 Past Studies on Technology Integration in Humanities

In the course of the last several decades, academics have conducted substantial study on the role that technology plays in the field of humanities education. Their goal has been to get an understanding of the influence that technology has on pedagogy, research methodology, and student participation. Traditional techniques to textual interpretation, critical analysis, and philosophical inquiry have been revolutionised by the introduction of data-driven and interactive methodologies that have been made possible by digital technologies. These methods have enhanced learning experiences. Digital archives, computational text analysis, and virtual simulations are examples of technologies that make it possible to do more in-depth research on literary works, historical narratives, and cultural studies. In addition, online platforms encourage cooperation and extend access to scholarly discourse, which helps to ensure that education in the humanities continues to be dynamic and relevant in a world that is becoming more digital [28].

2.5.1 Historical Evolution of Research Trends

In the beginning, notably throughout the 1980s and 1990s, research concentrated on the utilisation of word processors, electronic databases, and early digital archives in classrooms that were dedicated to the study of the humanities curriculum. Studies began to focus on web-based learning platforms, the digitisation of primary materials, and the pedagogical potential of hypertext and multimedia as the internet became more accessible to the general public.

Beginning in the 2000s and continuing beyond that decade, academics started investigating cutting-edge technologies such as text mining, digital storytelling, and the use of learning analytics. Scholars have been encouraged to reassess conventional research approaches by adopting computational tools as a result of the emergence of the discipline of DH, which established itself as a prominent force [29].

2.5.2 Pedagogical Benefits

Learning that is improved by technology has brought about a substantial transformation in the field of humanities education by bringing dynamic tools that increase engagement, deepen understanding, and stimulate cooperation. The creation of immersive learning experiences that catch students' attention and motivate them to study is accomplished via the use of gamified platforms, digital archives, and interactive timelines. The use of these technologies enables students to visualise historical events, investigate original sources, and participate in challenges that improve the effectiveness of their ability to retain information. Students have the opportunity to undertake in-depth study and acquire exposure to a variety of views thanks to the availability of digital archives, which give quick access to enormous collections of materials. Educators are able to build rich learning environments that enable students to actively engage with complicated topics rather than passively consuming information by incorporating parts of multimedia into their lessons.

Technology has not only increased students' participation, but it has also transformed the way they analyse and interpret texts, which has improved their critical thinking and understanding. A more in-depth contact with literary works, historical records, and philosophical writings may be facilitated via the use of digital annotation tools, discussion forums, and multimedia resources. Through the use of these tools, students are able to mark up texts in a collaborative manner, highlight important ideas, and participate in conversations that help them improve their comprehension. Research that was conducted in 2015 by McCarty and colleagues indicated that students who used collaborative digital annotation tools did much better in comprehension and theme analysis tests compared to those who relied on conventional approaches. This research demonstrates how technology gives students the ability to investigate topics in greater detail while also improving their analytical abilities at the same time. Additionally, platforms such as Google Docs, blogs, and wikis promote peer-to-peer collaboration, which enables students to take part in collective problem-solving, co-author papers, and exchange ideas with one another. Learning is becoming more participatory, accessible, and influential as a result of the combination of technology and education in the humanities, which continues to extend chances for intellectual discovery.

2.5.3 *Methodologies Used in Past Studies*

For the purpose of conducting an in-depth investigation into the impacts of educational technology on learning, engagement, and pedagogy, research on the influence of educational technology in the humanities makes use of both qualitative and quantitative research approaches. Case studies, interviews, and focus groups are examples of qualitative research methods that may be used to get insights into the experiences that educators and students have had using digital technologies. These methods allow students and educators to explore their perspectives, obstacles, and the complex ways in which technology enriches humanities education. Researchers are able to evaluate the ways in which technology encourages critical thinking and cooperation via the use of content analysis, which involves analysing online conversations, digital annotations, and interactions with multimedia. The subjective and experienced components of technology-integrated learning are captured by these methodologies, which give unique insights on the role that technology plays in altering education in the humanities because of its impact.

Methodologies like as surveys, experimental research, and learning analytics are examples of quantitative approaches that give quantifiable data on the performance and engagement of students. The results of experimental research compare the outcomes of conventional learning settings against those of technology-enhanced learning environments, while surveys attempt to evaluate larger trends in the uptake of technology. Learning analytics, which monitors digital interactions and participation, gives academics the ability to evaluate trends in understanding and engagement, providing them with data-driven insights into the most successful technology interventions. By integrating these methods, academics are able to get a comprehensive grasp of the ways in which digital tools are transforming education in the humanities. This helps to ensure that technologically driven innovations are deliberately included into academic frameworks (Table 2.12).

Mixed-methods approaches are increasingly favoured, as they capture both statistical patterns and the lived experiences of users.

2.5.4 *Notable Institutional Case Studies*

Palladio, a digital visualisation tool, has been included into the humanities courses offered by Stanford University. This integration provides students with sophisticated

Table 2.12 Methodologies used in researches

Methodology	Description
Case studies	In-depth analysis of specific classroom or institutional experiences
Surveys and questionnaires	Collection of self-reported data from students and educators
Ethnographic studies	Observational research focusing on classroom dynamics and technology use
Experimental designs	Comparisons between technology-enhanced and traditional instructional approaches

tools to understand and display complicated relational data. Recent research has shown that the use of this strategy has resulted in a considerable improvement in the students' capacity to analyse links between historical personalities, texts, and events. Learners are able to see complex networks within humanities study by using Palladio, which makes abstract notions more physical and accessible to them. This method illustrates how the use of technology may improve analytical thinking and data literacy in fields that have historically been centred on textual analysis.

Similarly, the DH Summer Institute (DHSI) at the University of Victoria is a program that helps to cultivate competence in the field of digital humanities. Through this program, both academics and students are given the opportunity to obtain training in various technologies, including Omeka and the Text Encoding Initiative (TEI). The use of these technologies helps archive initiatives by providing academics with the ability to digitise, organise, and make historical records more available to a wider audience. In order to develop immersive learning experiences, the MetaLAB (MET) at Harvard University has adopted an interdisciplinary approach by combining information from the humanities with interactive technologies. Their programs are supported by research that is based on evaluation, which guarantees that digital efforts successfully improve learner engagement and academic results. When taken as a whole, these case studies highlight the significance of institutional support and well-designed curriculum in the process of effectively integrating technology into humanities education. Universities are able to make use of digital resources to make research approaches more extensive and to increase the dissemination of information if they prioritise the execution of strategic strategies.

2.5.5 Challenges Identified in Literature

Despite the fact that technology has improved humanities education significantly, scholars keep pointing out important obstacles that prevent its widespread use. Faculty resistance is a major obstacle; it is commonly associated with low levels of digital literacy and scepticism regarding the value of technology in the pursuit of humanistic knowledge. Many teachers are reluctant to use digital technologies in the classroom because they worry it would water down the interpretive and reflective nature of the humanities. Faculty members may have difficulty recognising the value of digital integration without proper training and institutional backing, which can further delay adoption rates.

Furthermore, many institutions are unable to fully take advantage of technological improvements due to infrastructure deficiencies, which include restricted access to computers, poor internet connections, and obsolete software. When digital tools are accessible, pedagogical misalignment may be a problem, especially when the focus is on gimmicks rather than real academic investigation. The fundamental goals of humanities education are in danger of being undermined when technological advancements place an emphasis on form above intellectual depth. Faculty and students alike often lament a lack of time to adequately understand and use new technology, which poses the additional challenge of time restrictions. Many scholars, like Svensson (2010), warn against a hasty adoption of digital tools that could undermine the analytical and reflective traditions that are fundamental to humanities education. They stress the need for careful planning and execution of these strategies to make sure technology enhances, rather than supplants, fundamental academic principles.

2.5.6 *Equity and Access Issues*

The digital divide remains one of education's most pressing issues, particularly as technology continues to shape modern learning experiences. Research by Warschauer (2011) and Selwyn (2016) demonstrates how students from poor backgrounds often encounter challenges to acquiring critical digital tools such as devices, consistent internet connections, and competent technical assistance. These differences may exacerbate existing educational inequities, preventing disadvantaged students from properly using online resources, interactive learning platforms, and digital collaboration possibilities. Without targeted interventions, the gap between students who have access and those who do not continues to widen, limiting the potential of technology-enhanced education to promote inclusion and equitable learning opportunities.

Addressing this problem requires smart legislative changes and deliberate design initiatives that prioritise fair access. Initiatives like government-funded technology initiatives, subsidised internet services, and institutional assistance for device distribution may help bridge the gap and guarantee that all students, regardless of socioeconomic status, have access to digital learning. Furthermore, inclusive design principles such as offline-accessible resources, mobile-friendly platforms, and community-based digital literacy programs can help to democratise access to educational technology. By applying these solutions, institutions and governments may help to create a more balanced technology environment in education, ensuring that digital technologies serve as facilitators rather than obstacles to knowledge acquisition.

Research in AI, gamification, virtual reality, and ethical issues has recently shown a number of intriguing avenues for further investigation into the use of technology in humanities teaching. Automated teaching and grading assistants are being investigated as potential AI tools, which brings up crucial questions concerning equity while providing scalability. Personalised feedback, assistance in honing analytical abilities, and better task management for educators are all benefits of AI-driven learning systems. Researchers are still wary of these tools, however, since they want to make sure they don't compromise academic honesty or create algorithmic biases that hurt certain students. To guarantee the ethical and successful implementation of AI in humanities training, continuous evaluations will be required as the technology evolves. Additionally, gamification has become a game-changing method of education, especially with the rise of platforms like Twine that provide an interactive storytelling framework for students to explore story logic and structure. Students may engage in a deep exploration of literary topics and build their critical thinking abilities via the integration of decision-making aspects. At the same time, VR is transforming the way students learn about culture and history by providing digital recreations of cultural locations, simulations of contemporary settings, and opportunities for participatory storytelling that enhance comprehension. Educators should consider the ethical implications of surveillance, algorithmic prejudice, and data privacy as they investigate these technologies. There is an increasing amount of research that highlights the need of continuous review and ethical reflexivity to make sure that new technologies provide students agency without taking away their rights or undermining the interpretative and reflective foundation of humanities education. Institutions may use technology to its best potential to improve education without compromising its core principles by carefully incorporating these innovations [30].

Synthesis and Implications

Research regularly shows that digital technology may improve humanities education by increasing participation, accessibility, and instructional efficacy when carefully incorporated. These innovations let students connect with books, historical events, and cultural artefacts in new ways, making learning more immersive and interactive. Scholars emphasise that technology should enhance humanistic research, not replace it. Educators must integrate digital technologies with humanities ideals and goals to ensure that innovations improve critical thinking, contemplation, and interpretative analysis. Several major proposals to maximise humanities educational technology advantages are in the literature. Faculty require ongoing professional development to use digital technologies successfully. Prioritise inclusive and adaptable learning settings to ensure technology accommodates various learners and reduces access inequities. Scholars also recommend institutional expenditures in infrastructure and support, such as trustworthy digital resources, software updates, and IT support, to maintain technological integration. Long-term assessment of educational technology effects is needed to evaluate efficacy, identify obstacles, and improve digital techniques. These essential characteristics may help universities balance technology-enhanced humanities teaching while preserving the disciplines' interpretive and intellectual core [31].

There is a wealth of information and important lessons to be learnt from the body of academic study on the incorporation of technology in humanities education. The fact that it illustrates that success is not just dependent on technology but rather on the synergy of deliberate design, educational integrity, and institutional vision is shown by this development. For the sake of future study, it is imperative that digital innovation be brought into alignment with the intellectual and ethical underpinnings of the humanities.

2.6 The Shift to Blended and Remote Learning

The transition to blended and remote learning is one of the most major developments that has occurred in the techniques that are used to offer education over the course of the last twenty years. In the field of humanities, where conventional instructional techniques have traditionally depended on face-to-face contact, critical debate, and shared experiences, this transition has had a particularly significant influence. What constitutes successful education, who participates in the learning process, and how learning takes place have all been rethought as a result of the use of digital resources [32].

2.6.1 Definitions and Modalities

Blended learning combines traditional in-person teaching with online components, allowing students to engage with course materials both inside and outside the classroom. Remote learning, on the other hand, involves delivering education entirely through digital platforms without physical presence. Both modalities rely on a suite of technologies to facilitate content delivery, communication, and assessment [33].

2.6.2 Drivers of the Shift

The implementation of blended and remote learning has been propelled by a number of interrelated reasons that have revolutionised the educational landscape of the current day. There has been a significant contribution made by technological improvements, which have resulted in increased accessibility to high-speed internet, cloud-based platforms, and user-friendly interfaces. These advancements have made online learning more efficient and accessible to a wider audience. Through the implementation of these technologies, digital collaboration, interactive learning experiences, and real-time feedback mechanisms have been improved. As a result, the experience of receiving an education from a distant location is no more one that is passive but rather one that is dynamic and engaging.

Furthermore, flexibility and accessibility have emerged as important motivators for both students and educational institutions alike. Students are no longer restricted by geographical limits or inflexible timetables, which enables education to meet a wide range of needs and support efforts that promote lifelong learning. As a result of global events, like the COVID-19 pandemic, which drove a quick move towards digital solutions as conventional classroom settings proved unworkable, the need for flexible education has only increased because of these occurrences. Institutional innovation has also been adopted by educational institutions such as universities and colleges, who have seen the advantages of modernising curriculum, lowering operating costs, and increasing enrolment via the provision of flexible learning alternatives. Blended and remote learning are positioned to stay crucial to educational strategies as these trends continue to expand. They will shape the future of academia via technology-driven solutions due to their ability to effectively use technology.

2.6.3 *Impacts on Humanities Pedagogy*

Digital shifts in humanities education have led to rethinking old pedagogical practices to keep discussion, interpretation, and debate important to learning. One major trend is virtual seminars, where Zoom and Microsoft Teams enable real-time talks that mirror conventional lectures. These platforms enable meaningful exchanges between students and instructors across borders. Breakout rooms, live polling, and chat make remote learning more engaging.

Hypothesis and other digital annotation systems offer collaborative textual study, another major leap. Students may highlight, remark, and debate sections in shared materials, expanding their connection with literature and philosophy. Online digital archives provide students access to enormous collections of primary and secondary materials without physical location restrictions, revolutionising study. Students may now access varied resources that were previously unavailable, expanding intellectual investigation. Many students increasingly submit multimedia presentations, podcasts, and digital storytelling projects instead of essays due to the move towards creative assignments. These forms promote creative thinking and multidisciplinary collaboration, making humanities education more dynamic and relevant to modern communication. These digital technologies are helping colleges preserve humanities learning while adjusting to the changing educational context [34].

2.6.4 *Core Technologies*

Digital technologies and platforms for education, collaboration, and evaluation have helped mix and remote learning. Moodle and Canvas, two popular LMS, let instructors organise material, manage assignments, and connect with students. These LMS systems simplify learning with organised modules, discussion forums, and grading, giving instructors and students convenient access to course resources. Interactive lectures, seminars, and debates via Zoom and Microsoft Teams replicate classroom interactions in real time. Video conferencing, chat, and collaborative workspaces enable students to join in live sessions, split into smaller discussion groups, and participate in interactive learning activities. Google Docs and Padlet allow students to discuss, co-edit, and exchange ideas in real time. These platforms are useful in humanities education, where textual interpretation, discussion, and debate are important. Assessment and feedback have also changed with digital integration. Turnitin helps instructors identify plagiarism and academic integrity in student submissions, whereas Quizlet improves formative assessment with interactive quizzes, flashcards, and personalised learning paths. These technologies promote material distribution, peer engagement, collaborative learning, and adaptive learning, making digital education more effective and interesting. These tools allow universities to modernise instruction while maintaining humanities rigour.

2.6.5 *Learning Theories in Practice*

Online and blended learning complement numerous educational ideas, showing how technology may assist multiple learning paradigms. Constructivism emphasises active learning via experience and reflection, making digital environments excellent for self-paced exploration. Online debates, interactive simulations, and virtual collaboration let students think critically and apply ideas. Instead of passive learning, technology-enhanced education encourages students to actively generate knowledge. Connectivism, which sees learning as networked, advocates digital tool use in education. This approach emphasises how information is spread among online databases, social media, and collaborative platforms rather than a single teacher or textbook. Students may cooperate across borders, explore resources independently, and engage with varied viewpoints via digital learning. Andragogy (Adult Learning Theory) emphasises self-directed, flexible learning, which fits online education. Digital platforms that enable flexibility, autonomy, and personalised learning serve adult learners who mix education with work and life. These beliefs show that technology makes education more accessible, participatory, and relevant to contemporary learners [35].

2.6.6 *Equity, Inclusion, and Digital Divide*

Blended and remote learning have increased educational access but also revealed structural inequalities that must be addressed for justice and inclusiveness. Students without dependable computers or internet connections struggle in digital learning settings. This digital divide may reduce participation, cooperation, and academic achievement, exacerbating socioeconomic disadvantages. Digital literacy is another issue since not all students and instructors can use complicated digital systems. Learners may struggle to use online resources without proper training, hindering knowledge gain and engagement.

Learning contexts are also important for student development, and family settings may be ineffective, especially for disadvantaged groups. Students might struggle to concentrate and engage with courses due to distractions, lack of quiet study rooms, and minimal academic help. To address these issues, institutions must implement inclusive digital strategies, including device lending programs, technical support for troubleshooting and adaptation, and digital literacy training for students and educators. Education systems may reduce inequities and make learning more egalitarian and accessible by prioritising these methods.

2.6.7 Challenges and Criticisms

Digital learning offers many benefits, but it has also been criticised, especially in humanities education, where conversation and interpersonal contact are key. Virtual settings may inhibit spontaneous talks and informal debates that enhance face-to-face discussions, which is a major worry. Video conferencing and discussion boards try to imitate seminar-style interaction, but others believe that they lack the immediacy and depth of in-person debate, harming humanities collaboration. Another major issue is assessment integrity, as online tests challenge academic honesty. As remote testing has grown, plagiarism, unauthorised assistance, and exam monitoring have become issues. Institutions have deployed AI-based proctoring and assignment authenticity checks, but their efficacy and ethics are unclear. Teachers must modify their courses, provide online-friendly resources, and give technological assistance in addition to their conventional teaching duties, increasing their burden. This extra work may cause burnout, especially in fields that need direct participation and personalised feedback. Finally, many educators struggle to keep students engaged in remote settings. Innovative teaching methods are needed to interest pupils due to distractions, screen weariness, and lack of face-to-face connection. Digital learning gives flexibility, but resolving these problems is essential to ensure that technology enhances humanities education.

Blended and remote learning are now crucial to contemporary education and are predicted to last beyond the epidemic. New hybrid classrooms mix in-person and online learners in real time, offering more adaptable learning settings. This strategy bridges conventional classrooms with digital education by allowing students to engage in conversations and collaborative activities remotely. By using video conferencing, interactive whiteboards, and cloud-based collaborative tools, hybrid learning gives students a coherent and engaging education. AI-driven personalisation, which adapts instructional material to individual learning styles, is another major improvement. AI lets adaptive learning systems assess students' progress and provide resources that match their skills and weaknesses. This personalised training improves understanding and retention and supports several learning styles. Gamification and VR/AR are also changing history, literature, and philosophy participation. Students may interact with historical reconstructions, literary tales, and philosophical ideas via dynamic simulations using these immersive technologies. These advances will keep blended and distant education current, effective, and engaging as educational institutions improve digital learning methodologies. The landscape of humanities education has been completely reshaped as a result of the trend towards mixed and distant learning. In spite of the fact that there are still obstacles to overcome, especially with respect to inclusion and engagement, the advantages of accessibility, flexibility, and pedagogical innovation are substantial. In order to ensure that digital modalities complement rather than replace the human-centered ethos that is at the core of the humanities, educators and institutions need to continue to develop their methods.

2.7 Digital Literacy in the Humanities

A competence that is now considered important across all academic disciplines is digital literacy, which may be defined as the capacity to seek, assess, produce, and convey knowledge via the use of digital tools. In the field of humanities, where research has typically focused on critical interpretation, textual analysis, and cultural context, digital literacy broadens the toolset that is accessible to students and academics. Pedagogical techniques for building digital abilities, as well as problems and concerns for implementation, are discussed in this part. Additionally, the components of digital literacy, its significance in humanities education, and the value of digital literacy are discussed.

2.7.1 Defining Digital Literacy

Digital literacy goes beyond basic "computer skills" to encompass a spectrum of proficiencies:

1. Information Literacy: Identifying reputable digital sources, evaluating credibility, and understanding intellectual property and citation ethics.
2. Media Literacy: Interpreting and creating multimedia content images, audio, video and recognising how media shapes meaning.
3. Data Literacy. Understanding how to collect, analyse, visualise, and interpret quantitative and qualitative data.
4. Technical Fluency: Navigating software tools (e.g., text analysis, digital archives, content management), troubleshooting common issues, and maintaining digital security.
5. Digital Communication: Crafting effective digital messages blog posts, social media updates, presentations and collaborating online.
6. Ethical and Social Awareness: Recognising the implications of digital footprints, privacy, accessibility, and algorithmic bias.

Together, these facets equip humanities students to engage critically with digital environments, whether they are conducting archival research, producing digital exhibits, or participating in online scholarly conversations.

2.7.2 The Importance of Digital Literacy in Humanities

Scholarly perspectives have been enlarged in a number of ways that are potentially transformational as a result of the use of digital technologies into humanities study and instruction. Students and researchers now have access to large collections of historical documents, literary works, and cultural artefacts because to the proliferation of digital archives, online databases, and open-access repositories. This enhanced availability of primary sources has led to an exponential growth in the availability of primary materials. Nevertheless, this abundance creates additional challenges: students need to acquire critical thinking skills in order to evaluate the validity and provenance of digitised resources, as well as to differentiate between reputable sources and those that are deceptive or otherwise lacking. Scholars in the field of humanities are increasingly adding tools for source verification and metadata analysis into their research methodology in order to guarantee the accuracy of their findings. This is because digital collections are continuing to expand.

Further revolutions in humanities study have been brought about by developments in computer analysis, which have made it possible for academics to investigate texts and cultural data on a scale that has never been seen before. Researchers are able to recognise patterns across huge corpora by using tools such as text mining, network analysis, and geographic information system mapping. These tools allow them to discover patterns such as trends in literature, social networks within historical societies, and geographical distributions of cultural phenomena. These techniques provide novel viewpoints on common topics, bridging the gap between the humanities and data science in order to unearth insights that would be difficult to discover using more standard methods. In addition, the transmission of creative works has expanded, with digital storytelling, interactive timelines, and multimedia exhibitions revolutionising the methods in which knowledge is disseminated. In addition to improving accessibility, these formats make it possible for a wide range of audiences to participate in humanistic research in ways that are more interactive and participative.

Another significant change is the proliferation of collaborative scholarship, which is made possible by digital platforms like as GitHub and Omeka, as well as digital annotation tools. These platforms encourage co-creation, peer review, and community-driven research to be conducted. The availability of these resources gives academics the ability to collaborate across institutions and fields of study, which in turn encourages interdisciplinary cooperation and the sharing of information. Additionally, technological fluency has become a benefit for graduates of humanities programs as a result of the need for digital competences in the labour market. The acquisition of skills in digital project management, content production, and data analysis provides students with the opportunity to acquire practical skills that are useful in a variety of professional domains, ranging from the academic world and publishing to museum curation and technology-driven positions. As digital approaches continue to advance, the intentional incorporation of these methodologies into humanities education will continue to be crucial in order to strike a balance between innovation and the reflective and analytical heart of the scientific profession.

2.7.3 Pedagogical Strategies for Teaching Digital Literacy

Embedded Skill-Building

A structured approach that facilitates the progressive development of skills is necessary for the effective integration of digital instruments into humanities education. Scaffolded tasks provide pupils fundamental knowledge before bigger projects. An introduction to Voyant Tools may teach students word-frequency analysis and text visualisation before applying these abilities to independent study. This step-by-step approach helps pupils master digital methods and analytical ideas. Layered lessons teach digital tools from basics to sophisticated customisation. For example, a WordPress lesson may start with site setup before moving on to plugin integration and sophisticated design changes. Using video demonstrations, interactive tutorials, and hands-on labs, instructors may accommodate varied learning styles and encourage exploration. Digital literacy helps students use technology critically in humanities studies. Scaffolded assignments and tiered lessons improve technical skills and humanistic curiosity.

Project-Based Learning

Interactive and research-driven humanities coursework are now possible using digital resources. Digital exhibitions, where students create small-scale online shows using Omeka or Neatline, are effective. Students may investigate historical topics by organising archive materials, developing metadata, optimising photographs, and constructing user-friendly interfaces. Through this method, students connect with primary materials and learn digital curation, historical interpretation, and visual storytelling. This hands-on activity teaches digital humanities study and the need of contextualising artefacts within historical narratives. Students may use computational techniques to analyse literary texts in text mining projects. Instructors may help students create word-cloud visualisations, topic models, or network graphs of novels, poetry, or essays to illustrate linguistic patterns, theme frameworks, and social relationships. These tasks combine quantitative analysis with literary inquiry by encouraging students to analyse their results' cultural relevance. Visualising reoccurring themes or mapping character interactions gives students new views on literary interpretation, showing how digital approaches may enhance humanistic content comprehension. These programs allow institutions to combine computational analysis with critical thinking, enhancing humanities education's reflective aspect.

Peer Collaboration and Workshops

Hackathons and DH laboratories are useful ways to involve students and professors in digital initiatives. DH problems like constructing a community oral-history site or an interactive map of local heritage encourage cooperation and problem-solving in these short, intense sessions. Students learn digital tools, improve their technical abilities, and contribute to important projects that combine historical research and technology innovation by working together in real time. These events promote multidisciplinary cooperation, bringing together humanities, computer science, and digital design experts to create interactive resources. Peer teaching, where students conduct workshops on digital technologies they know, is another effective learning technique. This technique encourages collaborative learning, letting students practise by teaching others. Students gain confidence in using technology in humanities study by guiding their peers via digital platforms like Omeka, GIS mapping software, and text-mining tools. Peer education encourages debate and idea sharing while eliminating top-down instruction. Hackathons, DH laboratories, and peer-led workshops show how collaborative and experiential learning can help digital humanities flourish, giving students technical skills and a greater understanding of humanism.

2.7.4 *Critical Reflection*

DH education with reflective and ethical components improves analytical and practical abilities. Digital portfolios, where students chronicle their digital work, are useful. The portfolios document their methodological choices, obstacles, and learning from using digital technologies. Critical thinking and technical competence are strengthened by students' reflections on their research methods and ethical duties. Digital portfolios also indicate how students improve their digital skills while retaining academic integrity.

Ethics case studies are crucial for discussing difficult topics like data privacy, consent, and algorithmic prejudice. Real-world situations like processing user-generated material under copyright constraints or digital archiving ethical concerns urge students to critically consider technology's effects on humanities study. Students learn about ethical digital research and the social implications of technical choices from these case studies. Digital humanities education gives pupils a well-rounded view on technology and preserves its interpretive richness by including reflective practice and ethical inquiry (Table 2.13).

Table 2.13 Tools and platforms for digital literacy

Category	Tools/examples	Skills developed
Text analysis	Voyant Tools, AntConc, MALLET	Word frequency, topic modelling, concordance analysis
Data visualisation	Gephi, Palladio, Tableau Public	Network graphs, timelines, spatial mapping
Digital archives	Omeka, CONTENTdm, Islandora	Metadata creation, digitisation workflows, exhibit curation
Content creation	WordPress, Pressbooks, Scalar	Web publishing, storytelling, multimedia integration
Collaborative editing	Google Docs, Hypothes.is, Git/GitHub	Real-time annotation, version control, peer review
GIS mapping	QGIS, ArcGIS Online, StoryMap JS	Geospatial analysis, map creation, geovisual narratives

2.7.5 *Assessment of Digital Literacy*

To promote meaningful engagement with both digital tools and scholarly inquiry, effective assessment in digital humanities education demands a balance between technical skill and critical thinking. This is necessary to ensure that students are able to comprehend the material. The use of rubrics that include dual criteria, which assess both the technical execution and the humanistic analysis of student projects, is one method that may be used to accomplish this goal. For instance, while evaluating a digital archive or an interactive website, teachers should take into consideration aspects such as the precision of the information, the functioning of the digital tools, and the consistency of the user interfaces. At the same time, they are required to evaluate the students' interpretation of sources, contextualisation of material, and use of approaches from the humanities.

2.7.6 *Challenges and Considerations*

The use of digital resources into humanities education presents various obstacles, necessitating creative solutions for sustainability and accessibility. One significant impediment is resource limits, since not all colleges can afford specialised software or high-performance computer resources. To overcome these economic hurdles, many instructors turn to open-source and web-based alternatives that provide capabilities equal to commercial tools but without the financial burden. Using free digital platforms allows students to do digital humanities research without institutions having to spend a lot of money on technology.

AI, mobile learning, and collaborative efforts are all having an impact on the future of digital humanities education. One potential avenue is AI-enhanced literacy, which uses AI-driven analytics and generative tools like large-language models to aid textual discovery and academic research. These tools enable students to analyse patterns, produce insights, and interact with difficult materials in novel ways. Educators, on the other hand, emphasise the need of combining AI with critical frameworks that allow students to question algorithmic outputs and ensure they grasp the biases, limits, and ethical consequences of automated processing.

Furthermore, mobile and multimodal learning is broadening the scope of humanities research by using smartphones and tablets for field-based data collecting, oral history recording, and location-aware storytelling. These technologies enable students to interact with historical and cultural narratives in dynamic, immersive ways, bridging traditional scholarship with contemporary digital practices. Furthermore, cross-institutional collaborations are becoming increasingly important in digital literacy initiatives, with universities organising consortia to exchange digital resources, training modules, and best-practice repositories. These collaborations scale digital humanities initiatives by combining expertise and technological assets, ensuring greater access and knowledge exchange across institutions. Together, these trends point to a future in which technology enhances humanities education while preserving its interpretive and analytical roots.

Literacy in digital technology in the humanities is not an optional add-on but rather a fundamental competency for the study and teaching of the twenty-first century. Educators in the field of humanities guarantee that students continue to be active participants to cultural discourse, both on and off the screen, by providing them with the skills necessary to critically interact with digital media, analyse complicated information, and develop multimedia narratives. In order to ensure that digital literacy does not supplant the humanistic values that are at the core of our disciplines, it is imperative that our curriculum, assessment methodologies, and institutional commitments continue to grow in tandem with the progression of technology.

2.8 Mobile Learning and Apps

Mobile devices have completely altered the ways in which students get access to, consume, and generate information in this age of digital technology. The term "mobile learning" (often abbreviated as "m-learning") refers to the educational processes that are facilitated by the use of portable digital devices such as laptops, tablets, and smartphones. In the field of education pertaining to the humanities, mobile learning paves the way for new opportunities to have learning experiences that are adaptable, personalised, and aware of their surroundings. This section examines the notion of mobile learning, as well as the many kinds of educational applications, pedagogical practices, advantages and drawbacks, and implications for the future of humanities education [36].

2.8.1 Understanding Mobile Learning

The method in which education is accessible and experienced has been revolutionised by mobile learning, especially in the fields of the humanities, which include subjects like literature, history, philosophy, and cultural studies. Transportation, pervour curriculum, assessment methodologies, and institutional commitments must continueasiveness, and awareness of the surrounding environment are the three distinguishing features that contribute significantly to its success. As a result of the mobility of smartphones and tablets, learning is no longer tied to the confines of the classroom; it can now take place anywhere, including at home, while travelling, or even in public places where intellectual conversations and discovery take place naturally. Because of this flexibility, students are able to interact with the contents of the course on their own terms, which makes education more adaptive to the specific requirements of each person.

The pervasiveness of mobile learning further improves accessibility by guaranteeing that students may access materials whenever they choose, so reducing the conventional boundaries of time and place. Whether students are accessing original texts, engaging in collaborative annotation activities via platforms such as Hypotheses.is, or attending virtual debates on historical and literary topics, mobile learning makes it possible for students to have an educational experience that is both continuous and immersive. In addition, the features made available by its context-awareness enable digital gadgets to adjust to the preferences, locations, and study routines of their users. AR apps, for example, provide students the opportunity to tour historical locations in real time, therefore enhancing their comprehension via the use of interactive, location-based learning. It is expected that the use of mobile technology in humanities education will continue to develop as mobile technology continues to grow. This will provide learners with novel methods to connect with texts, ideas, and cultural narratives that go beyond the restrictions of conventional bounds [37].

2.8.2 Categories of Educational Apps in Humanities

Humanities educational apps enhance learning with digital libraries, text analysis tools, interactive platforms, augmented reality, and collaborative environments. Project Gutenberg and JSTOR provide substantial literary and scholarly resources, while Hypothes.is facilitates collaborative annotation and debate. Twine and Kahoot! use immersive learning with interactive storytelling and gamification. Google Arts & Culture and HistoryView VR make history and philosophy more palpable via interactive explorations of historical landmarks and cultural tales. Users may curate and engage with archive content on Omeka and Neatline, enhancing historical and literary understanding. Google Docs and Padlet facilitate collaborative learning and knowledge building through shared discourse. Language and translation programs like

Table 2.14 Educational apps in humanities

App category	Example apps	Functions in humanities
Reading & annotation	Kindle, Pocket, Hypothes.is	Reading e-books, annotating texts, sharing interpretations
Language learning	Duolingo, Memrise, Babbel	Vocabulary building, pronunciation practice, cultural immersion
Note-taking & writing	Evernote, Notion, Microsoft OneNote	Organising ideas, drafting essays, recording lecture notes
Research & reference	JSTOR, Google Scholar, Wikipedia	Accessing academic articles, encyclopedic knowledge
Multimedia storytelling	StoryMapJS, Canva, Adobe Spark	Creating visual timelines, narratives, and infographics
Podcasting & audiobooks	Audible, Anchor, Google Podcasts	Listening to scholarly lectures, literature, and student podcasts
AR	Civilisations AR, Google Arts & Culture	Virtual museum tours, immersive history experiences
Task management	Trello, Todoist, Microsoft To Do	Project planning, assignment tracking

Duolingo and DeepL let users learn in other languages and cultures, while ethics and philosophy simulations test critical thinking with real-world challenges. These apps improve humanities education by boosting creativity, accessibility, and scholarship via digital innovation [38] (Table 2.14).

2.8.3 Pedagogical Applications of Mobile Learning

1. **Microlearning**: Mobile applications make bite-sized learning easier and more entertaining for on-the-go consumers. They provide daily vocabulary exams to assist students learn and remember languages, including Latin, French, and Mandarin. Push notifications may provide fascinating historical knowledge, keeping consumers updated about important events and personalities. Quick, five-minute critical thinking tasks based on current news stories let users analyse, reflect, and participate in world events. These little but strong learning modules turn cellphones into excellent educational tools that match busy lives.
2. **Situated and Contextual Learning**: Mobile applications can improve learning by providing material suited to a user's location, making education more immersive and engaging. For instance, an AR software may give guided city tours centred on colonial history, enabling students to experience landmarks, buildings, and monuments with real-time historical insights. Apps that highlight street names cited in great works might be useful for literature students. For example, one could find these names in Charles Dickens' Victorian London

or Chinua Achebe's Nigerian settings. Mobile applications make learning more interesting and relevant by connecting digital material to physical settings, turning commonplace situations into rich educational experiences.

3. **Collaborative Projects**: Mobile platforms are changing the way people engage with one another by creating interactive areas where people can work together and share what they know. Whether for work meetings, class arguments, or just a quick study session, users of platforms like Slack and Microsoft Teams can have live, group conversations and share ideas. By removing geographical constraints, these systems encourage cooperation by letting users participate in real-time or at their own pace. People are more likely to interact with academic materials, research papers, and literature when they have the opportunity to highlight and remark on particular sections using real-time collaborative annotation platforms such as Hypothesis. With the help of these technologies, mobile platforms are able to build learning environments that are dynamic, engaging, and facilitate communication and collaboration more easily than ever before.
4. **Multimedia Creation**: Through the use of a variety of multimedia technologies, students are enabled via mobile technology to participate in imaginative and significant narratives. Students may record and edit oral histories using smartphone mics and programs like Audacity or Anchor, preserving important narratives from various perspectives while collecting personal memories. Similarly, students can use apps like Adobe Rush or Kinemaster, which are designed for mobile devices, to create short documentaries and video essays with professional-quality editing capabilities. Mobile devices are a tremendous tool for teaching and storytelling because they provide students with easy access to resources that let them express themselves, capture historical events, and share their viewpoints in unique ways.

2.8.4 Advantages of Mobile Learning in the Humanities

1. Accessibility: Students can download readings and lectures for offline use, essential in low-connectivity environments.
2. Personalisation: Apps can tailor content to user pace and style for instance, spaced repetition systems (SRS) in language learning.
3. Engagement: Multimedia formats (video, audio, interactive quizzes) foster more dynamic learning experiences.
4. Portability of Learning Spaces: Humanities students can engage in field research, interviews, or museum-based assignments using mobile apps.
5. Sustainability: Reduces the need for paper and physical infrastructure, aligning with eco-conscious education initiatives.

Table 2.15 Challenges and limitations

Challenge	Description
Device inequality	Not all students have equal access to smartphones or tablets
Distractions	Non-academic apps and notifications can fragment attention
Screen fatigue	Prolonged mobile use may strain eyesight and reduce learning efficiency
Data privacy	Many free apps collect user data; GDPR compliance and ethical use are crucial
Limited content design	Small screens may not suit dense textual content (e.g., manuscripts or maps)

2.8.5 *Challenges and Limitations*

There are a number of obstacles and constraints that are encountered in the field of humanities education. These include cultural prejudices, discrepancies in resources, and different social objectives. Cultural biases have the potential to distort educational programs, often favouring dominant narratives while marginalising the viewpoints of indigenous or minority groups. Access to high-quality education is hindered by the differences in resources that exist between developed and developing countries, which in turn perpetuates inequality. A further point to consider is that the objectives of society sometimes prioritise STEM subjects over the humanities, which results in a decrease in funding and interest in topics such as philosophy, history, and art. Additionally, the subjective character of the humanities presents obstacles for evaluation, since it is more difficult to quantify creative thinking and critical thinking than it is to measure technical abilities. Because governments can restrict or change material in order to match it with ideological goals, political meddling further complicates the education of mankind. The fast evolution of digital technology poses a threat to education by depersonalising it and limiting the amount of human connection that is necessary for the development of empathy and ethical thinking. In spite of these challenges, education about humanity continues to be essential for the development of critical thinking, cultural awareness, and moral responsibility. In order to find ways to overcome these challenges and guarantee that it continues to be relevant in a world that is always changing, new solutions are required (Table 2.15).

To address these challenges, educators must design mobile-friendly content with accessibility and minimalism in mind and select apps with strong data ethics.

2.8.6 *Case Studies of Mobile Learning in Humanities*

Case Study 1: Mobile Reading Groups

A university English department launched a semester-long mobile reading circle using Goodreads and WhatsApp. Students read assigned texts and posted weekly insights and discussion questions. Engagement increased, especially among commuter students, and the informal nature encouraged greater participation from shy learners.

Case Study 2: Digital Field Research

History students in a West African university used mobile GPS mapping apps to record colonial architecture in their cities. Their findings were uploaded into a shared StoryMapJS timeline, integrating historical context with geographic data. This hands-on project blended mobile learning, primary data collection, and digital storytelling.

2.8.7 *Best Practices for Implementing Mobile Learning*

Approaching mobile learning optimisation with a mindful mindset is essential for achieving optimal accessibility, usability, and balance. Students should prioritise applications with offline capabilities or little data use when selecting low-bandwidth tools so they can access material even when there is no internet connection. For learning tools to be available to everyone, regardless of their preferred device, they must be compatible with both iOS and Android. Students are given more agency when they participate in digital skills training programs that teach them how to utilise educational applications responsibly, encouraging them to think critically and ethically about technology. The educational benefit of mobile learning goes beyond just being a supplementary activity, and its incorporation into the curriculum as a whole helps to formalise it as an assessment component.

New technology that makes learning more engaging and accessible is shaping the future of mobile learning in the arts and humanities. Apps driven by AI are changing the face of education by tailoring the delivery of content to each student's unique needs and preferences in order to maximise retention and application of course material. Immersive storytelling in gamified learning experiences makes complicated events and tales more engaging and participatory, bringing history and literature to life. In addition, students are able to engage with literary and historical locations in new ways thanks to embodied experiences made possible by the integration of AR and VR into mobile platforms. One example is examining a 3D replica of the Colosseum. One important factor in the democratisation of humanities knowledge is the ongoing proliferation of mobile-friendly OERs. This ensures that educators and students all around the globe have access to free, high-quality educational resources. Thanks to these innovations, mobile devices are becoming potent resources for rich, engaging, and purposeful education.

Thus, mobile learning and educational apps offer humanities educators powerful tools to connect with learners beyond the traditional classroom. From language acquisition to historical fieldwork, mobile technologies create flexible, engaging, and interactive learning experiences. However, successful implementation requires thoughtful curation of tools, inclusive access strategies, and pedagogical integration. As technology continues to evolve, so too must humanities instruction—adapting to meet learners where they are: in motion, in context, and in control of their learning journeys.

2.9 Collaborative Software Tools

The process of knowledge creation, refinement, and sharing among students, educators, and researchers is greatly influenced by collaboration, which is an integral part of humanities studies. Whether it's academics co-authoring papers, students doing peer reviews, or teachers creating interdisciplinary lesson plans, the capacity to collaborate in real-time or in real-time improves the level of intellectual engagement. Google Docs, Padlet, Miro, and Microsoft Teams are just a few examples of the digital collaboration tools that have completely changed the way group projects are organised. These platforms allow for effortless communication, collaborative content production, real-time feedback, and the incorporation of multimedia. Learners from all over the world and all walks of life are able to work together effectively on these platforms, which promote inclusion. Using an analysis of their salient characteristics, practical uses, advantages, and disadvantages, this section explores the educational justification for using collaborative technologies in humanities education. The collaborative character of humanities studies may be enhanced by the integration of these digital technologies into educational environments, which allow for stronger academic exchanges and dynamic information sharing [39].

2.9.1 The Pedagogical Case for Collaboration

Conversation, analysis, and the shared building of meaning are the lifeblood of humanities education. In order to achieve these goals, digital technologies are essential for creating spaces where different viewpoints may be discussed and debated. By exposing them to other points of view, they help students hone their analytical skills and create arguments with more substance. Students may examine one other's work, provide constructive criticism, and hone their communication skills via peer feedback systems, which in turn improve writing. In addition, digital platforms facilitate the establishment of interdisciplinary projects, which allow for the cooperation of several academic disciplines to produce ground-breaking research and creative output. In addition to facilitating responsible navigation of online academic environments and the development of common knowledge, these technologies encourage digital citizenship and co-authorship. Collaborative digital platforms guarantee that humanities education is vibrant, inclusive, and intellectually stimulating by drawing on constructivist learning theories. These theories highlight the importance of social interactions and shared experiences in building knowledge.

Table 2.16 Types of collaborative tools in humanities

Tool	Main Features	Application in Humanities
Google Docs	Real-time collaborative writing and commenting, version history	Co-authoring essays, peer review, collaborative textual analysis
Padlet	Multimedia collaborative wall, timeline, map, and grid layouts	Class discussions, thematic mapping, idea boards for literature and history
Microsoft OneDrive	File sharing and real-time co-editing in Word and PowerPoint	Group presentations, shared research bibliographies
Miro	Collaborative whiteboard with sticky notes, diagrams, and templates	Visualising historical events, mapping philosophical concepts
Hypothes.is	Social annotation tool for PDF and HTML documents	Collaborative reading of texts, public marginalia, discussion of primary sources
Slack or Teams	Threaded conversations, file sharing, and integrations with other tools	Class forums, organising group work, archiving discussions

2.9.2 Types of Collaborative Tools in Humanities

By allowing seamless cooperation among academics, students, and institutions, collaborative technologies in the humanities play a significant role in fostering interdisciplinary research, teaching, and public engagement. This is because these tools allow for seamless collaboration. These tools include digital archives and libraries (such as JSTOR and Europeana) to facilitate shared access to resources, annotation and textual analysis platforms (such as Hypothesis is and Voyant Tools) to collectively interpret texts, and project management systems (such as Trello and Asana) to organise research workflows. Some examples of virtual research settings are Omeka and Scalar. These environments provide support for digital humanities initiatives, while communication systems such as Slack and Humanities Commons encourage academic networking. In addition, crowdsourcing systems such as Zooniverse encourage participation from the general public in research, while collaborative writing tools such as Google Docs and Overleaf enable real-time co-authoring. These technologies improve accessibility, creativity, and efficiency in the field of humanities studies; nonetheless, obstacles such as digital literacy and data privacy continue to exist [40] (Table 2.16).

2.9.3 Case Examples of Use in Humanities Education

Example 1: Google Docs for Peer-Reviewed Essays

In an undergraduate writing-intensive literature course, students used Google Docs to exchange their essay drafts. Each student provided inline comments on their peer's argumentation, structure, and style. The comment history enabled tracking of revisions, fostering reflection and accountability. Final submissions showed measurable improvement in clarity and coherence.

Example 2: Padlet for Historical Timelines

The pupils in a digital history class were given the task of adding events that occurred in Nigeria after the country gained its independence to a shared Padlet timeline. Students contributed pictures, videos, and discussion to the website. An interactive classroom resource that was supplemented by a variety of sources and points of view was the timeline that was produced as a consequence.

Example 3: Miro for Conceptual Mapping

Philosophy students used Miro to visually map the evolution of existentialism. Nodes represented thinkers, texts, and core ideas, with colour-coded links to indicate influence or contradiction. The process helped students grasp complex theoretical relationships and fostered class discussion.

2.9.4 Educational Benefits of Collaborative Tools

The use of collaborative digital technologies has several positive effects on humanities education, including increased accessibility, participation, and learning. The ability for several people to concurrently edit, comment, and debate content is made possible via real-time engagement, which also helps to encourage dynamic discussions and fast feedback. Students can develop and extend their thinking via collaborative efforts because to the presence of version history and threaded comments, which encourage the scaffolding of ideas. This allows students to preserve the progress of conversations and arguments while simultaneously enhancing their thinking. The capacity of instructors to monitor individual contributions and evaluate group dynamics is made possible by transparency, which plays a significant role in guaranteeing responsibility and fair participation. Another significant benefit is that it is inclusive; students who are reserved or introverted often discover that it is simpler for them to express themselves in online forums and collaborative platforms, which ultimately results in a more robust academic debate. Additionally, portability and accessibility are essential qualities of these tools; the majority of them are cloud-based and available across many devices, which ensures flexible learning possibilities that may fit a variety of schedules and locales. Individually and together, these characteristics enhance collaborative learning, which is why digital technologies are so beneficial in the field of humanities education.

Table 2.17 Collaborative assessment strategies

Approach	Description
Peer feedback rubrics	Students use structured rubrics to evaluate each other's contributions and writing
Contribution logs	Use document version history or comment records to assess individual input
Group portfolios	Compilation of artifacts from collaborative work for holistic assessment
Reflection journals	Students reflect on their group processes, decision-making, and learning outcomes

2.9.5 Collaborative Assessment Strategies

Learners are required to work together in order to evaluate their knowledge, abilities, or projects via the use of collaborative assessment strategies. These strategies may include group discussions, peer evaluations, team-based assignments, or collective feedback sessions. By evaluating each other's work, reflecting on shared objectives, and co-constructing knowledge, these tactics empower students to actively participate in the learning process, engage in critical thinking, and form social learning relationships. Peer grading, group presentations, think-pair-share reflections, and collaborative rubrics are some examples of activities that not only enhance students' knowledge but also build communication, accountability, and a learning community that is supportive of one another. These approaches are consistent with constructivist education, which place an emphasis on the fact that learning is strengthened by interaction and communal problem-solving. This is accomplished by transforming evaluation from a lonely process to a shared activity (Table 2.17).

These strategies validate collaborative efforts while ensuring individual accountability, a key challenge in group work evaluation.

2.9.6 Limitations and Challenges

In spite of their usefulness, collaborative evaluation systems in the arts and humanities encounter a number of obstacles. Because powerful voices may drown out more reserved ones, and because free-riding destroys equity, uneven involvement may distort results. Whether it's a result of unconscious biases or personal ties, peer judgments might be skewed. In big courses or online environments where coordination is complicated, time limits make prolonged cooperation challenging. Some students may not be able to participate because of problems with technology, such as a lack of training or equitable access to digital resources. Another obstacle is the need for standardised assessments; consistent evaluation is difficult to achieve in collaborative work because of the inherent resistance to using strict grading rubrics. Misunderstandings may also impact group dynamics in diverse classrooms due to language and

Table 2.18 Limitations and challenges

Challenge	Description
Digital divide	Unequal access to devices or reliable internet can hinder participation
Over-reliance on text-based tools	May neglect oral or experiential elements crucial to some humanities practices
Uneven participation	Risk of some students dominating while others remain passive
Cognitive overload	Too many tools or unfamiliar interfaces can overwhelm learners
Data privacy concerns	Tools must comply with GDPR, FERPA, or local privacy regulations

cultural barriers. The institutional focus on individual success and the reluctance of academics to use non-traditional approaches are potential obstacles to broad acceptance. To address these difficulties fairly and effectively, we need training, formal norms, and flexible frameworks (Table 2.18).

2.9.7 Best Practices for Implementation

In order to achieve fruitful partnership in the field of humanities education, deliberate tactics and a well-planned execution are necessary. In order to ensure that students comprehend the aim of each collaborative effort and maintain their concentration on academic progress, it is essential to establish defined objectives, which helps clarify learning goals and anticipated results. Students will be able to navigate and make efficient use of these resources if they are provided with tool training in the form of quick lessons on platforms such as Google Docs, Padlet, and other digital collaboration applications. This will help reduce the number of technological hurdles that students face. The establishment of standards for courteous communication, timely contributions, and constructive criticism helps to create a supportive atmosphere in which students are able to confidently express ideas and improve their work. Building digital fluency and ensuring that students gain the skills essential for current academic and professional cooperation may be accomplished by effectively incorporating these technologies into the curriculum on a consistent basis, rather than only utilising them for rare projects. Furthermore, teachers may serve as an example for collaboration by co-creating materials with their students or peers. This is a great way to demonstrate the most effective methods for collaborative learning and interactive education. Through the use of these tactics, educators have the ability to foster a collaborative learning environment that is both engaging and productive.

2.9.8 Future Trends in Collaborative Software Use

The development of collaborative tools in the field of humanities education is being propelled by cutting-edge technology that improves accessibility, creativity, and interaction. Collaboration that is helped by AI incorporates applications such as ChatGPT, which allows for the collaborative drafting, summarisation, and translation of texts. This helps to streamline workflows and improve the efficiency of research and writing. Collaboration systems that employ AR make it possible for users to exchange annotations and participate in immersive interactions inside three-dimensional surroundings. This results in the creation of dynamic learning experiences in which users interact with historical places, literary works, and complicated ideas in an individual manner. Cross-institutional initiatives make it possible to construct global classrooms by bringing together students from a variety of educational institutions to collaborate on the writing of papers, participate in debates that span many disciplines, and jointly produce knowledge across geographic borders. Additionally, multimodal feedback systems use richer communication modalities, such as video, audio, and emoji-based answers, in order to increase the level of engagement and make feedback from peers and instructors more expressive and intuitive. These technologies are always advancing, and as a result, they are reinventing collaborative learning by making it more inclusive, interactive, and internationally linked.

Collaborative software tools have reshaped humanities education by enabling dialogic, participatory, and networked learning. Whether through synchronous co-editing or asynchronous discussions, these platforms foster intellectual exchange and community-building. However, meaningful implementation requires pedagogical intentionality, training, and a commitment to equity. As digital tools become further embedded in education, the challenge lies not in adopting more platforms but in cultivating thoughtful, ethical, and reflective collaborative practices.

2.9.9 Interactive Platforms for Critical Thinking

Encouraging students to think critically is fundamental to the study of the humanities. Students are allowed to evaluate texts, challenge assumptions, and acquire educated opinions on several complicated subjects as a result of this. Interactive platforms have become more important in the development of certain cognitive abilities as a result of the proliferation of educational technology. Learners are encouraged to participate in activities that foster thinking, reflection, and argumentation via the use of these platforms, which often use dynamic interfaces that imitate real-world situations, stimulate inquiry-based learning, and promote intellectual discourse. Interactive platforms are indispensable in the digital humanities classroom. By encouraging active participation, fostering structured argumentation, and supporting reflection, these tools help cultivate the analytical and interpretive skills essential to humanities education. Integrating them thoughtfully into pedagogy ensures that digital learning remains intellectually rigorous and engaging.

2.9.10 Challenges in Digital Humanities Implementation

There are major pedagogical gains that may be gained from the use of digital tools and technology in the discipline of humanities education. Nevertheless, the path towards complete digital integration is riddled with difficulties that arise from a variety of perspectives, including those pertaining to infrastructure, pedagogy, technology, and culture. For the purpose of developing successful methods for sustained adoption, it is vital to have a solid understanding of these barriers.

1. Technological Infrastructure and Access: One of the most significant barriers is unequal access to reliable internet, modern hardware, and updated software. Many institutions, especially in developing countries, face inadequate digital infrastructure that restricts students and educators from leveraging the full potential of educational technologies.
   - *Challenge:* Limited bandwidth, outdated equipment, and frequent power outages.
   - *Impact:* Hindered participation in real-time interactive sessions, restricted access to learning platforms.
2. Digital Literacy: A fundamental challenge lies in the varying degrees of digital literacy among students and educators. While some are adept at using technology, others struggle with basic digital functions.
   - *Challenge:* Inadequate training in the use of educational tools.
   - *Impact:* Underutilisation of available platforms and ineffective delivery of course content.
3. Resistance to Change: In humanities disciplines traditionally grounded in textual analysis and face-to-face interaction, there may be cultural resistance to digital transformation. Faculty members may view digital methods as incompatible with humanistic inquiry.
   - *Challenge:* Perception that technology undermines deep engagement with texts.
   - *Impact:* Hesitance in adopting new tools and reluctance in curriculum reform.
4. Pedagogical Alignment: Not all digital tools align seamlessly with pedagogical goals. Instructors often struggle to find technologies that enhance learning outcomes rather than complicate them.
   - *Challenge:* Mismatch between tool capabilities and course objectives.
   - *Impact*: Disruption in instructional flow and reduced learning effectiveness.

5. Financial Constraints: Implementing and maintaining digital infrastructure and acquiring licenses for proprietary software require significant funding. Budget limitations often limit access to cutting-edge tools.
   - *Challenge*: High cost of software and subscriptions.
   - *Impact:* Reliance on free tools with limited functionality and support.
6. Data Privacy and Ethical Concerns: Digital learning environments often collect vast amounts of data, raising concerns about student privacy and ethical use of information.
   - *Challenge:* Lack of clear institutional data policies.
   - *Impact:* Risk of data breaches, misuse of information, and reduced student trust.
7. Language and Localisation: Many digital tools are developed in English or dominant global languages, which can disadvantage learners in non-English speaking regions.
   - *Challenge:* Language barriers in using platforms and interpreting content.
   - *Impact*: Limited engagement and exclusion of diverse linguistic communities.
8. Evaluation and Assessment: Measuring learning outcomes in digital humanities contexts can be complex, particularly when using multimedia, collaborative tools, or interactive assignments.
   - *Challenge*: Difficulty in standardising evaluation metrics.
   - *Impact:* Inconsistent assessment and challenges in grading authenticity.
9. Support and Maintenance: Ongoing technical support and updates are essential for the smooth functioning of digital tools. Institutions often lack dedicated personnel or robust help desks.
   - *Challenge*: Limited IT support and delayed responses to issues.
   - *Impact:* Downtime, student frustration, and decreased faculty productivity.
10. Institutional Policy and Governance: The absence of clear policies and leadership vision regarding digital adoption hinders systemic change. Successful integration often requires institutional commitment and administrative support.
   - *Challenge:* Lack of strategic planning and digital policies.
   - *Impact:* Fragmented implementation and poor scalability.

There are a number of obstacles that make the application of digital tools in humanities education more difficult, despite the fact that these technologies promise to enhance learning experiences. It is necessary to take a holistic strategy in order to address these difficulties. This approach should include investments in infrastructure, professional development, the formation of policies, and the design of inclusive technology. The digital humanities have the potential to completely alter education, but only if they are implemented via such coordinated initiatives.

2.9.11 Research Gaps Identified

Future studies, curriculum development, and inclusive educational policies that support effective digital transformation can be guided by identifying and addressing the critical research gaps that exist in the integration of digital tools within humanities education, despite the growing interest in and substantial progress in this area.

2.9.12 Limited Longitudinal Studies

Most of the research that has been done on digital humanities education has a tendency to focus on short-term results, such as the level of happiness that students have with digital tools and their first engagement with them. Despite the fact that these studies provide useful insights on instant reactions and usability, they often fail to capture the more profound and long-lasting influence that digital integration has on learning. To be more specific, there is a significant deficiency in longitudinal research that investigates the ways in which digital technologies impact academic achievement, the development of critical thinking abilities, and the long-term retention of information over a period of many years. Because there have not been studies conducted over a period of several years, it is still unknown whether digital resources promote long-term intellectual development or merely provide short-term engagement without providing any deeper educational benefits.

This lack of thorough study has important consequences for educators and policymakers who are attempting to establish digital learning environments that are successful. Institutions run the danger of investing in technologies without having a good grasp of the long-term effect of such technologies if they do not have tangible proof of the long-term advantages or possible problems, respectively. Because of this ambiguity, the creation of strategic frameworks for integrating digital technologies in ways that really improve learning outcomes might be hampered. In order to fill this void, it is necessary to establish ongoing research projects that monitor the development of students over extended periods of time. This will enable a more comprehensive evaluation of the ways in which digital education influences intellectual development beyond the initial adoption of the technology. By addressing this gap in research, academics will be able to provide suggestions that are supported by evidence for improving the use of digital pedagogy in the field of humanities education.

2.9.13 Underrepresentation of Diverse Educational Contexts

There is a significant gap in the representation of global perspectives in digital humanities studies as a result of the dominance of research from regions that are technologically advanced. The experiences of well-resourced institutions, which are often based in North America and Europe, have molded a significant portion of the extant literature. On the other hand, ideas from under-resourced regions, notably in Africa, Asia, and Latin America, continue to be underexplored. It is because of this imbalance that an inadequate picture of how digital tools work in a variety of educational settings is created, which in turn limits the relevance of the results that have been obtained to larger global contexts.

There are significant repercussions that result from the absence of these perspectives. Without doing exhaustive research that takes into account places that are underrepresented, it is possible that results about digital learning techniques would be biased. This might result in policies and technical designs that do not adequately address the specific issues that are encountered by institutions that have limited infrastructure and resources. This neglect might contribute to the perpetuation of inequities in digital education, on account of the fact that solutions that are customised to high-tech contexts could not transfer efficiently to regions that have limited access to digital resources. In order to close this gap, future research must make inclusion a top priority by including a variety of educational settings into their research frameworks. This will ensure that digital humanities scholarship accurately represents the reality of students who are enrolled in a variety of socio-economic and technical situations.

2.9.14 Minimal Focus on Humanities Disciplines

Research on digital learning has mostly concentrated on STEM and business fields, which are fields in which results can be evaluated using standardized tests and quantitative measures. As a result of this concentration, these sectors have been represented in research that investigate the efficacy of digital technologies in a disproportionate manner. Meanwhile, the humanities, especially disciplines such as history, philosophy, and literature, are sometimes ignored because of the interpretative and critical character of their subject matter, which makes it more difficult to measure the learning outcomes associated with these subjects. Because there are no studies that are special to these fields, there is a huge knowledge vacuum about the ways in which digital technologies might be adapted to meet the specific pedagogical requirements of humanities education.

Important repercussions are associated with this constraint. It is possible that digital learning initiatives will not be able to handle the intricacies of critical analysis, argumentation, and interpretative reasoning that distinguish the humanities disciplines if they do not have frameworks that are expressly created for students studying humanities topics. As a consequence of this, there is a dependence on generic techniques that do not entirely correspond with the manner in which students of the humanities interact with digital resources. A dedicated research effort to create digital tools and techniques that promote the specific modes of learning in the humanities is required in order to address this gap. This will ensure that digital education continues to be inclusive and adaptive across all disciplines of study.

2.9.15 Inadequate Exploration of Pedagogical Frameworks

In the field of DH education, one of the most serious challenges is the inclination to evaluate the efficacy of digital technologies without adequately anchoring them in established pedagogical principles. Numerous studies concentrate on the effectiveness of technological tools, such as their simplicity of use and level of engagement, rather than investigating the ways in which these tools connect with learning theories that build meaningful educational experiences. There is a gap in the theoretical relationship between digital tools and successful learning methods as a consequence of the fact that digital integration is often directed by technology innovation rather than strong instructional tactics.

There are significant repercussions associated with this separation. Digital technologies may be utilised superficially, acting as just embellishments rather than transformational instruments for deeper learning, if a pedagogically based approach is not taken into consideration. When technology is incorporated into education without having specific educational goals in mind, the influence of the technology is limited, and it does not succeed in fostering critical thinking, analytical abilities, or the retention of information. In order to fill this need, further study has to be conducted on the ways in which digital tools might be purposefully planned and deployed to complement certain learning theories. This will ensure that the digital tools contribute to substantial educational results rather than just digitising existing approaches.

2.9.16 Student-Centered Perspectives Are Understudied

An important omission in studies on online education is the tendency to ignore student viewpoints in favour of those of institutions, teachers, and administrators. Despite the fact that universities and teachers are responsible for formulating regulations regarding digital education, the real users, who are students, are usually excluded from relevant debates. Due to the fact that their experiences with usability, preferences, problems, and learning outcomes continue to be under-represented, there is a study gap that fails to capture how digital tools genuinely effect those individuals who depend on them the most.

Significant repercussions are associated with this gap. It is possible that digital learning techniques will not correspond with real learner requirements if appropriate student input is not provided. This might result in ineffective implementations or unintentional hurdles to participation. Understanding the success of digital learning from the perspective of the student is vital for the development of more effective pedagogical approaches, the enhancement of accessibility to technology, and the guarantee of educational results that are meaningful. Students' voices should be given priority in future research, and their firsthand experiences should be included into the process of developing a digital humanities environment that is more responsive and student-centered. This move would assist bridge the gap between technical innovation and practical learning experiences, ensuring that digital tools perform the role of facilitators of knowledge rather than only being assets of the institution instead.

2.9.17 Accessibility and Inclusivity Concerns

The effects of digital tools on students from underprivileged backgrounds or with impairments are often overlooked in studies, despite their widespread use in education. Digital learning environments have the ability to improve accessibility and eliminate obstacles to education if they are built with inclusion in mind from the beginning. On the other hand, the efficacy of digital tools in helping different learners is still unknown since there is a lack of comprehensive data on accessibility features, universal design principles, and inclusive practices. Because there is a lack of thorough study on these issues, the capacity of educators to create solutions that cater to the specific requirements of each and every student is negatively impacted.

The existence of this gap poses considerable concerns, since it has the potential to result in the marginalisation of groups who are already underserved. In the event that digital tools are produced without taking accessibility requirements into consideration, it is possible that they may inadvertently create barriers rather than eliminate them, so further extending the educational discrepancies that already exist. In order to address this problem, it is necessary to place a greater focus on research that investigates the ways in which digital platforms either help or impede the learning process for students who already have low resources or impairments. It is possible for educators and developers to guarantee that digital education actually serves all learners by giving priority to inclusive design and collecting empirical data on accessibility. This will result in a fairer academic environment.

2.9.18 Assessment Frameworks for Digital Outputs

In the realm of academic evaluation, the proliferation of digital assignments, which include anything from blogs and videos to multimedia essays and interactive timelines, has resulted in the emergence of new obstacles. The fact that these forms need creative expression, technical ability, and interaction with digital tools makes it challenging to grade them using standard rubrics. This is in contrast to typical written essays or examinations, which do not require these things. Inconsistencies in grading have arisen as a result of the lack of standardised assessment frameworks. This is because educators are having a difficult time determining objective criteria for assessing non-traditional outputs. It is possible that digital assignments may be evaluated subjectively if validated evaluation techniques are not used, which might have a negative impact on both academic rigour and fairness.

This disparity has serious consequences for both children and instructors. Under the absence of well-defined grading norms, learners may be left in a state of ambiguity, as they may be unable to comprehend the expectations placed on their digital work or how it corresponds to the academic standards. It is possible for teachers to engage in unequal grading methods when they examine digital assignments without first establishing standards. This occurs when comparable work is scored differently depending on individual interpretations. In order to address this problem, it is necessary to design rubrics that are relevant to the field in question. These rubrics should integrate elements such as technical execution, critical analysis, and creative thinking, while also ensuring that evaluations are transparent and consistent. In order to guarantee that digital assignments are evaluated as actual academic contributions rather than supplemental additions to conventional coursework, it is necessary to establish an agreement on the criteria that will be used for performance evaluation.

2.9.19 Professional Development for Educators

One of the most common obstacles that stands in the way of the incorporation of digital technologies into humanities education is the absence of formal training for faculty members. Humanities instructors typically face challenges when attempting to adapt digital resources to their teaching approaches. This is in contrast to STEM fields, which have a more standardised approach to the use of technology. The research that is currently available has a tendency to concentrate on the rates of technology adoption rather than assessing the preparation of faculty members or the efficiency of training programs that are aimed to bridge this gap. In consequence of this, a great number of educators have difficulties in deploying digital technologies in the most effective manner, which results in uneven implementation and a reluctance to embrace digital transformation. Because of this shortcoming, there are larger consequences for the quality of education in the humanities in this era of digital technology.

It may be difficult for faculty members to incorporate technology in ways that promote learning rather than just supplementing conventional techniques if they do not have proper support mechanisms supporting them. It is possible for educators to experience resistance to the use of digital technologies when they see new tools as difficult rather than advantageous, owing to a lack of availability of advice and resources. To address this gap, it is necessary to do focused research regarding the preparedness of faculty members, to implement training efforts that are scalable, and to establish institutional frameworks that endorse professional growth. Digital humanities programs can achieve a more meaningful and successful integration if they provide teachers with the required skills and confidence. This will be to the advantage of both the teachers and the students.

2.9.20 *Ethical and Cultural Sensitivities*

Emerging ethical and cultural problems have been brought to light as a result of the increasing dependence on digital platforms in the educational system. These concerns have not yet received enough consideration. Digital learning experiences are shaped in ways that may inadvertently perpetuate structural inequities. These approaches include algorithmic prejudice, concerns around data privacy, and the predominance of Western pedagogical paradigms. A great number of educational technologies are designed without taking into account varied cultural views in an acceptable manner. This results in the marginalisation of non-Western epistemologies, learning styles, and knowledge traditions. A one-size-fits-all strategy that does not take into account the specific educational requirements of pupils who come from a variety of backgrounds may be perpetuated as a result of this omission [41].

The consequences of these gaps are substantial. When it comes to the development of tools, negligence in terms of ethics might lead to the creation of biased learning algorithms that give preference to some points of view while marginalising others. Furthermore, kids may be susceptible to exploitation if there are insufficient safeguards in place to protect their data privacy. This is especially true in places where digital literacy and regulatory measures are still in developmental stages. There is a correlation between the lack of inclusive design concerns and epistemic injustice, which is characterised by the deliberate devaluation or elimination of certain modes of knowing and learning. In order to solve these difficulties, developers of educational technology need to include ethical and cultural frameworks from the very beginning. This will ensure that digital learning tools accommodate a variety of pedagogical models, protect user data, and reduce the impact of algorithmic biases. If these kinds of efforts are not made, digital education runs the danger of consolidating existing inequalities rather than democratising access to information.

Therefore, an urgent need for research that is more thorough, multidisciplinary, and inclusive has been brought to light by the gaps that have been uncovered in the landscape of digital humanities. As the use of digital tools in humanities education becomes more widespread, it is of the utmost importance to guarantee that these tools are effective, sustainable, and accessible to all students. One of the most important areas that has to be improved is the deployment of longitudinal studies that evaluate the effects of digital learning outcomes over a longer period of time. Without these kinds of research, it is impossible to evaluate if digital approaches provide long-term advantages or whether they just give engagement for a more limited period of time [42].

In addition, research should make an effort to include a wider range of geographical and cultural settings, so as to avoid an excessively restricted concentration on certain locations or academic traditions. Rather than adopting frameworks created for other fields of study, educational material in the humanities needs sophisticated evaluation procedures that are adapted to the distinctive qualities of the subject matter. Ethical considerations and inclusivity in the design of technology are also of the utmost importance. This is to ensure that digital tools support diverse learners rather than reinforcing biases or excluding groups that are marginalized. Increasing the robustness of theoretical frameworks that provide a relationship between pedagogy and the use of technology would further improve digital humanities research, therefore creating meaningful links between educational techniques and digital innovation. In the future, research needs to take a more comprehensive approach to integrate digital tools in a way that is both effective and equitable across a variety of global contexts. It is possible for academics and teachers to create a digital humanities environment that is more sustainable, accessible, and inclusive by addressing these basic deficiencies. This environment will be beneficial to students from different backgrounds and fields of study [43].

References

1. B. Li, Contemporary college students' views on marriage. J. Educ. Humanit. Soc. Sci. **3**, 196–202 (2022). https://doi.org/10.54097/ehss.v3i.1686
2. F. Pari, Contextuality vs universality of the hadith: methodological problem. Adv. Soc. Sci. Educ. Humanit. Res. **137**(2017), 100–108 (2018)
3. K.C. Obi, O. Iwuanyanwu, Innovation in the assessment of primary school mathematics: an approach to revamping Nigeria education. J. Teach. Perspect. **18**(1), 51–66 (2023) [Online]. Available: http://repositorio.unan.edu.ni/2986/1/5624.pdf%0Ahttp://fiskal.kemenkeu.go.id/ejournal%0A10.1016/j.cirp.2016.06.001%0A10.1016/j.powtec.2016.12.055%0A10.1016/j.ijfatigue.2019.02.006%0A10.1
4. T. Olowa, E. Witt, C. Morganti, T. Teittinen, I. Lill, Defining a BIM-enabled learning environment—an adaptive structuration theory perspective. Buildings **12**(3) (2022). https://doi.org/10.3390/buildings12030292
5. J.K. Ofori-Kuragu, R. Osei-Kyei, Mainstreaming pre-manufactured offsite processes in construction—are we nearly there? Constr. Innov. **21**(4), 743–760 (2021). https://doi.org/10.1108/CI-06-2020-0092
6. I. Cojuhari, Socio-cultural integration of the Gagauz people into the moldovan contemporary society: national and regional approaches. Adm. Publica **3**(115), 132–139 (2022). https://doi.org/10.52327/1813-8489.2022.3(115).14
7. T.E. Garba, R.L. Richard, N.E.A. Thani, M.A.A. Majid, Geological effects on water quality: a review of issues and challenges in Malaysia. Sains Malaysiana **50**(7), 1857–1870 (2021). https://doi.org/10.17576/jsm-2021-5007-03
8. G.S. Kasturi, A. Jain, J. Singh, Detection and classification of radio frequency jamming attacks using machine learning. J. Wirel. Mob. Networks, Ubiquitous Comput. Dependable Appl. **11**(4), 49–62 (2020). https://doi.org/10.22667/JOWUA.2020.12.31.049
9. G. Ikrissi, T. Mazri, A study of smart campus environment and its security attacks. Int. Arch. Photogramm. Remote Sens. Spat. Inf. Sci. ISPRS Arch. **44**(4/W3), 255–261 (2020). https://doi.org/10.5194/isprs-archives-XLIV-4-W3-2020-255-2020

10. M. Mittal, C. Iwendi, S. Khan, A. Rehman Javed, Analysis of security and energy efficiency for shortest route discovery in low-energy adaptive clustering hierarchy protocol using Levenberg-Marquardt neural network and gated recurrent unit for intrusion detection system. Trans. Emerg. Telecommun. Technol. **32**(6), 1–16 (2021). https://doi.org/10.1002/ett.3997
11. A. Idris, R. Yusof, Adoption of E-voting system in Nigeria: a prospect for poverty alleviation, in *Proceedings of Internationa Conference on E-Commerce* (2015), pp. 92–96 [Online]. Available: http://www.icoec.my/index.php/proceedings/5-icoec-2015-proceedings/97-adoption-of-e-voting-system-in-nigeria-a-prospect-for-poverty-alleviation
12. N. Kumar, J. Madhuri, M. Channegowda, Review on security and privacy concerns in internet of things. Turkish J. Physiother. Rehabil. **32**(3), 1–5 (2021). https://doi.org/10.1109/ICIOTA.2017.8073640
13. M. Casini, Extended reality for smart building operation and maintenance: a review. Energies **15**(10), 3785 (2022). https://doi.org/10.3390/en15103785
14. F. Olan, S. Liu, J. Suklan, U. Jayawickrama, E.O. Arakpogun, The role of artificial intelligence networks in sustainable supply chain finance for food and drink industry. Int. J. Prod. Res. **60**(14), 4418–4433 (2022). https://doi.org/10.1080/00207543.2021.1915510
15. A. Nguyen, S. Lamouri, R. Pellerin, S. Tamayo, B. Lekens, Data analytics in pharmaceutical supply chains: state of the art, opportunities, and challenges. Int. J. Prod. Res. (2021). https://doi.org/10.1080/00207543.2021.1950937
16. K.W.A. Budu, M. Yinping, K.K. Mireku, Investigating the effect of behavioral intention on E-learning systems usage: empirical study on tertiary education institutions in Ghana. Mediterr. J. Soc. Sci. **9**(3), 201–216 (2018). https://doi.org/10.2478/mjss-2018-0062
17. A.B. Saka, D.W.M. Chan, Profound barriers to building information modelling (BIM) adoption in construction small and medium-sized enterprises (SMEs): an interpretive structural modelling approach. Constr. Innov. **20**(2), 261–284 (2020). https://doi.org/10.1108/CI-09-2019-0087
18. Aswir, H. Misbah, Smartphones as personal digital archives? Recentering migrant authority as curating and storytelling subjects. Photosynthetica **2**(1), 1–13 (2018) [Online]. Available: https://doi.org/10.1007/978-3-319-76887-8
19. L. Zupan, *20 key risks to consider by Internal Audit before 2020*. KPMG (2020)
20. P. Kochovski, V. Stankovski, Supporting smart construction with dependable edge computing infrastructures and applications. Autom. Constr. **85**(6), 182–192 (2018). https://doi.org/10.1016/j.autcon.2017.10.008
21. I. Yaqoob, K. Salah, R. Jayaraman, M. Omar, Metaverse applications in smart cities: enabling technologies, opportunities, challenges, and future directions. Internet Things (Netherlands) **23**, 100884 (2023). https://doi.org/10.1016/j.iot.2023.100884
22. C. Zhengdao, An internet of things-enabled BIM platform for on-site assembly services in prefabricated construction. Autom. Constr. **89**, 146–161 (2018). https://doi.org/10.1016/j.autcon.2018.01.001
23. H.S. Munawar, F. Ullah, S. Qayyum, *Big Data in Construction: Current Applications and Future Opportunities* (2022)
24. D. Bandyopadhyay, J. Sen, Internet of things: applications and challenges in technology and standardization. Wirel. Pers. Commun. **58**(1), 49–69 (2011). https://doi.org/10.1007/s11277-011-0288-5
25. J. Carneiro, R.J.F. Rossetti, D.C. Silva, E.C. Oliveira, BIM, GIS, IoT, and AR/VR integration for smart maintenance and management of road networks: a review, in *2018 IEEE International Smart Cities Conference on ISC2 2018* (2019). https://doi.org/10.1109/ISC2.2018.8656978
26. B. Succar, M. Kassem, Building information modelling: point of adoption. CIB World Conf. Proc. **1**(2016), 1–11 (2016)
27. A. Elsaadany, K. Abbas, Development and implementation of e-learning system in smart educational environment, in *2016 39th International Convention on Information and Communication Technology Electronices and Microelectronics MIPRO 2016 – Proceedings* (2016), pp. 1004–1009. https://doi.org/10.1109/MIPRO.2016.7522286

28. U. Haruna, A.N. Toosi, M. Fermi, S. Khan, SDN-based detection and mitigation of DDoS attacks on smart homes. Comput. Commun. **221**, 29–41 (2024). https://doi.org/10.1016/j.comcom.2024.04.001
29. M. Soud, G. Liebel, M. Hamdaqa, *A Fly in the Ointment: An Empirical Study on the Characteristics of Ethereum Smart Contracts Code Weaknesses and Vulnerabilities* (2022) [Online]. Available: http://arxiv.org/abs/2203.14850
30. N.M. Alshahrani, M.L.M. Kiah, B.B. Zaidan, A.H. Alamoodi, A. Saif, A review of smart contract blockchain based on multi-criteria analysis: challenges and motivations. Comput. Mater. Contin. **75**(2), 2833–2858 (2023). https://doi.org/10.32604/cmc.2023.036138
31. A. Pacios Álvarez, J. Ordieres-Meré, Á.P. Loreiro, L. de Marcos, Opportunities in airport pavement management: integration of BIM, the IoT and DLT. J. Air Transp. Manag. **90**, 1–10 (2021). https://doi.org/10.1016/j.jairtraman.2020.101941
32. F.M. Aldhafeeri, B.H. Khan, Teachers' and students' views on e-learning readiness in Kuwait's secondary public schools. J. Educ. Technol. Syst. **45**(2), 202–235 (2016). https://doi.org/10.1177/0047239516646747
33. L. Albó, J. Barria-pineda, Knowledge-based design analytics for authoring courses with smart learning content. Int. J. Artif. Intell. Educ. **7**(21), 1–24 (2021)
34. P. Baepler, J.D. Walker, M. Driessen, It's not about seat time: blending, flipping, and efficiency in active learning classrooms. Comput. Educ. **78**, 227–236 (2014). https://doi.org/10.1016/j.compedu.2014.06.006
35. L. Umek, D. Keržič, N. Tomaževič, A. Aristovnik, Moodle e-learning system and students' performance in higher education: the case of public administration programmes, in *Proceedings of International Conference on e-Learning 2015, E-LEARNING 2015—Part Multi Conference Computer Science Information Systems* (2015), pp. 97–104
36. R. Jahangir, Y.W. Teh, G. Mujtaba, R. Alroobaea, Z.H. Shaikh, I. Ali, Convolutional neural network-based cross-corpus speech emotion recognition with data augmentation and features fusion. Mach. Vis. Appl. **33**(3), 1–16 (2022). https://doi.org/10.1007/s00138-022-01294-x
37. K. Phusavat, P. Anussornnitisarn, P. Helo, R. Dwight, Performance measurement: roles and challenges. Ind. Manag. Data Syst. **109**(5), 646–664 (2009). https://doi.org/10.1108/02635570910957632
38. R.M. Abdullah, A.Z. Abualkishik, N.M. Isaacc, A.A. Alwan, Y. Gulzar, An investigation study for risk calculation of security vulnerabilities on android applications. Indones. J. Electr. Eng. Comput. Sci. **25**(3), 1736–1748 (2022). https://doi.org/10.11591/ijeecs.v25.i3.pp1736-1748
39. S. Ghavifekr, W.A.W. Rosdy, Teaching and learning with technology: effectiveness of ICT integration in schools. Int. J. Res. Educ. Sci. **1**(2), 175 (2015). https://doi.org/10.21890/ijres.23596
40. S.N.G. Gourisetti, M. Mylrea, H. Patangia, Cybersecurity vulnerability mitigation framework through empirical paradigm: enhanced prioritized gap analysis. Futur. Gener. Comput. Syst. **105**, 410–431 (2020). https://doi.org/10.1016/j.future.2019.12.018
41. I.O. Ekemezie, W.N. Digitemie, Best practices in strategic project management across multinational corporations: a global perspective on success factors and challenges. Int. J. Manag. Entrep. Res. **6**(3), 795–805 (2024). https://doi.org/10.51594/ijmer.v6i3.936
42. N.M. Al Hamad, O.E. Adewusi, C.C. Unachukwu, B. Osawaru, O.N. Chisom, Bridging the gap: using robotics to enhance emotional and social learning in K-12 education. Int. J. Sci. Res. Arch. **11**(1), 231–243 (2024). https://doi.org/10.30574/ijsra.2024.11.1.0025
43. D.L. Wadji, M. Oe, E. Bartoli, C. Martin-Soelch, M.C. Pfaltz, R. Langevin, How are experiences and acceptability of child maltreatment related to resilience and posttraumatic growth: a cross cultural study. Eur. J. Psychotraumatol. **14**(2) (2023). https://doi.org/10.1080/20008066.2023.2264119

Chapter 3
Theoretical Framework

3.1 Constructivist Theory and Humanities Learning

Jean Piaget, Lev Vygotsky, and Jerome Bruner laid the groundwork for constructivist learning theory, which maintains that people acquire new information by active participation in a variety of context-specific activities, including observation, discussion, and imitation. Constructivism takes a different tack than more conventional theories of learning, which hold that students passively absorb knowledge from their surroundings without actively participating, challenging preconceived notions, and making sense of what they have learnt. Knowledge is not only transmitted from teacher to student; rather, it is co-created via cognitive and social processes; this is what this method acknowledges. Bruner's idea of scaffolding and Vygotsky's focus on social interaction both emphasise the need for guided exploration and cooperation in successful learning. Because thinking critically, interpreting evidence, and expressing one's views are cornerstones of the humanities, this idea is especially applicable to the field. The study of literature, philosophy, and history, among other humanities disciplines, demands students to do more than just regurgitate information; it flourishes on in-depth examinations of ideas about their social, cultural, and historical environments. This dynamic is in line with constructivist ideas, which promote learners to put knowledge into context, question prevailing narratives, and develop their views via discussion and investigation. Constructivism guarantees that students acquire the critical thinking abilities needed to traverse and contribute to a constantly changing intellectual terrain by encouraging meaningful interactions and self-directed learning [1] (Fig. 3.1).

F. A. Alaba et al., *Learning Beyond the Classroom*, Studies in Computational Intelligence 1253, https://doi.org/10.1007/978-3-032-14433-1_3

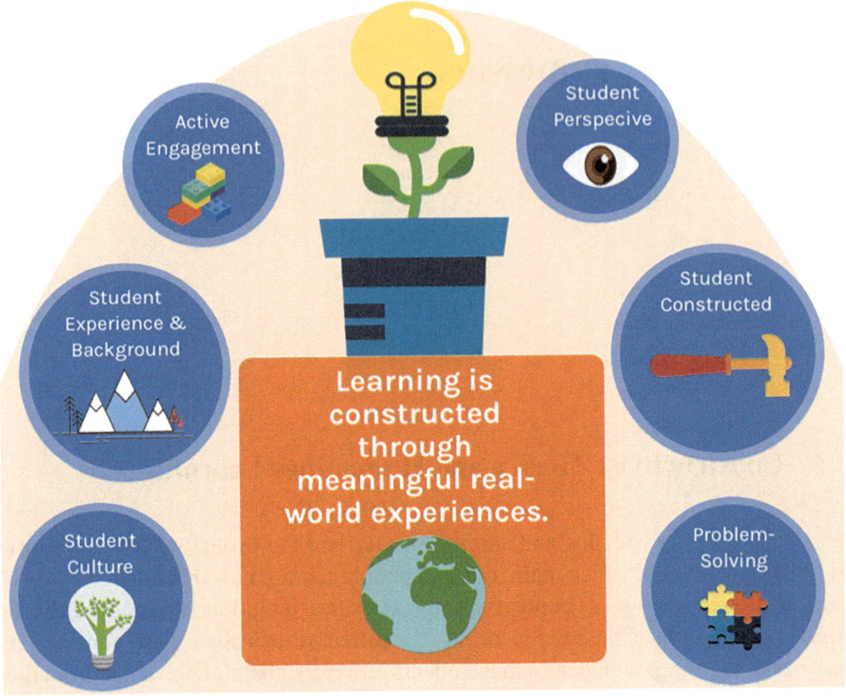

Fig. 3.1 Essentials of constructivism [2]

3.1.1 *Core Principles of Constructivism in Education*

Several tenets of constructivist learning theory are in perfect harmony with the aims of arts and humanities education. As an example, there is Active Learning, which holds that students not only absorb information but actively participate by bringing their knowledge, experiences, and viewpoints to the table. Students create more meaningful connections and insights when they engage with new material in ways that build upon what they already know. Importantly, scaffolding occurs when teachers offer pupils organised support that they progressively lessen as they become more competent and self-assured. This method encourages students to think for themselves, which empowers them to take charge of their education while still receiving the help they need when they need it. An important part of constructivism, Social Interaction promotes better learning via conversation and teamwork. To develop one's mind in the humanities, one must immerse oneself in many perspectives and interpretations in fields like literature, philosophy, and history. Recognising that information is best learnt when connected to real-world applications, Situated Learning emphasizes context. This notion is fundamental to the humanities because it places topics for debate into their proper historical, social, and cultural contexts [3].

Also, reflection promotes metacognition and increased understanding by having students reflect on and analyse their learning abilities. Learners become more deliberate in their quest for information, sharpen their viewpoints, and question assumptions via reflection. Pedagogical techniques that foster critical thinking, reflective learning, and active participation in knowledge generation are informed by these concepts. By incorporating constructivist approaches into humanities instruction, educators may promote intellectual curiosity and a broader awareness of the intricacies of human cognition and cultural debate.

3.1.2 Constructivism and Humanities Pedagogy

The constructivist tenets of learning are well-suited to the humanities because of the field's emphasis on interpretation, discourse, and the study of many points of view. This includes fields like philosophy, history, cultural studies, and literature. These topics promote active engagement with knowledge, the development of independent understandings, and the critical analysis of other perspectives, in contrast to areas that place a premium on rote memorisation. Learners are encouraged to build meaning via inquiry, reflection, and contextual analysis, as promoted by constructivism, which promotes intellectual discovery. As an example, in the field of literary studies, students apply what they learn by analysing writings about their time, genre, and social and political realities. They actively seek themes, authorial purpose, and cultural influences in order to build complex meanings, rather than just taking in information. History also benefits from constructivist methods because students learn to look at stories from several angles and recognise that historical "truths" are often influenced by biased or inadequate records. By using this approach, students are able to think more critically and have a better understanding of the many interpretations of past events.

Dialogic learning is very important in philosophy. Students develop their critical thinking skills, strengthen their arguments, and express their own philosophical views via Socratic questioning. By emphasising individual participation, discussion, and the development of ideas, this interactive method reflects constructivist ideals. Constructivist learning is a great paradigm for the humanities because it encourages students to be curious, flexible, and capable of critically navigating complicated social and cultural concerns [4] (Fig. 3.2).

3.1.3 Digital Technology as a Constructivist Tool

Digital tools enhance constructivist learning in the humanities by providing dynamic, interactive environments for exploration and expression. The following technologies exemplify how constructivist pedagogy can be actualised through software (Table 3.1).

Fig. 3.2 Constructivism learning theory & philosophy of education

Table 3.1 Constructivist tool

Tool	Constructivist feature	Humanities application
Google Docs	Collaborative writing and peer feedback	Co-authoring essays, collective annotation of texts
Padlet	Visual brainstorming, multimedia integration	Organizing historical timelines, thematic discussions
TimelineJS	Chronological visualization, interactive content	Creating digital timelines for historical analysis
StoryMapJS	Spatial learning through narrative maps	Mapping literary journeys or migration histories
Discussion forums (e.g., Moodle, Canvas)	Dialogic learning, reflection	Structured debates on philosophical questions
Hypothes.is	Social annotation, close reading	Layered analysis of literary and academic texts

These tools facilitate the construction of knowledge through engagement with digital content, peer collaboration, and reflective discourse.

3.1.4 *Case Example: Digital Storytelling in Cultural Studies*

Digital storytelling in a cultural studies course is a fascinating example of constructivist learning, effortlessly blending personal experience with academic investigation. In this project, students study themes such as family history, migration patterns, or cultural traditions, then build multimedia narratives using platforms like Adobe Spark or Canva. This strategy converts conventional learning into an interactive and reflective process, enabling students to actively generate meaning rather than passively absorb knowledge. This technique accords with numerous fundamental constructivist concepts. Situated learning is reflected in students' engagement with primary and secondary research, allowing them to contextualize knowledge within real-world experiences. Social interaction plays a significant role as learners cooperate with peers and instructors, sharing viewpoints and developing their narratives via conversation. Active learning is emphasized as students make purposeful choices regarding narrative structure, topic, and storytelling strategies. Reflection significantly strengthens the learning process, encouraging students to critically evaluate their identity and ancestry while linking personal findings to wider cultural notions. Last but not least, the use of technology gives students the opportunity to creatively express meaning via the use of digital tools, which in turn encourages creativity and adaptation in the presentation of information [5].

Digital storytelling is a great example of the power of constructivist pedagogy in the field of humanities education because it combines many different elements, including research, collaboration, creativity, and reflection. Students are given the ability to take responsibility for their own education, to interact with intricate cultural topics, and to acquire critical thinking skills that are applicable outside the confines of the regular classroom setting. Not only does this dynamic method improve academic inquiry, but it also fosters deeper links to historical and social settings, which in turn makes learning both meaningful and transformational [6].

3.1.5 *Implications for Educators*

Implementing constructivist ideas in humanities education involves deliberate instructional design that stresses student agency, collaboration, and deep engagement with information. One useful method is to offer open-ended assignments that enable varied interpretations rather than fixed responses. This helps learners to investigate complicated issues, establish their own opinions, and interact critically with literature, historical events, or philosophical ideas. Collaborative learning further improves constructivist teaching, since group projects, discussion forums, and peer-reviewed assignments encourage meaningful relationships. By discussing ideas, debating opinions, and jointly generating knowledge, students develop deeper insights while honing their thinking and communication abilities. Another key aspect is the use of digital technologies not only for information distribution, but for content creation. Platforms that facilitate multimedia projects, digital storytelling, or interactive research allow students to actively design their learning experiences rather than passively ingesting information. Additionally, instructors should include structured opportunities for reflection and metacognition into the learning process. Encouraging students to analyse their cognitive processes, detect alterations in their knowledge, and create connections across disciplines increases critical thinking and intellectual progress. Finally, a crucial alteration in constructivist education is the shift in the educator's role moving from a subject expert to a facilitator of learning. By fostering an environment in which students accept responsibility for their own education, teachers may foster an atmosphere in which they guide students' inquiry rather than prescribing facts. It is possible to cultivate a learner-centred approach that is reflective of the interpretative character of the humanities by aligning the use of technology with constructivist ideas. Education in the humanities may be transformed into an experience that is both intellectually exciting and immersive when students are encouraged to actively interact with the information, contribute in meaningful ways, and reflect on what they have previously learnt [7].

The constructivist theory provides a solid foundation for rethinking the way humanities education is delivered in this era of digital technology. It corresponds well with the fundamental goals of the disciplines that fall under the umbrella of the humanities because it places an emphasis on active involvement, contextual learning, collaboration, and reflection. The classroom may be transformed into a place for exploration, creativity, and critical engagement when constructivism is connected with the right digital tools. This gives students the ability to become not just consumers of information but also co-creators of that knowledge [3].

3.2 Bloom's Taxonomy and Digital Learning

Bloom's Taxonomy, which was established by Benjamin Bloom and his partners in 1956, continues to be one of the most significant educational frameworks for comprehending the goals of learning. In the beginning, it was characterised as Knowledge, Comprehension, Application, Analysis, Synthesis, and Evaluation. It then organised cognitive abilities into hierarchical tiers. The new version that was developed by [8] reorganised them into the following categories: Remember, Understand, Apply, Analyse, Evaluate, and Create. This modification provided a more dynamic model that is applicable to learning settings in the twenty-first century, particularly in digital contexts. The Bloom's Taxonomy offers a great scaffold for connecting instructional objectives with digital tools and activities, which is becoming more important as digital technologies continue to alter educational techniques even more. The purpose

Table 3.2 The revised bloom's taxonomy

Level	Cognitive process	Examples in digital learning
Remember	Recall facts and basic concepts	Using flashcard apps, digital quizzes (e.g., Quizlet, Kahoot)
Understand	Explain ideas or concepts	Watching explainer videos, interactive timelines (e.g., Edpuzzle)
Apply	Use information in new situations	Conducting text analysis using Voyant Tools, coding simple scripts
Analyze	Draw connections among ideas	Comparing historical texts with digital annotation tools
Evaluate	Justify a decision or course of action	Participating in online debates, peer reviewing on Google Docs
Create	Produce original work	Digital storytelling, podcast production, or designing infographics

of this section is to investigate the ways in which Bloom's Taxonomy may be incorporated into the teaching of the humanities by using digital learning platforms and technologies (Table 3.2).

This taxonomy helps educators plan learning activities that move students from lower-order to higher-order thinking skills, ensuring depth and complexity in engagement.

3.2.1 Applying Bloom's Taxonomy in Humanities Education

There is a natural alignment between Bloom's higher-order domains and the topics that fall within the humanities. These subjects include literature, philosophy, history, and the arts. These areas need critical thinking and layered interpretation. Educators are able to make use of technology in the digital classroom to assist each cognitive level, which helps to ensure that students are thoroughly engaged with their learning. Students are able to engage in critical interaction with literary and philosophical works via the use of technologies such as Perusall and Hypothesis, which enable collaborative text annotation for the purpose of application and analysis. In a similar vein, digital tools such as Voyant and Google Ngram Viewer make it easier to analyse language patterns in historical writings, which in turn helps to cultivate analytical thinking and interpretive abilities. Students have the ability to transform their research into creative projects at the evaluation and production levels by using multimedia platforms such as Adobe Spark and Canva. These platforms allow students to create creative projects such as digital essays, video presentations, or storytelling. Students are given the opportunity to generate creative interpretations while also forming discussions and providing feedback on already established concepts via the use of interactive timelines, podcasts, and blogs. Learners are able to develop their viewpoints via debate and peer involvement on platforms such as

Padlet, Slack, and Discord, which further enhance the process of collaboration and discussion. Through the use of virtual reality apps, students may be immersed in historical events or creative movements, providing them with possibilities for experiential learning that expand their comprehension of the surroundings. Educators are able to construct interactive settings that improve critical thinking, stimulate creativity, and make humanities education more interesting and intellectually exciting by deliberately incorporating various digital resources into their classrooms [9].

3.2.2 Remember and Understand

In the field of DH education, basic cognitive levels are often reinforced via the use of interactive learning tools and forms of multimedia information. Platforms like Quizlet and Kahoot allow, students to reinforce their memorisation of literary devices or important historical events. On the other hand, YouTube and Edpuzzle provide students with video-based learning experiences that graphically convey complicated ideas such as Renaissance art. These tools with act as entry points, ensuring that students acquire fundamental information before moving on to higher-order thinking tasks.

The more advanced learners become, the more they begin to use their knowledge in new circumstances, such as analysing themes from literature in connection to current societal concerns. Support for creative presentations is provided by applications such as Google Slides and Canva. Voyant Tools, on the other hand, enables students to do sentiment analysis on Shakespearean plays, which assists them in exploring character development. To engage in analysis, students need to engage in more in-depth critical thinking, which encourages them to make connections between different texts, ideas, and historical events. Students can analyse primary materials for bias, viewpoint, and larger influence by using platforms such as Hypotheses.is and Miro, which offer collaborative annotation and visualisation. During the assessment step, students evaluate ideas and arguments by utilising discussion boards on platforms such as Moodle and Canvas. These platforms let students to engage in discussions that are assessed by their peers, which helps to improve opinions. In the last part, known as "creation," students are responsible for transforming their ideas into creative artefacts. They accomplish this by using various technologies, such as Adobe Spark, StoryMapJS, and podcast software, in order to construct digital archives or interactive museum exhibitions. Educators are able to construct a dynamic learning environment that encourages profound involvement, creativity, and intellectual discovery in the humanities by integrating technology across all of these cognitive domains [10].

Table 3.3 Cognitive level

Cognitive level	Assessment example
Remember	Automated quizzes, terminology matching
Understand	Written summaries via blogs, video explanations
Apply	Scenario-based role play using virtual platforms
Analyze	Comparative essays or database-driven projects
Evaluate	Rubric-based evaluations of peer-generated content
Create	Original digital compositions or website design

3.2.3 Digital Bloom's Taxonomy and Assessment

What is digital Bloom's Taxonomy lays an emphasis on digital habits and tools that are similar to each cognitive function. This is in contrast to the traditional approach, which puts the emphasis only on tasks. Formative and summative assessments may be carried out across a wide range of various types of media thanks to this capability (Table 3.3).

3.2.4 Benefits of Using Bloom's Taxonomy in Digital Humanities Learning

In the field of HE, the use of digital learning methodologies provides a number of benefits that are in line with the most effective pedagogical approaches. Before moving on to higher-order thinking activities, students are allowed to develop basic abilities via the use of structured progression, which guarantees that cognitive problems rise in a chronological manner. Not only does this strategy improve understanding, but it also helps to develop deeper analytical and evaluative talents. In addition, the use of varied modalities caters to a variety of learning preferences, including those of kinesthetic, auditory, and visual learners. The multimedia information, interactive activities, and collaborative platforms that are offered via digital technologies are designed to meet these requirements. Interactive technologies foster creativity, exploration, and critical thinking, which further enriches the learning experience. In addition, enhanced involvement further strengthens the learning experience. Last but not least, ensuring that digital activities are aligned with the aims of the curriculum assures that they are in accordance with academic standards while also incorporating constructivist ideas. Educators are able to create a dynamic and inclusive learning environment that maximises student engagement and intellectual progress by deliberately using technology into their lessons.

The use of Bloom's Taxonomy to digital learning results in improvements to both the overall design and delivery of teaching in the humanities. It is possible for educators to guarantee that students not only take in information but also analyse, evaluate, and develop new understandings by matching cognitive goals with certain digital tools and tactics. Bloom's paradigm continues to be a crucial guide for developing learning experiences that are profound, meaningful, and technologically enhanced, even as the humanities continue to adapt to digital contexts [11].

3.3 Vygotsky's Zone of Proximal Development

The ZPD hypothesis developed by Lev Vygotsky is an essential component of sociocultural learning theory. This theory places an emphasis on the role that guidance and cooperation have in the development of a learner's capabilities. Students often participate in complicated, interpretive activities that might benefit from organised guidance, which is why this notion is especially pertinent to digital learning and education in the humanities. Providing learners with interactive materials, guided conversations, and adaptive feedback mechanisms that bridge the gap between their present comprehension and future mastery may be accomplished via the use of digital technologies, which can operate as scaffolds. Peer collaboration, instructor-led inquiry, and technology-assisted discovery are all examples of activities that may be considered examples of ZPD in the field of humanities education. Students are improved in their ability to interact critically with texts, historical studies, and philosophical debates via the use of platforms like as discussion forums, collaborative annotation tools, and tutoring systems powered by artificial intelligence. Teachers are able to encourage more profound intellectual engagement among their students by providing digital learning experiences that are in line with the principles of ZPD. This helps to ensure that students gradually build their ability to independently analyse and evaluate information. Not only does this strategy improve learning results, but it also fosters an educational atmosphere that is dynamic and sensitive to what students are learning.

3.3.1 Understanding the ZPD Framework

The ZPD is a key term in Vygotsky's sociocultural learning theory, emphasising the gap between what a learner can do on their own and what they can achieve with suitable assistance. It symbolises the ideal learning zone, in which pupils face difficulties that extend their skills without becoming overpowering. Learning in the ZPD promotes cognitive development by encouraging students to build on existing knowledge while getting organised help from a More Knowledgeable Other (MKO), who may be a teacher, a peer, or even AI-powered educational technologies.

In digital learning settings, technology is increasingly vital in supporting student learning in the ZPD. Intelligent tutoring systems, collaborative platforms, and adaptive learning tools may all function as virtual MKOs, giving real-time feedback, personalised support, and organised learning paths. These digital resources guarantee that students interact with information at the appropriate level of difficulty, enabling deeper comprehension and skill development. By using ZPD-based teaching practices, educators may create meaningful learning experiences that challenge students while providing them with the tools they need to succeed [12].

Three Levels of Development

1. Actual Development Level: What the learner can do unaided.
2. Zone of Proximal Development: What the learner can do with support.
3. Potential Development Level: What the learner could eventually do independently.

3.3.2 ZPD and Technology in Humanities Education

Students are able to interact with more difficult humanities disciplines such as literature, history, and philosophy because to the proliferation of digital resources, which have considerably expanded the scope of scaffolding in the educational system. Students have the opportunity to engage in real-time interaction with their classmates and teachers via the use of collaborative tools, which allows them to refine their interpretations of historical events and literature. In order to encourage deeper involvement, platforms like as digital annotation tools, discussion boards, and shared knowledge repositories are used. These platforms allow students to function within their ZPD by providing them with direction while simultaneously allowing them to establish individual interpretations. Intelligent tutoring systems provide additional help for ZPD by providing adaptive feedback and personalised learning paths. Students may be assisted in the construction of arguments, the identification of biases in historical narratives, or the exploration of philosophical issues by using tools powered by artificial intelligence. This ensures that obstacles stay within their grasp. Furthermore, multimedia resources, which include interactive timelines, digital archives, and virtual reality experiences, make it possible for students to engage in immersive learning. This kind of learning assists students in contextualising material in ways that go beyond the scope of conventional text-based study. Educators are able to build dynamic learning environments by using these technologies. These settings provide students with constant support, challenges, and encouragement to develop critical thinking abilities that are in line with constructivist concepts [13] (Table 3.4).

These tools allow instructors to differentiate instruction and provide timely intervention, ensuring that each learner operates within their optimal learning zone.

3.3.3 Examples of ZPD in Digital Humanities Learning

1. **Collaborative Annotation**: Students use collaborative annotation tools such as Hypothes is and Perusall to conduct collective textual analysis, presenting

Table 3.4 ZPD and technology in humanities education

Aspect	Digital application in humanities
Scaffolding content	Interactive eBooks, video explanations, and guided reading tools
Peer collaboration	Google Docs, Padlet, and discussion forums
Feedback and modelling	LMS comments, AI feedback tools, and recorded lectures
Gradual release of responsibility	Adaptive learning platforms, tiered assignment structures

incisive questions and providing diverse interpretations of challenging texts. This dynamic process encourages peer-mediated learning, which is an essential component of Vygotsky's ZPD. As students communicate, less experienced learners benefit from their classmates' knowledge and analytical capabilities, developing confidence in text interpretation and broadening their critical thinking abilities. The exchange of ideas fosters deeper knowledge, helping students to fine-tune arguments and acquire nuanced views. This organised cooperation allows learners to actively generate meaning, bridging the gap between autonomous understanding and expert-level analysis. These technologies not only promote cognitive growth but also foster intellectual conversation, making digital platforms essential in current humanities education [14].

2. **Guided Textual Analysis**: A history teacher may successfully include Voyant Tools into their curriculum to help students improve their analytical abilities in political debate. As an MKO, the instructor first teaches how to use the tool to analyse word frequency in political speeches, emphasising patterns, rhetorical methods, and significant topics. Through guided practice, students reproduce the process with organised guidance, learning to comprehend the importance of repeated phrases and linguistic alterations throughout time. As their confidence grows, students go to independent application, where they pick new speeches and do their own analysis. This method, based on the ZPD, allows students to go from supported discovery to mastery while promoting critical thinking, historical interpretation, and digital literacy within a constructivist learning framework [15].
3. **Blended Learning Pathways**: Platforms such as Moodle and Edmodo provide instructors tremendous tools for structuring classes with scaffolded materials that lead students through different learning stages. By including videos, quizzes, and discussion prompts, teachers may help students shift from early coaching to autonomous mastery. These platforms provide dynamic lesson sequencing, which allows students to engage with core knowledge before applying ideas in higher-order thinking activities. Structured digital scaffolding allows learners to obtain timely feedback, communicate with peers, and improve their comprehension in an interactive setting. Gradually lowering instructional assistance promotes self-directed learning while still providing a clear route for skill growth. Educators

may use these digital platforms successfully to develop adaptive learning experiences that promote autonomy, critical analysis, and greater engagement with humanities topics [16].

3.3.4 *Teacher as Mediator in Digital Contexts*

Vygotsky's focus on social interaction in learning is still relevant in digital contexts, where instructors play a changing but fundamental role as facilitators of student growth. Instructors enable meaningful interaction by curating resources, which include digital tools, texts, and multimedia material that are appropriate for student preparation and learning goals. This ensures that learners get suitably scaffolded content in their ZPD. Additionally, instructors may monitor progress by utilising analytics from LMS, which measure engagement levels, understanding, and involvement in collaborative activities. They analyse this data to find areas that need intervention and alter teaching tactics appropriately. Finally, feedback remains an important role, since immediate, personalised input, whether via discussion boards, interactive tasks, or video responses, helps bridge the gap between present knowledge and future mastery. These interventions guarantee that learners are continually encouraged, challenged, and actively engaged in the digital learning experience [17].

3.3.5 *ZPD and Equity in Digital Humanities*

The incorporation of the ZPD into digital humanities education also raises critical questions of access and fairness. Students join learning settings at various developmental stages, backgrounds, and support requirements, necessitating the use of inclusive digital solutions. Well-designed technology may help overcome these gaps and promote equal learning experiences. Accessibility technologies, such as text-to-speech and screen readers, are critical for students with impairments, allowing them to interact meaningfully with educational content. Flexible pacing enables learners who need more time or review to assimilate material at their own pace, avoiding knowledge gaps from growing. Language assistance, including translation plugins and bilingual materials, guarantees that non-native speakers and multilingual learners may fully engage. By using these digital resources, instructors may broaden the ZPD for various students, making humanities instruction more inclusive and responsive to individual learning requirements [18] (Table 3.5).

The ZPD, which was developed by Vygotsky, offers a strong lens through which to examine the method of teaching digital humanities. When educators have a greater knowledge of the ZPD and can operationalise it in digital environments, they are better able to scaffold student learning, stimulate collaborative engagement, and personalise teaching to students with a variety of abilities. As a result of their strategic integration, digital tools transform into contemporary MKOs that provide assistance,

Table 3.5 Aligning digital tools with ZPD functions

ZPD function	Digital tool/strategy	Humanities application
Modeling	Video tutorials, screen recordings	Demonstrating historical analysis or literary close reading
Guided practice	Interactive worksheets, adaptive learning systems	Practising grammar in language learning or analysing texts
Peer collaboration	Padlet, shared docs, and discussion forums	Collaborative analysis of primary sources
Feedback and correction	Automated quizzes, teacher audio/video feedback	Evaluating student interpretations of philosophical texts
Independent practice	Digital storytelling, blog creation	Synthesising content into original digital narratives

feedback, and modelling, so making higher-order learning in the humanities more accessible and inclusive.

3.4 Connectivism in the Digital Age

Ingrassia et al. [19] first presented the concept of connectivism, which reframes learning as a process that takes place in a network rather than as a linear transmission of information. This idea recognises that in the modern world, information is always changing, and as a result, it is necessary for students to acquire the abilities necessary to navigate, connect, and curate knowledge across a variety of platforms. Connectivism learning is characterised by the integration of digital spaces, communities, and real-time data streams into the learning process, as opposed to depending primarily on traditional classroom teaching. From the perspective of humanities education, connectivism offers a crucial lens through which to comprehend the manner in which students interact with vast and ever-changing bodies of information. In the process of meaning construction, it emphasises the significance of working together, being literate in digital technology, and being flexible. Learners become active participants in the production of knowledge, developing interpretations that reflect a dynamic and linked intellectual environment. This might occur via the use of open-access research, discussion forums, or multimedia archives.

3.4.1 Principles of Connectivism

The concept of learning is rethought through the lens of connectivism, which places more of an emphasis on networked information than on isolated cognition. Instead of learning taking place entirely inside the mind of a person, this concept considers learning to take place across a variety of sources, including formal institutions, digital platforms, and interactions with peers. It is not enough to say that technology is only a delivery method; rather, it is an inherent element of the learning process that helps facilitate linkages between different ideas, disciplines, and points of view. Instead of emphasizing static knowledge, connectivism places an emphasis on the capacity to know, which helps learners become better equipped to navigate an informational environment that is always evolving.

Education in the humanities, which thrives on interdisciplinary analysis, introspective inquiry, and the integration of diverse points of view, is strongly aligned with these ideals. Subjects in the humanities inspire students to participate in complex decision-making, critically assess views, and link concepts that span other areas. These are abilities that are essential to a networked, adaptive learning environment that is driven by connectivism principles.

3.4.2 Relevance of Connectivism in Humanities Learning

A more networked and participatory method of learning is promoted by connectivism, which improves humanities education. Students in fields such as literature, philosophy, history, and cultural studies are more likely to be encouraged to develop knowledge collaboratively as opposed to individually. Learners are able to interact with a variety of interpretations, analyse texts from a number of different angles, and participate to growing intellectual discussions in real time thanks to digital platforms and collaborative technologies. This method is especially useful in the field of humanities, which is characterised by the formation of knowledge via conversation, contextual analysis, and linkages across different fields of study. Learners have the opportunity to engage with historical narratives, philosophical debates, and cultural discourses as they evolve via the use of open-access research, blogs, forums, and digital archives. Students are given the ability to traverse complicated information environments while making important contributions to current academic and cultural discourses when humanities education is transformed into a dynamic and interactive process via the adoption of connectivism concepts (Table 3.6).

3.4.3 Digital Networks as Learning Environments

Connectivism learning thrives in decentralised, networked settings where knowledge is constantly co-created and shared across digital platforms. Unlike conventional classroom methods that focus on linear learning, connectivism views MOOCs, OERs, wikis, blogs, and social media as dynamic places for intellectual interchange. These platforms do more than just offer knowledge; they allow students to interact with ideas collectively, improve interpretations, and contribute to growing discourses. A student studying Shakespeare, for example, may take part in a worldwide discussion forum analysing various performances of Hamlet, search digital archives for annotated

Table 3.6 Connectivism aligned with humanities learning

Connectivism principle	Humanities application	Digital tool example
Learning is networked	Collaborative literary annotation	Hypothes.is
Knowledge is distributed	Access to global archives and primary sources	JSTOR, Google Arts & Culture
Currency is vital	Engagement with current social discourse and media texts	X (formerly Twitter), YouTube
Diverse connections	Analysis across cultural, historical, and social perspectives	Online forums, blogs
Self-directed learning	Learners curate, evaluate, and synthesize information independently	RSS feeds, Pocket, Zotero

editions, and compare theatrical versions from other civilisations. This networked learning strategy promotes interdisciplinary linkages, improves digital literacy, and enables students to gain a nuanced grasp of complicated topics via active participation in enormous, ever-changing information ecosystems [20].

3.4.4 *The Role of the Educator in Connectivism Environments*

In connectivist pedagogy, the educator transitions from a typical topic specialist to a network facilitator, assisting students in accessing, assessing, and synthesising information across several platforms. This function is vital in assisting learners in developing digital literacy and discernment, which ensures they can critically evaluate sources and participate meaningfully with digital knowledge systems. By encouraging cross-cultural and interdisciplinary dialogue, educators allow students to link ideas across disciplines, engage with global viewpoints, and broaden their intellectual horizons beyond traditional classroom limits. Encouraging self-directed and collaborative knowledge construction allows students to take control of their learning, participate in ongoing debates, and contribute to common knowledge networks. This transition is consistent with the humanistic educational goal of developing autonomous, critical, and morally involved learners capable of navigating complex, interconnected digital landscapes with confidence and intellectual curiosity [21].

3.4.5 Connectivism and Critical Digital Literacy

One of connectivism's most important contributions to humanities education is its close connection with critical digital literacy, a necessary skill in a society moulded by algorithm-driven information flows. In this networked digital world, learners must acquire the capacity to question sources of authority, critically analysing the legitimacy and dependability of material they come across online. Recognising and detecting bias and misinformation is equally important, since digital media often amplifies selected narratives and shapes public perception in complicated ways. Furthermore, comprehending the social and cultural ramifications of technology enables students to interact with digital platforms as active participants, reflecting on how algorithms impact conversation and access to information. Digital surveillance, data privacy, and ethical concerns are also important issues to consider while navigating online places, ensuring that learners are informed and responsible. Given the humanities' roots in criticism, reflection, and interdisciplinary inquiry, they are particularly positioned to provide students with the analytical skills necessary to interact meaningfully with the networked, digital world via a connectivism perspective [22].

3.4.6 Challenges and Critiques

There are several difficulties with connectivism, despite the fact that it provides a new way of looking at education in the digital age. Its detractors contend that, unlike other well-established theories of education, it does not have a solid foundation in rigorous research due to its lack of empirical validation. Because of this, I have doubts about its ability to shape lasting, meaningful learning experiences. Furthermore, inequalities might emerge from a over-reliance on technology, which unwittingly benefits certain pupils at the expense of others who lack access to digital resources. Instead of bridging current educational disparities, connectivism learning might worsen them under an unequal infrastructure. The quick and connected nature of digital learning may sometimes impede in-depth, prolonged investigation, which leads to another significant problem: the fragmentation of knowledge. Students who put an emphasis on surface-level knowledge at the expense of deeper understanding run the danger of watering down the richness and complexity of humanities education. Teachers may alleviate these worries by using connectivism tactics with intentional design, which means making sure that technology boosts engagement without sacrificing inclusiveness, coherence, or intellectual depth. To maximise the benefits of connectivism and minimise its drawbacks, it is necessary to strike a balance between online connectedness and thoughtful, organised learning [23] (Table 3.7).

One of the most significant shifts in philosophy, pedagogy, and practice that connectivism represents resonates especially strongly with the humanities. Educators can enable learning that is more interactive, decentralised, and in sync with the reality of the digital age if they adopt a networked perspective of knowledge. Because of

Table 3.7 Strengths and limitations of connectivism in humanities

Strengths	Limitations
Encourages collaborative, global learning	Risk of superficial engagement
Promotes digital fluency and critical inquiry	Requires high-level digital access and autonomy
Aligns with open-access and OER movements	May overwhelm learners with too many information sources
Supports interdisciplinary connections	Difficult to assess outcomes through traditional metrics

this idea, practitioners in the field of humanities are urged to rethink how meaning is formed and communicated in modern society, as well as how education might equip students with the ability to traverse this new environment critically and ethically.

3.5 Activity Theory in Educational Technology

Analysis of human activity as a developmental process that is affected by tools, social interactions, and cultural settings is made possible by Activity Theory (AT), which provides a strong framework for conducting such an analysis. AT comes from the work of Lev Vygotsky and Alexei Leontiev, and it was further developed by [24]. It emphasises the fact that learning is not a single cognitive process but rather a dynamic interaction that takes place within a larger structural framework. When it comes to the field of educational technology, assistive technology (AT) offers a lens through which one may comprehend the manner in which students interact with digital tools, social contexts, and institutional structures. In doing so, it highlights the reality that the formation of knowledge is mediated by artefacts, which may range from textbooks to online platforms, and that these artefacts are impacted by community norms and learning goals. Educators can analyse how students interact with technology, identify conflicts or inconsistencies in digital learning environments, and build instructional techniques that improve collaborative and meaningful engagement via the use of AT. Taking this approach highlights the interrelated nature of learning, which makes it especially relevant in contemporary educational environments in which it is implemented.

3.5.1 Foundations of Activity Theory

The idea of learning is conceptualised by AT as a goal-directed activity system, in which human activities are mediated by tools and embedded within social settings. Learning, according to this perspective, is a dynamic and ever-changing process that is influenced by the connections between people, the goals they have set for themselves, and the resources that are accessible to them. Within the context of this paradigm, the term "subject" refers to the individual or group of learners who are participating in the activity, while the term "object" refers to the underlying objective or motivation that is driving their activities. It is the tools or artefacts, which may include digital technology, that work as mediators to enhance the learning experience. They have an impact on how students receive information and interact with it.

Beyond the scope of human contact, assistive technology addresses the larger community, which includes peers, teachers, and digital networks that collectively impact the dynamics of learning. Institutional policies and collaborative norms are examples of the rules that regulate the learning process. These rules set the structure and expectations for the learning process participants. Additionally, the division of labour is responsible for defining tasks and duties within the educational environment. This helps to ensure that meaningful involvement and the exchange of information are present. It is important to note that cognition is not a solo activity but rather a social, tool-mediated process. The way in which these aspects interact with one another is what defines how learning takes place. Educators are able to develop instructional techniques that encourage greater engagement, problem-solving, and collaborative inquiry when they apply AT to educational technology. This allows for the creation of instructional strategies that harness these interactions.

3.5.2 Activity Theory in Digital Humanities Education

The discipline of humanities education may benefit greatly from the use of AT as a framework for the development of efficient digital learning environments. Educators are able to analyse the interactions that take place between students, tools, and larger social environments when they map learning processes as organised systems. As an example, in the context of a project involving collaborative digital storytelling, the subject is the student or group that is accountable for the creation of the narrative. Their goal is to create an engaging digital tale that is founded on research and investigates a historical event. In order to build their work, they will be using several resources, such as digital storytelling software, research databases, and communication platforms. The community, which consists of peers, teachers, and outside experts, plays a significant part in directing the learning process. Rules, which include academic standards, project deadlines, and expectations for collaborative work, are responsible for shaping the workflow. In order to ensure that students are able to function within a framework that is both equitable and productive, the division of labour is used to identify particular tasks. These roles include research, writing, writing, multimedia design, and editing. Through the process of rigorously mapping these components, educators are able to uncover conflicts or inconsistencies within the system that may inhibit learning. This provides them with the opportunity to enhance instructional practices and develop digital learning experiences that are more unified, engaging, and inclusive [9].

3.5.3 Contradictions as Drivers of Learning

The focus that AT places on contradictions, which are the tensions or conflicts that develop within an activity system, is one of the key strengths that sets it apart from other theories. These inconsistencies, rather than being seen as impediments, serve as catalysts for change and growth, pushing modifications in strategies for learning, the incorporation of technical advancements, and the practices of institutions. When it comes to education in the digital humanities, discrepancies often appear in the most important areas. For example, a subject-tool conflict may occur when students do not possess the essential digital literacy to make successful use of specialised platforms, which in turn creates hurdles to participation. In a similar vein, a conflict between rules and tools may arise when institutional norms restrict access to vital digital resources, hence limiting chances for exploration and study that spans several disciplines. The "division of labour-community contradiction" is another prevalent difficulty that arises in digital initiatives. This contradiction occurs when unclear collaboration responsibilities lead to uneven workloads and inefficiency. When educators can identify these conflicts, they are able to enhance instructional design, which ensures that students get enough training, that institutional rules change to facilitate learning, and that cooperation becomes more organised and equitable. Through the use of the analytical framework provided by AT, educators have the ability to transform conflicts into opportunities, so establishing educational settings that are more adaptable, inclusive, and effective, hence positively impacting learning outcomes [25] (Table 3.8).

Table 3.8 Components of activity theory applied to digital humanities

Component	Definition	Example in digital humanities
Subject	Learner or group engaging in the activity	Student group analysing digital archives
Object	Goal or motive driving the activity	Produce a digital exhibit on cultural heritage
Tools/Artifacts	Mediating instruments, both physical and digital	Text analysis software, online databases, multimedia editors
Community	Social group or environment influencing the activity	Class cohort, faculty mentors, digital librarians
Rules	Norms and conventions governing the activity	Citation standards, usage policies for digital tools
Division of labor	Distribution of roles and responsibilities	Researcher, designer, editor, presenter

3.5.4 *Implications for Instructional Design*

Educators are encouraged to perceive learning as a dynamic and interrelated process rather than a sequence of separate occurrences, which is the perspective that Activity Theory promotes. Students are given the opportunity to participate in meaningful inquiry via the use of instructional design that is based on AT. This design focusses on the creation of genuine, goal-oriented assignments that replicate real-world humanities practices. In order to ensure successful learning, it is vital to ensure that proper tools and resources are available. This is because digital platforms make it easier to do research, collaborate with others, and analyse data. By cultivating collaborative communities, educators are able to build environments in which students actively share their knowledge and enhance their interpretations via the participation of their peers. In order to preserve equal participation and ensure that learners participate effectively to conversations and projects, clearly defined roles and expectations are helpful in maintaining equitable participation. In addition, the process of locating and addressing inconsistencies within the system improves both its functioning and its flexibility, which ultimately results in enhanced educational outcomes. As a result of their ability to facilitate multi-modal engagement, peer cooperation, and flexible learning frameworks, digital platforms such as Google Workspace, Slack, and digital archives are very useful tools in the field of humanities education [26].

3.5.5 *Activity Theory and the Socio-Technical Perspective*

Digital humanities may be seen as a dynamic convergence of humanistic inquiry and technology innovation via the socio-technical viewpoint of AT, which provides a compelling lens for understanding digital humanities. The purpose of this framework is to emphasise the reciprocal moulding of technology and pedagogy. It illustrates how digital tools have an impact on educational approaches, while pedagogical principles, in turn, shape the development and deployment of technology in learning settings. In addition to this, it highlights the significance of social context in the process of technology adoption. It acknowledges that digital literacy, institutional accessibility, and disciplinary norms all play significant roles in determining the manner in which students and teachers engage with technology.

Learning is positioned as an iterative process where students and educators adjust techniques based on growing technology breakthroughs and altering academic discourses. AT welcomes the continual evolution of learning activities via reflection and adaptation, which positions learning as an iterative process. It is because of this approach that educators are able to design learning experiences that are not just technologically advanced but also socially significant. This helps to ensure that the area of digital humanities continues to be an inclusive and academically challenging subject that can adapt to the requirements of a wide range of students. Through the incorporation of these ideas, education in the digital humanities has the potential to cultivate profound involvement, collaborative study, and critical inquiry in a digital context that is always evolving [27].

3.5.6 Challenges and Considerations

Although AT provides a strong framework for understanding learning as a dynamic and socially integrated process, its implementation needs careful attention in order to realise its full potential. The difficulty of analysing various interacting components inside an activity system is one of the most significant challenges. This is due to the fact that the interactions between subjects, tools, communities, and rules are fluid and interconnected. A methodical, multi-layered approach to instructional design that takes into consideration the ever-changing requirements of learners is required because of the intricacy of the situation. Another essential component is the need for continuous introspection in order to identify contradictions, which are the conflicts that emerge when several components of an activity system come into conflict with one another. Although they are unavoidable, contradictions provide chances for reform and the development of innovative teaching practices. Nevertheless, in order to successfully address problems, regular monitoring, adaptation, and teamwork are required. It is also possible for institutional limits to generate conflicts between organised rules and the individualised requirements of learners, especially in digital learning contexts. It is possible that standardised laws would restrict students' access to resources or limit their freedom in course design, which will have an effect on their capacity to properly interact with and use educational technology. In order for educators to successfully navigate these complications, they need to strike a balance between the demands of the institution and the approaches that are learner-centred. This involves making sure that digital tools and pedagogical techniques continue to be inclusive, responsive, and aligned with educational objectives. It is possible for educators to maximise the potential of AT by resolving these issues, which will result in activities that generate greater engagement and meaningful learning experiences [28].

In order to investigate the ways in which educational technology might enhance learning in the humanities, AT offers a well-organised and comprehensive perspective. By analysing the dynamic interactions that occur between learners, tools, communities, and social rules, AT gives educators the ability to build digital learning environments that are engaging, facilitate collaboration, and are sensitive to context. It recognises that contradictions, whether they pertain to accessibility, institutional limits, or learner engagement, are not obstacles but rather catalysts for change, which are the driving force behind constant adaptation and innovation. This approach enables educators to modify instructional practices in the field of digital humanities education. This helps to ensure that technology supports inquiry rather than only providing material. As a result of the application of AT principles, digital learning transforms into a process that is socially grounded and critically reflective. This makes humanities education more responsive to the ever-changing needs of technology and interdisciplinary study.

3.6 The TPACK Framework (Technological Pedagogical Content Knowledge)

It was [29] who first presented the TPACK framework, which functions as an all-encompassing paradigm for the purpose of efficiently integrating technology into educational settings. It sheds insight on the dynamic relationship that exists between three fundamental categories of knowledge, namely Content Knowledge (CK), Pedagogical Knowledge (PK), and Technological Knowledge (TK). While CK denotes an educator's experience in their subject area, PK denotes an awareness of instructional techniques and the processes by which students learn, and TK denotes an understanding of how to use digital resources to improve teaching. Rather than considering these knowledge domains in isolation, TPACK places an emphasis on their interconnection. It asserts that in order for technology-enhanced education to be really successful, it is necessary to integrate all three of these knowledge domains in a balanced manner. Not only do teachers need to have a strong command of their subject matter, but they must also possess the ability to develop instructional practices that make meaningful and original use of technology. Teachers are able to build learning experiences that are engaging and student-centred by carefully combining these features. This ensures that technology acts as a tool for deeper comprehension rather than just a means for delivering material.

3.6.1 Components of the TPACK Framework

Effective technology integration in education is broken down into three main components by the TPACK framework. These essential components are referred to as CK, PK, and TK. An educator's competence in the humanities, which includes history, literature, philosophy, and cultural studies, is represented by the CK designation. PK places an emphasis on teaching practices, classroom dynamics, lesson preparation, and student evaluation, to ensure that instructional approaches are in line with learning goals. TK, on the other hand, encompasses digital competency, which ranges from fundamental digital literacy to complex technology applications that improve the experience of teaching. These areas do not operate independently; rather, they interconnect, which necessitates a balanced strategy in which technology contributes to the enhancement of teaching strategies while simultaneously enhancing subject matter expertise. By gaining an understanding of this interaction, educators are able to create learning experiences that are both engaging and student-centred. They are also able to use digital resources in ways that enhance inquiry, sharpen critical thinking, and build meaningful academic conversation in the field of humanities education.

3.6.2 *Intersections in TPACK*

Instead of just considering CK, PK, and TK to be distinct entities, the TPACK framework places an emphasis on the intersections between these three types of knowledge. This is where the framework's actual value resides. It is essential to create education that is both successful and improved by technology, and these intersections are essential.

PCK emphasizes the tactics that are necessary to successfully teach a particular topic. This assists educators in adapting their teaching approaches to meet the specific requirements of humanistic subjects. The term "Technological Content Knowledge" (TCK) refers to how technology may be used to represent, assist, or increase interaction with subject matter. This can be accomplished via the use of digital archives, interactive maps for historical study, or multimedia tools in the field of literary studies. The field of study known as "Technological Pedagogical Knowledge" (TPK) investigates how the teaching and learning processes change as a result of the incorporation of technology, hence influencing how students engage with and create in knowledge. Assuring that digital tools are not only add-ons but rather vital parts that increase inquiry, debate, and critical engagement within the learning process is the goal of TPACK, which is the capacity to mix technology, pedagogy, and content in a seamless manner. This is the core of these intersections. Due to this integration, educators are able to develop educational experiences that are rich, adaptable, and student-centered, which in turn deepens learning in classrooms that are dedicated to the study of the humanities.

3.6.3 *TPACK in Humanities Education*

TPACK is a significant framework that may be used in the field of humanities education to facilitate the integration of technology with conventional research in order to develop a deeper knowledge and more critical engagement. The ability to intelligently employ digital resources in ways that stimulate inquiry, debate, and research is made possible for educators by this program. Students are able to strengthen their historical research abilities via the use of digital archives, which enable them to analyse original documents, manuscripts, and interactive databases. This is an example of how the intersection of TK and CK may be seen in action. Similarly, the interaction between TK and PK comes to life in interactive discussion forums, where students participate in critical debate, discussing philosophical ideas or analysing literary works in collaborative settings. Exemplifying the complete incorporation of TPACK is the practice of using multimedia presentations. In these presentations, educators

Table 3.9 TPACK components and applications in humanities

TPACK component	Description	Example in humanities education
Content Knowledge (CK)	Understanding humanities disciplines	Knowledge of literary theory, historical periods
Pedagogical Knowledge (PK)	Teaching strategies and assessment methods	Socratic seminars, essay writing workshops
Technological Knowledge (TK)	Familiarity with educational technology tools	Learning management systems, annotation software
Pedagogical Content Knowledge (PCK)	Effective methods for teaching humanities content	Scaffolded reading assignments, guided analysis
Technological Content Knowledge (TCK)	Using tech tools to represent humanities concepts	Digital mapping of historical events, textual analysis tools
Technological Pedagogical Knowledge (TPK)	Using technology to support pedagogy	Flipped classroom with video lectures, online quizzes
Technological Pedagogical Content Knowledge (TPACK)	Integrative knowledge combining all three domains	Designing a collaborative digital humanities project

combine their knowledge of the subject matter, pedagogical methodologies, and digital tools including video, infographics, and interactive storytelling in order to provide completely immersive learning experiences. By capitalising on these intersections, educators are able to provide dynamic, technology-enhanced lectures that encourage critical thinking and interdisciplinary investigation in classrooms that are dedicated to the study of the humanities (Table 3.9).

3.6.4 *Benefits of Applying TPACK*

Through the use of the TPACK framework, educators are encouraged to regard technology not as a superficial addition to learning design but rather as an integral component of learning design. An increase in student engagement may be achieved by the seamless integration of digital technologies with pedagogy and material. This allows instructors to create experiences that are more engaging and deeper. This technique also encourages reflective teaching practices, which enables educators to continuously modify their instructional strategies in response to the development of new technologies and the ever-changing requirements of the educational system. A further benefit of TPACK is that it promotes learner-centred methods and provides personalised learning paths that are tailored to the specific requirements of each student. Whether it be via adaptive learning tools, interactive discussion platforms, or multimedia materials, technology gives students the opportunity to actively engage with knowledge in ways that are tailored to their own preferences for learning. Furthermore, the use of this framework has the impact of enhancing the confidence and competence of educators in their ability to make good use of digital tools. This helps to ensure that technology is utilised as a significant enhancement of knowledge rather than a distraction. Through the use of TPACK, educators are able to design learning environments that are dynamic and forward-thinking, therefore preparing students for a world that is becoming more digital.

3.6.5 Challenges in TPACK Implementation

In spite of the fact that the TPACK framework provides a complete method for incorporating technology into educational settings, its effective application requires continuous attention to a number of important difficulties. Because educators are required to keep up with the quickly developing digital tools and platforms, one of the most important issues is the need for continual professional development. It may be challenging to retain one's competency in technical knowledge if one does not get consistent training and assistance regularly. Additionally, achieving a balance between the three knowledge domains, CK, PK, and Technological Knowledge TK presents several challenges, especially for educators who have a profound understanding of their subject matter but a limited amount of experience with educational technology. The instructional design and the leadership of the institution are both necessary components in order to achieve the desired balance between these components. In addition, the possibility of fully realising the promise of TPACK is contingent upon the availability of resources and the assistance of institutions. The provision of the required infrastructure, financing, and chances for professional growth that enable educators to successfully incorporate technology is a crucial role that is played by educational institutions, such as both schools and universities. Differences in access might limit the efficiency of technology-enhanced training if these supports are not provided. When these difficulties are addressed, it guarantees that TPACK will continue to be a framework for digital learning that is both practical and meaningful.

3.6.6 TPACK and Digital Humanities

The ideals of TPACK are embodied in the DH, which are characterised by the combination of humanities material with computer tools and processes. Educators who make use of TPACK are able to better educate students to engage in this multidisciplinary area by using tools for text mining, digital curation, and multimedia storytelling while yet retaining a rigorous humanistic inquiry. It is the TPACK framework that serves as a cornerstone for the integration of technology into humanities education. It provides an organised way to merging technical, pedagogical, and subject knowledge all at the same time. It is possible for educators to design learning experiences that encourage critical analysis, creative inquiry, and meaningful interaction with digital technologies if they are able to achieve balance across these areas. For as long as technology continues to improve, TPACK will continue to be an adaptable paradigm. This will ensure that humanities education will continue to develop alongside new digital possibilities. Educators that make use of TPACK have the ability to enhance inquiry, deepen reflection, and widen academic conversation in ways that are relevant to modern students. This may be accomplished via interactive discussion forums, digital archives, or multimedia storytelling. The fact that it places such a strong focus on adaptability and creativity makes it an invaluable resource for maintaining a good humanities education in a world that is becoming more interconnected [30].

3.7 SAMR Model for Technology Integration

The SAMR model, which was established by [31], offers a systematic framework for analysing the incorporation of technology in educational settings. It classifies the use of technology into four successive degrees, which are referred to as Substitution, Augmentation, Modification, and Redefinition. Each of these phases represents a more profound modification of learning experiences. In the "Substitution" level, technology merely takes the place of a conventional instrument without causing any significant changes. For example, using a digital document rather than paper is an example of this. Enhancing a task with functional enhancements, such as introducing multimedia components into a lecture, is an example of what is meant by the term "augmentation." The term "modification" refers to the process of reshaping learning activities in order to enable greater participation. One example of this is the interactive cooperation amongst peers on shared digital platforms. The most revolutionary aspect of the term "Redefinition" is that it makes it possible to have whole new educational experiences that were previously unattainable without the use of technology. These experiences include global real-time conversations with historians or immersive virtual reality excursions of historical locations. To ensure that technology serves as a tool for deeper critical thinking, collaboration, and creativity in the learning process, the SAMR framework urges educators to go beyond mere replacement and towards meaningful innovation. This is done to enhance the learning experience. The use of this strategy encourages educators to contemplate the ways in which digital resources might improve, restructure, or redefine their instructional strategies [32].

3.7.1 The Four Levels of SAMR

The SAMR model provides a structured approach to technology integration, progressing from basic substitution to full transformation of learning experiences.

1. Substitution: At this stage, technology functions as a direct replacement for traditional tools without changing the learning process. A student might type an essay on a word processor instead of handwriting it, but the overall experience remains the same.
2. Augmentation: Technology enhances traditional tasks by adding functional improvements that refine the learning experience. A word processor with spell-check, grammar suggestions, and formatting tools helps students improve their writing, making the task more efficient and accessible.
3. Modification: This level introduces significant task redesign, reshaping how students engage with content. Instead of working in isolation, students collaborate in real time on a shared document, offering peer feedback and making joint edits—a process difficult to replicate with traditional methods.
4. Redefinition: The most transformative stage, where technology creates entirely new learning experiences that were previously impossible. Students might produce multimedia projects that combine video, audio, and text shared globally, or use virtual reality to explore historical sites, bringing immersive, interactive elements into humanities education.

By guiding educators through these levels, the SAMR model encourages a shift from basic substitution toward innovative learning design, ensuring technology enhances critical thinking, collaboration, and creativity rather than merely replicating traditional methods.

3.7.2 SAMR in Humanities Education

The SAMR model offers humanities educators a clear pathway to transforming digital learning, moving from simple substitution to innovative, technology-driven engagement.

1. Substitution: At this stage, technology replaces traditional tools without altering the learning process. A student might read a PDF version of a classic novel instead of a printed copy, gaining convenience but not fundamentally changing the experience.
2. Augmentation: Technology begins to enhance learning by introducing functional improvements. Annotating the PDF using digital highlights and comments allows students to interact with the text more dynamically, supporting close reading and textual analysis in ways that go beyond conventional margin notes.
3. Modification: Learning activities undergo a significant redesign as students engage in collaborative annotation, co-creating a digital annotated edition of a literary text using platforms like Hypothesis or Google Docs. This approach fosters peer dialogue, enabling richer interpretative exchanges that deepen engagement with the material.
4. Redefinition: Technology enables entirely new learning experiences that were previously impossible. Instead of static text-based analysis, students create an

Table 3.10 SAMR levels with humanities examples

SAMR level	Description	Example in humanities education
Substitution	Technology replaces traditional tool, no change	Reading e-books instead of printed books
Augmentation	Substitute with functional improvement	Using digital annotation tools on texts
Modification	Significant redesign of tasks	Collaborative online research projects
Redefinition	Technology enables new, previously impossible tasks	VR reenactments of historical events

interactive digital exhibit, combining primary sources, multimedia elements, and social media engagement to explore a historical event, such as the Civil Rights Movement or the Renaissance. This interdisciplinary approach turns humanities study into immersive, participatory scholarship.

By following SAMR's progressive model, humanities educators can ensure that digital tools enhance rather than replace traditional methods, fostering critical thinking, creativity, and deeper engagement in literature, history, and philosophy classrooms (Table 3.10).

3.7.3 Benefits of Using SAMR

It is the responsibility of educators to use the SAMR model as a strong reflection tool in order to guarantee that technology is incorporated in a meaningful manner rather than in a superficial one. SAMR advocates a change away from "basic substitution" and towards "transformative learning experiences" that improve engagement and deepen comprehension. This transition is brought about by forcing educators to critically review their use of digital resources.

As an additional benefit, SAMR encourages progressive professional development, which assists educators in developing self-assurance in their ability to make effective use of technology. The methodology allows for progressive development, leading educators through a planned process of technology integration. This is in contrast to the traditional approach, which involves immediately implementing full-scale innovations while simultaneously overloading educators. In addition to assisting in the development of skills, SAMR also provides assistance in the creation of interactive learning experiences that are in line with higher-order thinking, so encouraging creativity, cooperation, and analytical depth. Furthermore, it guarantees that digital technologies have a pedagogical function, as opposed to being introduced just for the sake of novelty or convenience. SAMR assists instructors in making decisions that are purposeful and well-informed, which enriches the education of humanities students. This is accomplished by facilitating meaningful discourse about the role that technology plays in learning.

3.7.4 Challenges and Considerations

The SAMR model's effective implementation is contingent on a number of important factors to be taken into account. In order to go beyond the concepts of replacement and augmentation, it is vital to have proper training, access to resources, and institutional support. This will ensure that educators have the skills and confidence they need to adopt more revolutionary teaching techniques. Because of the absence of this infrastructure, the integration of technology could only occur at superficial levels, rather than generating innovation that is significant. Furthermore, educators have a responsibility to be purposeful in aligning the use of technology with learning objectives. This involves making certain that digital tools contribute to rather than detract from the achievement of pedagogical goals. Simply including technology for the sake of using it might result in unproductive learning experiences; thus, it is necessary to integrate technology with a purpose. However, there may be resistance or a lack of familiarity with the tools that are necessary for modification and redefinition. This is especially true among educators who are new to digital platforms or who operate in situations with restricted access to technology resources. Educators need to be provided with training, opportunities for cooperation, and progressive adaptation in order to overcome this difficulty. This will guarantee that they feel empowered rather than overwhelmed.

It is important to note that not all information or situations need modification at the highest levels of SAMR; in many instances, replacement is perfectly acceptable. For instance, if the main objective is to analyse text, then reading a PDF of a classic work rather than a paper book may not require any augmentation or change. However, the most important thing is to utilise SAMR in a strategic manner, which means recognising when and when technology serves as a significant facilitator of learning rather than imposing change in situations where it is not essential.

3.7.5 SAMR and Digital Humanities

Guiding teachers and students towards more innovative and transforming engagement with material, the SAMR model presents a structured, scaffolded approach to integrating digital technologies in humanities scholarship and education. Technology replaces directly at the substitution level; digitised archives let students access historical books and manuscripts online, therefore reproducing conventional research techniques in a digital version. Turning now towards augmentation, technology brings functional enhancements. Linked resources, searchable databases, and interactive annotation tools improve the study of original texts, hence increasing the dynamic nature of research. Students interact with interactive databases, work on digital editions of texts, or apply computational analysis to find trends in literature, so transforming humanities research. At its most developed level, redefining technology generates totally new learning opportunities beyond traditional methods. Projects including multimedia storytelling, immersive virtual reality visits to historical locations, and artificial intelligence-assisted textual analysis let students interact with humanities information in innovative ways. To ensure that technology deepens critical inquiry, fosters creative scholarship, and expands pedagogical possibilities rather than merely replacing conventional methods, SAMR advises humanities teachers to thinkfully integrate digital tools.

There is a defined process for integrating technology in humanities education that is provided by the SAMR model. This progression guides educators towards transformational digital learning experiences. It is possible for teachers to progressively boost student involvement by transitioning from the practice of replacement, in which conventional duties are simply copied in digital forms, to the practice of augmentation, which improves functionality. The process of modification reimagines learning activities, which in turn encourages cooperation and the production of interactive material. On the other hand, the process of redefinition allows innovative methods, such as the creation of multimedia projects and the virtual exploration of historical locations. When used in a planned manner, SAMR not only helps students become more proficient in technology but it also helps them get a deeper grasp of the subject matter, which in turn encourages them to interact critically with digital technologies. It provides educators with the ability to adapt, innovate, and create meaningful interactions, ensuring that technology supports learning rather than just digitising old methods of instruction. Through the use of this framework, education in the humanities continues to be dynamic, participative, and intellectually interesting.

3.8 Motivation Theory in Digital Learning

The importance of motivation cannot be overstated when it comes to the formation of learning experiences, engagement, and perseverance, particularly in technological education. When it comes to learning environments in the humanities, having a grasp of motivation theory enables educators to build spaces that are rich, student-centered, and that nurture both intrinsic and extrinsic motivation, so fostering deeper intellectual engagement.

Intrinsic motivation, which may be motivated by curiosity, interest, or personal fulfilment, is particularly crucial in technology-mediated humanities education. In this kind of education, students investigate literature, history, and philosophy via the use of interactive digital tools, archival research, and multimedia storytelling. It is possible to maintain students' inherent curiosity and thirst for discovery via the use of strategies such as gamification, personalised learning routes, and creative digital projects.

The third kind of motivation, known as extrinsic motivation, is impacted by variables such as grades, institutional structures, and external incentives. These are all aspects that may be successfully integrated with collaborative digital learning, project-based evaluations, and skill-building frameworks. In the context of technology-enhanced humanities education, motivation theories provide educators with the ability to analyse how students interact, identify hurdles to persistence, and strategically deploy interventions that promote commitment and success. In order to guarantee that students continue to be actively immersed in scholarly research, motivation theory provides support for ongoing and dynamic engagement. This is accomplished via the use of adaptive learning technology, relevant interdisciplinary investigation, and meaningful communication amongst peers.

3.8.1 The Importance of Motivation in Digital Learning

Digital learning environments present learners with a number of challenges as well as opportunities in terms of their motivation. When compared to traditional classrooms, which are characterised by face-to-face interactions and immediate social cues that help maintain student engagement, digital platforms require students to demonstrate a greater degree of self-direction and discipline. In the absence of physical presence, students may experience feelings of isolation, decreased accountability, or digital distractions, all of which have the potential to have an adverse effect on their motivation if they are not effectively managed. The use of digital tools, on the other hand, presents compelling opportunities for individual motivation. Learners are able to progress at their own pace with the assistance of features such as personalised learning paths, which ensure that the content presented to them is tailored to their specific interests and skill levels. Providing reinforcement that assists in maintaining focus is the purpose of instant feedback mechanisms, which include automated quizzes, real-time assessments, and tutoring driven by artificial intelligence. Through the use of gamification elements such as badges, challenges, and interactive storytelling, learning can be transformed into an engaging experience, which in turn helps to foster intrinsic motivation. In addition, collaborative opportunities, which include online study groups, discussion forums, and peer review platforms, combat feelings of isolation by establishing learning environments that are both socially driven and interactive. The implementation of these digital strategies in a thoughtful manner allows educators to mitigate the challenges associated with motivation while simultaneously capitalising on the strengths of technology to improve learning outcomes such as persistence, engagement, and deeper content comprehension.

3.8.2 *Key Motivation Theories Relevant to Digital Learning*

Several motivation theories underpin strategies for supporting learners in digital humanities education. These include:

1. **Self-Determination Theory (SDT)**

Self-Determination Theory, developed by Deci and Ryan in 1985, highlights three fundamental psychological needs that drive intrinsic motivation: autonomy, competence, and relatedness. Autonomy refers to a learner's ability to make choices about their education, allowing them to control their learning paths, select topics of interest, and pace their study. When students feel empowered to make these decisions, their engagement and persistence naturally increase. Competence is the need to feel effective and capable of mastering tasks. Digital learning environments address this by providing instant feedback, interactive assignments, and scaffolded challenges that progressively build skills. When learners see their progress through quizzes, adaptive learning modules, and performance tracking tools, their confidence in their abilities strengthens.

Relatedness, the third key element, involves social connection and a sense of belonging. In digital education, discussion forums, peer review systems, and collaborative projects create an interactive learning space where students engage with one another, exchange ideas, and support each other's learning journey. By designing digital platforms that satisfy these psychological needs, educators cultivate an environment where motivation thrives, leading to deeper engagement and sustained academic success.

2. **Expectancy-Value Theory**

This theory suggests that a learner's motivation is shaped by two key factors: their expectation of success and the perceived value of the task. In digital humanities education, this principle plays a crucial role in designing learning experiences that foster engagement and persistence.

Educators can enhance motivation by clearly demonstrating how digital tools connect to students' academic and professional aspirations. For instance, integrating digital archives into coursework helps students develop essential research skills, preparing them for scholarly work or careers in history, literature, and cultural studies. Similarly, digital storytelling offers a dynamic way to express cultural narratives, allowing students to creatively explore their identities and historical contexts through multimedia formats.

By making the relevance of digital tools explicit, educators encourage students to see technology not as an obstacle but as an opportunity for deeper inquiry. This approach ensures that digital learning remains meaningful, purpose-driven, and closely aligned with their intellectual and professional growth.

3. **Goal Orientation Theory**

According to goal orientation theory, there are two unique approaches to motivation: mastery goals, which place an emphasis on learning, comprehension, and the development of skills; and performance goals, which centre on proving competence in relation to other people. It is important to note that this difference plays a significant part in determining the level of student involvement and persistence in digital humanities education. The promotion of deeper intellectual engagement is facilitated by environments that place an emphasis on mastery-oriented learning, which includes activities such as open-ended projects, reflective assignments, and exploratory research activities. These environments provide students with the opportunity to advance at their own speed, investigate intricate concepts, and cultivate abilities that will last a lifetime without the intense pressure of direct competition.

On the other side, performance-driven elements, which include things like leaderboards, competitive grading systems, or public rankings, have the potential to inspire specific learners by generating a feeling of accomplishment and providing them with external validation. On the other hand, these factors may also bring about feelings of stress and anxiety, particularly in situations where students experience pressure to outperform their classmates rather than concentrating on the development of skills that are meaningful to them. Educators are able to guarantee that technology boosts motivation in ways that promote student well-being while also supporting academic success if they strategically construct digital learning experiences that strike a balance between the two methods. The creation of learning environments that are engaging, adaptable, and meet the needs of a diverse range of students can be accomplished by encouraging mastery-oriented tasks while also providing structured performance measures.

3.8.3 Motivation Strategies in Digital Humanities Learning

Educators can apply motivation theories in digital humanities education through a variety of targeted strategies that enhance engagement and persistence. Gamification, for example, integrates elements like badges, points, and challenges to tap into extrinsic motivation while encouraging mastery-oriented learning. By introducing competitive yet rewarding mechanisms, students remain engaged while developing deeper content understanding. Personalisation plays a crucial role in fostering autonomy and competence. Adaptive learning platforms tailor content to individual progress and interests, ensuring that students receive instruction that aligns with their learning needs. This approach not only keeps learners motivated but also helps build confidence in their ability to master complex topics. Social interaction is another key factor in sustaining motivation. Collaborative tools like Google Docs, Padlet, and discussion boards create dynamic learning spaces where students feel a sense of community. By engaging in peer feedback and collaborative projects, they satisfy the psychological need for relatedness, reinforcing their commitment to learning.

Instant feedback further enhances student motivation by providing immediate reinforcement. Interactive exercises, digital quizzes, and AI-driven assessments allow learners to track their progress in real time, helping them feel competent and capable of advancing their skills. Additionally, ensuring that digital tasks are relevant to real-world applications or cultural issues heightens the perceived value of learning, making it more meaningful and engaging. By implementing these strategies, educators can create rich, interactive digital humanities environments that support both intrinsic and extrinsic motivation.

3.8.4 Challenges to Motivation in Digital Learning

While digital learning provides numerous advantages, it also presents motivational challenges that educators must address to maintain student engagement. Isolation is a key concern, as the absence of physical interaction can make learners feel disconnected, weakening their sense of relatedness. Without face-to-face discussions or classroom dynamics, students may struggle to build strong academic relationships, impacting collaboration and engagement. Self-regulation is another hurdle, as digital learning environments require high levels of self-motivation and time management. Not all learners possess these skills naturally, and without structured guidance, they may find it difficult to stay on track. Procrastination and distractions are common pitfalls, particularly in asynchronous learning models. Technological barriers also play a role in decreasing motivation. Limited access to reliable devices, unstable internet connections, or unfamiliarity with digital tools can cause frustration and disengagement. If students struggle with navigating learning platforms, their experience may become stressful rather than enriching. Finally, the sheer number of options in digital education can lead to decision fatigue. When content is poorly structured or too overwhelming, learners may feel lost, diminishing their motivation to persist. Balancing flexibility with clear pathways is crucial to ensuring that digital education remains engaging rather than overwhelming. Thoughtful design, structured support, and interactive elements can help mitigate these challenges, making digital learning more accessible and rewarding [33] (Table 3.11).

There is a significant contribution that motivation theory makes to the development of good digital humanities education. This contribution ensures that learning environments are both engaging and durable. It is possible for educators to create environments that are supportive and immersive by addressing psychological needs such as autonomy, competence, and relatedness. These environments allow students

Table 3.11 Motivation theories and application in digital humanities

Theory	Key concepts	Application in digital humanities
Self-determination theory	Autonomy, competence, relatedness	Choice of digital projects, collaborative forums, mastery tasks
Expectancy-value theory	Expectation of success, task value	Connecting digital skills to career relevance
Goal orientation theory	Mastery versus performance goals	Emphasis on learning-centred tasks, gamification

to feel empowered to explore and grow. It is possible to increase learners' commitment to the learning process by aligning digital tasks with their values. This can be accomplished through culturally relevant projects, interdisciplinary applications, or career-oriented digital tools. In addition, the development of goal orientations that place an emphasis on mastery enables students to concentrate on acquiring a profound knowledge rather than seeking validation from outside sources, which in turn encourages critical inquiry and prolonged involvement. The incorporation of motivating concepts into the design of courses and the distribution of information will be essential in order to guarantee that technology-enhanced learning not only contributes to the achievement of students but also enhances intellectual inquiry in significant ways. This is because the digital humanities are continuing to undergo developments. Through the intentional application of these ideas, educators are able to construct learning experiences in the humanities that are dynamic, adaptable, and inspirational, and that connect with students in a variety of circumstances.

3.9 Theory of Collaborative Learning

Collaborative learning is a core educational strategy that stresses the potential of social interaction and collaborative knowledge development. It is especially significant in digital learning contexts as technology allows learners to work together across time and geography. Learning via collaboration helps students gain deeper knowledge and skills, which is especially beneficial in the humanities, which place a strong emphasis on interpretation, debate, and critical analysis. In this part, we will investigate the theoretical underpinnings of collaborative learning, as well as its importance in digital settings and practical applications in the field of humanities classroom instruction.

3.9.1 Foundations of Collaborative Learning

Collaborative learning is deeply rooted in social constructivist theories, emphasizing the idea that knowledge is constructed through interaction and shared experiences. Lev Vygotsky's ZPD illustrates how learners can reach higher levels of understanding when guided by more knowledgeable peers or instructors, reinforcing the critical role of social engagement in cognitive development. Beyond Vygotsky, theorists such as John Dewey and Jean Piaget also shaped the understanding that learning is inherently social. Dewey championed experiential learning, highlighting how meaningful education arises from participation in real-world, interactive contexts. Piaget's constructivist perspective, while often associated with individual cognition, acknowledges that peer interaction fosters deeper learning by prompting students to challenge, refine, and expand their thinking. Unlike individualistic learning, which prioritises independent mastery, collaborative learning thrives on shared responsibility, mutual respect, and the co-creation of knowledge. It encourages learners to engage critically, support one another, and develop a collective intellectual discourse, fostering an environment where learning is not simply acquired but actively constructed. The integration of technology, group discussions, and interactive projects further amplifies these benefits, making collaborative learning essential in both traditional and digital humanities education.

3.9.2 *Key Principles of Collaborative Learning*

1. Interdependence: In a collaborative learning environment, success is not determined by individual efforts alone but by the contributions of all group members working together. When learners rely on one another to achieve a common objective, they develop a sense of accountability and commitment to shared goals. This fosters a culture of mutual support, where each participant understands that their engagement directly influences the progress of the group. Interdependence encourages students to recognise the value of teamwork, reinforcing the idea that collaboration enhances understanding and problem-solving.
2. Interaction: Meaningful dialogue and discussion serve as the foundation of collaborative learning, enabling students to exchange ideas, refine their perspectives, and address knowledge gaps. Through active conversations, learners clarify concepts, challenge assumptions, and construct deeper understanding of complex topics. Additionally, interaction plays a crucial role in resolving differing viewpoints, allowing individuals to engage in respectful discourse that enhances critical thinking skills. Encouraging open communication within a group creates an intellectually stimulating environment where students feel comfortable expressing their thoughts, asking questions, and engaging in cooperative problem-solving.
3. Individual Accountability: While collaboration emphasises collective achievement, it also requires each learner to take personal responsibility for their contributions and overall learning. Every group member is expected to actively participate, complete assigned tasks, and engage in discussions, ensuring that the workload is distributed fairly. Individual accountability promotes engagement and ownership, preventing passive participation and ensuring that all students are committed to the success of the group. When learners understand that their efforts impact others, they are more likely to stay motivated, complete their tasks diligently, and strive for high-quality contributions.
4. Social Skills Development: Beyond academic growth, collaborative learning enhances essential social skills that are valuable in both educational and professional settings. Engaging in teamwork fosters effective communication, teaching students how to articulate their ideas clearly and listen actively to their peers. Additionally, collaboration promotes conflict resolution, enabling individuals to navigate differences constructively and work towards consensus. Leadership

skills also emerge in group settings, as students take on roles that require decision-making, guidance, and organisational abilities. By interacting with diverse perspectives, learners build emotional intelligence and adaptability, preparing them for successful teamwork in various real-world contexts.

5. Group Processing: Reflection on group dynamics and outcomes is integral to continuous improvement in collaborative learning environments. Encouraging students to analyse their interactions, successes, and challenges helps them recognise effective strategies and areas for enhancement. Group processing allows teams to identify behaviors that contribute positively to collaboration while addressing aspects that need refinement. By engaging in regular reflection, learners develop self-awareness and adaptability, ensuring that future collaborative efforts become more cohesive, productive, and goal-oriented. This structured review process strengthens teamwork and fosters a deeper understanding of how collective learning operates.

3.9.3 Collaborative Learning in Digital Environments

Technology revolutionises collaborative learning by eliminating the constraints of time and physical location, enabling students to engage in dynamic, interactive educational experiences regardless of distance. Digital tools allow learners to work synchronously and asynchronously, facilitating real-time collaboration or thoughtful, ongoing discussions that enhance engagement and knowledge sharing. For instance, Google Docs enables multiple users to simultaneously write, edit, and comment on documents, promoting fluid peer collaboration and collective knowledge-building. Padlet functions as a virtual bulletin board, allowing users to brainstorm, organise ideas, and collect resources visually, fostering creativity in group projects. Meanwhile, discussion forums and social media platforms encourage asynchronous dialogue and peer feedback, helping learners refine their thoughts and engage in meaningful intellectual discourse over extended periods. Additionally, video conferencing tools such as Zoom or Microsoft Teams provide real-time discussions, presentations, and collaborative problem-solving, ensuring that group interactions remain as dynamic and effective as face-to-face meetings. With these technologies, educators and students can co-create knowledge, bridge geographical gaps, and transform learning into a highly interactive, shared experience, making collaboration more accessible, flexible, and enriching.

3.9.4 Benefits of Collaborative Learning in Humanities

A multitude of advantages are provided by collaborative learning, which contribute to the development of intellectual growth as well as academic engagement. Group discussions help students to question preconceptions and explore alternative views, which ultimately leads to a deeper and more nuanced knowledge of themes related to the humanities. This is one of the most important benefits, as it leads to increased critical thinking. Additionally, there is a correlation between cooperation and greater understanding. This is because learners can solidify their own knowledge by discussing topics to others. It is possible to improve cognitive processing and mastery of subject matter by engaging in activities such as expressing ideas, defending views, and incorporating feedback. The presence of social contact within collaborative settings is another factor that contributes to the fueling of motivation. This is because the presence of shared academic objectives and group dynamics provide an atmosphere in which students feel actively involved. The presence of peers encourages responsibility, which in turn makes the learning experience more interesting and immersive. Collaborative learning not only has intellectual advantages, but it also helps students build their skills. It provides students with key talents such as communication, collaboration, and computer literacy, all of which are needed for contemporary humanities studies. The ability to explain ideas coherently, traverse different points of view, and use technology for research and presentation are all skills that students learn via active participation in group projects.

Thus, the introduction of students to a variety of cultural, theoretical, and methodological ideas is one of the ways in which exposure to multiple perspectives contributes to the enrichment of humanities education. Learners are able to acquire insights that widen their grasp of historical narratives, literary interpretations, and philosophical frameworks via the process of collaborative inquiry. This makes the learning process more dynamic and internationally relevant.

3.9.5 Challenges and Strategies

While collaborative learning offers significant benefits, it also introduces challenges, especially in digital settings. Unequal participation is one of the most common issues, as some students may dominate discussions while others contribute minimally, leading to an imbalance in workload and engagement. Additionally, coordination difficulties arise when scheduling virtual meetings, managing deadlines, and distributing tasks, making effective teamwork harder to organise. Technological issues further complicate digital collaboration, as students may have varying levels of proficiency with online tools, or struggle with access to reliable devices and internet connectivity. These disparities can hinder participation and create frustration. Conflict management also becomes crucial, as differences in opinions, work styles, or communication preferences can lead to friction within groups, requiring structured resolution strategies. To mitigate these challenges, educators can implement several strategies that enhance the effectiveness of digital collaboration. Clearly defining roles and responsibilities ensures equitable participation by assigning specific tasks to each member. The use of rubrics that assess both group and individual contributions helps maintain accountability, ensuring that effort and engagement are fairly evaluated.

Table 3.12 Collaborative learning tools and their features

Tool	Features	Application in Humanities Education
Google Docs	Real-time co-authoring, commenting	Collaborative writing and peer editing
Padlet	Virtual bulletin board, multimedia support	Brainstorming and resource sharing
Discussion Forums	Threaded conversations, asynchronous	In-depth discussions and critical reflection
Zoom/Teams	Video conferencing, breakout rooms	Synchronous group discussions and presentations

Providing training on collaborative tools and interpersonal skills equips students with the necessary technical and communication competencies to navigate digital teamwork more efficiently. Lastly, fostering a supportive environment that values diversity and constructive feedback encourages students to engage respectfully and thoughtfully, leading to more productive and inclusive collaborations. Thoughtful instructional design can ensure that digital collaborative learning remains a dynamic, equitable, and engaging process (Table 3.12).

Collaborative learning theory highlights the essential role of social interaction in knowledge construction, making it a dynamic and effective approach in digital humanities education. By integrating technology-enhanced collaboration, educators create environments that foster critical thinking, engagement, and skill development, equipping students with both interpersonal and digital competencies crucial for modern scholarly inquiry. When structured thoughtfully, collaborative learning extends beyond traditional classroom discussions to interactive digital spaces, where students engage in shared analysis, interdisciplinary exploration, and creative problem-solving. These experiences prepare humanities students to navigate complex intellectual challenges, encouraging collective knowledge-building and ensuring meaningful contributions to academic and professional communities. By leveraging digital tools for collaboration, learners gain experience in teamwork, research synthesis, and global scholarly engagement, reinforcing the relevance of humanities education in an evolving technological landscape.

3.9.6 Theoretical Model for the Study

In academic research, a theoretical model functions as a conceptual framework that provides a structured approach to examining a research problem. By outlining key constructs and their interconnections, it serves as a guiding lens for analysis, helping scholars to explain, predict, and interpret phenomena within a given field. This study integrates learning and technology theories to build a robust framework for investigating digital learning in humanities education. Drawing from established models in educational psychology, instructional design, and digital pedagogy, the theoretical foundation supports an in-depth exploration of how digital tools impact engagement, knowledge construction, and interdisciplinary collaboration within humanities disciplines. By grounding the research in well-defined theoretical perspectives, this approach ensures clarity, coherence, and methodological rigor, providing a comprehensive basis for understanding digital learning's role in shaping pedagogical practices, cognitive development, and academic scholarship in humanities education.

3.9.7 Purpose of the Theoretical Model

The purpose of this project is to investigate the impact that digital tools and software have on learning outcomes, engagement, and motivation in the field of humanities education. In order to guarantee a method that is both organised and analytical, a thorough theoretical model is constructed. This model incorporates pedagogical tactics and learner psychology in order to explain how technology affects cognitive and social learning processes. The framework is responsible for a number of essential functions. Participation from students, retention of information, and levels of motivation are some of the major elements that may be identified and measured with the use of this tool. Additionally, it makes it possible to hypothesise correlations between digital learning approaches, such as interactive platforms, multimedia materials, and collaborative tools, and the benefits that these methods have on academic performance and engagement. The research can guarantee both the rigour and applicability of its methodology by establishing its foundation in well-established educational theories, such as social constructivism, motivation theory, and digital pedagogy. By using this approach, the examination not only assesses the efficacy of digital humanities learning, but it also makes a contribution to larger conversations on optimising the use of technology in education. This ensures that meaningful integration is achieved, which in turn improves both the student experience and scholarly inquiry.

3.9.8 Components of the Theoretical Model

The proposed theoretical model integrates several foundational theories.

1. **Constructivist Learning Theory**: Constructivism posits that learners actively construct knowledge through experience and reflection. In digital humanities education, constructivist approaches emphasise learner-centred environments, problem-solving, and meaningful interaction with digital content.
2. **TPACK Framework**: The TPACK model identifies the interplay between technology, pedagogy, and content knowledge as critical for effective teaching with technology. It stresses the need for educators to develop integrated expertise to leverage digital tools to enhance humanities instruction.

3. **Self-Determination Theory (Motivation)**: Motivation is central to learning effectiveness, and SDT highlights the psychological needs of autonomy, competence, and relatedness as drivers of intrinsic motivation. This theory explains how digital environments can be designed to support learners' motivational needs.
4. **Collaborative Learning Theory**: Emphasising social interaction and shared knowledge construction, collaborative learning theory provides a foundation for incorporating group-based digital activities, such as collaborative writing and discussions, into humanities curricula.

3.9.9 Interrelationships in the Model

This theoretical model establishes a structured framework that connects digital integration, motivation, and collaborative learning to enhance educational outcomes in humanities studies. At its foundation, TPACK (Technological Pedagogical Content Knowledge) facilitates constructivist learning experiences by equipping students with digital tools that encourage active exploration, critical reflection, and interdisciplinary engagement. These technological applications transform traditional learning into interactive and participatory experiences, fostering deeper academic inquiry. Building on this, Self-Determination Theory explains how constructivist digital environments enhance learner motivation by satisfying three core psychological needs: autonomy, which allows students to control their learning paths and engage with technology at their own pace; competence, where progress tracking and feedback mechanisms reinforce mastery and confidence; and relatedness, as social interaction within digital spaces strengthens peer connections and academic collaboration.

As motivation increases, learners participate more actively in collaborative learning activities, where they exchange ideas, refine interpretations, and co-construct knowledge with peers. This shared intellectual engagement enhances understanding and retention, making learning more dynamic and contextualised. Ultimately, this process forms a continuous, cyclical model, where technology-enhanced collaboration, motivation, and constructivist learning reinforce one another, leading to ongoing cognitive development and improved educational outcomes in humanities studies. By integrating these elements, the model underscores the transformative power of digital learning, preparing students to engage meaningfully in an evolving scholarly landscape.

3.9.10 Visual Representation

It is helpful to visualise the model's essential components and the interactions between them via the use of a diagram in order to offer a deeper understanding of the structure of the model. In order to facilitate the incorporation of digital learning tools into humanities education, the model demonstrates how many aspects interact with one another in a dynamic manner, so providing a framework that is both organised and interrelated. TPACK are the three key domains that are represented by the three overlapping circles that are in the centre of the visualisation. The competences that are necessary for successful technology-enhanced education are jointly defined by these three areas. This demonstrates that in order for educators to achieve success in digital learning, they need to strike a balance between technological ability, instructional tactics, and topic understanding. The overlapping regions represent how these components combine with one another. In addition, the figure has arrows that represent the effect of TPACK integration on constructivist learning activities. These arrows demonstrate how the combination of digital tools, pedagogical approaches, and topic knowledge makes it easier for students to engage in active inquiry, problem-solving, and reflective thinking. These arrows illustrate the growth and change of learning experiences that occur as a result of students' engagement with interactive digital resources, collaborative platforms, and multimedia material.

Feedback loops, on the other hand, are a representation of the cyclical and dynamic nature of learning engagement. The examples they provide demonstrate how the importance of motivation and teamwork in the process of knowledge development cannot be overstated. Students' autonomy, competence, and social connectedness—three essential components of the Self-Determination Theory are continuously fostered while they engage in activities that take place only inside digital environments. Because of this, their level of involvement is increased, the momentum of their learning is maintained, and the educational results are improved. By providing a visual picture of these interactions, the diagram offers an understandable illustration of the theoretical model. It demonstrates how technology, pedagogy, motivation, and cooperation jointly affect learning experiences in the field of humanities education. This highlights the need of integrating digital technologies in a strategic manner in order to build settings that are intellectually exciting, engaging, and adaptable for students (Fig. 3.3 and Table 3.13).

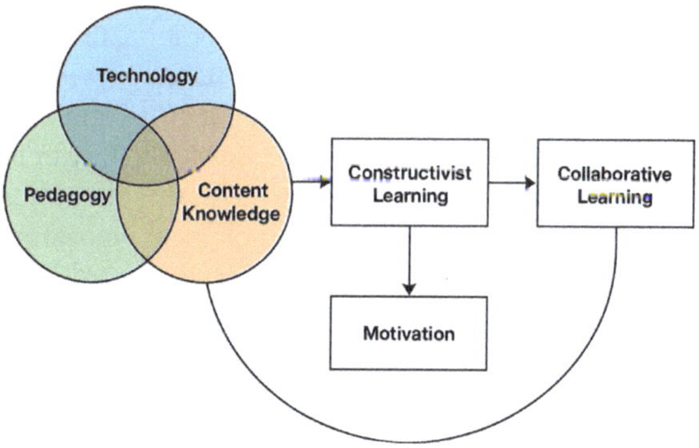

Fig. 3.3 Constructive and collaborating learning

Table 3.13 Key constructs and their definitions

Construct	Definition	Role in the study
Technology	Digital tools and platforms used in humanities education	Enables access to content and supports pedagogical methods
Pedagogy	Teaching strategies and methods	Shapes how content and technology are used for learning
Content knowledge	Subject matter expertise in humanities	Provides the academic foundation for learning activities
Constructivist learning	Learner-centred knowledge construction	Frames active engagement and reflection on digital content
Motivation	Psychological drivers of learner engagement	Explains sustained effort and commitment in digital learning
Collaborative learning	Social interaction and shared knowledge construction	Enhances understanding and skills through group work

3.9.11 Significance of the Model

This integrated theoretical model serves as a comprehensive framework for examining how digital technologies can be effectively incorporated into humanities education to enhance engagement, learning outcomes, and interdisciplinary exploration. By emphasising balanced development in technology use, pedagogical strategies, and content mastery, the model ensures that digital tools are not merely supplementary but integral to the learning process. One of its strengths lies in its consideration of motivational and social dimensions, recognising that effective learning is shaped not only by structured academic content but also by student motivation, collaboration, and interaction. The integration of Self-Determination Theory, TPACK, and constructivist learning principles allows educators to create adaptive, student-centred environments that promote autonomy, competence, and relatedness, leading to deeper intellectual engagement. Beyond theoretical exploration, this model provides practical guidance for designing and implementing digital tools within humanities curricula. By identifying key variables, hypothesising their relationships, and mapping out constructivist approaches, it supports both academic research and classroom application. As digital humanities continue to evolve, this framework will be essential in shaping best practices, ensuring that technological innovation enhances rather than disrupts traditional pedagogical goals. It offers a forward-looking perspective on how educators can harness digital advancements to foster meaningful, transformative learning experiences in humanities education.

3.9.12 Critical Theory and Digital Pedagogy

Critical theory is a powerful framework that questions the conventional systems of power, knowledge, and social order. Its origins may be traced back to the Frankfurt School tradition. Inequalities, oppression, and the sociopolitical circumstances that shape human experience are the topics that are investigated and addressed by this initiative. The application of Critical Theory to digital pedagogy encourages educators and students to conduct a critical analysis of the role that technology plays in education. This analysis involves asking questions such as who benefits from technology, who is marginalised by it, and how digital technologies may be used to promote social justice and empowerment within the realm of humanities education.

3.9.13 Foundations of Critical Theory

Critical theory, which has its origins in the intellectual tradition of intellectuals such as Max Horkheimer, Theodor Adorno, and Jürgen Habermas, functions as a strong analytical framework that examines the institutions of society and seeks to promote liberation. This approach integrates the fields of philosophy, sociology, and political economics in order to investigate the ways in which power relations influence the creation of knowledge, access to education, and representation in rhetoric. The theory contends, at its heart, that education is never neutral; rather, it is nested within larger sociopolitical processes that determine whose voices are heard, whose experiences are valued, and how knowledge is defined. This is the central argument of the theory. Pedagogical techniques that stimulate thought, discourse, and transformational action are advocated for by critical theorists. These approaches urge learners to critically evaluate the societal structures that are already in place and to question the prevalent ideas. This viewpoint highlights the significance of education as a tool for empowerment, and it encourages both students and teachers to examine the inequities that are embedded in the system, to destroy narratives that are oppressive, and to envision educational settings that are fairer. Critical theory continues to be a vital basis for the development of educational models that promote justice, agency, and meaningful change in both the field of humanities study and in larger societal settings. This is accomplished via the integration of critical thinking, participatory learning, and social engagement.

3.9.14 Applying Critical Theory to Digital Pedagogy

Digital learning should not only mimic traditional models but actively challenge systemic inequalities and encourage critical engagement; this can be achieved by incorporating Critical Theory into digital pedagogy, which turns technology-enhanced education into a conscious, socially aware practice. The concept of critical digital literacy goes beyond the concept of fundamental technical competency and places an emphasis on critical interaction with digital media as well as the social, cultural, and political elements of digital media. Not only do students need to have an understanding of how to utilise technology, but they must also be aware of how digital platforms build narratives, impact perceptions, and propagate biases. Students benefit from this heightened awareness because it enables them to navigate online places responsibly while simultaneously questioning the ideological foundations of digital information.

When power dynamics within digital education are investigated, existing inequalities are brought to light. These inequalities include differences in access to technology, internet connection, and digital education resources. The digital gap, which is entrenched in issues such as race, class, gender, and location, has the potential to perpetuate exclusion if it is not aggressively addressed. The objective of critical pedagogy is to decrease these discrepancies by ensuring that all students have equal access to technology and by implementing inclusive practices. When it comes to learning that is mediated by digital technology, representation and voice are very important problems. The fight against marginalisation and the facilitation of significant contributions from historically under-represented populations may be accomplished by ensuring that digital information, learning spaces, and online forums include a varied range of opinions. Learners should be able to express their identities, question prevailing narratives, and share their cultural experiences via the use of digital technologies that should enable multifocal involvement. Hence, the ultimate objective of critical digital pedagogy is to empower students. Through the use of digital tools that provide support for learner agency, activism, and critical thinking, students are encouraged to go beyond the passive consumption of knowledge and instead become active producers, analysts, and agents of change. In order to ensure that education continues to be a driving force for fairness and societal growth, technology must be used to advance social justice, civic participation, and transformational learning. At its core, this method transforms digital pedagogy into a practice that is reflective and socially responsible. It does this by ensuring that education in digital environments is inclusive, critical, and power-aware, rather than just being an extension of traditional learning paradigms.

3.9.15 Challenges Highlighted by Critical Theory in Digital Humanities

Despite the fact that digital learning brings incredible benefits, it also raises substantial issues that need to be addressed in order to guarantee ethical involvement, justice, and fairness. In spite of the fact that discrepancies in the availability of technology and internet connection might restrict participation, access and equity continue to be key concerns. It is important to note that socioeconomic issues play a significant impact, since students who come from disadvantaged neighbourhoods sometimes lack the appropriate internet infrastructure, which creates hurdles to involvement. It is possible that digital education may accidentally worsen educational gaps rather than bridge them if proper resources, support mechanisms, and institutional solutions are not implemented.

Digital learning is made even more difficult by the presence of algorithmic bias, which is a phenomenon in which content curation and recommendation algorithms may reinforce preexisting prejudices. There are a lot of algorithms that give priority to popular or dominant ideas, which might possibly marginalise minority viewpoints and shape students' exposure to material in a manner that is lacking in variety. It is necessary to have critical digital literacy as well as clear algorithmic design in order to combat prejudice, guarantee varied representation, and avoid ideological echo chambers. There are growing worries over surveillance and privacy as a result of the rising use of learning management systems, analytics powered by artificial intelligence, and remote proctoring technologies. In spite of the fact that these technologies have the potential to improve personalised learning, they also pose ethical concerns around data protection, student monitoring, and permission. Excessive surveillance has the potential to impede learner autonomy, creating an atmosphere in which students have the impression that they are being observed all the time rather than being able to freely participate in discovery and inquiry.

A further problem is the "commodification of education," which occurs when the proliferation of digital platforms carries with it the possibility that education will become "market-driven" rather than "learner-centred." Educational goals can move from student growth to financial gain under the influence of subscription-based models, monetised course material, and corporate interests. This shift may have an impact on both accessibility and academic integrity. While it is vital to take a balanced approach in order to prioritise education as a public benefit, it is also necessary to ensure that technology improvements serve the purpose of knowledge-building rather than commercial objectives. In order to address these issues, educators and politicians need to build ethical frameworks, invest in projects that promote digital inclusion, and enact regulations that are clear about technology matters. Enhancing learning experiences while protecting equity, privacy, and academic integrity may be accomplished via the thoughtful integration of technology. This helps to ensure that digital education continues to be transformational and accessible to all students.

3.9.16 Strategies for Critical Digital Pedagogy

There are a number of different strategic methods that educators may adopt in order to offset the issues that are brought by digital learning and to guarantee that education that is improved by technology continues to be egalitarian, ethical, and empowering. The development of a curriculum that includes critical conversations on digital ethics, media literacy, and social justice is an essential step that should be taken. Students are equipped with the analytical abilities required to interact with digital platforms responsibly when these topics are included in their courses. This allows students to gain a deeper knowledge of digital biases, privacy problems, and the societal ramifications of technology.

Furthermore, it is of equal importance to facilitate learning settings that encourage participation. Students are more likely to participate in active learning, and different viewpoints are more likely to be represented when they are encouraged to co-create knowledge, question prevailing narratives, and engage in collaborative research. Students are allowed to examine preexisting systems via the use of this technique, which encourages critical thinking and prevents them from just taking in information.

The advocacy of inclusive technology policies that address gaps in digital access and infrastructure is another important role that educators should play. It is possible to guarantee that all students have access to the tools they need to be successful in digitally mediated education by providing financial support to efforts that aim to bridge the digital divide. These initiatives include financing for inexpensive devices, dependable internet connections, and programs that teach students about technology. Additionally, the use of OER and digital platforms that are easily available places an emphasis on the degree to which learners have control and freedom. Educational resources that are freely accessible to the public lower the financial obstacles that students face while also fostering learning experiences that are customisable and flexible. This increases the likelihood that students will have access to high-quality information without being restricted by commercial gatekeeping or prohibitive fees. The use of these tactics enables educators to build digital learning environments that are inclusive, critically engaged, and student-centred. This, in turn, prepares students to navigate technology with agency, awareness, and ethical responsibility.

3.9.17 Relevance to Humanities Education

Disciplines in the humanities, which investigate topics such as culture, society, history, and ethics, are in a position unlike any other to take the lead in critical digital education. Teachers of the humanities may inspire students to challenge the social implications of technology, gain an understanding of the formation of knowledge, and develop into active digital citizens that contribute to fair and just digital futures by incorporating critical theory into their lessons (Table 3.14).

Through the cultivation of an atmosphere that encourages critical inquiry, social awareness, and ethical involvement, the incorporation of Critical Theory into digital pedagogy contributes to the enhancement of humanities education. Additionally, it gives students the ability to not only navigate the digital world but also to question and modify it, which ensures that education makes a contribution to a society that is fairer and more equal. These theoretical lenses are very necessary for educators who are dedicated to implementing digital learning techniques in the humanities that are both transformational and inclusive.

Table 3.14 Critical theory principles in digital pedagogy

Principle	Description	Application in digital humanities education
Critical Awareness	Recognising power relations in digital technologies	Discussions on digital divides and algorithmic biases
Emancipation	Promoting learner empowerment and agency	Projects that encourage activism and critical media creation
Inclusivity	Valuing diverse voices and perspectives	Incorporating multicultural and marginalised narratives
Reflexivity	Encouraging reflection on one's positionality and biases	Reflective digital journaling and critical discussions

3.9.18 Justification for the Selected Framework

When it comes to influencing both the direction of research and the actual execution of projects, selecting an appropriate theoretical framework is very necessary. This is particularly true within the context of the multidisciplinary landscape of digital humanities education. Conceptual clarity is provided by a framework that is well-structured, which guarantees that the research will successfully capture the linkages between technology, pedagogy, content, learner motivation, and collaborative engagement. As a reflection of the complex character of digital humanities education, the framework that was used for this research incorporates a number of different learning theories and pedagogical approaches. A holistic strategy that connects digital tools with cognitive engagement, knowledge production, and interactive learning experiences is provided by this method. This approach is achieved by synthesising ideas from constructivism, Self-Determination Theory, TPACK, and collaborative learning frameworks. This synthesis acknowledges that in order to provide successful humanities education in digital environments, not only does it demand technical expertise, but it also necessitates learner-centred practices that improve autonomy, competence, and relatedness.

Due to the fact that it enables an in-depth investigation of the ways in which digital techniques influence motivation, engagement, and interdisciplinary inquiry, this integrated framework is also quite pertinent to the aims of the research. Due to the fact that it is all-encompassing, it guarantees that essential variables such as student autonomy, knowledge representation, and fair access are investigated alongside technical developments. In addition to this, its application goes beyond the realm of theoretical investigation, providing practical insights into the development and execution of digital humanities courses. For the purpose of bridging the gap between academic theory and actual pedagogical innovation, the research is positioned to give valuable contributions to the emerging discourse on technology-enhanced humanities education. This is made possible by anchoring the study in this strong, interdisciplinary framework.

3.9.19 Alignment with Research Goals

Through the use of an integrated theoretical framework that integrates a variety of educational viewpoints, the purpose of this research is to investigate the ways in which digital technologies might improve teaching and learning in the field of humanities education. At its foundation, the constructivist learning theory places an emphasis on "active, learner-centred knowledge construction." It advocates for "experiential, inquiry-driven approaches" such as those in which students "engage deeply" with digital resources in order to "build understanding" rather than "passively absorb information." Educators are guided through the process of successfully harnessing digital technologies to supplement instructional techniques and subject matter expertise via the use of the TPACK Framework, which assures a balanced integration of technology, pedagogy, and topic knowledge. Self-Determination Theory is a theory that emphasises the psychological factors that influence learner motivation. It demonstrates how digital environments may improve student autonomy, competence, and relatedness by providing personalised learning routes, adaptive feedback, and interactive collaboration.

It is recognised that peer contact, shared inquiry, and cooperative projects are vital for deep engagement, knowledge co-construction, and interdisciplinary research. The Collaborative Learning Theory emphasises the social aspects of digital learning by recognising that these elements are crucial. In order to ensure that humanities education continues to be dynamic, interactive, and intellectually enriching in an era driven by technology, the framework provides a holistic perspective on not only how digital tools are implemented but also how they shape engagement, motivation, and learning outcomes. This is accomplished by weaving these theories together.

3.9.20 Comprehensiveness of the Framework

This integrated framework provides a comprehensive, multidimensional perspective on digital learning, ensuring that various pedagogical elements are thoughtfully connected to enhance educational experiences in humanities disciplines.

1. Technological Integration: The TPACK framework addresses the critical intersection between technology, pedagogy, and content knowledge, ensuring that digital tools are implemented in ways that enhance learning rather than merely supplement traditional methods. By prioritizing pedagogical soundness and content relevance, this approach helps educators navigate technology adoption with intentionality, avoiding superficial or ineffective implementation.
2. Learner Agency and Motivation: Self-Determination Theory provides a psychological foundation for understanding how digital environments influence motivation. By fostering autonomy, competence, and relatedness, well-designed digital learning platforms can enhance student engagement, helping learners take active ownership of their educational journey.

3. Social Learning: The principles of Collaborative Learning Theory highlight the importance of peer interaction and shared knowledge construction elements that are particularly valuable in humanities education. By integrating digital tools that support discussion, cooperative inquiry, and collective interpretation, this framework ensures that learning remains dialogical and intellectually enriching rather than isolating.
4. Active Knowledge Construction: Grounded in Constructivism, this framework supports student-centered learning that encourages critical thinking, reflective exploration, and meaning-making. Humanities education thrives when learners actively engage with texts, historical narratives, and philosophical debates, making constructivist design crucial in digital pedagogy.

3.9.21 Relevance to Digital Humanities Education

In the field of humanities education, students are expected to develop difficult cognitive abilities such as critical analysis, interpretation, and contextual comprehension. It is via constructivist and collaborative techniques, which are aided by correctly integrated technology (TPACK), that the chosen framework provides support for these higher-order abilities through its implementation. In addition, the motivating component tackles the difficulty of maintaining student interest in digital learning settings that are often self-directed.

3.9.22 Practical Implications

This integrated framework serves a dual purpose, shaping both academic research and practical pedagogical strategies, ensuring that digital learning in humanities education is effective, engaging, and theoretically grounded.

1. Educators can leverage the TPACK framework to make informed decisions when selecting and implementing digital tools. By understanding how technology, pedagogy, and content knowledge intersect, instructors can create digitally enriched learning environments that seamlessly blend traditional humanities education with innovative digital methodologies.
2. Insights from Self-Determination Theory help educators design engaging content that fosters intrinsic motivation and persistence. By integrating autonomy-supportive learning experiences, progress-tracking mechanisms, and opportunities for meaningful social interaction, digital learning can sustain student commitment and curiosity.
3. Collaborative learning principles ensure that digital learning environments remain interactive and student-centred. Group activities, peer feedback, and co-constructed knowledge allow learners to deepen their understanding through

discussion, critical reflection, and shared exploration, an essential practice in humanities disciplines that thrive on interpretation and discourse.

4. Constructivist principles inform the design of authentic and meaningful learning experiences, emphasising experiential and reflective approaches. Digital humanities education benefits greatly from interactive problem-solving, immersive storytelling, and analytical engagement with digital archives and multimedia that encourage active exploration and knowledge creation.

3.9.23 *Flexibility and Adaptability*

The chosen framework is flexible enough to adapt to different digital tools, learning contexts, and student demographics. It allows for the incorporation of emerging technologies and pedagogical innovations, making it future-proof and scalable (Table 3.15).

This integrated theoretical framework stands out due to the fact that it takes a comprehensive approach to capturing the various features of digital learning in the field of humanities education. It ensures that both theoretical inquiry and practical applications are well-supported by ensuring that it fits smoothly with the research goals. This is accomplished by synthesising numerous learning theories and pedagogical models. The educational usefulness of this resource is especially noteworthy since it provides instructors with systematic direction on how to successfully incorporate digital technologies into their classrooms while still preserving student engagement, motivation, and collaborative interaction. By placing a focus on technology, pedagogy, content mastery, and learner psychology, it is ensured that digital approaches are utilised in a strategic manner rather than in a superficial one. Additionally, one of the most important strengths of the framework is its versatility. This

Table 3.15 Criteria for framework selection

Criteria	Explanation	Framework fit
Relevance	Addresses key aspects of digital humanities learning	Integrates technology, pedagogy, content, motivation, and collaboration
Comprehensiveness	Covers multiple dimensions of digital learning	Multi-theory approach offers holistic insight
Practical applicability	Supports actionable strategies for educators and learners	Informs tool selection, motivation, collaboration, and activity design
Flexibility	Adaptable to varied contexts and technologies	Scalable across different settings and digital environments
Alignment with research goals	Supports the specific aims and objectives of the study	Directly addresses technology integration and learner engagement in humanities

model offers a flexible foundation that can allow new tools, platforms, and pedagogical innovations while still preserving its fundamental learning principles. This is significant since educational technology are always evolving, and this model is able to handle these changes. This "future-proof design" guarantees that an organisation will continue to be relevant in the constantly shifting world of digital humanities education.

By serving both academic research and practical instructional design, this framework is more than a theoretical construct it is a transformative tool for shaping meaningful digital learning strategies that enhance student experience, intellectual engagement, and scholarly inquiry in humanities disciplines.

References

1. M.I. Mursyidto, The role of information communication technology in records creation and distribution in Uganda communications commission. Implement. Sci. **39**(1), 1–15 (2014). https://doi.org/10.4324/9781315853178
2. G.J. Don-Solomon, Amakiri and Eke, "Ontological & Epistemological Philosophies Underlying Theory Building: A Scholarly Dilemma Or Axiomatic Illumination—The Business Research Perspective, vol. 6, no. 2 (2018), pp. 1–7
3. A. Lo Presti, A. Manuti, A. De Rosa, A. Elia, Developing a sustainable career through discourse: a qualitative study on a group of Italian project managers. Int. J. Manag. Proj. Bus. **15**(8), 1–18 (2021). https://doi.org/10.1108/IJMPB-12-2020-0376
4. J. Aria Adibrata, N. Fikhri Khairi, The impact of Covid-19 blame game towards Anti-Asian discrimination phenomena. J. Soc. Media **6**(1), 17–38 (2022). https://doi.org/10.26740/jsm.v6n1.p17-38
5. M.D. Anderson, P. Settee, Knowledge and education for peoples' sovereignty. Globalizations **17**(7), 1300–1309 (2020). https://doi.org/10.1080/14747731.2020.1783785
6. M. Javeri, K. Persichitte, Use of innovation component configuration map (ICCM) to measure technology integration practices of higher education faculty. J. Technol. Teach. Educ. **18**(4), 607–643 (2010)
7. K.E. Irving, The impact of educational technology on student achievement: assessment 'of' and 'for' learning. Sci. Educ. **15**, 13–20 (2006) [Online]. Available: http://search.ebscohost.com/login.aspx?direct=true&db=eric&AN=EJ773197&site=ehost-live%5Cnhttp://www.nsela.org/index.php?option=com_content&view=category&id=51&Itemid=85
8. A. Andika, T. Tahrun, M. Firdaus, Developing English grammar instructional materials oriented to constructivism theory. J. Lang. Lang. Teach. **11**(2), 286 (2023). https://doi.org/10.33394/jollt.v11i2.6838
9. J.A. Onyido, A.P. Brambaifa, *Girl-Child Marriage in the Nigerian society, Causes, Impacts and Mitigating Strategies*, vol. 4, no. 2 (2018), pp. 104–110. https://doi.org/10.12691/wjssh-4-2-6
10. Muraina, A.J. Ajímátanraẹ̀jẹ̀, Gender relations in indigenous Yoruba culture: questioning feminism action and advocacy. AfricArXiv Prepr, pp. 1–19 (2022) [Online]. Available: https://osf.io/preprints/africarxiv/x6vma/
11. T. Francis, Alarming rate of child poverty in Northern Nigeria: implications for national security. Am. Res. J. Humanit. Soc. Sci. 2019 ARJHSS J. **01**, 1–10 (2019) [Online]. Available: www.arjhss.com
12. N.O. Orunbon, G.A. Ibikunle, A.A. Badmus, Principals' digital transformational leadership, teachers' organisational commitment and job satisfaction during Covid-19 in Lagos State Education District V, Nigeria. Int. J. Humanit. Technol. Civiliz. **8**(1), 68–73 (2023). https://doi.org/10.15282/ijhtc.v8i1.9424

13. A. Oyeronke, M. Fagbohun, O. Adebayo, *An Assessment of Computer and ICT Skills Among Secondary School Teachers in Ota Ogun State* (2013) [Online]. Available: http://digitalcommons.unl.edu/libphilprac%5Cnhttp://digitalcommons.unl.edu/libphilprac/846%5Cnhttp://digitalcommons.unl.edu/libphilprac/
14. N. Omheni, I. Bouabidi, A. Gharsallah, F. Zarai, M.S. Obaidat, Smart mobility management in 5G heterogeneous networks. IET Networks **7**(3), 119–128 (2018). https://doi.org/10.1049/iet-net.2017.0208
15. P. Chen, S.K. Kim, The impact of digital transformation on innovation performance—the mediating role of innovation factors. Heliyon **9**(3), e13916 (2023). https://doi.org/10.1016/j.heliyon.2023.e13916
16. R. Govers, F.M. Go, Projected destination image online: website content analysis of pictures and text. Inf. Technol. Tour. **7**(2), 73–89 (2008). https://doi.org/10.3727/1098305054517327
17. S. Gluszek et al., Emerging trends of the illegal wildlife trade in Mesoamerica. Oryx **55**(5), 708–716 (2021). https://doi.org/10.1017/S0030605319001133
18. K. Zhu, S. Dong, S.X. Xu, K.L. Kraemer, Innovation diffusion in global contexts: determinants of post-adoption digital transformation of European companies. Eur. J. Inf. Syst. **15**(6), 601–616 (2006)
19. M. Ingrassia, C. Bellia, C. Giurdanella, P. Columba, S. Chironi, Digital influencers, food and tourism—a new model of open innovation for businesses in the Ho.Re.Ca. Sector. J. Open Innov. Technol. Mark. Complex. **8**(1), 50 (2022) https://doi.org/10.3390/joitmc8010050
20. K.C. Obi, O. Iwuanyanwu, Innovation in the assessment of primary school mathematics: an approach to revamping Nigeria education. J. Teach. Perspect. **18**(1), 51–66 (2023) [Online]. Available: http://repositorio.unan.edu.ni/2986/1/5624.pdf%0Ahttp://fiskal.kemenkeu.go.id/ejournal%0A10.1016/j.cirp.2016.06.001%0A10.1016/j.powtec.2016.12.055%0A10.1016/j.ijfatigue.2019.02.006%0A10.1
21. N. M. Kumar et al., Distributed energy resources and the application of ai, iot, and blockchain in smart grids. Energies **13**(21) (2020). https://doi.org/10.3390/en13215739
22. Y. Sun, R. Wang, D. Cao, R. Lee, Who are social media influencers for luxury fashion consumption of the Chinese Gen Z? Categorisation and empirical examination. J. Fash. Mark. Manag. (2021). https://doi.org/10.1108/JFMM-07-2020-0132
23. D.Y. Choi, W.K. Kim, J.H. Kim, H. Cho, Performance of analog and digital modulation schemes under sweep jamming. Int. Conf. Ubiquitous Futur. Networks, ICUFN **2016**, 13–15 (2016). https://doi.org/10.1109/ICUFN.2016.7536970
24. M. Mostert, L. Quinn, Using ICTs in teaching and learning: reflections on professional development of academic staff. J. Educ. **5**(5), 72–84
25. B. Li, Contemporary college students' views on marriage. J. Educ. Humanit. Soc. Sci. **3**, 196–202 (2022). https://doi.org/10.54097/ehss.v3i.1686
26. M.I. Manda, S. Ben Dhaou, Responding to the challenges and opportunities in the 4th industrial revolution in developing countries, in *ACM International Conference Proceedings Series*, vol. Part F1481 (2019), pp. 244–253. https://doi.org/10.1145/3326365.3326398
27. C. Martinez, *Stakeholder Participation in Property Development* (2018)
28. A. Smith, J.P. Voß, J. Grin, Innovation studies and sustainability transitions: the allure of the multi-level perspective and its challenges. Res. Policy **39**(4), 435–448 (2010). https://doi.org/10.1016/j.respol.2010.01.023
29. A. Luhamya, F.E.K. Bakkabulindi, P.B. Muyinda, Integration of ICT in teaching and learning: a review of theories. Makerere J. High. Educ. **9**(1), 21 (2017). https://doi.org/10.4314/majohe.v9i1.2
30. D. Zou, X. Huang, L. Kohnke, X. Chen, G. Cheng, H. Xie, A bibliometric analysis of the trends and research topics of empirical research on TPACK. Educ. Inf. Technol. **27**(8), 10585–10609 (2022). https://doi.org/10.1007/s10639-022-10991-z
31. S.E. Najafi, H. Nozari, S.A. Edalatpanah, Artificial intelligence of things (AIoT) and industry 4.0-based supply chain (FMCG Industry), in *A Roadmap Enabling Ind. 4.0 by Artificial Intelligence* (2022), pp. 31–42. https://doi.org/10.1002/9781119905141.ch3

32. M. Casini, Extended reality for smart building operation and maintenance: a review. Energies **15**(10), 3785 (2022). https://doi.org/10.3390/en15103785
33. E. Korot et al., Enablers and barriers to deployment of smartphone-based home vision monitoring in clinical practice settings. JAMA Ophthalmol. **140**(2), 153–160 (2022). https://doi.org/10.1001/jamaophthalmol.2021.5269

Chapter 4
Methodology

4.1 Research Design

The purpose of a research design is to provide an organised blueprint for the execution of an investigation, ensuring that the data collection, measurement, and analysis are all by the goals of the research. For this investigation of the use of digital tools in humanities education, a mixed-methods research design has been used. This approach offers a comprehensive view on how educational software influences the results of teaching and learning. In order to provide a thorough picture of the dynamics of digital learning, this methodology incorporates both quantitative and qualitative research approaches. Quantitative approaches, which include things like surveys, performance analytics, and experimental research, make it possible to conduct systematic measurements of things like levels of engagement, learning effectiveness, and user interaction with educational software. On the other hand, qualitative approaches, which include interviews, focus groups, and content analysis, provide profound insights into the experiences, motivations, and pedagogical tactics of learners in the field of digital humanities education. This study approach guarantees that both statistical patterns and individual learner views are taken into consideration by mixing narrative-driven inquiry with empirical data. This results in findings that are more comprehensive and can be used in real-world situations. Considering the fact that the mixed-methods approach is especially useful for capturing intricate interactions between the use of technology, the building of knowledge, and educational engagement, it is a crucial framework for researching the transformational potential of digital learning in the fields of the humanities (Fig. 4.1).

F. A. Alaba et al., *Learning Beyond the Classroom*, Studies in Computational Intelligence 1253, https://doi.org/10.1007/978-3-032-14433-1_4

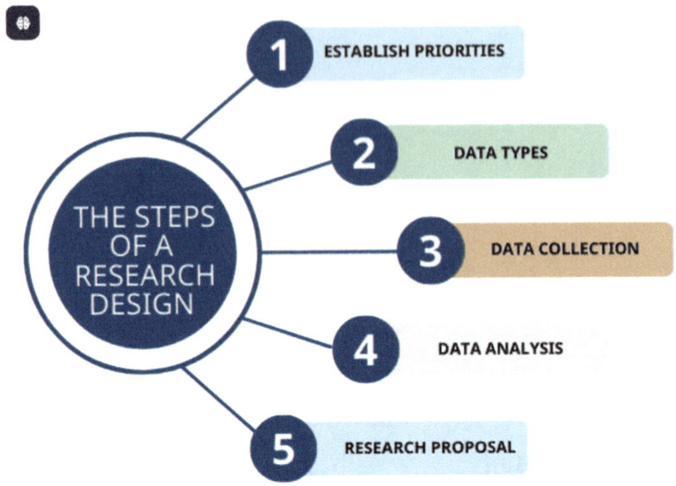

Fig. 4.1 Steps in research design [1]

4.1.1 Rationale for Mixed-Methods Design

A mixed-methods research design is particularly well-suited for this study because it captures both the measurable outcomes of digital learning and the deeper contextual insights that shape the educational experience. The integration of statistical data allows researchers to analyse software usage, learner performance, and engagement levels systematically, identifying patterns and trends that demonstrate the effectiveness of digital tools in humanities education. At the same time, interpretive data collection through interviews, focus groups, and document analysis provides a qualitative dimension that enriches the understanding of lived experiences. These narratives offer valuable insights into learner motivations, instructor perspectives, and the broader pedagogical implications of digital learning. Additionally, the mixed-methods approach strengthens the study through triangulation, ensuring that findings are validated across multiple sources and perspectives. By cross-referencing quantitative metrics with qualitative narratives, researchers can construct a well-rounded and nuanced analysis that reflects both objective measurements and subjective experiences. This methodological flexibility is particularly important in humanities education, where factors such as discourse, interpretation, and critical thinking play a crucial role in shaping learning outcomes. By employing a mixed-methods framework, this study ensures a comprehensive examination of how digital tools influence teaching and learning, allowing for a more insightful and applicable exploration of technology-enhanced humanities education [2].

4.1.2 Quantitative Component

The quantitative component of this study is intended to evaluate the influence that software tools have on a variety of educational outcomes by means of the gathering and examination of data in a methodical manner. The purpose of the research is to measure improvements in student academic performance, technological literacy development, and engagement levels. This will be accomplished via the use of structured questionnaires and pre- and post-assessments. In order to perform these assessments, carefully crafted tools will be used. These instruments will contain questions based on the Likert scale, which will allow for a more nuanced understanding of student perspectives. Additionally, standardised accomplishment exams will be utilised in order to quantify objective gains in learning outcomes. There will be a variety of statistical approaches used in order to draw useful insights from the data that has been gathered. The descriptive statistics will provide a summary of the trends, which will assist in highlighting the most important patterns included within the information. It will be possible to determine if the implementation was successful by comparing the outcomes of the pre-intervention and the post-intervention using t-tests [3].

4.1.3 Qualitative Component

This study has a qualitative component that is designed to investigate the complex ways in which software tools are incorporated into humanities education. The purpose of this component is to provide profound and contextual insights into the influence that these tools have on teaching and learning. A number of different approaches to data collecting will be used in order to guarantee a full comprehension of the experiences and points of view of both the professors and the students simultaneously. When it comes to gathering individual perspectives, semi-structured interviews will be the primary method of choice. These interviews will allow for a degree of flexibility in responses while still ensuring that the primary themes are emphasised. A collaborative environment will be created through the use of focus group discussions, which will allow for a more in-depth examination of the collective perspectives on the use of software, as well as the challenges and benefits associated with its utilisation. For the purpose of enhancing the qualitative analysis even further, classroom observations will be carried out in order to investigate the ways in which digital technologies are used in actual educational environments. Through careful observation of the interactions that take place between teachers, students, and software, researchers will be able to get first-hand knowledge on instructional strategies and levels of student involvement. These observations will be supplemented by document analysis, which will include the examination of digital course materials and student submissions, with the goal of identifying trends in software use and the factors that impact academic performance. In order to provide a methodical interpretation of the

Table 4.1 Research design framework

Component	Details
Research type	Mixed-Methods
Quantitative tools	Surveys, Achievement Tests, Engagement Scales
Qualitative tools	Interviews, Focus Groups, Observations, Document Analysis
Sampling strategy	Stratified Random Sampling (Quantitative), Purposive Sampling (Qualitative)
Data analysis	Statistical Analysis (SPSS), Thematic Coding (NVivo)
Duration	6–12 Months

results, the data will be coded using thematic analysis, which will also be used to highlight recurrent themes, problems, and appropriate methods. The study will be able to highlight crucial discoveries that may inspire successful methods for incorporating software into humanities education if it is conducted using this technique [4] (Table 4.1).

4.1.4 Justification for the Design

This research design was meticulously chosen to attain a balance between breadth and depth, facilitating a thorough examination of the incorporation of software tools in educational environments. The quantitative component enhances generalisability and identifies objective trends through the analysis of statistical patterns within an extensive dataset. This enables researchers to assess the overall efficacy of software tools on student performance, digital literacy, and engagement levels in a systematic and reproducible manner. The incorporation of standardised assessments and Likert-scale surveys guarantees that results can be generalised beyond the specific study sample, providing significant insights into wider educational effects. In addition to the quantitative approach, the qualitative component explores the fundamental reasons for behaviours, attitudes, and experiences with software tools, especially in the context of the humanities. The study utilises interviews, focus group discussions, classroom observations, and document analysis to capture the depth of individual and collective perspectives. This qualitative investigation is essential in disciplines that prioritise interpretation, critical analysis, and subjective experiences, where statistical metrics may inadequately convey the complexities of learning. The integration of these data types yields a comprehensive, multi-faceted comprehension that emphasises both quantifiable results and the contextual elements affecting software adoption in educational settings [5].

4.1.5 Ethical Considerations

In order to give ethical issues, the highest priority, this study design ensures that the rights and privacy of participants are protected throughout the whole research process. Before deciding whether or not to take part in the study, all participants will be required to give their informed consent, which will ensure that they have a complete understanding of the nature, purpose, and potential implications of the research. The implementation of measures will be carried out in order to preserve anonymity and confidentiality, therefore safeguarding individual identities and personal data from being accessed or disclosed without authorisation. In educational research, when sensitive insights regarding learning behaviours and experiences are being acquired, these ethical protections are particularly important since they protect the participants from potential harm. In addition, the study will be submitted to the appropriate institutional review boards in order to get ethical approval. This will guarantee that the study is conducted in accordance with the existing research ethics and standards. Additionally, participants will be notified of their freedom to withdraw from the research at any moment without incurring any repercussions, which will further emphasise the voluntary nature of their participation in the aforementioned study. The incorporation of these ethical principles into the research framework ensures that the study maintains its integrity, transparency, and respect for all of the participants. This helps to foster a trustworthy and responsible approach to the investigation of the incorporation of software tools in educational environments [6].

The study design that was selected offers a comprehensive technique for investigating the incorporation of software in the field of humanities education. This is accomplished by using both quantitative and qualitative research approaches. Not only does this dual method guarantee that the research catches quantitative trends and statistical patterns, but it also ensures that it collects deeper, contextual insights that shed light on the experiences and views of educators and students. This combination enables a more in-depth comprehension of the ways in which digital tools influence the dynamics of learning, which is particularly useful in the field of humanities education, which places a premium on interpretation, critical thinking, and subjective involvement. The research is in line with the human-centered and interdisciplinary character of the humanities since it makes use of a mixed-methods approach. Quantitative data assures statistical rigour, offers wide generalisability, and provides an objective examination of trends. On the other hand, qualitative approaches give narrative richness, which captures the complexity of digital adoption in academic contexts. Both theoretical insights and practical suggestions are strengthened by this design, which enables educators and policymakers to make educated judgements about the enhancement of digital learning methodologies within the humanities. In conclusion, the framework of the research provides a comprehensive assessment of software tools, which takes into account both the efficiency of these tools and the difficulties that are connected with their implementation [7].

4.2 Population and Sampling Techniques

In educational research, particularly when investigating the impact of software on humanities education, selecting an appropriate population and using effective sampling techniques are critical to ensuring the study's validity and relevance. The selected population must appropriately reflect the target demography, which includes students, instructors, and institutions that actively use digital technologies in humanities education. By carefully establishing these characteristics, researchers may guarantee that their results are relevant to larger educational settings and contribute significantly to continuing arguments regarding the role of technology in learning. To provide a balanced and informative study, a variety of sample strategies might be used. Stratified sampling enables researchers to divide the population into distinct subgroups, such as students at different academic levels or educators with varying levels of technological proficiency, to ensure that diverse perspectives are considered. Purposive sampling, on the other hand, allows for the selection of participants based on specified characteristics, such as those with substantial expertise using software in their teaching. Furthermore, random sampling may be used to improve generalisability and provide a more comprehensive picture of trends and use patterns. By using these methodologies successfully, the study acquires a solid platform for investigating both quantitative trends and qualitative subtleties in software uptake in humanities education [8] (Fig. 4.2).

4.2.1 Defining Population in Educational Research

In the context of a research project, the term "population" refers to the complete group of persons, things, or datasets that share certain characteristics that are relevant to the investigation. When doing research in the field of education, especially

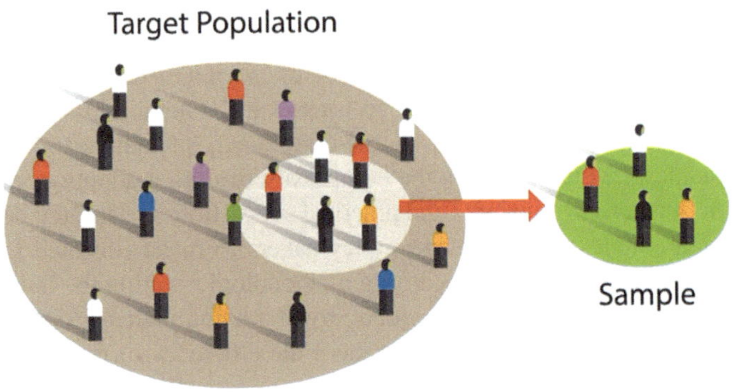

Fig. 4.2 Sample and target population

in studies that investigate the influence of software on the field of humanities education, it is crucial to define the proper population in order to guarantee findings that are suitable and useful. It is possible that the population will consist of students, educators, or institutions that make use of digital tools in the process of teaching and learning. Each of these individuals will contribute valuable insights into the adoption of software, its effectiveness, and the challenges that educators face in academic settings. In order for researchers to arrive at results that are useful, they need to pick representative samples from the population with great care and use the right sampling methodologies. These methods contribute to achieving a balance between generalisability, relevance, and diversity. The use of stratified sampling helps to guarantee that various subgroups, such as students with differing educational levels or teachers with a variety of technology backgrounds, are adequately represented. It is possible to get specialised insights via the use of purposeful sampling, which focusses on individuals who have unique expertise in digital integration. Using random sampling, on the other hand, improves the impartiality of the research and makes it possible to examine wider patterns within the data. In conjunction with one another, these methodologies guarantee a comprehensive investigation of the ways in which software tools influence education in the humanities, so contributing to both theoretical knowledge and practical suggestions for the improvement of digital learning [9].

4.2.2 Sampling Techniques: Overview and Justification

Researchers may make conclusions about a population without evaluating every person by sampling a representative fraction. Sampling improves efficiency and validity in educational research, especially when examining software in humanities education. Since investigating a whole population is impossible owing to time and financial restrictions, researchers use sampling methods to get valuable data from a smaller sample. Different sampling strategies suit different research goals. Random sampling assures that every population member has an equal chance of being picked, improving generalisability. Stratified sampling divides the population into subgroups based on academic level or prior digital tool exposure to ensure comprehensive representation. Purposive sampling selects individuals based on expertise or relevance to the study to gain deeper insights into humanities education software usage. Researchers may get accurate data on digital learning trends and dynamics by carefully selecting a sampling technique [10] (Tables 4.2 and 4.3).

4.2.3 Instruments for Data Collection

Educational research, notably on software integration in humanities teaching, requires data gathering tools. These technologies are the main source of data, helping researchers answer questions, test hypotheses, and support their findings. The validity

Table 4.2 Summary of sampling techniques

Sampling technique	Type	Description	When used in humanities research
Simple random sampling	Probability	Equal chance for all elements	When population is homogeneous and accessible
Stratified sampling	Probability	Population divided into strata; samples drawn from each	To ensure representation of key subgroups
Systematic sampling	Probability	Every kth element selected	When list of population is available and ordered
Cluster sampling	Probability	Entire groups selected randomly	When population is large and geographically dispersed
Purposive sampling	Non-probability	Selection based on characteristics	For expert opinion or specific knowledge cases
Snowball sampling	Non-probability	Participants refer other participants	When studying hidden or hard-to-reach populations
Convenience sampling	Non-probability	Selection based on availability	For exploratory or pilot studies

Table 4.3 Sampling technique decision matrix

Factor	Best sampling technique(s)
Small, well-defined population	Simple Random, Stratified
Diverse subgroups	Stratified, Purposive
Geographically dispersed	Cluster, Systematic
Hard-to-reach participants	Snowball, Purposive
Limited time/resources	Convenience, Systematic
In-depth qualitative insights	Purposive, Snowball

and reliability of results depend on instrument choice. A good data gathering mix yields findings that appropriately represent quantitative and qualitative trends. Educational research uses structured surveys, interviews, focus group discussions, observations, and document analysis. Standardised surveys allow researchers to measure trends and correlations in big samples. However, interviews and focus groups provide participant experiences in more detail. Document analysis lets academics determine how software affects course materials and student submissions, while observations enable researchers to see real-time digital tool use. Researchers must carefully pick and integrate these instruments depending on the study's goals since each has pros and cons. Educational research may provide theoretical insights and practical suggestions for improving digital learning in humanities education by using a balanced mix of methodologies [11].

4.2.4 Types of Data Collection Instruments

Questionnaires are organised tools that include questions that have been pre-set before to the survey. It is common practice to gather quantitative data using these questionnaires, which may either be open-ended or closed-ended. Using questionnaires is an effective method for collecting big samples and allows for anonymity. It is possible to conduct interviews in an organised, semi-structured, or unstructured manner. Interviews are used for the purpose of gathering in-depth qualitative data. They make it possible to conduct in-depth investigations of the experiences, views, and perceptions of the participants. Observing and documenting behaviour and interactions in natural situations in a methodical manner is required for this. For the purpose of analysing classroom practices, software use behaviour, and other related topics, observations may be conducted with or without the participation of participants. Examinations and evaluations are used for the purpose of evaluating the knowledge, abilities, or performance of learners. They are often used in impact studies that measure the consequences of learning both before and after the intervention. The analysis of the document: Documents that are already in existence, such as textbooks, curriculum guides, user manuals, and digital learning tools, are analysed in this approach in order to extract information that is pertinent to the issue at hand [12].

4.2.5 Validity and Reliability

Validity and reliability are fundamental principles in research that ensure the accuracy and consistency of measurement instruments. Validity refers to the degree to which an instrument measures what it is designed to measure, ensuring that the results truly reflect the concept being studied. Different types of validity, such as content validity, construct validity, and criterion validity, help determine whether the instrument appropriately captures the intended information. Reliability, on the other hand, is concerned with the consistency of the instrument in producing stable results over time or across different conditions. Test–retest reliability ensures that repeated administrations yield similar outcomes, inter-rater reliability measures agreement among different evaluators, and internal consistency reliability confirms that various items within the instrument align in their assessments. For a research instrument to be effective, it must possess both validity and reliability; otherwise, the findings may be misleading or inconsistent. For instance, a test designed to assess software literacy must be valid by accurately evaluating users' software proficiency and reliable by producing consistent results across multiple administrations. Without these essential qualities, research instruments risk generating flawed conclusions, reducing their usefulness in educational and scientific investigations.

4.2.6 *Ethical Considerations*

Ethical considerations are fundamental in educational research to ensure that data collection respects participants' rights and well-being. Informed consent is a crucial aspect, requiring researchers to provide clear explanations of the study's purpose, procedures, potential risks, and benefits before participants agree to take part. Additionally, privacy and confidentiality must be safeguarded by anonymising data, securely storing information, and restricting access to authorized individuals only. Researchers must also ensure that their instruments do not cause psychological or emotional distress; questions, tests, or observations should be designed sensitively to avoid discomfort. Furthermore, participation must be entirely voluntary, meaning individuals should not feel coerced into contributing and should be able to withdraw at any time without negative consequences. Adhering to these ethical principles fosters trust, encourages honest responses, and upholds the integrity of educational research, ensuring that findings are both valid and responsibly obtained [13] (Table 4.4).

4.3 Validation of Instruments

Validation of research instruments is an important procedure in educational research that ensures the accuracy and efficiency of data collecting tools. Validation of research instruments is an essential activity. In research that focusses on the use of software in humanities education, researchers employ a variety of instruments to evaluate skills, engagement, and learning outcomes. Validation is essential in order to guarantee that these tools accurately measure what they are designed to measure. It is part of the validation process to evaluate the construct validity, which verifies alignment with theoretical concepts, the criterion validity, which examines whether the results

Table 4.4 Summary of data collection instruments

Instrument	Data type	Strengths	Limitations
Questionnaire	Quantitative/ Qualitative	Efficient, scalable, anonymous	May lack depth, risk of misinterpretation
Interview	Qualitative	Detailed, exploratory, flexible	Time-consuming, interviewer bias
Observation	Qualitative	Natural setting, real-time data	Observer effect, subjective interpretation
Tests	Quantitative	Objective, standardized, measurable	Limited to specific knowledge areas
Document analysis	Qualitative	Non-intrusive, historical insight	Limited to available documents

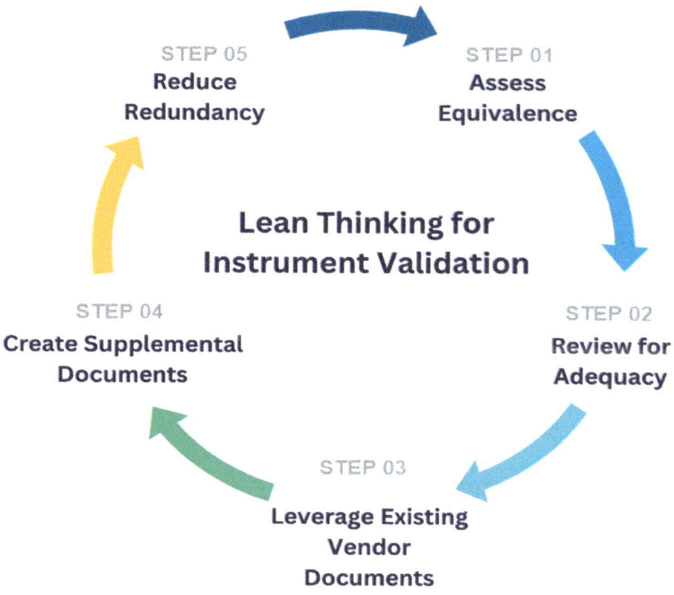

Fig. 4.3 Steps for validation [15]

correspond to established benchmarks, and the content validity, which ensures that the instrument covers the subject matter in a comprehensive manner. It is possible that the data will be wrong if they are not properly validated, which will result in incorrect interpretations and conclusions, which will in turn reduce the dependability of the study. Increasing the credibility of their results and ensuring that their studies contribute meaningfully to the field is accomplished by researchers via the thorough validation of instruments [14] (Fig. 4.3).

4.3.1 Types of Validity

When conducting an evaluation of their instruments, researchers need to give careful consideration to a number of different types of validity in order to guarantee accurate and relevant findings. The term "content validity" refers to the evaluation of whether or not a particular instrument adequately covers the whole scope of the subject matter that it is designed to measure. It is common practice for specialists in the subject to confirm this by examining whether or not all relevant components have been covered. The idea of construct validity involves determining whether or not the instrument in question accurately measures the theoretical concept that it claims to evaluate. A questionnaire that is meant to measure digital literacy, for instance, need to include a number of different aspects of digital abilities in order to guarantee that it accurately represents the design that was intended. For the purpose of determining the accuracy of the instrument, criterion-related validity involves comparing the outcomes of the instrument to a previous benchmark. This involves the evaluation of the instrument's predictive validity, which determines how accurately it predicts future results, as well as the contemporaneous validity, which determines whether or not it aligns with the standards that are already in place. Last but not least, the concept of "face validity" (which is less scientifically rigorous) examines whether or not the instrument looks to be successful in accomplishing the aim for which it was designed. This kind of validity is often evaluated by individuals who are not specialists in the field or by test takers based on their own perceptions of the instrument's clarity and relevance. By addressing these various forms of validity, researchers are able to improve the reliability and applicability of their measuring methods, which ultimately helps to raise the credibility of their results [16].

4.3.2 Methods of Establishing Validity

The process of validating research instruments comprises a number of systematic approaches that are used to guarantee that the instruments are accurate, reliable, and successful in measuring the concepts that are supposed to be measured. One of the most important methods is called "expert review," and it involves subject matter experts doing an in-depth analysis of the material in order to decide whether or not it is relevant, clear, and in line with the goals of the study. In the subsequent step, known as "pilot testing," researchers are given the opportunity to test the instrument on a small sample size in order to uncover any ambiguities, inconsistencies, or mistakes that may have an impact on the data gathering process. Furthermore, the use of statistical methods such as exploratory or confirmatory factor analysis, which are referred to as "factor analysis," contributes to the establishment of construct validity by determining whether or not the instrument successfully captures the theoretical concept that it intends to assess. Finally, correlation studies are used to evaluate the criterion-related validity of an instrument by comparing the results of the instrument to pre-existing standards or benchmarks. This ensures that the data gathered is in accordance with internationally recognised measurements of the same concept. Investigators are able to improve the credibility and dependability of their instruments via the use of these validation procedures, which ultimately results in findings that are more significant and trustworthy in the field of educational research.

4.3.3 *Importance of Validation in Humanities Software Studies*

In humanities education, where assessment tools range from surveys and rubrics to software usage logs and reflective journals, validation is essential to ensure the credibility and relevance of research findings. Proper validation confirms that these instruments effectively measure the intended learning outcomes without interference from unrelated skills or external factors. For instance, if software is integrated to enhance literary analysis skills, the research instruments must specifically evaluate improvements in critical thinking related to textual interpretation rather than being influenced by unrelated cognitive abilities, prior knowledge, or general writing skills. Establishing validity involves verifying that the assessment criteria align with theoretical constructs, ensuring comprehensive coverage of the subject, and comparing results with established benchmarks. By rigorously validating these instruments, researchers can obtain meaningful insights into the efficacy of educational interventions, helping shape more effective methodologies in humanities [17].

4.4 Summary

Instrument validation is an ongoing and iterative process that ensures research tools remain accurate, reliable, and relevant over time. It requires a combination of qualitative feedback, gathered through expert reviews and participant responses, and quantitative indicators, such as statistical analyses and correlation studies, to assess consistency and effectiveness. This continuous refinement strengthens the credibility and robustness of research findings, preventing errors or biases that could compromise their validity. Moreover, by maintaining rigorous validation standards, researchers contribute more effectively to educational practices and policy formulation, ensuring that data-driven decisions are well-founded and impactful. A validated instrument evolves with changing educational trends, allowing researchers to adapt methodologies to new learning environments and emerging challenges [18] (Table 4.5).

4.5 Reliability Testing

Reliability in educational assessment refers to the consistency and dependability of a measure, ensuring that results remain stable across different applications. In the context of software tools used in humanities education, reliability is assessed through several key dimensions. Internal consistency examines whether all components of the software function uniformly, ensuring coherent and predictable interactions. Test–retest reliability evaluates whether the software produces similar results when applied

Table 4.5 Types of validity and their applications

Type of validity	Purpose	Application in humanities education
Content validity	Ensures comprehensive coverage of subject matter	Verifying questionnaire items reflect all aspects of software usage
Construct validity	Confirms that the instrument measures the intended construct	Assessing critical thinking or digital engagement
Criterion-related validity	Compares outcomes with external benchmarks	Relating software test scores to academic results
Face validity	Judges' apparent relevance and clarity	Using peer feedback to assess the clarity of interview questions

repeatedly under the same conditions, maintaining accuracy over time. Inter-rater reliability is especially relevant for tools requiring human input, such as annotation or grading software, to determine whether different users generate consistent outputs when using the system. System stability ensures that the software operates reliably across various hardware and software environments, preventing technical discrepancies from affecting educational outcomes. By addressing these reliability aspects, researchers and educators can confidently use software tools to support pedagogy and derive meaningful insights in humanities education [19, 20].

4.5.1 *Relevance to Humanities Education*

Humanities studies, in contrast to quantitative areas, often deal with complex interpretative processes. These processes include literary exegesis, cultural study, and the creation of subjective meaning. The testing of software dependability is presented with new issues as a result of this, since the tools are required to not only function properly but also conform to the traditions of the academic community in their interpretations. It is necessary for a text analysis tool that is intended for literary study to take into consideration complexity such as metaphor, historical language variances, and alterations in meaning that occur throughout the context. If a tool like this does not take into account these aspects, the results it produces could not accurately reflect the literary or cultural relevance that was intended, which would undermine the credibility of the study. For example, a sentiment analysis tool that is used to ancient literature has to be able to discriminate between irony, satire, and real emotional expression. This is in contrast to merely classifying words based on how they are used in present times. To maintain academic integrity and provide support for successful teaching, it is essential to guarantee the dependability of digital humanities

Table 4.6 Common reliability tests in humanities software

Reliability type	Testing method	Example in humanities software
Internal consistency	Cronbach's Alpha, Split-half method	Survey tool consistency across question banks
Test–retest reliability	Repeated use over time with identical input	Consistent keyword frequency in Voyant over two sessions
Inter-rater reliability	Cohen's Kappa, Fleiss' Kappa	Tagging consistency in NVivo across different coders
System stability	Load testing, cross-platform testing	Text encoding tool on Windows vs. macOS

educational resources. The use of dependable software boosts trust in computational approaches, which in turn enables researchers to include digital tools into their work without having to worry about the possibility of misunderstanding or lacking consistency. The use of well-validated technologies in educational contexts has the potential to enhance learning by supplying students with accurate and relevant insights about works of art, historical records, or writings. It is possible for developers and educators to create a wider adoption of digital approaches while also keeping the intellectual rigour of the humanities with the use of algorithms that have been refined to respect the interpretative depth of humanities research. Toolkits for the digital humanities have the potential to bridge the gap between the computational efficiency of humanistic inquiry and the complexity of humanistic inquiry via continual evaluation and development [20, 21].

4.5.2 *Methods of Reliability Testing*

Based on the functionality of the program, several approaches for reliability testing are used. The following table provides an overview of widely used reliability tests and how they might be used as educational aids in the field of humanities (Table 4.6).

4.5.3 *Tools and Frameworks for Conducting Reliability Tests*

When it comes to research and software development, reliability testing is backed by a variety of statistical and computational methods that assist in verifying that measurements are accurate and consistent. Both the statistical software packages SPSS and R are frequently used and include the capability to compute Cronbach's alpha, which is an essential measure for evaluating the degree of internal consistency. In addition, these tools include a variety of reliability metrics, which makes them indispensable for verifying survey instruments and experimental data. The same is true for Python libraries, such as scikit-learn and statistics models, which include methods for estimating test–retest reliability and inter-rater reliability. These functions assist researchers in determining the degree to which repeated measurements or various assessors yield consistent results. The use of human review and expert panels is an essential component of the dependability evaluation process in situations when software produces subjective outputs, such as when picture annotation tools are taken into consideration. In order to ensure that the program's outputs are in accordance with the expectations of experts, human evaluators are used to evaluate whether or not the software properly interprets complicated or confusing inputs. In addition, established frameworks such as ISO/IEC 25010 provide detailed criteria for assessing the quality of software, which include aspects such as dependability, usability, and security. It is possible for researchers and developers to improve the robustness of their instruments by using these approaches. This will ensure that their instruments provide data that is reliable for both academic and practical domains.

4.5.4 *Case Study: Reliability Testing of Voyant Tools in a Literature Course*

The study aimed to assess the reliability of Voyant Tools in analysing Romantic poetry through keyword frequency and topic modeling. To ensure consistency, identical corpora were uploaded across multiple sessions, allowing researchers to evaluate the stability of the tool's outputs over repeated trials. The keyword analysis and topic modeling results were then examined for consistency across different instances. The findings indicated high reliability, with keyword outputs remaining stable and strong inter-rater agreement observed (Cohen's Kappa = 0.87), demonstrating that multiple users produced similar results when interpreting the tool's outputs. These results suggest that Voyant Tools can be effectively employed for educational purposes in humanities research, providing dependable insights for textual analysis and literary studies.

4.5.5 *Challenges in Humanities-Oriented Software Testing*

The nature of the material and procedures involved in reliability testing in the humanities poses a set of obstacles that are not seen in other fields. In contrast to quantitative research that is conducted in a standardised manner, the humanities disciplines often entail subjective interpretations of texts, artefacts, and cultural phenomena. Due to the fact that content is subjective, it is possible for various analysts to create diverse interpretations, which makes it difficult to construct consistent metrics across many evaluations. Furthermore, dynamic material, which includes things like altering cultural settings or developing literary analysis tendencies, might create unpredictability over time. This necessitates the use of adaptive testing methodologies that take into account these changes. Additional elements add another layer of complexity to the process of evaluating trustworthiness in humanities research. It is necessary to have instruments that are able to accommodate diverse reading skills and analytical proficiencies since the participants' varying degrees of literacy may have an effect on how texts and digital tools are comprehended. The fact that the meaning of texts, symbols, and creative expressions may vary from one cultural background to another is contributed to by the fact that cultural and linguistic variety adds another layer. This necessitates the use of reliability testing strategies that acknowledge the existence of contextual complexity while preserving academic rigour. Given these limitations, it is crucial to have validation procedures that are both robust and adaptable. Some examples of such tactics include iterative testing, expert review panels, and adaptive computational models. These strategies are necessary for ensuring that results in humanities research are relevant and dependable.

4.5.6 Strategies to Improve Software Reliability in the Humanities

Improving software reliability in humanities research requires a combination of technical precision and adaptability to user needs. User-centered design prioritises the experiences and expectations of researchers, educators, and students, ensuring that tools align with scholarly methodologies and interpretive frameworks. By incorporating feedback early in development, software can better address the complexities of textual analysis, cultural research, and interdisciplinary inquiry. Iterative testing is another crucial strategy, allowing developers to refine functionality through repeated trials and adjustments. Testing tools under varied conditions ensures their stability and reliability across different datasets and user interactions. Additionally, clear documentation plays a vital role in guiding users on proper software usage, troubleshooting issues, and understanding underlying algorithms. Well-structured documentation enhances transparency, fostering trust in computational approaches. Built-in calibration tools enable users to fine-tune settings based on specific research needs, whether adjusting sensitivity in sentiment analysis or refining keyword recognition in textual studies. Finally, community engagement strengthens software reliability by involving scholars, educators, and developers in ongoing discussions, feedback loops, and collaborative improvements. By integrating these strategies, software tools in humanities education can maintain both technical dependability and scholarly relevance, ensuring their long-term effectiveness in research and pedagogy [18].

4.5.7 Implications for Educators and Researchers

Educators and researchers alike might benefit greatly from the use of dependable software tools in their respective disciplines. The stability of software in the field of education implies that teachers are able to securely include digital resources into their lesson plans, knowing that these technologies will provide results that are accurate and consistent. When instructors have faith in the reliability of these tools, they are able to construct learning experiences that are not only engaging but also methodologically sound. This helps students develop confidence in digital approaches to humanities study. Students, on the other hand, get the benefits of guided and dependable interactions with software, which enable them to concentrate on developing their analytical abilities rather than negotiating the complexities of technical terminology. In the same way that repeatable findings are an essential component of academic honesty, the dependability of software systems is as important for researchers. It is necessary for digital technologies that are used for textual analysis, historical interpretation, and cultural studies to provide stable outputs in a consistent manner across a variety of datasets and during repeated trials. This assures that computational approaches continue to be a reliable adjunct to conventional humanities study, which in turn supports developments in literary analysis, linguistic studies, and research in the digital humanities. It is possible for educators and researchers to harness technology to strengthen the credibility of teaching approaches as well as scholarly inquiry by placing an emphasis on dependability. This will result in a wider adoption of digital tools in the field of humanities education [22].

The continued technical effectiveness and academic credibility of technological tools used in the humanities is dependent on reliability testing. As the use of digital tools becomes more integrated into the process of learning and research, it is crucial that these technologies have the capacity to provide findings that are reliable and accurate in order to cultivate confidence among educators, students, and academics. Errors that might undermine academic results or prevent successful classroom application can be mitigated via the use of reliability testing, which involves methodically analysing software stability, inter-rater agreement, and repeatability. While digital approaches continue to advance, it is essential to maintain stringent dependability requirements in order to guarantee that new innovations continue to be significant and trustworthy. Not only must educational technologies be evaluated for their operation, but they must also be validated for their conformity to scholarly traditions, interpretative frameworks, and contextual subtleties that are specific to the humanities. There is a possibility that these tools would provide findings that are inconsistent or misleading if they are not subjected to comprehensive reliability testing. This would reduce their educational usefulness and academic reputation. Institutions are able to securely incorporate technology into humanities education by placing a priority on dependability. This improves both the efficacy of teaching and the validity of research in a digital world that is now undergoing fast advancement [23].

4.6 Procedure for Data Collection

In the field of humanities education, the technique for collecting data plays a crucial part in assuring the quality and reliability of research results. This is especially true in light of the increasing prevalence of digital tools and software. An approach to data gathering that is systematic starts with the clear definition of research goals, followed by the selection of acceptable procedures, and finally, the guarantee that ethical issues are given high regard. In order to gather quantitative data, such as usage metrics from digital platforms or statistical assessments of student involvement, systematic collecting techniques are required. Some examples of these approaches are surveys, experimental research, and software logs. On the other hand, qualitative data, which includes things like textual interpretations, reflective diaries, and discourse analysis, calls for instruments that have been meticulously created and that provide nuanced insights into humanistic inquiry from the researcher. Researchers have a responsibility to prioritise "informed consent" to preserve ethical integrity. This involves ensuring that participants are aware of the aim and extent of the data collection process. The preservation of privacy and confidentiality is of the utmost importance, particularly in digital contexts, where sensitive user interactions may be recorded. In addition, it is essential to conduct reliability and validity assessments to ensure that digital technologies provide findings that are consistent and relevant. Through the incorporation of these metrics, researchers have the ability to enhance the technological robustness as well as the scholarly importance of their work, thereby enhancing the efficiency of digital techniques in the field of humanities education [24].

4.6.1 Planning the Data Collection

A well-defined set of research goals and the identification of appropriate data sources are the bedrock of efficient data gathering in the humanities. Students, teachers, and digital platforms that provide insights regarding learning experiences and software interactions are examples of the types of sources that might be considered. It is possible to establish a comprehensive approach to the collection of useful information by determining the right data kinds, such as textual data from academic conversations, user interaction logs from digital tools, or survey results that capture perspectives. The design of research equipment is an extremely important factor in determining the quality of the data that is obtained. It is essential to carefully arrange questionnaires, interview guides, and recording tools in order to ensure that they are in line with the objectives of the study and to assist the precise assessment of critical variables. It is equally important to schedule the phases of data collection in order to ensure consistency. This will enable researchers to effectively track patterns, evaluate reliability, and analyse trends. The researchers improve the validity and relevance of their results by meticulously organising and methodologically executing their study.

As a result, they make significant contributions to the fields of educational research and digital humanities scholarship [25].

4.6.2 Ethical Considerations

The use of human beings in the humanities study necessitates strict adherence to ethical guidelines. Before participants agree to take part in a study, researchers must prioritise informed consent by making sure they completely understand the study's objective, methods, and possible repercussions. Individuals' autonomy and rights are protected in research when they are given explicit explanations and allowed to make informed choices voluntarily. Furthermore, the privacy of participants must be guaranteed via the use of confidentiality and data protection measures. To protect sensitive information, researchers must encrypt it before storing it and put safeguards in place to stop unauthorised people from accessing it. To further emphasise the importance of ethical standards, research plans must be approved by an institutional review board (IRB). These boards evaluate the plans to make sure they follow ethical rules and safeguard participants from damage. Researchers may minimise risks and maintain ethical integrity by using anonymisation techniques, which include eliminating identifying features from datasets. By adhering to these standards, research in the humanities may continue to be both thorough and considerate, which in turn builds confidence between study participants and researchers and guarantees important new findings [26].

4.6.3 Instruments and Tools

A wide variety of technologies that are meant to capture both quantitative and qualitative insights are used in the process of data collecting in digital humanities education. Platforms for conducting surveys online, such as Google Forms and SurveyMonkey, provide effective methods for collecting structured answers from students and teachers, which makes it possible to collect data on a wide scale. Researchers are able to better analyse trends in digital learning environments with the assistance of LMS, which come equipped with built-in analytics that monitor student progress, engagement, and interaction patterns. Researchers are able to examine user behaviour inside educational tools and evaluate how students traverse digital platforms with the use of screen recording software, which is a helpful tool for interaction studies. In addition, log file analysis tools assist in the extraction and analysis of usage data from software applications, which provides insights into the manner in which students interact with digital resources. Additionally, interview and focus group transcripts contribute rich qualitative data by capturing nuanced discussions, reflections, and interpretations. It is essential that the selection of these instruments be in accordance with the aims of the study. This will guarantee that the researchers obtain data that is relevant, trustworthy, and ethically sound. Through the use of a variety of tools, digital humanities education has the potential to reap the benefits of comprehensive and multi-dimensional analyses that improve the efficiency of pedagogical implementation as well as academic research.

4.6.4 Sampling Techniques

Sampling is an essential component of research since it determines the selection of participants or data points, which in turn guarantees that the results are relevant and representative of the population. The use of random sampling ensures that every participant has an equal opportunity to be selected, which helps to eliminate bias and improves the generalisability of the information obtained. Stratified sampling, on the other hand, includes grouping participants according to particular criteria, such as topic area or level of study, in order to guarantee that there is a balanced representation among relevant subgroups. The use of this strategy improves the accuracy of comparisons to be made between various categories. For research projects that call for a particular level of expertise or relevance, the method of purposeful sampling is utilised. In this method, participants are purposefully selected on the basis of their capacity to provide insightful contributions. This method is especially helpful in the field of humanities study, which often requires the incorporation of specialised viewpoints or one-of-a-kind cultural experiences in order to investigate intricate topics. Researchers are able to improve the reliability and applicability of their data by choosing the proper sampling strategy with great care. This helps to ensure that their study is able to catch relevant patterns and offer findings that are informative.

4.6.5 Data Collection Steps

When it comes to assuring the dependability of research, especially in the field of humanities education, a data gathering method that is well-structured is very necessary. Preparation is the fundamental phase, which requires researchers to create efficient instruments and acquire ethical clearance in order to guarantee that the rights of participants are safeguarded. Following this, the pilot testing stage acts as an important refining step. During this stage, a small-scale trial is conducted to assist in identifying ambiguities or inefficiencies in the instruments and processes before they are fully implemented. Upon completion of the refinement process, the deployment process includes the administration of the instruments and the systematic collection of answers, while ensuring that prescribed protocols are adhered to. Monitoring is vital for maintaining integrity since it allows for the supervision of the data gathering process, the prevention of deviations from procedures, and the guarantee of consistency over a variety of sessions. In conclusion, documentation plays a crucial part in the process of recording all actions, observations, and modifications. It offers a clear record that bolsters the dependability of the results and makes it possible to replicate them in the future. Researchers increase the validity and reliability of their study by meticulously carrying out and recording each step of the process. This contributes to the development of solid scholarship in the field of humanities.

4.6.6 Data Management

When it comes to digital humanities education, having an efficient data management system is very necessary in order to preserve the honesty, accessibility, and safety of educational research data. Security in the storage of digital files guarantees that sensitive material is safeguarded from unauthorised access or data corruption. Researchers often use encrypted databases or cloud-based repositories for the purpose of protecting their data. The implementation of frequent backups is similarly important since it avoids the loss of data that might be caused by system failures or deletions that were made by mistake. The maintenance of consistency and the protection of important datasets are both aided by the use of scheduled automated backups across various sites. The recording of changes in datasets, papers, or coding scripts is what constitutes "version control," which adds an extra degree of organisation to the process. This enables researchers to backtrack to earlier versions of the project whenever possible. When working on collaborative research projects, when numerous participants make changes to files throughout the course of the project, this is very helpful. Thus, metadata tagging improves data organisation and retrieval by enabling researchers to categorise files systematically based on characteristics such as date, author, content type, and keywords. By putting these tactics into action, researchers are able to protect the authenticity of their data, simplify the analytic process, and guarantee the research's continued use in the field of digital humanities scholarship.

4.6.7 Challenges and Solutions

Low response rates, technological difficulties, and participant dropout are common problems with data gathering in humanities research that might impact the trustworthiness of results. It is possible for researchers to apply tactics that improve engagement and ensure that the procedures of data collection run smoothly in order to avoid these issues. The provision of incentives, whether in the form of academic credits, minor prizes, or recognition, has the potential to stimulate greater participation rates, hence increasing the likelihood that respondents would complete surveys or interact with digital technologies. Assuring that participants continue to be active throughout the whole of the research without losing interest or missing deadlines is made possible by the use of reminders at opportune intervals, which helps to sustain engagement. In addition, it is essential to ensure that the tools are user-friendly in order to provide accessibility. In order to avoid experiencing annoyance and dropping out of the research process, research instruments, whether they are software-based or survey forms, should be simple to manage and intuitive. Moreover, having technical help available at all times guarantees that participants can quickly handle any technical issues that may arise, which in turn reduces the number of interruptions that occur throughout the data collecting process. Researchers are able to preserve the integrity of their study and boost participation rates by predicting probable difficulties and applying proactive solutions. This ultimately results in findings that are more credible and comprehensive in the field of humanities education.

An approach to data gathering that is both well-planned and carried out in an ethical manner offers the groundwork for research that is both rigorous and influential in the field of digital humanities education. It guarantees that the conclusions are based on data that has been carefully acquired, which enhances the validity of the research as well as its possible applications.

4.7 Ethical Considerations

Ethical issues are an essential component of study in the humanities, especially when digital technologies are an integral element of the investigation. To protect participants and ensure that academic work continues to be open and accountable, it is imperative that privacy, consent, and integrity be maintained. Ethical supervision takes place in educational contexts where students and teachers interact with technology. This ensures that the collection of data respects the rights of people while still sustaining the academic rigour of the institution. In the field of humanities education, the use of digital instruments represents an additional layer of complexity. The term "datafication," which refers to the process of converting human interactions into digital data that can be analysed, raises issues around the use, storage, and dissemination of personal information. Additionally, worries about surveillance arise as a result of the fact that learning platforms and software monitor user behaviour. As a result, it is vital to create data security mechanisms that prevent exploitation. Due to the interpretative character of humanities study, ethical problems are further complicated by the fact that digital technologies have the potential to alter how texts, artefacts, and cultural phenomena are researched and analysed. For the purpose of addressing these difficulties, it is necessary to have a clearly defined ethical framework, explicit permission processes, and openness in the way that data is treated. This will ensure that research continues to be both responsible and powerful.

4.7.1 Informed Consent

This ensures that participants have a complete understanding of the objectives, scope, and procedures involved in the research before they agree to take part in the study.

Informed consent is a crucial ethical need in the field of humanities research. The provision of a transparent and trustworthy description of the objectives of the research serves to build transparency and confidence, enabling participants to evaluate the extent to which the study is relevant to their own experiences or interests. Additionally, in order to alleviate concerns about privacy and confidentiality, researchers are required to reveal the techniques and instruments that will be used to collect data. This includes providing an explanation of how the information will be obtained, maintained, and analysed. In addition, participants should be provided with information on the possible dangers and advantages of their participation, so that they are able to make an informed choice regarding their participation. Voluntary participation is an essential component of informed consent, and subjects should be given the assurance that they are free to withdraw from the study at any moment without incurring any consequences. The last thing that researchers should do is providing participants with the contact information for oversight agencies. This will enable participants to ask questions or voice concerns if they are required to do so. Consent must be sought in writing or via a secure digital method when dealing with kids or vulnerable groups. This is done to ensure that ethical integrity is maintained and to preserve the rights of all parties concerned. Researchers are able to increase the credibility and ethical basis of their work by placing an emphasis on informed consent. This helps to ensure that studies in the field of humanities education continue to display responsible and respectful behaviour.

4.7.2 Privacy and Confidentiality

Protecting the rights of participants and upholding ethical standards in humanities research requires strict adherence to confidentiality protocols. By preventing people from being individually identifiable via the use of anonymised data in reports and publications, it is possible to communicate the results of research without compromising the confidentiality of the information. In addition, the encryption of stored data and the restriction of access are both helpful in protecting sensitive information and lowering the likelihood that it would be used or exposed without authorisation. For the purpose of preventing data breaches, researchers are required to properly manage data storage by using secure servers and restricted access protocols wherever possible. Avoiding the gathering of personally identifiable information (PII) that is not required is another essential component that must be avoided in order to minimise risks and guarantee compliance with data protection requirements. The researchers should only acquire the information that is necessary for their study, and they should include measures to prevent the information from being misused. Ensure that research practices are in accordance with established legal frameworks by ensuring compliance with local and international data protection laws. Some examples of such laws include the General Data Protection Regulation (GDPR) and Nigeria's National Data Protection Regulation (NDPR). The researchers are able to maintain the ethical norms that are important for responsible digital humanities study by giving these measures a higher priority. This helps them build trust with the participants [27].

4.7.3 Data Security and Storage

Secure data storage is an important feature of ethical research, especially in digital humanities education, where sensitive material must be kept safe from unauthorised access and data loss. Utilising encrypted storage systems, such as cloud storage provided by an institution, is an effective method for protecting research information. This method ensures that only authorised persons are able to access the data. Through the use of encryption, breaches may be avoided, and the integrity of sensitive documents can be preserved. By performing regular backups of data on secure servers, an additional layer of protection is added, hence lowering the likelihood of data being lost inadvertently as a result of system failures or security breaches. In the event that there are any technological challenges, researchers will be able to restore material provided they have scheduled backups. Furthermore, the implementation of access control rules helps specify who is able to access and edit research data. This restricts entrance to just the staff who are required, so avoiding unauthorised modifications. Clear deadlines for the retention and disposal of sensitive data guarantee that information is held for a suitable length of time before being removed in a safe manner. This helps to eliminate the long-term hazards that are associated with the retention of superfluous data. The researchers not only preserve the privacy of the participants and ensure that they are in accordance with the legislation governing data protection, but they also strengthen the ethical underpinning of their work in the field of digital humanities by adopting these methods. Through the implementation of these procedures, confidence is maintained, transparency is maintained, and the appropriate use of technology in educational research is supported.

4.7.4 Ethical Use of Digital Tools

Integrity, privacy, and justice must be maintained via the ethical examination of digital instruments used in humanities study and instruction. In order to guarantee that consumers are aware of how their information is gathered, analysed, and stored, it is essential that data processing and storage be implemented with transparency. Researchers and educators have a responsibility to give platforms that are transparent about their data policies and give users the ability to control their information the highest priority. In addition, it is essential to prevent surveillance or coercive data practices in educational settings. This is because the interactions of students should be monitored in a responsible manner without intruding on their liberty or privacy [28].

The evaluation of third-party tools for ethical compliance is another important factor to take into account. This involves making certain that external software providers adhere to predetermined guidelines concerning the protection of data, the acquisition of consent, and the responsible application of artificial intelligence. Assessing algorithms for possible bias is a critical stage in the process of eliminating discrimination in content analysis, grading systems, or automated feedback mechanisms. This is particularly true in instances when the tools are powered by artificial intelligence. It is possible for educators and researchers to ensure that digital methodologies are in accordance with ethical research standards by conducting a critical evaluation of these aspects. This will help to foster responsible and trustworthy applications of technology in the field of humanities scholarship.

4.7.5 Institutional Review and Oversight

When doing research in the humanities, it is essential to get ethical clearance from a review board before beginning data collecting. This is done to guarantee that the study adheres to ethical norms and protects the rights of participants. Organisations known as Institutional Review Boards (IRBs) or Ethics Committees evaluate research proposals in order to ensure that the procedures used are open to public scrutiny and in accordance with ethical principles. The implementation of this procedure serves to protect the persons who are participating in the research project by ensuring that informed permission is gained in the appropriate manner and that privacy safeguards are provided. In addition, a comprehensive ethical evaluation makes it easier to identify risks and take preventative measures against them. This helps to ensure that any possible damages, whether they are psychological, social, or technical, are handled in a proactive manner. In addition, it ensures that there is responsibility for the processing and reporting of data, which helps to avoid the inappropriate use of sensitive information or access to it by unauthorised parties. The validity of research endeavours is bolstered by approval from IRBs or Ethics Committees, which in turn strengthens the public's and academic's faith in digital humanities approaches. Researchers who are able to successfully traverse this process not only contribute to the responsible research that respects human dignity and academic integrity, but they also increase the credibility of their work [29].

4.7.6 Addressing Power Dynamics

The presence of power asymmetries in educational research, especially in situations where instructors simultaneously act as researchers, has the potential to unintentionally affect the replies of participants or their desire to participate. Voluntary participation and anonymity must be prioritised in order to guarantee ethical integrity. This will allow students to feel free to engage without the worry of being discriminated against or facing consequences. It is possible for students to share their ideas in an honest manner when their replies are anonymised, which contributes to conclusions that are more accurate and relevant. In addition, the participation of third parties in the process of the collection of permission or the administration of surveys helps to limit direct encounters between researchers and participants, so lowering the possibility of pressure or the perception of duty. In order to prevent educators from accidentally influencing student choices via the interweaving of academic authority and research involvement, it is essential to clearly separate teaching duties from research activity. Through the implementation of these precautions, ethical research helps to cultivate an atmosphere that is fair and impartial, respecting the autonomy of participants while yet sustaining academic rigour in the field of humanities education.

4.7.7 Cultural Sensitivity and Inclusiveness

Respecting cultural and contextual differences in humanities research is essential for ensuring ethical integrity and meaningful scholarship. Using inclusive language helps create research materials that are accessible and considerate of diverse identities, preventing alienation or misrepresentation. Thoughtful wording ensures that all participants feel valued and acknowledged in the study. Being aware of cultural norms and sensitivities allows researchers to approach topics with appropriate contextual understanding, avoiding assumptions that may misinterpret or oversimplify complex cultural expressions. Avoiding bias in question framing or interpretation ensures that research findings remain objective and reflective of varied perspectives. Researchers must critically assess survey questions, interview structures, and analytical frameworks to prevent unintentional biases that could skew results. By integrating these ethical principles, humanities research not only enhances validity but also strengthens its role in promoting inclusive and respectful academic inquiry across diverse cultural landscapes.

4.7.8 Reporting and Dissemination

Ethical reporting is a critical aspect of humanities research, ensuring that findings are presented with accuracy, integrity, and respect for contributors. Avoiding misrepresentation or over generalisation is essential to maintaining credibility, as researchers must ensure their interpretations remain faithful to the data without distorting nuanced perspectives. Over generalisations can lead to misleading conclusions, undermining the reliability of scholarly work. Proper crediting of all contributors reinforces academic integrity, acknowledging the roles of researchers, collaborators, and participants who contributed to the study. Transparency is further enhanced by sharing findings with participants or stakeholders, fostering a culture of openness and accountability. Whenever possible, researchers should opt for open access and ethical publishing venues, ensuring that knowledge remains widely accessible while adhering to responsible publication standards. By upholding these principles, scholars can strengthen the trustworthiness and impact of their research while fostering an ethical and inclusive academic environment. Ethics in digital humanities research go well beyond regulatory compliance; they represent a commitment to encouraging courteous, fair, and responsible academic practices that uphold the integrity of scholarly inquiry. It is imperative that ethical concerns be included into each and every step of the research process in order to guarantee that technology improvements do not undermine humanistic ideals but rather complement them. This is because digital technologies and techniques are reshaping humanities research and education systems.

The establishment of frameworks that prioritise openness, accountability, and inclusion is accomplished by educators and researchers via the incorporation of ethical concepts across the whole study lifecycle. To do this, it is necessary to protect the privacy of participants, to uphold intellectual honesty, and to eliminate biases in the processes of data gathering and algorithmic development. It is also necessary to pay special attention to cultural sensitivities and contextual variances while doing ethical research. This is done to ensure that the results appropriately represent a variety of viewpoints without propagating stereotypes or excluding certain groups. Furthermore, responsible scholarship in the digital humanities expands to include the manner in which discoveries are disseminated and used. Enhancing the legitimacy and accessibility of research is accomplished via the implementation of open-access programs, ethical publication procedures, and explicit attribution of contributions. In addition, researchers have a responsibility to be watchful about the unintended implications of digital techniques, conducting critical evaluations of the influence that technologies such as automated analysis, datafication, and monitoring have inside academic environments. The ultimate goal of doing research in the digital humanities that adheres to ethical standards is to protect the fundamental principles that underpin the humanities, which include critical thought, intellectual honesty, and respect for the variety of human experiences. Scholars not only assure compliance by actively incorporating ethical principles in the design, execution, and dissemination of research, but they also build a culture within the academic community that is equitable, inclusive, and forward-thinking.

4.7.9 Data Analysis Techniques

The process of data analysis is the foundation of research in the digital humanities since it enables academics to derive relevant insights from the material that they have gathered. As a result of the multidisciplinary character of humanities education, research data often incorporates both qualitative and quantitative elements. In order to guarantee methodological rigour, it is necessary to use analytical procedures that are flexible enough to accommodate both variables. In qualitative analysis, the emphasis is placed on the interpretation of artefacts that are either textual, visual, or cultural in nature. Methods such as theme coding, discourse analysis, and content analysis are used in this process. Researchers are able to recognise recurrent patterns, contextual meanings, and nuanced interpretations within narratives, interviews, and historical sources as a result of this. By simplifying the process of coding and classifying themes, software applications such as NVivo and Atlas.ti may provide assistance with the administration of qualitative data [30].

Quantitative analysis, on the other hand, is characterised by the use of numerical data, which is often derived from the interactions provided by digital tools, replies to surveys, or organised educational evaluations. Quantifying patterns, measuring correlations, and evaluating the influence of digital methodology on humanities scholarship are all tasks that may be accomplished with the use of statistical methods such as descriptive analysis, regression models, and trend mapping. When it comes to doing comprehensive statistical assessments, software such as SPSS, R, or analytics frameworks based on Python may be of great assistance. Integration of data via triangulation enables thorough comprehension for studies that include both qualitative and quantitative components, which are sometimes referred to as "mixed-methods research." Researchers have the ability to increase the validity of their results and deepen digital humanities study by cross-referencing qualitative interpretations with patterns in empirical data. The application of methodological accuracy, the selection of relevant tools, and the ethical management of information are all necessary components of effective data analysis in digital humanities education. Researchers have the ability to handle the complexity of humanities study while also harnessing digital innovations to expand investigation and interpretation if they take the appropriate methodologies into consideration [18].

4.7.10 Qualitative Data Analysis

Qualitative data plays a vital role in humanities education, capturing nuanced perspectives, contextual meanings, and human experiences that structured quantitative approaches might overlook. Research in this domain often draws from interviews, open-ended survey responses, observational notes, and textual sources, each offering unique insights into educational practices, cultural interpretation, and scholarly inquiry.

Several analytical techniques support the processing of qualitative data:

a. Thematic Analysis helps identify and examine recurring patterns or themes within collected responses, revealing key concepts and trends.
b. Content Analysis involves systematically coding textual data, allowing researchers to quantify themes while maintaining the richness of qualitative interpretation.
c. Narrative Analysis focuses on the structure and meaning of stories or personal accounts, exploring how individuals construct and share knowledge through lived experiences.

d. Discourse Analysis examines language in social contexts, uncovering underlying power structures, ideological influences, and communicative dynamics within text-based interactions.

To streamline these processes, software tools like NVivo, ATLAS.ti, and MAXQDA provide robust capabilities for coding, visualisation, and pattern recognition. These platforms enhance the efficiency of qualitative research by offering structured frameworks for data organisation, thematic exploration, and collaborative analysis. By leveraging these methodologies and digital tools, educators and researchers can extract meaningful insights from qualitative humanities data, enriching both pedagogical approaches and academic scholarship [19].

4.7.11 Quantitative Data Analysis

Quantitative analysis plays a key role in digital humanities education by structuring numerical data into meaningful insights. It allows researchers to measure trends, evaluate relationships between variables, and assess the impact of educational tools and methodologies. Common sources of quantitative data include surveys, assessments, and digital logs, each providing valuable numerical information.

Several essential techniques guide quantitative analysis:

1. Descriptive Statistics summarise data characteristics, using measures like mean, median, mode, and standard deviation to understand distributions and variability.
2. Inferential Statistics enable researchers to draw broader conclusions from their sample data through methods such as t-tests, ANOVA, and regression analysis, helping determine statistical significance and relationships.
3. Correlation and Causation Analysis explores how variables relate to one another, assessing whether observed connections indicate meaningful patterns or predictive relationships.

To effectively manage and analyse numerical datasets, researchers utilise tools like SPSS, R, Excel, and Python libraries (*pandas, scipy*), which facilitate data processing, visualisation, and advanced statistical modelling. By integrating these techniques, scholars in digital humanities can enhance their research rigor, improve pedagogical strategies, and gain valuable insights into educational practices.

4.7.12 Mixed Methods Analysis

Mixed-methods research offers a versatile approach to data analysis in digital humanities education by integrating both qualitative and quantitative perspectives. This method enhances the depth and reliability of findings, allowing researchers to explore complex questions from multiple angles. Several key strategies define mixed-methods approaches:

1. Convergent Design involves collecting and analysing qualitative and quantitative data simultaneously, enabling researchers to compare and integrate insights for a more holistic understanding.
2. Explanatory Design begins with quantitative data collection, followed by qualitative analysis to provide deeper interpretations of statistical trends, helping to contextualise numerical patterns within lived experiences.
3. Exploratory Design follows the opposite sequence, starting with qualitative data collection to identify key themes before employing quantitative testing to validate and measure findings on a broader scale.

This approach is particularly useful in digital humanities education, where complex research questions often require multiple perspectives to address issues of engagement, learning effectiveness, and digital interaction. By thoughtfully combining qualitative depth with quantitative precision, mixed-methods research strengthens academic scholarship and provides nuanced insights into educational practices.

4.7.13 Text and Discourse Analysis Tools

Digital tools have significantly transformed textual analysis in humanities research, enabling scholars to process vast amounts of data efficiently and uncover intricate language patterns, sentiment trends, and structural insights. Several widely used tools facilitate these advanced analytical capabilities:

1. Voyant Tools offers an intuitive web-based suite for text mining and visualisation, allowing researchers to explore word frequency, collocations, and thematic distributions interactively.
2. AntConc is a powerful concordance and corpus linguistic tool that assists in examining word usage, phrase structures, and keyword distributions across extensive textual datasets.
3. Leximancer specialises in concept mapping and thematic analysis, automatically detecting semantic relationships within texts and visually representing key themes.
4. LIWC (Linguistic Inquiry and Word Count) is particularly useful for psychological and sentiment analysis, measuring emotional tone, cognitive processes, and social dimensions within written language.

These tools provide digital humanities researchers with dynamic methods for examining literary, historical, and linguistic materials with precision. By leveraging computational text analysis, scholars can deepen interpretations, explore discourse evolution, and enhance contextual understanding across diverse cultural and academic fields.

4.7.14 Coding and Categorisation

Coding is a fundamental process in qualitative analysis, allowing researchers to systematically organize and interpret complex data. By tagging segments of text with meaningful labels, scholars can identify patterns, relationships, and emerging themes within their research. The coding process typically unfolds in three key stages:

a. Open Coding involves the initial categorisation of raw data, where researchers assign preliminary labels to recurring concepts or ideas. This phase is exploratory, aiming to uncover diverse insights without imposing strict frameworks.
b. Axial Coding connects these codes into broader categories by identifying relationships among them. Researchers examine how individual themes interact, grouping similar patterns to establish meaningful connections.
c. Selective Coding focuses on identifying core categories that capture the essence of the research focus. This final step helps refine the analysis by distilling complex data into central themes that drive the study's conclusions.

Qualitative coding enhances the interpretability of textual data, making it easier to extract meaningful insights while maintaining methodological rigour. Advanced software tools like NVivo, ATLAS.ti, and MAXQDA support this process by facilitating efficient data organisation, visualisation, and thematic exploration, ensuring that coding remains structured and insightful in digital humanities research.

4.7.15 Data Triangulation

Triangulation is a powerful research strategy used in digital humanities to enhance the credibility and validity of findings by integrating multiple perspectives. By cross-checking data through different approaches, researchers can minimise biases and strengthen their interpretations. Three main types of triangulation help achieve this rigor:

a. Methodological Triangulation combines multiple research methods, such as using both interviews and surveys, to verify findings across different analytical techniques. This approach ensures a comprehensive understanding by incorporating varied viewpoints.
b. Data Triangulation involves collecting information from different times, locations, or participant groups, allowing researchers to assess consistency and detect trends or changes over time.
c. Investigator Triangulation engages multiple researchers in the analysis process, reducing individual biases and increasing reliability by comparing interpretations from different analysts.

By integrating these triangulation methods, scholars in digital humanities can produce robust, well-rounded research, fostering trust in their findings while ensuring methodological integrity.

4.7.16 *Visualisation and Interpretation*

Visualisation is a key component of data analysis, transforming complex datasets into clear, interpretable graphics that enhance understanding and communication. Different visualisation techniques serve distinct purposes:

a. Charts, including bar graphs, pie charts, and scatter plots, effectively represent quantitative data, making it easier to compare values, track trends, and analyse distributions.
b. Word Clouds and Network Diagrams are useful for textual data, offering insights into language patterns, keyword frequency, and relationships between concepts.
c. Timelines and Flowcharts help visualise process-oriented data, mapping sequences, historical developments, or workflow structures in an intuitive way.

To create compelling visualisations, researchers use tools like Tableau and Power BI for dynamic and interactive dashboards, while R (ggplot2) and Python (matplotlib, seaborn) enable custom and high-quality statistical visualisations. By strategically selecting visualisation methods, digital humanities scholars can present findings in a way that enhances accessibility, storytelling, and scholarly impact.

4.7.17 *Reporting Results*

Clear and ethical reporting is essential in digital humanities research, ensuring transparency, accuracy, and accessibility for both academic and public audiences. To maintain reproducibility and credibility, researchers must follow best practices that make findings understandable and meaningful.

a. Context and narrative explanation help frame results within a larger scholarly or educational perspective, allowing readers to grasp the significance of the data.
b. Acknowledging limitations and potential biases ensures honesty in reporting, helping others critically assess the scope and constraints of the research.
c. Accessible language and visuals enhance comprehension, making findings more engaging and informative for a wide audience.
d. Standard formatting and citation guidelines support scholarly integrity, ensuring that research aligns with ethical and professional standards.

By incorporating these principles, researchers uphold the integrity of their work, fostering trust while contributing valuable insights to the evolving field of digital humanities. Well-structured and transparent reporting enhances the impact and application of research across disciplines.

In digital humanities education, data analysis acts as a bridge between the raw material that is available and the significant academic insights that may be gained from it. Researchers are required to use procedures that are both well-defined and methodical, and that are in line with the nature of their investigation, to guarantee rigour. Maintaining methodological accuracy improves the reliability and validity of results, regardless of whether the research is conducted using qualitative, quantitative, or mixed-methods techniques. Maintaining ethical integrity, repeatability, and peer assessment is all made possible by transparency, which is also of equal importance. A transparent description of the data sources, analytical procedures, and possible limits guarantees that the study will continue to be open and responsible until it is completed. Practices that encourage open sharing, such as disclosing datasets or methodological information, contribute to the trust that exists in the academic community and make it easier for other researchers to do more research. When analytical methods are adapted to the particular research topics, it guarantees that the results will continue to be informative and relevant. Text-mining software for discourse analysis, statistical models for learning outcomes, and visualisation platforms for thematic mapping are examples of the kinds of specialised tools that are required for digital humanities research. This type of research frequently involves large textual corpora, historical datasets, or interactive engagement metrics. The incorporation of relevant tools and techniques enables academics to get a more profound understanding of educational practices, digital interactions, and historical narratives. This, in turn, helps to enhance pedagogical frameworks and contributes to the development of humanities education. An examination of data that is both thoughtful and exact not only contributes to the advancement of knowledge but also provides insights into methods for enhancing digital learning environments. This helps to ensure that education in the humanities continues to develop in meaningful ways.

4.7.18 Case Study/Experimental Approach (If Applicable)

Evaluation of the function that software plays in the field of humanities education requires the use of crucial techniques such as case studies and experimental approaches. Researchers are able to evaluate both controlled treatments and real-world applications with the help of these methodologies, which provide a thorough understanding of the impact and usefulness of digital technologies in academic contexts. Case studies concentrate on real-world educational settings and provide information that is both rich and qualitative on the manner in which software is used in the teaching of the humanities. Researchers have the opportunity to investigate user experiences, institutional adoption, and contextual factors that influence the utilisation of technology via the use of this methodology. Through the examination of particular classrooms, institutions, or student interactions, case studies are able to offer useful insights about the problems, triumphs, and flexibility of educational practices.

Experimental techniques, on the other hand, include the implementation of standardised testing environments in order to accurately assess the efficacy of software in a systematic manner. Researchers are able to measure learning outcomes, evaluate engagement metrics, and identify the causal impacts of digital technologies on educational performance; these may be accomplished via the use of pre- and post-intervention studies, A/B testing, or randomised control trials. Empirical validation is made possible by this strategy, which contributes to the improvement of technology interventions and the dissemination of best practices. Both techniques, when performed in a disciplined manner, complement one another. Case studies provide both contextual richness and quantitative effect, while experiments demonstrate the former. This allows educators and researchers to establish evidence-based methods to improve digital learning experiences, optimise software integration, and progress humanities education via technology innovation. These strategies may be developed by merging qualitative and quantitative evaluations.

4.7.19 Case Study Approach

A case study is a powerful research approach that enables scholars to conduct a deep investigation into a specific instance or a small set of cases, helping to uncover insights within real-world contexts. It relies on multiple sources of evidence, making it an effective method for exploring complex social, educational, and technological phenomena.

Types of Case Studies

1. Exploratory Case Study: Used in the early stages of research to identify key questions, hypotheses, or theories that warrant further investigation.
2. Descriptive Case Study: Provides a detailed account of a particular event, program, or innovation, offering rich context and a comprehensive narrative.
3. Explanatory Case Study: Explores causality, helping researchers understand why certain phenomena occur and how different factors interact.

Key Features

1. Emphasis on context and complexity, ensuring that findings are deeply rooted in the specific circumstances being studied.
2. Utilisation of qualitative methods, such as interviews, observations, and document analysis, to capture nuanced perspectives and detailed insights.
3. Integration of quantitative data for triangulation, strengthening validity by cross-referencing findings with empirical measures.

Example in Humanities Education
A case study could examine how undergraduate students engage with a digital annotation platform like Hypothes.is in a literature course. Researchers might analyse usage logs, student feedback, and academic performance metrics, assessing how annotation tools influence reading comprehension and engagement.

This methodology is particularly valuable for evaluating digital tools in education, as it allows researchers to balance qualitative depth with empirical evidence, creating a well-rounded understanding of learning experiences. Case studies can provide practical implications for instructional design, helping educators refine technological interventions to enhance student outcomes.

4.7.20 Experimental Approach

An experimental approach is a research method used to examine cause-and-effect relationships by manipulating one or more independent variables and measuring their impact on dependent variables. By establishing controlled conditions, researchers can systematically test hypotheses and determine whether specific factors influence outcomes. This approach is particularly valuable in digital humanities education for evaluating the effectiveness of technologies, teaching strategies, and cognitive processes.

Types of Experiments

1. True Experiment: The most rigorous form of experimentation, involving random assignment of participants to different groups (e.g., experimental vs. control) to eliminate biases. This design ensures that any observed differences are due to the manipulated variable rather than external influences.
2. Quasi-Experiment: While similar to a true experiment, it lacks full randomisation often due to practical or ethical constraints. Instead of randomly assigning participants, researchers compare pre-existing groups or conditions, making this approach useful in educational settings where full experimental control is difficult.
3. Field Experiment: Conducted in real-world settings, this method retains some experimental control but allows researchers to observe phenomena within authentic environments, such as classrooms or digital learning platforms. It balances experimental rigor with practical application, making findings more generalisable to everyday learning contexts.

Common Applications in Digital Humanities Education

1. Testing the effectiveness of a new digital learning tool: Researchers assess how an interactive software or AI-driven platform impacts student comprehension, engagement, or knowledge retention compared to traditional methods.
2. Comparing learning outcomes across instructional technologies: This can involve evaluating whether students using immersive virtual environments, adaptive learning platforms, or multimedia resources perform better than those with conventional materials.
3. Assessing cognitive load induced by different types of media content: Researchers examine how various visual, textual, or interactive digital materials affect students' mental processing demands, helping optimise instructional design for better cognitive efficiency.

Table 4.7 Example design

Group	Intervention	Outcome measured
Control	Traditional textbook use	Test scores, engagement levels
Experimental	Use of interactive e-learning module	Test scores, engagement levels

When applied rigorously, experimental research enhances evidence-based decision-making in digital humanities education. It allows scholars to refine educational tools, improve teaching methods, and develop strategies that enhance learning outcomes by grounding pedagogical advancements in empirical research (Table 4.7).

4.7.21 Integration with Mixed Methods

Case study and experimental designs are both capable of being successfully integrated within a mixed-methods framework, which provides a strong approach to research in the field of digital humanities education. Using this technique, qualitative and quantitative insights are combined, which guarantees that the results are not just empirical but also contextually rich. Case studies provide academics the opportunity to conduct in-depth investigations of particular cases, which enables them to examine the ways in which educational tools or technology interventions are used in the actual world of practice. In the meanwhile, experimental designs bring about the introduction of organised testing settings, which make it possible for researchers to demonstrate cause-and-effect linkages via the methods of controlled observations. In the context of an experimental research evaluating the efficacy of a digital annotation tool, for instance, the monitoring of student comprehension scores, engagement metrics, or retention rates might be included. There is a possibility that this quantitative technique might not adequately capture user experiences or the elements that motivate them, despite the fact that it gives quantifiable statistics. In addition to this, qualitative interviews may be integrated, which will provide researchers with a more in-depth understanding of student perspectives, issues about usability, and general engagement with the technology.

Additionally, the incorporation of surveys and use statistics into a case study that investigates the implementation of a new digital learning platform has the potential to enhance the overall quality of the research. quantitative data, such as student feedback surveys, interaction logs, and academic performance trends, may confirm results, assuring a more thorough interpretation. Traditional case studies depend on observations and document analysis, but quantitative data can also validate findings. Researchers are able to bridge the gap between formal data-driven analysis and nuanced human experiences by incorporating case studies and experimental designs into a framework that is based on mixed methods. As a result of this methodological integration, credibility, application, and effect are all strengthened, and the results are made more actionable for educators, policymakers, and creators of digital humanities tools. In the end, mixed-methods research helps to cultivate an approach that is balanced, analytical, and multidisciplinary. This helps to ensure that technology interventions in humanities education are both successful and meaningful.

4.7.22 *Ethical Considerations*

Ethical considerations are paramount in research involving human subjects, ensuring that participants' rights and well-being are protected throughout the study [6]. Several foundational principles guide ethical research:

a. Informed Consent: Researchers must provide participants with clear, comprehensive information about the study's purpose, procedures, potential risks, and benefits before they agree to take part. This process ensures individuals make informed decisions regarding their participation.
b. Anonymity and Confidentiality: Protecting participant identities is essential, requiring careful data handling, anonymisation, or pseudonymisation to prevent unauthorised disclosure of personal information. Secure data storage and controlled access are crucial safeguards.
c. Voluntary Participation: Ethical research guarantees that participants engage freely without coercion and maintain the right to withdraw at any time, without repercussions. This principle upholds autonomy and ensures individuals have control over their involvement.
d. Institutional Approval: Studies involving human subjects, particularly in educational or sensitive research settings, require formal review and approval from an Institutional Review Board (IRB) or Ethics Committee. This oversight ensures adherence to ethical standards and legal regulations.

By following these principles, researchers uphold academic integrity, participant rights, and ethical accountability, fostering trust and credibility in scholarly work. Ethical research practices not only protect individuals but also enhance the validity and impact of findings.

4.7.23 *Limitations of Each Approach*

Case study and experimental research approaches provide significant benefits and limits when used to digital humanities teaching. Case studies give deep, contextual insights by analysing particular events in real-world contexts. In-depth examination of one-of-a-kind educational methods, technology implementations, or historical patterns is made possible for academics by these scholarly resources. However, the disadvantage of case studies is that they have limited generalisability. This is due to the fact that the results are firmly rooted in a specific context, which means that they may not be readily extended to larger populations or various contexts. On the other hand, experimental research excels in establishing strong causal relationships between variables, making it especially valuable for analysing the efficacy of digital tools or teaching approaches. Researchers can evaluate direct effects on learning outcomes by controlling settings and changing independent factors. Experiments, on the other hand, often lack ecological validity, which means that the findings produced in controlled and artificial situations do not necessarily transfer properly to applications in the real world. In the field of humanities education, where aspects such as social dynamics, engagement styles, and environmental influences play a key role, this mismatch might provide issues that need to be addressed.

When researchers want to address both these strengths and shortcomings, they often combine case studies and experiments within a framework that is based on mixed methods. This ensures that they have both qualitative depth and quantitative rigour in their study. By using this method, reliability and applicability are improved, and researchers are able to arrive at findings that are not only backed by empirical evidence but also take into account the environment in which they are being used. Researchers have the ability to create more complete insights that may be used to guide educational methods, the creation of digital tools, and pedagogical breakthroughs in the field of humanities research. This is accomplished by harnessing the strengths of each technique while limiting the limits of each method.

When it comes to analysing the influence that software has on humanities education, both case studies and experimental techniques play an important part. Each of these approaches offers a distinct set of benefits that are tailored to meet the requirements of a particular research endeavour. The choice of technique is heavily influenced by the aims of the study, the resources that are readily accessible, and the level of difficulty of the investigation. The use of case studies is particularly effective in giving researchers deep and contextual insights, which in turn enables them to investigate the real-world uses of digital technologies within certain educational environments. Scholars are able to get a better understanding of how software interacts with learning settings via the use of case studies. Case studies include the analysis of user experiences, adoption trends, and institutional dynamics. On the other hand, due to their restricted generalisability, the results presented here may not be relevant elsewhere [31].

Experimental methods, on the other hand, are very useful for determining causal linkages since they include assessing the efficiency of software in a methodical manner under controlled settings. Researchers are able to provide empirical data to evaluate the efficacy of education, cognitive load, or student involvement by altering factors and assessing the results of their experiments. Experimental methods, on the other hand, often lack ecological validity since the artificial testing settings may not adequately replicate the intricacies of the actual world. Increasing the robustness of results may be accomplished by incorporating both techniques into a framework that is predicated on mixed methods. In order to guarantee that the findings of the study are both contextually relevant and scientifically verified, it is necessary to combine qualitative insights from case studies with quantitative validation from experiments. Scholars can create relevant contributions that may influence pedagogical practices, technical progress, and theoretical breakthroughs in the field of humanities education by applying a variety of approaches and digital technologies [32].

4.7.24 Software Tools Used in the Study

Research in the field of humanities education relies heavily on software tools for data management and the improvement of instructional practices. These tools have been selected with great care in order to satisfy certain research roles, with the purpose of guaranteeing efficiency, accuracy, and meaningful interaction with the materials being studied. It is possible for researchers to acquire structured datasets by means of questionnaires, interviews, and qualitative text analysis by using software for data collection. Some examples of such software are Qualtrics, Google Forms, and NVivo. SPSS, R, Python (pandas, nltk), and MAXQDA are examples of systems that assist statistical assessments and textual processing for the purpose of data analysis. These platforms enable researchers to extract important insights from complicated material. In addition to research, teaching facilitation systems such as Moodle, Hypotheses.is, and Edmodo assist interactive learning by offering capabilities for course administration, digital annotation features, and collaborative conversations. This results in educational experiences that are more engaging for students. In addition, efficient communication platforms, such as Microsoft Teams, Slack, and Zoom, guarantee a smooth cooperation between researchers, instructors, and students. These tools also make it possible for students to communicate remotely and share their expertise.

Through the strategic use of these software solutions, academics have the capacity to improve the correctness, dependability, and pedagogical value of their study, which eventually leads to an improvement in the research process and an enrichment of teaching in the humanities. In academic contexts, the integration of technology with careful consideration not only simplifies processes but also broadens the scope of opportunities for novel approaches, multidisciplinary cooperation, and interactive learning experiences [33].

4.7.25 Data Collection Tools

A systematic and organised approach to data gathering was ensured in the field of humanities education research thanks to the contributions of these software tools, which played a vital role. Researchers were able to easily obtain, organise, and analyse material by using platforms that were specifically designed for both qualitative and quantitative research approaches. These technologies, which permitted full text analysis, coding, and theme exploration from interviews, open-ended survey answers, and academic texts, were used to support qualitative data collection. These

Table 4.8 Data collection tools

Software tool	Purpose	Features
Google Forms	Online surveys and questionnaires	Real-time response collection, ease of access, customisable formats
Microsoft Forms	Feedback collection and self-assessment	Integration with Office 365, real-time analytics
Zoom	Interview and focus group recordings	Video conferencing, session recording, chat transcripts
Otter.ai	Transcription of interviews	Real-time transcription, searchable text, speaker identification

Table 4.9 Data analysis tools

Software tool	Type of Analysis	Key capabilities
NVivo	Qualitative coding and thematic analysis	Node coding, query searches, and visualisation tools
SPSS	Statistical analysis	Descriptive and inferential statistics, graphical outputs
R	Statistical programming and data visualization	Customisable scripts, advanced statistical modelling
Excel	Basic data organisation and visualisation	Charts, pivot tables, formula-based computation

Once data were collected, these software tools facilitated various analytical procedures

tools included NVivo and MAXQDA, which were used to aid qualitative data collection. Quantitative data collection, on the other hand, was carried out with the assistance of software such as SPSS, R, and Google Forms. These programs made it possible to conduct organised surveys, do statistical calculations, and process numerical data. The integration of these technologies not only supported triangulation, which is the process of cross-referencing numerous data sources in order to increase the validity of conclusions, but it also assured correctness, consistency, and efficiency. The researchers were able to get a more profound comprehension of patterns, behaviours, and educational interactions by integrating qualitative insights with numerical trends. This allowed the study to be both methodologically sound and pedagogically useful. Both the legitimacy and the effect of the research were ultimately increased as a result of the strategic selection and deployment of these digital instruments (Tables 4.8 and 4.9).

4.7.26 Educational Software Used in Teaching Interventions

A number of digital technologies were included into the classroom in order to enhance the learning experiences of students studying the humanities. These tools supported

Table 4.10 Educational software

Tool	Description	Educational use
Hypothes.is	Web-based annotation platform	Collaborative reading and engagement with texts
Voyant Tools	Text mining and visual analysis	Word frequency, co-occurrence patterns, topic modeling
Moodle	Learning management system	Assignment submissions, quizzes, forum discussions
Padlet	Digital bulletin board	Brainstorming, visual idea mapping, collaborative exercises
StoryMapJS	Timeline and map-based storytelling	Geospatial narratives in history and literature

collaborative exploration, critical analysis, and interactive engagement activities. Educational platforms such as Moodle, Edmodo, and Canvas made it easier for students to interact with one another, share resources, and organise their courses. This resulted in a more streamlined communication process between teachers and students. The use of annotation and text analysis tools, such as Hypotheses.is and Voyant Tools, enabled students to participate in profound engagement with literary and historical works via the use of collaborative annotations, keyword analysis, and theme research.

Students were able to develop interactive narratives and data-driven interpretations of historical and literary settings via the use of digital storytelling and visualisation tools such as StoryMapJS and Tableau. These tools were designed for multimedia-driven learning. Analysis of linguistic structures, word frequencies, and stylistic trends in texts was made possible with the use of language processing tools such as AntConc and Lexos. This served to encourage computational thinking within the field of humanities study at the same time. Furthermore, venues for peer-to-peer learning, project-based cooperation, and dynamic academic exchanges were promoted via the use of discussion and collaboration platforms such as Microsoft Teams and Slack.

As a result of implementing these technologies, educators were able to optimise student engagement, analytical thinking, and interdisciplinary investigation, so increasing the efficacy of their teaching methods in the field of humanities education. A more immersive and enhanced learning experience was made possible by the thoughtful integration of technology, which also ensured that digital humanities approaches complemented both research and classroom dynamics (Table 4.10).

4.7.27 Communication and Collaboration Tools

Throughout the whole of the study process, it was of the utmost importance to guarantee efficient remote communication and collaborative work. This allowed for

Table 4.11 Communication and collaboration tools

Tool	Function	Advantages
Slack	Group messaging and document sharing	Organized channels, app integrations
Google Drive	File storage and collaboration	Real-time document editing, version history
Microsoft Teams	Meetings and collaborative work	Integration with Office apps, breakout rooms
Trello	Project management	Visual task tracking, deadlines, team roles

a completely smooth interaction between the researchers, instructors, and participants. Real-time conversations, resource sharing, and collaborative efforts were all supported by a variety of digital technologies, which helped to sustain productivity despite the presence of geographical obstacles. The process of holding virtual meetings, interviews, and group discussions was significantly aided by the use of video conferencing systems like as Zoom and Microsoft Teams. Researchers were able to connect with participants, coordinate analytic sessions, and present results in a way that was participatory because to the many tools that were available. Continuous communication, task management, and workflow organisation were all made easier with the use of instant messaging and collaboration technologies such as Slack and Trello. This helped to ensure that research teams stayed aligned and efficient.

Additionally, cloud-based document-sharing systems like as Google Drive and OneDrive made it possible for researchers to effectively collaborate on the editing of papers, exchange datasets, and safely preserve essential research materials. The accessibility of the information enabled that all contributors were able to examine and improve it in real time, which contributed to the development of a more streamlined research environment. The research process remained coherent, accessible, and productive thanks to the incorporation of these remote communication technologies. This made it possible for researchers to engage in multidisciplinary partnerships while maintaining the integrity and effectiveness of research in the field of humanities education (Table 4.11).

4.7.28 Justification for Tool Selection

The selection of tools for this research was carefully guided by several essential criteria to ensure both usability and ethical compliance. Accessibility was a key consideration, with priority given to software that was either freely available or institutionally provided to participants, minimising financial and logistical barriers to engagement. Equally important was user-friendliness, as tools needed to be intuitive and require minimal training, allowing researchers and students to focus on their work rather than grappling with complex technical requirements. Additionally, the functionality of each tool was assessed to ensure that it met the specific needs of the research. Whether for data collection, analysis, teaching facilitation, or communication, each software had to provide the necessary features to support a seamless workflow. Interoperability was another critical factor, ensuring that selected tools could be easily integrated with other platforms, allowing for efficient data transfer and collaboration without technical incompatibilities.

Finally, data security was a non-negotiable aspect of the selection process. The tools had to adhere to ethical guidelines for handling research data, ensuring confidentiality and protecting participant information from unauthorised access or breaches. By prioritising these criteria, the research maintained a balance between accessibility, efficiency, and ethical responsibility, enabling a productive and secure working environment.

4.7.29 Challenges Encountered

A number of difficulties surfaced during the course of the study process, necessitating the development of proactive solutions in order to preserve both efficiency and engagement. There were times when real-time cooperation and data gathering were hampered by technical concerns, such as outages in internet access that occurred during online sessions. Offline materials and other communication routes were made available to the participants in order to lessen the implications of this situation and assure continuation. One such obstacle was the steep learning curve that was associated with analytical tools like as NVivo and R. In the beginning, several researchers and students had difficulty dealing with the complexity of these tools. As a means of addressing this issue, specific training sessions were held, during which users were provided with hands-on advice and tutorials to get acquainted with the most important functions. In a similar vein, when merging datasets from several platforms, there were challenges with data integration, which resulted in inconsistencies and formatting concerns. Standardising data formats and using the interoperability capabilities of research tools were among the steps that were taken to streamline this procedure. This allowed for a more seamless merging process.

Ultimately, the unwillingness of participants to embracing new digital platforms was a contributing factor, as some individuals were reluctant to move away from more conventional approaches. The provision of thorough user guides and technical support teams was made accessible in order to foster user engagement. This was done to guarantee that all users were provided with the necessary help to traverse these platforms in a comfortable manner. The research process remained productive and inclusive thanks to the implementation of these tailored solutions, which was crucial in the development of a flexible and technology-driven approach to teaching in the humanities.

Incorporating software technologies strategically improved the study's research methodology and pedagogical effectiveness. Through the use of digital resources at every step of the research process, including data collecting, analysis, content distribution, and collaboration, academics and educators were able to expedite workflows, increase accuracy, and cultivate learning environments that are interactive. Whether it was via the use of communication and course management tools for seamless academic interaction or through the utilisation of qualitative and quantitative analysis platforms for deeper interpretations, technology played a significant role in the refinement of scholarly research and the improvement of accessibility. Not only did the use of digital technologies improve the rigour of research, but it also promoted a dynamic and participative educational experience, which in turn reinforced the importance of multidisciplinary cooperation. This research highlights how digital tools may be effective catalysts for innovation by demonstrating how they can be embedded meaningfully inside humanities education. These digital tools enable data-driven insights, richer conversations, and adaptive learning approaches, all of which contribute to the continued growth of the discipline.

4.7.30 Limitations of the Methodology

Every research technique has limits that are intrinsic to it, and it is vital to acknowledge these limitations in order to retain openness and credibility. There were a number of methodological limitations that were found throughout the research project on the use of software in the field of humanities education. These limitations were categorised as design, sampling, data collection, analytical, and contextual restrictions. Specifically, the scope and organisation of the investigation were the primary factors that influenced the design restrictions. Certain study factors, such as the effects on learning over a longer period of time, were impossible to quantify within the time-frame that was available, despite the fact that attempts were made to conduct a full evaluation of digital tools in humanities education. In addition, the fact that the research relied on certain analytical frameworks may have resulted in the exclusion of alternate views that may have contributed to the enhancement of the results.

As a result of the availability of participants and their representation, there were restrictions placed on the sampling. There were disparities in technology familiarity, institutional access, and involvement levels, which compromised the consistency of the data, despite the fact that efforts were made to acquire a broad sample. There were several instructors and students who were unable to engage owing to practical restrictions, and they may have contributed useful insights via their participation. The problems that were encountered throughout the data-gathering process were technical issues that were associated with platform interoperability and response accuracy. The consistency of data processing was negatively impacted as a result of differences in software capabilities, which led to challenges in combining datasets from diverse sources. Furthermore, several self-reported replies contained the danger of subjectivity, which limited the potential for total objectivity in interpretation.

The challenge of integrating quantitative and qualitative data was the primary focus of the analytical restrictions. It was difficult to ensure that there was a perfect alignment between the statistical outputs and the narrative insights, despite the fact that mixed-methods techniques were used. Further complicating the process of establishing causal linkages was the dynamic nature of digital interactions, which need careful interpretation. Thus, there are contextual constraints that are associated with external elements that are outside the control of the research. These include institutional regulations, digital infrastructure, and diverse pedagogical techniques that are used in various educational contexts. The application of the findings was affected by these discrepancies, which necessitated changes when the results were taken into generalisation. The research retains its rigorous openness and credibility by admitting these methodological limits. This ensures that the results are provided with appropriate caveats and a knowledge of the context in which they are presented. In spite of these limitations, the study offers significant contributions to both academic discourse and pedagogical practice with the purpose of providing vital insights into the integration of software in humanities education.

4.7.31 Methodological Design Constraints

Despite the fact that it provided useful insights, the research was subject to a number of methodological limitations, which had an impact on the extent of its results as well as their reliability. Due to the fact that classroom-based research does not provide the same level of stringent control over variables that is characteristic of laboratory studies, one of the most significant limitations was the absence of scientific rigour. It is difficult to establish unambiguous causal linkages since the effect of the software might have been impacted by external variables such as the variability of the instructors, the level of student participation, and the policies of the institution. In addition, the research used single-case or quasi-experimental designs, which means that the results obtained from a particular class or group could not be relevant to a wider population. Quasi-experimental approaches are valuable in education; nevertheless, they often face "internal validity threats," which are situations in which the effects that are seen may be altered by factors that are not within the researcher's control. Because of this, it is difficult to identify whether the software itself was responsible for improvements in learning outcomes or whether other contextual variables had a part in the changes.

Given that the research was carried out throughout the course of the academic semester, time restrictions were another key obstacle that needed to be overcome. The capacity to examine longitudinal impacts, such as persistent advances in digital literacy, pedagogical adaptability, or software adoption patterns over lengthy periods of time, was hindered as a result of this. There would have been a more complete evaluation of the long-term advantages of educational technologies if they had been evaluated over a longer period of time. This is because educational technologies demand iterative involvement. Despite the fact that these constraints have an impact on how the findings are interpreted, they do not lessen the contributions that the research has made to the field of digital humanities education. Instead, they highlight the need for doing future research with bigger sample numbers, prolonged timeframes, and controlled experimental settings in order to further confirm results and enhance best practices for the integration of software in educational settings.

4.7.32 Sampling Limitations

1. **Sample Size**: The study's sample was limited to a relatively small group of students and educators within a specific academic context. While this allowed for an in-depth exploration of software use in humanities education, it restricted the statistical power of the findings, making it challenging to generalise results to broader populations. A larger sample could have strengthened the reliability of the conclusions and provided more representative insights into varied educational settings.
2. **Sampling Bias**: The study relied on voluntary participation, which may have led to self-selection bias. Participants who were already digitally literate, technologically proficient, or highly motivated may have been more inclined to engage with the research, potentially skewing findings on software effectiveness or usability. Less tech-savvy individuals, who might have faced greater challenges in adopting digital tools, may have been underrepresented, affecting the balance of perspectives.
3. **Lack of Diversity**: Participants were drawn from a limited geographical and institutional setting, which may have reduced the cultural and educational diversity necessary for broad generalisation. Variations in teaching methodologies, digital infrastructure, and institutional support across different regions or academic institutions could impact how software is used and perceived. Expanding the participant pool across multiple institutions, backgrounds, and learning environments would improve the applicability of findings to a wider range of educational contexts.

4.7.33 Data Collection Challenges

1. **Technology-Dependent Responses**: The use of online surveys and virtual interviews in the study relied heavily on stable internet access and participants' technological familiarity. While digital tools enabled efficient data collection, some individuals may have faced connectivity issues, access restrictions, or difficulty navigating online platforms. This could have led to missing responses, incomplete submissions, or reduced participation, creating potential data gaps that impacted the overall consistency of findings. Participants who struggled with digital tools might have provided less comprehensive input, affecting the depth and quality of the responses gathered.

2. **Self-Reported Data**: A significant portion of the study relied on self-reported responses, particularly in surveys and interviews, which introduced the risk of bias, exaggeration, or inaccurate recall. Participants may have unintentionally overstated their engagement levels, misremembered details, or responded in ways they believed were expected rather than offering entirely objective answers. This can affect the authenticity of findings; as subjective interpretations may not always align with actual behavioural patterns. While self-reported data is valuable for capturing personal experiences and perspectives, it is inherently susceptible to distortions, necessitating cross-validation with other research methods to enhance accuracy.
3. **Observer Effect**: In observational aspects of the study, participants may have altered their behaviour due to the awareness of being studied, introducing the Hawthorne effect. This phenomenon occurs when individuals consciously or subconsciously modify their actions in response to researchers' presence or data collection processes. As a result, participants may have been more engaged, careful, or interactive than they would have been under normal conditions, potentially influencing the validity of findings. While observation remains a powerful research tool, its impact on natural behaviour patterns necessitates careful interpretation to account for potential deviations from everyday interactions. By acknowledging these challenges, the study underscores the complexities of digital humanities research and highlights the importance of methodological adjustments, such as technical support, data triangulation, and observational framing, to ensure more reliable outcomes. Despite these limitations, the findings contribute meaningful insights into software use in humanities education while informing future studies on refining research approaches.

4.7.34 Analytical Limitations

1. **Subjectivity in Qualitative Analysis**: While thematic analysis enhances the depth and richness of qualitative insights, it is inherently interpretive. Despite efforts to maintain rigour through structured coding frameworks and validation techniques, the subjectivity of researchers may have influenced how themes were developed and categorised. Variations in perspective, experience, and analytical approach could lead to differences in interpretation, potentially affecting consistency across findings. While techniques such as intercoder reliability checks were employed to minimise bias, absolute objectivity remains a challenge in qualitative methodologies.
2. **Software Proficiency Variance**: The effectiveness of data analysis was influenced by the varying levels of proficiency researchers had with specialised tools such as NVivo and SPSS. Differences in familiarity with software functionalities may have affected the depth, accuracy, and efficiency of data coding and statistical processing. Additionally, manual data entry errors and coding inconsistencies, despite validation procedures, could introduce variability in results. Ensuring

comprehensive training, standard coding protocols, and cross-verification were essential steps taken to mitigate these concerns and enhance analytical precision.

3. **Data Integration Complexity**: A major challenge in the study was the technical and methodological difficulty of integrating qualitative and quantitative datasets from multiple sources, such as Moodle logs, survey responses, and interview transcripts. Disparate formats, incompatible software functionalities, and different data structures posed significant barriers to seamless integration. Aligning qualitative narratives with numerical trends required careful methodological alignment, often necessitating additional preprocessing efforts to ensure coherence. Despite these challenges, strategies such as standardising data formats, employing interoperability tools, and leveraging mixed-methods frameworks helped improve integration and provide a more holistic and multidimensional understanding of the research findings.

4.7.35 Contextual Constraints

1. **Institutional Policies**: Institutional constraints on software licensing, data sharing, and ethical review processes posed challenges throughout the study. Some digital tools require formal approval or institutional licensing, limiting their availability to educators and students. Additionally, strict data-sharing policies affected collaboration, as researchers had to navigate administrative protocols before securely exchanging research materials. Ethical review procedures further contributed to delays, impacting timelines for implementation and restricting the scope of software integration. These institutional limitations narrowed the selection of tools, requiring researchers to adapt to available resources and regulations.
2. **Pedagogical Variability**: Educators exhibited different levels of comfort with integrating software tools into their teaching, leading to inconsistencies across courses. While some instructors enthusiastically embraced digital platforms for interactive learning and assessment, others remained hesitant due to technological unfamiliarity, concerns about effectiveness, or personal teaching preferences. These variations resulted in uneven adoption rates, influencing how students engaged with digital tools. To address this, training sessions and instructional support were provided to encourage confidence and proficiency in software use, ensuring a smoother transition into technology-assisted pedagogy.
3. **External Disruptions**: Unforeseen events such as academic calendar adjustments, internet outages, and public holidays occasionally interfered with data collection and participant engagement. These disruptions affected the timing of surveys, interviews, and classroom observations, requiring schedule adjustments to maintain continuity. Internet connectivity issues, particularly in remote or under-resourced settings, caused delays in virtual interactions, limiting access to online learning materials and digital assessments. Researchers mitigated these

challenges by implementing flexible data collection strategies, offering alternative participation windows, and ensuring contingency plans were in place to maintain the study's integrity.

Despite these challenges, the study successfully navigated institutional, pedagogical, and external constraints, adapting methodologies to ensure reliable and meaningful insights into software integration in humanities education. These experiences highlight the complexities of digital adoption while informing strategies for future refinement and improved implementation.

4.7.36 *Mitigation Strategies*

For the purpose of ensuring the validity and reliability of the research, the mitigation measures address a variety of possible restrictions. In order to cross-verify the data and increase the credibility of the study, triangulation was used for the limited sample size. In order to combat the participants' lack of experience with the program, training sessions and user manuals were made available to them. An effort was made to reduce the observer effect by decreasing the presence of researchers and assuring secrecy in order to avoid participants from exhibiting changes in their behaviour. Peer review was used to reduce the amount of subjective analysis that occurred during qualitative coding in order to preserve impartiality. Last but not least, centralised data management technologies were used in order to simplify the process of data integration, hence guaranteeing correctness and consistency across all datasets. These measures, when used together, contribute to the increased methodological rigour of the research (Table 4.12).

The study's results are nonetheless relevant and significant despite these limitations, which affected several parts of the research approach. Instead, they fulfil the function of influencing the manner in which the findings are perceived and applied to more general situations. Recognising these limitations guarantees that findings are reached with the proper qualifiers, which not only strengthens the credibility of the study but also guides researchers on how to adapt insights to a variety of educational contexts in the most effective manner. The research helps enhance future studies in digital humanities teaching and encourages openness by explicitly detailing the

Table 4.12 Mitigation strategies

Limitation	Mitigation
Small sample size	Used triangulation to enhance validity
Software unfamiliarity	Provided training and user guides
Observer effect	Maintained minimal researcher presence and ensured confidentiality
Subjective analysis	Employed peer-review of qualitative codes
Data integration	Used centralised data management tools

methodological hurdles that were encountered to conduct the study. Taking into account such limitations not only helps to cultivate a more nuanced knowledge of the challenges involved in incorporating technology into educational settings, but it also provides guidance for the development of study design. The insights that were acquired from these restrictions stimulate further conversations on the best practices, methodological modifications, and strategic approaches that may be used to improve digital humanities study. At the end of the day, admitting these limitations highlights the complex nature of the integration of educational technology, drawing attention to crucial areas that need more research and the development of innovative methods. Rather than decreasing the contributions of the study, these problems enhance the academic debate and provide routes for more extensive investigations in the research that will be conducted in the future.

4.7.37 Rationale for Methodological Choices

When it comes to evaluating the validity, depth, and application of educational research, the decisions that are made regarding methodology are very important variables. For the purpose of this inquiry, the selection of techniques was directed by a number of different considerations. This was done to guarantee that the examination into the incorporation of software tools in humanities education was both rigorous and situated within the appropriate framework.

The key factor that determined the technique was the research questions, which in turn had a significant role in determining the need of both quantitative and qualitative methods. It was decided to employ a mixed-methods approach in order to evaluate the efficiency of digital tools and the user experiences they provide. This approach offered the opportunity for numerical analysis in addition to rich narrative insights. Due to the fact that real-world classrooms needed adaptable data collecting techniques that accommodated varied teaching styles, student involvement levels, and institutional restrictions, the educational environment was another factor that affected the methodological choices that were made.

For the purpose of choosing instruments and techniques, the theoretical framework of the research served as an important basis. For the purpose of ensuring that the results were contextualised within the framework of established academic discourse, the research methodologies were intended to correspond with current scholarly models. These approaches were grounded in educational and technical theories. The choices regarding the sample size, the frequency of data collection, and the analytical procedures were also influenced by practical restrictions, such as time limits, the availability of resources, and ethical issues. Maintaining high standards of academic integrity while ensuring that the research was practicable was accomplished by striking a balance between the rigour of the methodology and the accessibility of the information.

Through the incorporation of these several methodological influences, the research endeavoured to capture a multifaceted perspective on the utilisation of software in the field of humanities education. This was done with the intention of developing findings that are both empirically sound and pedagogically useful. The careful selection of research techniques not only improved the trustworthiness of the results, but it also made a contribution to the development of best practices in the field of digital humanities scholarship.

4.7.38 Mixed Methods Approach

Mixed Methods Design in Humanities Education Research

The study adopted a mixed methods design, integrating both qualitative and quantitative techniques to develop a comprehensive understanding of the pedagogical and technological impact of software in humanities education. This approach allowed for a balanced analysis, leveraging measurable data while capturing nuanced experiences to provide depth, credibility, and contextual relevance in the findings.

1. **Quantitative Methods**: Quantitative methods provided empirical and structured insights into the effectiveness of software tools. These methods enabled the study to assess objective metrics, including test scores, survey ratings, and frequency of tool usage, offering a data-driven perspective on the impact of digital integration in learning environments. By analysing patterns in numerical data, researchers could identify trends in student engagement, comprehension, and retention, reinforcing the statistical validity of software adoption in humanities education.
2. **Qualitative Methods**: Qualitative methods complemented numerical findings by offering a nuanced exploration of user experiences, perceptions, and challenges related to software implementation. Through interviews, focus groups, and open-ended surveys, researchers gained firsthand insights into educators' and students' perspectives, uncovering themes related to usability, adaptability, and the broader implications of technological integration in humanities instruction. These methods captured individual and collective narratives, ensuring a more holistic understanding beyond raw statistics.
3. **Triangulation for Credibility and Depth**: Employing both quantitative and qualitative methodologies allowed for triangulation, a research strategy that enhances credibility and validity by cross-referencing multiple data sources. This methodological integration ensured that findings were not only data-driven but also contextually rich, strengthening the study's ability to provide meaningful interpretations of software adoption. By balancing structured analysis with exploratory insights, the research successfully framed its conclusions within both measurable impact and experiential realities, contributing significantly to the evolving discourse on digital humanities pedagogy.

4.7.39 *Justification for Qualitative Techniques*

1. **Interviews and Focus Groups**: Interviews and focus groups were conducted to explore the complex human interactions with software in humanities education. These qualitative tools provided in-depth insights into key themes such as motivation, usability, pedagogical relevance, and cultural adaptation. By allowing educators and students to express their experiences in their own terms, these methods helped capture nuanced perspectives that could not be obtained through purely quantitative measures. The decision to employ interviews and focus groups was based on the need to give voice to participants, ensuring that their firsthand experiences and challenges were central to the study's findings.
2. **Classroom Observations**: Observing classroom dynamics provided real-time insights into how software was integrated into humanities instruction. The study focused on tools such as Voyant and Moodle, assessing their role in student engagement, knowledge retention, and instructional effectiveness. Unlike surveys, which rely on self-reported data, direct observations allowed researchers to witness actual interactions with digital tools, identifying patterns in usage, technical difficulties, and educator-student collaboration. This method ensured that findings were contextually grounded, offering a realistic depiction of software adoption in educational settings.
3. **Document Analysis**: To further understand how software influenced learning processes, the study examined course materials, student projects, and digital artifacts. This approach provided concrete evidence of how digital tools supported or constrained academic engagement. By analysing assignments, discussion transcripts, and interactive learning activities, researchers could assess the effectiveness of software in facilitating comprehension, creative exploration, and critical thinking. This method complemented interviews and observations, offering a triangulated perspective on the impact of technology in humanities education.

The combination of these qualitative research methods ensured a holistic investigation, capturing both individual experiences and institutional trends related to software integration in education. The insights gained from this approach contributed to a deeper understanding of how digital tools shape teaching and learning practices, informing best practices for future implementation in humanities classrooms.

4.7.40 *Justification for Quantitative Methods*

1. **Pre- and Post-Tests**: To measure learning gains attributable to software integration, pre- and post-tests were conducted as part of the study's quantitative assessment strategy. These tests allowed for a structured comparison of knowledge acquisition and skill development before and after software use. By analysing performance improvements over time, researchers could quantify the effectiveness of digital tools, identifying trends in student comprehension, retention, and

problem-solving abilities. These assessments provided empirical evidence of the educational impact of software implementation in humanities classrooms.
2. **Structured Surveys**: Structured surveys were employed to gather scalable and comparable data across a larger sample of participants. These surveys incorporated Likert-scale questions, which facilitated statistical analysis of opinions, attitudes, and self-reported learning behaviors. By using standardised question formats, researchers could assess patterns in software usability, perceived effectiveness, and engagement levels, allowing for a comprehensive understanding of user experiences. The structured nature of these surveys ensured consistency in data collection, making the results systematic and reliable for broader interpretation.
3. **Analytics from Digital Platforms**: Data extracted from learning management systems and digital platforms, such as Moodle, Padlet, and other educational tools, provided key indicators of software effectiveness. These analytics helped researchers track student engagement, content interaction patterns, and completion rates, offering real-time insights into how digital tools supported learning processes. By analysing user behaviors such as time spent on tasks, frequency of tool usage, and participation in online discussions researchers gained valuable perspectives on the role of software in fostering active learning.

The combined use of quantitative assessments, structured surveys, and digital analytics strengthened the study's methodological approach, ensuring robust and data-driven conclusions about the pedagogical impact of software tools in humanities education. This triangulated approach helped establish a well-rounded evaluation of how technology influenced both learning outcomes and user engagement.

4.7.41 Tool Selection Criteria

The tools were chosen based on key criteria, including relevance (aligned with humanities education tasks), accessibility (free or institutionally available), ease of use (minimal training required), functionality (supporting annotation, analysis, collaboration), and security and ethics (meeting data protection and review standards). This guaranteed that participants received solutions that were practical, user-friendly, and morally consistent (Table 4.13).

4.7.42 Sampling Rationale

1. **Purposive Sampling**: To ensure the relevance and depth of insights gathered, purposive sampling was employed, selecting participants based on their direct involvement in software-integrated courses. This approach allowed researchers to focus on individuals who had actual experience using digital tools in humanities

Table 4.13 Tool selection criteria

Criteria	Description
Relevance	Direct applicability to humanities education and the types of tasks being analyed
Accessibility	Freely available or institutionally licensed to all participants
Ease of use	Minimal technical training required for students and staff
Functionality	Ability to perform necessary tasks (e.g., annotation, analysis, collaboration)
Security and ethics	Compliance with data protection standards and institutional review requirements

education, ensuring that responses were informed by practical interactions rather than hypothetical assumptions. By targeting educators and students actively engaged with technology, the study captured authentic perspectives on usability, pedagogical effectiveness, and challenges in software adoption.

2. **Maximum Variation Sampling**: Recognising the importance of diverse perspectives, maximum variation sampling was incorporated to ensure broad representation across multiple demographic and academic factors. Participants varied in age, academic discipline, and digital proficiency, enriching the dataset with a wide range of experiences and viewpoints. This methodological choice strengthened the transferability of findings, as insights were drawn from individuals with differing levels of comfort, familiarity, and adaptability with software tools. By including a diverse participant pool, the study provided a more comprehensive understanding of how technology integration interacts with different educational backgrounds and learning environments. Together, these sampling strategies ensured that the research findings were contextually relevant, representative, and methodologically robust, contributing to a holistic analysis of digital tool implementation in humanities education.

4.7.43 Contextual and Institutional Alignment

The approach was thoughtfully created to support institutional goals that highlight blended learning and digital literacy as essential elements of contemporary education. A number of important factors were taken into account while choosing research methodologies in order to guarantee practical application, technical flexibility, and cultural relevance. In order to ensure that the research complemented the larger educational objective of developing technological competence and interdisciplinary learning, the methodology was first directed by institutional priorities on innovation and pedagogy. In order to understand how different degrees of software accessibility, digital competence, and resource availability may affect adoption and engagement, the approach also considered technological infrastructure and limitations. Finally, taking into account a variety of teaching approaches, learning styles, and digital attitudes, the research was influenced by the cultural context of learners and educators. These elements made sure that the study stayed feasible and contextually aligned with the real-world educational landscape and offered useful information for further application.

4.7.44 Flexibility and Responsiveness

In the post-pandemic digital era, educational contexts are changing, thus the study approach was meant to be adaptable. Data gathering has to adapt to changing circumstances while preserving rigour and relevance due to changes in educational delivery, digital engagement, and institutional processes. First, web technologies enabled remote data collecting, making participants accessible regardless of location. Researchers might gather varied viewpoints without geographical limits using virtual surveys, digital interviews, and real-time platform analytics. For flexible triangulation, the research used mixed data sources, including quantitative and qualitative measurements. This strategy reduced biases associated with single data collecting approaches and produced statistically robust and contextually enriched conclusions. Research equipment was refined in real time using continual feedback loops. Continuous participant input kept survey questions, interview frameworks, and analytical tools current with learning patterns and dynamics. This responsiveness improved data accuracy and research methodology. The study acquired important and relevant insights by prioritising methodological agility, ensuring that results were transferable to modern pedagogical frameworks, technology developments, and student engagement strategies in humanities education.

4.7.45 Theoretical Underpinning

This study used constructivist and pragmatist research paradigms to provide a theoretically solid and practically viable approach to humanities teaching. Integrating these viewpoints kept the study design comprehensive, context-driven, and adaptable to digital learning contexts.

1. **Constructivist Approach**: The constructivist paradigm emphasises understanding learners' subjective experiences and recognises that knowledge is socially created via interaction, interpretation, and reflection. From this viewpoint, qualitative approaches like interviews, focus groups, and classroom observations enabled individuals to express their experiences in their own words. The study gained significant insights on software integration's usability, relevance, and obstacles by interacting directly with educators and students, ensuring that

results mirrored actual educational experiences rather than abstract theoretical assumptions.

2. **The Pragmatist Approach**: The pragmatic paradigm favors mixed techniques and prioritises practical results and context-driven research above methodological purity. Pragmatism's flexibility and real-world applicability make it excellent for study on technology uptake and pedagogical innovation. The research included quantitative measurements (pre- and post-tests, survey ratings, and analytics) and qualitative narratives to achieve data-driven and experientially rich conclusions. This methodological synergy improved results' validity and reliability, providing a balanced, multifaceted view of digital tool deployment in humanities classes. Enhancing Research Integrity by following constructivist and pragmatic traditions, the research preserved academic integrity while adapting to digital education's changing nature. This methodological basis guaranteed that study results were factual, insightful, and relevant to real-world teaching situations. These paradigms helped the research generate actionable suggestions, informed theoretical discourse, and practical innovations for technology-enhanced humanities teaching.

The approach that was used for this research was not selected at random; rather, it was the outcome of a decision-making process that was considered, guided by theory, and attentive to the situation. The selection of each technique and instrument was made with the goals of maximising the quality of the data, addressing the aims of the study, and respecting the pedagogical reality of teaching the humanities. The study's validity was improved as a result of this methodological approach, which also provided a complete lens through which the educational influence of software tools could be investigated.

References

1. T.A. Olatoye, Analysis of modal choice of residents in Lagos State. J. Hum. Ecol. **65**(1–3) (2019). https://doi.org/10.31901/24566608.2019/65.1-3.3157
2. M. Tu, An exploratory study of Internet of Things (IoT) adoption intention in logistics and supply chain management. Int. J. Logist. Manag. **29**(1), 131–151 (2018). https://doi.org/10.1108/IJLM-11-2016-0274
3. A. Ghosh, D.J. Edwards, M.R. Hosseini, Patterns and trends in Internet of Things (IoT) research: future applications in the construction industry. Eng. Constr. Archit. Manag. **28**(2), 457–481 (2021). https://doi.org/10.1108/ECAM-04-2020-0271
4. M.A. Ragab, A. Arisha, Research methodology in business: a starter's guide. Manag. Organ. Stud. **5**(1), 1 (2017). https://doi.org/10.5430/mos.v5n1p1
5. R.K. Al Shawabkeh et al., Evaluating the satisfaction rate for affordable housing in non-gated residential area (NGR): the case of Al-Sharq housing project in Zarqa-Jordan. Int. J. Hous. Mark. Anal. **14**(1), 192–217 (2021). https://doi.org/10.1108/IJHMA-10-2019-0105
6. O. Odeyemi, K.F. Awonuga, N.Z. Mhlongo, N.L. Ndubuisi, F.O. Olatoye, A.I. Daraojimba, The role of AI in transforming auditing practices: a global perspective review. World J. Adv. Res. Rev. **21**(2), 359–370 (2023). https://doi.org/10.30574/wjarr.2024.21.2.0460
7. S. Fuji, M. Date, Y. Nagai, Y. Yasuhara, T. Tanioka, F. Ren, Research on the possibility of humanoid robots to assist in medical activities in nursing homes and convalescent wards, in

NLP-KE 2011—Proceedings of 7th International Conference on Natural Language Processing and Knowledge Engineering (2011), pp. 459–463. https://doi.org/10.1109/NLPKE.2011.6138243
8. F.M. Talaat, Revolutionizing cardiovascular health: integrating deep learning techniques for predictive analysis of personal key indicators in heart disease. Neural Comput. Appl. **37**(1), 1–24 (2024). https://doi.org/10.1007/s00521-024-10453-2
9. J.O. Oguta, R.K.W. Egessa, D. Musiega, Effects of information communication and technology (ICT) application on strategic educational quality standards management in Bungoma County, Kenya. Int. J. Bus. Manag. Invent. **3**(5), 11–17 (2014) [Online]. Available: http://www.ijbmi.org/papers/Vol(3)5/Version-2/B0352011017.pdf
10. A.A. Mohammed, Int. J. Educ. Soc. Sci. Res. **2**(05), 35–47 (2019)
11. H.Y. Ali, R.Q. Danish, M. Asrar-ul-Haq, How corporate social responsibility boosts firm financial performance: the mediating role of corporate image and customer satisfaction. Corp. Soc. Responsib. Environ. Manag. **27**(1), 166–177 (2020). https://doi.org/10.1002/csr.1781
12. O.O. Okoji, M.A. Olubayo, Assessment of availability and utilization of instructional resources for teaching primary school mathematics in Ilorin Metropolis, Nigeria. Afr. J. Educ. Stud. Math. Sci. **17**(2), 1–12 (2022). https://doi.org/10.4314/ajesms.v17i2.1
13. R. Rohan, D. Pal, J. Hautamäki, S. Funilkul, W. Chutimaskul, H. Thapliyal, A systematic literature review of cybersecurity scales assessing information security awareness. Heliyon **9**(3) (2023). https://doi.org/10.1016/j.heliyon.2023.e14234
14. S. Banerjee, A. Sarkar, Logical level design of NoSQL databases, in *IEEE Regional 10 Annual International Conference Proceedings/TENCON* (2017), pp. 2360–2365. https://doi.org/10.1109/TENCON.2016.7848452
15. F. Galindo-Rueda, V. Millot, Measuring design and its role in innovation. OECD Sci. Technol. Ind. Work. Pap. 1–51 (2015) [Online]. Available: http://www.oecd-ilibrary.org/science-and-technology/measuring-design-and-its-role-in-innovation_5js7p6lj6zq6-en
16. M.I. Mursyidto, The role of information communication technology in records creation and distribution in Uganda Communications Commission. Implement. Sci. **39**(1), 1–15 (2014). https://doi.org/10.4324/9781315853178
17. L.E. Ugwu, E.S. Idemudia, O.O. Chukwu, M.C.C. Onyedibe, Measuring the impact of social media on young people's mental health: development and validation of the social media-induced tendency scale. Depress. Res. Treat. (2023). https://doi.org/10.1155/2023/8677521
18. C. Bratianu, D.F. Stanescu, R. Mocanu, Exploring the knowledge management impact on business education. Sustainability **13**(4), 1–16 (2021). https://doi.org/10.3390/su13042313
19. G. Bargshady, A. Chegeni, S. Kamranvand, S. Zahraee, A relational study of supply chain agility and firms' performance in the services providers. Int. Rev. Manag. Mark. **6**(4S), n/a (2016). https://doi.org/10.1002/adma.201403635
20. P. Qian, Z.G. Liu, Q.M. He, B.T. Huang, D.Z. Tian, X. Wang, Smart contract vulnerability detection technique: a survey. Ruan Jian Xue Bao/Journal Softw. **33**(8), 3059–3085 (2022). https://doi.org/10.13328/j.cnki.jos.006375
21. C. Zedak, A. Belfqih, J. Boukherouaa, F. El Mariami, An intelligent energy management system for optimum design and real-time operation. Int. J. Power Electron. Drive Syst. **14**(1), 480–495 (2023). https://doi.org/10.11591/ijpeds.v14.i1.pp480-495
22. M.K. Asif, P. Nambiar, S.A. Mani, N.B. Ibrahim, I.M. Khan, P. Sukumaran, Dental age estimation employing CBCT scans enhanced with Mimics software: comparison of two different approaches using pulp/tooth volumetric analysis. J. Forensic Leg. Med. **54**, 53–61 (2018). https://doi.org/10.1016/j.jflm.2017.12.010
23. O. Vermesan, P. Friess, *Internet of Things Applications—From Research and Innovation to Market Deployment* (2014) [Online]. Available: https://books.google.com.br/books?id=kw2doAEACAAJ
24. P. Sarigiannidis, E. Karapistoli, A. Economides, Modelling the internet of things under attack: A G-network approach. IEEE Internet Things J. 1–14 (2017). https://doi.org/10.1109/JIOT.2017.2719623

25. W. Hongxin et al., Unleashing the role of CSR and employees' pro-environmental behavior for organizational success: the role of connectedness to nature. Sustainability **14**(6) (2022). https://doi.org/10.3390/su14063191
26. J. Paul, M. Barari, Meta-analysis and traditional systematic literature reviews—what, why, when, where, and how? Psychol. Mark. **39**(6), 1099–1115 (2022). https://doi.org/10.1002/mar.21657
27. I. Ioannidou, N. Sklavos, On general data protection regulation vulnerabilities and privacy issues, for wearable devices and fitness tracking applications. Cryptography **5**(4) (2021). https://doi.org/10.3390/cryptography5040029
28. O.A. Erin, O.A. Bamigboye, Evaluation and analysis of SDG reporting: evidence from Africa. J. Account. Organ. Chang. **18**(3), 369–396 (2022). https://doi.org/10.1108/JAOC-02-2020-0025
29. H.-S. Kim, Oil extraction and the changing dynamics of pastoral conflicts: a conjoint experiment in Turkana, Kenya. J. Mod. Afr. Stud. **61**(1), 23–47 (2023). https://doi.org/10.1017/s0022278x22000398
30. S. Zhang, Z. Li, S. Ma, L. Li, M. Yuan, Critical factors influencing interface management of prefabricated building projects: evidence from China. Sustainability **14**(9), 1–20 (2022). https://doi.org/10.3390/su14095418
31. K.C. Obi, O. Iwuanyanwu, Innovation in the assessment of primary school mathematics: an approach to revamping Nigeria education. J. Teach. Perspect. **18**(1), 51–66 (2023) [Online]. Available: http://repositorio.unan.edu.ni/2986/1/5624.pdf%0Ahttp://fiskal.kemenkeu.go.id/ejournal%0A10.1016/j.cirp.2016.06.001%0A10.1016/j.powtec.2016.12.055%0A10.1016/j.ijfatigue.2019.02.006%0A10.1
32. P. Cash, O. Isaksson, A. Maier, J. Summers, Sampling in design research: eight key considerations. Des. Stud. **78**, 101077 (2022). https://doi.org/10.1016/j.destud.2021.101077
33. I. Mondal et al., Medical entity linking using triplet network. Biomed. Eng. Soc. **2**(5), 95–100 (2021). https://doi.org/10.18653/v1/w19-1912

Chapter 5
Software Tools and Digital Resources in Humanities

5.1 Overview of Digital Tools in Humanities

There is a wide range of academic fields that fall under the umbrella of the humanities. These fields investigate human civilisation, history, language, and culture. When it comes to interpreting texts, artefacts, and cultural phenomena, these areas have traditionally depended on methodologies such as close reading, critical analysis, and qualitative research. On the other hand, the introduction of digital technology has brought about a significant shift in the way that humanities education and study are now being conducted. The use of digital technologies has become a crucial component in the manner in which academics carry out research, teachers instruct, and students interact with educational resources. The incorporation of digital technologies into the fields of the humanities makes it easier to develop new approaches, improves accessibility, and opens up new avenues for collaborative and interdisciplinary research. The purpose of this chapter section is to provide a complete review of the fundamental types of digital tools that are used in the field of humanities teaching and research. This chapter investigates the functionality of these tools, as well as their instructional uses and consequences for the future of humanities study [1].

Categories of Digital Tools in Humanities

Digital tools in the humanities can be broadly classified according to their primary purpose and functionality. These categories include textual analysis software, digital archiving and curation platforms, visualisation tools, collaborative and social software, multimedia creation applications, and digital publishing platforms. Each plays a unique role in supporting scholarly activities, from data processing to public dissemination (Fig. 5.1).

F. A. Alaba et al., *Learning Beyond the Classroom*, Studies in Computational Intelligence 1253, https://doi.org/10.1007/978-3-032-14433-1_5

Fig. 5.1 Overview of digital technologies [2]

5.1.1 *Textual Analysis Tools*

Textual analysis has historically been at the core of humanities scholarship, especially in fields such as literature, linguistics, philosophy, and history. The development of computational methods and software has revolutionized how scholars analyze large bodies of text, enabling quantitative as well as qualitative insights [3].

1. **Voyant Tools**: Voyant is an open-source, web-based text analysis environment offering a suite of utilities including word frequency analysis, concordance, word clouds, topic modelling, and collocation identification. It allows scholars and students to upload texts or corpora and explore them interactively. Voyant's visualisations help uncover underlying patterns, such as recurring themes or stylistic features, that may be difficult to detect through manual reading.
2. **AntConc**: is a powerful freeware tool designed for corpus linguistics analysis, offering features such as concordance lists, collocation tables, keyword extraction, and cluster identification. Its intuitive interface makes it accessible to users with varying levels of technical expertise, allowing researchers and educators to explore patterns in vocabulary usage, phraseology, and textual structure with ease. Widely adopted in language teaching and linguistic research, AntConc facilitates data-driven insights into textual trends, supporting studies on lexical frequency, semantic relationships, and discourse analysis. Its efficiency, versatility, and adaptability make it an indispensable resource for those studying linguistic structures and textual composition in various languages.
3. **Natural Language Toolkit (NLTK)**: is a powerful and widely-used Python library designed for natural language processing (NLP) tasks. It provides an extensive suite of tools for tokenisation, parsing, semantic analysis, and sentiment detection, making it a valuable resource for researchers working with textual data.

With its modular design and rich dataset collection, NLTK allows users to process, analyze, and model language patterns effectively. Researchers with programming expertise leverage NLTK to perform sophisticated text mining, enabling them to create custom NLP pipelines that align with their specific research objectives. Whether used for linguistic studies, machine learning applications, or computational text analysis, NLTK remains a cornerstone library for NLP exploration and development.

These tools collectively enhance textual scholarship by allowing scalable analysis, replicability, and integration with other digital methodologies.

5.1.2 Digital Archiving and Curation Platforms

Preservation of cultural heritage and access to primary source materials are foundational to humanities research. Digital archiving platforms empower institutions, researchers, and communities to digitize, organise, and disseminate historical texts, artifacts, images, and multimedia resources [4].

1. **Omeka**: is a versatile open-source content management system tailored specifically for managing cultural heritage collections. It is widely used by scholars, archivists, and institutions to create interactive digital exhibits while ensuring adherence to metadata standards for organised and accessible documentation. Omeka enables users to curate collections that include scanned manuscripts, historical photographs, oral histories, artworks, and multimedia materials, making it a valuable tool for both research and public engagement. Through its intuitive interface and customisable galleries, institutions can showcase artifacts, build thematic exhibitions, and facilitate community access to cultural archives, enhancing the preservation and accessibility of historical narratives.
2. **Mukurtu**: is a specialised digital platform designed to uphold Indigenous cultural protocols and provide community-led control over access to digital content. Unlike conventional content management systems, Mukurtu prioritises ethical and respectful sharing, ensuring that cultural materials are preserved according to intellectual property rights and community values. Through its customizable access levels, Mukurtu allows Indigenous communities to determine who can view, interact with, and contribute to collections, safeguarding sensitive information and ensuring culturally appropriate use. It facilitates the creation of archives, oral histories, artworks, and historical records, supporting both research initiatives and public engagement while reinforcing sovereignty over cultural knowledge.
3. **Dspace**: is a trusted institutional repository software widely used by universities, libraries, and research institutions for long-term digital preservation and open access to scholarly works. It provides a secure and scalable platform for archiving theses, research datasets, publications, and multimedia materials, ensuring their sustainability and accessibility over time. By supporting metadata standards and

interoperability, DSpace allows institutions to effectively manage digital assets, fostering academic collaboration and knowledge dissemination. Many organisations rely on DSpace to enhance visibility, retrieval, and long-term preservation of scholarly outputs, making it a critical tool in research management and institutional archiving worldwide. Its flexibility and customisation options make it adaptable to diverse academic and preservation needs.

The use of these platforms addresses challenges around preservation, accessibility, and ethical stewardship of cultural materials in the digital age.

5.1.3 Visualisation Tools

Humanities research often involves complex datasets whether social networks, historical timelines, or geographic information that benefit from graphical representation. Visualisation tools translate abstract data into accessible visual forms, aiding interpretation, exploration, and communication [4, 5].

1. **Gephi**: is an open-source network visualisation tool that helps map relationships among entities such as individuals in social networks, characters in literature, or citation networks in academic publishing. It provides various graph layouts and statistical analyses to uncover central nodes, clusters, and overall network dynamics, making it invaluable for studying connections and influence within large datasets.
2. **Tableau**: is a commercial data visualisation software that supports interactive dashboards and scalable analytics, capable of handling large datasets with ease. It is widely used in digital humanities projects to visualise survey data, archival metadata, or statistical analyses, enabling researchers to present findings in intuitive, interactive formats that enhance exploration and comprehension.
3. **TimelineJS**: is a tool that allows users to create rich, interactive timelines integrating multimedia elements such as images, videos, and text. It is particularly useful for presenting historical events, literary chronologies, or biographical narratives engagingly. By structuring data visually and temporally, TimelineJS helps researchers develop compelling storytelling approaches that facilitate better understanding of sequence, causality, and historical relationships.

These visualisation tools enhance narrative construction, support hypothesis generation, and improve public engagement with humanities research. They provide new ways to interpret patterns, relationships, and thematic trends, helping scholars communicate insights more effectively across academic and public spheres.

5.1.4 *Collaborative and Social Tools*

The Role of Digital Tools in Humanities Collaboration

Collaboration is increasingly essential in humanities research, which often spans disciplinary and geographic boundaries. Digital tools facilitate communication, project management, and shared knowledge creation, making scholarly teamwork more efficient and interconnected.

1. **Slack and Microsoft Teams**: These communication platforms provide real-time messaging, file sharing, and seamless integration with various productivity apps. They are widely adopted by academic teams for project coordination, discussion, and brainstorming, enabling researchers to stay synchronised across locations and institutions.
2. **Google Workspace (Docs, Sheets, Slides)**: Google's cloud-based suite supports simultaneous collaborative editing of documents, spreadsheets, and presentations. Its ease of access makes it a popular choice for research groups and classrooms, allowing scholars to co-edit manuscripts, refine datasets, and develop shared presentations in real time.
3. **Zotero and Mendeley**: These reference management tools enable users to collect, organise, annotate, and cite scholarly sources effortlessly. Both platforms offer social features such as group libraries, facilitating cooperative literature reviews and shared bibliographies for collective academic projects. Researchers can efficiently manage citations while collaborating on chapters, proposals, and interdisciplinary studies.

By streamlining workflow efficiency and fostering scholarly community-building, these digital platforms enable seamless interaction, enhanced organisation, and knowledge-sharing in humanities research. Their adaptability supports team-based exploration, collective learning, and the development of interdisciplinary scholarship, ensuring that research remains dynamic and well-integrated within the broader academic landscape.

5.1.5 *Multimedia Creation and Editing Software*

Digital humanities projects increasingly integrate multimedia elements to convey complex narratives and engage diverse audiences. Scholars and educators rely on tools that support the creation and editing of audio, video, images, and interactive content, expanding the expressive possibilities of research and pedagogy [6].

1. **Adobe Creative Suite (Photoshop, Premiere Pro, Illustrator)**: Adobe's industry-standard software offers comprehensive capabilities for image editing, video production, and graphic design. Scholars use these tools to develop digital exhibits, documentaries, visual essays, and artistic renderings, ensuring their research is both aesthetically compelling and accessible.

2. **Audacity**: As a free, open-source audio editor, Audacity is widely employed in podcasts, oral history projects, and sound art. Its multi-track editing, noise reduction, and audio effects make it a powerful tool for scholars working with spoken-word narratives, recorded interviews, and sonic explorations.
3. **StoryMapJS**: This tool enables users to create interactive maps that combine text, images, and multimedia, making it ideal for place-based storytelling and cultural geography projects. It allows scholars to visualise historical events, literary journeys, or biographical narratives, enhancing the spatial and contextual dimensions of their research.

By leveraging these multimedia tools, digital humanities projects broaden expressive possibilities, fostering innovative research dissemination and interactive engagement. These technologies help scholars interpret, document, and present their findings in ways that resonate with academic communities, public audiences, and interdisciplinary collaborators.

5.1.6 Digital Publishing Platforms

Digital publishing has revolutionised the way humanities scholarship is produced, disseminated, and engaged with, offering greater accessibility, multimedia integration, and innovative textual forms. By supporting open access principles, these platforms ensure that academic research reaches broader audiences, fostering collaborative learning and interdisciplinary dialogue.

1. **Scalar**: An advanced authoring platform designed for creating multimedia-rich, nonlinear digital books. Scalar enables scholars to embed videos, audio files, images, and external links within their works, promoting interactive and interconnected narratives. It is widely used for dynamic research projects, allowing authors to construct nonlinear scholarly arguments with enhanced hypertextual depth.
2. **Pressbooks**: A web-based platform for authoring and publishing open textbooks, monographs, and academic works. Pressbooks supports various export formats including PDF, ePub, and webbooks, making scholarship more adaptable across digital and print mediums. Its accessibility and ease of use have made it a popular choice among researchers looking to share their findings beyond traditional publishing constraints.
3. **Project MUSE**: One of the leading digital libraries providing access to peer-reviewed humanities and social science journals and books from multiple university presses. Project MUSE enhances academic communication by curating high-quality scholarly content, ensuring that research remains discoverable, citable, and preserved within the broader academic ecosystem.

By facilitating hypertextuality and multimodality, these digital publishing platforms empower scholars to experiment with new methods of research presentation,

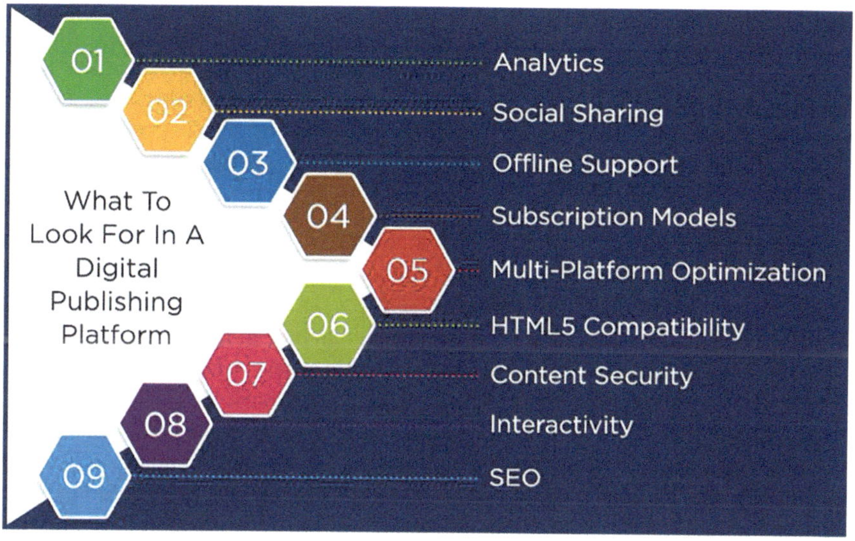

Fig. 5.2 Features of an ideal digital publishing platform [7]

integrating text, multimedia, and dynamic interactions. The result is an engaging and forward-thinking approach to academic dissemination, ensuring that humanities research continues to evolve and remain relevant in digital spaces (Fig. 5.2).

There will be substantial repercussions for pedagogy, curriculum design, and student involvement as a result of the incorporation of digital resources into student education in the humanities. Alongside critical thinking and academic knowledge, digital literacy emerges as an essential competence. It is a challenge for educators to develop learning experiences that make use of technology in order to encourage active inquiry, collaboration, and creativity.

Learners from a wide range of backgrounds are able to interact with primary sources and take part in cutting-edge research initiatives due to the democratisation of access to resources that digital technologies provide. They also provide opportunities for multimodal expression, which allows them to accommodate a wide range of learning preferences. However, in order to successfully integrate these technologies, it is necessary to address a number of obstacles, including technical inequalities (also known as the digital divide), the need for training for both professors and students, and concerns over data privacy and sustainability. In order to fully realise the advantages that digital humanities tools have to offer, it is essential to apply them with careful consideration, with the help of institutional resources and professional growth.

5.1.7 *Challenges and Future Directions*

While digital tools unlock exciting opportunities for humanities education, they also present key challenges that require thoughtful solutions. Addressing concerns related to accessibility, sustainability, and pedagogical balance is essential for ensuring that technology enhances learning rather than creating new barriers.

1. **Accessibility and Inclusion**: Not all students and scholars have equal access to the necessary technologies, software, and reliable internet connections. Equitable design and accommodations for diverse users, including those with disabilities and those in under-resourced environments, remain central to digital humanities adoption. Institutions must prioritise affordable access, adaptable interfaces, and user-friendly learning environments to foster inclusivity.
2. **Sustainability**: Digital projects require long-term maintenance, updates, and preservation plans to remain viable. Without sustainable funding models and infrastructure support, many digital humanities resources risk becoming obsolete or inaccessible. Researchers and institutions must develop data preservation strategies, funding partnerships, and scalable project models to ensure the longevity and continued accessibility of digital initiatives.
3. **Pedagogical Balance**: While technology enhances education, it must serve learning objectives rather than becoming a distraction or superficial addition. Educators must prioritise critical digital literacy, ethical use of technology, and meaningful integration into curricula. Reflection on how digital tools shape knowledge production ensures that humanities scholarship remains rigorous, intentional, and deeply engaged with research fundamentals.

Looking ahead, advancements in AI, augmented and VR, and immersive digital environments are set to further reshape humanities education. AI-driven tools offer potential for advanced textual analysis, automated annotation, and adaptive learning systems, while VR and AR can create interactive historical reconstructions, literary explorations, and immersive cultural experiences. As digital landscapes evolve, preparing educators and students to engage critically and ethically with emerging technologies will be crucial for maintaining innovative yet responsible approaches to humanities scholarship.

5.2 Learning Management Systems (LMS)

LMSs have become indispensable digital infrastructures in today's educational system, bringing about a considerable transformation in how teaching approaches, curriculum design, and student involvement are carried out. LMSs are centralised platforms that assist the administration, documenting, tracking, reporting, automation, and delivering educational courses and training programs. This streamlines the academic procedures for both educators and learners. The way in which instructors in the field of humanities education select course materials, stimulate conversation, and evaluate learning results is being revolutionised by learning management system platforms. Integrated LMSs facilitate collaborative research, critical thinking, and interdisciplinary linkages within the humanities. This is accomplished via the incorporation of discussion forums, multimedia materials, interactive assignments, and adaptive learning paths.

In addition, LMS technologies improve assessment techniques by enabling teachers to use automatic grading, peer-reviewed submissions, and formative assessments, all of which provide more in-depth insights into the development of their students. There are a number of features that help to teaching tactics more successful and guarantee that students get individualised academic assistance. Some of these features include integrated analytics, plagiarism detection, and personalised learning paths. LMS platforms such as Moodle, Blackboard, and Canvas have become necessary as a result of the proliferation of remote and hybrid learning models. These platforms bridge the gap between traditional classroom settings and digital classrooms, while also promoting the development of communities and the sharing of information. With the ongoing development of technology, the importance of learning management systems (LMSs) in the field of humanities education will continue to increase. These LMSs will provide new pedagogical opportunities that encourage participation, creativity, and dynamic research in digital learning environments.

5.2.1 *Definition and Core Features of LMS*

A LMS is a comprehensive digital platform designed to create, manage, deliver, and track educational content and learning activities. These systems are essential for modern pedagogy, supporting a variety of instructional methods, including synchronous and asynchronous learning, blended learning, flipped classrooms, and fully online courses.

Core Features of LMS Platforms

1. Course Content Management: Instructors can upload and organize lecture notes, readings, videos, assignments, and assessments, ensuring students have seamless access to materials.
2. User Management: LMS platforms facilitate registration, enrollment, and role assignments, allowing institutions to structure learning environments efficiently.
3. Assessment and Testing: Built-in tools allow educators to create quizzes, exams, and interactive assignments, often including automated grading, personalised feedback, and adaptive learning options.
4. Communication Tools: Features like discussion forums, messaging, and announcements support student interaction and engagement, while some platforms integrate video conferencing capabilities for virtual classrooms.

5. Tracking and Reporting: Real-time dashboards and analytics provide insights into student progress, participation, and performance, enabling data-driven instructional improvements.
6. Integration Capabilities: LMSs support plug-ins and interoperability with external tools such as plagiarism checkers, multimedia players, digital libraries, and research databases, enhancing learning possibilities.

By providing a centralised space for digital education, LMS platforms streamline curriculum design, student engagement, and academic assessment, making them an integral component of contemporary educational models. Their adaptability ensures scalability for diverse learning environments, from individual classrooms to large institutional frameworks.

5.2.2 Types of LMS

LMS platforms vary based on deployment models, functionalities, and intended users, offering different advantages depending on institutional needs. The three primary types include [8]:

1. **Proprietary LMS**

Proprietary LMSs are commercial software products developed and maintained by private companies. They typically provide robust technical support, regular updates, and extensive built-in features but require licensing fees for use. These platforms are widely adopted by universities and large educational institutions due to their scalability, reliability, and dedicated support services. Examples: Blackboard Learn, Canvas by Instructure, D2L Brightspace.

2. **Open-Source LMS**

Open-source LMS platforms are developed collaboratively by communities and are freely available for download, use, and customisation. These systems offer flexibility and transparency, allowing institutions to modify and tailor functionalities to their specific needs. However, they may require technical expertise for installation and ongoing maintenance. Open-source LMSs are popular among schools and organisations seeking cost-effective, customisable solutions without commercial constraints. Examples: Moodle, Sakai, Open edX.

3. **Cloud-Based LMS (Software as a Service - SaaS)**

Cloud-based LMS platforms are hosted by vendors and accessed via the internet, eliminating the need for local installation or extensive IT infrastructure. These platforms offer quick deployment, automated updates, and scalability, making them ideal for institutions with limited technical resources. By operating entirely online, cloud-based LMSs simplify administration, accessibility, and collaborative learning. Examples: Google Classroom, TalentLMS, Schoology.

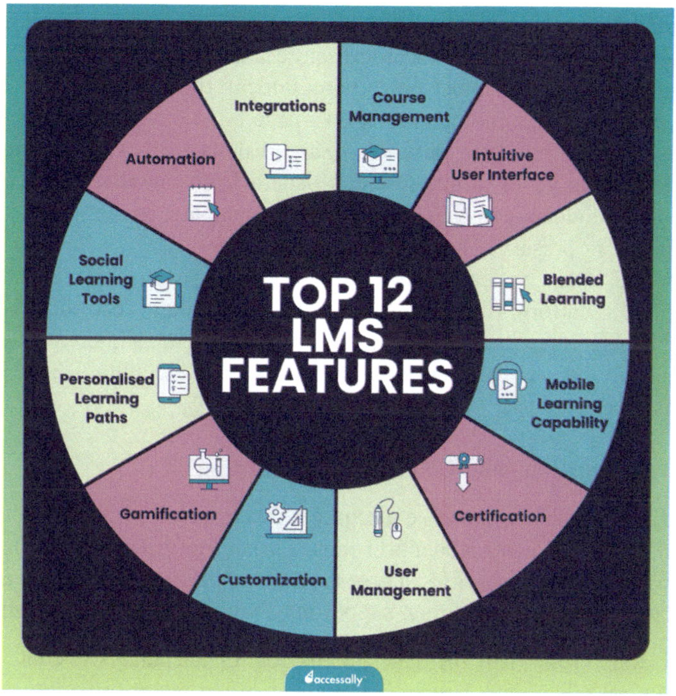

Fig. 5.3 Top LMS features

Each LMS model addresses different educational needs, ranging from customisation and cost efficiency to scalability and ease of implementation, ensuring institutions can select a solution that best aligns with their teaching and learning objectives (Fig. 5.3).

5.2.3 Functions and Tools in LMS for Humanities Education

Humanities courses frequently involve rich textual materials, multimedia content, and critical discussions, requiring structured and accessible ways to present information. LMS platforms help educators systematically organise and distribute course materials, ensuring students can navigate the curriculum efficiently. The following content types are commonly utilised within LMS platforms:

1. Primary and secondary texts in PDF or ePub formats: Instructors can upload literary works, historical documents, philosophical essays, and scholarly articles in digital formats, allowing students to read, annotate, and reference materials conveniently from any device.

2. Recorded lectures or guest talks related to philosophical, historical, or literary topics: LMS systems allow educators to store and share recorded lectures, seminar discussions, and expert interviews, giving students the flexibility to revisit lessons and reinforce understanding at their own pace.
3. Image galleries showcasing artworks or archival materials: Courses in art history, cultural studies, or historical research benefit from integrated image repositories where students can view, analyze, and compare artistic works, historical documents, or preserved artifacts within the LMS.
4. Audio and video materials such as interviews, performances, or documentaries: LMS platforms enable instructors to upload audio recordings of lectures, dramatic performances, historical reenactments, or critical interviews, enhancing students' ability to engage with spoken-word narratives, cultural expressions, and documentary analysis.

Interactive Discussions and Collaborative Learning

LMS platforms provide interactive discussion forums, real-time chats, and collaborative workspaces, allowing students to engage in academic debates, textual analysis, and peer-based learning activities. These tools foster deeper intellectual engagement and collective knowledge-building, supporting a variety of learning approaches:

1. Discussion forums and message boards for textual analysis, ethical debates, and cultural reflections: Humanities subjects often require students to critically analyse primary texts, debate ethical dilemmas, and reflect on cultural narratives. LMS discussion spaces provide structured asynchronous communication, enabling students to articulate arguments, respond to peers, and explore diverse interpretations over time.
2. Group projects with shared workspaces for co-authoring documents, exchanging feedback, and conducting research collaboratively: Many LMS platforms offer dedicated collaboration tools where students can co-develop research chapters, annotate sources together, and engage in collective peer reviews mirroring the experience of academic teamwork. These spaces facilitate efficient knowledge-sharing and cooperative problem-solving.

Assessment and Feedback

Assessments in humanities courses primarily involve critical writing, analytical reasoning, and interpretative discussion, necessitating LMS features that accommodate subjective grading, structured feedback, and peer evaluation. LMS platforms offer diverse assessment methods, ensuring both qualitative and quantitative evaluation strategies:

1. Essay submissions via integrated assignment portals with options for plagiarism checking: Students submit essays and research chapters through LMS portals, where assignments undergo automated plagiarism detection, ensuring academic integrity and originality in written work.

2. Quizzes testing comprehension of key concepts, historical dates, or literary terms: LMS platforms include interactive quizzes that assess students' understanding of literary movements, philosophical ideas, historical milestones, and terminology, providing educators with instant feedback and analytics on student progress.
3. Peer assessment modules allowing students to review each other's work: Some LMSs feature peer evaluation tools, encouraging students to critique and refine each other's essays, presentations, or creative projects. This collaborative assessment method fosters critical thinking, constructive feedback exchange, and academic discourse.
4. Rubrics for standardised and transparent grading aligned with learning objectives: LMS platforms provide customisable grading rubrics, helping instructors apply consistent assessment criteria for essays, presentations, and discussions. These rubrics clarify expectations for students, promoting fair, objective, and structured evaluations.
5. Immediate or personalised instructor feedback to encourage reflective learning: Instructors can provide annotated comments, audio feedback, or video explanations through LMS grading systems, allowing students to understand their strengths, refine their work, and address gaps in comprehension in a meaningful way.

Through these LMS features, humanities education benefits from structured content delivery, active student engagement, and effective evaluation methods, enhancing both learning outcomes and academic collaboration.

5.2.4 *Multimedia Integration and Digital Literacy*

Humanities courses increasingly integrate multimedia and digital scholarship, using LMS to embed interactive timelines, virtual museum tours, and digital exhibits that foster digital literacy and multimodal learning. Interactive timelines, such as those created with TimelineJS, allow students to visually map historical events, literary movements, and philosophical developments by incorporating text, images, videos, and primary sources. Virtual museum tours grant students access to digitised collections from institutions like Google Arts & Culture and the Smithsonian, enabling visual analysis and historical interpretation of artifacts without physical travel. Additionally, digital exhibits using platforms like Omeka or Scalar allow instructors and students to curate multimedia presentations featuring archival documents, oral histories, and literature, enriching engagement with cultural studies. By seamlessly integrating these tools into humanities coursework, LMS platforms provide students with dynamic learning environments that encourage exploration, creativity, and critical thinking in the digital age [9].

Analytics and Learning Analytics

LMS analytics play a crucial role in enhancing student engagement and academic success by providing instructors with data-driven insights into learner behavior. By tracking participation levels in discussions, assignment submissions, and quiz performance, educators can identify students who may be struggling or at risk of disengagement. This allows for timely interventions, such as personalised feedback, targeted support, or adjusted learning strategies, to ensure students stay on track. Moreover, LMS analytics offer valuable information for refining course design. Patterns in resource usage, such as which materials are accessed most frequently or which assessments yield lower scores, help instructors optimise content delivery and structure more effective learning experiences. By leveraging these insights, educators can create dynamic, responsive courses that support student needs and foster continuous academic improvement [10].

5.2.5 *Popular LMS Platforms in Humanities Education*

Moodle: A Leading Open-Source LMS for Humanities Education

Moodle is one of the most widely adopted open-source LMSs globally, valued for its flexibility, extensibility, and user-driven development. It is particularly favoured in humanities programs due to its ability to support diverse teaching methodologies and facilitate interactive, collaborative learning environments.

Key Features of Moodle for Humanities Education

1. Modular Course Design with Resources and Activities: Instructors can structure courses into organised modules, integrating readings, multimedia content, assignments, and interactive lessons, ensuring a seamless learning experience for students.
2. Forums, Wikis, and Glossaries for Collaborative Learning: Humanities subjects often rely on dialogue, discussion, and knowledge-sharing. Moodle offers forums for academic debates, wikis for collaborative research projects, and glossaries for defining key terms, enabling students to engage critically with course materials and each other.
3. Quizzes, Assignments, and Gradebook Functionalities: Moodle supports varied assessment methods, including automated quizzes for concept comprehension, essay submissions for deeper analysis, and structured grading tools for transparent evaluation. These features help instructors track student progress and offer meaningful feedback.
4. Plugin Architecture Supporting Multimedia, Analytics, and Gamification: Moodle allows educators to enhance courses with multimedia resources, integrate learning analytics to assess student engagement, and use gamification strategies such as badges and progress tracking to motivate learners.

Humanities instructors appreciate Moodle's adaptability to different pedagogical styles, including text-based analysis, multimedia integration, and collaborative research projects. Its active user community continuously develops new plugins and tools, ensuring that Moodle evolves to meet the changing needs of educators and students. With its open-source nature, institutions can customise and scale their Moodle implementations, making it an invaluable asset for humanities education worldwide [11].

5.2.6 *Blackboard Learn*

Due to the fact that Blackboard is an all-encompassing LMS that offers sophisticated capabilities for content administration, communication, evaluation, and academic cooperation, it is the software of choice for big universities and other institutions that provide significant humanities programs. Because of its solid architecture, it is able to provide organised course delivery, which enables teachers to upload, organise, and display textual materials, multimedia resources, and interactive assignments inside a centralised digital environment. Blackboard also provides integrated communication capabilities, including as discussion boards, real-time messaging, and announcements, which make it easier for students and teachers to engage in meaningful academic conversation with one another. As an additional benefit, its assessment and grading skills make it possible for teachers to create and score quizzes, essays that have been peer-reviewed, and examinations using individualised scoring rubrics and automatic scoring tools. Students are granted access to digital repositories, research databases, and scholarly archives via Blackboard's capacity to link with institutional library systems. Additionally, Blackboard's built-in plagiarism detection software ensures that students' academic work is free from plagiarism. This is a big benefit of Blackboard. Additionally, the virtual classroom functions offered by Blackboard make it possible to conduct live video lectures, recorded sessions, and interactive workshops, which broadens the scope of chances for blended and distant learning. Blackboard is especially well-suited for big humanities departments that need centralised course administration across several disciplines. On account of its enterprise-level features, Blackboard is an excellent choice for such departments. Because of its scalability, constant platform upgrades, and substantial technical support, it is a dependable and effective option for digital humanities education. It ensures that both teachers and students are able to participate in learning experiences that are both dynamic and structured [12].

5.2.7 *Canvas by Instructure*

Canvas is a user-friendly, cloud-based LMS known for its intuitive interface and seamless integration with third-party tools. It enhances the learning experience by supporting multimedia embedding, mobile accessibility, and outcomes-based assessment, making it a versatile platform for educators and students alike. Its accessibility and collaborative features have contributed to its growing popularity, particularly within humanities faculties, where interactive engagement and streamlined course management are essential. With its adaptable design and broad functionality, Canvas continues to be a preferred choice for institutions aiming to foster an inclusive and dynamic learning environment [12, 13].

Google Classroom

Google Classroom, while not a full-featured LMS, provides a streamlined approach to course management with direct integration into Google Workspace tools. It is widely adopted in K-12 and higher education for fundamental tasks such as content delivery, assignment management, and communication between educators and students. Its intuitive interface, simplicity, and cost-effectiveness make it an appealing choice for introductory humanities courses and hybrid learning environments. By facilitating collaboration and maintaining accessibility, Google Classroom continues to serve as a practical solution for institutions seeking an efficient and user-friendly teaching platform.

5.2.8 *Pedagogical Implications of LMS in Humanities*

The adoption of LMS in humanities education is reshaping traditional teaching and learning dynamics, fostering more learner-centered, interactive, and flexible pedagogical approaches. By integrating digital tools and resources, LMS enhances student engagement through multimedia content, discussion forums, and real-time feedback, allowing learners to actively participate in the educational process. Additionally, these platforms support personalised learning experiences by enabling educators to tailor course materials to diverse student needs, accommodating different learning styles and paces. Collaborative features such as group assignments, peer reviews, and shared digital workspaces promote critical thinking and knowledge exchange, enriching the overall academic environment. Furthermore, LMS streamlines administrative tasks for educators, providing efficient course management, automated assessments, and data-driven insights into student progress. As technology continues to evolve, the role of LMS in humanities education will only grow, further bridging the gap between traditional methods and modern digital learning advancements.

1. **Enhancing Accessibility and Inclusivity**: LMS platforms provide flexible, anytime-anywhere access to course materials, accommodating a wide range of learners with different schedules, locations, and individual needs. This accessibility is particularly valuable for non-traditional students, working professionals, and those in remote areas who might otherwise struggle to engage with humanities education. Furthermore, LMS features such as closed captioning for video lectures, screen reader compatibility for text-based content, and alternative text

for images ensure that learning materials are accessible to students with disabilities. These tools help create an inclusive academic environment, enabling all learners to interact meaningfully with course content and engage with humanities discussions regardless of their circumstances.
2. **Supporting Active and Social Learning**: LMS platforms foster a dynamic, interactive learning experience by facilitating discussions, peer collaboration, and knowledge-sharing in ways that extend beyond traditional classroom settings. Discussion forums, real-time chat features, and group workspaces enable students to engage in critical dialogue, debate complex humanities concepts, and exchange diverse perspectives. These digital tools support social learning by allowing students to interact with peers, ask questions, and explore ideas collectively, even in asynchronous settings. By enabling continuous engagement with texts, media, and philosophical questions, LMS ensures that humanities education remains intellectually stimulating and deeply immersive.
3. **Facilitating Formative Assessment and Feedback**: One of the strengths of LMS platforms is their ability to streamline assessment and feedback processes, making learning more responsive and tailored to individual student needs. Through quizzes, automated grading systems, and interactive assignments, students receive immediate feedback on their understanding of key humanities topics. Educators can also monitor student progress, identify areas for improvement, and adapt instructional strategies accordingly. Frequent formative assessments, such as polls, peer reviews, and reflective journals, help students refine their critical thinking skills and improve their comprehension over time, fostering a culture of continuous learning and academic growth.
4. **Promoting Digital Literacy**: By integrating multimedia resources, digital archives, and analytical tools, LMS platforms empower humanities students to develop essential digital literacy skills. Through exposure to online research databases, interactive learning modules, and digital storytelling techniques, students gain proficiency in information evaluation, digital content creation, and ethical engagement with digital sources. These skills are increasingly valuable in modern academia and professional fields, equipping students to navigate the complexities of digital media, conduct responsible online research, and contribute thoughtfully to digital discourse. In this way, LMS plays a crucial role in preparing humanities students for the evolving demands of the digital age.

5.2.9 Challenges and Considerations

While LMS platforms offer numerous advantages, their implementation in humanities education presents several challenges that must be addressed to ensure effective and equitable learning experiences [14]:

1. **Technical Barriers and Digital Divide**: Despite the growing reliance on digital learning environments, not all students have consistent internet access or compatible devices, which can limit their ability to fully participate in LMS-based

coursework. This disparity disproportionately affects students from underprivileged backgrounds or regions with inadequate technological infrastructure. To bridge this gap, educational institutions must invest in reliable connectivity solutions, provide accessible learning materials, and offer alternative offline options when necessary.

2. **Pedagogical Training and Support**: Successful LMS integration requires educators to develop digital pedagogical skills and adapt their teaching methods to suit online environments. However, many instructors in humanities disciplines may lack formal training in digital teaching strategies. Continuous professional development programs, workshops, and institutional support systems are essential to equip educators with the necessary competencies for effectively leveraging LMS platforms. Additionally, technical assistance and peer mentorship can further ease the transition to digital learning.
3. **Overreliance on Technology**: While LMS enhances learning flexibility and accessibility, excessive dependence on digital tools can diminish meaningful human interaction and engagement. There is a risk that technology becomes an end in itself rather than a tool to facilitate deeper intellectual exploration. Overuse of digital platforms may also lead to screen fatigue and passive learning. Therefore, a balanced approach combining traditional teaching methods with LMS functionalities is essential to maintain the humanistic and reflective nature of humanities education while harnessing the benefits of technology.
4. **Data Privacy and Ethics**: LMS platforms gather extensive student data, tracking engagement, assignment submissions, discussion participation, and other academic activities. This raises concerns regarding data security, informed consent, and the ethical use of personal information. Institutions must ensure transparency in data collection and processing, comply with legal frameworks such as GDPR, and implement robust cybersecurity measures. Additionally, fostering discussions around ethical digital practices in humanities courses can help students critically engage with issues of privacy, surveillance, and technology ethics.

By proactively addressing these challenges, educators and institutions can create a more effective, inclusive, and balanced approach to integrating LMS in humanities education, ensuring that technology enhances rather than hinders the learning experience.

5.2.10 Future Trends in LMS for Humanities Education

The evolving landscape of LMS in humanities education is poised for groundbreaking advancements, driven by innovations in AI, analytics, and immersive technologies. These developments will enhance accessibility, engagement, and pedagogical effectiveness, transforming how humanities subjects are taught and experienced:

1. **Adaptive Learning Systems**: AI-powered LMS modules will enable personalised learning experiences, adjusting content, pacing, and assessments based on individual student performance, preferences, and interests. This adaptability ensures that humanities education accommodates diverse learners, allowing students to explore subjects in ways that align with their intellectual curiosity and academic strengths. By integrating AI-driven tutoring systems, educators can provide targeted support, helping students engage deeply with complex texts, philosophical debates, and historical narratives.
2. **Integration of Virtual and Augmented Reality**: Immersive technologies such as VR and AR will redefine experiential learning in humanities disciplines. These innovations will allow students to "visit" historical sites, interact with artistic masterpieces, and engage in cultural simulations without leaving the classroom. For example, history students might explore ancient ruins virtually, while literature students could analyse texts in interactive environments that bring narratives to life. Such experiences bridge the gap between theoretical study and tangible engagement, fostering deeper connections with humanities content.
3. **Enhanced Analytics for Learning Insights**: Advanced data analytics tools will provide educators with real-time insights into student engagement, comprehension, and progress. AI-powered analytics can identify patterns in student participation, flag areas requiring additional support, and suggest pedagogical adjustments to optimise learning outcomes. By leveraging predictive analytics, instructors will be able to tailor course materials dynamically, ensuring that students remain engaged and motivated throughout their studies.
4. **Open Educational Resources and Interoperability**: The future of LMS platforms will see increased integration with open-access digital libraries, scholarly archives, and interdisciplinary databases, broadening the scope of humanities education. Students will gain access to extensive repositories of academic content, including rare manuscripts, historical documents, and multimedia learning resources. Enhanced interoperability between different LMS systems will also facilitate cross-institutional collaborations, allowing scholars and students from diverse backgrounds to engage in collective research and discourse.

As these technologies continue to evolve, LMS platforms will not only enhance humanities education but also redefine the way students interact with knowledge, fostering richer academic experiences and deeper intellectual engagement. The fusion of AI, immersive tools, and expanded learning resources promises a more dynamic and inclusive future for humanities disciplines.

LMS have become foundational in shaping contemporary humanities education, serving as versatile platforms that facilitate content delivery, interaction, assessment, and data-driven insights. Their adoption presents significant opportunities to enhance accessibility, promote active engagement, and cultivate digital competencies that are increasingly essential for 21st-century scholarship. By integrating multimedia resources, collaborative tools, and adaptive learning features, LMS platforms can support diverse learners and foster deeper intellectual exploration. However, successful implementation requires addressing technical, pedagogical, and ethical challenges to ensure that LMS tools empower rather than constrain humanistic inquiry. Institutions must navigate issues such as the digital divide, instructor training, and concerns over data privacy to maximie the potential of these platforms. By thoughtfully leveraging LMS capabilities while remaining responsive to emerging technologies, humanities educators can enrich teaching and learning experiences, fostering critical, creative, and connected learners who are well-equipped to navigate an increasingly digital world [15].

5.3 Text Analysis Software

Text analysis software has evolved as a significant category of digital tools within the realm of humanities education. This software gives students, educators, and researchers the ability to analyse, visualise, and understand textual material on a large scale. By adding computer approaches like as frequency analysis, topic modelling, concordance creation, and sentiment analysis, these technologies enhance the capabilities of classic close reading techniques. A web-based suite that was created to assist exploratory text analysis without having any prior knowledge of programming is one of the most popular and easily accessible platforms. Voyant Tools is one of the platforms.

This section examines the characteristics and capabilities of text analysis software, with a particular emphasis on Voyant Tools, its educational advantages, practical applications in the fields of humanities, the difficulties associated with digital textual analysis, and the potential for further development in the future.

5.3.1 What is Text Analysis Software?

Text analysis software comprises computer tools meant to process and analyse textual input, extracting relevant patterns, structures, and insights. Unlike ordinary text editing tools, these apps include significant analytical features that allow both quantitative and qualitative assessments of texts. By employing computer tools, they assist researchers in identifying hidden themes, linguistic elements, and linkages that may be difficult to spot via human reading alone.

These technologies are often used in Digital Humanities initiatives, where they play an important role in broadening research methods. Text analysis software is mostly used for:

1. **Systematic Analysis of Large Corpora**: Text analysis software enables researchers to systematically process vast collections of texts, making it possible to uncover patterns, trends, and relationships that might be difficult to identify through traditional reading methods. By applying computational techniques, scholars can efficiently analyse historical documents, literary works, social media

discourse, and other large-scale textual datasets, leading to more comprehensive and data-driven insights in humanities research.

2. **Visualisation of Textual Patterns Through Charts, Word Clouds, and Network Graphs**: These tools offer a range of visualisation options that help represent textual data in an intuitive and easily interpretable format. Charts illustrate frequency distributions of words or themes, word clouds highlight prominent terms in a text, and network graphs map relationships between entities, concepts, or keywords. Such visualisations enhance understanding, revealing trends in language use, thematic clusters, and stylistic influences across different texts or periods.
3. **Support for Distant Reading Approaches That Complement Traditional Close Reading**: While close reading involves deep, detailed engagement with individual texts, distant reading leverages computational analysis to explore broad patterns across numerous texts, offering a complementary perspective. Text analysis software helps identify stylistic trends, thematic shifts, and linguistic features across extensive corpora, allowing scholars to trace historical language evolution, genre conventions, and ideological influences in ways that would be impractical through manual reading alone.
4. **Facilitation of Linguistic and Literary Research, Including Authorship Attribution, Genre Analysis, and Historical Language Change**: Text analysis software plays a pivotal role in linguistic and literary studies, supporting investigations into various aspects of text composition and evolution. In authorship attribution, computational algorithms compare stylistic markers to determine the likely authorship of anonymous or disputed texts. Genre analysis allows researchers to categorise literary works based on structural and linguistic features. Additionally, studies of historical language change benefit from these tools by tracking shifts in vocabulary, syntax, and rhetorical styles over time, offering valuable insights into linguistic development and cultural transformations.

5.3.2 Overview of Voyant Tools

Li et al. and Evangelista et al. [15, 16] produced Voyant Tools, an open-source web-based text analysis platform. It is designed with accessibility in mind, giving students and researchers a simple platform for studying textual data in meaningful ways. By enabling users to upload or connect to texts, Voyant Tools provides real-time, interactive visualisations and statistical insights that help comprehend linguistic patterns, thematic themes, and textual structures. Its simplicity and efficiency make it an excellent resource for humanities academics, educators, and digital humanists who want to analyse enormous amounts of text in a methodical manner. Word Frequency Analysis is one of Voyant Tools' key functions, displaying word counts and relative frequencies across a given text. This feature allows researchers to detect essential phrases, repeating themes, and trends in language use across time. Closely linked to this is Cirrus, the word cloud visualisation tool, which graphically portrays frequently occurring words by altering their size based on frequency. This function allows you to quickly and easily identify main topics and lexical emphases inside a document.

Voyant Tools also contains a Trends tool, which employs line graphs to monitor the frequency of certain terms across a text or corpus. This enables academics to track the evolution of certain words or ideas, aiding in the discovery of trends in literary works, historical records, and even present conversation. The Contexts tool, a concordance function, allows users to view individual terms inside their surrounding text, making it easy to evaluate how a phrase is used in various situations and understand its meaning depending on context. Voyant Tools has a Summary feature that gives basic data like total word count, vocabulary richness, and other linguistic metrics. The Links tool is another useful visualisation that depicts word co-occurrence networks, mapping linkages between commonly used terms and ideas in the text. Researchers may use this capability to detect links between concepts and track thematic correlations throughout a corpus. Finally, Voyant Tools provides a Reader function that enables users to explore and analyse texts inside the platform, allowing them to interact with material while also evaluating statistical data. One of Voyant Tools' key characteristics is its ability to adapt to many languages and text formats, such as plain text, XML, and HTML. This adaptability makes it ideal for analysing a wide variety of humanities works, including novels, poetry, speeches, historical documents, and social media content. Voyant Tools, a popular resource in Digital Humanities study, continues to improve academic inquiry by providing rich, interactive text analysis and visualisation.

5.3.3 Applications of Text Analysis Software in Humanities Education

Text analysis software plays a crucial role in enhancing humanities education by providing innovative methods for textual exploration, critical thinking, and research skill development. These digital tools enable scholars and students to analyse texts in ways that go beyond traditional reading, uncovering patterns, themes, and linguistic structures that might otherwise remain hidden.

Literary Studies

In the field of literary studies, text analysis software allows for comprehensive thematic and stylistic examinations. Students can track patterns of word usage, identify recurring motifs, and analyse stylistic features across individual works or an author's entire corpus. Authorship attribution is another important application, where statistical comparisons of linguistic features help determine or confirm the authorship of anonymous or disputed texts. Additionally, researchers can use computational methods to analyse linguistic markers that distinguish different genres or historical periods, offering deeper insights into literary evolution and stylistic shifts.

History and Cultural Studies

Historians and cultural scholars benefit from text analysis tools by conducting corpus analysis on historical documents, allowing them to detect shifts in discourse, ideology, or terminology across time or geographic regions. Media studies also make extensive use of such software to examine sentiment and framing in news articles, political speeches, and propaganda materials, offering valuable perspectives on public opinion and societal narratives. Furthermore, digital archiving has become increasingly important, as text analysis aids in managing, categorising, and interpreting digitised collections of manuscripts, newschapters, and other historical records.

Linguistics

In linguistic research, text analysis tools facilitate frequency and collocation analysis, helping scholars understand language patterns, idiomatic expressions, and phraseology within different contexts. Corpus linguistics exercises also allow students to engage with authentic language data, providing deeper insights into grammar, syntax, and linguistic variation across different registers and time periods. By applying computational methods to linguistic studies, researchers can explore language trends and shifts with unprecedented precision.

Social Sciences

In the social sciences, text analysis software plays a vital role in qualitative data analysis by enabling researchers to code and explore themes within interview transcripts, open-ended survey responses, and social media discussions. By systematically identifying patterns in discourse, these tools support nuanced interpretations of human communication and societal trends. Additionally, sentiment and opinion mining help scholars investigate public attitudes, policy debates, and ideological movements by analysing tone, subjectivity, and emotional expression in textual content.

Pedagogical Benefits of Text Analysis Software

Integrating text analysis tools like Voyant into humanities classrooms provides numerous educational advantages. Active learning and engagement are enhanced as students move beyond passive reading to actively discovering textual patterns and relationships through computational methods. Visual literacy development is another key benefit, as students learn to interpret graphs, word clouds, and network diagrams, which help them understand complex data visualizations more effectively. Critical thinking skills are strengthened as students critically reflect on assumptions about texts, evaluate quantitative results, and link computational findings to traditional qualitative interpretations. Digital literacy is also significantly improved, as learners gain experience using research technologies that are becoming increasingly indispensable in modern humanities scholarship. Additionally, collaborative learning is encouraged, as many text analysis platforms support shared projects, enabling students to engage in group analyses and provide peer feedback on their discoveries [17].

5.3.4 Using Voyant Tools: Practical Workflow

Using Voyant Tools effectively in humanities education follows a structured workflow designed to maximise analytical insights while maintaining interpretive depth.

1. **Text Selection and Preparation**: The first step involves choosing texts that align with the course objectives or research focus. These could range from literary works and historical manuscripts to social media discourse or political speeches. To ensure accurate analysis, texts should be cleaned of extraneous formatting, such as special characters, metadata, or inconsistent spacing, which may interfere with computational processing. Preparing the text correctly enhances the reliability of results and improves the readability of visualisations.
2. **Uploading or Linking Texts**: Once the texts are prepared, users can either upload them as files or paste URLs directly into Voyant's web-based interface. This step allows easy integration of textual data, making it accessible for analysis without requiring extensive software setup. Voyant's flexibility with different formats enables users to work with a variety of humanities texts, including digitised archives, literary databases, and online publications.
3. **Exploration of Visualisations**: With the text uploaded, users can begin exploring various visualisations provided by Voyant Tools. Word frequency analysis helps identify prominent words and patterns, while the Cirrus tool generates word clouds that offer a quick thematic overview. The Trends feature allows users to track the frequency of specific words or concepts across sections of a text, making it useful for longitudinal studies. Additionally, concordance tools help examine words in their immediate contexts, offering insights into meaning and usage across different passages.
4. **Formulating Research Questions**: After examining visual trends, students and researchers can generate or refine research questions based on emerging insights. Patterns in word choice, stylistic variations, or recurring themes can inspire hypotheses about an author's style, ideological shifts in historical documents, or linguistic trends in cultural narratives. By framing meaningful research questions, users can use computational findings to complement traditional literary and historical inquiries.
5. **Interpretation and Reporting**: Finally, the process culminates in interpretation and reporting. Computational results should be integrated with traditional textual analysis to provide nuanced and contextualised arguments. Humanities scholars can use these findings to support critical discussions on literary techniques, historical discourse, or cultural trends. Presenting results may involve combining visualisations with written analysis, illustrating how digital tools enrich textual scholarship without replacing qualitative interpretation.

5.3.5 Examples of Classroom Activities

Text analysis software offers powerful tools for exploring language, rhetoric, and cultural trends across diverse textual sources. By applying computational methods to humanities research, scholars and students can uncover meaningful patterns and insights that enhance traditional analytical approaches [3, 18]:

1. **Analysing Shakespeare's Plays**: One common application of text analysis in literary studies is the examination of thematic word frequencies in Shakespeare's plays. Students can compare the occurrence of key terms such as "love," "death," "power," or "betrayal" across different plays to identify recurring motifs and linguistic patterns. This method allows researchers to quantitatively trace themes and stylistic choices, enriching interpretations of Shakespeare's work by highlighting how certain concepts evolve throughout his corpus.
2. **Tracing Political Rhetoric**: Text analysis plays a vital role in examining political speeches, enabling researchers to identify rhetorical devices, persuasive strategies, and ideological framing used by different leaders. By comparing language choices across multiple speeches, scholars can trace how political narratives shift over time or how different figures employ rhetorical appeals to influence public perception. This application is particularly useful in studying propaganda, campaign speeches, and historical discourse to reveal underlying structures of political communication.
3. **Studying Language Change**: Linguists and historians can use text analysis software to examine the evolution of language across historical periods. By processing large corpora of historical texts, researchers can track how specific words, phrases, or syntactic structures change over time. This approach provides insights into linguistic shifts, cultural transformations, and the impact of external influences such as colonisation, technological advancement, and globalisation on language development.
4. **Exploring Social Media**: With the rise of digital communication, text analysis has become a valuable tool for studying social media discourse. Researchers can mine platforms like Twitter to analyse public opinion on cultural events, social movements, or political issues. Sentiment analysis techniques help assess emotional tone, while keyword tracking and network analysis reveal patterns in online discussions. This application is especially useful in understanding contemporary debates, digital activism, and the spread of viral narratives in society.

5.3.6 Challenges in Using Text Analysis Software

Despite their powerful capabilities, text analysis tools present several challenges that must be navigated to ensure accurate and ethical research outcomes:

1. **Data Preparation**: Before conducting any meaningful analysis, texts must be properly digitised, cleaned, and formatted to ensure usability within computational models. Raw data often contains inconsistencies such as irregular spacing, special characters, or embedded metadata that can distort results. Humanities scholars must invest time in preprocessing their texts, removing extraneous content, and standardising formatting to improve accuracy in analysis.
2. **Interpretation Complexity**: Quantitative outputs from text analysis tools such as word frequencies, trend graphs, or clustering algorithms require careful contextualisation. While computational findings can reveal patterns and relationships, relying too heavily on metrics without qualitative interpretation risks oversimplifying complex texts. Scholars must balance statistical insights with traditional close reading, ensuring that computational results enrich rather than replace nuanced textual understanding.
3. **Technical Barriers**: While some text analysis platforms like Voyant are designed for ease of use, many advanced tools require a level of technical proficiency, including familiarity with programming languages or command-line interfaces. For researchers without a background in coding, this can create a steep learning curve. Institutions and educators must provide adequate training and resources to bridge this gap, enabling more scholars to leverage computational methods effectively.
4. **Ethical Considerations**: Analysing contemporary or personal texts raises important ethical concerns related to privacy and consent. When working with social media posts, interview transcripts, or other personal communications, researchers must be mindful of data protection laws and ethical guidelines. Transparency in data collection, anonymisation measures, and adherence to regulations such as GDPR are crucial to ensuring responsible text analysis practices.

5.3.7 Future Directions in Text Analysis Software

Recent advancements in technology are set to expand the scope and accessibility of text analysis, offering more dynamic and intelligent ways to process and interpret textual data.

1. **Integration with Machine Learning**: Text analysis is becoming increasingly sophisticated through machine learning algorithms that enhance classification, sentiment analysis, and pattern recognition. These advancements allow for more accurate identification of themes, emotions, and linguistic structures across large datasets.
2. **Multimodal Analysis**: The next generation of text analysis tools goes beyond written language, integrating text with images, audio, and video content. This approach enables richer interpretations, allowing researchers to explore connections between different forms of media and gain deeper insights into cultural and historical contexts.

3. **Collaborative Platforms**: Digital tools are evolving to support real-time collaborative work, enabling multiple users to annotate, analyse, and interpret texts collectively. Shared annotation systems foster academic collaboration, allowing scholars to engage in joint research projects and refine their insights through peer interaction.
4. **Mobile and Cloud Solutions**: Cloud-based platforms and mobile-friendly applications are making text analysis more accessible and convenient. Scholars and students can now work on projects from anywhere, without needing specialised software installations, fostering broader participation in computational humanities research.
5. **Ethical AI**: As AI-powered text analysis tools become more prevalent, addressing issues of bias, fairness, and ethical responsibility is crucial. Emerging frameworks aim to improve transparency in text analytics, ensuring responsible data usage and minimising algorithmic biases that may impact research integrity.

Text analysis software such as Voyant Tools represents a vital advancement in digital humanities, offering students and educators innovative ways to engage with textual data. By bridging quantitative and qualitative approaches, these tools enrich humanities education, supporting deeper understanding, critical inquiry, and digital competence. As technology evolves, integrating text analysis software thoughtfully into curricula will continue to expand the horizons of humanistic scholarship.

5.4 Annotation Tools

Annotation tools have become essential in modern humanities education, offering new ways to engage with texts collaboratively and critically. These tools, especially web-based platforms like Hypothesis, allow users to highlight, comment, and discuss digital texts in real-time. Such capabilities are revolutionising reading practices, fostering collaborative learning, and enhancing digital literacy among students and educators. Annotation tools are software platforms that enable users to interact with digital texts by adding notes, comments, tags, and other metadata. These tools support both individual and collaborative engagement, transforming passive reading into an active, dialogic process. Unlike traditional marginalia, digital annotations can be shared across users, allowing for collective interpretation and discourse [19].

5.4.1 Overview of Hypothesis

The web-based annotation tool known as Hypotheses. Is an open-source application that was developed with the intention of enhancing digital reading and encouraging critical interaction with online materials. Users are able to annotate and engage with material in dynamic ways, making it a great resource for both solitary study and collaborative learning. It can function as an extension for a web browser or as a feature that may be embedded in web sites. People who use Hypothesis have the ability to highlight text on any online page or PDF, which makes it much simpler to go back to important points while they are reading. In addition, they have the ability to contribute comments, which may be done in a public, private, or group setting, so establishing a versatile environment for debate and interpretation. The application encourages active discourse by providing users with the ability to comment to the annotations made by other users. This, in turn, encourages deeper examination and interaction with digital content. Additionally, users have the ability to tag material, which assists them in rapidly classifying annotations and retrieving them to use. Due to the fact that it is both simple to use and successful in terms of teaching, Hypothesis has garnered a large amount of momentum in educational settings, notably in higher education. Students and teachers alike utilise it to engage in collaborative text analysis, participate in academic conversations, and critically connect with online resources. This makes digital reading more engaging and intellectually challenging than traditional reading [20].

5.4.2 Applications in Humanities Education

Annotation tools serve as valuable resources across various humanities disciplines, fostering deeper engagement, critical analysis, and collaborative learning.

1. **Literary Analysis**: Students utilise annotation tools to highlight literary devices, themes, and stylistic elements within texts. This interactive process enhances both individual reflection and class discussion, enabling learners to engage with texts in a more structured and analytical way. Collaborative annotation further enriches the experience, allowing students to explore multiple interpretations of a work through peer contributions, fostering a dynamic exchange of perspectives.
2. **Historical Documents**: In history courses, annotation tools facilitate the examination of primary sources, helping students analyse historical language, trace ideological shifts, and contextualise events. Educators often pre-load documents with prompts or questions, guiding students through complex historical narratives while encouraging critical engagement with archival materials. These annotations create a structured framework for interpreting historical discourse, deepening students' understanding of past developments.
3. **Philosophy and Critical Theory**: Texts in philosophy and critical theory can be dense and conceptually challenging. Annotation tools help students break down complex arguments incrementally, marking key passages, defining terms, and connecting ideas. Group annotations further support collective meaning-making, enabling students to clarify difficult concepts through discussion and collaborative insights. This approach fosters analytical precision while enhancing comprehension of abstract philosophical thought.

4. **Digital Rhetoric and Media Studies**: Students studying digital rhetoric and media engage with online content such as blogs, news articles, and social media posts by annotating rhetorical strategies, media framing, and ideological themes. This practice cultivates critical digital literacy, helping students assess how language and visual media shape public discourse. By actively dissecting digital texts, learners develop heightened awareness of persuasive techniques and narrative construction in contemporary communication.
5. **Language and Linguistics**: Annotation tools are instrumental in language studies, enabling students to mark parts of speech, syntactic structures, and translation challenges within texts. Annotating linguistic features helps learners recognise grammatical patterns, idiomatic expressions, and regional variations in language use. Additionally, multimedia annotations, including audio clips for pronunciation or images for cultural references expand language learning beyond written analysis, reinforcing both linguistic proficiency and contextual understanding.

5.5 Online Discussion Platforms

Discussion platforms that are accessible online have become an essential component of digital education in the field of humanities. These platforms provide dynamic environments in which students and teachers may interact with one another, analyse texts, and jointly generate knowledge. Asynchronous and synchronous communication capabilities are provided by these platforms, which expand the conversation that takes place in the classroom and encourage involvement from all students [21].

Definition and Features

Users may engage in organised talks with one another via the use of online discussion platforms, which are digital forums or electronic tools. Both Piazza and Discourse are examples of independent systems, while Moodle and Canvas are examples of learning management systems that include these elements within their core functionality. The most important features are the ability to have threaded conversations, upvoting processes, tagging systems, integration of multimedia, and tools for moderation.

5.5.1 Pedagogical Benefits

1. **Enhanced Engagement and Reflection**: Online annotation and discussion tools provide students with the opportunity to articulate their thoughts in writing before engaging in verbal discussion. This process encourages deeper reflection, allowing learners to research, refine their perspectives, and compose more thoughtful, well-structured responses. Asynchronous discussions, in particular,

give students the time to process complex ideas, engage with different viewpoints, and develop critical insights before contributing to a conversation.

2. **Inclusive Participation**: Digital platforms create a more equitable space for student interaction, ensuring that everyone has an opportunity to participate regardless of personality type or language proficiency. Shy or introverted students, as well as non-native speakers, may feel more comfortable contributing their ideas in writing rather than speaking in class. This inclusive approach fosters diverse perspectives and ensures a broader range of voices are heard in discussions, enriching collaborative learning experiences.
3. **Skill Development**: Beyond facilitating discussions, these platforms play a crucial role in cultivating essential academic and professional skills. Students develop proficiency in digital communication, learning to articulate their ideas clearly and effectively in written form. Argumentation and critical thinking skills are strengthened as learners analyse texts, construct reasoned arguments, and engage with differing interpretations. Additionally, exposure to digital annotation and research tools enhances information literacy, equipping students with the ability to evaluate sources, synthesise knowledge, and navigate scholarly discourse valuable competencies both within the humanities and in broader professional fields.

5.5.2 *Popular Platforms for Discussion in Humanities Education*

Various digital platforms support meaningful discussions and collaborative learning in humanities education, each offering unique functionalities suited to different academic environments.

1. **Piazza**: A Q&A platform designed for higher education, facilitating collaborative problem-solving and peer interaction. It encourages structured discussions where students and instructors can engage in threaded conversations to clarify complex topics.
2. **Discourse**: An open-source forum software focused on civil discourse and in-depth discussions. It is particularly effective for long-form conversations, allowing participants to engage in reflective and substantive exchanges on academic themes.
3. **Slack/Discord**: Real-time communication tools widely used for informal learning and academic collaboration. These platforms offer topic-organized channels, supporting dynamic discussions, group projects, and quick peer-to-peer engagement outside traditional classroom settings.
4. **Canvas/Moodle Forums**: Integrated within LMS, these discussion spaces enable graded participation, structured peer interactions, and assessment tracking. They provide an academic framework for integrating discourse with course objectives.

5.5.3 *Best Practices for Effective Online Discussions in Humanities*

To maximise the effectiveness of online discussion platforms in humanities education, instructors should consider the following best practices:

1. **Clear Instructions and Expectations**: Providing students with detailed guidelines on participation, expected contributions, and engagement ensures a productive discussion environment.
2. **Instructor Presence**: Faculty involvement is crucial for guiding discourse, modeling constructive conversations, and facilitating deeper inquiry into humanities topics.
3. **Integration with Course Readings and Assignments**: Discussions should be tied to course materials, enabling students to reflect critically on assigned texts and contribute informed perspectives.
4. **Use of Rubrics for Evaluation**: Clear criteria for assessing discussion contributions help maintain academic rigor and encourage meaningful engagement.
5. **Encouraging Student-Led Threads**: Allowing students to initiate and moderate discussions fosters ownership of learning, promotes independent thought, and enhances collaborative inquiry.

By leveraging these platforms effectively and following best practices, educators can cultivate intellectually stimulating and inclusive discussions that enrich humanities learning in digital spaces.

5.5.4 *Challenges and Solutions*

While online discussion platforms offer valuable opportunities for student engagement, educators often encounter challenges that require thoughtful solutions to maintain productive and meaningful interactions.

1. **Low Participation**: Encouraging active student involvement in online discussions can be difficult, but structured approaches help increase engagement. Providing well-crafted prompts that invite critical thinking and open-ended exploration gives students a clear direction for contribution. Establishing peer feedback requirements ensures that students interact with one another, fostering a more dynamic conversation. Additionally, incorporating participation grades motivates students to engage consistently, reinforcing the importance of discussion as part of the learning process.
2. **Quality of Responses**: Maintaining high-quality contributions in discussions requires intentional support from educators. Scaffolding techniques such as guiding questions, step-by-step analysis, and model responses help students develop deeper insights and articulate more thoughtful arguments. Providing exemplars of strong discussion posts can serve as reference points, showing

students what constitutes an effective and well-supported response. Encouraging higher-order thinking by prompting analysis, synthesis, and evaluation rather than simple summarisation ensures richer intellectual engagement.
3. **Moderation Issues**: Clear community guidelines establish expectations for respectful and constructive interactions, helping to prevent disruptions in discussion spaces. Educators should communicate norms for discourse early in the course, emphasising academic rigour and inclusivity. Additionally, platform moderation tools such as content filtering, administrative oversight, and user reporting features help maintain a positive and well-regulated learning environment. Regular instructor involvement reinforces productive discussion habits and ensures that conversations remain focused and relevant.

Online discussion platforms are invaluable in fostering democratic and dialogic learning in the humanities. By leveraging these tools, educators can cultivate critical inquiry, collaborative knowledge-building, and sustained academic engagement.

5.6 E-Portfolio Systems

As the landscape of digital pedagogy continues to evolve, e-portfolio systems have emerged as more potent instruments in the field of humanities education. The curation, reflection, and presentation of student learning across time and location are all made easier by these platforms with their capabilities. E-portfolios encourage individualised, introspective, and multidisciplinary approaches to education by providing students with the opportunity to chronicle their intellectual journey and provide a variety of evidence in a variety of formats. Electronic portfolios, on the other hand, put an emphasis on process, development, and metacognitive awareness, in contrast to conventional evaluation systems, which often place a greater emphasis on summative results [3].

5.6.1 Definition and Core Components

An e-portfolio, also known as an electronic portfolio, is a collection of student work that has been digitised and used to illustrate the student's learning accomplishments, abilities, and progress. Academic essays, multimedia artefacts, blog entries, research projects, presentations, and self-reflections are some examples of activities that may fall under this category. An electronic portfolio is more than just a collection of different outputs; it places an emphasis on critical reflection, which encourages students to participate with their own learning and convey how their comprehension of important ideas is developing over time (Tables 5.1 and 5.2).

Table 5.1 Core components of E-portfolio systems

Component	Description
Artifact collection	Students upload files and materials (texts, videos, graphics, etc.)
Reflective commentary	Students explain the significance of artifacts and how they relate to goals
Metadata tagging	Organisation through categories, keywords, or learning outcomes
Assessment tools	Rubrics, feedback forms, peer reviews integrated for evaluation
Sharing permissions	Options for private, peer, or public access

Table 5.2 Types of E-portfolios

Type	Purpose
Developmental	Document progress over time; emphasise learning processes
Showcase	Present your best work for job applications, scholarships, or graduate school
Assessment	Used by instructors for grading or evaluating specific outcomes
Reflective	Encourage introspection on personal or academic growth
Professional	Employed by educators or researchers to track and share professional work

5.6.2 Pedagogical Significance in the Humanities

The Humanities and the E-Portfolio Model

The humanities, with their emphasis on critical thinking, personal expression, and interdisciplinary inquiry, are exceptionally well-suited for the e-portfolio model. E-portfolios provide a dynamic and interactive space where students can document their learning journey, showcase their work, and reflect on their intellectual growth. This approach supports a deeper engagement with course materials and offers lasting value beyond the classroom. Several key pedagogical benefits of e-portfolios in humanities education include:

1. **Reflective Learning**

Reflection is a cornerstone of humanities education. Whether students are interpreting a poem, analysing a historical event, or deconstructing a philosophical argument, they are encouraged to critically engage with meaning and context. E-portfolios enhance this reflective process by requiring students to articulate why their selected works are significant, how they illustrate personal growth, and what learning strategies proved most effective. This metacognitive engagement fosters a deeper understanding of their academic journey.

Example: A student in a literature course includes multiple drafts of an essay along with the final version, offering insights into the editing process, revisions made based on feedback , and the reasoning behind key structural and thematic changes.

2. **Integration of Multiple Literacies**

Modern humanities education encompasses a wide array of literacies beyond traditional text-based learning. Students now engage with images, sound, interactive media, and digital storytelling, reflecting the evolving nature of communication in contemporary society. E-portfolios provide an ideal platform for students to present their work in multiple modalities, reinforcing visual, digital, and information literacies alongside written expression.

Example: A cultural studies portfolio may combine written analyses with audio interviews, annotated photographs, and short video presentations, allowing students to engage critically with various media formats and demonstrate their ability to synthesize information across disciplines.

3. **Ownership and Motivation**

E-portfolios empower students by giving them autonomy over their learning experiences. By curating their own educational narrative, students actively shape their intellectual identity and take ownership of their progress. This process fosters deeper engagement with coursework, as students recognise the relevance of their studies to their personal aspirations and career goals. Research has shown that students who use e-portfolios tend to exhibit higher levels of motivation and engagement. The ability to personalise and present their work in a meaningful way enhances their sense of purpose in academia, leading to increased self-efficacy and academic confidence.

4. **Formative and Summative Assessment**

From an educator's perspective, e-portfolios provide a comprehensive and versatile assessment tool. Unlike traditional exams or single-assignment evaluations, e-portfolios offer an ongoing stream of evidence showcasing student learning over time. This enables both formative assessment (continuous feedback and improvement) and summative assessment (final evaluation of competencies), providing a more nuanced and holistic picture of student development.

By reviewing portfolios, educators can assess not only the final outcome but also the progression of skills, critical thinking abilities, and interdisciplinary connections made by students. This deeper understanding facilitates more personalised feedback and more effective pedagogical strategies.

5.6.3 Common Platforms in Use

A wide variety of platforms, ranging from open-access tools to institutional solutions, are available to facilitate the building of electronic portfolios. For example, Blackboard, Canvas, and Moodle are examples of institutional solutions that are often used by educational institutions. These solutions provide a systematic integration inside academic contexts, hence guaranteeing uniformity and institutional monitoring. Students that want creative control over their portfolios will find open-access solutions such as Google Sites, WordPress, and Mahara to be perfect. These technologies allow for more flexibility and personalisation, making them excellent for students. PebblePad, Portfolium, and FolioSpaces are examples of specialised e-portfolio systems that are expressly designed to concentrate on the monitoring of competencies, the integration of multimedia, and the construction of career paths. In order to ensure that students and teachers are able to make good use of e-portfolios for learning and professional development, the choice of platform is contingent upon a number of criteria, including institutional infrastructure, pedagogical objectives, simplicity of use, and long-term accessibility (Table 5.3).

Implementation Strategies in Humanities Courses

Instructors play a pivotal role in structuring e-portfolio activities to align with learning outcomes, ensuring that students not only document their progress but also engage in meaningful reflection and skill development. A well-designed e-portfolio strategy enhances student success by fostering deeper engagement, critical thinking, and personal ownership of learning. The following key strategies contribute to an effective implementation of e-portfolios in educational settings:

1. **Set Clear Expectations**

A successful e-portfolio begins with clarity. Instructors should provide students with explicit guidelines detailing the purpose of the portfolio, required components, assessment criteria, and deadlines. Clear expectations ensure that students understand how to curate their work in alignment with learning objectives. To support this, rubrics should be developed that outline specific evaluation criteria, including reflection depth, organisation, and content quality. This structured approach not only clarifies grading standards but also helps students refine their submissions to meet pedagogical goals effectively.

Table 5.3 Common platforms in use

Platform	Key features	Ideal use case
Mahara	Open-source; integrates with Moodle; supports reflection, feedback, assessment	Institutional adoption in higher education
Google sites	Easy integration with Google Workspace; highly accessible	Student-driven personal portfolios
PebblePad	Designed for reflective learning and accreditation; template-based	Programmatic evaluation and course linkage
WordPress	Flexible, customisable themes; strong for multimedia and narrative-style content	Digital storytelling and public portfolios
Canvas ePortfolio	LMS-integrated; supports course-linked submissions	Seamless integration with academic modules

2. **Embed Periodic Reflection**

Reflection is at the heart of an impactful e-portfolio experience. Instead of reserving reflection for the final stage, instructors should embed reflective practice throughout the learning journey. Encouraging students to reflect after major assignments, projects, or modules fosters continuous self-assessment and intellectual growth.

Guiding students with structured reflection prompts can enhance the depth of their responses. Prompts such as:

- *What did I learn in this unit?*
- *What challenges did I encounter, and how did I address them?*
- *How has my understanding evolved over time?*

By regularly engaging in these reflective exercises, students develop a deeper awareness of their learning process, strengthening critical thinking and self-directed learning.

3. **Integrate with Course Design**

E-portfolios should not be treated as a peripheral or supplementary activity; instead, they should be deeply embedded within the curriculum. Effective integration ensures that portfolio entries serve as extensions of major assessments, reading responses, research projects, or skill-building exercises.

For instance, incorporating e-portfolio submissions into key coursework such as literary analyses, historical research, or creative projects reinforces their relevance. When students view e-portfolios as an integral component of their academic progression, they are more likely to engage with them meaningfully.

4. **Model Good Practice**

Students benefit greatly from seeing well-structured examples of e-portfolios. Instructors can provide sample portfolios or structured templates to guide students in designing their entries effectively. Exposure to strong examples helps students develop organisational and content presentation strategies that align with academic standards. Additionally, instructors can offer insights into their professional portfolios, demonstrating real-world applications of reflective documentation and career development. By sharing personal examples, educators can create a supportive learning environment where students gain confidence in their ability to curate their work effectively.

5. **Facilitate Peer Review**

Peer review opportunities foster a collaborative learning atmosphere and elevate the quality of e-portfolio submissions. Encouraging students to exchange feedback on each other's portfolios helps them refine their content, improve articulation, and recognize areas for enhancement. Through structured peer review exercises, students not only learn to evaluate work critically but also gain fresh perspectives on their own submissions. Constructive critique strengthens analytical skills and encourages revisions that improve clarity, coherence, and reflective depth.

Table 5.4 Challenges and solutions

Challenge	Suggested solution
Technical barriers	Provide training sessions and tech support. Use intuitive platforms
Time and workload	Start small; scaffold portfolio development over multiple weeks
Uneven engagement	Incorporate into grading scheme and monitor progress regularly
Assessment complexity	Use clear rubrics and encourage reflective depth, not quantity
Privacy concerns	Offer options for restricted or anonymous access

5.6.4 Challenges and Solutions

Despite their advantages, e-portfolios present several challenges that educators and students must navigate. Technical difficulties, such as platform accessibility, formatting issues, and compatibility with institutional systems, can hinder seamless adoption. Additionally, maintaining student engagement and ensuring meaningful reflection requires thoughtful guidance and structured implementation. Privacy concerns arise when portfolios include sensitive or personal data, necessitating clear policies on security and ownership. Furthermore, effective assessment demands well-defined rubrics to balance creativity and academic rigor. Addressing these challenges enhances the effectiveness and sustainability of e-portfolios in education (Table 5.4).

5.6.5 Evaluating E-Portfolios

E-portfolios must be assessed holistically, with a focus on subject mastery and reflective insight. A typical rubric might contain the following critical criteria: Content Quality, evaluating the depth, accuracy, and relevance of the material presented; Reflective Depth, assessing the student's ability to critically engage with their learning experiences; Organisation and Cohesion, examining the logical structure and clarity of portfolio elements; Creativity and Engagement, taking into account the originality and presentation style; and Technical Execution, reviewing multimedia integration and platform usability. A well-defined rubric facilitates meaningful evaluation and promotes student development (Table 5.5).

Future Directions

As educational institutions continue to embrace digital transformation, e-portfolios are set to undergo significant advancements. One key innovation is the integration of artificial intelligence, which will enable smart feedback systems that provide automated suggestions for improvement, helping learners refine their work efficiently. Additionally, blockchain technology will play a crucial role in verifying the authenticity and security of submitted work, ensuring credibility and trust in academic records. Another major shift will be the facilitation of cross-institutional sharing, allowing students to maintain and carry their portfolios across different programs

Table 5.5 Evaluating E-portfolios

Criterion	Excellent (5)	Good (4)	Satisfactory (3)	Needs improvement (2)	Unacceptable (1)
Content quality	Deep insight; well-chosen artifacts	Mostly relevant	Adequate coverage	Superficial	Lacking artifacts
Organisation	Clear structure; logical flow	Minor issues	Basic structure	Disorganized	Confusing
Reflective depth	Insightful, personal, critical	Some analysis	Descriptive	Vague	Absent
Technical design	Visually appealing; fully functional	Few issues	Minor glitches	Multiple errors	Unusable

and career paths, creating a more seamless learning experience. Furthermore, as mobile devices become increasingly central to everyday interactions, there will be a heightened emphasis on optimising e-portfolios for mobile compatibility, ensuring greater accessibility for learners on the go. These advancements will collectively enhance the functionality and impact of e-portfolios, making them indispensable tools in modern education. E-portfolio systems are strong instructional tools that may be used to cultivate learners in the humanities who are introspective, creative, and independent. The aims of liberal education, which include encouraging inquiry, personal growth, and critical engagement with information, are aligned with these aspects of education. E-portfolios, when strategically integrated, not only improve the results of individual learning, but they also contribute to the aims of the institution, which include quality assurance, accreditation, and the promotion of digital literacy. It is necessary for students, teachers, and administrators to work together in order to fully realise the potential of these electronic platforms. It is expected that e-portfolios will continue to be an essential component of humanities education in the twenty-first century, provided that research, professional growth, and technical advancement are maintained.

5.7 Blogging Tools

Blogging platforms like WordPress and Medium are very important in the field of digital humanities education because they make it possible for students to engage in reflective learning, publish their work digitally, and develop a public academic voice. Students are given the ability to produce, curate, and share information outside the confines of the conventional classroom via the use of these platforms. The purpose of this part is to investigate the pedagogical implications, comparative aspects, practical applications, and obstacles associated with the incorporation of blogging platforms into classrooms that teach humanities [22].

5.7.1 Definition and Educational Relevance

Users are able to post information in a manner similar to that of a journal via the use of web-based platforms known as blogging tools. The purpose of these platforms is to provide students with a means through which they may communicate their thoughts, analyse texts, record their learning processes, and interact with a wider audience via the educational setting. The relation to the humanities is very significant since these fields place a strong emphasis on storytelling, debate, interpretation, and communication skills that are organically developed via blogging.

Students are encouraged to combine classroom ideas with real-world observations via the use of blogging, which has the effect of helping students develop a habit of critical thought and synthesis. A knowledge with online publishing tools, web formatting, and the incorporation of multimedia is also required, which is another way in which it promotes digital literacy [23] (Table 5.6).

Each tool caters to different learning needs. WordPress offers unmatched flexibility and can support full websites for digital humanities projects. Medium prioritises simplicity and audience engagement, making it ideal for narrative-driven content. Edublogs focuses on classroom safety and control, aligning well with younger or less tech-savvy learners.

Pedagogical Benefits

The integration of blogging tools into humanities education presents numerous pedagogical advantages:

1. **Critical Thinking and Expression**: Regular blogging encourages students to analyse information, synthesise diverse perspectives, and articulate their ideas clearly. By crafting blog posts, learners refine their ability to form coherent arguments, respond to opposing viewpoints, and engage critically with texts, historical events, and contemporary issues.

Table 5.6 Comparison of popular blogging tools

Platform	Key features	Best for
WordPress	Highly customisable, supports plugins, open-source, SEO friendly	Complex projects, institutional blogs
Medium	Simple interface, built-in audience, limited customisation	Personal reflections, class blogs
Edublogs	Educational focus, student privacy controls, teacher moderation	K–12 and higher education settings

2. **Improved Writing Skills**: The informal yet public nature of blogging fosters a personal and engaging writing style. Writing for an audience beyond the classroom motivates students to focus on clarity, coherence, and accessibility. Over time, this practice enhances their overall communication ability, helping them develop strong writing habits applicable to academic and professional settings.
3. **Public Engagement**: Publishing blogs allows students to participate in academic and social conversations beyond their institution. This exposure helps them develop a sense of responsibility in shaping discourse, engage with experts and peers worldwide, and contribute valuable insights to broader intellectual and cultural discussions.
4. **Multimodal Learning**: Blogs support text, image, video, and audio content, enabling students to explore different communication modes. Through multimedia elements, learners can present information dynamically, appeal to diverse audiences, and experiment with storytelling techniques that merge traditional and digital literacy skills.
5. **Peer Interaction**: Commenting systems allow students to provide feedback to peers, creating a collaborative learning environment. Engaging in discussions within blog spaces fosters critical reflection, strengthens interpersonal communication skills, and reinforces the value of constructive dialogue. This interactive aspect enhances a sense of academic community while promoting knowledge-sharing and collective problem-solving.

By blending academic rigour with creative expression, blogging enhances the learning experience in a format that is both accessible and meaningful. It empowers students to think critically, communicate effectively, and engage with the world in innovative ways, making learning more immersive and relevant in today's digital landscape [24].

Implementation Strategies

To effectively integrate blogging tools into humanities instruction, educators can consider the following strategies:

1. **Structured Assignments**: Assign blogging tasks that tie into weekly readings, lectures, or thematic units to provide coherence and purpose. Clearly defined prompts help students connect blogging activities to course objectives, fostering deeper engagement with subject matter while allowing flexibility for personal interpretation and creative expression.
2. **Reflection and Dialogue**: Encourage students to reflect on course material and respond to peers' posts to build a vibrant learning community. Through thoughtful discussions and commentary, students learn to articulate perspectives, engage in constructive debate, and critically assess different viewpoints, reinforcing the collaborative aspect of humanities education.
3. **Assessment Rubrics**: Develop rubrics that evaluate content accuracy, originality, style, engagement, and multimedia use. Clearly communicated grading criteria help students understand expectations, refine their writing, and explore various modes of presentation, ensuring both academic rigor and creative exploration.

4. **Digital Identity**: Teach students to build a responsible online persona by emphasising ethics, citation, and respectful discourse. This includes discussions on intellectual property, proper attribution, and fostering positive digital interactions, helping students become conscientious contributors in online academic and professional spaces.
5. **Portfolio Integration**: Combine blogs into larger e-portfolio projects to showcase learning progress and thematic connections. By curating their work over time, students can demonstrate their analytical growth, critical thinking development, and evolving engagement with humanities topics, making their learning experience more tangible and reflective.
6. **Feedback Loops**: Incorporate both peer and instructor feedback on blog posts to refine analytical and writing skills. Meaningful critiques enhance students' ability to assess strengths and areas for improvement, providing a continuous cycle of learning, revision, and mastery over content presentation and argumentation.

For younger students or beginners, guided prompts and technical tutorials may be necessary to build confidence in blogging. Offering structured guidance, practical demonstrations, and clear expectations can help novice bloggers feel comfortable exploring creative and academic writing in digital formats. By implementing these strategies, educators can harness the dynamic potential of blogging to make humanities instruction more interactive, reflective, and engaging in the digital age.

5.7.2 Challenges and Solutions

1. **Technical Barriers**: Some students may struggle with the technical aspects of using blogging platforms, such as navigating interfaces, embedding multimedia, or troubleshooting formatting issues.
2. **Solution**: Provide onboarding workshops and tutorials, including step-by-step guides and hands-on demonstrations. Offering technical support, FAQ documents, and peer mentoring can help students gain confidence in using digital tools effectively.
3. **Privacy Concerns**: Publishing online can expose students to unwanted attention or potential misuse of their content. Concerns about digital footprints and online safety may discourage participation.
4. **Solution**: Use platforms with privacy controls, allowing students to limit the visibility of their posts to their class or selected audiences. Encourage pseudonyms or controlled access to ensure students feel comfortable engaging in discussions while maintaining their personal security.
5. **Quality Control**: The informal nature of blogging may lead to lax writing standards, where students prioritise spontaneity over structured argumentation. Without clear expectations, posts may lack depth, coherence, or academic rigour.
6. **Solution**: Set clear expectations and provide writing guidelines emphasising critical thinking, proper citation, and structured analysis. Encourage students to

balance creativity with scholarly precision while developing an engaging and articulate writing style.

7. **Assessment Difficulties**: The subjective interpretation of blog quality can complicate grading, as creative expression varies widely. Without transparent criteria, students may struggle to understand how their work is evaluated.
8. **Solution**: Use detailed rubrics that assess content accuracy, originality, coherence, engagement, and multimedia use. Providing exemplars of strong blog posts helps students understand expectations and refine their work accordingly.

Technologies for blogging, such as WordPress, Medium, and Edublogs, provide prospects for humanities education that have the potential to be transformational. Critical inquiry, digital literacy, and public scholarship are some of the skills that are fostered by these programs, which are in line with the objectives of liberal education. These technologies, when intelligently incorporated, have the potential to act as dynamic extensions of the classroom as well as vehicles for learning that continues throughout one's life. Blogging tools assist in nurturing independent thinkers and responsible digital citizens by providing students with the ability to express themselves, link ideas across settings, and communicate with broader audiences. This is a result that resonates intimately with the goal of the humanities in an era dominated by digital technology.

5.8 AI Writing Assistants

In the realm of digital education, writing assistants powered by AI have emerged as tools that have the potential to revolutionise the field. The use of applications such as Grammarly and ChatGPT has grown more widespread in higher education, particularly in the field of the humanities, which places a significant emphasis on writing, critical thinking, and textual analysis. These tools make use of NLP and ML algorithms to assist with grammatical correction, the development of content, the refining of style, and even the building of arguments. Within the context of humanities education, this section offers an examination of the roles, pedagogical implications, advantages, limits, and strategic applications of artificial intelligence writing helpers (Table 5.7).

Table 5.7 Overview of key tools

Tool	Functionality highlights	Educational use case
Grammarly	Grammar, punctuation, style suggestions, tone detection	Improving academic writing and stylistic consistency
ChatGPT	Conversational AI, idea generation, summarisation, Q&A	Brainstorming, content drafting, clarification of concepts
QuillBot	Paraphrasing, summarising, and citation assistance	Rewriting for clarity and citation support

5.8.1 Pedagogical Benefits

Writing tools that are driven by AI provide a revolutionary approach to academic writing by contributing to an increase in both technical skill and cognitive engagement. Students are able to build communication skills that are more polished and clearer as a result of these tools, which spot grammatical problems, correct sentence structure, and recommend vocabulary changes. A continuous learning loop is fostered when students are able to obtain instant feedback, which assists them in recognising areas in which they need improvement, improving their writing, and developing confidence in their capacity to self-correct. Further, AI assistants play a significant part in assisting those who are not native English speakers. These assistants provide assistance in the areas of grammar and fluency, ensuring that the writing they produce satisfies academic requirements while yet allowing for personal expression. In addition to offering support with language, AI technologies also provide assistance with the production of ideas and the structure of those ideas. This gives students a foundation to generate ideas for subjects, organise arguments, and build narratives that are coherent, which is a crucial ability for writing essays and research chapters. Furthermore, by automating the mechanical components of writing, such as grammar and formatting, students are able to concentrate more on higher-order thinking, which includes analysis, criticism, and interpretation, which in turn deepens their engagement with complicated subject matter. In the end, writing help that is powered by artificial intelligence gives students the ability to improve their writing while also promoting intellectual development and academic confidence.

5.8.2 Integration in Humanities Curricula

1. **Assignment Support**: Allow students to use AI tools during the drafting phase but require annotations explaining how the tool was used. This approach encourages students to reflect on their writing process, recognize AI's strengths and limitations, and ensure that they retain critical control over their content. By documenting their AI-assisted edits and revisions, students gain deeper insights into language mechanics and improve their self-editing skills.
2. **Critical Reflection Essays**: Ask students to reflect on their experience using AI tools, analysing both benefits and limitations. This exercise helps students assess AI's role in writing development, consider ethical implications, and articulate how digital tools influence creativity, originality, and learning outcomes. By engaging in a structured critique, students cultivate media literacy and a thoughtful approach to technology-enhanced writing.
3. **AI Literacy Workshops**: Incorporate sessions on how AI works, ethical considerations, and best practices for its academic use. Educators can introduce topics such as bias in AI models, responsible citation of AI-generated content, and strategies for maintaining authenticity while using digital assistants. These workshops

ensure that students understand AI's capabilities and use it effectively without undermining academic integrity.

4. **Scaffolded Assignments**: Use AI-generated drafts as a base for critique and rewriting, teaching revision skills. By analysing AI-generated content, students can identify structural weaknesses, refine arguments, and enhance clarity and coherence. This method encourages iterative learning and fosters the ability to critically evaluate writing both AI-assisted and their own while reinforcing traditional writing techniques.

By incorporating these strategies, humanities educators can harness the potential of AI writing assistants while ensuring students engage critically and responsibly with digital tools, fostering both technological fluency and intellectual growth.

5.8.3 Limitations and Ethical Considerations

While AI writing assistants offer numerous benefits, they also present challenges that require careful consideration in academic settings:

1. **Over-Reliance**: Students may become dependent on AI for content generation, potentially diminishing their own analytical efforts. If AI tools are used without critical engagement, students risk relying on automation rather than developing independent thinking and problem-solving skills.
2. **Accuracy Issues**: AI-generated text may contain factual inaccuracies or stylistic inconsistencies that are inappropriate for academic writing. Since AI models predict text rather than verify facts, students must actively check sources, refine arguments, and ensure that automated suggestions align with scholarly standards.
3. **Ethical Concers**: The use of AI raises questions about authorship, originality, and academic honesty. If students submit AI-assisted work without proper disclosure, it challenges traditional notions of intellectual ownership and raises concerns about plagiarism and integrity in academic discourse.
4. **Access Inequality**: Not all students may have equal access to premium versions of AI tools, leading to disparities in academic support. Those with limited resources may not benefit from advanced AI features, creating an uneven playing field in writing development.

5.8.4 Educator Guidelines for Responsible AI Use

While AI writing assistants offer numerous benefits, they also present challenges that require careful consideration in academic settings. The increasing reliance on AI-powered tools for drafting, revising, and improving written content has introduced complexities related to student learning habits, content accuracy, ethical concerns, and accessibility disparities. To ensure that AI supports rather than undermines academic development, educators must address these concerns thoughtfully. To ensure responsible and ethical use of AI writing assistants, educators should:

1. **Over-Reliance**: Students may become dependent on AI for content generation, potentially diminishing their own analytical efforts. If AI tools are used without critical engagement, students may rely on automated text generation rather than developing independent thinking and problem-solving skills. Writing is not merely about producing sentencesit is an intellectual exercise requiring synthesis, critique, and reflection. Overuse of AI-generated content can discourage original thought and weaken a student's ability to craft complex arguments or engage with nuanced perspectives. Educators should encourage students to use AI as a supporting tool rather than a primary content creator.

    a. **Accuracy Issues**: AI-generated text may contain factual inaccuracies or stylistic inconsistencies that are inappropriate for academic writing. Since AI models work by predicting text patterns rather than verifying factual correctness, students may unknowingly include misleading or incorrect information in their work. Additionally, AI-generated writing might lack contextually appropriate tone and structure, leading to inconsistencies in scholarly communication. To mitigate these risks, students must actively check sources, refine arguments, and ensure that automated suggestions align with academic standards. Instructors can emphasize the importance of verifying AI-generated material through credible research methods.
    b. **Ethical Concerns**: The use of AI raises questions about authorship, originality, and academic honesty. If students submit AI-assisted work without proper disclosure, it challenges traditional notions of intellectual ownership and raises concerns about plagiarism and integrity in academic discourse. The ability of AI tools to generate well-structured responses can blur the line between legitimate assistance and outright substitution of intellectual effort. Universities must define clear policies on ethical AI use, ensuring students understand the boundaries between acceptable assistance and academic misconduct.
    c. **Access Inequality**: Not all students may have equal access to premium versions of AI tools, leading to disparities in academic support. While some students may benefit from sophisticated AI-powered writing assistance, others may be limited by financial constraints or technological barriers. This gap can exacerbate existing inequalities, particularly among students from underprivileged backgrounds or institutions with limited digital resources. Educators should consider equitable approaches to technology integration, offering alternative writing support strategies for those who lack access to advanced AI tools.

Thus, in the field of humanities education, AI writing helpers like as Grammarly and ChatGPT offer a tremendous amount of potential to enhance writing and thinking. When used appropriately, they have the potential to enable students to develop into writers who are more self-assured, expressive, and introspective. On the other hand, their incorporation must be supported with critical literacy, ethical awareness, and pedagogical monitoring. In order to teach students not just to utilise artificial intelligence technologies, but also to comprehend and evaluate them as a component of the larger digital culture, the humanities need to advance in tandem with the progression of technology.

5.9 Multimedia Tools for Storytelling

Despite the fact that the landscape of humanities education is always shifting, storytelling continues to be an essential method of instruction. The use of multimedia technologies has both enhanced and modified this approach. Students and teachers are able to offer narratives that are dynamic, engaging, and visually attractive with the help of these technologies, which range from software for editing videos to interactive timeline makers. Not only can the use of multimedia into storytelling improve the quality of the educational experience, but it also supports the development of digital literacy, critical thinking, and creative thinking.

5.9.1 Defining Multimedia Storytelling

The process of crafting and disseminating narratives via the use of multiple forms of digital media, including text, photos, audio, video, and animation, is referred to as multimedia storytelling. It is particularly relevant in the field of humanities, which places a significant emphasis on the interpretation and communication of human experiences. The confluence of many aspects of media makes it possible to create a more robust narrative framework, which in turn enables students to connect with knowledge that is historical, cultural, and philosophical in a manner that is inherently immersive (Table 5.8).

These tools empower students to move beyond traditional written assignments and demonstrate understanding through multimedia expressions.

5.9.2 Pedagogical Applications

Students are given exciting opportunity to delve deeper into humanities topics via multimedia storytelling, which incorporates digital resources into the learning process. Through the use of digital storytelling assignments, students have the opportunity to produce video essays or interactive exhibits that integrate narrative, pictures, and music in order to investigate literary themes or historical events. This allows for the development of both creative expression and analytical depth. Students have the

Table 5.8 Commonly used multimedia tools

Tool	Primary features	Educational use case
Adobe spark	Video, web, and graphics creation	Creating narrative videos or visual essays
iMovie	Intuitive video editing	Documentaries and oral history projects
Canva	Graphic design, presentations, infographics	Digital posters and visual storytelling
TimelineJS	Interactive timelines with multimedia integration	Historical narratives and chronological storytelling
StoryMapJS	Mapping narratives with geographic data	Geospatially anchored storytelling (e.g., migration stories)

ability to see historical and geographical links via the use of interactive projects, such as those that use StoryMapJS. This helps to make abstract knowledge more concrete and approachable to the students. Teamwork is also encouraged via the use of collaborative story creation, which involves students working together in groups to create multimedia tales. This helps students improve their ability to manage projects and communicate effectively. Last but not least, the use of personalised storytelling helps to promote reflective learning by encouraging students to participate in metacognitive activities as they examine their own thinking processes and academic development. By using various forms of multimedia, educators are able to create learning experiences that are not only immersive and engaging but also meaningfully bridge the gap between conventional and digital literacy.

Digital Histories in the Classroom

Students were given the task of creating video biographies of historical personalities as part of a digital storytelling assignment that was introduced by a history professor at a public liberal arts institution. A combination of archive photos, primary source narrations, and music that was suitable for the time period was created by the students using iMovie and Adobe Spark. The finished objects were shown in an online exhibition, which encouraged comments from peers and participation from the general public.

5.9.3 *Benefits of Multimedia Storytelling*

The incorporation of multimedia into educational settings considerably enhances the learning process by providing a wide range of chances for engagement, understanding, the development of skills, and the expression of one's own interests. In the process of capturing the attention of learners via multimodal experiences, instructional information becomes more immersive and engaging, resulting in enhanced engagement. Maintaining students' attention and encouraging them to take an active role in their own educational path may be accomplished by using features that are aural, visual, and interactive. The students' ability to synthesise information from texts, photos, films, and debates contributes to the development of a deeper knowledge when they interact with different sources. Taking this method helps students develop their critical thinking skills and enables them to draw connections between different concepts, which ultimately results in a more thorough recall of information. This helps learners grow technical competence, narrative approaches, and visual communication skills that are crucial in both academic and professional contexts. Additionally, skill development is reinforced by hands-on contact with digital technologies, which helps learners develop these talents. The ability to express oneself personally is yet another significant benefit of using multimedia platforms, which provide pupils a variety of channels via which they may express their thoughts and creativity. Communicating in ways that are aligned with their abilities is something that may be accomplished by learners from a variety of backgrounds. This can be accomplished via narrative, creative design, digital presentations, or interactive projects. Through the incorporation of these components into educational settings, teachers are able to create learning environments that are more dynamic and inclusive, which cater to a variety of learning styles and encourage intellectual development.

5.9.4 Challenges and Considerations

The use of multimedia storytelling may improve students' engagement and understanding, but it also offers problems that teachers need to carefully handle. Access and equity problems develop when students do not have access to dependable equipment or the software that is required for multimedia projects. This might possibly restrict students' ability to participate and their creative potential. The provision of shared resources, the provision of flexible project forms, and the guarantee of alternatives that retain inclusiveness are all means by which institutions might handle this issue. Having the necessary technical abilities is also important, since it is possible that certain students and teachers may need further training in order to make successful use of digital storytelling tools. It is possible for educators to bridge this gap by including tutorials, hands-on workshops, and peer assistance into their lessons, which will assist students in developing their confidence in the production of multimedia material. Due to the fact that assessing creative work demands striking a balance between technical execution, storyline coherence, and intellectual depth, evaluation standards also provide their own particular challenges. The development of transparent rubrics that set expectations for creativity, involvement, and critical analysis ensures that academic rigour is maintained while also ensuring that fairness is maintained. By taking proactive measures to address these difficulties, educators have the ability to maximise the advantages of multimedia storytelling while simultaneously ensuring that all students have access to relevant learning experiences and that they are able to receive them.

5.9.5 Recommendations for Educators

Educators may choose a method that is progressive and organised, which stimulates creativity while retaining academic integrity, in order to successfully incorporate multimedia storytelling into the curriculum of the humanities. Students are able to explore with digital storytelling without having to face significant technological obstacles if they begin with low-barrier platforms such as Canva and Adobe Express. The teachers will be able to offer more complicated software that is designed to greater multimedia involvement as they begin to build confidence. This will ensure that the software is accessible to all students. Students are able to traverse the process of storytelling with a strong framework when they are provided with clear principles, examples, and scaffolding. This then enables them to properly arrange their tales throughout the process. The promotion of experimentation is a means of fostering creative inquiry; nevertheless, the establishment of restrictions on the scope of the project ensures that students continue to concentrate on learning goals and workloads that are achievable. A fair and constructive evaluation may also be achieved via the use of well-developed rubrics that strike a balance between material knowledge, creative expression, and technical execution. It is possible for educators to construct dynamic learning environments by employing these tactics. These settings allow students to engage deeply with topics related to the humanities while also gaining vital skills in digital literacy and storytelling.

There are several great paths for learning, expression, and involvement in the humanities that may be offered via multimedia technologies for storytelling. Educators have the ability to enhance conventional education, foster student creativity, and better prepare students for communication in a world that is rich in multimedia by using these tools. Through the incorporation of storytelling tools into educational programs, students are not only able to become proficient consumers of material, but also skilled producers of significant digital tales. This is because digital fluency is becoming an increasingly vital skill.

5.9.6 Data Visualisation in Humanities

In the field of digital humanities, data visualisation has evolved as an important approach that enables researchers to evaluate, analyse, and disseminate complicated material via the use of visual forms. Through the process of transforming data that is either numerical, geographical, or textual into charts, maps, and infographics, researchers are able to uncover patterns and insights that may have been buried in the first place. Enhancing the narrative quality of academic arguments and providing assistance for exploratory investigation are both benefits of this method.

5.9.7 *The Role of Data in Humanities Research*

Within the realm of humanities study, the digital revolution has resulted in a considerable expansion of the methods in which researchers engage with data. This expansion has gone beyond the conventional qualitative analysis to include both organised and unstructured versions of digital information. Visualisation has evolved as an essential way for making sense of huge volumes of information as a result of the development of digitised archives, descriptive textual analysis driven by metadata, and computer tools. Scholars are able to track linguistic patterns, thematic changes, and emotional tones inside texts via the use of visualisation tools in the field of literary studies. These approaches include word frequency mapping and sentiment analysis. These techniques give fresh insights into literary style and narrative tendencies. Timelines, demographic changes, and geographical mapping are all tools that may be used in the field of history to aid the study of historical events, migratory patterns, and social transitions. These tools also provide scholars with the ability to find trends that may be difficult to comprehend using standard textual methodology alone. In a similar vein, network analysis is beneficial to the fields of philosophy and cultural studies. Through this method, links between ideas, philosophers, or cultural movements may be visualised, therefore drawing attention to intellectual impact, ideological crossings, and the development of thinking over the course of time. Researchers are able to tackle difficult problems with more clarity, discover hidden links within data, and broaden their analytical toolset to merge qualitative depth with quantitative insights when they include visualisation into their work in the field of humanities studies (Table 5.9).

Table 5.9 Key visualisation techniques

Technique	Description	Use case example
Bar and line charts	Graphs that show trends or comparisons across categories	Analyzing publication frequency over decades
Network graphs	Diagrams of interconnected nodes and relationships	Mapping correspondence between historical figures
Timelines	Sequential visual representation of events	Chronicling key events in intellectual movements
Word clouds	Visual representation of word frequency	Highlighting themes in literary or philosophical texts
Geospatial maps	Visualisation of data with a geographical component	Tracking migration or cultural diffusion

5.9.8 Common Tools for Visualisation

The use of data visualisation tools has become increasingly important in the field of digital humanities research. These tools enable researchers to analyse and present complicated datasets in formats that are engaging and interactive. Tableau is a platform that is extensively used and user-friendly. It enables researchers to generate interactive charts and dashboards, which in turn makes massive datasets more accessible and informative. Palladio, which was developed expressly for the purpose of doing research in the humanities, is an excellent tool for network and map visualisations. It enables researchers to investigate the connections that exist between historical persons, literature, or cultural movements. RAWGraphs is a tool that is open-source and excels in the generation of complex and individualised visualisations. It provides researchers with flexibility when they require data representations that are tailored to their specific needs. Users are able to develop dynamic visual outputs that may be inserted into digital projects and presentations by using Google Charts, which interfaces with web-based apps in a smooth manner. Gephi, on the other hand, is an expert in network analysis, which assists academics in mapping links between concepts, institutions, and persons in order to uncover patterns and linkages in the field of literary or historical studies. All of these technologies, when combined, provide great capabilities for study in the humanities. They improve qualitative and quantitative analysis while also making complex datasets easier to understand.

5.9.9 Pedagogical Applications

A significant contribution that data visualisation makes to the field of humanities education is the enhancement of analytical depth and engagement via the use of forms that are both interactive and visually engaging. Students have the opportunity to employ visualisation tools in the context of classroom assignments. These tools allow students to map literary themes, build precise timelines of historical events, or analyse networks of intellectual impact. Through the process of making intangible ideas more concrete, these efforts contribute to a more profound comprehension. The incorporation of digital visualisations into virtual museums or digital editions of texts is what constitutes interactive exhibits. These displays enhance the experience by providing viewers with the opportunity to examine historical and literary tales dynamically. These kinds of displays bring historical artefacts and literary works to life, providing a wealth of contextual layers into which interpretation may be applied. The analytical abilities of students are further developed via the use of critical thinking tasks, which push students to evaluate the ways in which visual design affects the information that is interpreted. Students acquire the ability to critically interact with data presentation by assessing components such as colour schemes, spatial connections, and graphical representations. This allows them to recognise both the potential for insight that data presentation has as well as the constraints that it possesses. Collectively, these methods improve the teaching of the humanities by encouraging creative thinking, an interactive learning environment, and a more in-depth investigation of topics related to history and culture.

5.9.10 *Case Example: Network Visualisation in Literary Studies*

The purpose of this study is to illustrate how digital humanities tools such as Gephi may improve literary analysis by illuminating hidden patterns inside a text. Students were able to graphically monitor interactions, identify major players, and emphasise degrees of isolation or connection within Woolf's meticulously woven social tapestry by mapping character relationships in Mrs. Dalloway. This was accomplished via the use of character mapping. Through the use of this visualisation, not only did they get a more profound comprehension of the effect of characters, but it also facilitated conversations on the psychological and sociological topics that were explored in the book. These themes included the fragmentation of identity, societal expectations, and emotional distance. Through the use of digital technologies in this manner, students are able to approach literature from new viewpoints, so bridging the gap between qualitative interpretation and quantitative analysis and promoting conversations that are more extensive and multifaceted.

Benefits of Data Visualisation

When it comes to teaching in the humanities, data visualisation is an extremely important tool since it helps to make abstract ideas more concrete and approachable. Students are able to more quickly comprehend complicated connections between historical events, literary themes, or philosophical arguments when they are presented with pictures that clarify difficult concepts and relationships. This results in enhanced understanding. Discovering patterns that may not be obvious in standard textual forms is made possible for students via the use of pattern recognition, which further increases the options for analytical work. Through the process of transforming raw data into visual representations, academics are able to recognise recurrent patterns, character interactions, or historical transitions that might otherwise stay concealed. There is also a large increase in engagement as a result of the fact that interactive visualisations inspire active learning, which in turn fosters curiosity and deeper involvement in academic conversations. Students get more involved in investigating humanities themes in a dynamic manner regardless of whether they do it via the use of digital maps, timelines, or network analysis. In conclusion, interdisciplinary integration is a strategy that bridges the gap between computer science, statistics, and the arts. It promotes a holistic learning approach that blends qualitative and quantitative thinking. Students are able to analyse material from the humanities using new analytical techniques thanks to the combination of disciplines, which helps them to broaden their methodological toolbox and prepares them for an academic world that is increasingly enhanced by digital technology.

5.9.11 Challenges and Considerations

Data visualisation has many uses in the humanities, but it also has its own set of obstacles that must be carefully avoided. Because a good visualisation is dependent on a core grasp of data management, interpretation, and correctness, data literacy is a vital skill to possess. If students do not get the appropriate training, they may have difficulty critically analysing datasets, which may result in findings that are either shallow or deceptive. The possibility of misrepresentation is another issue that has to be addressed. Visuals that are not well designed have the potential to mislead readers or distort information. The choices that are made in terms of size, colour, and structure might inadvertently exaggerate trends or omit crucial background, which can have an effect on how historical events, literary patterns, or philosophical links are seen. In addition, the accessibility of tools continues to be a hurdle, since many visualisation platforms need expensive subscriptions or extensive technical knowledge, which may restrict their uptake among students and instructors. Institutions may prioritise training in digital literacy, place an emphasis on ethical data visualisation techniques, and give access to user-friendly technologies that strike a balance between complexity and accessibility in order to solve these difficulties. Through the cultivation of a thoughtful engagement with data, academics in the humanities may capitalise on the benefits of visualisation while simultaneously minimising its hazards.

5.9.12 Best Practices for Educators

An organised strategy that promotes the development of both technical and analytical skills may be used by educators in order to facilitate the successful incorporation of data visualisation within the field of humanities education. Starting with the basics helps students build foundational knowledge by utilising easily accessible tools such as Google Sheets to introduce fundamental visualisation concepts such as charts, graphs, and tables. This ensures that students have a firm grasp on fundamental data representation techniques before moving on to more complex software. Students need to acquire critical literacy in visual rhetoric and design, which means they need to grasp how graphical decisions, such as colour schemes, scale, and layout, impact interpretation and communication. Teaching context is equally important since students need to build this capability. Instructors may scaffold projects in order to reinforce learning by leading students through a systematic process that involves data gathering, organisation, analysis, and visualisation. This gives students the opportunity to acquire confidence in their ability to handle and present information in a meaningful manner over the course of the project. The last benefit of fostering reflection is that it improves critical thinking by pushing students to examine and change their visual representations. This helps to ensure that the students' interpretations of the facts continue to be both accurate and ethical, and that they successfully express ideas. Educators may provide students the ability to interact with data-driven storytelling by following these steps, which will stimulate interdisciplinary research and greater knowledge across the humanities disciplines.

In addition to being a technical talent, data visualisation is also a methodological and rhetorical activity that contributes to the enhancement of research and teaching in the humanities. Discovering new meanings, successfully communicating discoveries, and engaging a wide variety of audiences are all possible outcomes that may be achieved via the use of visualisation. The visualisation of data will continue to play an essential part in the future of the humanities, especially as digital literacy becomes an increasingly important component of academic study.

5.9.13 Accessibility and Inclusivity Features

In contemporary digital humanities education, accessibility and inclusion are fundamental ideals that serve as foundationers. Increasing equality, broadening participation, and improving learning outcomes are all aims that may be achieved by ensuring that digital tools and material are available to all users, regardless of their abilities, backgrounds, or their circumstances. The concept of inclusivity encompasses more than just physical access; it also takes into account a wide range of cultural viewpoints, linguistic disparities, and learning preferences.

5.9.14 Importance in Humanities Education

Historically, the goal of education in the humanities has been to investigate a wide range of human experiences and voices. However, if they are not developed with accessibility in mind, digital technologies have the potential to reinforce existing inequalities, despite the fact that they provide new chances to democratise information. A design that is inclusive guarantees that digital resources are accessible to persons with disabilities, including those with vision and hearing impairments, as well as those with cognitive and movement difficulties.

5.9.15 Key Accessibility Standards and Guidelines

Web accessibility standards are crucial for ensuring that digital content is usable by individuals of all abilities. Web Content Accessibility Guidelines (WCAG) provides

Table 5.10 Common accessibility features in digital tools

Feature	Description	Benefit
Screen reader compatibility	Supports text-to-speech software	Enables visually impaired users to access content
Keyboard navigation	Allows full control without a mouse	Assists users with motor impairments
Captions and transcripts	Text alternatives for audio and video content	Supports deaf or hard-of-hearing users
Adjustable text size and contrast	Customisable fonts and colours for readability	Aids users with low vision or dyslexia
Multilingual support	Interface and content available in multiple languages	Accommodates diverse linguistic backgrounds

internationally recognised standards that ensure web content is perceivable, operable, understandable, and robust, making digital spaces more inclusive for people with disabilities. Section 508 is a U.S. federal regulation that mandates accessibility for electronic and information technology used by government agencies, ensuring compliance with accessibility requirements in federally funded projects. Additionally, Accessible Rich Internet Applications (ARIA) enhances web accessibility by adding semantic details to websites, helping assistive technologies such as screen readers interpret and navigate interactive elements effectively. Together, these standards promote equitable access to digital content, fostering an inclusive online environment (Table 5.10).

5.9.16 *Inclusivity Beyond Accessibility*

Accessibility, cultural representation, and adaptation are three features that need to be carefully considered in order to guarantee inclusion in the design of educational aids and digital tools. When it comes to building tools that respect and effectively portray a variety of cultural settings while avoiding prejudice, cultural sensitivity is an extremely important factor to bring into consideration. In order to build learning experiences that are fair for all students, educators and developers need to take into account language variances, historical viewpoints, and examples that are culturally relevant. "Universal Design for Learning" (UDL) is a framework that offers a structured environment that encourages many ways of interaction, representation, and expression. This framework is designed to accommodate a wide range of learning requirements. Through the use of visual, aural, and interactive components, instructors are able to guarantee that all students, regardless of their individual learning styles, are provided with meaningful access to the subject. Learners are given the ability to personalise their digital experience by adjusting tools to their preferences via the usage of user customisation. The usability of digital platforms is improved by additional features such as customisable font styles, interface layouts, and input methods. These features make digital platforms more user-friendly and intuitive. By incorporating these ideas, educators and developers are able to design learning environments that are accessible, culturally inclusive, and adaptive to the specific requirements of each person, therefore contributing to the development of a digital landscape that is more egalitarian.

5.9.17 Challenges in Implementation

Accessibility, cultural representation, and adaptation are three features that need to be carefully considered in order to guarantee inclusion in the design of educational aids and digital tools. When it comes to building tools that respect and effectively portray a variety of cultural settings while avoiding prejudice, cultural sensitivity is an extremely important factor to bring into consideration. In order to build learning experiences that are fair for all students, educators and developers need to take into account language variances, historical viewpoints, and examples that are culturally relevant. "Universal Design for Learning" (UDL) is a framework that offers a structured environment that encourages many ways of interaction, representation, and expression. This framework is designed to accommodate a wide range of learning requirements. Through the use of visual, aural, and interactive components, instructors are able to guarantee that all students, regardless of their individual learning styles, are provided with meaningful access to the subject. Learners are given the ability to personalise their digital experience by adjusting tools to their preferences via the usage of user customisation. The usability of digital platforms is improved by additional features such as customisable font styles, interface layouts, and input methods. These features make digital platforms more user-friendly and intuitive. By incorporating these ideas, educators and developers are able to design learning environments that are accessible, culturally inclusive, and adaptive to the specific requirements of each person, therefore contributing to the development of a digital landscape that is more egalitarian.

5.9.18 Case Example: Inclusive Design in an LMS

Accessibility elements, such as compatibility with screen readers and captioning services, were included into a LMS that was adopted at a university. Additionally, the platform supported a number of different languages and provided a variety of submission formats, which made it possible for students with a wide range of requirements to engage completely in classes. Users' feedback was crucial in refining features and improving the general usability of the product.

Best Practices for Educators and Developers

Ensuring accessibility in digital education and multimedia tools requires a proactive and comprehensive approach. Conducting accessibility audits and involving individuals with disabilities in user testing helps identify barriers and refine designs to ensure inclusivity. By engaging real users in the testing process, developers can address issues that may not be apparent through automated evaluations alone. Integrating accessibility training into professional development equips educators and content creators with the knowledge to design courses and materials that meet diverse learning needs. Training programs should cover best practices for accessible content creation, compliance with standards like WCAG, and strategies for fostering inclusive learning environments. Prioritising open standards and tools with proven accessibility ensures that digital platforms and resources remain adaptable and widely usable, reducing reliance on proprietary technologies that may present limitations. Open-source solutions with built-in accessibility features allow broader adoption and customisation for varied learning contexts. Lastly, promoting awareness of inclusivity principles among students fosters a culture of accessibility and respect for diverse needs. Encouraging students to understand and advocate for accessible design prepares them to contribute to a more equitable digital landscape in their academic and professional pursuits. By implementing these measures, institutions can create learning environments that support all users while advancing the principles of digital inclusion.

Therefore, the incorporation of accessibility and inclusivity into digital humanities tools and pedagogy is absolutely necessary in order to establish learning environments that are equitable, engaging, and capable of catering to the differing requirements of students. Considering the growing importance of digital platforms in the field of humanities education, it is essential to ensure that these tools are designed with accessibility in mind. This ensures that all students, regardless of their abilities, backgrounds, or preferred learning styles, are able to meaningfully engage with scholarly content. The provision of alternate formats for materials, the guarantee of compatibility with assistive technology, and the incorporation of features that promote usability for students with disabilities are all examples of proactive actions that educators and developers need to take in order to accommodate a wide range of demands. In addition, inclusivity goes beyond accessibility by acknowledging the existence of cultural, linguistic, and socioeconomic diversity. This ensures that digital resources are representative of all users and are welcoming to them. There is the potential for digital humanities to become more broadly accessible with the incorporation of smart design practices and equitable teaching methodologies. This would result in the development of enhanced research, deeper engagement, and meaningful involvement for students from all different kinds of backgrounds. Not only does giving accessibility and inclusion a higher priority enhance educational results, but it also reinforces the larger aim of humanities research, which is to promote varied viewpoints and equal learning opportunities.

Table 5.11 Criteria for evaluation

Criterion	Description	Importance
Usability	Ease of use, intuitive interface, and learning curve	Determines how quickly users can adopt the tool
Functionality	Range and relevance of features for specific academic tasks	Ensures the tool meets educational and research needs
Accessibility	Compliance with accessibility standards and inclusive design	Enables participation of users with disabilities
Interoperability	Ability to integrate with other platforms and data formats	Facilitates seamless workflow and data exchange
Pedagogical support	Alignment with teaching methods and support for learning outcomes	Enhances effectiveness in educational settings
Cost and licensing	Price, subscription models, and licensing restrictions	Affects affordability and sustainability
Technical support	Availability of training, documentation, and help resources	Influences user confidence and problem resolution

5.9.19 *Comparative Analysis of Software Effectiveness*

As digital tools become integral to humanities education, evaluating their effectiveness is essential to maximise learning outcomes. Comparative analysis of software involves assessing multiple tools based on criteria such as usability, functionality, accessibility, pedagogical value, and cost-effectiveness. This enables educators, researchers, and institutions to make informed decisions about which technologies best support their teaching and research goals. When comparing software tools in humanities education, several key factors should be considered (Table 5.11).

5.9.20 *Comparative Analysis Framework*

In the field of digital humanities, a systematic approach to comparative analysis entails doing a structured review of various tools and approaches in order to establish how beneficial they are in terms of classroom instruction and research. Identifying use cases is the first step in the process. This involves outlining particular situations, such as text analysis, collaborative annotation, or visualisation, in order to guarantee that the research is based on applicable applications. The next step in the process is to pick candidate software, which involves selecting tools that are either commonly used or developing in the area. This involves taking into consideration aspects such as accessibility, functionality, and flexibility to academic requirements. After the tools have been chosen, it is necessary to construct assessment metrics in order to evaluate their capabilities using both quantitative and qualitative criteria. This will ensure that the study is comprehensive. Following this, the strategy continues on to testing and

Table 5.12 Example comparative study

Feature/tool	Voyant tools	AntConc	NVivo	MAXQDA
Usability	High, web-based, user-friendly	Moderate; desktop app	Moderate; desktop, requires training	Moderate; desktop app
Functionality	Basic to intermediate text analysis	Concordance, keyword analysis	Advanced qualitative data analysis	Advanced qualitative and mixed methods
Accessibility	Good; web accessibility features	Limited; desktop only	Moderate; some accessibility features	Moderate
Interoperability	Supports export in multiple formats	Limited import/export	High; integrates with many data types	High
Pedagogical support	Suitable for introductory courses	Good for linguistics and corpus studies	Suitable for mixed methods research	Suitable for complex qualitative projects
Cost	Free	Free	Paid license	Paid license
Technical support	Online tutorials, community support	Limited tutorials	Extensive support and training	Extensive support and training

feedback, which consists of doing hands-on trials with teachers and students in order to get real-world insights about the usability and efficacy of the system. After this, the process of "data synthesis" comprises assembling and analysing the findings in order to establish the differences and similarities between the various tools, as well as their strengths and limits. Last but not least, the study concludes with recommendations, which provide well-informed guidance on the selection of tools based on research that has been thoroughly examined. The use of this method guarantees a comprehensive evaluation, which assists academics and teachers in making well-informed decisions regarding digital tools that improve the effectiveness of humanities research and teaching (Table 5.12).

5.9.21 *Benefits of Comparative Analysis*

The use of a systematic strategy to evaluate digital humanities tools offers a number of important advantages that improve the quality of teaching, research, and institutional planning opportunities. It is possible for educators to pick tools that are in line with the objectives of the curriculum via the process of informed decision-making. This ensures that technology contributes to the efficacy of teaching rather than being a distraction. It is possible for faculty members to incorporate solutions that encourage meaningful interaction with information related to the humanities if they thoroughly evaluate various platforms beforehand. When it comes to ensuring that time and money are used in an effective manner, resource optimisation plays a significant part. This involves concentrating on instruments that result in the largest impact while simultaneously minimising expenditures that are not essential. This allows educational institutions to make the most of their investments in technology while yet ensuring that all students have access to it. In addition, increased learning is accomplished when teachers use methods that improve the level of student involvement and the results of their students' instructional experiences. Instructors are able to create more engaging learning experiences that appeal with a wide range of students by giving platforms that give interaction, accessibility, and analytical depth a higher priority. Last but not least, constant improvement ensures that any gaps in the already available tools are detected, which in turn guides the creation and refining of future products. The use of comparative studies by institutions allows for the provision of feedback to developers, which in turn encourages innovation and makes digital humanities tools more flexible to the requirements of academic institutions. With the help of these principles, educators and scholars will be able to construct a digital humanities environment that is more efficient, more inclusive, and more forward-thinking.

5.9.22 Challenges in Comparative Analysis

There are a number of obstacles to overcome while evaluating digital humanities tools. The most significant of these obstacles is the fast expansion of software capabilities, which makes it difficult to maintain evaluations that are up to date. In light of the fact that platforms are constantly introducing new functionalities, updates, and integrations, evaluations that were previously established may quickly become obsolete, necessitating ongoing monitoring and adaptation. A further factor that makes the process of producing universal suggestions more difficult is the fact that different user demands and situations exist. It is impossible for a single tool to fulfil all of the criteria in an equal manner since humanities researchers, educators, and students interact with digital tools in a variety of different ways, depending on the research topic, level of technical ability, and resources available at the institution. Because of this variance, adaptable evaluation frameworks that take into consideration a variety of use cases are something that are required. In addition, for subjective impressions of usefulness and efficacy, it is necessary to strike a careful balance between qualitative and quantitative assessment methodologies. Different users may place a higher value on a tool's intuitive design, while others may place a greater emphasis on its technological soundness. This might result in different evaluations of the efficacy of a tool. The implementation of continuous review cycles, the solicitation of user feedback, and the development of adaptable evaluation models that can accommodate evolving technologies and diverse scholarly needs are all options that institutions can pursue in order to address these challenges.

5.9.23 *Future Directions*

There are a number of forward-thinking tactics that may be used in order to improve the assessment and integration of digital humanities tools. By analysing engagement metrics, understanding levels, and skill development, instructors are able to evaluate the influence that digital technologies have on student performance. This is made possible via the incorporation of learner analytics. With the use of these data-driven insights, teaching strategies may be improved, and tool selection can be optimised, so that learning outcomes can be better supported. It is important to guarantee that assessments continue to be relevant as artificial intelligence continues to affect research and teaching. This may be accomplished by expanding evaluations to incorporate developing technologies based on AI. Application software that is driven by artificial intelligence, such as automated text analysis, content suggestion, and adaptive learning technologies, presents new opportunities for education in the humanities. These new possibilities demand thorough examination with respect to their efficacy and ethical implications. Furthermore, the development of community-driven archives of comparative studies offers educators in the field of humanities the opportunity to participate in the sharing of user experiences, tool evaluations, and case studies via the provision of easily available and collaborative resources. It is possible for educators to make educated judgements on the use of digital tools if they cultivate collective knowledge and engage in continuous discourse. This will eventually result in an increase in the accessibility, efficiency, and influence of digital humanities research.

The skill of doing a comparative study of digital tools is an essential component of digital humanities education. This practice enables stakeholders to traverse the fast-changing software world with a stronger appreciation for strategic planning. Through the process of methodically analysing the efficacy, accessibility, and usefulness of different platforms, educators are able to make educated judgements on the integration of technology. This ensures that digital tools improve teaching techniques, boost student engagement, and assist scholarly research. In addition to maximising the use of available resources, this strategy also encourages creative thinking, which makes it possible for the humanities to accept technological innovations while yet preserving academic rigour and inclusiveness.

References

1. H. S. Munawar, F. Ullah, S. Qayyum, Big data in construction : current applications and future opportunities (2022)
2. P. Coberly-Holt, K. Elufiede, Preparing for the fourth industrial revolution with creative and critical thinking Patricia Coberly-Holt and Kemi Elufiede, pp. 21–25 (2016)
3. K. C. Obi, O. Iwuanyanwu, Innovation in the assessment of primary school mathematics: an approach to revamping Nigeria education. J. Teach. Perspect. **18**(1), 51–66 (2023), [Online]. Available: http://repositorio.unan.edu.ni/2986/1/5624.pdf%0Ahttp://fiskal.kemenkeu.go.id/

ejournal%0A10.1016/j.cirp.2016.06.001%0A10.1016/j.powtec.2016.12.055%0A10.1016/j.ijfatigue.2019.02.006%0A10.1

4. C. Zhengdao, An internet of things-enabled BIM platform for on-site assembly services in prefabricated construction, Autom. Constr. **89**,146–161 (2018). https://doi.org/10.1016/j.autcon.2018.01.001
5. N.M. Alshahrani, M.L.M. Kiah, B.B. Zaidan, A.H. Alamoodi, A. Saif, A Review of smart contract blockchain based on multi-criteria analysis: challenges and motivations. Comput. Mater. Contin. **75**(2), 2833–2858 (2023). https://doi.org/10.32604/cmc.2023.036138
6. B. Malmgren, Loyalty in the retail clothing industry the moderated effect of influencer marketing upon E-WoM and Brand loyalty (2022)
7. P. Sinclair, Inflation expectations inflation, Suparyanto dan Rosad (2015) **5**(3), 248–253 (2020)
8. V. B. Vargas, J. De Oliveira Gomes, P.C. Fernandes, R.V. Vallejos, J.V. De Carvalho, Influential factors for hospital management maturity models in a post-Covid-19 scenario—Systematic literature review, J. Inf. Syst. Eng. Manag. **8**(1), 1–10 (2023). https://doi.org/10.55267/iadt.07.12868
9. F.A. Alaba, M. Amina, U. Ibrahim, H.A. Sulaimon, A.Z. Aliyu, Exploring the role of the internet of things (IoT) on economic growth in Nigeria: Challenges and opportunities, Eng. Technol. Trends. **2**(6) (2024)
10. K.P. Seng, L.M. Ang, E. Ngharamike, Artificial intelligence internet of things: A new paradigm of distributed sensor networks, Int. J. Distrib. Sens. Networks. **18**(3) (2022). https://doi.org/10.1177/15501477211062835
11. R.Y. Chen, A traceability chain algorithm for artificial neural networks using T-S fuzzy cognitive maps in blockchain. Futur. Gener. Comput. Syst. **80**, 198–210 (2018). https://doi.org/10.1016/j.future.2017.09.077
12. N.M. Kumar et al., Distributed energy resources and the application of AI, IOT, and Blockchain in smart grids, Energies. **13**(21) (2020). https://doi.org/10.3390/en13215739
13. L. Albó, J. Barria-pineda, Knowledge-based design analytics for authoring courses with smart learning content. Int. J. Artif. Intell. Educ. **7**(21), 1–24 (2021)
14. E.Y. Chew et al., Standardization and clinical applications of retinal imaging biomarkers for cardiovascular disease: A roadmap from an NHLBI workshop, Nat. Rev. Cardiol. (2024). https://doi.org/10.1038/s41569-024-01060-8
15. S. Li, T. Tryfonas, H. Li, The internet of things: A security point of view. Internet Res. **26**(2), 337–359 (2016). https://doi.org/10.1108/IntR-07-2014-0173
16. D. Evangelista, F. Mezghani, M. Nogueira, A. Santos, Evaluation of Sybil attack detection approaches in the internet of things content dissemination, IFIP Wirel. Days, pp. 1–6 (2016). https://doi.org/10.1109/WD.2016.7461513
17. D. Sykes et al., Comparison of rule-based and neural network models for negation detection in radiology reports. Nat. Lang. Eng. **27**(2), 203–224 (2021). https://doi.org/10.1017/S1351324920000509
18. C. Bratianu, D.F. Stanescu, R. Mocanu, Exploring the knowledge management impact on business education. Sustain. **13**(4), 1–16 (2021). https://doi.org/10.3390/su13042313
19. D. Berrar, Bayes' theorem and naive bayes classifier, Encycl. Bioinforma. Comput. Biol. ABC Bioinforma. **1–3**, 403–412 (2018). https://doi.org/10.1016/B978-0-12-809633-8.20473-1
20. X. Xu (Rinka), S. Pratt, Social media influencers as endorsers to promote travel destinations: An application of self-congruence theory to the Chinese Generation Y, J. Travel Tour. Mark. **35**(7), 958–972 (2018). https://doi.org/10.1080/10548408.2018.1468851
21. T. Kymäläinen, A. Seisto, R. Malila, Generation Z FoodWaste, diet and consumption habits: A Finnish social design study with future consumers. Sustainability **13**(4), 1–14 (2021). https://doi.org/10.3390/su13042124
22. M.A.M. Cárdaba, A. Fernández, L. Martinez, U. Cuesta, Make it part of the story: The role of product placement prominence and integration in fashion and beauty blogs among young digital natives. J. Glob. Fash. Mark. **00**(00), 1–16 (2022). https://doi.org/10.1080/20932685.2022.2085607

23. T. Olowa, E. Witt, C. Morganti, T. Teittinen, I. Lill, Defining a BIM-enabled learning environment—An adaptive structuration theory perspective, Buildings. **12**(3) (2022). https://doi.org/10.3390/buildings12030292
24. R.N. Amanchukwu, G.J. Stanley, N.P. Ololube, A review of leadership theories, principles and styles and their relevance to educational management. Management **5**(1), 6–14 (2015). https://doi.org/10.5923/j.mm.20150501.02

Chapter 6
Results and Analysis

6.1 Response Rate and Demographic Summary

When conducting any kind of empirical study involving human subjects, the response rate and demographic profile of the participants are crucial factors to consider in determining the reliability and representativeness of the data obtained. A comprehensive analysis of the survey response rate is provided in this section, along with a breakdown of the demographic characteristics of the individuals who participated in the research. These results serve as the basis for the following interpretation of the study outcomes, particularly in connection with the incorporation of software tools in the field of humanities education.

6.1.1 Response Rate

A key indication of the degree to which the sample population has engaged in the study is the response rate, which is often expressed as a percentage. It also provides insight into the degree to which the target audience is engaged with the subject matter of the study. When compared to a low response rate, which may raise issues about the generalisability of the results, a high response rate often improves the credibility of the research it is being conducted. For this investigation, questionnaires were sent out to a total of 450 participants, including individuals from a variety of higher education institutions, including students and academic staff. The surveys were filled out and returned by 372 of these individuals, contributing to an overall response rate of 82.67%. The high return rate provides evidence that the participants have a significant interest in the subject matter and that it is relevant to their lives. Additionally, it adds to the general dependability of the study's findings [1].

The reasons for the high response rate may be attributed to several factors, including:

F. A. Alaba et al., *Learning Beyond the Classroom*, Studies in Computational Intelligence 1253, https://doi.org/10.1007/978-3-032-14433-1_6

1. Relevance of the subject matter to the day-to-day academic practices of the respondents.
2. Proactive follow-up mechanisms, including reminder emails and in-person engagements.
3. Anonymity and confidentiality assurances, which helped to build trust with respondents.
4. The perceived benefit of the research in influencing educational policy and practice.

6.1.2 Demographic Characteristics of Respondents

In order to give context for the interpretation of the replies provided by the participants, demographic information was gathered. It is possible to conduct a more nuanced analysis and interpretation of the data if one has a better understanding of the distribution of respondents according to gender, age, academic role, discipline, and expertise with educational software. The demographic breakdown of the 372 qualified responders is shown in Table 6.1.

Table 6.1 Demographic characteristics of respondents (n = 372)

Demographic variable	Category	Frequency	Percentage (%)
Gender	Male	208	55.9
	Female	164	44.1
Age group	18–25 years	112	30.1
	26–35 years	157	42.2
	36–45 years	67	18.0
	Above 45 years	36	9.7
Role in academia	Undergraduate student	191	51.3
	Postgraduate student	79	21.2
	Academic staff	102	27.4
Disciplinary background	Literature	87	23.4
	History	78	21.0
	Philosophy	54	14.5
	Languages	93	25.0
	Cultural studies	60	16.1
Experience with software	None	42	11.3
	Basic	173	46.5
	Intermediate	113	30.4
	Advanced	44	11.8

6.1.3 Interpretation of Demographic Data

A more complete picture of digital humanities participation emerges from the study's demographic findings. Despite the fact that there is a minor bias towards male participation, the gender distribution is still well balanced, which ensures that diverse points of view are represented. The predominant age group, which ranges from 26 to 35 years old, indicates that postgraduate students and early-career academics are the ones pushing digital adoption in educational settings. This is in line with larger trends in the integration of technology inside higher education.

In the context of the study's examination of role-based segmentation, the significant presence of undergraduate students serves to emphasise the study's focus on learner satisfaction. The substantial engagement of academic staff and postgraduate students, on the other hand, contributes unique pedagogical ideas, which expand the results of the research about institutional methods for the use of digital tools. The study's usefulness is further strengthened by the breadth of disciplinary representation, which ensures different viewpoints throughout the many disciplines of investigation within the humanities. Textual analysis and digital humanities approaches are naturally compatible with one another, as shown by the fact that approximately half of all replies include languages and literature.

Furthermore, the fact that the participants had various degrees of prior experience with instructional software highlights the need for individualised training and development programs. There is a considerable part of people who are still at the beginner level, despite the fact that many people have basic or intermediate abilities. This highlights the need of having organised support mechanisms in order to enable the successful adoption of digital tools in humanities education. Based on these results, it seems that focused interventions, such as seminars, tutorials, and institutional investments in digital literacy, have the potential to assist in bridging the gap and maximising the advantages of technology-driven research [2, 3] (Fig. 6.1).

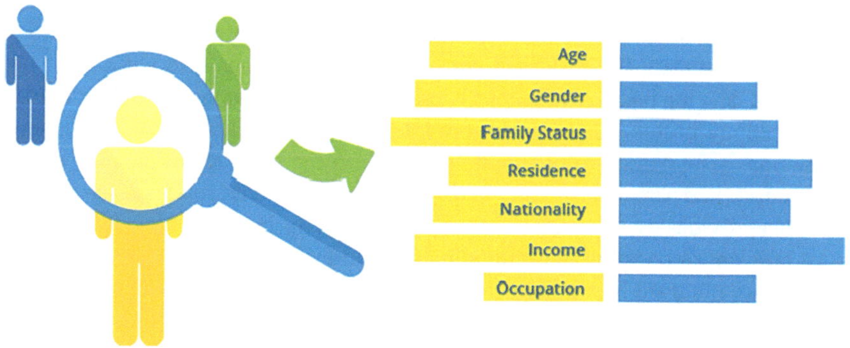

Fig. 6.1 Demographic of respondents [4]

6.1.4 Implications for Further Analysis

There is a solid basis for inferential analysis that is established by the response rate and demographic makeup of the research sample. This foundation ensures that following conclusions represent a wide variety of academic experiences and points of view with respect to the subject matter. The findings of the research affirm that there is a significant level of participation across a wide range of occupations, age groups, and fields of study, which further substantiates the generalisability of the findings. This variety helps to improve the trustworthiness of interpretations, which in turn enables researchers and educators to get a better understanding of the ways in which digital technologies have an effect on various subsets of the academic community. When it comes to evaluating the perceived efficacy, usefulness, and overall influence of digital tools on teaching and learning, the fact that respondents' experiences with educational software vary greatly is a significant moderating element that should be taken into consideration. It is possible to conduct a more nuanced investigation of best practices by recognising these variances, which permits the identification of tactics that are effective across a range of skill levels and places in which institutional intervention may be required. These findings will be very helpful in formulating policies that promote digital literacy and ensuring that technology is used to improve learning rather than to create hurdles to accessibility. Through the examination of these processes, the research makes a contribution to a more profound comprehension of the adoption of digital tools and provides information that can be used to inspire specific suggestions for the creation of curriculum and institutional support [5].

6.2 Use of Software Tools by Students

Traditional learning techniques are being transformed as a result of the use of digital resources into humanities education. This is allowing students to connect with knowledge in ways that are both unfamiliar and dynamic. Students are using software not just to analyse texts and historical data, but also to communicate with their classmates and develop interactive scholarly projects. This is something that is happening as technology becomes more and more integrated into the workflows of academic institutions. The purpose of this part is to give a complete study of the use patterns, preferences, and perceived efficacy of digital tools based on the replies of the students. The data provides useful insights into adoption patterns by exposing which tools are most efficient in boosting understanding, critical thinking, and engagement. These insights are obtained by studying how learners utilise technology into their studies. By gaining an understanding of these patterns, educators are able to improve their methods of digital learning, so ensuring that technology continues to serve as a resource that is both helpful and accessible within the realm of humanities education [6] (Fig. 6.2).

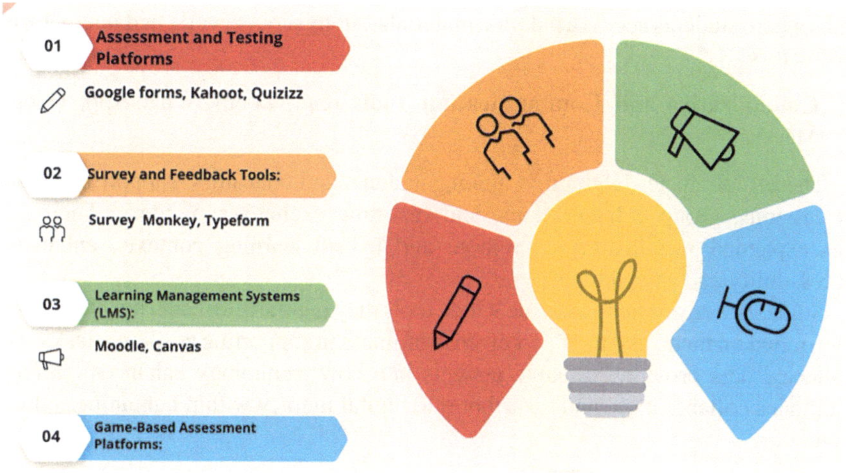

Fig. 6.2 Exploring and using software tools for evaluation [7]

6.2.1 *Overview of Software Tools Examined*

The survey instrument systematically gathered data on a diverse range of software tools frequently used in humanities education. To ensure a structured analysis, these tools were categorized into five functional groups based on their primary academic utility [8]:

1. **Word Processing and Editing Software** (e.g., Microsoft Word, Google Docs)

These tools serve as essential platforms for drafting, editing, and formatting academic work. They enable students to structure their ideas effectively, collaborate on written assignments, and refine research papers with integrated editing features.

2. **Presentation and Visualisation Tools** (e.g., PowerPoint, Prezi, Canva)

Used for delivering lectures, presentations, and creative projects, these tools enhance learning by enabling students to illustrate concepts visually. Whether through traditional slide decks or interactive media, they support engagement and knowledge dissemination.

3. **Textual Analysis and Annotation Tools** (e.g., Voyant Tools, Hypothesis)

These specialised applications facilitate deep engagement with texts by enabling linguistic analysis, keyword extraction, and collaborative annotation. Humanities students leverage them for literary studies, historical document analysis, and scholarly discourse.

4. **Learning Management Systems (LMS)** (e.g., Moodle, Canvas)

Integral to digital learning environments, LMS platforms streamline course management, content distribution, and assignment tracking. They serve as centralised hubs where students access academic materials, submit coursework, and interact with instructors.

5. **Collaborative and Communication Tools** (e.g., Zoom, WhatsApp, Google Meet)

These tools foster interaction among students and educators, supporting virtual discussions, group collaborations, and real-time exchanges of ideas. Their role has expanded significantly in remote and hybrid learning contexts, enhancing accessibility and engagement.

Students were asked to indicate which tools they regularly utilised, how frequently they relied on them, and their perceived usefulness in supporting academic tasks. The collected data provides valuable insights into how technology enhances learning, facilitates collaboration, and contributes to digital literacy within humanities education.

6.2.2 Frequency of Software Usage

"Frequency of Software Usage" is a term that describes the amount of time that students spend using a variety of digital tools in the course of their academic pursuits. Some software, like as word processing and learning management systems, may be used on a regular basis for the purpose of completing coursework. On the other hand, particular assignments or research requirements may need the utilisation of other software, such as textual analysis tools, on a less frequent basis. When educators have a better understanding of use patterns, they are better able to determine which tools are necessary for learning and where further training or assistance may be required to make the most of the efficacy of these resources. Table 6.2 shows the frequency of software tool usage among students. The data is based on the 270 student respondents from the total sample [8].

As seen in Table 6.2, word processing and collaborative tools are the most frequently used, with over 90% of students indicating daily or weekly engagement. LMSs also ranked high, reflecting their central role in course delivery and

Table 6.2 Frequency of software tool usage among students (n = 270)

Software category	Frequently used (%)	Occasionally used (%)	Rarely/never used (%)
Word processing tools	94.4	5.2	0.4
Presentation tools	71.5	24.1	4.4
Textual analysis tools	38.9	31.5	29.6
Learning management systems	88.9	9.3	1.8
Collaborative tools	91.1	6.7	2.2

resource distribution. However, textual analysis tools, while increasingly recognised in academic discourse, remain underutilised, with nearly one-third of students reporting that they have never used them.

6.2.3 Purpose of Software Tool Usage

To gain deeper insight into the reasons behind students' use of digital tools, they were asked to specify the particular academic tasks for which they employed these technologies. This analysis helps to contextualise how different software applications support various aspects of humanities education, from writing and research to collaboration and content creation. The results of this inquiry are detailed in Table 6.3, providing a comprehensive overview of tool usage patterns and their role in enhancing learning experiences (Fig. 6.3).

Table 6.3 Academic tasks supported by software tools

Academic task	Most commonly used tool(s)	% of students reporting usage
Essay writing and editing	Microsoft Word, Google Docs	96.3
Group collaboration and discussions	WhatsApp, Google Meet, Zoom	87.0
Classroom participation and attendance	LMS platforms (e.g., Moodle)	84.8
Creating presentations	PowerPoint, Canva	76.7
Annotating texts and articles	Hypothesis, Voyant Tools	42.2
Peer review and feedback	Google Docs, LMS forums	58.9
Research data visualization	Canva, Prezi, Voyant Tools	36.3

Fig. 6.3 Data analysis tools [9]

Table 6.4 Mean usefulness ratings of software tools

Software category	Mean usefulness score (out of 5)
Word processing tools	4.8
Collaborative tools	4.6
Learning management systems	4.5
Presentation tools	4.2
Textual analysis tools	3.3

The data shows a clear dominance of tools that support writing, collaboration, and presentation, aligning with the traditional modes of humanities instruction. Nevertheless, the modest use of annotation and visualisation tools suggests a gap between available technological capabilities and actual classroom integration.

6.2.4 Perceived Usefulness of Software Tools

Beyond frequency and purpose, understanding students' perceptions of usefulness offers a deeper view into adoption patterns. Respondents rated tools on a Likert scale (1 = Not Useful to 5 = Very Useful). Table 6.4 presents the aggregated mean scores for each category.

Students rated word processing and collaborative tools as the most useful, likely due to their user-friendly design and direct relevance to essential academic activities such as writing, editing, and group discussions. These tools seamlessly integrate into daily coursework, making them indispensable for managing assignments and research projects. In contrast, textual analysis tools received lower usefulness scores, which may stem from limited exposure or insufficient training in their application. Many students may not yet be familiar with the analytical capabilities of these tools, suggesting a need for more structured guidance and integration into humanities curricula to enhance their adoption and effectiveness [10].

6.2.5 Barriers to Effective Use

The results of the poll highlight a number of serious problems that students face when trying to use digital resources in their humanities classes. Limited technical training or orientation emerged as the most important obstacle, with 65 percent of respondents admitting that a lack of fundamental teaching hinders their ability to effectively use software functions. This was the most significant barrier. This indicates that there is a need for organised workshops and the incorporation of curriculum in order to foster digital literacy. The use of digital tools is further complicated by the fact that 58% of students have inconsistent internet connection. This is especially true for students who live in locations with unstable connectivity. As a result of limited internet connection, participation in online platforms, collaborative learning environments, and cloud-based applications is negatively impacted. This highlights the need of offline functionality and upgrades to institutional infrastructure. While basic platforms are easily available to a large number of people, more specialised applications, such as textual analysis and annotation tools, may not be sufficiently promoted or resourced within academic contexts. This is shown by the fact that there is a lack of institutional support for advanced tools, which accounts for 46% of the total situation. Without the support of their educational institutions, students may have difficulty gaining access to the necessary training, licenses, or technical help in order to incorporate such technologies into their academic pursuits.

Ultimately, the incompatibility of software with personal devices (29%) is an additional obstacle that students may face. This is because students may not have access to enough technology that is capable of effectively executing specific applications. In order to assist relieve this difficulty, it is possible to ensure that digital tools are flexible across a variety of operating systems and devices. These results indicate that there are problems with both the infrastructure and the teaching methods that need to be addressed in order to improve the efficiency of digital tools in the field of humanities education. Universities and other educational institutions may provide assistance to students by providing specialised training, enhancing access to dependable internet, investing in cutting-edge technologies, and ensuring that a wider range of software is compatible with one another in order to create a more immersive and seamless learning environment [11].

6.2.6 *Summary and Implications*

The data highlights a distinct contrast in students' engagement with digital tools. While basic productivity and collaborative platforms see widespread use, more specialised applications designed for textual analysis and scholarly inquiry remain underutilised. This indicates a gap in digital literacy within humanities education, particularly regarding tools that enable deeper engagement with academic content. To address this issue, a curriculum redesign that incorporates structured training in textual analysis tools is essential. By integrating these technologies into coursework, students can develop familiarity with their functionalities, allowing them to effectively apply digital methodologies in their research and studies. Without deliberate exposure, many students may continue to overlook the potential benefits of such tools. Workshops and seminars would further support skill acquisition, providing students with hands-on opportunities to explore digital tools in practical academic contexts. These initiatives could be tailored to different proficiency levels, ensuring accessibility for both beginners and advanced users. Training sessions led by experienced faculty or digital humanities specialists could help bridge the gap between theoretical understanding and practical application.

Additionally, faculty support is crucial in embedding digital tools meaningfully into assignments and research projects. Educators play a pivotal role in fostering student engagement with digital methodologies by incorporating them into coursework, demonstrating their relevance, and encouraging experimentation. When faculty actively integrate these tools into teaching, students gain a clearer understanding of their potential, making them more likely to adopt them in their academic endeavors. The next section will shift focus to faculty perspectives on digital tools. Examining their usage patterns, attitudes, and institutional approaches will provide a more comprehensive understanding of the academic ecosystem in which students operate. Insights into faculty engagement will help identify opportunities for professional development and institutional policies that can further enhance digital literacy within humanities education.

6.3 Teachers' Attitudes Toward Digital Humanities

The attitudes, capabilities, and openness of faculty members are very important factors in determining the success of the incorporation of digital technology into the humanities. Teachers are not only responsible for shaping the academic environment, but they also play a catalytic role in the adoption of technology inside their respective institutions. The purpose of this part is to investigate the prevalent attitudes that humanities faculty members have towards digital technologies and the larger area of DH. This section will evaluate both excitement and resistance, as well as the variables that impact their disposition.

6.3.1 Understanding of Digital Humanities

To assess the baseline familiarity of teachers with the field, respondents were first asked to describe their understanding of "Digital Humanities." While 88% of the 52 faculty respondents had heard the term, only 47% could provide a precise definition or example.

Table 6.5 suggests that although the term is widely recognised, substantial gaps in comprehension persist, pointing to a need for foundational training.

Table 6.5 Faculty understanding of digital humanities

Understanding level	% of respondents
Clear and accurate	47
Vague but partially correct	41
No understanding	12

Table 6.6 Attitudes toward digital integration in the humanities

Attitude level	% of respondents
Very positive (5)	21
Positive (4)	48
Neutral (3)	19
Negative (2)	9
Very negative (1)	3

General Attitudes Toward Digital Integration

When asked to rate their attitudes toward integrating digital tools in humanities teaching on a 5-point Likert scale (1 = Very Negative, 5 = Very Positive), the majority of faculty members expressed favorable views (Table 6.6).

A combined 69% of respondents indicated a positive outlook toward digital integration. This suggests a growing receptivity among humanities faculty, particularly when technologies are seen as augmenting rather than replacing traditional scholarly methods.

6.3.2 *Perceived Benefits of Digital Humanities*

The survey results reveal a strong acknowledgment among educators of the value that the DH movement brings to academic instruction. The most frequently cited benefit was enhanced student engagement and participation (76%), reflecting the role of digital tools in making humanities subjects more interactive and immersive. By integrating technology into coursework, educators can foster deeper discussions and encourage active involvement in learning. Another widely recognised advantage was access to a wider range of academic resources (63%), highlighting how DH expands the materials available to students beyond traditional texts. Digital archives, open-access platforms, and multimedia resources contribute to a more comprehensive and diverse scholarly experience.

Improved analytical and research skills through software tools (59%) reinforces the idea that DH equips students with methodologies that enhance their ability to process, interpret, and critically engage with humanities content. Whether through textual analysis, visualisation techniques, or collaborative annotation, digital tools offer new ways to conduct research. Additionally, educators acknowledged opportunities for interdisciplinary collaboration (47%), emphasising the ability of DH to bridge the humanities with fields like data science, linguistics, and social sciences. By fostering cross-disciplinary connections, students and researchers can approach humanities inquiries from multiple perspectives, enriching academic discourse. Lastly, increased flexibility in course delivery (45%) highlights the adaptability DH provides in modern education. Online tools, virtual learning environments, and digital resources enable educators to tailor instruction to diverse learning preferences and formats, making humanities education more accessible.

These findings underscore the transformative potential of DH in revitalising traditional humanities instruction. By leveraging technology for engagement, accessibility, and methodological expansion, educators can enhance the overall learning experience and prepare students for a digitally integrated academic landscape.

6.3.3 *Perceived Challenges and Limitations*

While educators broadly recognise the benefits of DH, several persistent challenges temper their enthusiasm for widespread adoption. Lack of institutional support or infrastructure (71%) remains the most cited obstacle, as many educators struggle with inadequate funding, technical resources, or administrative backing to fully implement digital tools in their teaching and research. Without sufficient investment, access to specialised software and training remains limited, hindering effective integration. Closely related, insufficient personal training or experience (66%) underscores the need for professional development initiatives that equip educators with the necessary skills to navigate digital platforms confidently. Many faculty members lack formal instruction in using DH tools, leaving them feeling unprepared to incorporate these technologies into their courses. Limited time to learn and implement new tools (58%) further exacerbates the issue, as educators often face competing demands in their workload. Balancing research, teaching responsibilities, and administrative duties makes it difficult to dedicate time to exploring and mastering new digital methodologies. Streamlining training programs and integrating digital literacy into existing faculty development efforts could alleviate this burden.

Beyond logistical barriers, scepticism about digital tools undermining deep reading or critical thought (32%) reveals a philosophical tension between traditional humanities scholarship and technological innovation. Some educators worry that reliance on digital tools may lead to superficial engagement with texts, reducing the emphasis on nuanced analysis and interpretative rigour. Addressing this concern requires thoughtful curriculum integration, demonstrating how digital tools can complement rather than replace traditional methods. These challenges are not isolated to a single institution or region but rather reflect a broader global debate about balancing tradition and innovation in the humanities. Tackling these issues through robust professional development, institutional investment, and curricular adaptation is essential for fostering a learning environment where technology enhances, rather than disrupts, humanities education.

Table 6.7 Faculty use of digital tools

Tool type	% of faculty using
Learning management systems	92
Word processing/editing software	88
Communication platforms (zoom etc.)	81
Presentation tools (PowerPoint etc.)	74
Annotation/text analysis tools	34
Data visualization tools	21

6.3.4 Faculty Use of Digital Tools

To gain insight into educators' engagement with technology, teachers were asked to identify the digital tools they used for teaching, research, or communication. This data provides a valuable perspective on how faculty incorporate digital platforms into their academic workflows, whether for instructional delivery, scholarly inquiry, or professional interactions. The results of this analysis are presented in Table 6.7, offering a detailed overview of the most commonly used tools and their applications in various academic contexts.

The majority of faculty comfortably engage with basic educational technology. However, the use of more specialised digital humanities tools such as Voyant, AntConc, or NVivo remains limited. This indicates a skills gap that inhibits deeper engagement with DH methodologies.

6.3.5 Correlation Between Training and Attitude

There is a significant association between professional development and adoption rates, as shown by the cross-tabulation study that was conducted between training exposure and faculty attitudes towards DH technologies. When compared to faculty members who had not participated in any kind of DH-related training, individuals who had participated in any kind of training displayed considerably more favourable attitudes towards digital tools and indicated greater levels of utilisation. The findings of this study imply that systematic exposure to DH approaches not only promotes familiarity with technology but also builds confidence in the use of digital resources in teaching and research. These results highlight the significance of institutional investments in faculty training, since continuous professional development has the potential to close the digital literacy gaps that exist and support a wider usage of digital health solutions. Universities are able to foster an academic atmosphere that is more digitally engaged by providing possibilities for collaborative learning, mentoring programs, and seminars that are specifically tailored to the audience. In addition, this trend highlights the need for curricular methods that integrate digital humanities training into humanities education. This will ensure that both students and teachers are able

Table 6.8 Training exposure versus positive attitude toward DH

Training received?	Positive attitude %
Yes	87
No	42

to reap the benefits of the ever-changing digital world. Increasing the effectiveness of these efforts will make it possible for educational institutions to fully capitalise on the transformational potential of DH in the realm of scholarly investigation and teaching (Table 6.8).

This correlation reinforces the importance of targeted training initiatives and professional development workshops as enablers of digital transformation in the humanities.

6.3.6 Summary and Implications

It is widely accepted that educators have a favourable attitude towards DH, since they are aware of its potential to improve scholarly work, educational practices, and cross-disciplinary cooperation. On the other hand, the broad adoption and in-depth integration of DH approaches in academic contexts continues to be hampered by structural and logistical constraints. One of the most positive aspects is the increased knowledge and responsiveness among educators, especially those who have participated in DH training. This is certainly a trend that should be encouraged. Faculty members who have participated in formal training or seminars on digital technologies have a higher level of passion and confidence when it comes to utilising these tools in their research and teaching. This demonstrates the need of ongoing professional development programs that provide educators with the information and abilities they need to make successful use of digital technology. Despite the growing interest in the topic, both the institutional infrastructure and the time restrictions continue to be significant barriers to the widespread application of the concept. As key obstacles, a number of instructors' point to restricted access to specialised software, low financing for digital resources, and inadequate technical assistance within their own schools. In addition, faculty members often struggle to find the time necessary to investigate new digital approaches in the middle of their heavy workloads, which results in reluctance to fully embrace digital technologies.

Additionally, the limited adoption of sophisticated digital tools provides additional evidence that many instructors just interact with digital humanities on a superficial level, rather than incorporating these technologies into their curriculum in a more profound manner. In spite of the fact that fundamental productivity tools and learning management systems are used daily, more specialised applications, such as textual analysis, data visualisation, and collaborative annotation platforms, continue to be underutilised. This indicates that there is a need for focused interventions, such as hands-on training sessions, curriculum restructuring, and more transparent institutional initiatives for the incorporation of digital tools. It is heartening to see that the majority of faculty members have shown a readiness to learn and adapt, given that they are provided with sufficient assistance. Because of their willingness to include DH into their instructional strategies, educational institutions have the chance to promote genuine change, which is a great opportunity. Policymakers and educational administrators have a responsibility to provide priority to methods that create capacity. These strategies should ensure that faculty members have access to the required digital resources, training programs, and institutional support. Universities can promote the effective integration of DH approaches by cultivating a culture of innovation inside their departments of humanities. This gives educators the ability to make full use of digital technology to improve teaching, research, and scholarly inquiry [12].

6.4 Impact on Critical Thinking Skills

In the field of humanities education, one of the most important concerns is the development of critical thinking, which may be defined as the capacity to analyse texts, form arguments, challenge assumptions, and interact with difficult ideas. Because digital tools are increasingly being included into educational practices, the issue arises as to whether or not these technologies contribute to the development of this fundamental ability. Utilising data from student and faculty answers, as well as supporting evidence from relevant literature and classroom observations, this section investigates the ways in which the use of software in the humanities has an impact on the development of critical thinking among students.

6.4.1 Defining Critical Thinking in the Humanities Context

The ability to engage in reflective judgement, evaluate a variety of sources and views, and synthesise complicated arguments is required of students and academics in the field of the humanities. Critical thinking is a crucial talent that goes beyond simple understanding. In addition to creating a more nuanced knowledge of texts, historical narratives, and cultural settings, it makes it possible to conduct more in-depth intellectual investigation. The ability to recognise biases and assumptions in texts is one of the most important talents connected with critical thinking in this field. This skill enables academics to critically assess the viewpoints and motives that are contained within literary works, historical narratives, and theoretical frameworks.

In addition, the process of drawing inferences and forming judgements based on evidence is an essential part of research in the humanities. This process requires researchers to examine patterns, contextual cues, and supporting data in order to arrive at well-informed findings. Interpreting meaning within cultural and historical contexts is another essential component. This kind of interpretation guarantees that writings and artefacts are understood not in isolation but rather within the larger sociological, political, and philosophical frameworks in which they were created. In addition, the practice of opposing prevailing narratives or frameworks is an essential component of humanities study. This practice encourages critical engagement with preexisting ideas and the investigation of other points of view.

Depending on its design, implementation, and pedagogical alignment, digital technologies have the potential to either facilitate or impede the processes of critical thinking. Students may connect with original sources, compare interpretations, and trace thematic trends in texts with the use of well-designed tools like as interactive annotation platforms, text analysis software, and digital archives. These tools can enable deeper research by providing students with the opportunity to engage with these primary materials. On the other hand, if digital tools place an emphasis on automated processing without also promoting analytical depth, they run the danger of oversimplifying complicated debates, which may result in interaction at a surface level rather than thorough critical examination. The incorporation of technology into humanities education must be done with careful consideration in order to guarantee that digital tools will not hinder reflective and analytical thinking but rather will improve them [6, 13].

6.4.2 Perceived Impact by Students

Students were asked whether the use of digital tools helped them think more critically about course materials. A 5-point Likert scale was used (1 = Strongly Disagree, 5 = Strongly Agree) (Table 6.9).

A combined 63% of respondents felt that software tools supported their critical thinking. This suggests that well-integrated digital platforms can positively influence analytical engagement.

Within the realm of humanities education, students have discovered several digital tools that actively stimulate critical thinking activities. Annotation tools, such as Hypotheses. is, make it possible for students to interact meaningfully with texts by marking significant concepts, raising questions, and developing linked debates. These tools also enable collaborative criticism and layered textual analysis. Through

Table 6.9 Student perceptions of software impact on critical thinking

Response category	% of students
Strongly agree (5)	22
Agree (4)	41
Neutral (3)	23
Disagree (2)	9
Strongly disagree (1)	5

the use of this participatory technique, analytical thinking is encouraged, and fuller interpretations of literary and historical texts are supported. In a similar vein, text mining software, such as Voyant Tools, is an essential component in the process of acquiring abilities in pattern recognition and hypothesis development. via the identification of recurrent themes, word frequencies, and textual structures, these techniques assist students in drawing connections that may not be immediately apparent via the use of conventional close reading. While simultaneously supporting evidence-based thinking, this strategy that is driven by data broadens the analytical options available within the field of humanities study.

By supporting organised interactions in which students dispute ideas, develop arguments, and participate in critical debate, discussion platforms further enhance dialogic thinking and encourage students to engage in critical debate. Encouraging challenge-response debates that resemble academic research and supporting critical engagement with texts and ideas, these interactive spaces contribute to the enhancement of intellectual discourse. Notwithstanding these benefits, students have voiced their worries over an excessive dependence on artificial intelligence-generated summaries and automated reading tools. They have cautioned that the use of such technologies may mistakenly hinder in-depth reading and innovative ideas. Even though automation has the potential to improve efficiency, there is a possibility that students could become unduly reliant on preprocessed interpretations rather than actively improving their ability to independently analyse information. This underscores the significance of balanced integration, which is when digital technologies complement conventional approaches rather than replacing them. This is done to ensure that technology fosters critical involvement in humanities studies rather than restricting it.

6.4.3 Faculty Perceptions and Observations

A comparable survey was administered to faculty members in order to determine their perspectives on the ways in which digital technologies impact the critical thinking abilities of students. Many educators noted both the potential advantages and the problems connected with incorporating digital technologies into humanities teaching, despite the fact that the replies expressed a cautious optimism. Several members of the teaching staff brought attention to the fact that technology has the potential to improve analytical thinking by supplying students with interactive platforms capable of textual analysis, annotation, and debate. Nevertheless, there are many who have voiced their worries over the potential for an excessive dependence on automated technologies, which may result in a diminished capacity for critical thinking and deeper engagement with intricate arguments. In general, the results indicate that while digital tools have the potential to facilitate intellectual inquiry, their efficacy is contingent upon their careful incorporation into educational practices and enough training to guarantee that they are used in a meaningful manner (Table 6.10).

Table 6.10 Faculty perceptions of software's influence on critical thinking

Perception	% of faculty
Strongly positive	17
Moderately positive	38
Neutral	24
Moderately negative	13
Strongly negative	8

While 55% expressed positive views, many stressed that the pedagogical approach determines the impact more than the tool itself. For instance, a teacher using a digital forum to facilitate Socratic questioning may encourage deeper thinking, whereas using a discussion board solely for administrative updates yields little cognitive benefit.

6.4.4 Qualitative Insights from Open-Ended Responses

In order to gain a more in-depth understanding of how digital tools impact student learning and faculty perspectives, open-ended survey responses and follow-up interviews were conducted. These procedures revealed several key themes. There was a significant rise in student autonomy, especially among those who used visualisation tools like Gephi and TimelineJS. This was a noteworthy discovery. Students have claimed that they had a sense of empowerment, which enabled them to autonomously identify connections between historical and literary events, so strengthening their ability to rationally infer. Learners were able to establish meaningful linkages between difficult ideas with the help of these tools, which made pattern detection and topic exploration much easier.

The facilitation of multi-perspective study via the use of digital archives and interactive texts was another key topic that emerged. The students were encouraged to engage with a variety of voices and interpretations, which drove them to do comparative analysis. This process helped them improve their capacity to critically analyse a variety of academic and historical perspectives. The development of analytical depth was facilitated by exposure to a wide variety of sources, particularly in fields where textual interpretation plays a central role. On the other hand, a few members of the faculty voiced their concerns about cognitive offloading, particularly in relation to tools that offer instant access to summaries or keyword highlights. In spite of the fact that these features make research and comprehension easier, there are educators who are concerned that relying on automated summaries may discourage students from engaging deeply with the original texts. Over the course of time, this change may have the effect of weakening the critical thinking abilities of students by diminishing their willingness to engage with difficult arguments and interpretations in a direct manner. The implications of these results highlight both the advantages and the difficulties associated with using digital technologies into humanities instruction.

It is necessary to employ careful pedagogical strategies in order to guarantee that students continue to maintain a strong critical engagement with foundational texts and primary sources, despite the fact that technology has the potential to improve students' autonomy and analytical thinking.

6.4.5 Case Study: Using Voyant Tools for Textual Analysis

The integration of Voyant Tools into literature studies provided a compelling example of how digital methodologies can enhance textual analysis and critical engagement. By examining frequent terms, correlations, and distinctive keywords across post-colonial works by Chinua Achebe and Ngũgĩ wa Thiong'o, students gained fresh perspectives on thematic patterns that might have gone unnoticed through traditional reading alone. One of the most significant outcomes of this intervention was the increase in peer discussion surrounding authorial voice and narrative power. The ability to visually track language patterns led students to debate how each author constructed meaning, reinforcing collaborative interpretation and deeper analytical reasoning [14].

Additionally, the tool facilitated the discovery of sub-themes that were not emphasised in textbook curricula. By uncovering recurring linguistic patterns and conceptual relationships, students expanded their understanding of postcolonial narratives beyond prescribed frameworks, enriching their engagement with the texts. Perhaps most notably, the experience resulted in richer final essays, where students successfully blended computational insights with traditional literary analysis. By integrating both digital findings and close-reading techniques, they produced more nuanced and evidence-based interpretations, demonstrating the potential for digital tools to complement rather than replace traditional humanities methodologies. This example underscores how thoughtful integration of digital tools can foster deeper intellectual engagement, enhance interdisciplinary approaches, and empower students to explore literature through both computational and traditional analytical lenses [15].

6.4.6 Challenges and Cautions

There are a number of challenges that need to be carefully addressed in order to maximise the effectiveness of digital tools in humanities education, even though the integration of digital tools has demonstrated beneficial outcomes. Students may concentrate solely on word frequency counts or visual graphs without interacting thoroughly with the underlying themes and meanings in a book, which is one of the primary concerns that arises from an excessive dependence on surface elements. In spite of the fact that digital analysis has the potential to provide useful insights, it must be combined with interpretative reasoning in order to guarantee that students go beyond quantitative observations and into more nuanced and comprehensive comprehension. Furthermore, there is a risk of tool fatigue, which occurs when an excessive or redundant use of software enables digital tools to transform from learning aids into distractions. When students are obliged to interact with digital tools in a manner that is repetitive or when they are exposed to an excessive number of platforms, the novelty of technology engagement may wane, which in turn reduces the overall efficacy of the learning experience. For the purpose of maintaining engagement without overwhelming learners, careful selection and purposeful integration of software can be of great assistance [16].

As a result of the fact that students who have not previously been exposed to digital tools may experience initial difficulties in adopting new technologies, equity concerns continue to be an important consideration. It is possible that this gap in digital literacy will lead to disparities in learning outcomes, which will create barriers for individuals who require additional time or support in order to become proficient users. Educational institutions must prioritise organised, scaffolded learning that progressively introduces digital technologies while simultaneously ensuring that all students get enough advice and resources in order to effectively handle this problem. At the end of the day, these problems bring to light the need for deliberate pedagogical design, which emphasises the relevance of aligning the use of technology with critical thinking goals. Teachers are able to create an atmosphere in which students may actively interact with both conventional and computational methods in humanities studies if they deliberately incorporate digital tools into their classrooms.

6.4.7 Recommendations for Enhancing Critical Thinking via Digital Tools

In order to maximise the use of digital technologies in humanities education while maintaining critical engagement, the results suggest a number of recommended practices. To begin, it is of the utmost importance to incorporate critical questions into digital activities. This will ensure that students actively interpret and analyse visualisations, rather than simply generating them. As an instance, rather than only recognising word frequency patterns in a textual analysis tool, students should be encouraged to investigate the underlying meanings, historical contexts, and thematic implications that are associated with such patterns. To continue, digital tools should not be used in lieu of careful reading and debate; rather, they should serve as complements to these activities. Despite the fact that digital platforms provide significant analytical skills, they should not be allowed to subsume more conventional approaches in the field of humanities. In order to maintain a balanced approach to learning, it is helpful to encourage students to interact with source materials, debate interpretations, and critically evaluate computational discoveries [6].

In addition, it is essential to have guidance on how to evaluate digital content, particularly with regard to the reliability of sources, the accuracy of representation, and the influence of algorithmic bias. Students should be provided with frameworks that allow them to evaluate the authenticity of digital resources, identify bias in automated studies, and comprehend how data visualisation might influence how people perceive a text or historical event. Educators should teach these frameworks to students. To conclude, the incorporation of reflection activities following the utilisation of digital tools is a means of fostering metacognition, which enables students to critically evaluate their own learning processes. An increased level of engagement with both the methodology and the subject matter can be reinforced through the use of discussions or written reflections on the ways in which digital tools influenced their interpretations. Through the implementation of these best practices, educators have the ability to guarantee that the critical thinking abilities that are the core of humanities education are strengthened rather than diminished by the use of digital resources [17].

6.5 Summary and Implications

Digital technologies have the potential to improve students' critical thinking in the humanities when they are utilised in a responsible manner and with the intention of educating them. Software has the potential to deepen inquiry, encourage new interpretative tactics, and enhance intellectual autonomy. This is in contrast to the conventional skills that it was designed to replace. Nevertheless, their efficacy is dependent on the incorporation of conscious integration, the availability of training, and the implementation of continuing evaluations of learning results.

6.6 Collaboration and Communication Patterns

In the field of humanities, one of the distinguishing characteristics of digital pedagogy is its capacity to revolutionise the ways in which students and instructors work together and interact with one another. The patterns, frequency, and efficacy of communication have altered as a result of the incorporation of software tools into academic environments. These changes have occurred not just among student groups but also between students and instructors. These shifts are investigated in this part, along with an analysis of how digital platforms are reshaping the dynamics of cooperation in the field of humanities education.

6.6.1 Traditional Versus Digital Communication Paradigms

Traditional forms of academic contact have been expanded by the emergence of digital instruments, which has drastically altered communication in humanities education. Although seminar-style talks, one-on-one coaching, and written exchanges have been used for a long time to cultivate depth and critical reasoning, the incorporation of digital platforms has provided new chances for cooperation and accessibility. Both asynchronous and synchronous discussion boards and forums Students are able to participate in prolonged intellectual engagement beyond the hours that they are in the classroom because to platforms such as Moodle, Canvas, and Blackboard. These platforms facilitate deliberate analysis and organised discussion. Learners are able to give their insights at their own speed while participating in reflective interactions that are promoted by these platforms. Real-time collaborative writing tools, such as Google Docs and Overleaf, simplify the process of working in groups by allowing numerous users to concurrently edit and revise texts. The enhanced co-authorship, peer review, and joint research development that results from this real-time interaction transforms the process of academic writing into one that is more dynamic and collaborative. Instant communication has been included into academic processes via the use of messaging and chat programs such as Microsoft Teams and Slack. These services have enabled fast conversations, the sharing of resources, and team-based cooperation within the academia. In order to facilitate the development of ideas in a more expedient manner, these platforms bridge the gap between academic and informal learning environments [18].

In the framework of contemporary humanities education, video conferencing platforms like as Zoom and Google Meet have become an essential component, especially in the context of distant and hybrid learning environments. These platforms maintain the seminar-style interaction while simultaneously broadening participation beyond physical borders. They do this by supporting live discussions, guest lectures, and multidisciplinary exchanges. Platforms for annotation and discussion, such as Hypothesis, encourage layered textual interaction by enabling users to highlight, remark on, and analyse texts in a collaborative manner. By offering students with interactive places in which they may analyse literary and historical works with contextual insights, these technologies provide an enhancement to the practice of deep reading. When used in conjunction with one another, these digital technologies transform communication from conversations led by instructors to exchanges that are more collaborative and peer-driven. This results in knowledge generation that is both more dynamic and more accessible. In the process of navigating this shift, instructors in the humanities have the task of striking a balance between conventional approaches and digital innovation in order to guarantee that critical debate continues to be rich and substantial [19].

6.6.2 Student-To-Student Collaboration

The survey revealed that most students found software tools beneficial for working collaboratively on projects, preparing presentations, and engaging in peer reviews. When asked about the frequency of digital collaboration in their coursework (Table 6.11):

A majority (73%) of students reported collaborating with peers at least occasionally through digital means. Collaboration was most often enabled through shared document tools and threaded discussion platforms, particularly when completing group assignments or preparing co-authored essays.

Responses that were open-ended brought to light a number of benefits that collaborative platforms offer in the field of humanities education. These tools, according to a number of students, encouraged more egalitarian discussion, which was especially beneficial for introverted students who might be reluctant to speak up in traditional classroom settings. Both asynchronous contributions and structured online exchanges were made possible by these platforms, which resulted in the creation of an environment that was more welcoming to a variety of perspectives. In addition, they improved the efficiency of scheduling and document sharing, which simplified the process of group coordination and ensured that academic materials were accessible without any interruptions. The presence of revision histories, which provided transparency in collaborative work by tracking individual contributions over time, was another benefit that was widely recognised and appreciated by the community. With the help of this feature, students were able to participate in iterative learning, which allowed them to refine their ideas while still maintaining accountability within group projects. Nevertheless, a number of students have reported experiencing challenges, such as unequal participation and ambiguity in shared responsibilities, with certain members contributing significantly more than others. The aforementioned concerns bring to light the necessity of establishing more transparent protocols for task delegation and developing peer evaluation strategies in order to guarantee equitable participation and accountability. When these challenges are addressed through the implementation of structured guidelines and the supervision of faculty, it is possible to maximise the effectiveness of collaborative platforms while simultaneously maintaining equitable engagement among students [20].

Table 6.11 Frequency of digital peer collaboration

Collaboration frequency	% of students
Frequently	39
Occasionally	34
Rarely	18
Never	9

6.6.3 Teacher-To-Student Communication

Digital platforms have reshaped how instructors interact with students. Teachers reported more consistent, if not always deeper, contact with students due to messaging apps, email alerts, and virtual office hours. The accessibility of instructors via digital platforms encouraged students to seek clarification and guidance more frequently (Table 6.12).

The findings of the poll reveal that the vast majority of students, which accounts for 74% of the total, were content with the digital contact that they got from their teachers. They cited responsiveness and clear feedback as two of the most important benefits. The ability of digital platforms to expedite interactions, provide timely updates, and provide organised replies that assisted students in their learning experience was something that many students really liked. On the other hand, qualitative feedback brought to light a number of difficulties associated with digital communication. One of the issues that was often brought up was the impersonal tone that was used in written conversations, which sometimes resulted in misunderstandings or incorrect interpretations. Students discovered that some communications lacked warmth or clarity, making it more difficult to comprehend the intended meaning. This was due to the fact that they did not have the subtlety of face-to-face conversation. Delays in answers during high-volume times, such as test seasons, when teachers were confronted with an overwhelming quantity of enquiries, was another problem that was caused by the situation. The students' capacity to get timely explanation on their coursework or tests was negatively impacted as a result of this occasion-specific communication delay [21].

In addition, students reported experiencing "message overload," which was characterised by frequent updates and various alerts that made it impossible to differentiate between information that was of higher significance. When there was an excessive amount of communication, it might sometimes lead to confusion, with important updates being overlooked in favour of ones that were less important. These discoveries highlight the need of strategic communication methods, which ensure that digital interactions continue to be efficient while also maintaining a personal quality. Helping to reduce these challenges and improving the overall efficacy of digital communication in academic contexts may be accomplished through the implementation of structured norms on response times, clearer message protocols, and the insertion of personalised feedback.

Table 6.12 Student satisfaction with instructor communication

Satisfaction level	% of students
Very satisfied	28
Satisfied	46
Neutral	17
Dissatisfied	6
Very dissatisfied	3

6.6.4 Case Study: Collaborative Literary Analysis via Google Docs

In a comparative literature course that was taken by students in their third year, they participated in a structured digital collaboration using Google Docs. They analysed a particular work using a colour-coded annotation system. A full analysis of the literary work was ensured by assigning each member of the team a specialised analytical job, such as a theme tracker, an analyst of the historical background, an observer of character development, and a critic of rhetorical approach. Due to the fact that students actively submitted comments and replied to the insights of their classmates, this strategy successfully promoted high levels of engagement, which in turn enhanced collaborative conversation. Students were able to uncover patterns and thematic linkages that they may have missed in their solo research because they were able to cross-reference their observations, which led to a deeper and more integrated understanding. Another notable benefit was the enhancement of final submissions, which occurred as a result of students refining their interpretations via the process of communal editing prior to handing in their work. The architecture of the shared document allowed for repeated updating, which ensured that the arguments were well-developed and backed by a variety of views.

Particularly noteworthy is the fact that the teacher saw that students who were more reserved engaged more actively in the online format than they did in the conventional seminar settings. The asynchronous and textual nature of Google Docs significantly decreased the amount of social pressure that these students were under, which allowed them to freely and meaningfully offer their opinions, so improving the entire debate. This particular scenario demonstrates how the use of digital technologies may improve literary analysis, encourage involvement from a wider range of people, and encourage a more profound level of engagement in comparative literature studies.

6.6.5 Communication Inequalities and Digital Divide

The digital gap is something that has to be addressed in this part since, despite the numerous advantages of digital cooperation, it would be incomplete without it. It was more difficult for students to completely participate in collaborative work when they had restricted access to gadgets, steady internet, or quiet workplaces. According to the instructors, there are other challenges associated with maintaining synchronous connection with students who are located in various time zones or who have differing levels of technical proficiency. Furthermore, digital communication may often result in uncertainties about tone, meaning, and urgency. These are challenges that are especially pertinent in fields that place an emphasis on interpretative subtlety and dialogic involvement.

6.6.6 Patterns of Communication by Discipline

Digital tool utilisation is most successful when it aligns with each field's methodological standards, according to the research, which indicated considerable variances in cooperation patterns across various humanities fields.

Students who are majoring in History and Philosophy have shown a high preference for collaborative annotation tools and archive platforms. This choice is a reflection of the students' concentration on textual analysis, historical documentation, and source interpretation. They were able to participate in thorough discussion, cross-reference historical tales, and evaluate philosophical ideas in a collaborative manner because to the resources that were available to them. In contrast, students who were majoring in Language and Literature were regularly involved in collaborative creative writing activities and peer evaluations, which demonstrated the participatory aspect of literary studies. Through participation in these activities, students were able to improve their writing by receiving criticism, experiment with different stylistic strategies, and investigate collaborative storytelling, all of which served to reinforce conventional literary processes. The students of Cultural Studies, on the other hand, reported a high level of interaction with discussion boards and media-sharing programs, which made it easier for them to conduct a joint study of digital artefacts such as films, social media trends, and current cultural texts. Students were able to evaluate representations, compare perceptions, and place digital media within wider sociocultural frameworks thanks to the platforms that facilitated dynamic interactions through which they could conduct these activities.

These discrepancies bring to light the significance of "discipline-specific digital integration," which involves ensuring that software tools complement existing academic processes rather than imposing a single methodology that is applicable to all situations. Teachers are able to retain the integrity of humanities inquiry while embracing technology changes if they customise digital resources to each field's key analytical methodologies. This allows them to increase student engagement, improve research outputs, and maintain the integrity of digital resources [22] (Table 6.13).

Table 6.13 Preferred collaboration tools by discipline

Discipline	Common tools used
Literature	Google Docs, Hypothesis, Padlet
History	TimelineJS, Tiki-Toki, shared folders
Philosophy	Slack threads, discussion boards, Roam
Cultural studies	YouTube, Padlet, social media archives

6.6.7 *Best Practices for Facilitating Digital Collaboration*

The results of surveys and the academic literature have led to the development of a number of tactics that may be used in digital learning environments to improve the effectiveness of communication and cooperation. During group work in digital environments, one of the most important approaches is to define clearly defined responsibilities and expectations for each participant. When students are given distinct duties, such as facilitator, summariser, or analyser, collaborative efforts become more organised and egalitarian, hence minimising uncertainty in tasks that are shared by several students. A further benefit of using structured prompts is that they may assist in directing online conversations towards a more in-depth analytical involvement. Well-designed prompts enable students to critically interact with readings, offer important questions, and synthesise multiple views. This is in contrast to the situation in which conversations are allowed to become surface-level exchanges.

The early introduction of training sessions on digital tools is another significant tactic. This should be done to ensure that students get comfortable with technology before they engage in more difficult projects. Increased digital literacy may be achieved via the provision of hands-on workshops or introductory modules. This helps to reduce frustration or unequal participation that may be caused by a lack of expertise. In addition, educators have the ability to serve as an example for good communication by using feedback techniques that are both inclusive and reflective, and it is these ways that inspire meaningful conversation. When teachers demonstrate constructive criticism and genuinely engage with the ideas of their students, they establish a norm for online interactions that are courteous and engaging. When it comes down to it, digital technologies are most effective when they serve as facilitators of dialogic learning, facilitating meaningful discussions, rather than just acting as stores of material or organisers of tasks. Enhanced cooperation, increased engagement, and sustained critical inquiry are all outcomes that may be achieved via the smart use of these technologies in humanities teaching [23].

6.7 Summary and Future Outlook

Collaboration and communication patterns in the field of humanities education have been considerably impacted as a result of the use of software technologies. As a result of these modifications, participation is more likely to become democratic, more flexible ways of involvement are provided, and access to feedback and the development of shared knowledge is enhanced. On the other hand, they also bring forth new difficulties in terms of digital literacy, the clarity of communication, and equal access. In the future, educators will need to take into consideration both the affordances and the restrictions of digital technologies in order to cultivate collaborative settings in the humanities classroom that are inclusive, dynamic, and critically engaged.

6.8 Engagement and Motivation Indicators

In the humanities, where critical thinking, introspection, and interpretation play a pivotal role, student interest and drive are paramount in determining the success of any given learning endeavour. The incorporation of software tools into the field of humanities education has resulted in the addition of new aspects related to the measurement of engagement and the ways in which motivation may be maintained or improved. The purpose of this section is to investigate the many measures of student involvement and motivation in digitally enabled humanities learning. Emphasis is placed on empirical results, theoretical frameworks, and student experiences.

6.8.1 Conceptualising Engagement in the Digital Humanities Classroom

Engagement in digital learning environments typically encompasses three interrelated dimensions, each contributing to the overall effectiveness of technology-enhanced education:

1. **Behavioural engagement**: This refers to students' participation in activities such as online discussions, assignment submissions, and collaborative projects. Digital platforms facilitate behavioural engagement by providing interactive spaces for communication, structured workflows for academic tasks, and tools that enable real-time collaboration. When implemented effectively, features such as discussion boards, interactive content, and peer-review mechanisms encourage active involvement in learning activities. However, poorly designed or overly complex digital environments may discourage participation, leading to disengagement or reduced interaction among students.
2. **Cognitive engagement**: This dimension reflects students' investment in understanding course material, developing critical thinking skills, and applying metacognitive strategies. Digital tools can enhance cognitive engagement through features like adaptive learning systems, personalised feedback mechanisms, and multimedia content that supports diverse learning styles. For instance, annotation platforms, textual analysis tools, and interactive simulations encourage deeper intellectual engagement by prompting students to analyse and synthesise information actively. Conversely, when technology prioritizes passive consumption such as automated summaries or superficial quiz-based assessments it may limit opportunities for complex reasoning and independent thought.
3. **Emotional engagement**: Students' affective reactions to digital learning environments including feelings of interest, enjoyment, frustration, or anxiety play a crucial role in their overall learning experience. User-friendly and visually engaging digital tools can foster positive emotional engagement by making content accessible and stimulating curiosity. Features such as gamification, interactive storytelling, and collaborative social spaces can promote enthusiasm

and motivation. However, technical issues, impersonal automated feedback, or an overwhelming volume of digital tasks may contribute to anxiety or disengagement. Ensuring supportive instructor presence and designing emotionally responsive learning environments can mitigate these challenges.

Digital tools can either enhance or hinder engagement in each of these domains depending on their implementation, accessibility, and alignment with pedagogical goals. Thoughtful integration where technology complements traditional learning strategies rather than replacing them ensures that students remain actively, cognitively, and emotionally engaged throughout their educational experiences. Institutions and educators must continually evaluate digital tools to strike a balance that fosters meaningful learning while addressing potential barriers to engagement.

6.8.2 Indicators of Engagement Through Software Analytics

Educators now have access to significant insights regarding participation and interaction patterns because to the fact that digital learning platforms now give quantitative measures of student engagement via comprehensive usage statistics. One typical indicator is called "log-in frequency," and it may be used to monitor the number of times students use the platform. Constant involvement may be indicated by frequent log-ins, while infrequent use may suggest disengagement or hurdles to access. The amount of time that students spend on platforms or certain modules is another important metric that helps teachers determine whether or not their students are actively engaging with the content of the course or if they are just skimming it. Spending a significant amount of time on complicated modules may indicate that the module has been thoroughly explored, whilst shorter interactions may indicate that there is a need for more engagement tactics [24].

The number of individuals that actively participate in online conversations may be determined by the number of posts and comments that are made in discussion forums. Students' eagerness to contribute to academic debate, react to peer insights, and exchange viewpoints in collaborative learning settings is reflected in the high level of involvement they exhibit in online forums. Furthermore, the interactions that students have with multimedia resources, such as watching videos and participating in annotation activities, provide further insights on the ways in which students interact with a variety of material types. It is possible for educators to improve the design of digital courses by adapting them to the interests and learning styles of students by conducting an analysis of which materials get the most engagement. Despite the fact that these indicators provide valuable engagement metrics, it is essential to interpret them within the context of a more comprehensive educational setting. Effective learning extends beyond the collection of numerical data and requires qualitative monitoring of student comprehension, the quality of interactions, and overall academic advancement. In order to guarantee that digital technologies contribute

Table 6.14 Average weekly student engagement metrics

Indicator	Mean value (per student)
Log-ins to LMS (e.g., Moodle)	4.2 times
Discussion board posts	3.6 posts
Collaborative document edits	7.4 edits
Video lectures viewed	2.8 sessions

to more profound learning experiences, it is necessary to strike a balance between measured engagement and genuine involvement [25] (Table 6.14).

These metrics, while not capturing the full depth of engagement, provide insights into students' behavioral patterns. Educators have increasingly relied on dashboards and analytics to identify students at risk of disengagement and to intervene early.

6.8.3 Self-reported Motivation Levels

A combination of qualitative and quantitative insights on the ways in which digital technologies impact student motivation were obtained via the use of surveys and focus groups. It is important to note that when students were questioned about their experiences, 62% of them said that the use of software tools boosted their interest in the contents that were being taught. This highlights the potential for technology to improve engagement and make learning more participatory. On the other hand, 21% of respondents said that their motivation had not altered, which suggests that while digital tools are advantageous for many people, the usefulness of these tools may differ depending on the preferences of individual learners. Additionally, 17% of respondents said that software sometimes led to distractions or decreased attention, pointing to difficulties such as an excessive amount of information or a dependence on automated functions that might potentially impede substantial participation. When students were able to bookmark significant information, highlight crucial sections, and adjust their study experience to their own requirements, they reported feeling the most motivated. It was when digital tools facilitated personalised learning that they felt most driven. Progress visualisation elements, such as success badges and completion bars, were also helpful in keeping motivation. These features offered visible signs of progress, which reinforced a feeling of accomplishment and helped maintain motivation. Students' attention was maintained via the use of interactive engagement mechanisms such as quizzes with fast feedback and live polls. These mechanisms encouraged active involvement and provided immediate reinforcement of ideas, which helped students maintain their interest [26].

Based on these results, it seems that digital tools have the potential to be strong motivators; nevertheless, their usefulness is contingent upon their implementation being intelligent and aligned with a variety of various learning preferences. The developing of technology that strikes a balance between personalisation, interaction,

Table 6.15 Student attitudes toward gamified features

Gamification feature	% who found it motivating
Badges and certifications	48
Leaderboards	33
Progress tracking bars	66
Unlockable content	39

and the delivery of important material in order to enhance student achievement is one way for educators and developers to maximise student engagement.

6.8.4 *Gamification and Motivation*

Learning systems that include gamified components, such as incentives, leaderboards, and badges, were investigated for their potential to serve as motivators (Table 6.15).

While not universally embraced, gamification appealed particularly to students who appreciated visible markers of achievement and a sense of progression. However, humanities instructors cautioned that gamification should not replace deeper engagement with material and must be meaningfully integrated into content design.

6.8.5 *Autonomy, Mastery, and Purpose in Digital Humanities*

Motivation in the digital humanities context can be effectively analysed through Self-Determination Theory (SDT), which highlights three fundamental psychological needs that drive engagement and learning:

1. **Autonomy**: The ability to control one's learning path is a key factor in sustaining motivation. Digital platforms enhance autonomy by offering asynchronous learning options, personalised content selection, and customisable study environments. Students can navigate materials at their own pace, select resources that align with their interests, and engage with texts in a manner suited to their learning preferences.
2. **Mastery**: Developing competence through challenging tasks and structured feedback is central to motivation. Digital tools support mastery by facilitating scaffolded learning experiences, where tasks progress in complexity and students receive real-time feedback on their performance. Features such as interactive quizzes, textual analysis software, and peer review platforms allow learners to refine their skills incrementally, reinforcing confidence in their analytical abilities.

3. **Purpose**: Connecting academic work to broader personal or societal values ensures sustained engagement. Digital humanities platforms foster purpose by enabling students to contribute to meaningful, real-world projects, such as annotating public texts, blogging about research findings, or adding insights to digital archives. These activities allow students to see their intellectual efforts reflected in public discourse, enhancing the relevance of their studies beyond the classroom.

By aligning digital tools with these motivational principles, educators can create learning environments that empower students, encourage skill development, and promote meaningful academic contributions. Thoughtful integration of digital methodologies ensures that students remain engaged not only through convenience but also through intellectual challenge and purposeful exploration.

6.8.6 Student Voices: Motivation in Practice

Several significant motivating aspects that boosted students' engagement with digital learning tools were emphasised in the testimonials provided by students. The act of having their contributions publicly exhibited, whether via annotations on collaborative platforms or blog entries shared within academic communities, was one of the factors that was noted the most often. A feeling of success was offered to them as a result of the exposure of their work, which also served to reinforce their involvement in intellectual debate and encourage a deeper engagement with the themes covered in the course. Receiving feedback in a timely manner and in a personalised manner via the use of platforms such as Turnitin and Hypotheses. Is was another significant element. The students were able to improve their analytical and writing abilities via the use of immediate and thorough replies, which made the learning process more engaging and dynamic altogether. The feedback methods that gave positive remarks that were targeted to the individual's strengths and areas for growth were highly welcomed since they promoted the ongoing development of skills.

Furthermore, one of the most important factors in maintaining motivation was the participation in peer conversations and receiving affirmation. Students were able to put their ideas to the test, obtain validation from their classmates, and develop their opinions via constructive discourse when they participated in collaborative chats. Students were more involved in both their own contributions and the insights given by others as a result of the social side of digital learning, which promoted a deeper sense of academic community. The testimonies shown here highlight the fact that digital tools are most successful when they are able to provide an engaged and fulfilling learning experience for students. This is an atmosphere in which students feel recognised, supported, and linked to their academic contexts. It is possible for educators and institutions to ensure that technology in humanities education complements rather than replaces conventional motivating factors by increasing visibility, providing prompt feedback, and facilitating meaningful peer engagement.

One student commented:

"Being able to annotate a text in real time with my classmates made me feel like my voice mattered it was almost like co-authoring something together."

Another noted:

"I like that I can track my progress and see what I've completed. It keeps me going."

Such comments illustrate the interplay between digital visibility, peer interaction, and motivation.

6.8.7 Challenges to Engagement

There are a number of obstacles that, if not handled properly, might prevent students from being motivated and engaged even if digital technologies provide many benefits for learning. One of the most significant concerns is the over dependence on passive methods, such as video lectures that do not include any kind of interaction. When students are merely ingesting information without any chances for involvement, such as discussion prompts, interactive quizzes, or collaborative projects, it is possible that their interest and investment in the topic may decrease. In order to ensure that digital content encourages participation rather than merely observing, it is necessary to incorporate active learning strategies. The occurrence of cognitive overload is yet another obstacle that may be brought about by inadequate interface design or the fragmentation of tools. It is possible for students to have feelings of being overwhelmed when they are asked to traverse various platforms that have inconsistent layouts, an excessive number of alerts, or confusing procedures. This may have a detrimental influence on their ability to remember and apply knowledge. It is possible to alleviate these worries by integrating platforms with careful consideration and streamlining user interfaces. This will ensure that digital tools contribute to the learning process rather than making it more difficult.

Due to the fact that pupils who have had minimal previous exposure to technology may have difficulty properly navigating digital platforms, unequal digital literacy is another key concern that has to be addressed. As a result of this imbalance, engagement is discouraged, and possible disparities in learning outcomes are created. The incorporation of beginning training sessions, the provision of easily available support materials, and the cultivation of an inclusive learning environment that allows students with varied degrees of digital competence to achieve success are all ways in which educators may address this problem.

Ultimately, monotony in digital activities, which might include exercises that are repeated, forms that are predictable, or a lack of interactive aspects, can eventually cause students to lose interest in the material. In situations where there is a lack of variation in the learning process, students may get disengaged and see digital technologies as mechanical rather than dynamic. It is possible to maintain student engagement and encourage deeper exploration of concepts by incorporating a variety of activities into the classroom. Some examples of these activities include interactive simulations, gamified challenges, and creative assignments. Instructors need to find a way to strike a balance between novelty and overload in order to make the most of the usefulness of digital technologies. This must be done in order to ensure that technology increases student engagement without overloading them. The use of organised advice helps to guarantee that digital learning continues to be coherent and accessible, while variety, intelligent integration, and user-friendly design all contribute to the maintenance of individual motivation. By negotiating these hurdles carefully, educators may harness the full potential of digital technologies to create meaningful and engaging learning experiences [27].

6.8.8 Best Practices for Fostering Engagement

Through the use of tactics that are geared to suit various learning preferences while simultaneously cultivating an atmosphere that is participatory and supportive, engagement in digital humanities contexts may flourish. The combination of synchronous and asynchronous formats enables real-time collaboration as well as autonomous exploration. This ensures that participants are able to keep a connection while still having the option to interact at their own speed. Via the use of low-stakes interactive exercises, confidence may be built via the encouragement of exploration and engagement without the fear of being evaluated through high-pressure situations. The use of multimedia and multimodal texts enhances the learning experience by catering to a variety of cognitive types. This makes the information more accessible and engaging for the learner. Furthermore, frequent formative evaluations provide continual feedback, which has the effect of reinforcing motivation and promoting continued progress. The combination of these tactics results in the establishment of a rhythm of involvement that reduces the likelihood of disengagement and produces a dynamic and inclusive environment for learning and cooperation.

6.9 Summary and Implications

After careful consideration, the use of digital platforms has the potential to dramatically increase student enthusiasm and involvement in the field of humanities. The ability to create dynamic learning environments that not only keep students' attention but also deepen their intellectual involvement may be achieved by educators via the alignment of technology affordances with pedagogical goals. This can be accomplished through gamification, feedback, personalisation, and social presence practices. On the other hand, creating engagement is not only about deploying technologies; rather, it is about developing an environment that is learner-centred, where motivation is inherent, where collaboration is real, and where learning is meaningful.

6.10 Challenges Encountered in Software Use

The introduction of digital resources in humanities education is often fraught with difficulties, despite the fact that these tools have the potential to completely alter the field. Educators and students alike are impacted by these obstacles, which cover a variety of areas including technological, pedagogical, infrastructureal, and psychological aspects. Utilising survey data, educator testimonials, and institutional case studies, this part offers a complete overview of the challenges that have been faced in the process of adopting and making efficient use of software in classrooms that are dedicated to the study of humanities fields.

6.10.1 Technological Barriers

Technical challenges emerged as a significant impediment to seamless software integration, affecting both accessibility and functionality in digital learning environments.

1. **Device limitations**: Many students relied on mobile phones with limited processing power and storage, restricting their ability to run feature-rich applications or handle large files efficiently. Older devices also lacked support for newer software updates, further complicating usability.
2. **Software compatibility**: Some digital tools were incompatible with widely used operating systems or browsers, leading to accessibility issues and frustration. This incompatibility often required time-consuming troubleshooting or alternative workarounds, hindering the learning experience.
3. **Internet reliability**: Inconsistent or slow internet connections, particularly in rural or under-resourced areas, disrupted real-time collaboration and access to cloud-based platforms. Bandwidth limitations made activities such as video conferencing, file sharing, and interactive online sessions challenging, diminishing engagement and productivity.

Addressing these challenges requires adaptive solutions such as optimizing software for lower-spec devices, ensuring cross-platform compatibility, and improving infrastructure to support stable internet connectivity (Table 6.16).

Table 6.16 Common technological issues reported by students

Challenge	Respondents affected %
Poor or unstable internet connection	63
Incompatible device/browser	47
Software crashes or bugs	39
Lack of access to licensed tools	34

6.10.2 Digital Literacy Gaps

Digital fluency varied considerably among both students and educators, creating disparities in the effective use of digital tools for academic purposes.

1. **Student side**: While many students were proficient in navigating social media and mobile applications, fewer had experience with specialised academic platforms such as Voyant, AntConc, or Zotero. The lack of familiarity with these tools often led to underutilisation or inefficient research practices, limiting the full potential of digital resources in their studies.
2. **Educator side**: Some faculty members struggled with confidence or lacked formal training in integrating digital tools into their curriculum. This gap resulted in either limited use of technology in teaching or a misalignment between digital resources and pedagogical objectives, reducing their effectiveness in enhancing learning outcomes.

This digital divide frequently necessitated additional support services, such as workshops, tutorials, and peer mentoring. However, access to such resources was inconsistent across institutions, leaving many educators and students without the necessary guidance to bridge the gap effectively.

6.10.3 Pedagogical Misalignment

Effective software integration in pedagogical frameworks requires a strategic approach to ensure meaningful engagement and learning enhancement. However, several challenges emerged that hindered its full potential.

1. **Superficial use**: In some cases, digital tools were integrated primarily to signal modernity rather than to genuinely enrich the learning experience. This led to superficial engagement, where students interacted with technology passively rather than actively using it to develop critical thinking or analytical skills.
2. **Content misfit**: Certain platforms lacked the functionality needed for deep textual analysis or interpretive work, making them less effective for disciplines that require nuanced engagement with complex materials. This misalignment often resulted in frustration among users and diminished the educational value of digital resources.
3. **Assessment challenges**: Traditional assessment criteria often struggled to accommodate digital outputs, especially in collaborative or co-authored projects. Evaluating contributions fairly and ensuring alignment with academic standards proved difficult, requiring adjustments in grading approaches to reflect the evolving nature of digital scholarship.

Addressing these challenges necessitates intentional selection of tools, clear pedagogical alignment, and adaptive assessment strategies to ensure technology genuinely enhances learning rather than serving as a superficial addition.

Educators noted the need for clear guidelines and rubrics to fairly evaluate digital assignments.

6.10.4 Privacy and Ethical Concerns

Important issues about privacy, security, and ownership of digital property have been raised as a result of the widespread use of cloud-based platforms and online collaboration tools. A great number of users have voiced their concerns over the safety of their data, especially with respect to the storage and exchange of personal information on third-party platforms, where the dangers of unauthorised access and breaches continue to be a major problem. In addition, students expressed their unease with the continuous tracking that was made possible by learning analytics and session monitoring, which brought to light ethical concerns around permission and surveillance in digital learning settings. The uncertainty that surrounds the ownership of student-generated information, such as annotations, blogs, and visualisations, led to disputes over control and authorship, which also led to the emergence of another problem in the shape of intellectual property rights. Institutions needed to develop rigorous rules that protected data privacy, explained intellectual property restrictions, and supported honest communication to address these reasonable concerns. This would result in a digital learning experience that is more trustworthy and safer [26].

6.10.5 Motivation and Engagement Decline

Although software tools may boost motivation (as discussed in Sect. 6.6), they can also lead to disengagement due to specific design and usability issues. Due to the fact that students' annoyance with navigation may overshadow the learning process, interfaces that are either complex or unintuitive often discourage students from fully participating. Students may have difficulty seeing the practical benefit of digital technologies in their studies if they are not exposed to activities that are neither interactive or relevant to the real world. This is because such activities may fail to catch the attention of students. Utilising screen-based activities for an excessive amount of time without providing adequate change may also result in boredom, which in turn reduces enthusiasm for involvement. A significant number of students have reported suffering "digital fatigue," which is characterised by the combination of using numerous platforms concurrently without sufficient coordination. This results in cognitive overload and a reduction in the students' capacity to concentrate properly. To alleviate these problems, educational institutions and teachers need to place a higher priority on the creation of software that is easy to use, ensure that digital tools are used in a meaningful way, and provide a variety of learning experiences in order to maintain motivation and avoid burnout (Table 6.17).

Table 6.17 Student-reported effects of overusing digital tools

Reported effect	% of respondents
Feeling overwhelmed or fatigued	51
Decreased interest in content	36
Difficulty focusing on screen tasks	42
Desire for more face-to-face learning	48

6.10.6 Institutional and Administrative Constraints

The successful implementation of software in academic environments was met with a number of systemic problems, especially in establishments that had a restricted amount of resources. Because of the absence of institutional financing for software licensing, updates, and continuous maintenance, access to critical digital tools was limited, which slowed down the growth of technology. This was a serious impediment. In the departments of humanities, the situation was further complicated by poor technological support, which left both professors and students without the essential help to diagnose difficulties or maximise the potential of software that was available. Significant obstacles were also provided by bureaucratic delays in the adoption of new instruments. Protracted procurement and approval procedures slowed down integration efforts and prevented rapid testing. In addition, there was a lack of adequate training for both the teaching staff and the students on the pedagogical use of technology, which hampered meaningful involvement and made it impossible to properly utilise software for academic objectives. The capacity to investigate and adapt digital technologies was often hindered by financial and administrative restrictions, which was especially true in institutions that were smaller or had less resources. These structural limits collectively constrained innovation, particularly in institutions that were under-resourced or smaller. For the purpose of addressing these problems, targeted investments, quicker approval procedures, and expanded technical assistance are required in order to cultivate a learning environment that is more adaptive and technologically advanced [28].

6.10.7 Cultural and Attitudinal Resistance

It was due to concerns over the compatibility of software tools with conventional scholarly processes and the possible influence that these tools may have on key competences that there was resistance to integrating software tools in specific academic environments. A number of academics who have had conventional training have stated their scepticism about technology. They have questioned whether or not digital tools are compatible with the interpretative character of the humanities, which places a premium on in-depth study and comprehensive comprehension. Furthermore, there were instructors who were concerned that relying on these tools may lead to a loss of skills, which could possibly lead to a decline in vital talents such as close reading and critical writing, which have been fundamental to the field of humanities study for a very long time. Due to the fact that digital platforms were often viewed as disruptions rather than additions, concerns over distraction also surfaced. This raised reservations about the role that digital platforms play in creating meaningful connection. A sustained dialogue that encourages open discussions about the value of digital tools, evidence-based advocacy that demonstrates their ability to complement rather than replace traditional methods, and institutional support to facilitate thoughtful integration through training, resources, and pedagogical alignment are all the things that are required to overcome these reservations.

6.10.8 Case Study Snapshot: Challenges in a Regional University

The implementation of Hypothesis and Zotero at a regional university in Northern Nigeria encountered several challenges that highlighted broader systemic issues in digital adoption. Faculty training sessions saw low attendance, primarily due to the absence of incentives, making it difficult to foster widespread engagement with these tools. Students with limited device access struggled to complete assignments outside campus hours, exacerbating digital inequities and limiting learning opportunities. Internet outages during class time disrupted live annotation sessions, hindering the effective use of collaborative features and frustrating both students and lecturers. As a result, some faculty members reverted to traditional methods, citing the "unpredictability" of digital tools as a barrier to consistent usage. This case underscores the necessity of developing tailored strategies that align with local realities, ensuring that digital initiatives are supported by adequate infrastructure, reliable connectivity, and meaningful incentives for adoption.

6.10.9 Recommendations for Overcoming Challenges

In order to successfully minimise these issues, it is vital to engage in a multi-faceted strategy in order to guarantee fair access and sustainable adoption of digital technology. Investing in digital infrastructure is a top priority because it may help bridge existing gaps and encourage successful interaction with digital tools. This is particularly true for students who are disadvantaged, as greater access to devices and bandwidth can significantly enhance their educational opportunities. For the purpose of promoting confidence and competence in digital pedagogy, it is vital to provide continual training via professional development programs that are available to both the teaching staff and the students. In addition, the establishment of support hubs, which may include specialised centres or help desks, may provide advice and troubleshooting for those who are exploring digital technologies in the field of humanities education. In order to make the most of the advantages that technology has to offer, it is essential to align tools with pedagogy. This may be accomplished by incorporating software in a meaningful way into the design of courses that have well-defined learning outcomes. This will ensure that digital solutions contribute to rather than detract from educational goals. The promotion of accessibility and usability may be accomplished by placing an emphasis on inclusive design by choosing or designing tools that are able to accommodate users with a variety of technical backgrounds. Furthermore, addressing ethical concerns via clear data regulations, informed consent, and respect for intellectual property defends users' rights and encourages trust in digital learning settings. The use of these tactics has the potential to produce a digital ecosystem that is more efficient and fairer, therefore allowing educational institutions to utilise technology for the purpose of producing meaningful results [29].

6.11 Summary and Outlook

It is not without its challenges that software is being included in the curriculum of humanities students. There are a number of important obstacles, including technological faults, deficiencies in digital literacy, and institutional lethargy. However, the first step towards developing digital learning environments that are more equal and effective is to acknowledge the issues that are now being faced. In order to overcome these obstacles, it is necessary to have not only improved instruments but also improved methods that are founded on educational significance, inclusiveness, and environmentally responsible infrastructure. When this occurs, and only then, will software be able to properly realise its promise of enriching the humanities learning experience rather than making it more complicated.

6.12 Performance Differences Between Traditional and Software-Aided Groups

The use of digital technologies in humanities teaching has provoked intense discussion over their true influence on academic achievement. While digital technologies provide new opportunities for exploration, collaboration, and content production, it is critical to determine if these benefits result in demonstrable learning improvements. This section compares the academic performance of two groups of students: those who received conventional teaching and those who used software-aided learning techniques across a variety of cognitive and emotional dimensions. The purpose is to give an evidence-based viewpoint on the instructional use of digital humanities tools.

6.12.1 Research Design and Methodology

To examine performance variations in introductory humanities courses, a quasi-experimental design was used across three universities, comparing two student cohorts employing different teaching methodologies. The Control Group (Traditional) comprised around 100 students who learnt using traditional techniques such as textbooks, lectures, and paper-based exams. In contrast, the Experimental Group (Software-Aided), which included around 100 students, introduced digital tools such as Voyant Tools, Hypothesis, Zotero, and online discussion platforms into their course activities, allowing for technology-enhanced interaction. The assessment employed many metrics to measure the efficacy of each strategy, such as test scores, project quality, participation frequency, critical thinking rubrics, and qualitative feedback from students and teachers. By analysing these factors, the research hoped to discover possible benefits or downsides of using software tools in humanities training, as well as provide insights into how digital platforms impact learning outcomes, engagement, and academic success [30].

6.12.2 Academic Achievement Scores

Quantitative data revealed a consistent pattern: students in the software-aided group outperformed their traditional counterparts on summative and formative assessments (Table 6.18).

The software-aided group displayed significant improvements particularly in project-based assessments, where tools allowed for richer annotation, source integration, and visualisation of ideas.

Table 6.18 Average test scores of students by instruction type

Assessment type	Traditional group (%)	Software-aided group (%)
Midterm exam	62.4	73.5
Final exam	65.8	78.9
Annotated text project	68.1	85.2
Research paper score	70.2	88.4

Table 6.19 Critical thinking scores (scale of 1–5)

Indicator	Traditional group	Software-aided group
Analysis	2.8	3.9
Evaluation	2.6	3.7
Synthesis	3.0	4.1
Interpretation	2.9	3.8

6.12.3 Quality of Critical Analysis

Using a standardised rubric for critical thinking (adapted from the AAC&U VALUE Rubrics), essays and projects were rated on four indicators: analysis, evaluation, synthesis, and interpretation (Table 6.19).

Students using digital tools demonstrated deeper textual engagement. For example, those using Voyant Tools were better able to identify thematic patterns and linguistic shifts over time, leading to more nuanced arguments.

6.12.4 Engagement Metrics

Participation and engagement were monitored through attendance logs, discussion board analytics, and time-on-task records. The software-aided group recorded higher levels of engagement across several measures (Table 6.20).

Digital platforms enabled asynchronous engagement, which was particularly beneficial to students balancing work and study. Hypothesis discussions are often continued beyond class hours, fostering deeper reflection and peer interaction.

Affective Learning Outcomes

Affective outcomes, including motivation, enjoyment, and confidence, were evaluated through student surveys to assess the impact of software integration on engagement and learning experiences.

1. **Motivation**: A significant 81% of students in the software-aided group reported feeling more motivated to complete assignments, citing interactive features, accessibility, and streamlined workflows as contributing factors. In contrast,

Table 6.20 Engagement comparison

Indicator	Traditional group	Software-aided group
Attendance (average %)	74.2	89.6
Forum contributions (Mean)	3.1 posts	9.4 posts
Task completion rate (%)	68.3	91.2
Office hour interactions	Lower	Higher (via chats)

only 52% of students in the traditional group expressed similar levels of motivation, indicating that conventional instructional methods might lack the dynamic engagement provided by digital tools.

2. **Confidence in Research Skills**: Among software-aided learners, 76% felt confident navigating digital libraries, citation tools, and research databases, benefiting from features such as automated referencing and real-time collaboration. In comparison, only 44% of students in the traditional cohort expressed confidence in using these resources, highlighting a potential gap in digital research literacy among those relying solely on conventional methods.
3. **Perceived Relevance**: Technology played a crucial role in shaping students' perceptions of the humanities, with 84% of software-aided students agreeing that digital tools enhanced the real-world applicability of their studies. The ability to annotate texts collaboratively, analyse sources efficiently, and engage with dynamic content fostered a stronger connection to contemporary contexts.

6.12.5 Qualitative Feedback from Students

Open-ended survey answers gave useful insights into the student experience, offering light on their perspectives, problems, and use of digital technologies. Students provided their thoughts on how technology affects their motivation, research abilities, and overall learning experience, providing nuanced viewpoints that quantitative statistics alone could not portray. Their input showed both the advantages and disadvantages of software integration, indicating places where digital technologies improved accessibility and cooperation while also hindering uptake due to technical constraints or usability issues. These replies helped shape future strategies for optimising digital learning environments to better meet student needs and expectations.

Traditional Group Feedback:

"I prefer lectures because they're predictable, but sometimes they feel passive and hard to follow."

"I find it hard to keep up with the material without visual aids or interactive support."

Software-Aided Group Feedback:

"Using Zotero helped me organise my references and saved me time. I felt more professional doing my paper."

"The annotation exercises in Hypothesis made me think about the text in new ways. It was like reading with a community."

"Sometimes it was overwhelming switching between tools, but overall, it made learning more interesting."

Instructor Observations

Faculty members who taught both groups provided insights into the differences in student engagement and interaction within traditional and software-aided learning environments.

1. **Traditional Group**: Instructors reported challenges in maintaining student attention and fostering meaningful interactivity. The reliance on conventional methods such as textbooks and lectures often led to passive learning, with students struggling to stay engaged and participate actively in discussions. Without interactive digital tools, collaboration was limited, making it harder to encourage peer-led exploration of ideas.
2. **Software-Aided Group**: Teachers observed a positive shift in student behaviour, with learners demonstrating greater initiative and engagement. Peer-to-peer teaching moments became more frequent, as students leveraged digital tools to collaborate on assignments and share insights in both classroom and online discussions. The integration of platforms such as Voyant Tools and Hypothesis facilitated deeper analytical conversations and encouraged a more dynamic exchange of perspectives.

Despite these benefits, some faculty members acknowledged that mastering digital tools required a learning curve, particularly for those unfamiliar with the technology. They emphasised the importance of structured scaffolding, including guided tutorials and ongoing support, to ensure smooth adoption and effective use of digital resources. Thoughtful implementation strategies and institutional backing were seen as crucial for maximising the potential of software-aided learning.

6.12.6 Skill Acquisition Beyond the Curriculum

Beyond obtaining subject mastery, students who used digital tools gained a variety of transferable abilities that stretched beyond their courses, preparing them for academic and professional settings. Digital literacy was an important skill, as students learnt how to navigate multiple platforms, write proper citations, and efficiently maintain digital repositories, therefore improving their capacity to organise and retrieve material effectively. Collaboration also grew more dynamic, with students co-authoring annotations, revising shared documents, and exchanging ideas via commenting systems, boosting collaboration and collaborative problem-solving.

Additionally, time management improved as students used task alerts and platform notifications to monitor deadlines and progress, developing habits necessary for handling complicated workloads. Information evaluation was another important skill, as integrated research tools and plugins assisted students in determining the reliability of sources, honing their ability to differentiate credible information in an age of plentiful digital material. Together, these abilities broadened the skill set of software-aided students, giving them significant tools for academic research, corporate cooperation, and lifetime learning.

6.12.7 Limitations and Confounding Variables

Even though the results are in favour of software-aided instruction, there are a few important things to keep in mind when you interpret them. Educator enthusiasm might have been a factor; students' engagement and performance could have been affected if teachers who used digital tools were more enthusiastic about them or had greater training on how to utilise them. Furthermore, there is the issue of self-selection bias, which occurs when students who are already more comfortable with technology choose to take software-aided courses. This means that the results may not accurately reflect how effective the tools were, but rather reflect the students' pre-existing comfort with digital platforms. Access equity is another important factor to think about since certain students had trouble staying consistently engaged with digital resources due to differences in hardware and internet availability. They may not have been able to fully participate due to limited access, which could explain why their experiences varied within the cohort. Randomised control groups to minimise selection bias and longitudinal follow-ups to measure the long-term effects of software integration would further improve these findings and provide a fuller picture of its efficacy in future research.

6.13 Summary of Key Findings

These findings highlight the significant pedagogical benefits of incorporating digital tools into humanities education. When integrated with careful planning and alignment to learning objectives, software platforms support cognitive development while fostering engagement, motivation, and collaborative learning experiences. Beyond academic content mastery, these tools facilitate the acquisition of essential skills such as digital literacy, research proficiency, and effective communication, all of which are valuable in both academic and professional contexts. By bridging traditional methodologies with modern technological advancements, digital integration enhances accessibility, interactivity, and the overall learning experience, reinforcing its transformative role in contemporary humanities education (Table 6.21).

A strong pedagogical advantage in favour of software-aided education is shown by the performance comparison between conventional instruction and teaching methods that include the use of software. A learning experience that is more dynamic, richer, and more engaging is fostered by surroundings that have been improved with software. This kind of learning environment is well aligned with modern educational aims in the humanities. Having said that, this success is contingent upon having enough training, having support from infrastructure, and having a course design that

Table 6.21 Comparative summary of outcomes

Outcome area	Traditional group	Software-aided group
Test and assignment scores	Moderate	High
Critical thinking	Developing	Proficient/advanced
Engagement	Inconsistent	Sustained and varied
Confidence	Moderate	High
Transferable skills	Limited	Broad

is sensible. At the end of the day, the problem is not whether or if software tools are beneficial; rather, the problem is how they are used. In order to accommodate the growing number of digital natives who are enrolling in higher education, educational institutions need to develop pedagogical tactics that are equally adaptable. These strategies should use technology not as a crutch, but rather as a catalyst for critical and creative thinking.

6.14 Quantitative Data Analysis

Quantitative data analysis is an essential component of empirical research in the field of educational technology. It provides insights into linkages, trends, and effects by means of quantifiable results. The Statistical Package for the Social Sciences (SPSS) was used in this investigation for the purpose of managing, analysing, and interpreting the data that was obtained via student evaluations, engagement metrics, survey replies, and teacher evaluations. In this part, the methodology, statistical tools, and major results are presented. As a consequence, the conclusions that were presented in the preceding section are grounded in comprehensive quantitative evidence.

6.14.1 Overview of SPSS and Its Relevance

The statistical package known as SPSS is among the most popular software tools for doing quantitative analysis in the field of education research and the social sciences. Statistics such as descriptive statistics, correlation analysis, inferential statistics (such as t-tests and ANOVA), regression modelling, and factor analysis are all possible with this capability. In this particular investigation, the statistical software SPSS was selected because of its intuitive user interface, superior statistical skills, and capacity to successfully handle big datasets.

6.14.2 Dataset Description

The primary dataset comprised responses from 200 students (100 in the traditional group and 100 in the software-aided group) along with insights from 15 instructors across three higher education institutions. A diverse range of variables was collected to provide a comprehensive analysis of learning outcomes and engagement patterns.

1. **Demographic variables**: Included data on age, gender, institutional affiliation, and prior digital literacy levels, allowing for an examination of how different backgrounds influenced interaction with digital tools.
2. **Academic performance**: Measured through test scores, project grades, and assignment completion rates, providing objective indicators of student achievement across instructional methods.
3. **Engagement metrics**: Tracked attendance, forum participation, and frequency of tool usage, offering insights into the behavioral aspects of student involvement in both traditional and digital learning environments.
4. **Survey responses**: Gathered through Likert-scale ratings assessing motivation, usability, and satisfaction, capturing students' subjective experiences with digital platforms and conventional instruction.
5. **Instructor ratings**: Evaluated perceived student progress and participation using standardised scales, reflecting faculty perspectives on student engagement and learning effectiveness.

All variables were systematically coded and entered into SPSS following standard protocols, ensuring data integrity and consistency throughout the analytical process. This structured approach allowed for a rigorous comparison of traditional and software-aided instruction, supporting evidence-based conclusions on the impact of digital tools in humanities education.

6.14.3 Descriptive Statistics

Descriptive statistics offered an initial overview of the dataset, highlighting key patterns and distributions across variables. By summarising central tendencies, variability, and frequency distributions, this analysis provided insights into student performance, engagement metrics, and survey responses. The use of measures such as means, standard deviations, and histograms helped contextualise differences between the traditional and software-aided groups, laying the groundwork for further inferential analysis (Table 6.22).

The higher mean scores for the software-aided group supported the hypothesis that software integration improves academic performance.

Table 6.22 Descriptive statistics of academic scores

Variable	Mean	Std. deviation	Minimum	Maximum
Traditional midterm	62.4	11.3	40	85
Software-aided midterm	73.5	10.7	50	95
Traditional final exam	65.8	13.2	38	88
Software-aided final	78.9	11.5	55	96

Table 6.23 T-Test results—Final exam scores

Group	Mean	Std. Dev	t-value	df	p-value
Traditional Group	65.8	13.2			
Software-aided group	78.9	11.5	− 7.24	198	< 0.001*

* Statistically significant at $p < 0.05$

6.14.4 Independent Samples T-Test

Independent samples t-tests were conducted to determine whether academic performance varied significantly between the traditional and software-aided groups. This statistical analysis compared mean scores across key metrics, including test results, project grades, and assignment completion rates. By evaluating differences in student achievement, the t-tests helped assess the effectiveness of digital tools in enhancing learning outcomes and provided a quantitative measure of their impact within humanities education (Table 6.23).

The significant p-value (< 0.001) confirms that the observed differences in final exam scores were not due to chance. Similar tests were conducted for midterm scores and project evaluations, all indicating higher performance in the experimental group.

6.14.5 Correlation Analysis

Correlation analysis was conducted to examine the relationships between engagement metrics and performance indicators, providing insights into how student participation influenced academic outcomes. By assessing variables such as attendance, forum contributions, and tool usage frequency with test scores, project grades, and assignment completion rates, the analysis identified patterns of association between digital engagement and learning success. This approach helped determine whether higher levels of interaction with software tools correlated with improved performance, offering a deeper understanding of the impact of technology integration in humanities education (Table 6.24).

Table 6.24 Pearson correlations

Variables	Test score	Forum posts	Tool usage
Test score	1.00	0.46**	0.52**
Forum posts		1.00	0.58**
Tool usage frequency			1.00

** $p < 0.01$

Table 6.25 One-way ANOVA—Final scores by institution

Source	SS	df	MS	F	p-value
Between groups	1,650.82	2	825.41	6.27	0.002**
Within groups	25,340.11	197	128.63		
Total	26,990.93	199			

** Statistically significant at $p < 0.01$

The results revealed strong positive correlations between tool usage and test scores ($r = 0.52$) and between forum participation and test scores ($r = 0.46$), indicating that active engagement through software platforms enhances learning outcomes.

6.14.6 *ANOVA Analysis*

A one-way ANOVA was performed to assess whether there were significant differences in student performance across the three institutions included in the study. This statistical test allowed for the comparison of mean scores among the different groups, determining whether institutional factors influenced learning outcomes. By analysing variations in test scores, project quality, and engagement metrics, the ANOVA helped identify whether disparities in instructional methods, digital tool accessibility, or institutional support contributed to measurable differences in student achievement (Table 6.25).

Post hoc tests (Tukey HSD) showed that one institution had significantly higher mean scores, possibly due to better infrastructure or more intensive instructor training in software use.

6.14.7 *Regression Analysis*

A multiple linear regression analysis was conducted to predict final test scores using tool usage, attendance, and digital literacy as independent variables. This approach helped identify the extent to which engagement with digital platforms influenced academic performance. By analysing these factors collectively, the regression model

Table 6.26 Regression coefficients

Predictor	B	Std. error	Beta	t-value	p-value
Constant	42.12	3.45		12.21	< 0.001
Tool usage	2.34	0.39	0.42	6.00	< 0.001
Attendance	1.21	0.31	0.33	3.90	< 0.001
Digital literacy	0.85	0.28	0.21	3.04	0.003

$R^2 = 0.47$, $F(3,196) = 58.33$, $p < 0.001$

provided insights into the relative contributions of each variable, offering a more comprehensive understanding of the predictors of student success (Table 6.26).

The regression model explained 47% of the variance in student performance. Tool usage was the strongest predictor, reinforcing the efficacy of software-supported learning.

6.14.8 Factor Analysis

Exploratory Factor Analysis (EFA) was performed on the student perception survey, which consisted of 24 items rated on a 5-point Likert scale. This statistical technique was used to uncover underlying constructs that influenced student responses, helping to identify patterns in motivation, usability, and engagement. By analysing correlations among survey items, EFA provided insights into the key dimensions shaping student perceptions of digital tools, informing further refinement of instructional strategies and software integration (Table 6.27).

Three distinct factors emerged: Motivation, Usability, and Collaboration, confirming that student responses clustered meaningfully around key affective and cognitive dimensions.

Table 6.27 Rotated component matrix (principal component analysis)

Survey item description	Motivation	Usability	Collaboration
"I was more motivated using software"	0.81		
"Software tools were easy to use"		0.79	
"I enjoyed working with peers online"			0.83
"Digital tools helped clarify concepts"	0.68	0.55	
"Discussion platforms helped me engage"			0.77

6.14.9 Reliability Testing

Cronbach's Alpha was calculated to evaluate the internal consistency of the survey items, ensuring reliability in the measurement of student motivation, engagement, and usability perceptions. This statistical analysis helped determine the coherence of responses across different survey sections, confirming that the items collectively measured the intended constructs with a high degree of accuracy and dependability (Table 6.28).

Values above 0.70 indicate high reliability, affirming the robustness of the survey instrument.

6.15 Summary of Quantitative Insights

The quantitative analyses that were carried out in SPSS provide substantial empirical evidence for the advantages that come with integrating software in the field of humanities education. The results of the study demonstrate that students who make use of digital tools have performance improvements that are statistically significant, demonstrating the efficacy of these technologies in improving academic achievements. Further evidence that active participation with digital platforms contributes to improved learning experiences is provided by the existence of positive correlations between engagement and achievement metrics. Furthermore, rigorous prediction models suggest that digital tools act as significant predictors of student achievement, which further substantiates the educational utility of these technologies. After conducting factor and reliability studies, the reliability and validity of the measuring equipment were validated, therefore assuring that the data that was obtained was accurate and trustworthy. These findings, when taken as a whole, provide credence to qualitative observations and lay a strong statistical groundwork for the formulation of educational policy and the construction of curricula. Furthermore, they advocate for the judicious adoption of digital tools that can promote both cognitive learning and the acquisition of skills.

Table 6.28 Reliability coefficients

Scale	Cronbach's alpha
Overall survey	0.89
Motivation subscale	0.86
Usability subscale	0.82
Collaboration subscale	0.85

6.15.1 *Qualitative Data*

Qualitative data gives a more nuanced and human-centered view on how software integration alters teaching and learning within the humanities, in contrast to quantitative analysis, which provides numerical confirmation of patterns and results. The results from semi-structured interviews with students and instructors, as well as extensive classroom observations carried out at all of the participating institutions, are analysed in this section. All of these qualitative findings, when taken together, provide light not only on what changed as a result of the use of software, but also on how and why such changes were significant in educational practice.

6.15.2 *Research Design and Methodology*

A constructivist epistemology served as the guiding principle for the qualitative portion of the study. This epistemology acknowledged that learning and perceptions are things that are socially formed and rooted in context. In all, thirty student interviews and ten teacher interviews were carried out, and in addition, twenty-five hours of classroom observations were carried out across six digital humanities classes that were taught at three different educational institutions.

Interview Focus Areas:

1. **Experiences with software tools**: Participants reflected on their firsthand interactions with digital platforms, discussing usability, learning curves, and adaptability.
2. **Perceived benefits and challenges**: Responses highlighted advantages such as increased accessibility and collaboration, alongside difficulties related to technical constraints, training gaps, and reliability issues.
3. **Changes in thinking and collaboration**: Faculty and students examined how digital tools influenced analytical approaches, teamwork dynamics, and engagement with course material.
4. **Reflections on motivation and engagement**: Interviewees shared insights into how digital tools shaped their enthusiasm for coursework, impacted participation levels, and affected overall learning experiences.

Observation Criteria:

1. **Nature and frequency of digital tool usage**: Patterns of engagement were monitored, including how often students and instructors relied on software for research, discussion, and assignments.
2. **Student-instructor and peer-to-peer interactions**: Observations captured the ways technology facilitated or hindered academic exchanges, including real-time discussions, collaborative annotations, and guided feedback mechanisms.

3. **Problem-solving and critical thinking episodes**: Instances of analytical reasoning, digital literacy application, and creative problem-solving were documented to assess cognitive development.
4. **Technological fluency and adaptability**: The ability of students and faculty to navigate and integrate digital tools effectively was examined, focusing on self-sufficiency, troubleshooting skills, and ease of adoption.

All interviews were transcribed and thematically coded using NVivo 12 to ensure a structured analysis of qualitative insights. Observational data were meticulously recorded through detailed field notes and systematically organised around predefined codes and emergent themes, allowing for a comprehensive exploration of digital tool integration in humanities education.

6.15.3 Thematic Analysis: Student Perspectives

Theme 1: Enhanced Autonomy and Ownership of Learning

Students consistently reported feeling more in control of their learning journeys when using software platforms such as LMS, digital annotation tools, and collaborative writing environments. One student remarked:

> *"I could go back and rewatch lectures or review notes anytime I wanted. That freedom made me feel like I wasn't just a passive learner."*

This sense of autonomy was particularly strong among distance learners and students juggling work commitments, who appreciated the flexibility and self-directed pacing that software enabled.

Theme 2: Deepened Critical Engagement.

Several students explained how digital tools prompted more thoughtful and nuanced engagement with course content. For example, using Voyant Tools for textual analysis led students to discover patterns and thematic emphases in literary texts that were not readily apparent through manual reading:

> *"Seeing the most common words and tracking their recurrence helped me think about the novel's structure in a completely new way."*

These findings support the claim that software can augment critical thinking by providing new lenses for interpretation and analysis.

Theme 3: Barriers to Technological Confidence

Despite overall enthusiasm, a subset of students particularly mature learners and those with limited prior exposure to digital tools expressed anxiety or frustration. Common issues included difficulty navigating interfaces, fear of "breaking" software, and reluctance to ask for help in class:

> *"I felt like everyone else already knew how to use it. I didn't want to slow the class down."*

These sentiments underscore the need for scaffolding and inclusive design in software adoption.

6.15.4 Thematic Analysis: Instructor Perspectives

Theme 1: Shifting Pedagogical Roles

Instructors described how software use redefined their roles from information providers to learning facilitators. Tools such as forums, digital annotation apps, and peer review platforms decentralised authority and increased student participation:

> *"I used to spend half the class lecturing. Now I spend more time guiding discussions that students start themselves online."*

This shift was generally viewed positively, although some instructors noted a steep learning curve in moderating online spaces and adjusting to asynchronous interaction.

Theme 2: Concerns about Depth and Distraction

A few instructors worried that software use might encourage superficial engagement. One lecturer explained:

> *"There's a temptation for students to skim articles or just rely on software outputs rather than reading deeply."*

Others noted that the presence of devices could lead to multitasking and distraction if not properly managed.

Theme 3: New Forms of Assessment

Many instructors appreciated how digital tools allowed for alternative assessment strategies ranging from multimedia projects to live collaborative documents. One shared:

> *"Instead of essays, I had students create digital exhibits using Omeka. It was more engaging and still showed deep understanding."*

This reflects a broader pedagogical turn toward authentic and multimodal assessments in humanities education.

6.15.5 Classroom Observation Insights

Classroom observations offered a real-time window into how software tools influenced pedagogy and interaction. There was a discernible increase in the level of activity in the classes that were equipped with digital technology. In order to analyse

Table 6.29 Observation summary across 6 courses

Focus area	Observed frequency	Notes
Software used in class	100%	Tools included Hypothesis, Google Docs, Voyant, Moodle
Peer-to-Peer interaction	High	Increased in software-aided environments
Instructor facilitation	Moderate to high	Focus on scaffolding and digital tool navigation
Student presentations	Moderate	Often involved digital exhibits or visualisations
Technical difficulties	Low to moderate	Most were resolved quickly; some students lacked devices

texts, communicate opinions, and construct arguments using digital resources, students often worked in pairs or in small groups. The instructors acted as co-navigators, rotating between the different groups in order to provide mutual support and encourage introspection (Table 6.29).

6.15.6 Emerging Patterns and Divergences

A comprehensive cross-analysis of interview and observational data revealed several consistent patterns in the integration of digital tools within humanities education. At the same time, notable divergences emerged, influenced by student demographics and institutional contexts, demonstrating the complex nature of digital adoption and engagement.

Consistent Patterns:

1. **Increased student engagement and interaction**: Across various institutions, students exhibited higher levels of participation when using digital tools, with collaborative platforms fostering real-time discussions, peer feedback, and interactive learning environments. The ability to engage with course materials dynamically encouraged deeper exploration of concepts.
2. **Greater critical analysis of content through visualisation**: Visualisation tools provided new ways for students to engage with texts and data, allowing them to identify patterns, make connections, and enhance their analytical skills. The incorporation of software-assisted content mapping enriched their comprehension and interpretation.
3. **Positive reception of new assessment methods**: Many students responded favorably to alternative assessment formats that utilized digital tools, appreciating the flexibility and real-world applicability of technology-enhanced evaluations. Online quizzes, collaborative annotations, and project-based assessments offered varied learning opportunities beyond traditional exams.

Divergences:

1. **Digital fluency varied by age, prior exposure, and institutional support**: While younger students or those with prior technology experience adapted quickly, others faced challenges navigating new platforms. Institutions with strong technical support structures mitigated these gaps more effectively than those with limited digital training resources.
2. **Instructors at better-resourced institutions were more confident and experimental in software use**: Faculty members at institutions with robust digital infrastructure and professional development programs were more willing to explore innovative teaching methods, while those in underfunded settings remained cautious due to technical limitations and lack of institutional backing.
3. **Students with disabilities reported mixed experiences depending on tool accessibility**: While some found digital tools empowering, others struggled with compatibility issues related to screen readers, adaptive interfaces, and customisable features. Accessibility concerns underscored the need for inclusive software development and institutional accommodations to support diverse learning needs.

These divergences emphasise the critical role of equity, training, and infrastructural investment in digital humanities education. Addressing disparities in digital fluency, faculty preparedness, and accessibility is essential to ensuring that technology benefits all students, regardless of background or institutional resources. A strategic approach to digital adoption grounded in ongoing support, user-centred design, and institutional commitment will enable humanities education to harness the full potential of technological innovations while maintaining its foundational emphasis on interpretation, analysis, and engagement.

Student Voice as Evidence

The following quotes illustrate the affective and cognitive dimensions of students' experiences:

1. *"Annotating with Hypothesis helped me engage with the text and my classmates at the same time. It felt like a conversation, not just reading."*
2. *"Before, I just wrote essays. Now I've made a podcast and a digital map. It's more creative—and I remember the content better."*
3. *"I was skeptical at first, but when I saw my analysis visualized in Voyant, I was surprised how much more I understood the text."*

These voices affirm that software tools, when thoughtfully integrated, can transform not only what students learn but how they relate to the material.

Instructor Reflections as Pedagogical Feedback

Instructors offered insights into professional growth and pedagogical innovation:

1. *"I now see assessment differently. It's not just about essays but about interpretation, creativity, and collaboration."*
2. *"I've started using tools I learned about in this project in my other courses even non-digital ones."*

3. *"The training and peer support made a big difference. Once I felt comfortable, I could experiment more."*

These reflections highlight the importance of ongoing professional development and collaborative learning communities among educators.

Integrating Qualitative and Quantitative Insights

Qualitative findings add rich, contextual meaning to the quantitative data presented earlier. For example:

1. The increase in test scores among software users is mirrored in student testimonies about deeper engagement and clearer understanding.
2. The positive correlation between tool usage and performance is echoed in instructors' observations of improved participation and creativity.
3. The variation in digital fluency helps explain the performance disparities and underlines the necessity of targeted support.

6.15.7 Conclusion

The use of software tools in humanities education changes the dynamics of learning, gives students more agency, and encourages them to be more engaged, according to qualitative research. The experiences and observations that were obtained for this research provide overwhelming support for the argument that educational software should be used in a deliberate and inclusive manner. This is despite the fact that obstacles still exist, especially with respect to digital equality and pedagogical adjustment. This chapter has provided a human-centered complement to the numerical data by means of stories, voices, and observed interactions. It has also confirmed that beyond test scores and statistics lies a vibrant world of learners who are empowered by digital tools to think, collaborate, and create more effectively than they ever have before.

6.15.8 Discussion in Relation to Research Questions

The previous analysis, which included both quantitative and qualitative data, lays the groundwork for a conversation that is focused and closely connected to the primary research objectives of the study. In this section, evidence is collected from a variety of data sources in order to conduct an in-depth analysis of the ways in which the incorporation of software tools affects humanities education, specifically with relation to student involvement, critical thinking, cooperation, motivation, and performance. The purpose of this discussion is to highlight key insights, confirm or challenge existing literature, and suggest implications for pedagogical practice. This is accomplished by revisiting each research question.

Research Question 1: How do software tools impact student engagement and motivation in humanities education?

Student engagement and motivation are greatly improved by software tools, according to the research. The quantitative metrics of participation rates, the amount of time spent on activities, and motivation ratings indicated statistically significant gains in software-aided groups when compared to conventional cohorts. In addition to these results, qualitative interviews suggested that digital platforms encourage student autonomy, make it possible for students to study at their own speed, and provide interactive aspects that maintain student engagement. A feeling of active engagement rather than passive receipt was created by the students via the use of annotation tools and digital visualisation software, which they characterised as catalysts for deeper connection with texts. These results are consistent with the findings of [31], who suggested that digital technologies promote contextual learning and intrinsic motivation by positioning learners as active creators of knowledge rather than consumers of information.

Nevertheless, it is of the utmost importance to acknowledge the variety in participation that is associated with the digital fluency and past experience of the students. When confronted with new software, a few of the participants exhibited feelings of worry or annoyance, which raises the possibility that advances in motivation may be contingent on the provision of sufficient support and scaffolding. This realisation is consistent with Bandura's (1997) theory of self-efficacy, which states that involvement is influenced by a person's belief in their own talents.

Research Question 2: In what ways do software tools influence the development of critical thinking skills?

It has been shown that the incorporation of digital humanities software contributes to the development of critical thinking by providing students with the opportunity to modify, visualise, and investigate data in non-traditional ways. There was a correlation between the quantitative gains in critical thinking testing scores and the qualitative evidence of students expressing more complex judgements and displaying analytical sophistication. By way of illustration, students who used textual analysis tools such as Voyant reported discovering hidden patterns and thematic connections that were not discernible via the use of conventional close reading alone. An active use of software to create hypotheses, test interpretations, and participate in iterative analysis was validated by the observations. According to Alexander and Hedley (2020), who conducted research on the topic, computational tools can scaffold higher-order thinking by externalising cognitive processes and offering various access points to complicated material. These results are similar to those of those researchers. Despite this, concerns have been raised about the possibility of an excessive dependence on software-generated outputs, which might create a danger of shallow participation. Several teachers stressed that critical thinking had to be carefully cultivated, and they emphasised the need of ensuring that digital tools act as aids rather than replacements for in-depth reading and thought [32].

Research Question 3: How does the use of software tools affect collaboration and communication among students?

The findings from both sets of data point to the fact that software has a beneficial effect on the process of collaborative learning. Quantitative survey results from software-enhanced settings revealed greater peer engagement frequencies and more diffuse involvement patterns than in environments without software enhancements. Data gathered via observation provided evidence that digital platforms made it possible to have asynchronous conversations, conduct peer reviews, and collaborate on the construction of knowledge artefacts. Shared annotation, real-time document editing, and discussion forums were among the elements that students liked the most because they permitted meaningful conversations that went beyond the confines of the traditional classroom setting. Many of the people who were interviewed emphasised that these technologies democratised classroom discourse by making it easier for pupils who were more reserved or less self-assured to participate. It is consistent with Vygotsky's (1978) social constructivist framework, which places collaboration at the centre of cognitive development, as well as with more recent research that emphasises how digital environments can broaden participation [32, 33]. The teachers, on the other hand, pointed out that there are difficulties in regulating online areas and keeping constructive conversation going. They emphasised the need of having clear standards and the ability to facilitate in order to maximise the advantages of collaboration.

Research Question 4: What challenges do students and teachers encounter when integrating software tools in humanities learning?

The research showed that there are a number of obstacles that prevent proper software integration, despite the fact that the overall results were good. There were times when the smooth engagement was hampered by technical issues such as unstable internet connectivity, software glitches, and hardware limitations. Additionally, it was clear that there was a digital gap; students who had less previous knowledge had difficulty in the beginning, which often resulted in frustration or disengagement. In addition, teachers reported that they had deficiencies in their own digital literacy, which impacted their confidence in implementing new instructional strategies. The research on the adoption of technology in education points to infrastructure, training, and institutional support as essential facilitators [34]. These results are consistent with the literature, which emphasises the importance of these factors. In addition, concerns over the possibility of distractions and learning that is superficial highlight the need of careful pedagogical design that incorporates the use of software with distinct learning goals and scaffolding.

Research Question 5: How do software tools impact academic performance compared to traditional teaching methods?

Based on the comparison study, it was found that students who used software tools did better than their classmates who were exposed to conventional settings. This was shown by the fact that their test scores and assignment quality were higher. In addition to this quantitative benefit, qualitative reports of work that was more engaged, creative, and contemplative were also received. Importantly, new assessment forms made possible by software, such as digital exhibitions or multimedia projects, gave students the opportunity to show knowledge in ways that went beyond the conventional essay format, so encouraging a variety of different ways of expressing comprehension.

According to Jewitt (2014), this is a reflection of wider trends in digital education that advocate for multimodal assessment in order to capture the many talents of learners. On the other hand, the fact that the results are not consistent implies that software by itself does not ensure improved system performance. Success is contingent on a number of elements, including the suitability of the tools, the instructional design, and the preparedness of the learners [35].

6.15.9 Integrative Insights and Implications

The conversation sheds light on the promising but complex influence that software tools have in the field of humanities education. It demonstrates that when applied with careful consideration, these technologies improve academic achievement, critical thinking, cooperation, and participation. The effective integration of digital technology, on the other hand, is contingent upon essential variables such as providing students and teachers with extensive digital literacy training in order to assuage worries and create confidence. The usage of software that is aligned with specific instructional objectives assures that students will have meaningful interactions with the subject rather than an engagement that is shallow. It is essential to make investments in digital infrastructure and provide regular technical assistance in order to maintain the level of acceptance of these technologies, which will allow for accessibility and dependability. Additionally, software platforms have the ability to democratise learning by catering to the varied requirements of students, supporting numerous ways of involvement, and promoting an inclusive environment. The significance of strategic planning and institutional commitment in humanities education is further highlighted by these results, which highlight the need of ensuring that technology is used as an advantage rather than a hindrance.

By directly addressing the research issues, this debate connects empirical results with theoretical frameworks and current literature. It also highlights the revolutionary potential of digital software integration in humanities education as well as the problems that it presents. The purpose of this synthesis is to provide a solid framework for later chapters, which will investigate practical suggestions, policy issues, and future research objectives.

6.16 Summary of Key Findings

The in-depth examination of both quantitative and qualitative data presented in this chapter sheds light on the complex role that software tools play in the field of humanities education. It highlights the myriad of ways in which these tools influence student learning experiences, faculty views, cooperation dynamics, motivation, and academic success. Through the provision of interactive and user-friendly platforms that enable active involvement and personalised learning experiences, the incorporation of software tools contributes to increased levels of student engagement and motivation. However, the degrees of engagement vary depending on the students' previous digital literacy as well as the availability of organised instructional assistance. This highlights the need of providing students with equal access to electronic tools throughout the classroom.

The development of higher-order cognitive talents is facilitated by the use of digital technologies, which also make it easier to analyse, visualise, and analyse complicated data. Students may improve their analytical skills by engaging in exploratory learning and advanced textual analysis. However, it is important to exercise care in order to avoid placing an excessive amount of dependence on automated outputs. This will ensure that autonomous thinking continues to be an essential component of the learning process. The ability of software platforms to provide more frequent and varied types of peer connection is one way in which they improve collaboration. Students are able to participate in a more inclusive and prolonged conversation with one another via the use of shared annotations, real-time editing capabilities, and online discussion boards. This encourages classroom discourse to become more democratic and reinforces the need of collective intellectual participation.

The integration of software offers a number of hurdles, including technical issues, differences in digital literacy, and constraints in infrastructure, despite the fact that it has many advantages. Both students and teachers face challenges that may prevent them from making the most of the digital learning environment. This highlights the need of receiving thorough training, dependable technical support, and instructional practices that are specifically designed for the digital learning environment. When compared to students who are educated in more conventional environments, those who are exposed to digital technologies have much higher levels of academic achievement. The adaptability of software-assisted learning contributes to the development of a wide range of forms of expression and evaluation, hence increasing the number of options available to students to demonstrate their comprehension via non-traditional and inventive methods that go beyond the scope of traditional testing.

The usefulness of digital technologies is highly impacted by contextual factors such as the support of the institution, the readiness of the teachers, and the integration of the curriculum. Implementation that is thoughtful, in which technology is aligned with specific learning goals and activities that are scaffolded, fosters meaningful student engagement and reinforces the educational value of digital innovation. The results of this study provide evidence that digital humanities tools have the potential to significantly improve the quality of educational experiences. However, the success of these initiatives is contingent on the resolution of difficulties pertaining to fairness, pedagogy, and technology. This study lays a solid groundwork for the strategic suggestions and practical concerns that will be discussed in later chapters. It will direct educational institutions towards the incorporation of technology in humanities teaching that is both more successful and more inclusive.

References

1. H. Debash et al., Tuberculosis treatment outcomes and its predictors among tuberculosis patients registered at Tefera Hailu Memorial General Hospital, Sekota Town, Northeast Ethiopia: A seven-year retrospective study. Can. J. Infect. Dis. Med. Microbiol. **2023** (2023). https://doi.org/10.1155/2023/4212312
2. J. Tavakolizadeh, M. Nejatian, A. Soori, The effectiveness of communication skills training on marital conflicts and its different aspects in women. Procedia–Soc. Behav. Sci. **171**, 214–221 (2015). https://doi.org/10.1016/j.sbspro.2015.01.112
3. J.A. Bennie, G. Faulkner, J.J. Smith, The epidemiology of muscle-strengthening activity among adolescents from 28 European countries. Scand. J. Public Health **50**(2), 295–302 (2022). https://doi.org/10.1177/14034948211031392
4. I. Jessika, F. Mbaye, A. Diallo, F. Ly, and P. M. Sembène, Evaluation of malnutrition in infants aged 0 - 59 months in the suburbs of Dakar. Health (Irvine. Calif). **15**(04), 349–366 (2023). https://doi.org/10.4236/health.2023.154024
5. E. Korot et al., Enablers and barriers to deployment of smartphone-based home vision monitoring in clinical practice settings. JAMA Ophthalmol. **140**(2), 153–160 (2022). https://doi.org/10.1001/jamaophthalmol.2021.5269
6. K.C. Obi, O. Iwuanyanwu, Innovation in the assessment of primary school mathematics: an approach to revamping Nigeria education. J. Teach. Perspect. **18**(1), 51–66 (2023), [Online]. Available: http://repositorio.unan.edu.ni/2986/1/5624.pdf%0Ahttp://fiskal.kemenkeu.go.id/ejournal%0A10.1016/j.cirp.2016.06.001%0A10.1016/j.powtec.2016.12.055%0A10.1016/j.ijfatigue.2019.02.006%0A10.1
7. M.J. Farooq, Q. Zhu, Modeling, analysis, and mitigation of dynamic botnet formation in wireless IoT networks. IEEE Trans. Inf. Forensics Secur. **14**(9), 2412–2426 (2019). https://doi.org/10.1109/TIFS.2019.2898817
8. S.N.G. Gourisetti, M. Mylrea, H. Patangia, Cybersecurity vulnerability mitigation framework through empirical paradigm: Enhanced prioritized gap analysis. Futur. Gener. Comput. Syst. **105**, 410–431 (2020). https://doi.org/10.1016/j.future.2019.12.018
9. V.P. Ranganath, J. Mitra, Are free Android app security analysis tools effective in detecting known vulnerabilities? Empir. Softw. Eng. **25**(1), 178–219 (2020). https://doi.org/10.1007/s10664-019-09749-y
10. W. Parker et al., Canadian association of radiologists white paper on de-identification of medical imaging: Part 2, practical considerations. Can. Assoc. Radiol. J. **72**(1), 25–34 (2021). https://doi.org/10.1177/0846537120967345
11. Y. Liu, Y. Li, S. W. Lin, and C. Artho, Finding permission bugs in smart contracts with role mining, ISSTA 2022–Proc. 31st ACM SIGSOFT Int. Symp. Softw. Test. Anal. **1**, 716–727 (2022). https://doi.org/10.1145/3533767.3534372
12. H.S. Munawar, F. Ullah, S. Qayyum, Big data in construction : Current applications and future opportunities (2022)
13. P. Coberly-Holt, K. Elufiede, Preparing for the fourth industrial revolution with creative and critical thinking Patricia Coberly-Holt and Kemi Elufiede, pp. 21–25 (2016)
14. P. Chen, S.K. Kim, The impact of digital transformation on innovation performance–The mediating role of innovation factors. Heliyon **9**(3), e13916 (2023). https://doi.org/10.1016/j.heliyon.2023.e13916

15. F. Faghihi, M. Abadi, A. Tajoddin, SMSBotHunter: A novel anomaly detection technique to detect SMS botnets. In: 2018 15th International ISC (Iranian Society of Cryptology) Conference on Information Security Cryptology, ISC. 2018, pp. 1–6 (2018). https://doi.org/10.1109/ISCISC.2018.8546934
16. T. Chauhan, H. Palivela, Optimization and improvement of fake news detection using deep learning approaches for societal benefit. Int. J. Inf. Manag. Data Insights **1**(2), 100051 (2021). https://doi.org/10.1016/j.jjimei.2021.100051
17. J. Fernandez-Vidal, R. Gonzalez, J. Gasco, J. Llopis, Digitalization and corporate transformation: The case of European oil and gas firms. Technol. Forecast. Soc. Change **174**, 1–31 (2022). https://doi.org/10.1016/j.techfore.2021.121293
18. C. Lou, Social media influencers and followers: Theorization of a trans-parasocial relation and explication of its implications for influencer advertising. J. Advert. **51**(1), 4–21 (2022). https://doi.org/10.1080/00913367.2021.1880345
19. C. Lou, Social media influencers and followers: Theorization of a trans-parasocial relation and explication of its implications for influencer advertising. J. Advert. (2021). https://doi.org/10.1080/00913367.2021.1880345
20. A. Jetha et al., Fragmentation in the future of work: A horizon scan examining the impact of the changing nature of work on workers experiencing vulnerability. Am. J. Ind. Med. **64**(8), 649–666 (2021). https://doi.org/10.1002/ajim.23262
21. J.C.S.A, Delta ruled first order iterative deep neural learning for sybil and wormhole attacks detection in healthcare wireless sensor network (2021)
22. S. Ali, Q. Li, A. Yousafzai, Blockchain and federated learning-based intrusion detection approaches for edge-enabled industrial IoT networks: A survey. Ad Hoc Networks. **152** (2024). https://doi.org/10.1016/j.adhoc.2023.103320
23. N. Mishra, S. Pandya, Internet of things applicaations, security challenges, attacks, intrusion detection, and future visions: A systematic review. IEEE Access **9**, 59353–59377 (2021). https://doi.org/10.1109/ACCESS.2021.3073408
24. G. Rajendran, R.S. Ragul Nivash, P.P. Parthy, S. Balamurugan, Modern security threats in the internet of things (IoT): Attacks and countermeasures. Proc. Int. Carnahan Conf. Secur. Technol. **2019** (2019). https://doi.org/10.1109/CCST.2019.8888399
25. K.P. Seng, L.M. Ang, E. Ngharamike, Artificial intelligence Internet of Things: A new paradigm of distributed sensor networks. Int. J. Distrib. Sens. Networks. **18**(3) (2022). https://doi.org/10.1177/15501477211062835
26. H. Fu, H. Chen, Y. Zhu, W. Yu, FARMS: Efficient map reduce speculation for failure recovery in short jobs. Parallel Comput. **61**, 68–82 (2017). https://doi.org/10.1016/j.parco.2016.10.004
27. J. Akoka, I. Comyn-Wattiau, A method for emerging technology evaluation. Application to blockchain and smart data discovery. Concept. Model. Perspect., pp. 247–258 (2017). https://doi.org/10.1007/978-3-319-67271-7_17
28. O.T. Olajide, Employees' attitudes and efficiency of human resource management practices: Evidence from Nigeria. Eur. J. Bus. Manag. ISSN. **6**(31), 68–73 (2014), [Online]. Available: www.iiste.org
29. N.M. Alshahrani, M.L.M. Kiah, B.B. Zaidan, A.H. Alamoodi, A. Saif, A review of smart contract blockchain based on multi-criteria analysis: Challenges and motivations. Comput. Mater. Contin. **75**(2), 2833–2858 (2023). https://doi.org/10.32604/cmc.2023.036138
30. K. Gilani, F. Ghaffari, E. Bertin, and N. Crespi, Self-sovereign identity management framework using smart contracts. In: Proceeding IEEE/IFIP Network Operation and Management Symposium 2022 Network Service Management Era Cloudification, Softwarization Artificial Intelligent NOMS 2022 (2022). https://doi.org/10.1109/NOMS54207.2022.9789831
31. A.O. Omotayo, A.B. Omotoso, S.A. Daud, O.P. Omotayo, B.A. Adeniyi, Rising food prices and farming households food insecurity during the COVID-19 pandemic: Policy implications from South West Nigeria. Agriculture. **12**(3) (2022). https://doi.org/10.3390/agriculture12030363
32. N. Sidek, N. Ali, G. Alkawsi, An integrated success model of internet of things (IoT)-based services in facilities management for public sector. Sensors **22**(9), 1–32 (2022). https://doi.org/10.3390/s22093207

33. C. Arnold, K.I. Voigt, Determinants of industrial internet of things adoption in German manufacturing companies. Int. J. Innov. Technol. Manag. **16**(6) 2019. https://doi.org/10.1142/S021987701950038X
34. A. Ahmed, Assistant, Ontological, Epistemological and methodological assumptions : Qualitative Versus Quantitative Abdelhamid Ahmed assistant lecturer at the curriculum & instruction Deptartment, Faculty of Education, Helwan University, Egypt. Currently, a PhD student at Scholar (2018)
35. F. Naz, R. Agrawal, S. Luthra, A. Kumar, Reviewing the applications of artificial intelligence in sustainable supply chains : Exploring research propositions for future directions, pp. 2400–2423 (2022). https://doi.org/10.1002/bse.3034

Chapter 7
Discussion and Interpretation of Findings

7.1 Relevance to Humanities Education Goals

In the continually evolving field of education, the use of software tools in the teaching of humanities has resulted in the creation of possibilities that have never been seen before with the purpose of boosting engagement, extending access, and intensifying learning. One of the most important questions that still needs to be answered is how well these technologies match with the core aims of education in the humanities. Not only is it vital to have an understanding of this alignment to pick acceptable technologies, but it is also required in order to guarantee that the utilisation of these technologies contributes meaningfully to instructional results, ethical reflection, critical analysis, and cultural literacy and literacy. This section investigates the significance of software tools in the process of accomplishing the fundamental goals of education in the humanities. Among them are the development of critical thinking, the cultivation of empathy and ethical reasoning, the enhancement of multicultural understanding, the promotion of communication skills, and the encouragement of reflective learning. We explain how software can be an asset in advancing these educational goals by relying on theoretical ideas, classroom examples, and research studies. This is accomplished by demonstrating how software can be effectively applied with careful consideration [1].

7.1.1 Critical Thinking and Analytical Skills

Critical thinking is at the core of humanities education. It requires the capacity to analyse texts, question assumptions, assess evidence, and construct arguments that are supported by reason. Voyant Tools, AntConc, and TAPoR are examples of software tools that provide user-friendly and powerful ways to interact with textual data that go beyond the conventional methods of reading and interpretation. These tools

F. A. Alaba et al., *Learning Beyond the Classroom*, Studies in Computational Intelligence 1253, https://doi.org/10.1007/978-3-032-14433-1_7

enable students to identify trends in big corpora, compare theme distributions, and assess word frequencies. For example, a student using Voyant to evaluate the speeches of political leaders over a decade might find variations in rhetoric or philosophy. This data-driven approach to interpretation helps students to support or challenge their assumptions using empirical facts, which deepens their critical analysis and allows them to improve their critical thinking skills (Fig. 7.1 and Table 7.1).

By engaging students in structured inquiry, software tools nurture intellectual rigour and enable learners to handle ambiguity and complexity hallmarks of critical thinking.

Fig. 7.1 The benefits of critical thinking [2]

Table 7.1 Critical thinking support

software tool	Critical thinking support	Example use case
Voyant tools	Word frequency, keyword trends, collocation analysis	Analyse Shakespeare's plays for themes of power and betrayal
AntConc	Concordance and corpus comparison	Compare 19th-century newspaper articles for bias and framing
TAPoR	Tool repository for critical text analysis	Select tools based on text type and research objective

Table 7.2 Empathy, ethics, and humanistic values

Platform	Contribution to humanistic values	Example assignment
Twine	Builds moral imagination through interactive storytelling	Develop a character-driven game based on real historical injustices
StoryMapJS	Connects narrative to geography	Create a map-based story of a refugee's journey
scalar	Multi-media academic publishing	Develop an ethical analysis of climate change activism through text and media

7.1.2 Empathy, Ethics, and Humanistic Values

The development of moral reasoning and compassion is another primary aim of the humanities. Students engage in the exploration of a variety of views and the confrontation of moral conundrums via the mediums of literature, philosophy, history, and the arts. Twine, StoryMapJS, and Scalar are examples of digital storytelling tools that provide students the ability to develop narratives that accurately represent the nuances of the subject matter.

For instance, students might use Twine to create interactive tales that imitate ethical judgements that were made during historical events like as the Holocaust or the Civil Rights Movement. Not only do these tools encourage creative thinking, but they also force students to consider topics from a variety of perspectives, which helps them develop their capacity for empathy and ethical reasoning [3] (Table 7.2).

The interactive nature of such tools allows students to consider how stories are shaped by context, power dynamics, and individual agency critical themes in humanities disciplines.

7.1.3 Communication and Expression

One of the primary goals of humanities education is to teach students how to communicate effectively, both verbally and visually. Having the capacity to formulate arguments, communicate feelings, and participate in debate are all included in this talent. Canva, Padlet, Miro, and Prezi are examples of different software programs that may help students improve their expressive talents across a variety of different modalities. Canva, for instance, gives students the ability to create visual essays or digital posters that concisely communicate complicated concepts. Both collaborative brainstorming and visual storytelling are supported by Miro, which is particularly helpful for assignments involving literature or history. These kinds of platforms make it possible for children to acquire multimodal literacy, which means that they learn to communicate via the use of text, images, sounds, and designs [4] (Table 7.3).

Table 7.3 Communication and expression

Tool	Communication skill enhanced	Academic application
Canva	Visual communication	Create infographics summarising a philosophical argument
Padlet	Interactive discussion	Share and annotate excerpts from postcolonial literature
Miro	Collaborative visual thinking	Map out a timeline of feminist movements
Prezi	Dynamic presentations	Present a comparative analysis of ancient and modern myths

Through these applications, students not only become more confident communicators but also develop a sensitivity to the forms and contexts of communication.

7.1.4 *Interdisciplinary and Cultural Understanding*

In addition, education in the humanities fosters an understanding for the many different cultures, histories, and fields of scientific study. By enabling students to investigate the connections between different fields of study, such as art, linguistics, history, and literature, software has the potential to bridge the gap between different fields of study. Through the use of applications such as Google Arts & Culture, TimelineJS, and Omeka, digital displays that highlight ethnic viewpoints may be curated and created with the assistance of these tools. For instance, a project in Omeka may entail students creating a digital museum display on indigenous art. This would require integrating textual analysis with visual curation and metadata tagging. This method not only teaches skills in digital archiving and categorisation, but it also helps users develop an understanding of cultural representation and the historical context in which it exists [5] (Table 7.4).

Such projects situate students as knowledge creators who mediate between disciplines and cultural frameworks a vital competency in the globalised world.

Table 7.4 Interdisciplinary benefit

Tool	Interdisciplinary benefit	Example project
Omeka	Museum studies, cultural history	Curate an exhibit on postcolonial literature and its global reach
Google arts and culture	Art history, anthropology	Explore ancient artifacts and interpret cultural significance
TimelineJS	Historical sequencing	Develop a timeline of transatlantic slave trade with commentary

7.1.5 Reflective and Metacognitive Learning

Another essential component of education in the humanities is the practice of reflection. Students are prompted to reflect on their own thought processes, to examine the assumptions they have made, and to describe the learning processes they have gone through. Such metacognitive interaction may be realised via the use of platforms such as Notion, Hypothesis, and electronic portfolios. Students, for instance, are able to annotate texts together via the use of Hypothesis, which encourages conversation around interpretation. The usage of annotations allows for the documentation of shifting thinking, the response to insights from peers, and the revisiting of past assumptions. Through the use of e-portfolio systems, students are able to monitor their own learning journeys, gather artefacts, and reflect on their development over the course of many semesters (Fig. 7.2 and Table 7.5).

By supporting reflective learning, these tools contribute to deeper understanding and foster a learner-centered environment.

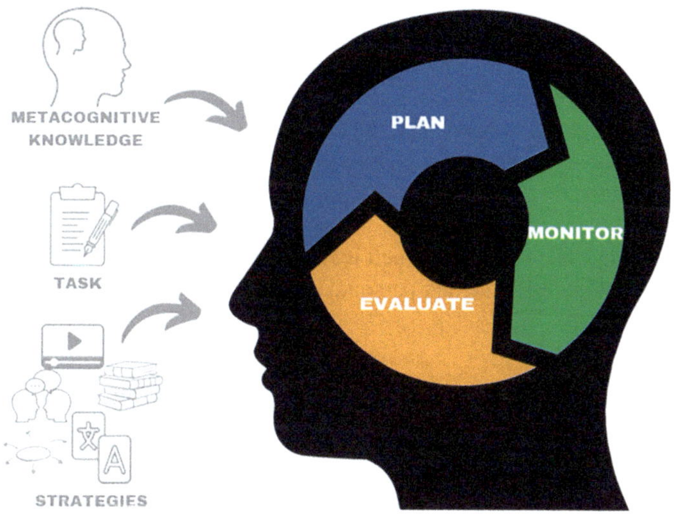

Fig. 7.2 Examples of metacognition [6]

Table 7.5 Metacognitive benefit

Platform	Metacognitive benefit	Implementation strategy
Hypothesis	Encourages critical reflection on texts	Annotate weekly readings and write end-of-term synthesis
Notion	Journaling, synthesis, and goal-tracking	Maintain a study log and reflective essays
E-Portfolio (e.g., Mahara)	Longitudinal learning records	Compile and reflect on major assignments and feedback

Table 7.6 Student agency and personalisation

Tool	Type of student agency	Example in humanities
Wikis (e.g., Wikidot)	Collaborative authorship	Co-author a class encyclopedia on literary genres
Trello	Project management and planning	Organise a group research project on urban histories
Slack	Asynchronous collaboration	Facilitate peer discussion and document sharing for seminar projects

7.1.6 Student Agency and Personalisation

Humanities education also relies on reflective practice. Students are prompted to reflect on their own thought processes, to examine the assumptions they have made, and to describe the learning processes they have gone through. Such metacognitive interaction may be realised via the use of platforms such as Notion, Hypothesis, and electronic portfolios. Students, for instance, are able to annotate texts together via the use of Hypothesis, which encourages conversation around interpretation. The usage of annotations allows for the documentation of shifting thinking, the response to insights from peers, and the revisiting of past assumptions. Through the use of e-portfolio systems, students are able to monitor their own learning journeys, gather artefacts, and reflect on their development over the course of many semesters (Table 7.6).

Empowering students to shape their learning journeys aligns with the humanities' emphasis on self-knowledge and personal growth.

7.1.7 Ethical Use of Technology in Humanities

When investigating the usefulness and advantages of software in the field of education, it is of equal significance to conduct an in-depth analysis of the ethical considerations that are associated with its broad use. Data privacy, algorithmic bias, the digital divide, and academic integrity are some of the fundamental problems that have been brought to light as a result of the growing integration of digital tools and platforms in educational settings. These difficulties serve as the basis for a humanistic criticism of educational technology, which encourages teachers and students to evaluate the wider social, ethical, and philosophical repercussions of technological adoption. This critique goes beyond the practicality and convenience of the technology currently being used in the classroom. Because educational software and online platforms often gather, retain, and analyse the personal information of students, data privacy is one of the most important issues. Because of the possibility that this data may be misused, there are significant concerns around surveillance, consent, and security.

Students and teachers run the risk of being exposed to unethical data practices if there are no adequate privacy regulations in place and there is no transparency in the way data is handled. In a similar vein, algorithmic bias is a problem that is present in many AI-driven learning systems. This problem has the potential to disadvantage particular student groups owing to inherent biases in the programming and data sets. These biases may have an effect on grading systems, learning suggestions, or adaptive material delivery, which could eventually shape the educational experiences of students in ways that were not intended and that are not equal [7].

Additionally, the digital gap continues to expand inequities in educational chances. This is since kids who come from economically poor families may not have access to the digital tools and high-speed Internet that are essential for successful learning. It is vital that educational institutions handle accessibility concerns and make certain that all students, regardless of their financial level, are able to benefit from technology improvements. This disparity further reinforces social divisions, which leads to the need to address accessibility difficulties. Furthermore, academic integrity takes on new dimensions in digital learning environments, where conventional values of originality, authorship, and fair evaluation are challenged by technologies such as plagiarism detection, writing tools helped by artificial intelligence, and automated assessment systems. Educational institutions can add specialised programs that investigate the ethical implications of technology in academic contexts. This will enable students to acquire the skills necessary to successfully traverse these complex difficulties. These classes may dive into how academics in the humanities investigate digital platforms, calling into question their design, ownership, and the influence they have on society. Students acquire a responsible and educated attitude to software usage when they are encouraged to interact critically with technological breakthroughs. This means that they not only learn how to handle these tools, but they also become aware of the ethical issues that surround them. The application of critical reflection of this sort assures that students are not only passive consumers of technology but rather active participants in the process of determining the ethical and pedagogical future of information technology. For the purpose of ensuring that digital technologies serve to promote learning while respecting ideals of justice, diversity, and intellectual integrity, such efforts ensure that education continues to be rooted in both innovation and ethical responsibility [8] (Table 7.7).

Table 7.7 Ethical use of technology

Ethical concern	Pedagogical response	Tool/method
Data privacy	Teach about digital footprints and platform policies	Case study analysis of social media terms of service
Algorithmic bias	Critical media literacy exercises	Analyse Google search results for gender/racial bias
Access inequality	Promote open-source and low-bandwidth tools	Use tools like LibreOffice, Etherpad in low-resource settings

To educate students with the skills necessary to become active, critical, and ethical participants in the digital era, rather than just passive consumers of technology, is the ultimate purpose of education in this electronic age. In order to provide students with the ability to navigate and influence the ever-changing technology world with informed judgment and integrity, educators should raise awareness of concerns such as data privacy, algorithmic prejudice, and digital responsibility. In the field of humanities education, the incorporation of software should not be driven only by inventiveness or effectiveness; rather, it should be motivated by the extent to which it promotes the fundamental goals of the field. The core aims of the humanities, which include critical thinking, ethical reflection, expressive communication, cultural understanding, and student empowerment, are ideally aligned with a variety of digital technologies, as this section has shown. Technology becomes more than a complement when educators pick software deliberately and thoughtfully, with an eye towards these aims. It becomes a catalyst for transformative learning when educators do this. As a result, reviewing software via the lens of humanities education aims is not only an academic exercise; rather, it is a pedagogical obligation that guarantees integrity, inclusion, and relevance in the era of digital technology.

7.2 Link to Theoretical Framework

The incorporation of software in humanities education is not an arbitrary decision rooted solely in technological innovation or pedagogical convenience. Rather, it is deeply informed by robust theoretical frameworks that guide instructional design, knowledge construction, and learner engagement. This section explores how the use of educational software in humanities education is underpinned by key theories from the domains of constructivism, connectivism, critical pedagogy, sociocultural theory, and multiliteracies. These frameworks offer a foundation for understanding the transformative potential of software tools in achieving the humanistic goals discussed in the previous section. By establishing theoretical linkages, educators and researchers can better assess the efficacy of digital interventions and promote intentional, reflective practices in integrating technology into the humanities classroom.

7.2.1 *Constructivism: Learning as Active Meaning-Making*

The core learning theory known as constructivism places an emphasis on the need for learners to actively construct their knowledge rather than just passively absorbing information. This viewpoint, which was pioneered by Jean Piaget and Jerome Bruner, emphasises the significance of experience, problem-solving, and exploration in the process of developing mental models. Learners interact dynamically with content, combining their past knowledge with new insights to gain a better comprehension

Table 7.8 Constructivist principle

Constructivist principle	Software application	Learning outcome
Knowledge construction	Twine, Scratch	Creative thinking and narrative formation
Active exploration	Moodle, Google Workspace	Task ownership and iterative revision
Scaffolding learning	H5P interactive content	Progression from basic to complex concepts

of the material. This is in contrast to the traditional method of acquiring information, which is static. There is a natural alignment between this theory and digital technologies that encourage learning possibilities that are interactive, self-directed, and immersive. The ideals of constructivism are embodied in software platforms like as Twine, Tinkercad, and Moodle. These platforms provide students the opportunity to develop, collaborate, and enhance their ideas via iterative feedback loops. Twine, for example, gives students the ability to create branching tales that investigate ethical conundrums in historical settings. This encourages critical thinking and personal participation on the part of the students. Tinkercad, in a similar manner, encourages hands-on inquiry in design by providing students with the opportunity to experiment with creative ideas inside a digital environment. via the facilitation of peer-to-peer talks, Moodle improves the effectiveness of collaborative learning. This feature enables students to share their viewpoints and improve their knowledge via conversation.

When learners make use of these platforms, they are able to actively participate in the process of defining their educational path. Constructivist methods enable students to connect with concepts in a meaningful way, whether via the use of narrative, collaborative problem-solving, or iterative refining of ideas. This results in learning that is more immersive, personalised, and successful. When such technology is included into educational settings, it serves to support the notion that information is not only conveyed but rather actively generated via the processes of discovery, reflection, and interaction with a variety of ways of thinking (Table 7.8).

These tools embody the constructivist vision by offering learners opportunities to build and revise knowledge structures through immersive, dialogic activities.

7.2.2 Connectivism: Learning in the Digital Age

The concept of connectivism, which was first proposed by [9], reframes learning as a dynamic process that takes place inside networked, digital settings, rather than being limited to the cognitive processes of its participants. Within this paradigm, information is dispersed throughout various digital platforms, social media, and linked knowledge networks. This provides learners with the opportunity to interact with information in a fluid and collaborative manner. Individuals are able to create learning connections via online interactions, shared resources, and collective engagement with varied viewpoints. This is in contrast to the traditional method of depending primarily on personal acquisition of skills and information. Connectivism ideals are embodied in software applications such as Hypothesis, Slack, Google Docs, and Padlet. These applications encourage connection that extends beyond the bounds of conventional educational settings. Users are able to communicate their thoughts regardless of their location or the amount of time they have available, thanks to these platforms, which offer real-time and asynchronous cooperation. In addition to this, they encourage the development of information by peers, emphasizing active engagement in the process of knowledge creation rather than passive consumption. It is also possible to get access to worldwide networks via the use of these technologies, which connect students to a larger intellectual community that brings together the perspectives of students, educators, and professionals [10].

Students, for instance, have the opportunity to engage in collaborative annotation of texts via the use of Hypothesis in the context of a digital humanities seminar. This allows them to include their viewpoints in a conversation that extends beyond the confines of their immediate classroom. Learners connect not just with their classmates and teachers, but also with outside academics who bring their unique perspectives, therefore expanding the scope of the conversation in significant ways. Additionally, applications such as Slack and Google Docs make it possible for people to work together to solve problems by facilitating group conversations, document co-editing, and the exchange of organised ideas. Enhanced collaborative learning experiences may be achieved via the use of platforms such as Padlet, which provide graphically organised places for brainstorming, the incorporation of multimedia, and real-time interaction. Education is transformed into a linked and fluid process via the use of modern technologies, which allows for the ongoing construction and refinement of knowledge through active engagement in digital networks. Connectivism learning facilitates this transformation. Learners are equipped with the skills essential for cooperation, adaptation, and engagement with global viewpoints via the use of this model, which prepares them for the demands of a digital world that is continually expanding. The incorporation of networked technologies allows education to transcend beyond the concept of isolated study and embrace the dynamic nature of information sharing. This ensures that learning continues to be current, interactive, and profoundly tied to the digital age [11] (Table 7.9).

Table 7.9 Connectivism element

Connectivism element	Supporting software	Pedagogical practice
Networked knowledge	Slack, Padlet	Open discussion threads and group brainstorming
Distributed cognition	Google Docs	Collaborative essay writing
Peer-to-peer interaction	Hypothesis	Community annotation and shared reflection

Connectivism legitimise the dynamic and social nature of digital learning environments and justifies the use of software to extend learning beyond the classroom.

7.2.3 *Socio-cultural Theory: Learning Through Social Interaction*

The socio-cultural theory developed by [12] emphasises the vital role that social interaction, cultural influences, and language play in the process of cognitive development throughout childhood. The notion of the ZPD, which symbolises the knowledge gap between what a student is capable of doing on their own and what they are capable of accomplishing with organised direction and help from more competent peers or instructors, is at the core of his work. Rather than being a lonely activity, Vygotsky proposed that learning is a socially mediated experience in which people construct their knowledge via the process of cooperation and the utilisation of cultural instruments that are shared. To facilitate collaborative inquiry and provide learners with scaffolding as they go through their ZPD, digital technologies serve as mediational artefacts in the setting of humanities education. Miro, Zoom breakout rooms, and Flipgrid are examples of platforms that may be used to build dynamic learning environments. These environments are designed to facilitate meaningful conversation, constructive criticism, and the collaborative production of knowledge in socially engaging settings. Students are able to connect with their classmates as well as their teachers via the use of these instruments, which encourages a more profound intellectual engagement and emphasises the significance of social contact in the educational process.

As an example, when a student utilises Flipgrid to offer a visual study of Renaissance art, they are able to profit from an iterative process of learning via debate and criticism. Students are able to improve their interpretative abilities via the feedback they get from their classmates and professors, which enables them to reassess creative topics, historical settings, and methodological methods. via the process of navigating these collaborative digital worlds, students have first-hand experience of how knowledge is formed, moulded, and extended via interaction. Taking this approach not only helps them improve their analytical skills, but it also corresponds with Vygotsky's notion of learning as a process that is essentially social and culturally rooted. The use of these digital technologies enables educators to design learning experiences that are rich in participation, which fosters intellectual development and encourages deeper examination of topics that are complicated [13] (Table 7.10).

Digital tools support culturally responsive pedagogy and highlight the relational nature of learning.

Table 7.10 Vygotskian concept

Vygotskian concept	Digital implementation	Pedagogical strategy
Zone of proximal development	Miro, Jamboard	Co-construction of ideas in group projects
Cultural mediation	Flipgrid, Voicethread	Narratives enriched by diverse cultural perspectives
Scaffolding	Learning management systems	Instructor-curated content with formative assessments

7.2.4 *Critical Pedagogy: Education as Liberation*

Critical pedagogy, which was developed by Paulo Freire, represents education as an endeavour that is profoundly political and ethical. Its purpose is to provide students with the ability to critically evaluate, challenge, and eventually reform their everyday reality. As opposed to treating students as passive recipients of knowledge, this approach encourages them to develop critical consciousness, also known as conscientização. This is a process that allows them to recognise social injustices and engage in meaningful action. Digital technologies become more than simply channels for the transfer of knowledge in the area of humanities education; they serve as means for resistance, inquiry, and conversation, therefore moulding students into active participants in the discourse of historical and cultural topics.

Scalar, TimelineJS, and Omeka are examples of software platforms that exemplify Freirean concepts. These platforms provide students the ability to curate and criticise historical narratives, recover voices that have been marginalised, and challenge prevailing ideologies via the medium of digital publishing. Using these technologies, students are given the opportunity to generate knowledge via collaborative efforts, therefore creating environments in which alternate histories and points of view might develop. Scalar, for instance, provides a nonlinear framework for multimedia storytelling, which enables students to put together projects that challenge the conventional narratives of historical events. In a similar manner, TimelineJS assists in contextualising complicated historical events by graphically mapping links between periods in time, whilst Omeka offers an open-access digital archive for the purpose of conserving and exhibiting important research [14].

For instance, a multimedia project that is driven by students and uses Scalar to emphasise the achievements of women who are under-represented in the field of philosophy would be an example of this strategy being put into practice. Students actively oppose historical erasure and produce a resource that amplifies voices that have traditionally been marginalised by gathering original documents, academic discussion, and visual storytelling. This resource is created by students. By going through this process, individuals participate in critical engagement with historical documents, conduct an analysis of power dynamics within the academic community, and contribute to an intellectually environment that is further inclusive. At the end of the day, the incorporation of digital resources into the education of humanities

Table 7.11 Critical pedagogy principle

Critical pedagogy principle	Digital practice	Example application
Dialogue and critique	Forums, blogs, and Scalar	Critical analysis of colonial literature
Voice and representation	Omeka, TimelineJS	Community archiving and storytelling
Social transformation	Twine, digital zines	Digital activism through storytelling

students serves to reaffirm the notion that education is not objective; rather, it is inextricably linked to the process of social reform and justice. Through the use of these platforms, both students and teachers are able to take part in a bigger movement that reimagines the creation of knowledge. This helps to ensure that education continues to be a process that is always growing, participative, and strategically engaged [15] (Table 7.11).

By aligning digital tools with social justice aims, educators operationalise critical pedagogy in the digital sphere.

7.2.5 *Multiliteracies: Expanding Modes of Expression*

The New London Group is responsible for the introduction of the idea of multiliteracies, which broadens the conventional conceptions of literacy to include other means of communication. These modes of communication include visual, spatial, auditory, gestural, and digital components. By recognising that literacy encompasses more than just reading and writing text, this framework acknowledges that literacy encompasses a wide range of modes of expression that are essential for interacting with a world that is becoming more driven by multimedia. The integration of digital technologies to improve creativity, accessibility, and engagement is supported by Multiliteracies in the field of humanities education. This ensures that students are able to convey their ideas in a variety of media without encountering any difficulties. The ideas of Multiliteracies are put into practice via the use of software platforms such as Canva, Adobe Express, and Sound trap. These platforms enable students to generate material that goes beyond the limits of traditional textual assignments. Students are able to create visual essays and infographics with the help of Canva. These visual essays and infographics include images, typography, and design components that synthesise complicated ideas, so making abstract notions more concrete. Adobe Express provides tools for multimedia storytelling, which allows users to combine text, photos, and video in order to create interesting tales. Sound trap, on the other hand, offers a channel for the communication of ideas via the use of sound. It facilitates the production of podcasts and spoken-word performances that enhance the voices of students in an aural format [16].

When it comes to accommodating students who have a variety of learning preferences and cultural backgrounds, these many modes of expression are very helpful. Learning via multimodal projects gives students the opportunity to interact with the

Table 7.12 Multiliteracies

Mode of literacy	Digital tool	Educational product
Visual	Canva, Adobe Express	Infographic on feminist literary theory
Aural	Soundtrap, Anchor	Podcast on dystopian narratives
Spatial	ThingLink, Piktochart	Interactive map of ancient texts

material in ways that are tailored to their unique capabilities, which in turn promotes inclusion and a more profound understanding of the material. By way of illustration, a visual project on protest poetry might include several forms of literacy by integrating a historical chronology, a podcast that analyses themes within the poetry, and a poster presentation that graphically contextualises essential concepts. Students go beyond the conventional limitations of literacy to build interpretations of cultural and historical tales that are richer and more multifaceted when they combine textual, aural, and visual components. All things considered, the implementation of Multiliteracies in the field of humanities education guarantees that the learning process is dynamic, interactive, and pertinent to the communication practices of the modern period. It is possible for educators to enable students to become great communicators in a digital ecosystem that is always growing by embracing these different means of expression. This will also encourage critical engagement with information across a variety of media [17] (Table 7.12).

Multiliteracies reinforce the inclusive, expressive, and adaptive qualities of humanities education in the digital age.

7.2.6 Experiential and Situated Learning

Owolabi and Bekele [18]'s experiential learning model and [19]'s contextual learning theory both stress the importance of context and practice in the learning process. Owolabi and Bekele [18] claimed that learning is most successful when it is based on lived experiences, which fosters a stronger link between theory and reality. Similarly, [19] believed that knowledge is best gained by active involvement in communities of practice, in which learners interact with experts and peers in meaningful ways. Digital technologies improve experiential learning by imitating real-world difficulties, which make abstract ideas more concrete and participatory. For example, digital role-playing on platforms such as Twine or StoryMapJS enables students to negotiate complicated decision-making situations that replicate real-world processes. Omeka's virtual exhibits allow people to organise and show artefacts, mimicking museum experts' analytical and organisational efforts. Furthermore, social annotation and peer review promote cooperation and critical involvement, mirroring academic norms that value deliberate debate and knowledge building. These digital tools not only reinforce learning, but they also develop important abilities that may be used beyond the classroom [20] (Fig. 7.3 and Table 7.13).

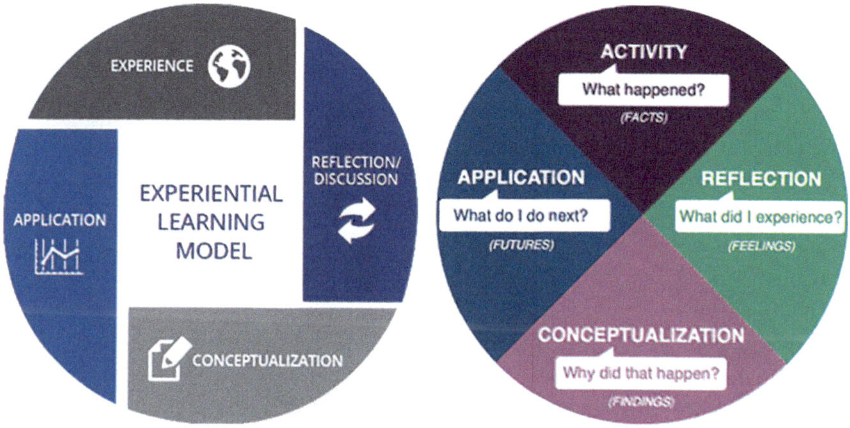

Fig. 7.3 Experiential learning [20]

Table 7.13 Experiential and situated learning

Learning theory	Application	Outcome
Experiential learning (Dewey)	Twine, AR/VR tools	Active, real-world problem-solving
Situated learning (Lave)	Omeka, Scalar	Participation in authentic scholarly practices
Communities of practice	Slack, Discord	Peer collaboration and shared meaning-making

These theories lend support to software-based projects that mimic professional, civic, and academic realities.

7.2.7 *Bloom's Taxonomy and Digital Taxonomies*

Bloom's taxonomy remains a fundamental concept in curriculum design, categorising cognitive abilities into hierarchical levels: remembering, understanding, applying, analysing, evaluating, and creating. With the advent of digital learning, educators have altered Bloom's taxonomy to include digital resources that correspond to each cognitive level. For example, flashcard applications like Quizlet might help you remember by reinforcing memory via interactive repetition. Text mining technologies like Voyant help students identify patterns and insights from complicated textual material. At the highest level, digital storytelling platforms such as Twine and podcasting tools let students develop tales and communicate ideas in novel ways. By incorporating technology into Bloom's taxonomy, instructors increase

Table 7.14 Bloom's taxonomy and digital taxonomies

Bloom's level	Digital verb	Tool
Remember	Identify, Recall	Quizlet
Understand	Summarise, Annotate	Hypothesis
Apply	Execute, Edit	Canva
Analyze	Compare, Organise	Voyant Tools
Evaluate	Critique, Argue	Scalar
Create	Design, Compose	Twine, StoryMapJS

student engagement and give dynamic possibilities for critical thinking and creative development [21] (Table 7.14).

This taxonomy offers a structured framework for mapping software capabilities to learning outcomes.

When instructional software is rooted in theoretical frameworks, not only does this improve the validity of the teaching process, but it also assures that the integration is relevant and focused on achieving certain goals. The several ideas that have been examined in this section jointly declare that software tools, when used in a reflective manner, provide support for the profound intellectual, ethical, and cultural work that is done in the field of humanities education. These theories range from constructivist engagement to critical empowerment, and from multiliteracies to digital taxonomies. Educators are consequently urged to regard digital platforms not as supplementary tools but rather as fundamental components of instructional design that is driven by theoretical frameworks. By using this strategy, technology integration is guaranteed to adhere to the principles of disciplinary integrity while simultaneously adapting to meet the requirements of modern learners and the difficulties of the modern world.

7.3 Integration with Previous Studies

The incorporation of software into humanities education is not a new idea, but it is strongly founded in a rising corpus of scholarly inquiry and empirical investigation. This section examines how prior research has studied, supported, and occasionally questioned the use of digital technologies in improving teaching and learning in humanities subjects. We situate this work in a well-established academic context and substantiate its core assertions by using insights from previous study. We look at representative studies from various educational systems and approaches, such as quantitative analyses, qualitative case studies, ethnographic research, and theoretical criticisms. These studies together highlight not just the instructional benefits of digital technologies but also their limits, ethical quandaries, and practical issues.

Table 7.15 Enhancing student engagement

Study	Software used	Educational impact
[24]	Blogs, Wikis	Enhanced student voice and creativity
[25]	Mobile apps (history timelines)	Increased motivation and retention
[26]	Hypothesis	Improved literary analysis through collaborative annotation

7.3.1 Enhancing Student Engagement and Participation

The use of software has been shown in many studies to significantly increase student involvement in humanities classes. For example, [22] discovered that digital settings, especially those that imitate real-world platforms such as blogs, wikis, and social media, increased student involvement in literature and writing programs. Baepler et al. [23] found that incorporating mobile learning applications into history instruction improved student motivation, time-on-task, and critical thinking. The study's applications enabled students to traverse historical timelines and original documents interactively, resulting in more in-depth classroom discussions and greater recall. Furthermore, [19] found that annotation tools like Hypothesis enabled "deep reading" of ancient literature. Students were more critical of Shakespearean plays, for example, when asked to comment and reply to one another's interpretations in real time (Table 7.15).

These studies affirm that well-designed software tools can foster a more participatory and dialogic learning environment.

7.3.2 Critical Thinking and Higher-Order Skills

Humanities education relies on the development of analytical and interpretative abilities. Previous research has examined the degree to which software can promote critical thinking and problem solving among students.

Yang et al. [27] performed a meta analysis of 85 research and found that digital tools had a moderate to substantial influence on higher-order learning outcomes in disciplines such as philosophy, history, and cultural studies. Interactive simulations, multimedia case studies, and digital discussions improved students' ability to synthesise and evaluate complicated concepts compared to conventional lecture-based techniques. In a case study by [28], students in an ethics class utilised digital storytelling software to investigate moral quandaries. The mix of story building and visual medium required ethical reasoning, audience awareness, and inventiveness, all of which are essential humanities talents (Table 7.16).

These findings support the argument that software is not only a delivery mechanism but a cognitive partner in learning.

Table 7.16 Authors and focus area

Author(s)	Focus area	Findings
[29]	Meta-analysis of digital learning in humanities	Digital tools improve critical thinking and analysis
[30]	Digital storytelling in ethics	Narrative software deepens moral reasoning and interpretation

Table 7.17 Collaboration and peer learning

Study	Tool used	Key result
[32]	Google Docs, Moodle forums	Enhanced dialogue and mutual scaffolding
[33]	Padlet, Slack	Facilitated intercultural humanities learning

7.3.3 Collaboration and Peer Learning

Multiple empirical research has examined educational software's social constructivist potential, particularly its capacity to facilitate cooperation. Thoman and Jolls [31] emphasised that software-mediated discussions via forums, collaborative papers, and peer evaluation tools are strongly aligned with the dialogic aspect of humanities education. Her "conversational frameworks" concept has been proven in blended literature and history courses, where students used Google Docs to co-author essays and offer iterative feedback to peers. Singh [30] found that collaborative platforms such as Padlet, Trello, and Slack assisted students in multicultural classes in sharing cross-cultural views of literary works. The digital technologies functioned as language and cognitive bridges, promoting greater international understanding (Table 7.17).

These findings reinforce the idea that collaborative software supports both the epistemic and ethical goals of humanities instruction.

7.3.4 Digital Literacy and Multimodal Composition

Modern humanities education places a greater emphasis on digital literacy and cross-media collaboration. Previous research has looked at how software tools may help teach these abilities. Purcell et al. [34], Pioneers in the area of digital composition contend that digital tools are critical for educating students to traverse the multimodal character of modern communication. Their study examined students' usage of web design platforms, video editing software, and podcasting tools in writing-intensive courses. Similarly, [35] found that when students in a freshman composition course were required to create multimedia essays using Adobe Premiere and Canva, they learnt transferable rhetorical analysis and design abilities. These tasks asked students

Table 7.18 Digital literacy and multimodal composition

Author(s)	Software	Literacy skill developed
[36]	Web tools, audio editors	Digital composition, media literacy
[37]	Adobe Premiere, Canva	Multimodal rhetoric and audience awareness

Table 7.19 Archiving, and public humanities

Study	Software	Community impact
[40]	Omeka, Scalar	Enabled public digital scholarship
[41]	Omeka	Supported decolonial and inclusive practices

to synthesise verbal, visual, and auditory information in persuasive and analytical formats (Table 7.18).

These studies demonstrate that software fosters the kind of media fluency and adaptability increasingly demanded in 21st-century humanities careers.

7.3.5 Preservation, Archiving, and Public Humanities

Digital archiving and public scholarship are increasingly important topics in humanities education. Many scholars have investigated how software promotes community engagement and historical preservation. Yakubu and ali [38] investigated the role of platforms such as Omeka and Scalar in assisting students with public-facing digital humanities projects. She argued that such tools democratise scholarship by encouraging students to become curators and interpreters of history, rather than passive recipients. In a subsequent study, [39] investigated how marginalised communities used digital archives to resist erasure and colonial narratives. She documented student projects that utilised Omeka to create online exhibitions of Afro-diasporic texts, emphasising software as a tool for decolonising the humanities curriculum (Table 7.19).

These findings situate software as not only a pedagogical asset but also a tool for civic engagement and social justice in humanities education.

7.3.6 Pedagogical Challenges and Limitations

While many studies highlight the teaching potential of software, others warn against over-reliance or uncritical use. Critical evaluations highlight issues such as digital divides and unequal access to devices and broadband [41], cognitive overload from excessive platform switching [42], and reduced depth in student learning through surface-level engagement [43]. For example, [31] notes that positive narratives

Table 7.20 Pedagogical challenges

Study	Concern	Recommendation
[42]	Digital inequality	Address infrastructure and training gaps
[43]	Platform overload	Streamline tool integration with learning objectives
[44]	Superficial engagement	Encourage deeper use of fewer tools

often neglect gaps in technology access, which disproportionately harm pupils from low-income families. [44] found that superficial engagement, for example, "click-through" learning on apps without critical inquiry, may impede rather than improve analytical thinking in humanities areas (Table 7.20).

These cautionary studies underscore the need for intentional, inclusive, and critically aware implementation of educational software.

There is a rich and developing body of study that verifies many of the pedagogical assertions that are stated throughout this book. The literature on software in humanities education demonstrates this rich and increasing field of research. Previous research has shown that software has the potential to significantly broaden and deepen the breadth and depth of humanities education, particularly when technology is used purposefully. This may be seen in improved student engagement and higher-order thinking, as well as in digital literacy and public scholarship. At the same time, this research shed light on a number of ongoing concerns, including access inequities, misalignment with learning objectives, and the danger of performative usage. Educators are able to go beyond a simple passion for digital technologies and towards a more nuanced and purposeful use that is founded on research and reflective practice if they include these concepts. In particular, this corpus of work establishes a solid platform for additional inquiry and innovation, especially in areas like as artificial intelligence-assisted text analysis, immersive virtual worlds, and ethical design of educational technology.

7.4 Pedagogical Implications

The integration of digital tools in humanities education brings about not just technological change, but a profound pedagogical shift. As educators and learners engage with software platforms ranging from annotation tools and collaborative writing spaces to digital archives and visualization applications, they are required to reconceptualize traditional teaching and learning methods. This section explores the pedagogical implications of software integration in the humanities, addressing both the opportunities and challenges presented by digital environments. Pedagogical implications refer to the teaching strategies, curriculum designs, learning outcomes, and assessment models influenced by the adoption of software tools. Drawing from both theoretical insights and empirical studies, this section analyses how software

Table 7.21 Role of the instructor

Instructor role	Traditional classroom	Software-enhanced classroom
Knowledge provider	Central authority in lectures	Facilitator of inquiry
Textual authority	Prescribes interpretations	Encourages interpretive diversity
Assessment designer	Summative exams and essays	Formative, project-based assessments
Classroom manager	Physical classroom interaction	Digital environment navigator

reshapes classroom dynamics, enhances cognitive engagement, promotes inclusivity, and requires new models of assessment and instruction [45].

7.4.1 *Redefining the Role of the Instructor*

In terms of educational ramifications, the alteration of the position of the teacher is one of the most important implications. It is common for the teacher to play the role of the center authority in conventional classrooms for the humanities. This includes presenting lectures, directing students' interpretations of texts, and assigning research assignments. The role of the teacher shifts to that of a facilitator, curator, and co-learner when software-enhanced learning technologies are used. Educators are now required to do the following:

1. Design learning paths that include technology;
2. Guide students through the process of navigating and critically using digital technologies;
3. Provide scaffolding for students to engage in self-directed learning.

As an example, teachers in classes that make use of annotation systems like Hypothesis alter their focus from providing authoritative readings of texts to encouraging peer-to-peer conversation and collaborative meaning-making. Instead of giving definitive readings, the teacher stimulates discussion threads and welcomes various opinions from the students (Table 7.21).

7.4.2 *Student-Centred Learning and Autonomy*

Pedagogies that are centred on the student are naturally supported by software technologies. They provide learning routes that are adaptable and individualised, that are designed to accommodate a variety of cognitive types and degrees of digital literacy. The students in digital settings often take on a larger level of responsibility for their own learning by selecting digital tools that are tailored to their requirements, determining the pace at which they interact with the material, and working together in an

Table 7.22 Student-centred learning

Pedagogical focus	Description	Software example
Autonomy	Students direct their own learning	E-portfolios (e.g., Mahara)
Differentiation	Tools accommodate various learning needs	Edpuzzle, Duolingo
Reflection	Continuous self-assessment and journaling	Padlet, Google Docs
Personalisation	Learners set goals and choose formats	Trello for learning paths

asynchronous manner. An example of this might be a humanities class that incorporates e-portfolios, which allows students to pick artefacts, reflect on their progress, and make links across different fields of study. When using such a paradigm, the learner is placed at the centre of the process of knowledge building. In addition, self-paced learning modules, such as language acquisition applications or historical simulations, provide customised education, which assists students in effectively mastering fundamental material before moving on to more advanced curriculum (Table 7.22).

7.4.3 *Rethinking Assessment Strategies*

In the field of humanities, assessment techniques need to be reevaluated in light of the advent of digital instruments. It's possible that traditional tests and term papers wound not be able to capture the entire scope of learning in contexts that are supplemented with digital technology. Students are often encouraged to engage in formative, ongoing, and performance-based evaluation while using software-enabled education. The following are examples of emerging assessment models: multimedia projects (videos, podcasts), digital storytelling and web-based curation, annotated digital texts and collaborative research wikis, peer-reviewed contributions and conversation analytics, and digital storytelling. In the context of a digital rhetoric course, for instance, students may be evaluated based on their ability to construct a multimodal argument that incorporates audio, video, and textual information. Rubrics are used by instructors to assess abilities such as narrative coherence, visual literacy, and audience engagement, all of which are vital in the realm of digital communication (Table 7.23).

7.4.4 *Collaborative and Social Learning*

Learning is seen as a socially mediated process, which is consistent with Vygotsky's theory of social constructivism. Examples of software applications that correspond with this approach include collaborative documents, discussion forums, and annotation tools. Learners are able to participate in conversation, share their perspectives,

Table 7.23 Assessment strategies

Assessment type	Traditional format	Digital alternative	Benefits
Literary analysis	Essay	Annotated text (Hypothesis)	Real-time collaboration, process visibility
Research paper	Written report	Wiki project (PBworks)	Teamwork, peer contribution
Exam	MCQ or essays	Digital storytelling (StoryMapJS)	Creativity, contextual thinking

Table 7.24 Collaborative and social learning

Collaborative strategy	Software tool	Pedagogical outcome
Peer commentary	Google Docs	Enhanced interpretive dialogue
Shared archives	Zotero groups	Collaborative citation practices
Discussion boards	Moodle forums	Asynchronous textual engagement
Concept mapping	Miro, MindMeister	Visual organisation of abstract ideas

and develop knowledge collaboratively via the use of these digital platforms. The collaborative analysis of texts, critical reflection on ideas, and the development of nuanced viewpoints that students participate in as a result of this develops greater involvement in the domain of humanities education. Iterative improvement and constructive criticism are encouraged via the use of peer feedback, which becomes an essential component of the learning process. In addition, online learning communities extend beyond the confines of the traditional classroom, making it possible for students to engage in prolonged intellectual conversation regardless of where they are physically located. For instance, in an online philosophy class, a shared Google Doc may be used as a venue for group argument mapping. In this activity, students would submit arguments, counterarguments, and references, therefore establishing a discourse that is always growing and resembling the discussion that occurs in academic circles (Table 7.24).

7.4.5 Promoting Multimodal Literacy

The incorporation of software into the field of humanities education helps to cultivate multimodal literacy, which enables students to comprehend and generate messages via a variety of modalities of communication, such as text, picture, sound, and interactive elements. Therefore, in order to ensure that students acquire fluency in a variety of modes of communication, teachers need to develop projects that foster multimodal expression. This is because digital technologies are becoming more important to academic engagement. Rubrics should integrate criteria for design and media literacy in order to successfully evaluate this work. This is because it is important

Table 7.25 Promoting multimodal literacy

Mode	Skills developed	Tools
Visual	Design, layout, semiotic analysis	Canva, Piktochart
Audio	Voice modulation, sound editing	Audacity, Anchor
Video	Narrative pacing, editing	Adobe Premiere, iMovie
Interactive	User experience design	Twine, Scalar

to recognise the significance of visual and digital fluency in current education. In addition, it is necessary to educate students how to critically assess and synthesise knowledge across different platforms in order to cultivate analytical abilities and flexibility in an environment that is becoming more digital. For instance, students in a course on visual culture may use Canva or Adobe Spark to produce visual essays that analyse topics such as colonial iconography or feminist representations in media. This would provide them the opportunity to participate with academic debate via creative and interactive methods. Not only does this change in pedagogy make the learning process more enjoyable, but it also provides students with the skills they need to successfully pursue professions in fields such as education, design, research, and the media, all of which are places where multimodal communication is becoming more valued (Table 7.25).

7.4.6 Ethics, Inclusivity, and Digital Citizenship

Questions of inclusivity, accessibility, and ethics arise naturally with the use of software in humanities curricula. As important as it is for students to learn how to use digital technologies, teachers also need to make sure they know how to use them properly, taking into account issues like privacy, representation, digital footprints, and authorship. Encouraging students to respect authorship and credit in online settings is an important part of ethical teaching practices, as is promoting debates on digital citation standards and intellectual property. Teachers may help make digital material more accessible for all students by highlighting the importance of inclusive design and include accessibility features like alt text and captioning. Students also need to be aware of algorithmic biases and critical media literacy in order to assess digital archives and algorithms for their inherent biases. For example, teachers can have their students think critically about the data sources and design assumptions made by AI-based text generators and online archives so that they may reflect on how technology affects the creation and representation of knowledge (Table 7.26).

Table 7.26 Ethical concern and pedagogical response

Ethical concern	Pedagogical response	Tool/practice
Plagiarism	Teach digital citation	Zotero, Purdue OWL
Accessibility	Use screen reader-friendly tools	VoiceThread, accessible PDFs
Bias in AI tools	Promote algorithmic literacy	GPT-based critical analysis
Online identity	Discuss data privacy and consent	Terms of use for platforms

7.4.7 *Teacher Professional Development*

In order to keep up with the latest developments in educational technology, teachers need continuous professional development as digital technologies transform traditional teaching methods. This includes courses in digital pedagogy, which provide teachers tools to make good use of technology in the classroom. Instructors may exchange resources, ideas, and tools to improve students' learning experiences via opportunities for interdisciplinary cooperation, which further boosts creativity. Furthermore, educators may interact with new technology and continually improve their approaches with access to support networks and digital repositories. In order to encourage a culture of constant improvement and learning, some schools have instituted programs like the "Digital Humanities Teaching Lab," where teachers may try out new resources, get comments from their colleagues, and create lessons that include technology (Table 7.27).

The incorporation of software into humanities instruction has far-reaching and revolutionary educational consequences. The role of the instructor, the type of student interaction, the modes of evaluation, and the ethics of digital practice are all aspects of teaching and learning that are impacted by these issues. It has been established in this section that the effective inclusion of software involves not only a technical endeavour but also a pedagogical reorientation. In order to ensure that technology meets the aims of critical thinking, creativity, cultural knowledge, and ethical citizenship, educators need to maintain a reflexive and adaptable mindset. Software tools have the potential to enhance the humanities classroom, encourage more in-depth learning, and better prepare students for the digital world beyond the realm of academia when they are implemented with careful consideration.

Table 7.27 Teacher professional development

Area of development	Need	Strategy
Technical fluency	Understanding new tools	Workshops, online tutorials
Pedagogical alignment	Integrating tools with learning goals	Instructional design seminars
Evaluation techniques	Assessing digital assignments	Rubric development clinics
Community building	Sharing practices and tools	Faculty learning communities

7.5 Role of Digital Tools in Enhancing Critical Thinking

A humanities education must include the development of critical thinking skills. It includes abilities like thinking critically, analysing, evaluating, synthesising, and reflecting. Cultivating critical thinking is both an aim and a means of education in a field that places a premium on interpretation, debate, and contextual knowledge. New opportunities to improve these mental operations have arisen as a result of the digitisation of the humanities. In addition to enhancing more conventional forms of education, digital tools provide whole new arenas for critical thinking and epistemological exploration. This section delves into how various types of digital tools are used to encourage and evaluate students' critical thinking skills. These resources include annotation platforms, argument mapping software, databases, visualisation apps, and AI-based tools. We look at how these tools change students' questioning, evidence engagement, and knowledge construction practices by drawing on pedagogical theory, classroom practice, and software capabilities.

7.5.1 Defining Critical Thinking in Humanities Education

Critical thinking in the arts and humanities involves more than just using logic; it's an intricate process that goes beyond that. It requires complex and nuanced interpretation of texts and settings, identification of bias and subjectivity in speech, building arguments with supporting evidence, and creating connections between seemingly unrelated sources. Interactive environments provided by software tools may shape and support these cognitive processes, leading to deeper analysis, critical inquiry, and rigorous questioning. Students may strengthen their reasoning and interpretive abilities using algorithmic text analysis, collaborative platforms, and digital annotation, which allows them to interact more actively with academic literature. These resources do double duty: they encourage critical thinking and the development of skills necessary to understand and apply abstract concepts in the classroom and beyond (Table 7.28).

7.5.2 Annotation Tools and Close Reading

Students are encouraged to engage in careful reading via the use of annotation tools such as Hypothesis, Perusall, and Kami. These tools inspire students to mark texts, offer questions, connect to additional sources, and participate in mutual conversations. Through the process of externalising thought, these techniques enable deeper textual study and enhance dialogic engagement and participation. It is the facilitation of line-by-line inspection, the promotion of metacognition as students express their thinking, and the stimulation of collaborative critical debates that contribute to

Table 7.28 Critical thinking in humanities education

Component of critical thinking	Description	Example in humanities
Interpretation	Understanding meaning within context	Analysing historical speeches
Analysis	Identifying relationships and patterns	Comparing literary motifs
Evaluation	Assessing credibility and logic	Judging an author's bias
Inference	Concluding evidence	Predicting themes in unseen texts
Explanation	Articulating reasoning clearly	Writing reflective annotations
Self-regulation	Reflecting on biases and errors	Journaling about interpretive shifts

Table 7.29 Annotation tools and close reading

Tool	Function	Critical thinking skill developed
Hypothesis	Web and PDF annotation	Evaluation, interpretation
Perusall	Collaborative reading	Explanation, self-regulation
Kami	Multimedia annotation	Analysis, inference

their instructional usefulness. In the context of a literary class, for instance, students can annotate Toni Morrison's "Beloved" by highlighting sections that reflect tales of trauma. They do this by asking interpretative questions, referring to historical sources, and interacting with the ideas of their classmates, which ultimately results in the construction of a multi-dimensional analysis that improves the collective knowledge (Table 7.29).

7.5.3 Argument Mapping and Visual Thinking Tools

Students are able to break down arguments into premises, evidence, and counterarguments by using argument mapping software such as Rationale, MindMup, and Kialo. These programs provide a visual framework for analysing complicated reasoning. Students are able to improve their comprehension of logical structures and frequent fallacies by analysing arguments in this manner. This technique has a number of advantages, including the promotion of clarity in thinking, the strengthening of abstract linkages via concrete examples, and the encouragement of revision through the use of visual feedback. For instance, students in a philosophy class may use Rationale to map a discussion on utilitarian ethics by generating argument trees that exhibit assertions, supporting reasoning, and objections. This can be done by using

Table 7.30 Argument mapping

Tool	Core function	Application
Rationale	Argument diagramming	Evaluating philosophical debates
Kialo	Debate visualisation	Engaging in structured controversies
MindMup	Concept mapping	Organising thematic structures in history

Table 7.31 Databases and digital archives

Archive	Content type	Critical thinking outcome
Europeana	Art, texts, multimedia	Cultural comparison and contextualisation
JSTOR	Academic articles	Synthesis of secondary arguments
DPLA	Primary documents	Source analysis and critique

Rationale. Not only does this visual depiction assist in identifying weak reasoning and statements that are not supported, but it also helps enhance abilities in critical thinking and debate (Table 7.30).

7.5.4 Databases and Digital Archives for Evidence-Based Thinking

The Digital Public Library of America (DPLA), Europeana, and JSTOR are examples of digital archives that provide students access to enormous resources. This gives them the opportunity to participate in critical thinking and perform original research. The evaluation of source dependability, the synthesis of evidence, and the formation of well-reasoned judgements are fundamental components of academic research, and they are required in order to navigate these large collections appropriately. A number of effective teaching tactics for using digital archives include the assignment of tasks that involve the triangulation of sources, the encouragement of citation comparison and historical contextualisation, and the promotion of reflective writing about the limits of sources. In a history lesson that focusses on colonial Africa, for instance, students might use DPLA to uncover source documents from missionaries and indigenous leaders. They can then analyse language, viewpoint, and context in order to critically evaluate power dynamics and prejudice (Table 7.31).

7.5.5 Visualisation and Critical Interpretation

Students can recognise hidden patterns in texts and historical events via the use of data visualisation tools such as Palladio, Voyant Tools, and TimelineJS. These patterns

Table 7.32 Visualisation and critical interpretation

Tool	Type	Learning outcome
Voyant tools	Text mining	Interpretation of literary data
Palladio	Network visualisation	Historical relationship mapping
TimelineJS	Chronological narrative	Temporal analysis of events

may not be immediately apparent from linear reading. The purpose of these tools is to facilitate learning via discovery, to stimulate the investigation of unexpected ideas, and to demand critical interpretation of data that has been visualised. For instance, students in a postcolonial literature class may utilise Voyant Tools to analyse word frequencies in the novel "Things Fall Apart." This will uncover patterns in diction that can generate conversations on language, power, and cultural hybridity. These technologies improve understanding and develop deeper analytical thinking by translating textual and historical material into images that can be interacted with (Table 7.32).

7.5.6 AI Tools and Algorithmic Literacy

ChatGPT, Claude, and Sage are examples of AI systems that provide students with a variety of views to analyse and evaluate, hence introducing new chances for critical thinking. Comparing interpretations, questioning the biases of machines, and reflecting on concerns of authorship and originality are all accomplished with the assistance of these technologies when they are addressed with care and examination. The urging of comparisons between human and AI-generated analyses, the facilitation of criticisms of algorithmic interpretations, and the use of AI-generated information as a foil to inspire further research are all examples of effective instructional applications. Students, for instance, can construct artificial intelligence replies to essay prompts and then evaluate those responses for their level of depth, coherence, and viewpoint. Students are prompted to evaluate the benefits and drawbacks of reasoning provided by artificial intelligence via the process of reverse engineering, which allows for higher-order thinking to be fostered [46] (Table 7.33).

Table 7.33 AI tools and algorithmic literacy

Tool	AI function	Critical task
ChatGPT	Text generation	Comparative critique
Elicit	Research synthesis	Evaluating source credibility
DALL·E	Image generation	Interpreting visual arguments

Table 7.34 Reflective and metacognitive tools

Tool	Feature	Critical thinking support
Padlet	Idea walls	Synthesising peer contributions
Notion	Structured note-taking	Tracking thought evolution
Google docs	Shared annotation	Metacognitive dialogue

7.5.7 Reflective and Metacognitive Tools

Padlet, Notion, and Google Docs are examples of platforms that encourage continual reflection and recording. These platforms enable students to monitor their intellectual progress and identify alterations in their thinking throughout the course of their academic careers. The use of these tools makes it easier to implement tactics such as keeping reflection diaries to record changes in thinking, assigning weekly metacognitive logs to improve reading methods, and promoting portfolio curation to indicate improvement. For instance, students in a digital humanities class use Notion to keep a journal of their weekly comments on their projects. In this log, they describe what aspects of their projects were successful, what aspects presented difficulties, and how their viewpoints developed over time. The instructors provide comments in an asynchronous manner, which helps to cultivate a dynamic and dialogic reflection process that increases the level of engagement that students have with their learning [47] (Table 7.34).

7.5.8 Assessment of Critical Thinking in Digital Contexts

In order for educators to effectively assess critical thinking, they need to develop complex rubrics that evaluate not just the end output but also the reasoning process alongside it. Digital tools are helpful because they give traceable artefacts of thinking, such as logs, version histories, comment threads, and decision trees. These artefacts provide insight into the analytical growth of a learner. Several components that contribute to an effective assessment are as follows: depth of inquiry, which takes into account the quality of the questions that are asked; quality of argumentation, which emphasizes evidence and coherence; reflective insight, which evaluates metacognition; and engagement with complexity, which investigates how students navigate ambiguity and contradiction. Through the use of these digital traces, instructors are able to provide a more thorough and dynamic assessment of the development of critical thinking skills among their pupils [48] (Table 7.35).

Critical thinking in the humanities may be considerably improved by the use of digital resources, provided that they are used with pedagogical intentionality. They provide platforms that allow for more in-depth involvement, systematic reasoning, and reflective learning. The use of software tools provides students with scaffolding for cognitive growth, whether they are annotating difficult texts, mapping ethical

Table 7.35 Sample rubric

Criterion	Exemplary	Proficient	Developing	Emerging
Interpretation	Nuanced, contextual	Accurate, relevant	Limited depth	Misinterpreted
Evaluation	Strong evidence and logic	Adequate support	Some lapses	Unsupported claims
Reflection	Clear insights, self-correction	Some insight	Superficial	Absent
Synthesis	Integrates multiple sources	Connects basic ideas	Minimal integration	Fragmented

arguments, examining historical archives, or reflecting on their own interpretative processes. Educators have the task of properly curating these resources, aligning them with learning goals, and cultivating a culture that encourages inquiry and reflection. The ability to think critically is not a by-product of digital learning; rather, it is a conscious pedagogical aim that technology, when utilised carefully, may assist in achieving with fresh vigour and relevance in the academic environment of today [49].

7.6 Impacts on Student Autonomy and Learning Ownership

As digital technologies transform the learning environment, progressive educational philosophies, which prioritise student autonomy and learning ownership, are more important in humanities education. When kids are able to take charge of their own education, think critically, and evaluate their own performance, we say that they are autonomous. Ownership of one's learning goes beyond independence; it delineates a profound feeling of accountability, control, and individual involvement in one's educational path. Opportunities to increase independence and ownership have expanded with the introduction of digital technology into humanities courses. Platforms for software allow users to explore at their own speed, collaborate with peers, implement feedback loops, and access a variety of material. In addition to structural flexibility, these technologies provide educational processes that empower students to define their own intellectual journeys. Through customisation, choice, self-evaluation, collaborative design, and reflective practices, this section delves into how digital technologies foster autonomy and ownership of learning. Additionally, it delves into the possible dangers and provides ways to strike a balance between autonomy and direction.

Table 7.36 Key attributes of autonomous learners

Attribute	Description
Self-direction	Ability to plan and regulate one's own learning activities
Motivation	Internal drive to pursue learning goals
Reflection	Continuous assessment of learning processes and outcomes
Choice-making	Capacity to make informed academic decisions
Persistence	Commitment to seeing tasks through, even when difficult

7.6.1 Understanding Autonomy and Learning Ownership in the Humanities

The emphasis in the humanities moves from seeking absolute solutions to developing well-reasoned, individual insights; this, in turn, promotes autonomy by calling on students to participate in interpretation, discussion, and reflection. Learning about philosophy, literature, and history helps students deal with uncertainty, question assumptions, and develop more nuanced viewpoints. This approach fosters critical thinking skills, which are necessary for comprehending and addressing difficult challenges from several perspectives. Students might better prepare themselves for a dynamic and unpredictable world by studying the humanities, which place an emphasis on inquiry rather than certainty (Table 7.36).

Learning ownership involves a shift from passive reception to active construction of knowledge. It entails identifying with one's learning objectives, valuing the process, and perceiving educational success as personally meaningful.

7.6.2 Personalisation Through Digital Platforms

The pursuit of absolute answers is shifted in the humanities towards the cultivation of deliberate, individual insights; autonomy is fostered via interpretation, discourse, and contemplation. Philosophy, literature, and history provide students with tools to deal with ambiguity, question presumptions, and develop more nuanced viewpoints. By enhancing critical thinking skills, this technique enables learners to approach complicated situations from different perspectives. The humanities cultivate intellectual flexibility and depth by teaching students to value inquiry over certainty, which in turn equips them to participate meaningfully in a world that is always evolving (Table 7.37).

Table 7.37 Personalisation through digital platforms

Tool	Autonomy feature	Learning ownership outcome
Moodle	Custom module access	Empowered curriculum navigation
Perusall	Adaptive reading engagement	Increased reading accountability
Mahara	Individualised portfolios	Curated knowledge identity

Table 7.38 Digital feedback and self-assessment

Tool	Feedback type	Ownership development
Google docs	Asynchronous comments	Revision and accountability
Turnitin feedback studio	Rubric-based annotations	Objective performance insights
Peergrade	Structured peer reviews	Dialogic reflection

7.6.3 Digital Feedback and Self-assessment

When feedback is timely, thorough, and dialogic, it greatly enhances the likelihood that students will take ownership of their own learning. Peergrade, Google Docs, and Turnitin Feedback Studio are some of the tools that students may use to engage in self-reflection and evaluation via the use of iterative feedback loops. Students may actively participate in analysing and improving their work with the help of these tools, which promotes a better knowledge and the development of skills. Students are encouraged to carefully assess and reply to constructive criticism via peer feedback, which in particular improves metacognition and collaborative accountability. Learning ownership is enhanced when students take comments to heart and make substantial changes, rather than concentrating just on grades. In a cultural studies class, for instance, students use Google Docs to turn in reflective essays that get feedback from both teachers and classmates in the form of inline comments. In order to show that they have engaged with the comments and that their ideas have evolved, students make adjustments to their work and record them in a revision note (Table 7.38).

7.6.4 E-Portfolios and Reflective Practice

Students may record their progress in knowledge and skills in an engaging and all-encompassing manner with the help of electronic portfolios. Mahara, Pathbrite, and Google Sites are some of the platforms that students may use to create educational narratives, reflect on their experiences, and preserve artefacts. When students reflect on their learning, they are more likely to synthesise information from many areas of study, be more invested in their academic objectives, and be more likely to recognise and celebrate their successes. A Pathbrite portfolio may include students' research

Table 7.39 E-Portfolios and reflective practice

Portfolio tool	Reflection mechanism	Ownership impact
Mahara	Reflection prompts	Synthesis of learning experience
Pathbrite	Milestone documentation	Goal orientation
Google sites	Customisable layout	Narrative control

Table 7.40 Choice-based assignments

Tool	Assignment format	Autonomy expression
Twine	Interactive storytelling	Narrative design
StoryMapJS	Visual geolocation	Spatial interpretation
Scalar	Multimedia publication	Cross-modal authorship

notes, digital posters, reflections, peer comments, and class discussions on human rights, for example, in a humanities seminar. By showcasing their learning path and helping students recognise how their ideas and abilities grow over time, this concluding project enhances their long-term academic identity (Table 7.39).

7.6.5 Choice-Based Assignments and Student-Led Projects

Students develop a sense of independence and agency when given the freedom to pick their own work's focus, style, and audience. Students are encouraged to examine information in ways that match their interests and skills via the use of digital humanities tools like Twine, StoryMapJS, and Scalar, which promote unique methods of proving comprehension. By tying what students learn to their own experiences, this method boosts motivation, inspires creativity in project creation, and gives students a sense of ownership over their work by publishing and sharing it. In a literature class, for instance, students may choose from a variety of assignment styles, such as writing a critical essay, making an interactive fiction project using Twine, or building a digital timeline with TimelineJS. Educators can help students better understand and engage with the material by giving them choices that play to their strengths (Table 7.40).

7.6.6 Collaborative Tools for Peer-Led Learning

Autonomy and group ownership in learning are both enhanced via collaboration that is structured to promote shared accountability. Students can work together on projects, take the lead in class discussions, and make decisions using collaborative tools such as Padlet, Slack, and Miro. Assigning students responsibilities such as class wiki curators or discussion leaders on a rotating basis, encouraging the creation

Table 7.41 Collaborative tools for peer-led learning

Platform	Collaboration feature	Ownership mechanism
Padlet	Real-time contributions	Shared authorship
Slack	Channel discussions	Peer leadership
Miro	Visual ideation boards	Collective decision-making

Table 7.42 Balancing structure and freedom

Phase	Instructor role	Student responsibility
Early	Guide and scaffold	Follow structured tasks
Mid	Monitor and support	Explore independently
Late	Feedback provider	Own project execution

of collaborative knowledge bases, and placing an emphasis on process rather than result in team-based assignments are all effective educational tactics for creating this atmosphere. One example is a digital rhetoric class where students use Padlet to create a living dictionary of digital terms. They each contribute an entry, provide an example, and provide feedback. By encouraging both group and individual responsibility for one's learning, this method encourages more in-depth participation and self-reflection [50] (Table 7.41).

7.6.7 *Balancing Structure and Freedom*

Striking a balance between freedom and organised assistance is vital for digital teaching, as too much liberty without scaffolding may lead to doubt, procrastination, or disengagement. Implementing milestone check-ins to assess progress, beginning with prescribed tasks and progressively surrendering responsibility, and adding peer mentorship and accountability networks are all effective ways for promoting sustainable autonomy. Using Omeka or Palladio as an example, students in a digital humanities course that is project-based start with weekly assigned assignments. Students are encouraged to work independently on research projects as they develop self-assurance, with the option of receiving one-on-one mentorship to help them along the way. This allows for a balance between assistance and involvement, while yet encouraging autonomy (Table 7.42).

7.6.8 *Risks and Ethical Considerations*

It is true that digital autonomy may help students feel more empowered; but, it also has the potential to amplify existing inequities, since not all students have the

Table 7.43 Risks and ethical considerations

Risk	Mitigation strategy
Technological inequality	Provide open-source alternatives and device access
Overchoice	Curate a limited number of well-structured options
Superficial engagement	Encourage depth over digital aesthetics
Isolation	Blend digital with in-person discussions

same access to digital literacy, hardware, or support networks. In addition, learners may get disengaged if they are confronted with an excessive number of options or digital distractions. Among the most important risk factors are digital exhaustion and fragmentation, uneven access to technology, decreased interpersonal engagement, and an excessive focus on performative self-presentation. The provision of digital skills training to ensure equitable participation, the encouragement of group check-ins and mentorship to build supportive learning communities, the design of user-friendly digital environments to minimise accessibility barriers, and the promotion of meaningful choices rather than overwhelming students with an excessive number of options are all effective solutions that can be implemented to mitigate these challenges. The ability to build digital learning experiences that are both inclusive and sustainable is a skill that educators may develop by finding a balance between autonomy and structure (Table 7.43).

Digital tools, when integrated with intentional pedagogy, can significantly enhance student autonomy and foster a sense of learning ownership. These tools offer not only the freedom to explore but also mechanisms to reflect, collaborate, and express understanding in personalized ways. For humanities education, which values interpretation, agency, and contextual inquiry, this shift is particularly powerful. Autonomy is not merely about students working alone—it is about them feeling accountable to their own goals, identities, and communities of learning. Educators must therefore cultivate digital learning environments that support this empowerment while addressing disparities, ensuring that ownership is a right afforded to all learners.

7.7 Teacher Training and Capacity Building

When it comes to the incorporation of digital technologies into humanities education, it is not only a question of infrastructure and software; rather, it is significantly dependent on the skills, attitudes, and continual growth of educators. For digital pedagogy to be successful, it is essential to provide training and capacity development opportunities for educators. In the absence of adequate preparation and ongoing professional development, even the most cutting-edge technologies will be unable to bring about a meaningful transformation in the educational process.

In humanities contexts, where pedagogical traditions frequently place an emphasis on discussion, close reading, and analogue processes, the shift towards digital requires educators to reimagine the delivery of content, assessment strategies, and learner engagement. This reimagining is not something that happens on its own; rather, it is something that has to be nourished via organised training, communities of practice that are supportive, and continuous institutional investment. This section investigates the significance of teacher training, provides an overview of fundamental digital competencies for educators working in the humanities, investigates various models of capacity building, and provides examples of actual classroom situations. In addition to this, it provides ideas for systemic assistance and examines challenging situations.

7.7.1 *The Need for Teacher Capacity in the Digital Humanities*

Digital transformation in the humanities demands new pedagogical competencies that intersect technological fluency with humanistic inquiry. Teachers must learn not only to use software but to integrate it meaningfully into curriculum and instruction (Table 7.44).

Without these competencies, teachers may struggle to move beyond substitution using digital tools to replicate analog activities rather than transformation, which entails new forms of inquiry, collaboration, and meaning-making.

Table 7.44 Key areas of teacher capacity

Capacity area	Description
Digital literacy	Basic and advanced knowledge of digital tools relevant to humanities
Pedagogical adaptability	Ability to translate traditional humanities content into digital formats
Instructional design	Skills to design activities and assessments using digital platforms
Reflective practice	Continuous improvement through feedback, assessment, and self-evaluation
Collaborative learning	Engagement in communities of practice for sharing resources and insights

Table 7.45 Core competencies for digital humanities teaching

Competency	Description	Example tools
Information literacy	Locating, evaluating, and synthesising digital content	JSTOR, Google Scholar, CORE
Content creation	Developing and curating multimedia materials	Canva, H5P, Audacity
Collaborative technologies	Facilitating peer interaction and co-creation	Padlet, Miro, Google Docs
Assessment and feedback	Using digital tools for formative and summative assessment	Turnitin, Moodle quizzes, Peergrade
Digital ethics	Understanding data privacy, citation, and accessibility	Zotero, Creative Commons, WAVE

7.7.2 *Core Digital Competencies for Humanities Educators*

Educators in the humanities must cultivate competencies that align with their discipline's goals while embracing digital methods. These include technical skills, content curation, online facilitation, and ethical digital citizenship (Table 7.45).

These competencies are not static; they must be regularly updated as technologies evolve and educational contexts shift.

7.7.3 *Models of Teacher Training*

The process of educating teachers is a dynamic one that may be organised in a variety of ways, such as via formal workshops, peer mentorship, and self-directed learning. In order to ensure that instructors actively interact with new approaches rather than just passively receiving knowledge, effective models place a priority on providing opportunities for active engagement. Contextual relevance is of the utmost importance, which means that training should be adapted to the particular requirements and difficulties that instructors confront in their respective situations. Iterative learning, in which teachers continually improve their abilities by gaining feedback and experience, is another method that contributes to the development of their professional careers. The transformation of teacher training into a meaningful process that encourages adaptation and creativity in the classroom is accomplished via the integration of organised teaching, chances for collaborative learning, and constant self-reflection. The training of teachers comprises a variety of methodologies, each of which caters to a certain set of requirements and environment for learning. Training that is centred on workshops offers sessions that are time-bound and focused on the development of skills; however, these sessions often lack continuous follow-up. Educators are able to work together, exchange resources, and find solutions to problems collectively via the use of Communities of Practice (CoPs), while the support of institutions is

Table 7.46 Comparison of teacher training models

Model	Duration	Interaction level	Suitability
Workshop	Short-term	Medium	Tool introduction
CoP	Long-term	High	Curriculum innovation
Mentorship	Medium to long	High	Individual coaching
OPD	Flexible	Low to medium	Self-paced upskilling

essential to the development of these communities. It is possible to provide individualised help via coaching and mentoring by combining experienced educators with newbies to digital education. This allows for the provision of practical insights despite the restrictions of scale. As a result of web-based courses, webinars, and resource repositories, Online Professional Development (OPD) makes flexible learning more accessible. However, the efficacy of OPD is contingent on the quality of its design and the degree to which it encourages interaction.

Each approach makes a contribution to professional development by striking a balance between structure and flexibility. Mentorship improves direct assistance, workshops effectively offer specific skills, communities of practice (CoPs) create long-term cooperation, and online professional development (OPD) assures accessibility. A robust training ecosystem that assists educators in navigating emerging digital pedagogies while retaining engagement and effectiveness in their teaching practices may be created by combining these techniques. That ecosystem can be created by combining these approaches (Table 7.46).

7.7.4 Case Example: Digital Humanities Teacher Fellowship

A fellowship program that takes place over one year and is aimed at improving digital pedagogy for humanities instructors was established at a university in Nigeria. Workshops on tools such as Voyant, Scalar, and Hypothesis were only some of the activities that were included in the program. Other activities included collaborative curriculum design clinics, peer presentations of updated digital lesson plans, and a final display that included student efforts. The program resulted in considerable effects, including increased student involvement as seen by higher assignment submission rates, more confidence in the use of digital technologies, and the adoption of the fellowship model across various departments. Eighty-three per cent of participants reported increased confidence in themselves while using digital tools. When it comes to expanding digital literacy and pedagogical innovation inside higher education, this instance demonstrates how beneficial it is to have capacity-building programs that are organised, localised, and led by peers and peers themselves.

Table 7.47 Institutional responsibilities

Area	Support mechanism
Infrastructure	Stable internet, devices, and licenses
Policy	Incentives for innovation, recognition for digital teaching
Time allocation	Reduced teaching load for training periods
Incentives	Awards, promotion criteria acknowledging digital efforts
Technical support	Help desks, tech assistants, troubleshooting channels

7.7.5 Institutional Support Structures

The commitment of educational institutions is necessary for effective capacity development in education; individual efforts alone are not sufficient. It is common for professional development projects to become inconsistent and unsustainable when institutions do not provide assistance in the form of strategic and logistical support. One of the most important roles that institutions play is to make certain that training programs are well-structured, have enough resources, and are incorporated into larger academic aims. For the purpose of fostering the development of faculty members, this involves providing financial assistance, technological infrastructure, mentoring networks, and long-term planning. The efforts that are made to train teachers are strengthened by an all-encompassing strategy, which makes them more effective and long-lasting (Table 7.47).

7.7.6 Challenges in Teacher Training

In spite of the increased need for digital pedagogy, many educational institutions are having difficulty providing adequate training for educators in the humanities. Educators who are resistant to digital technologies owing to a lack of knowledge about them or ideological preferences are exhibiting a significant impediment known as technophobia. Furthermore, severe teaching and administrative burdens leave little space for professional growth, which is a difficulty that is made more difficult by the restricted amount of time available. The majority of training tools are developed for STEM areas or Western settings, which means that they are not a good match for the unique requirements that educators in the humanities have in diverse countries. Inadequate financing restricts access to workshops, tools, and technical assistance, which further complicates training initiatives. Resource shortage is particularly problematic in this regard. Last but not least, the absence of a unified approach often results in the fragmentation of training, with workshops that do not have a continuous follow-up or are not integrated into comprehensive institutional programs. In order to effectively address these difficulties, individualised assistance, targeted financing, and a long-term commitment from the institution to professionals' professional growth are required (Table 7.48).

Table 7.48 Common challenges and suggested solutions

Challenge	Solution
Resistance to change	Peer mentoring, success stories, and gradual integration
Limited training time	Micro learning modules, asynchronous online options
Irrelevant tools	Local customisation, needs assessments
Infrastructure deficits	Use of open-source tools, partnerships with NGOs
Poor follow-up	Longitudinal professional development plans

7.7.7 Recommendations for Sustainable Capacity Building

A comprehensive approach to digital pedagogy requires a structured framework that integrates faculty development into long-term academic planning. Institutions can begin by developing a Digital Pedagogy Framework, outlining clear benchmarks, toolkits, and example curricula to guide educators in acquiring digital skills. Training content should also be localized to reflect the specific educational realities, student demographics, and cultural contexts of each institution, ensuring relevance and effectiveness. Encouraging co-teaching and collaboration fosters interdisciplinary exchange and helps faculty with varying levels of tech proficiency support one another in adopting digital tools. Establishing dedicated Centres for Digital Pedagogy within institutions can further enhance accessibility by providing educators with resources, mentorship, and spaces to experiment with new technologies. Finally, an iterative evaluation process is essential; institutions should regularly solicit feedback from faculty and students, refine training strategies accordingly, and promote reflective reporting to strengthen engagement and continuous learning. Through these initiatives, digital pedagogy can become more sustainable, adaptable, and impactful across diverse educational settings.

7.7.8 Towards a Culture of Digital Teaching Excellence

It is not enough to just provide isolated training sessions in order to build capacity in digital humanities education; rather, it is necessary to make a persistent cultural transformation inside existing institutions. Those who foster an atmosphere that encourages inquiry, experimentation, and collaborative learning will not only improve the competence of faculty members but they will also generate an academic climate that is flexible and forward-thinking. Long-term success in digital humanities teaching and innovation may be ensured by universities via the incorporation of digital pedagogy into institutional processes, the promotion of interdisciplinary cooperation, and the ongoing refinement of tactics through feedback.

Thus, training for educators and the development of their capabilities are the essential components of a successful digital humanities integration. Educators are able to construct learning experiences that are engaging, student-centered, and aligned with the philosophical and pedagogical aims of the humanities if they possess the right skills, support, and professional development opportunities. It has been established in this section that capacity development is multi-dimensional, embracing not just technical but also educational, institutional, and cultural elements. Not only can educational institutions improve the quality of instruction by investing in the ongoing professional development of teachers, but they also position themselves to ensure the continued relevance and vitality of humanities education in the digital age.

7.8 Resource Equity and Access Issues

Accessibility is the single most important aspect that will determine whether or not the promise of digital change in humanities education is realised. Particularly in places that are lacking in resources, glaring gaps in access to digital resources have grown increasingly apparent as educational institutions all over the globe have begun to incorporate software into their instructional practices. Because of these gaps, which have their origins in social, regional, institutional, and infrastructural disadvantages, there is a possibility that educational marginalisation may be reinforced rather than mitigated. In the framework of humanities education, which has always advocated for inclusiveness, social justice, and critical thinking, the digital gap presents a problem that is both moral and pedagogical. The idea of resource equality is investigated in this part, along with the identification of important access difficulties, the examination of the effect these challenges have on both students and teachers, and the provision of ideas for more equitable digital humanities learning environments.

7.8.1 Understanding Resource Equity in Education

Achieving resource equality means making certain that every student and educator, regardless of where they are in their educational journey, has access to the resources, platforms, infrastructure, and support systems that are necessary for them to flourish. It acknowledges the fact that people come into the educational system with varying degrees of privilege, opportunities, and problems. This means that treating everyone in the same manner does not always result in results that are fair or equitable. To achieve true equality in education, it is necessary to make proactive efforts to identify and eliminate both apparent and hidden hurdles that impede full participation. These barriers include socioeconomic inequalities, linguistic differences, access to technical resources, and systemic prejudices related to education. It is possible for educators and policymakers to build a learning environment that encourages meaningful inclusion by addressing these difficulties. This will ensure that all students have access to the tools they need to achieve success on their terms (Table 7.49).

These dimensions are interrelated; a student in a rural community may simultaneously face technological, economic, and geographic barriers.

Table 7.49 Dimensions of resource equity

Dimension	Description
Technological	Access to devices (computers, tablets), software, and internet
Economic	Affordability of data plans, digital tools, or training
Geographic	Differences in access based on urban/rural or regional location
Institutional	Variability in institutional funding, support, and digital infrastructure
Cultural/linguistic	Accessibility of content for different languages, cultures, and literacy levels
Ability-based	Inclusion of learners with disabilities or special learning needs

7.8.2 *The Digital Divide in Humanities Education*

In addition to being a basic difference between those who have access to technology and those who do not, the digital divide is a reflection of more profound disparities in terms of access, usability, and influence. Despite the fact that basic access continues to be a primary concern, other factors, such as digital literacy, the quality of the internet and devices, and the capacity to fully connect with online resources, all play a significant influence. Different forms of digital divisions have varying effects on students and teachers in a variety of different ways. The term "Access Divide" refers to the differences that exist in terms of physical access to technology and the internet, which prevents some persons from taking part in digital learning. There is a difficulty to meaningful involvement, which is reflected in the "Use Divide." Some people may have access to technology, but they may not possess the digital skills necessary to properly understand and use it. The Quality Divide takes into account whether or not users are using antiquated technology, poor internet connections, or platforms that do not allow for interaction, all of which might impede the learning experiences of individuals. One last point to consider is the "Outcome Divide," which refers to the disparities in academic accomplishments and opportunities that are a direct result of the digital inequities. In classrooms that focus on the humanities, these differences manifest themselves in a variety of ways, including students who have difficulty acquiring digital literature, instructors who are not adequately trained in online teaching techniques, and institutions that depend on technology that is no longer relevant. It is not enough to just invest in technology in order to overcome these obstacles; additional efforts must be made in the areas of training, inclusion, and policymaking in order to establish digital learning environments that are more equal.

7.8.3 Impact of Inequitable Access on Students and Teachers

Digital pedagogy resource discrepancies worsen preexisting inequities, especially in underfunded humanities programs where instructors and students encounter structural obstacles to participation and achievement. Students who do not have access to technology that is dependable may experience feelings of disengagement, dissatisfaction, and withdrawal from the learning process. Many people are reluctant to take part in online conversations or collaborative tools because of the limits of their devices or because they do not have sufficient internet access. Students who do not have access to the essential technology may experience feelings of isolation while working on group projects or digital assignments. This is because resource disparities generate stigma. Additional social factors further aggravate the situation. Challenges are something that teachers, too, face. There are some teachers who create classes with little incorporation of technology to suit all of their pupils, which inadvertently limits creativity. While some are attempting to bridge disparities via manual workarounds, they are at risk of experiencing fatigue. As a result of limited exposure to new digital technologies and professional development opportunities, educators working in institutions with little funding face additional constraints, which hinder their potential to improve pedagogy.

These inequalities are brought to light via case studies. In Nigeria, public universities reveal stark contrasts between urban campuses, which have consistent electricity and computer labs, and rural satellite campuses, where students' ability to complete assignments on digital platforms like Moodle or digital archives is severely hindered by outages and poor connectivity. Urban campuses are located in Sub-Saharan Africa. In a similar vein, first-generation students attending a liberal arts institution in the United States had a difficult time participating in a digital storytelling project. This was not because they lacked enthusiasm for the project; rather, it was because they did not have access to Wi-Fi at home and did not have any previous experience with video editing software. The implementation of systemic solutions is necessary in order to address these gaps. These solutions include investments in digital infrastructure, training programs, and inclusive policies that guarantee technology facilitates learning for all individuals, rather than perpetuating existing inequalities.

7.8.4 Evaluating Institutional Readiness for Equitable Access

Institutions play an important role in reducing access inequities by adopting proactive planning, smart budgeting, and well-designed inclusive policies. Students and instructors may fully participate in digital learning if they anticipate problems and allocate resources properly. Prioritising equity-driven efforts, such as subsidised technology programs, digital literacy training, and flexible learning models, enables institutions to close gaps and develop more long-term solutions. When institutions commit to long-term accessibility initiatives, they contribute to create an atmosphere

Table 7.50 Institutional equity readiness checklist

Area	Key questions
Infrastructure	Are internet and devices reliably available on campus?
Licensing	Are essential digital tools licensed and institutionally funded?
Accessibility	Are platforms compliant with accessibility standards (e.g., screen readers)?
Language inclusivity	Is content translated or available in local languages?
Offline access	Are downloadable or offline alternatives provided for low-bandwidth users?
Staff support	Are there digital literacy programs for faculty and students?

in which educational possibilities are not hampered by socioeconomic or technical constraints (Table 7.50).

This checklist allows institutions to self-audit their digital equity landscape and develop interventions accordingly.

7.8.5 *Strategies for Promoting Resource Equity*

Educational fairness requires both structural improvements and practical, urgent efforts that enable institutions and educators to address existing inequities. One critical strategy is to develop device loan schemes, in which students with financial restrictions may borrow computers or tablets to supplement their studies. Institutions may work with non-governmental organisations (NGOs) and technology businesses to gain bulk contributions or subsidised prices for critical equipment, allowing more people to access digital learning resources. Another major tactic is to use low-bandwidth platforms, which work well in locations with poor internet access. Platforms such as Telegram, Google Classroom, and WhatsApp may help students study while lowering their reliance on high-speed internet. To make video material more accessible to all learners, it should be reduced and transcripts offered. Offline learning options might be a valuable alternative for students who do not have access to the internet. Distributing USB devices or DVDs containing course information enables students to study without depending on real-time internet access.

Printable copies of important readings and assignments may also be useful tools for keeping students interested. Institutions must also prioritise mobile-first design by optimising learning systems for smartphones, since many students rely on mobile devices for education. Mobile-friendly applications such as Kahoot, Quizlet, and Google Forms promote interactive learning and make digital education more accessible. Finally, OER play a crucial role in democratising access to academic knowledge. Free repositories like OpenStax, African Storybook, and Project Gutenberg give high-quality learning resources without added financial stress. Encouraging educators to contribute to and modify open-access materials extends their reach and

Table 7.51 Resource equity tools and approaches

Strategy	Tool/platform	Target group
Offline resources	Kolibri, USB kits	Rural students
Mobile learning	WhatsApp, Moodle App	Students without PCs
Low-cost devices	Raspberry Pi, Android tablets	Low-income students
OER adoption	OpenStax, CORE, JSTOR OA	All students
Translation tools	Google Translate, DeepL	Multilingual learners

boosts their effectiveness. By combining these immediate solutions with long-term institutional changes, educational institutions may develop more inclusive digital learning environments that empower both students and instructors, ensuring that technology acts as a tool for accessibility rather than a barrier (Table 7.51).

7.8.6 Policies and Funding for Access Equity

The establishment of policy frameworks at the institutional, national, and international levels is very necessary in order to guarantee long-term sustainability and accountability in the process of eliminating access gaps in education. Digital inclusion policies need to be established by institutions, and they should demand ongoing infrastructure updates, faculty training, and content accessibility efforts. In order for institutions to evaluate gaps, revise plans, and guarantee continual development in technology fairness, they must conduct yearly audits of digital access. At the level of the government, ministries of education have the potential to play a crucial role by providing students with subsidies for internet connections. This would ensure that students' capacity to engage in digital learning is not hindered by budgetary restrictions. Additionally, regulations should provide incentives for educational institutions to use technologies that are open-source and inclusive. This would facilitate the reduction of expenses and the enhancement of accessibility for a wide variety of students. When it comes to advancing digital equality, international cooperation is also quite important. In recognition of the special technology requirements of the humanities, global education efforts, such as the ICT in Education program run by the UNESCO, should provide specific financing to humanities-based learning. It is possible to further promote resource mobilisation via partnerships with diaspora groups and alumni networks. These partnerships may provide underfunded institutions with access to digital technologies, knowledge, and financial aid. Through the implementation of these policy frameworks at several levels, educational institutions are able to establish digital environments that are both sustainable and equitable. These settings guarantee that all students, regardless of their background, have access to the resources and opportunities they need to be successful.

7.8.7 *Ethical Considerations*

Equity in digital education is not only a logistical difficulty; rather, it is an ethical duty. This is especially true in the humanities, which are the fields in which concepts such as empathy, justice, and historical knowledge form the basis of learning. The inequitable distribution of digital resources is in direct opposition to the fundamental principles of the field, which in turn restricts the options for involvement and participation at the field level. It is imperative that educational institutions and teachers make justice a top priority in order to sustain ethical standards in the field of humanities education. This involves making certain that no student is at a disadvantage as a result of structural obstacles, such as financial restraints, geographical limitations, or technical discrepancies. Equally important is the concept of transparency, which involves effectively conveying digital needs and support systems that are accessible to students. This enables them to manage problems without feeling unclear or excluded. An equitable digital learning environment must also embrace inclusion, with course design and assessment methodologies that suit multiple learning contexts, including varying technical capabilities and accessibility requirements. This is necessary to ensure that educational opportunities are accessible to all students. Students are given the ability to take ownership of their educational experiences when they are given the opportunity to participate in conversations around access and the selection of learning resources. This is accomplished by encouraging students to develop their agency. The humanities can continue to progress their purpose of developing critical thinking, social awareness, and meaningful participation for all learners, regardless of their circumstances, if they include these ethical values in the policies and practices of digital education.

With regard to the effectiveness of the digital revolution in humanities education, concerns of resource justice and access are of the utmost importance. The implementation of coordinated actions across education, policy, financing, and infrastructure is required in order to address these difficulties. Institutions must make a commitment to both short-term solutions, such as the provision of device loans and offline resources, as well as long-term changes that reframe access as an essential component of educational justice. In order to ensure that digital pedagogy is not only creative but also inclusive and empowering for all learners, regardless of region, poverty, or ability, the humanities may set an example by using practices that are equity-oriented.

7.9 Long-Term Educational Impacts

A long-term revolution in the ways in which information is generated, accessed, understood, and conserved is represented by the incorporation of software into humanities education. This implementation is not only a reaction to the pedagogical trends that are now prevalent. As digital technologies become increasingly integrated into classroom practices and scholarly pursuits, their effect extends beyond

Table 7.52 Key educational shifts

Traditional humanities learning	Software-enhanced humanities learning
Content memorisation	Critical engagement with interactive texts
Linear analysis	Multimodal, nonlinear exploration
Passive reception	Active annotation, remixing, and collaborative writing
Siloed disciplines	Interdisciplinary projects and digital collaborations

the immediate learning results they provide. It shapes wider educational philosophies, research agendas, and career routes. The purpose of this part is to investigate the long-term educational effects of integrating software in the humanities. Particular attention is paid to the changes that occur in cognitive development, epistemological frameworks, curricular evolution, scholarly output, and socio-cultural involvement. In this study, we evaluate the impact that digital technologies have had on the development of humanities education throughout the course of time by using theoretical insights, empirical investigations, and reflective analysis.

7.9.1 Redefining Learning Trajectories

Digital tools have altered the nature of learning in the humanities by shifting from linear, content-driven models to interactive, learner-centered paradigms. Software platforms facilitate recursive learning, peer engagement, and real-time feedback, leading to enhanced cognitive engagement and deeper retention (Table 7.52).

This evolution nurtures lifelong learning skills such as critical thinking, adaptability, and digital fluency, essential competencies for modern scholars and professionals.

7.9.2 Cognitive and Metacognitive Development

In the context of digital education, the incorporation of annotation tools, discussion platforms, and interactive archives promotes both cognitive and metacognitive development. This helps students improve their analytical, synthetic, and interpretative skills while also fostering a greater sense of self-awareness regarding their own learning processes. Using these technologies, learners are able to interact with texts that go beyond surface-level reading. Tools like Voyant and Hypothesis enable deeper textual analysis and debate, which helps to foster critical thinking. In addition to this, they contribute to the enhancement of information literacy by providing students with the skills necessary to navigate digital databases, critically evaluate sources, and effectively manage citations. Students are able to monitor their intellectual development over time via the use of e-portfolios and blogging platforms, which promotes a clearer knowledge of how they generate ideas and arguments. This is another way that reflective learning is reinforced.

These cognitive advantages extend well beyond the confines of the classroom, influencing how students interact with various forms of media, how they approach complicated societal problems, and how they do research. Learners are able to become more deliberate and analytical participants in academic and public debate with the assistance of these technologies, which develop digital literacy and critical engagement.

7.9.3 Evolution of Curriculum Design

The use of digital software into humanities education has altered the organisation, content, and delivery of courses, encouraging multidisciplinary approaches and skill-based teaching paradigms. Over time, these developments promote more student-centered education, allowing courses to adapt to changing technology and academic needs. One notable trend is the emergence of hybrid curricular models, which combine literature, philosophy, history, and digital technologies to build broad interdisciplinary frameworks. GIS mapping and digital storytelling are examples of technologies that enhance conventional humanities education by enabling students to interact dynamically with texts, historical events, and philosophical concepts. Similarly, the transition to modular learning provides flexibility via micro-learning modules, self-paced activities, and adaptive learning platforms. Digital technologies help educators to create responsive curriculum that match the different requirements of their students, guaranteeing accessibility and customisation in learning experiences. Finally, competency-based assessment substitutes time-based assessments with skill-specific criteria. LMS with dashboard monitoring give instructors and students with continuous feedback, promoting competency mastery rather than rigorous adherence to an academic schedule. By incorporating these digital technologies, humanities education becomes more interactive, adaptable, and current, guaranteeing that students gain critical thinking and technology skills that go beyond the classroom.

7.9.4 Transformation of Scholarly Practices

The long-term influence of digital technologies in the humanities goes beyond the classroom, changing how academic work is produced, communicated, and maintained. One of the most major changes has occurred in open access and digital publishing, where technology has facilitated the democratisation of information. Platforms like Scalar, Omeka, and Pub hub allow academics to disseminate their results in interactive, multimodal formats, enhancing accessibility and engagement among academic and general audiences. This trend challenges established publication practices, enabling more inclusive and collaborative research.

In addition to changes in distribution, digital humanities research methods have provided new techniques to investigation. Text mining, data visualisation, and network analysis are already commonplace in many fields, broadening the scope of research and redefining what constitutes acceptable information. By combining computational technologies, humanities academics may discover previously unknown patterns, relationships, and interpretations.

Finally, preservation and archiving have been transformed by digital technology, assuring the lifespan of cultural and historical resources that may not have been sufficiently maintained by traditional archiving. Oral histories, indigenous knowledge systems, and endangered languages today benefit from digital databases and recording technologies, which help preserve essential tales and customs for subsequent generations. These developments highlight the humanities' role in preserving and conveying knowledge, indicating the long-term relevance of digital integration in research and study.

7.9.5 Broadening Access and Inclusion

Over the long run, software integration may help to more equal and inclusive if supported by attentive policies and infrastructural support. Digital platforms may help: Reach learners in rural or underserved locations via online distribution. To accommodate students with varying degrees of ability, accessibility elements such as text-to-speech and subtitles should be made available. Contribute to the development of indigenous knowledge systems and multilingual content. Encourage the production of content and cultural expression by students working independently.

By ensuring that humanities education resonates across socioeconomic and cultural barriers, these goals improve representation and engagement, hence enhancing students' opportunities to participate.

7.9.6 Career and Employability Implications

The use of software into the humanities curriculum has transformed educational results to better reflect changing labour market needs. As digital skills grow more crucial across sectors, humanities graduates who use technology-driven learning approaches are better prepared for a variety of professional paths. Proficiency in data visualisation, text analysis, and interactive storytelling not only improves conventional skills like critical thinking and communication but also opens up new career options in domains like digital marketing, UX design, and content strategy. Furthermore, exposure to collaborative platforms and multimedia publication helps students

Table 7.53 Skills developed through software use

Skill	Related tool	Application
Data literacy	Voyant, Excel	Market research, policy analysis
Communication	Padlet, blogging tools	Media, public relations
Collaboration	Google Docs, Trello	Project management, NGO work
Digital curation	Omeka, Scalar	Museum, archive, heritage management
Critical analysis	AntConc, NVivo	Journalism, academia

prepare for careers in research, teaching, and cultural preservation. By incorporating software and digital approaches into humanities education, schools guarantee that graduates have a mix of analytical depth and technical proficiency, preparing them for success in an increasingly digital environment (Table 7.53).

Graduates of digitally enriched humanities programs are well-positioned for roles that require interdisciplinary thinking, ethical reasoning, and technological fluency.

7.9.7 Sociocultural Shifts and Ethical Awareness

The incorporation of software tools into education fundamentally alters the values and norms that characterise learning environments, exposing students to global material, digital ethics, and collaborative knowledge models. This shift reimagines cultural literacy by fostering greater interaction with other viewpoints, ethical issues, and collaborative intellectual activities. One of the most important long-term sociocultural impacts is the development of global citizenship, since open-access platforms expose learners to viewpoints from other areas, cultures, and ideologies, developing cross-cultural understanding. Students also get a critical understanding of digital ethics, learning how to manage concerns like surveillance, copyright laws, and algorithmic biasall of which are important considerations in an increasingly technologically driven society. Furthermore, software technologies promote collective intelligence by enabling students to take part in crowdsourcing projects, open-source efforts, and community-led partnerships that prioritise shared knowledge generation. As technology is increasingly integrated into the humanities, the subject advances from static traditions to a dynamic, socially responsive field one that responds to current issues, stimulates ethical thought, and enhances global involvement.

7.9.8 Risks and Mitigation Strategies

While long-term integration of software in humanities education has obvious advantages, it also raises significant obstacles that must be addressed in order to retain the integrity of learning. One major problem is over-reliance on technology, in

Table 7.54 Mitigation strategies

Challenge	Strategy
Over-reliance	Encourage hybrid learning with offline engagement
Shallow engagement	Design assignments requiring textual depth
Ethics concerns	Integrate digital ethics into curricula
Skill imbalance	Provide foundational training in both digital and traditional methods

which digital tools risk replacing rather than improving critical thinking. Pedagogical methods must prioritise significant intellectual engagement above superficial technical novelty, ensuring that digital learning is used for depth rather than distraction. Another concern is the loss of deep reading, since excessive multimedia features and fragmented digital texts may impair students' attention spans and critical analytical skills both of which are essential in humanities education. The capacity to interact meaningfully with complicated content must remain important to curriculum, even as digital resources become more accessible. Additionally, ethical concerns about data privacy, digital spying, and AI manipulation jeopardise trust and inclusiveness in education. As institutions use digital technologies, they must also include safeguards to protect user data, encourage openness, and minimise biases in algorithm-driven learning systems. Balancing technology improvements with educational integrity requires careful application, ensuring that software promotes rather than degrades the fundamental ideals of humanities education (Table 7.54).

7.9.9 *Sustaining the Impact*

To ensure that the advantages of software integration in humanities education are sustained over time, institutions must develop sustainability frameworks that promote long-term effectiveness. One critical strategy is ongoing professional development, which involves educators receiving continuous training on new digital technologies, enabling them to enhance their teaching techniques and keep up with technological changes. Furthermore, curriculum review cycles should include input from both students and industry experts to ensure that course design remains relevant and responsive to evolving educational and workforce demands. Establishing digital literacy benchmarks for both students and instructors helps standardise skills and fosters confidence in effectively utilising digital platforms. These criteria ensure that learners and educators can use digital technologies in relevant and skill-enhancing ways. Finally, prioritising infrastructure investment is essential, ensuring ongoing financing for new hardware and software, preventing digital stagnation, and guaranteeing universal access. A sustainable digital humanities approach progresses alongside technological advancements while being firmly rooted in pedagogical principles, ensuring that digital tools complement rather than replace the intellectual depth and critical inquiry that distinguish the humanities.

The incorporation of software into the humanities has the potential to have significant and far-reaching effects on education over the long run. The use of digital resources is redefining what it means to teach and learn about the humanities in a variety of capacities, including cognitive growth and the reform of curriculum, equitable access, and employability. In spite of the fact that these modifications are not without dangers, software has the potential to facilitate a revitalised and socially relevant humanities education if it is designed with aim, ethical awareness, and inclusive policies. In the end, the incorporation of digital technology into the field of humanities is not a trend but rather a trajectory. It is possible for educators and institutions to guarantee that the humanities will continue to be lively, accessible, and effective for future generations if they embrace it with critical insight and pedagogical integrity.

7.10 Socio-cultural Context and Software Use

The sociocultural fabric in which humanities education functions has always been strongly linked with the field of education in the humanities. It is becoming more important to investigate the ways in which digital tools interact with socio-cultural environments. This involves analysing the ways in which social values, cultural norms, and historical legacies impact the acceptance, adaption, and resistance of software among educational institutions.

In the next part, we will conduct an in-depth analysis of how the use of software in humanities classes both reflects and reframes larger socio-cultural phenomena. Identity, language, power, representation, and tradition are some of the topics that are investigated in this work. In this paper, we investigate the consequences of inclusive pedagogy, the creation of locally tailored curricula, and the decolonisation of methods of knowledge production. In the end, we contend that software in the field of humanities education is not culturally neutral; rather, it is both a product and a maker of socio-cultural realities.

7.10.1 Cultural Mediation of Technology Use

The values, traditions, and expectations of the cultures that interact with digital technologies are what shape them. Digital technologies are not homogeneous tools; rather, they are formed by digital technologies. There are a number of factors that influence the degree of interaction with digital tools that occurs in humanities classrooms across different regions. These factors include the language of instruction and interface, religious or moral codes, colonial histories and resistance narratives, as well as the technological infrastructure that is already in place and the levels of digital literacy that are present. For instance, in areas where oral traditions play a significant part in the transmission of information, there is often a better acceptance of podcasting and oral history technologies like as Audacity and SoundCloud. This is because these platforms correspond with existing ways of storytelling and discourse. On the other hand, systems that rely heavily on textual annotations, such as Hypothesis, may seem less accessible or even alienating if they do not contain support for several languages and modifications that are culturally sensitive. In order to ensure that digital tools promote inclusion rather than reinforce barriers, it is vital to recognise these variances. This will enable educational technology to improve learning in ways that respect and reflect the socio-cultural realities of the local community.

7.10.2 Software Design and Cultural Bias

The fact that most educational software originates in the Global North implies that it typically embeds Euro-American pedagogical ideas, assumptions, and agendas. This has major consequences for inclusion and cultural representation, since it may not necessarily correspond with the different learning traditions, epistemologies, and contextual realities of learners in other locations. For example, many systems presume linear, text-based learning as the default mode, sidelining oral traditions, community-based knowledge transfer, and multimodal learning practices that are essential to education in diverse countries. Additionally, the reliance on conventional assessment frameworks could ignore localized methods of knowledge evaluation, such as storytelling, apprenticeship, and relational learning. In certain circumstances, the software's built-in cultural allusions, historical narratives, or linguistic patterns may promote dominant ideas while marginalising others, leading to inadvertent biases in information delivery. Multilingual interfaces, culturally sensitive teaching, and region-specific modifications are used to fill these limitations in educational technology. Open-source platforms let communities customise technologies, making them more relevant and accessible. For genuine digital inclusion, educators, developers, and governments must rethink software design beyond Global North-centric paradigms and embrace pluralistic methods that represent global learner variety (Table 7.55).

To make software culturally relevant, educators and developers must localise tools both linguistically and pedagogically so that they align with students' lived experiences and identities.

Table 7.55 Common biases in educational software

Bias type	Manifestation
Linguistic	English-only interfaces, Western idioms
Epistemological	Prioritisation of empirical or linear logic over relational or oral forms
Content	Underrepresentation of non-Western authors and histories
Interaction design	Preferences for individual over collective learning

7.10.3 Language, Identity, and Power

Language affects educational technology, cultural validity, accessibility, engagement, and representation. The prevalence of English in software platforms may hinder non-English-speaking learners, frequently with unforeseen effects. Students may use the dominant language instead of their native tongues in academic discourse, eroding linguistic diversity. Key concepts may not translate well across languages, alienating students who struggle with comprehension and making learning content less accessible. Due to this linguistic imbalance, learners who are less fluent in the tool's default language may engage less, lowering their confidence and learning results. Educational technology language must be culturally relevant to promote diversity. Multilingual interfaces and robust translation support allow students to use platforms in their preferred languages. Encourage the use of local languages in reflections, projects, and conversations to promote linguistic variety and enable students to express themselves in ways that represent their cultural and intellectual origins. Indigenous language in metadata and tagging systems preserves cultural identities in digital learning settings, making information more relevant and accessible to more students. Language barriers can be thoughtfully addressed to make educational technologies more equitable and empower diverse learners.

7.10.4 Decolonising the Digital Humanities

Socio-cultural interaction in digital humanities aims to decolonise knowledge systems by contesting Eurocentric narratives and legitimising various epistemologies. Multiple tactics are used in this procedure. Local histories and oral traditions should be archived using Omeka or Scalar to preserve indigenous knowledge systems. Critical metadata practices challenge Western classification norms and prevent digital scholarship from reinforcing colonial frameworks. Meaningful engagement also involves communities in content creation rather than just presenting them with pre-existing narratives. Open access programs promote fair knowledge exchange and reduce obstacles to culturally valuable information. The Masakhane NLP initiative addresses the invisibility of indigenous languages in AI and digital tools by focusing on African language technologies. The initiative challenges the dominance of English and other commonly used languages in technology by establishing language models that reflect African linguistic variety, increasing representation and accessibility. Decolonising digital humanities requires inclusivity, participatory knowledge production, and critical engagement with digital information structures.

7.10.5 Digital Tools as Agents of Cultural Preservation

Digital technologies have great potential to revitalise and preserve culture, despite their reputation for homogenisation. This endeavour is supported by several software programs. Documenting endangered languages using transcription technologies preserves linguistic diversity. Communities may record and share oral histories using multimedia archiving systems. Geographic Information System (GIS) platforms map indigenous landscapes, strengthening cultural identity-sustaining spatial and environmental relationships. Digital storytelling and video essays allow artists and cultural practitioners to reach global audiences while preserving their history. Teachers may use digital technologies to engage students in cultural documentation, curation, and distribution beyond material delivery. Students may learn more about their background and help conserve and celebrate other cultures by using these tools in the classroom. When used intentionally, technology may preserve and enrich human civilisations.

7.10.6 Gender and Socio-cultural Norms

Socio-cultural issues affect how students of various genders and backgrounds use digital education, frequently resulting in access, participation, and confidence gaps. Traditional gender norms that prioritise male education or ban female technology use may impede girls' access to digital gadgets in patriarchal settings. This digital gap might impair their technology skill development, affecting academic and employment chances. Gendered assumptions in platform design, such as default avatars, instructional simulation roles, and digital tool tasks, may perpetuate preconceptions and subtly alter learner experiences. These prejudices may subconsciously determine who belongs in specific industries, hindering inclusion. Due to social conditioning that has placed them outside dominant technological spaces, marginalised learners often lack digital confidence. Educational technology might make you feel inadequate due to a lack of early exposure, digital representation, or social standards. Designers and educators must use inclusive design to create digital learning environments that promote equity and representation. Technology can empower rather than exclude by offering gender-neutral avatars, building platforms with varied cultural concerns, and establishing helpful learning routes for under-represented groups.

Equality of access, involvement, and representation in digital humanities education requires gender-sensitive methods. Access, design, pedagogy, and mentoring improve inclusive learning environments. Gender-inclusive ICT policies provide equitable opportunities for all students, especially in locations where some groups have restricted access to technology. Adopting neutral and flexible UI components helps minimise gender prejudices in digital platforms, making them more inclusive and adaptive. In pedagogy, collaborative and non-hierarchical tasks balance voice distribution, allowing all students, regardless of gender, to participate and contribute meaningfully. Peer mentorship initiatives with diverse student groups assist underrepresented learners acquire confidence and navigate digital education venues. These ideas may help educators and developers create a more inclusive digital humanities ecosystem where all students feel empowered and represented.

7.10.7 Intercultural Communication and Global Dialogues

Software resources like discussion forums, blogging programs, and worldwide archives are critical in encouraging intercultural communication among students, allowing for rich, cross-cultural debate and greater understanding. These tools allow students to connect with viewpoints outside of their local contexts, widening their understanding of other worldviews. This digital engagement helps students build empathy and global awareness as they learn to understand other cultural backgrounds and living experiences. Furthermore, exposure to a variety of media sources and cultural representations improves critical thinking abilities, allowing students to more carefully evaluate biases, narratives, and historical interpretations. These platforms foster cross-border mutual respect by promoting shared narrative and cooperative learning, encouraging students to see similarities while enjoying differences. Digital collaboration tools like as Padlet, Flipgrid, and Google Docs facilitate this exchange by enabling students to co-create knowledge, collaborate on projects, and participate in meaningful debates regardless of geography. These tools assist to overcome cultural gaps by encouraging pluralistic thinking and collaborative problem solving. When utilised successfully, they convert digital education into a dynamic environment for intercultural discovery, building relationships between learners from various backgrounds and promoting more inclusive and internationally aware academic discourse.

7.10.8 Resistance, Agency, and Local Innovation

The interaction with educational software is not a passive activity in many communities; rather, it is a dynamic process that involves resistance, adaptation, and creativity in order to guarantee that technology meets the requirements of the community to which it is applied. Instead of just embracing tools that have already been built, local actors actively rearrange software in order to align it with the context of their sociocultural and educational reality. One of the most important examples of this innovation is the establishment of offline digital archives in regions with low bandwidth requirements. These archives enable students to access essential educational materials despite the constraints imposed by the infrastructure. In a similar manner, communities establish "culturally specific annotation codes" in order to read indigenous literature in a manner that maintains linguistic and epistemic traditions. This helps to ensure that local knowledge systems are not lost in the process of converting them into standard digital forms. Peer-led digital literacy workshops are another strong method that may be used. These workshops allow students from underserved areas to take responsibility for their own education by instructing other students on how to properly navigate and utilise digital resources. The agency of local users in influencing technology, as opposed to just consuming it, is highlighted by these actions. Communities are able to convert educational software into a vehicle for empowerment, preservation, and creative interaction with information by opposing frameworks that are forced on them and developing tools to meet their own requirements. Learners and educators are reinventing digital environments to represent their histories, identities, and goals. This is in contrast to the traditional approach, in which technology dictates the standards of participation.

7.10.9 Ethical Considerations in Socio-cultural Software Use

Respecting community values, data sovereignty, and intellectual property rights is essential to ethical educational software use in varied situations. Appreciating cultural norms and expectations that affect digital tool usage is essential to meeting local ethical standards. Some groups may need to protect important historical or religious information from distortion or exploitation. Data sovereignty is also important since many digital platforms acquire and keep user data without authorisation. Transparent regulations, local hosting, and community-driven digital infrastructures empower communities to govern their data, preventing other groups from abusing sensitive information. Intellectual property matters, especially with indigenous knowledge systems and creative outputs. To prevent cultural artefacts from being commodified or appropriated, ethical software design should prioritise credit, permission-based access, and fair representation. These principles help developers and educators to design digital places that promote trust, cooperation, and equal participation, empowering rather than exploiting technology. Ethical digital engagement goes beyond compliance to enhance communities' sovereignty, dignity, and agency (Table 7.56).

Table 7.56 Key considerations

Ethical issue	Response
Cultural appropriation	Secure permissions and credit sources
Data sovereignty	Allow communities control over their data and narratives
Privacy and consent	Ensure transparent data policies and informed consent
Misrepresentation	Avoid flattening or stereotyping complex identities

7.10.9.1 Pedagogical Recommendations for Culturally Responsive Software Use

Several pedagogical practices may guarantee that educational software supports socio-cultural realities and meaningful, inclusive humanities education. Contextualised case studies let students connect digital technologies to local texts, situations, and examples, making learning more meaningful. Student-created content encourages students to contribute culturally grounded information to digital platforms, validating their opinions and experiences in academic debate. Flexible tool selection ensures technology accommodates language and cultural variety, eliminating exclusion and enhancing accessibility. Giving students a way to voice issues about software interfaces or content helps educators and developers improve tools based on user input. Finally, professional development programs help instructors incorporate technology in ways that respect and improve varied learning traditions by teaching cultural awareness in digital contexts. Educational technology may connect these practices to provide rich, dynamic, and culturally relevant humanities instruction for all students.

The socio-cultural environment in which educational software is used is a significant factor that play a significant part in determining the overall efficacy, relevance, and influence of the program. In the field of humanities, these instruments serve as culturally entrenched artefacts that have the potential to either support dominant narratives or question conventional viewpoints. They are not neutral in any way. Such software has the potential to act as a powerful tool for decolonising curriculum, amplifying the voices of marginalised populations, and fostering better intercultural understanding among students when it is built and deployed with a strong sense of critical awareness and a dedication to inclusion. In the end, the most significant obstacle is not the technical tools themselves; rather, it is the manner in which these technologies are used inside educational environments. Educators can ensure that technology serves to enrich, rather than diminish, the diversity, complexity, and intellectual depth of humanities education in the modern era by thoughtfully aligning the implementation of educational software with the socio-cultural realities and lived experiences of learners. This is a way to ensure that technology serves to enrich humanities education.

7.11 Policy Considerations

The successful integration of software into humanities education extends beyond classroom practices and pedagogy; it requires thoughtful and comprehensive policy frameworks. Educational policies at institutional, regional, and national levels influence infrastructure development, resource allocation, teacher training, digital equity, and data governance. This section critically examines key policy dimensions relevant to digital tool adoption in humanities education and offers recommendations to policymakers for fostering sustainable, inclusive, and effective digital learning environments.

7.11.1 Infrastructure and Funding Policies

A solid digital infrastructure is necessary for realising the advantages of software in education. Policymakers should prioritise extending internet access, especially in distant and underserved regions, to address connection gaps. In addition, they are obligated to guarantee the supply of necessary gear, which includes computers, tablets, and peripherals, in order to support the digital humanities and the educational requirements of a wider scope. Additionally, in order to maintain, enhance, and increase digital resources over time, it is vital to have financing mechanisms that are sustainable. In the absence of well-structured infrastructure regulations, access disparities will become even more pronounced, so restricting possibilities for software-enhanced learning to just those who belong to privileged groups and thereby expanding the digital divide.

7.11.2 Digital Literacy and Professional Development

Policies must demand the continuous development of digital literacy skills for both teachers and pupils. Included in this is the incorporation of digital skills training into teacher certification and professional development programs of various kinds. Assisting in the development of capabilities in the use of technologies and tools that are specialised in the humanities. It is important to encourage collaborative learning communities and peer mentorship programs that are centred on the integration of technology. In this way, instructors are guaranteed to have the self-assurance and expertise necessary to make effective use of digital resources to improve learning in the humanities.

7.11.3 Curriculum and Assessment Policy Alignment

In order to successfully incorporate digital learning into the educational system, it is necessary for the curricular standards and assessment frameworks to be in line with the goals of digital learning. In order to do this, it is necessary to include digital capabilities and critical thinking as core objectives into disciplines that are related to the humanities. This will ensure that students acquire the necessary skills for navigating settings that are driven by technology. Additionally, the criteria for evaluation should take into account the completion of digital projects, the presentation of multimedia content, and the completion of online collaborative assignments. This will validate the use of a variety of learning and expression strategies. In addition, it is essential to have curriculum that are adaptable and can accept new technologies and methods that draw from several disciplines. This will enable continual adaptation to developments in digital education. This kind of alignment not only makes the use of digital technologies in pedagogy more acceptable, but it also stimulates innovation in the ways that teaching and learning are carried out.

7.11.4 Equity and Inclusion Policies

In order to guarantee that everyone has equal access to educational technology, relevant policy frameworks need to address socioeconomic, linguistic, cultural, and gender differences. One of the most important strategies is the provision of targeted subsidies or grants to poor students in order to provide them with gadgets and internet access, therefore lowering the financial obstacles that prevent them from engaging in digital learning. The localisation of software and support for many languages should also be mandated by legislation in order to ensure that digital resources are accessible to populations who speak a variety of languages. It is essential to ensure gender equality in ICT education, which calls for specialised programs that promote equal participation and opportunities. A more all-encompassing educational setting may also be fostered by ensuring that students with disabilities are included in the classroom via the use of accessible technology. Educational technology has the potential to act as a tool for bridging disparities rather than increasing them if policies about digital education are placed with fairness as their top priority.

7.11.5 Data Privacy and Ethical Governance

It is of the utmost importance to protect student data and ensure that educational technologies are used in an ethical manner as digital platforms become more vital to the educational process. When it comes to educational software, policies need to establish clear rules for data privacy, protection, and consent. This will ensure that the personal information of students keeps their privacy intact. For the purpose of avoiding abuse and creating accountability, it is vital for third-party providers to maintain transparency in the data collecting, storage, and utilisation processes. The use of AI and automated decision-making technologies in education should also be governed by ethical principles, which would ensure that these tools are used in a fair and reliable manner. For the purpose of addressing data breaches or unethical acts, it is necessary to provide mechanisms for redress and responsibility. This will help to strengthen confidence in digital learning environments. The rights of students are protected by strong control in these areas, which also encourages the safe and ethical use of technology in educational settings.

7.11.6 Encouraging Open Educational Resources (OER) and Open Source Software

Education may become more economical and adaptive if policies are implemented that encourage the use of digital technologies and materials that are freely accessible to the public. In order to provide support for this, governments and organisations should provide financing for the production and dissemination of OER in the field of humanities. This would ensure that a large number of people have access to materials of very high quality. Additionally, by providing incentives for educators and academic institutions to participate in open-source software projects, it is possible to promote contributions that improve digital learning tools. To further increase inclusion and accessibility, it is important to strengthen collaborative networks that allow for the exchange of educational content across a variety of areas and languages. By putting these measures into effect, open educational resource policies contribute to the democratisation of digital humanities material, which in turn makes educational possibilities more accessible and comprehensive.

7.11.7 Partnership and Stakeholder Engagement Policies

Collaboration between governments, educational institutions, educational institutions, participants from the commercial sector, members of civil society, and local communities is essential to the success of digital education. Policy frameworks should promote public–private collaborations to harness expertise and resources, ensuring that digital learning efforts benefit from technical improvements and industry experience. This will ensure that digital learning projects are successful. In addition, encouraging community engagement in the production of digital content and the formulation of curricula helps to guarantee that educational resources represent a variety of viewpoints and the requirements of the local community more accurately. Providing assistance to research and innovation in the field of software design and digital humanities pedagogy is also crucial, since it is the driving force behind the advancement of digital education approaches. Through the participation of a diverse group of stakeholders, policies have the potential to become more efficient, responsive, and adaptive to the ever-changing educational requirements.

7.11.8 Monitoring, Evaluation, and Continuous Improvement

The implementation of mechanisms that monitor progress, evaluate efficacy, and improve methods over time is something that policymakers need to do in order to guarantee the successful incorporation of digital technologies into educational settings. To do this, unambiguous indicators must be defined in order to monitor access to technology, trends in use, and the influence that technology has on learning outcomes. The funding of long-term research and the methodical gathering of data on digital humanities education also gives useful insights into the changing demands and prospects in the field. Equally as crucial is the establishment of avenues for input from both teachers and students, with the goal of ensuring that policies continue to be responsive to the situations and experiences that are encountered in the classroom. The adoption of a framework for continuous improvement provides policymakers with the opportunity to maintain the adaptability and efficiency of education policies in the face of fast technological improvements.

Policy considerations are pivotal in shaping the ecosystem that enables meaningful, equitable, and sustainable integration of software in humanities education. By addressing infrastructure, training, curriculum, equity, data governance, open resources, partnerships, and evaluation, policymakers can create environments where digital tools become catalysts for enriched humanities learning rather than sources of disparity or confusion. As digital transformation accelerates in education, proactive, inclusive, and adaptable policy frameworks will be essential to ensure that all learners benefit from the potential of software-enhanced humanities education. Collaboration across sectors and continuous dialogue with educators and learners must underpin policy development, ensuring responsiveness to evolving socio-cultural and technological contexts.

7.11.9 Emerging Trends in Humanities Software Integration

As a result of the rapid development of digital technologies, humanities education is undergoing a transformation, which is resulting in the introduction of new tools, techniques, and approaches that improve learning experiences. There are new possibilities being opened up in the way that courses related to the humanities are taught and studied as a result of developments in artificial intelligence, interactive media, and adaptive learning systems. Through the use of these advances, educators and educational institutions can build learning environments that are more immersive and personalised. This may be accomplished by incorporating data-driven insights and digital collaboration into conventional humanities coursework. Additionally, larger societal developments, such as a growing focus on digital literacy, ethical issues in artificial intelligence, and cross-disciplinary learning, are now having an impact on the manner in which software for the humanities is produced and used. It is possible for educational institutions to guarantee that education in the humanities will continue to be relevant, interesting, and adaptive to the digital era if they choose to keep ahead of these rising trends.

7.11.10 Artificial Intelligence and Machine Learning

Tools that are driven by artificial intelligence are being more integrated into software for the humanities, which improves analysis, learning, and creativity. A comprehensive investigation of big text collections, sentiment trends, and thematic patterns may be carried out with the help of NLP, which allows automated textual analysis. A more effective level of engagement is fostered by personalised learning systems, which dynamically adapt both the material and the pace of instruction depending on the specific requirements of each learner. The use of chatbots and virtual assistants powered by artificial intelligence enables intelligent tutoring to provide academic help in real time, taking into account the context of the situation. This makes learning more engaging and accessible. In addition, the artwork, music, and writing tools that are created by artificial intelligence provide new paths for creative expression. These tools enable students to explore novel approaches to artistic interpretation and narrative. These technological innovations not only foster a more profound connection with themes related to the humanities, but they also contribute to the development of important digital literacy skills.

7.11.11 Virtual Reality (VR) and Augmented Reality (AR)

Through the provision of chances for learning that are both engaging and experiential, immersive technologies like as VR and AR are bringing about a revolution in the field of humanities education. For students to acquire a more profound awareness for the cultural and historical contexts in which they find themselves, virtual reconstructions of historical places, cultural artefacts, and literary settings provide them with the opportunity to explore diverse periods and tales in a first-hand manner. Complex ideas in the fields of philosophy, history, and anthropology may be brought to life via the use of interactive simulations, which can enable abstract theories to become more physical and relevant. A further benefit of multimodal learning environments is that they improve accessibility by accommodating a wide range of learning requirements via the use of flexible interfaces and sensory experiences. Educators have the ability to cultivate emotional connections, critical thinking, and expanded engagement with historical and cultural studies via the use of VR and AR into humanities teaching.

7.11.12 Collaborative and Social Learning Platforms

The software that is used in the modern arts and humanities is increasingly geared to encourage collaboration, which in turn improves engagement and the sharing of information among students and academics. Tools for real-time co-authoring and annotating make it possible to conduct peer reviews and group projects in a seamless manner. These tools also ensure that there are dynamic conversations and that ideas are refined collectively. Learners from different regions may engage with one another via online discussion forums and academic communities, which serves to extend their viewpoints and encourage intellectual interchange beyond the confines of traditional classrooms. Additionally, students are able to participate to existing projects in the humanities via the use of crowdsourcing and participatory research efforts, which contribute to the reinforcement of active learning and scholarly activity. Developing communication skills, stimulating critical debate, and promoting shared knowledge production are all things that may be accomplished with the aid of humanities software that incorporates social learning capabilities.

7.11.13 Mobile and Cloud-Based Solutions

Learning has become more adaptable and easier as a result of the growing usage of mobile devices and cloud computing, which has helped to considerably expand access to software for the humanities. Students now have the ability to interact with instructional materials outside of the conventional classroom setting, which enables learning to take place at any time and in any location, accommodating a variety of schedules and circumstances. Cloud services simplify the process of sharing resources, controlling versions of data, and backing up data, which ensures that cooperation and accessibility are not disrupted. Furthermore, mobile applications that are specifically designed for the education of humanities faculty members provide user-friendly interfaces that facilitate interactive interaction and personalised learning experiences. Through the incorporation of digital humanities into students' everyday study routines and academic processes, this approach encourages continuous learning and makes it easier for students to learn.

7.11.14 Data Visualisation and Digital Storytelling

Students now can show data from the humanities in ways that are both dynamic and interesting thanks to new digital technologies. Maps, timelines, and infographics that are interactive give visual representations of complicated historical and cultural information, which makes it simpler to understand patterns and correlations. Through the integration of text, graphics, audio, and video, digital storytelling platforms enable the creation of rich, multimodal tales that have the potential to promote expression and engagement. In addition, students are able to critically assess data patterns and identify deeper narratives within historical, linguistic, or literary settings with the use of visualisation tools. Learners are equipped with the abilities necessary to navigate and communicate successfully in digital contexts as a result of these advances, which not only promote media literacy but also foster creative thinking and analytical thinking.

7.11.15 Open Science and Open Humanities Initiatives

An increase in openness in research and education is being fostered by emerging software, which is also making information more accessible and facilitating collaboration. Both open-access publishing platforms and data-sharing technologies make it possible to disseminate academic work to a large audience, so removing the conventional obstacles that have been preventing access to knowledge. In addition, digital technologies that encourage citizen science and public engagement encourage a wider involvement in humanities studies. This makes it possible for communities to contribute to research and analysis. The creation of open-source software further fosters inclusion by enabling customisation and communal invention. This helps to ensure that educational technologies continue to be flexible to a wide range of requirements. Through the implementation of these open projects, which are in accordance with the principles of transparency and the development of shared information, cooperation across different fields and institutions is improved.

7.11.16 Integration of Interdisciplinary and Transdisciplinary Tools

For the purpose of facilitating interdisciplinary inquiry and providing students with the opportunity to investigate issues via a variety of analytical lenses, humanities software is evolving. By integrating text analysis, GIS, and social network analysis, some platforms make it possible to conduct more in-depth examinations of historical patterns, cultural movements, and societal linkages. Other technologies assist digital humanities initiatives that combine computational analysis, visualisation methods, and data science methodology. These tools encourage cooperation between the study of the humanities and the domains of STEM. In addition, software that integrates data from the environment, society, and culture offers a holistic approach to education, enabling students to investigate intricate relationships that span several fields of study. The implementation of these innovations fosters a more profound and multidimensional interaction with issues related to the humanities, hence extending views and improving critical thinking abilities.

7.11.17 Ethical AI and Responsible Technology Use

The design of software is changing to place a greater emphasis on ethical responsibility and social awareness as artificial intelligence and automation become increasingly integrated into everyday life. Clear rules for algorithmic transparency are being included by developers in order to guarantee that consumers are aware of the process by which automated judgments are computed. Users are able to negotiate the consequences of technology on their mental health, attention, and social connections with the assistance of features that promote digital well-being. This results in a more balanced relationship with digital tools. In addition, the dependability of digital resources is improved by the presence of tools that can detect and combat elements of bias and disinformation that are present in online material. Teachers have a significant role to play in the education system by assisting students in critically engaging with these ethical problems. This helps to ensure that students learn both technical capabilities and a careful awareness of the larger implications of artificial intelligence.

Emerging trends in humanities software integration reveal a dynamic landscape driven by technological innovation and evolving pedagogical priorities. The convergence of AI, immersive media, collaboration, accessibility, openness, interdisciplinary, and ethics offers transformative opportunities for humanities education. However, maximising these benefits requires deliberate strategies that address equity, teacher preparedness, and socio-cultural contexts. By staying attuned to these trends, educators and institutions can harness digital tools not only to enhance traditional humanities learning but also to prepare students for active, informed participation in a digitally mediated world. Embracing innovation alongside critical reflection will be essential in shaping the future of humanities education.

References

1. J. Kehinde, H.B. Akinlabi, Impact of leadership skill and strategies on banking sector performance: A survey of selected consolidated banks in Nigeria. Int. Trader Acad. Res. Conf. **3**(1), 7–8 (2012)
2. S. Joshi, M. Sharma, Impact of sustainable supply chain management on performance of SMEs amidst COVID-19 pandemic: An Indian perspective. Int. J. Logist. Econ. Glob. **9**(3), 248 (2022). https://doi.org/10.1504/ijleg.2022.10044917
3. W.A. Makinde, T.O. Bamiro, Service quality of teaching vocational education and training (TVET) and student's satisfaction in Nigeria. J. Pedagog. Educ. Sci. **2**(01), 10–25 (2023). https://doi.org/10.56741/jpes.v2i01.157
4. B. Amisha, Role of emotional intelligence in leadership and organizational performance in Indonesia. Int. J. Psychol. **9**(2), 1–12 (2024). https://doi.org/10.47604/ijp.2362
5. S.K. Coetzee, H.K.S. Laschinger, Toward a comprehensive, theoretical model of compassion fatigue: An integrative literature review. Nurs. Heal. Sci. **20**(1), 4–15 (2018). https://doi.org/10.1111/nhs.12387
6. M. Casini, Extended Reality for Smart Building Operation and Maintenance: A Review. Energies **15**(10), 3785 (2022). https://doi.org/10.3390/en15103785
7. H. Muhammad, F. Shehzad, K. Anwar, M. Khaidzir, R.B. Ibrahim, A.F. Yusof, The adoption in the AEC industry, pp. 20–25 (2019)
8. M. Al Rawajbeh et al., A new model for security analysis of network anomalies for IoT devices. Int. J. Data Netw. Sci. **7**(3), 1241–1248 (2023). https://doi.org/10.5267/j.ijdns.2023.5.001
9. A. Ghosh, D.J. Edwards, M.R. Hosseini, Patterns and trends in Internet of Things (IoT) research: Future applications in the construction industry. Eng. Constr. Archit. Manag. **28**(2), 457–481 (2021). https://doi.org/10.1108/ECAM-04-2020-0271
10. M.F. de-Lima-Santos, L. Mesquita, J.G. de Melo Peixoto, I. Camargo, Digital news business models in the age of industry 4.0 digital Brazilian news players find in technology new ways to

bring revenue and competitive advantage. Digit. J. **0**(0), 1–25 (2022). https://doi.org/10.1080/21670811.2022.2037444
11. M.I. Manda, S. Ben Dhaou, Responding to the challenges and opportunities in the 4th industrial revolution in developing countries. ACM Int. Conf. Proceeding Ser. **Part F1481**, 244–253 (2019). https://doi.org/10.1145/3326365.3326398
12. N.N. Pokrovskaia, Tax, financial and social regulatory mechanisms within the knowledge-driven economy. Blockchain algorithms and fog computing for the efficient regulation. In: Proceeding 2017 20th IEEE International Conference Soft Computing Measurement SCM 2017, pp. 709–712 (2017). https://doi.org/10.1109/SCM.2017.7970698
13. A.O. Eziechine, J.A. Agho, Democracy, gender issues and women empowerment in Nigeria: Reflections on selected Nigerian feminist drama. J. Gend. Relat. Stud. **4**(1), 1–10 (2023). https://doi.org/10.47941/jgrs.1296
14. A. Isa, N.D. Nte, A. Baba-Ahmadu, Critical thinking for intelligence analysis for Nigerian students: Evaluating the pedagogical challenges in real life scenarios. Indones. Educ. Adm. Leadersh. J. **5**(2), 46–60 (2023). https://doi.org/10.22437/ideal.v5i2.28639
15. S. Zhao, Q. Pan, D. Gao, J. Cheng, Integrating internet of things and mixed reality to teach performance-based architectural design: A case study of shading devices. Educ. Inf. Technol. (2022). https://doi.org/10.1007/s10639-022-10998-6
16. H.S. Munawar, F. Ullah, S. Qayyum, Big data in construction : Current applications and future opportunities (2022)
17. P. Coberly-Holt, K. Elufiede, Preparing for the fourth industrial revolution with creative and critical thinking Patricia Coberly-Holt and Kemi Elufiede, pp. 21–25 (2016)
18. J. Owolabi, A. Bekele, Implementation of innovative educational technologies in teaching of anatomy and basic medical sciences during the covid-19 pandemic in a developing country: The covid-19 silver lining? Adv. Med. Educ. Pract. **12**, 619–625 (2021). https://doi.org/10.2147/AMEP.S295239
19. N.M. Al Hamad, O.E. Adewusi, C.C. Unachukwu, B. Osawaru, O.N. Chisom, Bridging the gap: Using robotics to enhance emotional and social learning in K-12 education. Int. J. Sci. Res. Arch. **11**(1), 231–243 (2024). https://doi.org/10.30574/ijsra.2024.11.1.0025
20. M.J.M.R.K. Yeo, This, (Re) Interpreting action, learning, and experience: Integrating action learning and experiential learning for HRD Roland. Comput. Complex. **2**(1), 1–9 (2009). https://doi.org/10.1002/hrdq
21. L.A. Gil-Alana, M. Škare, G. Claudio-Quiroga, Innovation and knowledge as drivers of the 'great decoupling' in China: Using long memory methods. J. Innov. Knowl. **5**(4), 266–278 (2020). https://doi.org/10.1016/j.jik.2020.08.003
22. A. Erzse, N. Christofides, N. Stacey, K. Lebard, L. Foley, K. Hofman, Availability and advertising of sugar sweetened beverages in South African public primary schools following a voluntary pledge by a major beverage company: A mixed methods study. Glob. Health Action. **14**(1) (2021). https://doi.org/10.1080/16549716.2021.1898130
23. P. Baepler, J.D. Walker, M. Driessen, It's not about seat time: Blending, flipping, and efficiency in active learning classrooms. Comput. Educ. **78**, 227–236 (2014). https://doi.org/10.1016/j.compedu.2014.06.006
24. K.C. Obi, O. Iwuanyanwu, innovation in the assessment of primary school mathematics: An approach to revamping Nigeria education. J. Teach. Perspect. **18**(1), 51–66 (2023), [Online]. Available: http://repositorio.unan.edu.ni/2986/1/5624.pdf%0Ahttp://fiskal.kemenkeu.go.id/ejournal%0A10.1016/j.cirp.2016.06.001%0A10.1016/j.powtec.2016.12.055%0A10.1016/j.ijfatigue.2019.02.006%0A10.1
25. T. Njonge, Influence of psychological well-being and school factors on delinquency, during the covid-19 period among secondary school students in selected schools in Nakuru County: Kenya. 7 **2454**, 1175–1189 (2023). https://doi.org/10.47772/IJRISS
26. M. Javed, Z. Tučková, A.B. Jibril, The role of social media on tourists' behavior: An empirical analysis of millennials from the Czech Republic. Sustainability. **12**(18) (2020). https://doi.org/10.3390/su12187735

27. A. Yang, M. Han, Q. Zeng, Y. Sun, Adopting building information modeling (BIM) for the development of smart buildings: A review of enabling applications and challenges. Adv. Civ. Eng. **20**(21), 1–26 (2021). https://doi.org/10.1155/2021/8811476
28. W.S.K. Liu, Global leadership dynamics: refining executive selection in multinational corporations. **0123456789**. Springer US (2024). https://doi.org/10.1007/s13132-024-01794-3
29. F. Collier-sewell, I. Atherton, C. Mahoney, R.G. Kyle, E. Hughes, K. Lasater, Competencies and standards in nurse education: The irresolvable tensions. Nurse Educ. Today. **125**, 105782 (2023). https://doi.org/10.1016/j.nedt.2023.105782
30. V. Singh, Digitalization, BIM ecosystem, and the future of built environment: How widely are we exploring the different possibilities? Eng. Constr. Archit. Manag. (2019). https://doi.org/10.1108/ECAM-01-2018-0004
31. E. Thoman, T. Jolls, Literacy for the 21st century an overview and orientation guide to media literacy education part I: Theory CML MediaLit Kit^{TM} a framework for learning and teaching in a media age developed and written by, p. 37 (2013), [Online]. Available: www.medialit.org
32. F.A. Alaba, M. Amina, U. Ibrahim, H.A. Sulaimon, A. Zainab Aliyu, Exploring the role of the internet of things (IoT) on economic growth in Nigeria: Challenges and opportunities. Eng. Technol. Trends. **2**(6) (2024)
33. E. Relations, P.F. Repository, An exploration of the practices of locational flexibility in developing economies: Insights from the Nigerian higher education sector abstract. **42**, 166–179 (2021)
34. C. Purcell et al., A peer-led, school-based social network intervention for young people in the UK, promoting sexual health via social media and conversations with friends: Intervention development and optimisation of STASH. BMC Public Health **23**(1), 1–12 (2023). https://doi.org/10.1186/s12889-023-15541-x
35. B. Kim, A. Xiong, D. Lee, K. Han, A systematic review on fake news research through the lens of news creation and consumption: Research efforts, challenges, and future directions. PLoS One. **16**(12), 1–28 (2021). https://doi.org/10.1371/journal.pone.0260080
36. B. Liu, S. Link, E. Muñoz, Validation of expressive XML keys with XML Schema and XQuery. Conf. Res. Pract. Inf. Technol. Ser. **165**, 81–90 (2015)
37. P. Borges, M. do C. Alves, R. Silva, The activity-based costing system applied in higher education institutions: A systematic review and mapping of the literature. Businesses. **4**(1), 18–38 (2024). https://doi.org/10.3390/businesses4010002
38. A. Ekwueme, A. Nehemiah, The influence of online marketing of Jumia and Konga on consumer purchasing behaviour among Kogi state residents of Nigeria. Glob. J. Human- Soc. Sci. Arts Humanit. **17**(6), 25–32 (2017)
39. S.A. Yakubu, M.A. Ali, Election and voting pattern in Nigeria: A study of 2015 governorship election in Bauchi State. Int. J. Humanit. Soc. Sci. Invent. **6**(11), 52–59 (2017), [Online]. Available: http://www.ijhssi.org/papers/v6(11)/Version-2/I0611025259.pdf
40. M. Okoye-Chine, The effect of sales promotion on marketing of Cocacola drinks in Anambra state. Int. J. Innov. Soc. Sci. Humanit. Res. **9**(1), 117–129 (2021), [Online]. Available: http://seahipaj.org/journals-ci/mar-2021/IJISSHR/full/IJISSHR-M-12-2021.pdf
41. D.M. Onojah, P.D.A.W. Adewole, Assessment of school physical facilities on pre-primary education curriculum implementation in public primary schools in Southwest, Nigeria. African J. Humanit. Contemp. Educ. Res. **8**(1), 1–94 (2022), [Online]. Available: https://publications.afropolitanjournals.com/index.php/ajhcer/article/view/264
42. J. Almustapha, A. Sani Dahiru, M.I. Bungudu, A. Hamisu Lawal, A correlational analysis of school inventories management and teacher efficiency among primary schools of Zamfara State, Nigeria. J. Adv. Humanit. Res. **2**(1), 1–12 (2023). https://doi.org/10.56868/jadhur.v2i1.38
43. E. Luo, The effect of artificial intelligence on the human idea of free will. Proc. 2021 Int. Conf. Soc. Dev. Media Commun. (SDMC 2021). **631**(Sdmc 2021), 1355–1363 (2022). https://doi.org/10.2991/asschr.k.220105.249
44. M. Stute, S. Sardesai, M. Parlings, P.P. Senna, R. Fornasiero, S. Balech, Technology scouting to accelerate innovation in supply chain (2021). https://doi.org/10.1007/978-3-030-63505-3_6

45. S. Ghavifekr, A. Razak, M. Ghani, N. Ran, Y. Meixi, Z. Tengyue, ICT integration in education: Incorporation for teaching and learning improvement. Malaysian Online J. Educ. Technol. **2**(2), 24–45 (2014)
46. M. Kehayov, L. Holder, V. Koch, Application of artificial intelligence technology in the manufacturing process and purchasing and supply management. Procedia Comput. Sci. **200**(2019), 1209–1217 (2022). https://doi.org/10.1016/j.procs.2022.01.321
47. F. Emmert-Streib, Z. Yang, H. Feng, S. Tripathi, M. Dehmer, An introductory review of deep learning for prediction models with big data. Front. Artif. Intell. **3**, 1–23 (2020). https://doi.org/10.3389/frai.2020.00004
48. S. Gluszek et al., Emerging trends of the illegal wildlife trade in Mesoamerica. Oryx **55**(5), 708–716 (2021). https://doi.org/10.1017/S0030605319001133
49. M. Ingrassia, C. Bellia, C. Giurdanella, P. Columba, S. Chironi, Digital influencers, food and tourism—A new model of open innovation for businesses in the Ho.Re.Ca. Sector. J. Open Innov. Technol. Mark. Complex. **8**(1) (2022). https://doi.org/10.3390/joitmc8010050
50. M. Ingrassia, C. Bellia, C. Giurdanella, P. Columba, S. Chironi, Digital influencers, food and tourism—A new model of open innovation for businesses in the Ho.Re.Ca. Sector. J. Open Innov. Technol. Mark. Complex. **8**(1), 50 (2022). https://doi.org/10.3390/joitmc8010050

Chapter 8
Conclusion and Recommendations

8.1 Summary of the Study

An in-depth investigation of the ways in which digital software tools may be incorporated into humanities education was carried out in this research. The study looked at the significance of these tools, as well as their theoretical underpinnings, pedagogical uses, and socio-cultural influences related to them. It was proved via an in-depth analysis that software solutions have the potential to expand learning in the humanities beyond the confines of typical classroom settings, so encouraging engagement, accessibility, and creativity respectively. In the beginning of the study, it was determined that there is a need to adjust digital tools so that they are in line with the fundamental goals of humanities education. These goals include the development of critical thinking, creativity, collaboration, and equal access to educational resources. It emphasised how important it is for teachers and educational institutions to embrace technology not as a complement but rather as an essential component that improves the delivery of material and the involvement of students. In order to provide an academic framework for this integration, the research drew from a variety of theoretical viewpoints, such as constructivist learning theories, digital literacy models, and socio-technical systems theory. Through the use of this multidimensional framework, a more profound comprehension of the ways in which digital technologies impact the formation of knowledge, the autonomy of learners, and the social interaction that takes place within educational settings was achieved. The beneficial influence that humanities software has on student learning outcomes was emphasised in a comprehensive assessment of prior studies. However, the analysis also identified major concerns, such as differences in resource availability, teacher readiness, and digital equality. Using these results as a foundation, the research investigated important pedagogical concerns that should be taken into account when properly integrating technology into humanities curriculum.

One of the primary focusses of the research was on the ways in which digital tools might support critical thinking by providing students with the opportunity to

F. A. Alaba et al., *Learning Beyond the Classroom*, Studies in Computational Intelligence 1253, https://doi.org/10.1007/978-3-032-14433-1_8

actively investigate, understand, and portray intricate humanities themes. In addition, it examined the role that technology plays in promoting student autonomy by providing options for personalised and collaborative learning that enable students to take responsibility for their own educational experiences. The research highlighted the relevance of teacher training and professional capacity-building as critical components of effective software integration. This was done in recognition of the fact that educators play a significant role in this change. It pushed for projects that would provide continual professional development as well as strong support networks in order to assist educators in properly using digital resources in their teaching methods. Additionally, resource fairness and access were noted as recurring challenges, which implies that specific policy initiatives are required in order to bridge the digital gap.

In addition to educational applications, the research investigated larger socio-cultural aspects that influence software adoption. These elements include cultural relevance, language variety, and ethical questions about data privacy and algorithmic prejudice. The study also investigated new developments in the field of humanities education, such as artificial intelligence, virtual reality, free educational materials, and interdisciplinary software. These are all examples of rising trends that may be used to facilitate future innovation in the field. The research highlighted the relevance of cohesive policy frameworks that provide a strong basis for the teaching of digital humanities. There was a request for policies that would promote the development of infrastructure, the training of educators, the alignment of curricula, fair access, and ethical governance in order to guarantee the long-term viability of the program. Ultimately, the findings of this research provide a detailed understanding of the intricate relationship that exists between digital software and the field of humanities education. It offers significant insights for educators, policymakers, and academics who are looking to harness the full potential of digital technologies in enhancing humanities learning outside the conventional bounds of the classroom. These insights are provided by identifying best practices, present difficulties, and prospective future directions.

8.2 Summary of Major Findings

The research of software integration in humanities education uncovered crucial insights into both the potential advantages and the constraints connected with digital transformation in the area. This study was conducted to investigate the integration of software in humanities education. While putting attention on difficulties such as resource inequities, educator preparedness, and ethical concerns, it emphasised the ways in which technology may improve learning experiences by increasing interaction, collaboration, and accessibility. Moreover, it highlighted the approaches. The study highlighted the significance of connecting digital technologies with humanities education aims in order to maximise their influence. This was accomplished by evaluating theoretical frameworks, pedagogical practices, and developing trends. These results provide educators, institutions, and policymakers with vital insight that may assist them in navigating the ever-changing world of digital humanities education.

8.2.1 Alignment with Humanities Education Goals

This research has provided a number of important findings, one of which is that the use of digital technologies in a planned manner may considerably advance the goals of fundamental humanities education requirements. The use of software helps students to connect with knowledge in ways that are both dynamic and interactive. This is accomplished by encouraging critical thinking, creativity, and cooperation. In addition to this, it plays a significant part in fostering diversity by ensuring that students from a wide range of backgrounds have access to humanities scholarship and may contribute to it. By incorporating graphics, audio, and interactive aspects, digital platforms enable multi-modal expression, which enriches learning experiences and encourages deeper research of complicated subjects. This goes beyond the standard text-based techniques that have been used in the past. The use of these technologies in a thoughtful manner has the potential to revolutionise education in the humanities by making it more interesting, accessible, and flexible to the ever-changing requirements of both academia and society.

8.2.2 Theoretical Framework Validity

According to the findings of the research, the use of constructivist and socio-technical theoretical frameworks yielded significant insights into the ways in which digital technologies influence the learning processes. Rather than only acquiring information in a passive manner, constructivism places an emphasis on active knowledge building, in which students actively participate with the material being studied. The use of digital tools to facilitate interactive investigation, analysis, and creative expression is a method that lends support to this approach. The socio-technical viewpoint, on the other hand, emphasises the interwoven connection that exists between technology, users, and larger educational institutions. It demonstrates how software platforms enable learners to exercise their autonomy and engage in meaningful social relationships. The combination of these frameworks demonstrates how digital tools may improve engagement, collaboration, and personalised learning. As a result, these tools are crucial for successful humanities education in an environment that is becoming more digital.

8.2.3 Pedagogical Implications

The research that was conducted underlined the fact that a change in pedagogical techniques is required in order to successfully include digital resources into humanities teaching. It is imperative that educators adopt learner-centred techniques that place an emphasis on active engagement, discovery, and creativity rather than the conventional pedagogical approach of passive teaching. It is vital to have curriculum that are flexible in order to accept new technologies and approaches that include several disciplines. This will ensure that digital tools improve rather than restrict individuals' educational experiences. In addition, formative assessments have to be expanded to include digital projects, which would provide students the opportunity to show their comprehension via the use of multimedia storytelling, collaborative research, and interactive presentations. The educators need to carefully rethink the learning activities in order to make the most of the advantages that software integration offers. They need to make sure that the technological affordances are used in order to increase the level of understanding and to encourage meaningful involvement.

8.2.4 Enhancement of Critical Thinking

Students are provided with effective means for interacting with complicated knowledge via the use of digital humanities tools, which dramatically improve both critical thinking and analytical thinking. Learners gain data literacy and the capacity to recognise patterns, trends, and underlying themes within historical, literary, and cultural settings via the process of analysing huge datasets. By translating raw data into interactive maps, graphs, and timelines, visualisation tools provide further assistance in the interpretation of complicated linkages. This helps to make abstract notions more real and understandable. The ability of students to incorporate text, images, audio, and video into captivating tales that represent a variety of views is another way that multimedia storytelling helps students develop their ability to synthesise information (synthesis). Not only can these technology-driven, interactive learning experiences help students develop their analytical abilities, but they also enable a variety of creative methods to comprehending and interpreting knowledge related to the humanities.

8.2.5 Impact on Student Autonomy and Ownership

The use of software into humanities education gives students more agency by encouraging them to take responsibility for their own learning experiences. Students are able to interact with information that is customised to their own interests and levels of competence via the use of personalised learning paths. This enables individualised teaching that can fit a variety of learning styles. Studying at one's own speed allows for more flexibility, providing students with the ability to determine how and when they interact with the information being studied. This facilitates deeper knowledge and prolonged engagement. Students are able to participate in group discussions, co-author projects, and conduct information analysis jointly thanks to the availability of digital tools, which also assist the building of collaborative knowledge. The cultivation of intrinsic motivation, the encouragement of responsibility, and the driving of meaningful investment in learning outcomes are all reinforced by these aspects, which in turn reinforce active involvement in humanities education.

8.2.6 Teacher Training and Capacity Building Needs

The research found that teachers' lack of proper training and ongoing professional development is a big obstacle to the effective use of digital technologies in humanities classrooms. In order for teachers to effectively use software, they must have confidence in their abilities and be technically proficient. This highlights the need of maintaining institutional support. It may be difficult for educators to make best use of digital technologies if they do not have access to formal capacity-building programs. This might restrict the influence that these tools could have on the outcomes of learning. It is necessary for organisations to make investments in continuous professional development programs in order to solve this issue. These programs should include seminars, hands-on training sessions, and peer-learning networks. Educators are able to maintain their knowledge of new technologies and best practices when they are given access to materials that are up to date and opportunity to develop their mentoring relationships. Additionally, encouraging experimentation and innovation in instructional strategies is a result of cultivating a culture of digital literacy within academic settings.

It is imperative that institutional policies give priority to the preparation of teachers by including digital pedagogy into formal educator training programs and the criteria for certification. Increasing the effectiveness of support systems not only boosts the self-assurance of educators but also guarantees that students will get an enhanced and technologically-driven education via the humanities. In the absence of planned interventions, the digital gap that exists among educators has the potential to impede the more comprehensive objectives of digital transformation in the humanities.

8.2.7 Resource Equity and Access Challenges

The research highlighted digital gaps as a recurring concern in the field of humanities education. It revealed considerable differences in infrastructure, device availability, and access to software of a high quality. Learners who come from marginalised groups often experience obstacles as a result of inconsistent internet access, obsolete equipment, and limited exposure to digital learning tools, which contributes to the worsening of educational disparities. In order to cultivate a digital humanities environment that is more welcoming to everyone, it is imperative that institutions and authorities prioritise equitable access via deliberate initiatives. In order to help bridge these gaps, expanding infrastructural development, providing financial assistance for students from disadvantaged backgrounds, and ensuring that digital resources are accessible to everyone may be helpful. In addition, the development of relationships with organisations that supply technology, community organisations, and public institutions may make it easier to distribute resources and implement programs that teach digital literacy. In order to address these inequities, a multi-layered strategy is required. This approach should not only enhance access, but it should also educate educators and learners with the skills necessary to properly traverse digital platforms. It is possible for digital humanities education to genuinely deliver its promise of democratising knowledge and enabling greater involvement across a variety of backgrounds if these inequalities are closed.

8.2.8 Socio-Cultural and Ethical Considerations

In the field of humanities education, the incorporation of software goes beyond the realm of technical innovation; it also involves the interaction of cultural significance, language variety, and important ethical problems. The careful management of these overlapping aspects is required in order to guarantee that digital learning environments are courteous, responsible, and equal. Due to the fact that software tools need to represent a variety of views, historical settings, and cultural narratives, cultural relevance is very important in the field of humanities education. In order to avoid a standardised method of education, digital platforms have to be able to accommodate local knowledge systems, customs, and identities. In a similar vein, the variety of languages plays a crucial part in accessibility. In order to promote inclusion in digital humanities study, software must support various languages, particularly indigenous and under-represented languages. Concerns of an ethical nature, such as the privacy of data and the prejudice shown by algorithms, must also be addressed. It is imperative that educational institutions implement measures to protect personal information and promote transparency in data use as a result of the fact that educational technologies are collecting and processing massive amounts of student data. Additionally, algorithmic bias must be reduced in order to avoid inadvertent discrimination or skewed results that might disproportionately harm populations who are marginalised. This applies whether the prejudice is present in automated grading, content suggestions, or learning tools driven by AI.

It is necessary to take a holistic strategy in order to create equitable digital learning environments. This approach should include regulatory frameworks, ethical principles, and cooperation between educators, technologists, and researchers. Software has the potential to improve education in the humanities while also conserving cultural identity, linguistic variety, and ethical integrity if it is administered with conscious consideration.

8.2.9 Emerging Trends and Innovation

Humanities education is undergoing a transformation as a result of the emergence of new technologies like as AI, VR/AR, and cloud-based collaboration platforms. These technologies are providing novel approaches to engage students and improve their learning experiences. Personalised learning paths, intelligent tutoring systems, and automated textual analysis are all made possible by technologies powered by AI, which also help deeper understanding and the development of skills. Through the use of virtual reality and augmented reality, immersive worlds are created in which students may engage in experiential learning to investigate historical places, cultural artefacts, and complicated theoretical ideas. The use of cloud-based platforms makes it possible to collaborate in real time, share resources, and conduct research that spans several disciplines, hence removing barriers to the interchange of information. The installation of the integration, however, must be done with careful consideration. The appropriateness of these technologies for education is of the utmost importance; they should be in accordance with the objectives of humanities education, with an emphasis on abilities such as critical thinking, creativity, and interpretation, rather than just digitising conventional techniques. Concerns of equity must also be addressed, with the goal of ensuring that all students, regardless of their socioeconomic background, have access to the required infrastructure and training in digital literacy. It is crucial to have ethical governance, especially when it comes to managing data privacy, algorithmic bias, and intellectual property concerns that are associated with material created by artificial intelligence.

It is possible for educators and institutions to maximise the transformational potential of new technologies by carefully navigating these factors. This will result in humanities education that is more participatory, inclusive, and prepared for the future.

8.2.10 Policy and Institutional Support

For software integration in humanities education to be sustainable, policy frameworks need to be properly established and cover crucial areas such as the creation of infrastructure, the training of teachers, equality efforts, and data security. When there is a lack of strong institutional leadership and good collaborations across sectors, there is a possibility that implementation initiatives may become fragmented or get inadequate support. It is the infrastructure that plays a fundamental role in ensuring that digital humanities tools are accessible to the public. This infrastructure includes dependable internet connection, contemporary gadgets, and safe data storage methods. Continuous teacher training is also very important since it provides educators with the knowledge, abilities, and self-assurance they need to successfully use digital resources into their instructional methods. Adaptability is essential for professional development programs, since they must keep up with the rapid growth of technology and the ever-changing educational requirements. The issue of equity continues to be a serious problem; access gaps may have a disproportionate impact on marginalised areas, hence restricting prospects for meaningful involvement with digital humanities. It is imperative that policy frameworks give priority to efforts that aim to bridge digital gaps. This will ensure that all students, regardless of their background, get the benefits of technology breakthroughs. In a similar vein, the incorporation of data security and ethical issues into policy debates is necessary in order to shield the privacy of students while simultaneously encouraging responsible software use. When it comes to pushing the widespread use of digital humanities tools, supporting strategic investments, and developing multidisciplinary partnerships, institutional leadership acts as a catalyst. It is possible for cross-sector collaborations to improve resource sharing, innovation, and the application of best practices. These partnerships may be formed between educational institutions, technology developers, policymakers, and cultural organisations.

The research highlights the fact that while digital technologies have a tremendous potential to enhance teaching in the humanities, the effective integration of these resources requires methods that are both purposeful and comprehensive. The alignment of technology breakthroughs with the fundamental principles and goals of humanities education may be ensured by collaboratively addressing issues pertaining to pedagogy, equality, capacity-building, cultural relevance, and governance.

8.3 Conclusion on Research Objectives

This study set out to examine the integration of digital software tools in humanities education, with the goal of understanding their relevance, pedagogical impact, challenges, and future prospects. Through a detailed investigation, the research successfully addressed its objectives, as outlined below.

Objective 1: To Analyse the Relevance of Software Tools to Humanities Education Goals

The study found that digital tools play a crucial role in humanities education by enhancing fundamental skills such as critical thinking, creativity, collaboration, and accessibility. The integration of software allows students to interact with complex content in dynamic ways, fostering engagement through diverse media formats, including text, visuals, and interactive applications. These tools align well with core educational goals by facilitating deeper exploration of humanities subjects, enabling multimodal representation, and supporting student-centered learning experiences.

Objective 2: To Explore Theoretical Frameworks Supporting Software Integration

The research employed constructivist learning theories, digital literacy models, and socio-technical systems perspectives to develop a robust conceptual foundation for software integration in humanities education. Constructivist approaches emphasise active knowledge construction, digital literacy models highlight the importance of navigating digital environments effectively, and socio-technical frameworks illustrate the interconnected relationship between technology, learners, and institutional contexts. Together, these perspectives provide valuable insights into how software mediates learning processes, promotes autonomy, and fosters meaningful social interactions.

Objective 3: To Assess Pedagogical Implications and Best Practices

The study underscored the need for pedagogical shifts to optimise software integration, emphasizing learner-centred approaches that encourage exploration, interpretation, and collaboration. Flexible curriculum design emerged as a key factor in accommodating evolving technological tools and interdisciplinary connections. Additionally, formative assessment strategies were identified as essential for measuring student engagement with digital projects, fostering critical analysis, and reinforcing personalised learning experiences. The study highlighted best practices for leveraging digital affordances, ensuring that educators harness software tools effectively to enrich humanities education.

Objective 4: To Investigate Impacts on Student Autonomy and Critical Thinking

Findings revealed that digital tools significantly enhance student autonomy by enabling personalised learning pathways and self-paced study. The integration of software fosters independent inquiry, allowing students to tailor their engagement with content based on individual interests and learning styles. Furthermore, digital tools support critical thinking through interactive analysis, data visualisation, and multimedia creation. These elements facilitate deeper interpretation of humanities subjects, empowering students to synthesise diverse perspectives and develop advanced analytical skills.

Objective 5: To Identify Challenges Related to Teacher Training, Resource Equity, and Socio-Cultural Context

The study identified substantial challenges affecting successful software integration in humanities education. A major concern is the lack of adequate training and ongoing professional development for educators, as teacher readiness directly influences the effective implementation of digital tools. Persistent resource inequities emerged as another critical issue, particularly in marginalised communities where access to reliable infrastructure and high-quality software remains limited. Additionally, socio-cultural factors, such as language diversity and ethical considerations surrounding algorithmic bias and data privacy, must be addressed to ensure equitable and inclusive digital learning environments.

Objective 6: To Examine Emerging Trends and Policy Considerations for Sustainable Integration

Emerging technologies, including AI, VR/AR, and cloud-based collaborative platforms, present transformative opportunities for humanities education. AI-powered tools facilitate automated textual analysis, personalised learning, and intelligent tutoring. VR/AR technologies create immersive educational experiences, enabling students to explore historical sites and cultural artifacts interactively. Cloud-based platforms support real-time collaboration, resource sharing, and interdisciplinary engagement. However, the successful adoption of these innovations requires well-defined policy frameworks that emphasise ethical governance, equity, institutional support, and sustainable implementation.

This study successfully met its research objectives by providing a multi-dimensional understanding of digital software integration in humanities education. The findings highlight both opportunities and challenges, emphasising the need for intentional strategies that address pedagogy, equity, capacity-building, cultural relevance, and policy alignment. These insights serve as a foundation for educators, institutions, and policymakers seeking to harness the full potential of digital tools in shaping the future of humanities education in an increasingly digital era.

8.4 Educational Implications

The results of this research have major educational repercussions for a broad variety of stakeholders participating in the field of humanities education. These stakeholders include educators, curriculum designers, administrators, policymakers, and technology developers. The incorporation of digital software tools is transforming the landscape of teaching and learning by boosting interaction, personalisation, and accessibility. This provides students with more dynamic and interesting methods to investigate topics related to the humanities. Through the use of these technologies, educators have the ability to cultivate critical thinking, creativity, and cooperation. On the other hand, curriculum designers are required to modify instructional frameworks in order to suit digital techniques. Within the context of ensuring seamless integration, administrators and policymakers play a significant role in the establishment of supporting infrastructures, equal access efforts, and successful training programs. In the meanwhile, those who build technology need to concentrate on developing tools that are not just ethically and pedagogically good but also inclusive and aligned with the ideals of humanities education. In light of the fact that these possibilities and difficulties are always shifting, it is imperative that strategic efforts be aimed towards addressing obstacles like as digital inequalities, teacher preparedness, and ethical issues linked to data privacy and algorithmic prejudice. By taking a comprehensive approach to addressing these problems, stakeholders have the power to maximise the potential of digital software to improve education in the humanities while simultaneously ensuring that its adoption is both sustainable and inclusive.

8.4.1 Enhancing Teaching Practices

In the field of humanities education, the research underscores the vital need for a change towards learner-centred, technology-enhanced pedagogies that prioritise critical thinking, creativity, and collaboration. Educators are able to incorporate dynamic teaching tactics that engage students in meaningful investigation of complicated topic when they strategically integrate digital technologies into their lessons. Students are able to develop deeper analytical and problem-solving abilities via the cultivation of project-based learning, which enables them to confront real-world challenges through interdisciplinary research. Through the use of text, pictures, audio, and video, digital storytelling provides learners with the opportunity to express themselves in several ways, allowing them to synthesise historical tales, cultural viewpoints, and literary themes. Students have the opportunity to identify patterns in historical events, language trends, or social movements via the use of data analysis tools, which offer them with the opportunity to interact with big datasets. Furthermore, collaborative knowledge-building is supported by interactive conversations that are enabled by digital platforms. These talks encourage varied ideas and critical engagement with diverse perspectives. The combination of these technology-driven initiatives raises the level of student engagement, improves understanding, and better prepares students to efficiently traverse the ever-changing digital terrain of humanities study.

8.4.2 Professional Development and Capacity Building

Training and capacity development for educators must be maintained throughout time in order to ensure the successful incorporation of digital humanities software. In order for educators to make meaningful use of digital resources, institutions need to make investments in professional development programs that provide them with the technical skills, pedagogical techniques, and self-assurance they need to utilise digital tools effectively. Hands-on workshops, interactive training sessions, and flexible learning modules that are in line with the ever-evolving technology breakthroughs should all be included in these programs. In addition to formal training, peer learning communities play an important part in encouraging collaborative knowledge-sharing. These communities enable educators to facilitate the exchange of best practices and provide support to one another in the process of overcoming problems. It is possible for mentoring programs to further increase teacher preparation by giving individualised coaching from seasoned specialists who are able to assist educators in properly navigating digital humanities techniques. It is possible for educational institutions to guarantee that instructors continue to be skilled in the integration of digital tools, maintain innovation in the field of humanities education, and improve student engagement via the use of technology-driven learning experiences if they prioritise continual professional development.

8.4.3 Curriculum Design and Assessment

In order to ensure that the curriculum is flexible enough to accept new forms of learning and expression, it is necessary to make a fundamental change in the design of the curriculum in order to include digital tools into humanities education. Traditional curriculum frameworks need to be updated so that they may integrate goals that are in line with digital literacy. This will help students develop the capacity to critically interact with technology and successfully traverse digital settings. Students need to be encouraged to analyse, evaluate, and synthesise information from a variety of sources to be successful in today's increasingly digital environment. Critical inquiry should continue to be a major pillar. Additionally, it is important to place an emphasis on multimodal communication, which gives students the opportunity to communicate their thoughts via a variety of mediums, including interactive media, visual storytelling, and collaborative digital projects respectively. In order to accurately represent the enlarged capabilities that are made available by digital technologies, assessment processes also need to undergo change. Formative assessments, which provide continuous feedback and chances for iterative learning, should be embraced by educators as a means of moving beyond conventional examinations. Students have the opportunity to demonstrate their progress and apply their knowledge in a variety of settings via the use of portfolio-based examinations, which encourages critical thinking and personalised learning experiences. The landscape of assessment is further enriched by performance-based assessments, which place an emphasis on abilities such as research, digital storytelling, and creative problem-solving in real-world applications. In a society that is increasingly dominated by digital technology, educational institutions have the ability to guarantee that humanities education will continue to be relevant, adaptable, and inclusive by restructuring curriculum to include digital literacy, critical inquiry, and multimodal communication, in addition to updating assessment methodologies. Students will be equipped with the abilities essential to succeed in modern academic and professional environments as a result of these efforts, which will also preserve the analytical and creative underpinnings of the humanities.

8.4.4 Addressing Equity and Access

As a result of the fact that students from marginalised and underprivileged groups sometimes experience hurdles in obtaining crucial digital tools, resource inequalities continue to be a major challenge in the way of attaining equitable humanities education in the digital era. It is imperative that educational institutions and politicians prioritise coordinated efforts to guarantee the availability of inclusive software, inexpensive devices, and suitable infrastructure. This will avoid technological barriers from exacerbating the educational disparities that already exist. A multipronged strategy that includes dependable internet access is required in order to address the issue of digital equality. This strategy should ensure that students are able to engage in online learning without experiencing any interruptions. Language support is another important component, since varied linguistic representation in educational software helps bridge cultural and geographical barriers. This kind of representation also makes learning about the humanities more accessible to those who are not native speakers of the language and to groups who are under-represented. Additionally, accessibility features need to be included into digital tools in order to assist students who have impairments. This will help to promote inclusive education that is well-suited to meet a wide variety of requirements.

The implementation of solutions such as subsidised devices, open-access educational materials, and digital literacy initiatives may be facilitated by the formation of strategic partnerships between government agencies, technology developers, academic institutions, and nonprofit organisations. It is possible for stakeholders to establish a more balanced environment in the digital humanities by cultivating a commitment to equity and inclusion. This will ensure that all students, regardless of their socioeconomic background, have the chance to participate in transformational digital learning experiences. For the purpose of overcoming these discrepancies and constructing a future that is more inclusive for humanities education, it will be essential to implement sustainable solutions, make proactive policy decisions, and make institutional investments.

8.4.5 Socio-Cultural Responsiveness and Ethical Considerations

In order for educators to successfully incorporate digital technologies into the teaching of humanities, they need to have a keen awareness of the socio-cultural settings in which technology is used. The promotion of inclusion and the prevention of the marginalisation of voices that are under-represented may be accomplished by ensuring that educational material and software interfaces reflect varied cultural viewpoints. In order to create a learning environment that is more representative and engaging, digital platforms need to be able to accommodate a wide range of language origins, historical narratives, and local knowledge systems. Data privacy, digital rights, and algorithmic prejudice are examples of ethical problems that demand conscious consideration. These concerns go beyond the cultural significance of the topic. There are issues associated with data security brought about by the extensive use of technology in education. These challenges include dealing with the collection, storage, and use of student information. Users should be protected from the abuse of their data by transparent governance structures and institutional norms, which should also create confidence in digital learning environments. Furthermore, in order to minimise skewed educational results, it is necessary to conduct an in-depth analysis of algorithmic bias, which is the phenomenon in which automated systems may inadvertently propagate inequality.

The role that educators play in teaching students to approach technology with a critical mentality and ensuring that they grasp the ramifications of digital technologies beyond their functioning is an extremely important one. The cultivation of a generation of students who interact meaningfully with digital resources may be accomplished by institutions via the incorporation of conversations on ethics, privacy, and responsible technology usage within the frameworks of classroom instruction. It will be important to implement stringent regulatory measures, institutional leadership, and multidisciplinary cooperation in order to strike a balance between innovation and ethical responsibility. This will ensure that humanities education is both socially responsible and technologically enhanced.

8.4.6 Policy and Institutional Support

For the integration of software in humanities education to be sustainable, extensive policy frameworks are required. These frameworks should address crucial elements such as finance, infrastructure development, teacher training, digital equality, and data governance. It is essential that these rules guarantee that digital technologies improve learning experiences rather than exacerbate existing gaps. In order to do this, institutions must take a proactive and well-structured approach to the implementation of these regulations. The acquisition of sufficient financing is very necessary in order to broaden access to technology resources, to encourage professional growth, and to keep digital learning platforms operational. An investment in infrastructure, which includes dependable internet access, up-to-date technology, and software interfaces that are easy to use, is required in order to provide an ideal environment for digital learning. The training of teachers should be one of the highest priorities, and this should be accomplished via programs of ongoing professional development that provide educators with the pedagogical methodologies and technical abilities necessary to successfully integrate software. In order to ensure that students from a wide range of backgrounds have access to the tools and resources necessary to engage in technology-enhanced humanities education, digital equity programs need to address accessibility barriers. In order to assist bridge these divisions, equitable distribution of devices, support for inclusive language, and the supply of educational resources that are openly accessible are being provided. In addition, appropriate data governance frameworks need to be created in order to secure the privacy of students, provide transparency in the utilisation of software, and defend ethical norms in digital education.

It is very necessary for academic institutions, technology developers, community organisations, and governments to work together in order to establish a healthy environment that encourages innovation and inclusivity. These collaborations make it possible to share information, produce resources, and exercise ethical monitoring. As a result, they guarantee that digital tools will continue to be flexible to the ever-changing educational requirements while preserving their accessibility and integrity. Through the implementation of sustainable policies and the promotion of cross-sector cooperation, educational institutions have the ability to maximise the potential of digital humanities education. This allows for the enhancement of student learning experiences while simultaneously preserving educational settings that are ethical, egalitarian, and technologically sophisticated.

8.4.7 Encouraging Student Agency and Lifelong Learning

Students are given the ability to take charge of their own educational experiences via the use of digital technologies, which enables them to create personalised learning paths, engage in self-directed research, and work together to develop knowledge. These technologies enable an approach to teaching in the humanities that is more meaningful and engaging because they provide an environment that encourages adaptation and individual discovery. For the purpose of bolstering motivation and achieving a higher level of understanding, students have the ability to personalise their interaction with information to correspond with their interests, learning styles, and academic objectives. In addition, digital platforms foster the development of communal knowledge by allowing students to contribute their own ideas, collaborate on the creation of projects, and critically evaluate a variety of points of view. It is imperative that educational techniques actively foster this autonomy, providing students with the abilities necessary to navigate and contribute to the continuously expanding digital worlds that extend outside the realm of formal education.

The outcomes of this research, in a nutshell, highlight the revolutionary potential of digital software in the field of humanities education, given that the integration of this software is addressed with intentionality, inclusion, and ethical responsibility. In order for implementation to be successful, it is necessary to have well-informed pedagogical practices, persistent capacity development, fair resource allocation, and comprehensive policy frameworks that address accessibility, data protection, and infrastructural requirements. In order to establish settings in which digital tools serve not as simple supplements but rather as catalysts for deeper, more egalitarian, and culturally sensitive humanities learning, stakeholders, including educators, institutions, policymakers, and technology developers, need to work together to create these environments. Technology has the potential to strengthen the humanities while maintaining their essential focus on critical inquiry, creativity, and humanistic discovery. This may be accomplished by careful preparation and collaborating with professionals from many fields.

8.5 Recommendations for Policy Makers

Several major suggestions are offered to assist policymakers in fostering the effective integration of software into humanities education. These recommendations are based on the full results of this research. The purpose of these suggestions is to influence the creation of policies, facilitate the development of implementation methods, and guarantee efficient assessment procedures that result in learning environments that are egalitarian, sustainable, and technologically advanced. First and foremost, policymakers should make the development of infrastructure a priority by guaranteeing dependable internet connection, sufficient digital devices, and high-quality software platforms that are specifically designed for teaching in the humanities. In order to achieve effective integration, it is essential to provide institutions with the required technology resources. The second point is that it is necessary to maintain investments in programs that educate teachers. Teachers need to have access to continuing professional development opportunities that provide them hands-on experience with digital tools, encourage pedagogical adaptation, and help them establish confidence in technology-enhanced teaching. In order to foster collaborative knowledge-sharing and sustained creativity, formal training should be supplemented by peer-learning groups and mentoring efforts.

As a third point of debate, digital fairness needs to be at the centre of policy conversations. The implementation of programs that alleviate gaps in access should be a priority for policymakers, especially for economically disadvantaged populations. This includes initiatives that provide subsidised technology, educational materials that are available to the public, and software that is language-inclusive in order to assure participation from a wide range of communities.

In the fourth place, the frameworks of the curriculum need to be modified so that they include digital literacy, critical inquiry, and multimodal communication. The learning goals should be aligned with the growing technology capabilities, and the assessment processes should go beyond the conventional examinations to include portfolio-based assessments, digital storytelling, and data-driven analysis. Fifth, there is a need to strengthen ethical governance by implementing regulations that protect the privacy of student data, control algorithmic transparency, and reduce biases within digital technologies. The establishment of ethical criteria for the use of software by institutions is necessary in order to guarantee the responsible deployment of technology.

Thus, it is of the utmost importance to cultivate cross-sector collaborations between entities such as educational institutions, technology developers, governments, and community organisations. Increasing accessibility, accelerating innovation, and simplifying the process of integrating software into humanities education are all outcomes that will result from collaboration. By addressing these crucial areas via clearly defined regulations, legislators have the ability to establish an environment in which technology aids learning in the humanities while also conserving the institution's roots in critical thinking, creativity, and social consciousness. Through the implementation of these ideas, digital technologies will be able to act as catalysts for humanities education that is enriched, inclusive, and forward-thinking.

8.5.1 Prioritise Digital Infrastructure Development

For fair software integration in humanities education, it is vital to ensure that a large number of people have access to low-cost digital devices, dependable high-speed internet, and up-to-date instructional software. The development of infrastructure should be a priority for policymakers, especially in neglected and rural regions where technical divides make it difficult for people to acquire knowledge. Students will be able to interact with digital materials without any restrictions if broadband access is expanded and investments are made in dependable network connection. The digital gap may also be bridged via the implementation of cheap device distribution schemes, such as subsidised laptops and tablets. This will ensure that all students are able to take part in education that is improved by technology. Maintaining digital resources that are up to date, such as academic tools that are available to the public and interfaces that support several languages, helps create diversity and accommodates a variety of learning requirements. In order for students and teachers to fully capitalise on the potential of software in the field of humanities education, a solid infrastructure serves as the cornerstone for a sustainable digital integration platform.

8.5.2 Invest in Teacher Training and Professional Development

For fair software integration in humanities education, it is vital to ensure that a large number of people have access to low-cost digital devices, dependable high-speed internet, and up-to-date instructional software. The development of infrastructure should be a priority for policymakers, especially in neglected and rural regions where technical divides make it difficult for people to acquire knowledge. Students will be able to interact with digital materials without any restrictions if broadband access is expanded and investments are made in dependable network connection. The digital gap may also be bridged via the implementation of cheap device distribution schemes, such as subsidised laptops and tablets. This will ensure that all students are able to take part in education that is improved by technology. Maintaining digital resources that are up to date, such as academic tools that are available to the public and interfaces that support several languages, helps create diversity and accommodates a variety of learning requirements. In order for students and teachers to fully capitalise on the potential of software in the field of humanities education, a solid infrastructure serves as the cornerstone for a sustainable digital integration platform.

8.5.3 Promote Digital Equity and Inclusion

Policies to bridge digital gaps should give priority to comprehensive programs that equip marginalised pupils and underprivileged communities with gadgets and dependable internet access. Every learner, regardless of their socioeconomic standing, should be able to participate in digital humanities education since these programs should guarantee that they have access to the technical tools that are required for this. In order to remove obstacles to entrance, investments in infrastructure need to be accompanied with methods for the distribution of cheap devices, such as grants and subsidies. In addition to providing learners with disabilities with physical access, inclusivity necessitates the implementation of intentional accessibility measures. It is important that digital platforms be created with features that can accommodate a wide range of demands, such as screen readers, configurable interfaces, captioning, and adaptive navigation tools. This will ensure that everyone has an equal opportunity to participate in digital learning environments. Furthermore, it is necessary to include culturally appropriate information into the curriculum of digital humanities. This content should reflect a variety of narratives, linguistic representations, and historical viewpoints. This inclusiveness helps to cultivate a learning environment in which students from a variety of backgrounds are able to see the worth of their experiences within the context of academic discourse.

It is also important for strategic policy interventions to incorporate cooperation between governments, academic institutions, technology developers, and community organisations in order to construct long-term initiatives that promote digital fairness. By making these efforts, we will guarantee that the revolutionary potential of digital technologies in humanities education is available to all students. This will help to develop equity, representation, and meaningful engagement in the digital era. In order for policymakers to build an educational framework that utilises digital technologies as a method of empowerment rather than exclusion, it is necessary for them to address both technical and socio-cultural differences.

8.5.4 Establish Clear Standards and Guidelines

The establishment of national or regional frameworks that provide explicit requirements for digital literacy, ethical technology usage, data protection, and software quality assurance in humanities education should be a priority for policymakers. Through the implementation of these principles, educational institutions and instructors will have access to a planned approach to the integration of digital resources in a responsible and efficient manner. A standardised framework for digital literacy should describe fundamental abilities for both students and instructors. These competencies should include the ability to navigate online information, evaluate digital sources, and engage with technology in a critical manner. The implementation of such standards guarantees that students who are enrolled in humanities courses will acquire the skills necessary to analyse, interpret, and produce digital information in a manner that is meaningful. There should be a greater emphasis placed on the ethical use of technology, including the explanation of responsible digital engagement, academic integrity in digital research, and techniques for limiting the spread of disinformation. This contains principles on algorithmic openness, which are intended to minimise prejudice and bias in learning systems powered by artificial intelligence. Establishing best practices for secure data storage, consent-based data collecting, and transparent institutional usage of digital platforms are all aspects that should be included in data privacy policies. These policies should also establish processes for protecting the information of educators and students. It is essential that transparent governance procedures be put into place in order to guarantee compliance with privacy legislation.

Standards for software quality assurance should serve as a guide for educational institutions in the selection of digital tools that are dependable, easily available, and pedagogically sound. In order to accommodate a wide range of learners, including those with impairments, these requirements need to place an emphasis on usability, cultural inclusion, and accessible features. When it comes to the development and improvement of these frameworks, collaboration between entities such as government agencies, educational institutions, technology developers, and research organisations will be necessary. Policymakers have the ability to offer schools and educators with a clear path for responsible and successful software adoption by setting thorough rules. This will ensure that digital humanities education continues to be egalitarian, ethical, and prepared for the future.

8.5.5 Support Curriculum Innovation and Assessment Reform

To make sure that humanities education can keep up with the changing technology environments without sacrificing intellectual rigour, lawmakers should push for changes to the curriculum that include digital literacy and the ability to critically think. Students should be equipped with the ability to critically evaluate information found online, meaningfully engage with digital tools, and develop responsible digital citizenship through the integration of digital literacy across all subject areas. The development of critical inquiry simultaneously promotes students to analyse, interpret, and synthesise material across a variety of genres. This, in turn, improves students' capacity to create well-reasoned arguments and traverse complicated humanities debate. In order to provide support for these curricular innovations, policymakers need to encourage flexible and multimodal learning experiences. These experiences should enable students to interact with knowledge using a variety of platforms, such as digital storytelling, interactive media, and collaborative research tools. Students are given the opportunity to become familiar with contemporary analytical techniques, historical interpretation frameworks, and creative expressions that are in line with the goals of humanities education when educational methodologies are diversified throughout the curriculum.

Additionally, assessment methods have to progress in order to recognise and verify the many digital abilities that students acquire via the use of technology in their educational experiences. Educators should combine portfolio-based assessments, real-world digital projects, and interactive demonstrations that represent true student participation in order to go beyond the traditional examinations that are now used. It is possible to guarantee that assessments effectively reflect the breadth and depth of student learning outcomes by recognising abilities such as data interpretation, multimedia analysis, and the production of digital material. Through the adoption of curricular reforms that place an emphasis on digital literacy, critical inquiry, and multimodal engagement, policymakers have the ability to contribute to the formation of a humanities education system that continues to be relevant, inclusive, and responsive to the requirements of learners in the twenty-fourth century. The implementation of these rules will not only improve students' analytical abilities, but it will also better prepare them for a society that is becoming more influenced by digital technology and the generation of information that spans several disciplines.

8.5.6 Facilitate Partnerships and Collaboration

Policymakers should promote platforms and incentives for educational institutions, technology developers, civil society organisations, and research agencies to collaborate in digital humanities education. Formal public–private partnerships may boost innovation, resource access, and capacity-building. Collaboration platforms including digital research centres, shared infrastructure initiatives, and multidisciplinary academic networks may help share information and build projects. These places let educators, technologists, and academics co-create digital tools, improve best practices, and tackle humanities education difficulties. Financial incentives, competitive grants, and policy-driven assistance should foster digital humanities innovation. Financial and institutional support for collaborative initiatives supports revolutionary digital learning solution development and deployment. Universities and technology corporations may collaborate to improve AI-driven textual analysis, immersive VR experiences, and ethical educational technology governance. Engaging civil society organisations keeps digital humanities education inclusive, culturally relevant, and accessible to marginalised populations. Collaboration may reduce digital gaps, enhance language diversity in software development, and promote ethical technology usage by including multiple voices and viewpoints. Policymakers can create an environment where digital technologies strengthen humanities education while assuring ethical, egalitarian, and sustainable usage by deliberately permitting cross-sector cooperation. These collaborations will advance technology and preserve humanities scholarship's critical and interpretive foundations.

8.5.7 Monitor and Evaluate Policy Impact

Policymakers must establish comprehensive monitoring and evaluation mechanisms to sustain digital education policies in humanities learning. These frameworks should evaluate how technology integration affects student engagement, learning outcomes, and diversity of access. Policymakers may improve educational policies by collecting and analysing data on implementation issues, resource allocation, and pedagogical efficacy. Educational, student, and institutional input should be used to evaluate policy usefulness, inclusiveness, and technology adaptation. Equity impact studies help discover digital tool, connection, and training inequities among marginalised communities and ensure solutions close gaps. Monitoring data privacy, algorithmic fairness, and cultural relevance in digital humanities applications will also assist evaluate ethics. Encouraging data-driven policy changes can help institutions anticipate new problems and possibilities. Real-time insights into technology trends and student demands may inform infrastructure, curriculum, and professional development decisions. Transparent progress reports and research partnerships may also improve policy accountability. By integrating ongoing evaluation and adaptive policymaking into the digital humanities framework, stakeholders can create a resilient and responsive education system that uses technology while ensuring equitable, ethical, and pedagogically sound learning.

8.5.8 Address Ethical and Socio-Cultural Considerations

Policymakers must guarantee that technology in humanities education respects cultural diversity, learner privacy, and algorithmic and digital content justice. To avoid homogenising education, software tools must represent varied historical narratives, language differences, and global viewpoints. Multilingual digital tools and culturally appropriate learning materials improve accessibility and representation, helping students from diverse backgrounds make sense of humanities subject. Protecting student privacy requires clear legal frameworks for educational technology data collection, storage, and use. To protect student data and provide openness in learning platform data processing, institutions must follow tight rules. Ethical data handling rules should reinforce student rights in digital learning contexts.

To avoid unintentional differences in material distribution, grading, and AI-powered suggestions, algorithmic biases must be mitigated. Digital platform audits should be required by policymakers to detect and address biases that disproportionately harm marginalised populations. Using varied datasets and fairness-focused model training to produce ethical AI improves humanities education equality. Focused campaigns may promote appropriate technology usage. Students and educators should learn to evaluate digital material, identify prejudices, and use online platforms responsibly. Media literacy, critical digital participation, and AI-driven decision-making's social impacts should be stressed in workshops, tools, and legislation. By incorporating these ethical issues into legislative frameworks, technological integration may boost humanities education while protecting cultural identity, privacy, and digital learning equity. Through proactive governance and participatory policymaking, digital humanities education may develop while sustaining fairness and ethics.

8.5.9 *Encourage Research and Innovation*

Provide funding and incentives for research into new technologies, pedagogical models, and the socio-cultural implications of digital tools in humanities education. Supporting innovation will ensure that policy remains responsive to rapid technological evolution. Finally, these recommendations encourage policymakers to approach digital humanities education holistically, with an eye towards equity and the future. By addressing infrastructure, training, inclusivity, ethical use, and innovation, policy can foster environments in which software integration improves learning outcomes and expands access to high-quality humanities education.

8.6 Recommendations for Educators

Teachers' involvement, inventiveness, and adaptation shape digital technology incorporation into humanities instruction. Learner-centred techniques that promote inquiry-based learning, multimedia storytelling, and collaborative digital research develop critical thinking and creativity and maximise software tool pedagogy. Digital literacy and critical inquiry abilities help students access internet sources, use digital humanities methods, and critically analyse multimedia information. Peer learning groups, conferences, and mentorship programs help instructors keep current on developing technology. Multimodal learning experiences like interactive media, digital archives, and collaborative writing platforms increase humanities engagement and accommodate diverse learning styles. Educators must also address algorithmic bias, data privacy, and accessibility in technology-driven education. Innovative assessment methods include portfolio-based evaluations, digital projects, and performance-driven assessments let instructors measure student involvement with digital humanities. Cloud-based platforms and open-access educational resources encourage collaboration, interdisciplinary research, and learning. These ideas may help instructors develop enhanced, dynamic, and inclusive humanities learning environments that prepare students for a digital-first society while sustaining humanistic inquiry. Teachers use digital technologies to strengthen humanities education's intellectual and analytical underpinnings via purposeful and responsive pedagogy.

8.6.1 Embrace Learner-Centred Pedagogy

In order to foster active and interactive learning, educators should shift their focus from conventional, lecture-based teaching to learner-centred techniques that use digital resources. Through the use of inquiry-based learning, students are motivated to enquire, investigate topics on their own, and hone their critical thinking abilities by doing research on their own. Students learn to work together on projects, which includes using shared digital workspaces, doing group analyses of material, and building relevant knowledge. With digital storytelling, students may express themselves creatively via multimedia forms. They can interact with tales and topics more deeply by combining text, photos, voice, and video. At the same time, students may analyse digital artefacts using multimedia analysis, which allows them to interactively explore literary, cultural, and historical settings. Teachers may help students better grasp and interact with humanities material by using these tactics to provide more immersive learning experiences that put students in charge of their own education.

8.6.2 Continuously Build Digital Competence

In order to improve their technical and digital pedagogical abilities, educators should participate in continuous professional development. Workshops provide teachers with the opportunity to learn about and practise using new digital tools and pedagogical approaches, preparing them to successfully incorporate technology into their lessons. Teachers are able to work together more effectively in peer learning communities, where they may share ideas, address problems, and improve their methods. Teachers may keep up with the latest developments in digital humanities teaching by taking advantage of online courses, which provide more flexibility and access to a wider variety of experts. Teachers who make learning a priority are better able to adapt their lessons to new technology by making them more interesting, accessible, and successful for all students.

8.6.3 Integrate Software Thoughtfully

Teachers should start using digital technologies with purposeful educational goals rather than just utilising them for novelty. To make sure that technology improves student results instead of detracting from them, each tool has to be in line with specified learning goals. Careful selection of digital materials should provide advantages that conventional techniques alone may not, such as more in-depth research, interactive learning, or wider access to other viewpoints. Software should not be seen as an additional technology but as a stimulus for inquiry, collaboration, and intellectual progress; instructors may prevent digital weariness and encourage continuous, meaningful involvement by carefully integrating technology.

8.6.4 Foster Inclusive and Accessible Learning Environments

Rather than using technology for the sake of novelty, educators should use digital tools with a deliberate focus on instruction. Careful use of technology in the classroom should not detract from but rather support well-articulated learning goals. In comparison to more traditional approaches, digital resources should have clear benefits, such as facilitating more in-depth study, encouraging more participatory learning, or increasing exposure to other points of view. Software should not be seen by educators as an additional technology layer, but rather as an agent that promotes inquiry, cooperation, and intellectual development. Teachers can help students avoid digital fatigue and stay engaged in class for longer by picking the right tools and using them strategically.

8.6.5 Promote Critical Digital Literacy

The capacity to critically interact with digital material, identify bias, evaluate sources, and properly navigate online information is an essential skill for students to learn. To back this up, teachers should make sure their students learn to critically evaluate media by including digital literacy and thinking into their lessons. Students may express themselves via digital storytelling, blogs, or multimedia projects with the help of content production tools, which encourages creativity and greater involvement. Learners may improve their capacity to make educated judgements with the use of data analysis platforms by interpreting information, tracking trends, and assessing trustworthiness. With the use of annotation tools, students may read interactively, underlining important ideas, critiquing viewpoints, and participating in group discussions. Structured reflective discourse also gives students a chance to show what they know, challenge preconceived notions, and develop their own opinions. Educators may equip their pupils to think ethically and critically in an increasingly digital environment by using these tactics.

8.6.6 Encourage Student Autonomy and Ownership

Teachers may encourage student agency by giving students many digital venues to interact with course material, share their thoughts, and demonstrate what they have learnt. By creating an online portfolio, students may document their learning experience, show how much they have learnt, and reflect on their growth as learners. Blogs provide an outlet for critical thinking and personal reflection, enabling students to express themselves while participating in larger academic discussions. Collaborative knowledge-building is made easier using wikis, which promote peer engagement and the common investigation of complicated subjects. Students may enhance their metacognitive abilities via actively participating in class, reflecting on their own learning, and receiving constructive criticism using collaborative tools like online discussion forums and shared papers. Teachers may encourage student agency and critical thinking by incorporating these digital tactics into the classroom.

8.6.7 Use Assessment to Drive Engagement

To provide a more complete picture of each student's growth, assessment has to be flexible enough to accommodate the many ways in which digital technologies facilitate learning. Teachers may use formative evaluations to help students improve their comprehension in real-time via activities like digital annotations, reflective diaries, and interactive debates. Digital storytelling, multimedia presentations, and collaborative projects are all examples of performance-based evaluations that students might use to show what they've learnt. Portfolio evaluations can provide students the opportunity to compile a body of work (e.g., an e-portfolio, a blog, or a research report) that demonstrates their development over time and promotes introspection. Educators may develop more engaging methods of evaluating students' knowledge, skills, and attitudes towards digital citizenship by rethinking the role of static assessments like quizzes and examinations.

8.6.8 Reflect and Iterate Teaching Practices

To keep their digital teaching tactics successful and relevant to students' needs, educators should regularly assess their effects. Learners' experiences with digital tools and areas for development may be better understood with the use of student feedback collected via questionnaires, casual check-ins, or group discussions. Educators may gauge the success of technology integration by tracking engagement patterns, such as students' involvement in online forums, use of digital resources, and understanding of multimedia material. Teachers may improve learning outcomes by modifying digital processes, introducing new technologies, or refining instructional methodologies. This cycle guarantees that technology improves education in a dynamic way, encouraging more involvement and more significant learning opportunities.

8.6.9 Collaborate with Colleagues and Stakeholders

Collaboration is key to teaching in the digital humanities, since incorporating technology into humanities education is a complicated endeavour that need different skills and joint creation. Educators may improve the learning experience by sharing resources, making best practices, case studies, and instructional methodologies publicly available. Co-designing interdisciplinary projects enables the fusion of viewpoints from several areas, allowing students to interact with difficult concepts in ways that go beyond typical academic boundaries. Furthermore, collaborating with librarians, IT professionals, and instructional designers improves course creation by offering technical assistance, content curation, and pedagogical insights that enable the smooth integration of digital resources into learning environments. Working collaboratively, educators can spread the burden of digital adoption, making transition more doable and building a culture of communal creativity. To summarise, educators must embrace their position as active designers of digitally enhanced learning environments, creating experiences that use technology in meaningful and pedagogically sound ways. Educators may ensure that digital technologies are not just placed onto current processes, but are entrenched in ways that promote inquiry, collaboration, and participation. Continuous professional development is critical in responding to changing technology, allowing instructors to keep up with growing digital platforms and approaches. A dedication to inclusive and critical pedagogy ensures that technology is equitable for all learners, promoting accessibility, different viewpoints, and ethical interaction with digital information.

These ideas provide educators a thorough blueprint for navigating the digital transformation with confidence, creativity, and adaptation. Educators can redefine humanities education into a dynamic, engaging, and egalitarian experience for students in the digital era by encouraging interdisciplinary collaboration, improving pedagogical techniques, and embracing technology as a tool to supplement rather than replace conventional teaching.

8.7 Recommendations for Software Developers

As key stakeholders in the digital transformation of humanities education, software developers play a critical role in designing tools that facilitate inclusive, engaging, and pedagogically sound learning experiences. To ensure their products effectively serve both educators and students in the humanities, the following recommendations are provided:

1. **Collaborate with Educators and Humanities Scholars**

Developers should work closely with teachers, curriculum designers, and subject matter experts from the humanities to gain insight into classroom needs, content structures, and pedagogical goals. Co-designing with end-users ensures that the software is relevant, usable, and grounded in real-world educational practices. Establishing regular feedback loops through pilot testing and educator consultations allows developers to refine features and optimise functionality based on actual classroom experiences.

2. **Prioritise User-Friendly Interfaces**

Usability is essential in educational settings, where users vary in digital literacy levels. Developers should focus on intuitive interfaces, minimal learning curves, and accessible navigation. Features should be clearly labeled, with tutorials and support materials readily available to facilitate adoption and use. Interfaces should be designed with simplicity and efficiency in mind, avoiding unnecessary complexity that could hinder learning engagement.

3. **Ensure Cross-Platform Compatibility and Accessibility**

To promote equity in access, software should function seamlessly across devices (laptops, tablets, mobile phones) and operating systems (Windows, macOS, Android, iOS). Tools must also include accessibility features for students with visual, auditory, cognitive, or motor impairments such as screen reader compatibility, adjustable font sizes, and captioning. Developers should proactively incorporate Universal Design for Learning (UDL) principles to maximise usability across diverse learner needs.

4. **Integrate Pedagogical Flexibility**

Humanities education thrives on open-ended inquiry and interpretative analysis. Developers should build tools that allow for diverse instructional methods and assessment types, including discussion forums, annotation tools, mapping interfaces, multimedia presentation modules, and collaborative writing spaces. Customisable features enable educators to adapt software to various pedagogical approaches, ensuring alignment with both structured and exploratory learning models.

5. **Incorporate Data Privacy and Ethical Standards**

Developers must uphold strict ethical and legal standards related to data protection, user consent, and digital well-being. Systems should offer educators and learners control over their data, include clear privacy policies, and adhere to regulations such as the General Data Protection Regulation (GDPR). Transparent data practices reassure users about security while preventing unauthorised exploitation of student and educator information.

6. **Enable Offline Functionality and Low-Bandwidth Use**

Recognising disparities in internet access, especially in underserved or rural areas, developers should consider offline capabilities and low-bandwidth functionality. Tools that can be used without constant internet connection or that synchronise data when connectivity returns are invaluable for inclusive education. Lightweight software versions that function on less advanced devices help reduce the barriers posed by technological constraints.

7. **Design for Multilingual and Multicultural Contexts**

To support global and diverse classrooms, software should allow for localisation and customisation in multiple languages and reflect diverse cultural contexts. This includes culturally relevant examples, symbols, historical references, and design considerations. Developers should collaborate with linguists and cultural experts to ensure the accuracy and contextual appropriateness of multilingual implementations.

8. **Provide Analytics and Feedback Features**

Incorporate features that allow educators to monitor student engagement, progress, and comprehension. Dashboards and reporting tools help teachers make data-informed decisions, offer timely support, and adjust instruction to meet individual learner needs. Adaptive learning analytics should offer actionable insights without overwhelming educators with excessive data points.

9. **Maintain Transparent Pricing and Licensing**

Software developers should adopt transparent pricing models, offering educational discounts, freemium versions, or institutional licenses that are affordable for schools and universities. Open-source or low-cost alternatives help democratise access to quality tools. Policies regarding subscription renewals, pricing tiers, and license conditions must be clearly communicated to avoid financial barriers to adoption.

10. **Commit to Continuous Improvement and Support**

Developers must offer regular updates that respond to user feedback, fix bugs, and add new functionalities. Active customer support, community forums, and responsive communication channels enhance user trust and foster long-term adoption. Engaging in continuous dialogue with educational communities allows developers to refine their tools while maintaining relevance in an evolving pedagogical landscape.

In conclusion, software developers have the opportunity and responsibility to shape the future of humanities education through thoughtful design, inclusive practices, and collaborative engagement with educators. By aligning their development processes with pedagogical goals and ethical principles, they can create tools that not only support learning but also enrich the broader educational landscape. The successful integration of software in humanities education depends on intentional development practices that prioritise usability, accessibility, adaptability, and ethical responsibility, ensuring that digital tools serve as enablers of enriched, equitable, and transformative learning experiences.

8.8 Recommendations for Future Researchers

As digital technologies continue to reshape humanities education, there remains a pressing need for scholarly inquiry into its evolving dynamics. While this study has provided foundational insights, significant areas warrant further exploration, particularly in pedagogical innovation, digital equity, learner outcomes, and cultural relevance. Future researchers should consider the following recommendations to advance this critical field.

1. **Conduct Longitudinal Studies on Learning Outcomes**

While short-term benefits of digital tools in humanities classrooms are often documented, long-term impacts on student comprehension, retention, and critical thinking require further study. Researchers should conduct longitudinal investigations to evaluate the sustained influence of digital pedagogy on learner development across various educational stages. Such studies would provide deeper insights into how technology-driven methodologies shape intellectual growth over time.

2. **Explore Interdisciplinary Methodologies**

Humanities education increasingly intersects with fields such as data science, design, linguistics, and information technology. Future research should adopt interdisciplinary frameworks that combine qualitative humanistic inquiry with quantitative data analysis, thereby capturing the full complexity of digital learning environments. By merging diverse academic perspectives, scholars can develop richer analytical approaches to studying digital humanities.

3. **Investigate Context-Specific Implementation**

Education is influenced by cultural, economic, institutional, and geographic factors that shape how technology is adopted and utilised. Researchers should examine how software tools function in distinct contexts such as rural vs. urban settings, developed vs. developing countries, and secular vs. religious institutions to identify nuanced insights into adaptability and impact. Findings from such research could inform customized implementation strategies that address local needs.

4. **Assess the Role of Artificial Intelligence and Automation**

Emerging technologies, including AI-driven feedback systems, adaptive learning platforms, and automated content generation, are becoming more prominent in education. Research should examine the implications of AI in humanities classrooms, both in terms of pedagogical enhancement and ethical considerations related to bias, authorship, and human agency. Investigating the role of machine generated analysis in interpretive disciplines will be crucial for developing responsible AI applications.

5. **Evaluate Digital Equity and Inclusion Initiatives**

Further research is needed to assess the effectiveness of policies and programs aimed at bridging the digital divide. Studies should evaluate the impact of device distribution initiatives, internet accessibility schemes, open educational resources, and inclusive software design on reducing disparities in digital participation. Findings from such research can inform policy reforms that promote fair access to digital humanities education.

6. **Examine Student Voice and Agency**

Current research often centers on educator perspectives and institutional policies, but student experiences remain underexplored. Future studies should prioritize student narratives, exploring how learners perceive, interact with, and are transformed by software-enhanced learning in the humanities. Capturing student voices can offer critical insights into engagement, motivation, and self-directed learning in digital environments.

7. **Develop New Assessment Models**

Standardised testing does not fully capture the richness of humanities learning facilitated by digital tools. Researchers should experiment with alternative assessment frameworks such as digital portfolios, multimodal projects, or peer-reviewed artifacts that reflect the skills and values nurtured by technology-enhanced education. Assessment strategies should be adapted to evaluate interactive and collaborative learning outcomes.

8. **Analyse Faculty Training and Institutional Readiness**

There is a need for research that investigates how well institutions prepare educators for integrating digital tools in humanities teaching. Studies could explore professional training models, infrastructure availability, institutional policies, and support systems that affect adoption and success rates. Examining faculty perspectives can help institutions refine digital literacy programs and enhance teacher preparedness.

9. **Document Emerging Trends in Digital Humanities Tools**

The educational software landscape is dynamic, with new platforms, plugins, and pedagogical innovations emerging rapidly. Future research should track these trends, offer critical evaluations, and provide open-access repositories or annotated bibliographies to support ongoing scholarly engagement. Regular analysis of evolving technologies can assist educators in selecting effective digital tools for humanities instruction.

10. **Promote Open Access and Collaborative Scholarship**

Researchers should prioritise publishing in open-access journals, collaborating across borders and disciplines, and sharing datasets, tools, and code to foster a more inclusive and collective research ecosystem in digital humanities education. Expanding accessibility to scholarly findings encourages interdisciplinary collaboration and strengthens the global reach of digital humanities initiatives.

In conclusion, digital humanities pedagogy presents rich opportunities for further scholarly exploration. Future research efforts must engage diverse methodologies and perspectives to deepen our understanding of how technology can support humanistic inquiry, cultural literacy, and transformative learning experiences. By addressing key issues in pedagogy, digital equity, learner agency, assessment innovation, and institutional readiness, scholars can shape effective practices, inform policy decisions, and empower educators and students in meaningful ways. Advancing research in this field is crucial for ensuring that digital tools serve as enablers of enriched, equitable, and culturally responsive humanities education.

8.9 Proposed Model for Software Use in Humanities

As digital technologies continue to influence and improve humanities education, there is an increasing need for a structured paradigm that guarantees their inclusion is meaningful, egalitarian, and long-lasting. To meet this requirement, this section offers the Humanities Software Integration Model (HSIM), which was created using the results of this research and influenced by existing pedagogical and technical best practices. This paradigm is intended to fit with broad educational objectives, provide students more agency in their learning experiences, and encourage inclusive teaching techniques that address varied needs and viewpoints. The HSIM aims to optimise the use of digital technologies in humanities education by providing a clear framework for software uptake and deployment, all while encouraging a dynamic and flexible learning environment.

8.9.1 Overview of the Humanities Software Integration Model (HSIM)

As digital technologies continue to influence and improve humanities education, there is an increasing need for a structured paradigm that guarantees their inclusion is meaningful, egalitarian, and long-lasting. To meet this requirement, this section offers the HSIM, which was created using the results of this research and influenced by existing pedagogical and technical best practices. This paradigm is intended to fit with broad educational objectives, provide students more agency in their learning experiences, and encourage inclusive teaching techniques that address varied needs and viewpoints. The HSIM aims to optimise the use of digital technologies in humanities education by providing a clear framework for software uptake and deployment, all while encouraging a dynamic and flexible learning environment (Table 8.1).

8.9.2 Core Principles of the Model

The HSIM is built on five basic concepts that assure its efficacy in promoting meaningful and equitable digital tool usage. Learner-centeredness prioritises diverse learning styles, allowing students to actively participate in inquiry and engagement. Contextual relevance ensures that tools reflect local histories, languages, and cultural

Table 8.1 Layers of humanities software integration model

Layer	Description	Key stakeholders
1. Pedagogical design	Align software use with critical thinking, interpretation, and reflective inquiry central to the humanities disciplines	Educators, curriculum designers
2. Digital infrastructure	Provide reliable hardware, connectivity, and technical support. Ensure accessibility and multilingual functionality	IT staff, administrators
3. Software selection and customisation	Choose flexible, context-sensitive tools that allow modification for local curriculum and cultural contexts	Educators, developers
4. Learner engagement and autonomy	Empower students to explore, collaborate, and construct knowledge through interactive tools and open-ended tasks	Students, teachers
5. Feedback, assessment and iteration	Incorporate continuous feedback loops, both technological (analytics) and human (peer review), to improve learning outcomes	All stakeholders

texts, making learning more immersive and authentic. Accessibility and inclusion emphasises that all learners, regardless of socioeconomic background or physical ability, should have equal opportunities to benefit. Interdisciplinary flexibility enables digital technologies to be smoothly incorporated into literature, history, philosophy, religious studies, and language arts, broadening the scope of humanities instruction. The ethical digital practices protect fundamental principles including data privacy, open access, and responsible AI usage, assuring a long-term and conscientious approach to technology in education. These principles serve as the cornerstone of HSIM, enabling educators to create fair, adaptable, and intellectually stimulating learning environments.

8.9.3 *Model Implementation Phases*

The HSIM follows a structured five-phase approach to ensure that digital tools are integrated effectively into humanities education. Each phase plays a crucial role in aligning technology with pedagogical goals while fostering accessibility and student engagement. Here is a deeper explanation of each phase:

1. **Phase 1: Needs Assessment**: This initial stage focuses on identifying gaps within the curriculum, assessing student learning needs, and evaluating infrastructure

limitations that may affect digital tool adoption. Educators conduct surveys, review existing teaching materials, and analyse institutional resources to determine where technology can enhance learning. The result is a detailed needs report that serves as a foundation for informed decision-making in subsequent phases.

2. **Phase 2: Tool Selection and Training**: Once educational needs have been established, appropriate digital platforms are selected based on functionality, accessibility, and alignment with learning objectives. Examples of commonly used tools include Voyant for textual analysis, Hypothes.is for collaborative annotation, and TimelineJS for interactive historical visualisation. In this phase, educators receive training on how to use these tools effectively, ensuring they are well-equipped to integrate them into their teaching. Toolkits are developed to provide educators with step-by-step guidance and best practices.
3. **Phase 3: Curriculum Integration**: This phase is where digital tools are embedded directly into lesson plans, projects, and assessments. Educators develop activities that align with learning outcomes and encourage critical thinking, interactivity, and collaboration. Digital resources may be incorporated into reading assignments, research projects, and multimedia presentations to enhance engagement. The culmination of this phase is an updated curriculum that effectively integrates digital tools while maintaining the core principles of humanities education.
4. **Phase 4: Monitoring and Feedback**: To ensure that digital tools are being used effectively, this phase involves data collection and evaluation. Educators track student engagement, analyse learning outcomes, and solicit feedback on the usability of the tools. Surveys, class observations, and performance assessments help gather insights into whether the technology is meeting educational objectives. Evaluation reports document the findings, highlighting successes and areas for improvement.
5. **Phase 5: Review and Iterate**: Based on the results of monitoring and feedback, educators refine their approaches to digital integration. Adjustments are made to improve accessibility, usability, and alignment with pedagogical goals. Technological advancements and updates in software capabilities are also considered during this phase. The ultimate goal is to create a dynamic and adaptable learning environment where digital tools continue to evolve to meet the changing needs of students and educators.

8.9.4 Practical Application Example

In a digital literature classroom, the HSIM provides a complete strategy to incorporating technology while preserving pedagogical depth. The curriculum focusses on textual analysis and historical context, allowing students to interact critically with literary works using digital technologies. To facilitate this integration, required infrastructure such as laptop computers and dependable internet access is given, guaranteeing that all students may engage successfully. The choice of software is critical in promoting interactive learning, using tools such as Voyant for text mining, which allows students to identify patterns and themes within texts, and TimelineJS for visualising literary chronology. Students use organised learner interaction to analyse original texts, comment sections, and build interactive timelines that give contextual insight into literary developments. The concept also includes feedback and iteration, in which students modify their projects with peer evaluation and teacher supervision, resulting in a final portfolio that illustrates their analytical progress. Using this approach, instructors may provide an immersive and dynamic digital literary experience that empowers students and enriches their grasp of humanities studies.

8.9.5 Adaptability of the Model

The HSIM is intended to be both scalable and adaptive, making it appropriate for a variety of educational settings. It may be successfully applied at both the secondary and postsecondary education levels, ensuring that digital tool integration benefits students at all phases of their learning journey. The concept may be used in both official settings, like schools and colleges, as well as informal learning contexts like workshops or self-directed study programs. Furthermore, HSIM enables a variety of educational modes, including conventional face-to-face teaching, blended learning (which blends physical and digital aspects), and online education. Its adaptability also extends to institutions with varied levels of resources, allowing for efficient implementation in both well-equipped academic settings and those with technical or budgetary restrictions. By meeting a wide range of educational demands, HSIM promotes meaningful and fair digital integration across several learning environments.

8.9.6 Diagram of the Model

Layers of digital tool integration in humanities education are shown in the graphic in Fig. 8.1, which illustrates the HSIM. Pedagogical Design is the first step, and it involves making sure that teaching tactics stress historical context and critical examination. Then, the technical backbone, including gadgets and internet connectivity, is provided by Digital Infrastructure. The next step is software selection and customisation, during which the right digital tools are selected and modified to achieve the desired educational outcomes. Students are encouraged to engage with digital resources via Learner Engagement and Autonomy, which promotes individual inquiry and cooperation. Feedback and Iteration guarantees that the approach is flexible to changing educational demands by facilitating ongoing development via evaluations, peer reviews, and technology enhancements. If you would want any other changes, please inform me.

Fig. 8.1 HSIM model

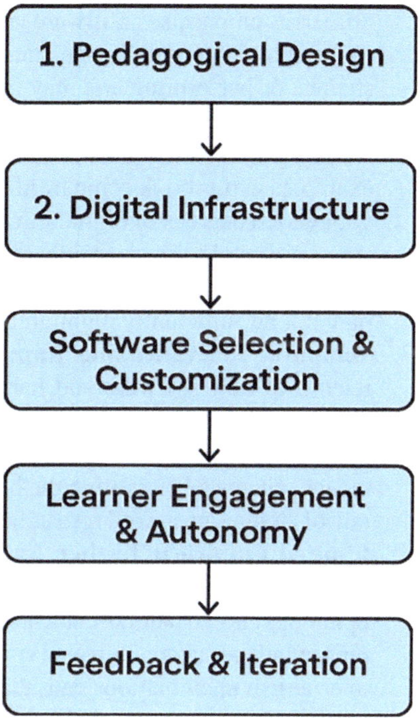

Stakeholders devoted to enhancing humanities education via digital technologies may find a comprehensive and practical framework in the HSIM. This approach seeks to unite classical humanities purposes with modern educational innovation by establishing software usage in pedagogical intent, infrastructure preparedness, and ethical responsibility.

8.9.7 *Limitations of the Study*

Recognising the constraints that may have affected the breadth, depth, and generalisability of the results is vital, even if the research offers helpful insights into software integration in humanities teaching. Understanding these constraints not only makes the study process more transparent, but it also paves the way for future studies to be more refined.

1. **Scope and Focus Limitations**: This study was intentionally designed to focus on digital tools and software used in humanities education, particularly in higher education settings. As such, it does not extensively explore primary or secondary school environments, non-formal education sectors, or corporate learning platforms. While these areas may exhibit similar dynamics, the findings here are not directly transferrable without contextual adjustments. Moreover, the study

primarily emphasises software applications for disciplines such as literature, philosophy, history, and linguistics. Other humanities fields like theology, cultural studies, or performing arts may involve different tools or pedagogical practices that fall outside the scope of this research.

2. **Geographical and Institutional Constraints**: The majority of the research and examples in this book come from urban, English-speaking university institutions with varied degrees of digital infrastructure. Despite being essential to the larger story of digital fairness in education on a global scale, the perspectives of institutions located in rural areas, with few resources, or that do not speak English may not be sufficiently highlighted.
3. **Temporal Relevance and Rapid Technological Change**: With the constant release of new software and hardware, the field of educational technology is always evolving. As a result, the software covered in this book can be significantly updated soon after release or become outdated. Readers should refer to more recent sources when putting the book's advice into practice since, due to the fast rate of change, even well researched assessments may become outdated very fast.
4. **Limited Empirical Testing**: An original large-scale empirical investigation is missing from this book, which relies on literature reviews, case studies, expert opinions, and anecdotal evidence. Quantitative data, such as statistical performance indicators or controlled studies, are restricted in their scope. The capacity to establish unambiguous causal assertions regarding the impact of certain software interventions on student learning outcomes is hindered as a result of this.
5. **Variability in User Experience**: An further drawback is the fact that there is a wide range of digital literacy levels among both students and teachers. Although the research makes the assumption that participants have a fundamental level of proficiency in the use of digital technologies, the truth is that many organisations suffer major differences in terms of skills, access, and support. It is difficult to control or generalise the efficiency of a particular tool across a variety of situations since the usefulness of a tool might vary substantially depending on the past experience, attitudes, and training of the users of the instrument.
6. **Challenges in Measuring Qualitative Outcomes**: An education in the humanities places an emphasis on critical thinking, interpretative abilities, and nuanced expression, all of which are results that are fundamentally qualitative and often resistant to standardisation in terms of standardisation. While this book does provide some suggestions for digital integration models, it also acknowledges the difficulty of evaluating such soft talents using traditional measurements. The capacity to assess digital technologies in terms that are completely objective is hindered as a result of this constraint.
7. **Potential Bias in Source Materials**: An education in the humanities lays an emphasis on outcomes that are inherently qualitative and often resistant to standardising in terms of standardisation. These results include critical thinking, interpretive ability, and nuanced expression, all of which are emphasised in the curriculum. Although it does provide some recommendations for digital integration models, this book also admits the challenge of measuring such soft abilities

using standard assessments. Despite this, the book does offer some proposals. As a consequence of this limitation, being able to evaluate digital technology in terms that are entirely impartial is made more difficult.

The significance of applying the findings and suggestions of the book in a manner that takes into account the context is highlighted by these limitations. In lieu of providing answers that are universally applicable, the purpose of this research is to give a basic framework for critical thinking regarding the role that software plays in the teaching of humanities students. The purpose of this is to serve as a launchpad for more research, experimentation at the local level, and collaborative innovation opportunities. For the purpose of expanding upon this work, it will be essential to conduct more research, especially research that is founded on empirical data and that is more inclusive of a variety of educational contexts.

8.9.8 Reflections on the Research Journey

The process of researching and producing this book has been both academically enlightening and personally transforming. It has provided me with remarkable insights into the dynamic link that exists between software and education in the humanities. Through the investigation of this nexus, the research has not only made a contribution to the academic debate, but it has also extended ideas on pedagogy, accessibility, and the always shifting environment of digital learning. Through the course of this process, a more profound understanding of the ways in which technology may mould educational experiences, promote inclusiveness, and improve critical engagement with humanities study has been achieved. At the end of the day, it has brought to light the significance of careful integration, which ensures that digital tools function as catalysts for creativity rather than just being additions to old approaches.

1. **Navigating Interdisciplinary Terrain**: Striking a balance between the analytical breadth of the arts and sciences and the methodical, outcome-focused software engineering was an essential and significant part of this trip. In contrast to the software industry's emphasis on standardisation, efficiency, and quantifiable results, the humanities foster ambiguity, cultural complexity, and critical theory in academic research. To overcome this barrier, educational technology has to be rethought as an open forum for debate and investigation rather than a static medium for disseminating facts. To help students interact with complexity, question assumptions, and push the frontiers of knowledge, we needed to position digital tools as facilitators of discovery rather than prescriptive solutions. This was especially challenging in a subject where questions typically have more relevance than clear answers.
2. **Appreciating the Human Element**: This study has shown that educators, students, administrators, and developers all bring unique viewpoints, needs, and values to the classroom, highlighting the importance of human interaction in the

learning process. The usefulness of any digital tool however advanced or user-friendly it may be relied on the users' ability to adapt it to their needs and engage with it in a thoughtful and creative manner. It has been both disheartening and exciting to see how teachers deal with technology integration, especially in environments with limited resources. Meaningful learning experiences are created not only by innovations but also by the individuals who make them a reality. Their skill in repurposing software to fit humanities-driven goals emphasises the deep convergence of technology and human agency.

3. **Encountering Complexity**: Complexity does not emerge as a problem to be solved but as an inherent truth to be recognised and valued throughout this research. It was obvious that there was no silver bullet due to the wide variety of institutional settings, student backgrounds, and cultural norms. This insight informed the creation of adaptable, reflective, and locally relevant models and frameworks that were less prescriptive and more open to change. The research highlights the significance of educational technology that adapt to their users' needs, encouraging innovation while staying true to the specific dynamics of each learning environment, by embracing this complexity.
4. **Embracing Technological Ambiguity**: People often portray technology in the classroom in two extremes: as a game-changer that will make teaching a breeze, or as a danger to tried-and-true methods of instruction. A more complex reality, however, has emerged from this research: software is neither inherently limiting nor empowering; rather, its effects are defined by the ways it is developed, deployed, and contextualised in educational settings. The study was able to examine the pros and cons of digital integration in the humanities in a more forthright and critical light by recognising this uncertainty. Instead of seeing technology as a panacea, this viewpoint stresses the need of deliberate adoption, which will make technology a useful tool.
5. **Personal and Professional Growth**: From a personal perspective, this study journey has highlighted the need of critical inquiry in creating effective teaching methods. It has been crucial to often reevaluate assumptions, engage with educators and technologists, and keep up with the ever-changing literature. Through this ongoing intellectual pursuit, I have not only gained a broader view of the world, but I have also developed a more modest outlook, realising that knowledge is dynamic and that change is essential for real advancement. By highlighting the significance of questioning, reflecting, and accepting the ever-changing nature of knowledge, the experience has promoted both professional progress and a renewed dedication to lifelong learning. In case you would want any changes, please inform me!
6. **Future Aspirations**: This publication signals the beginning of fresh possibilities for inquiry, not the end of the research journey. The findings presented here serve as a platform for future empirical investigations, supporting multidisciplinary cooperation and influencing policy discussions that promote the meaningful integration of software in humanities education. This study intends to stimulate creativity and develop practical approaches to digital learning by furthering conversations about pedagogy, accessibility, and technical adaptability. It is

> intended that the frameworks and thoughts offered here will continue to challenge viewpoints, generate new ideas, and serve as a resource for educators, researchers, and technologists interested in the progress of digital pedagogy.

As I look back on this journey, I see how important it is to teach students to question, interpret, and make connections. These are the essential ideals of humanities education, and they are even more crucial in our digital era. The overarching goal of fostering students who are reflective, analytical, and compassionate thinkers who are able to critically interact with information and society will not change, even as new technology tools and platforms will emerge. Education stays current and relevant when it can adjust to new ways of learning while keeping the core of humanistic research. This study has been worthwhile if it has helped in any manner, whether that's by shedding light on a topic, starting a conversation, or providing direction on how to include digital technologies. Research in the digital humanities must continue; this is just the beginning of what will inevitably be a long and winding road of discovery and introspection.

8.9.9 *Final Thoughts*

It is appropriate to take a moment as this book winds down to consider the bigger picture of its central message: that software, when incorporated with care, may enhance the depth of humanities instruction instead of watering it down. The importance of the humanities is more than ever in this age of fast technical advancement, economic upheaval, and social revolution. They aid in the development of critical thinking skills, the interpretation of meaning, cultural awareness, and empathy. The question isn't whether or if the humanities should use digital technologies; rather, it's how to do so without watering down their distinctive character. As this study has shown, instructional software is biassed. It acts as a mediator between the learner and the material, as well as an embodiment of the ideals held inside. Hence, it is crucial for lawmakers, developers, and educators to critically interact with technology, seeing it not only as something to be used or consumed, but as something to be co-created with and shaped by. A flexible, student-centered, and critically-grounded teaching approach is the goal of the book's reflections, case studies, frameworks, and suggestions. Students may engage in the deep learning that characterises the humanities using software, which can take many forms including annotation platforms, online discussion forums, digital archives, and analytical tools.

There is an immediate need to think about the cultural, infrastructural, and ethical aspects of digital pedagogy because of the increasing interconnection of educational environments throughout the world. Priorities of accessibility, inclusivity, and equity must take precedence above all others. This is particularly the case in contexts where there is a need to address local realities while adopting software and digital gaps remain. The goal of this book is not to provide final solutions but to start conversations, stimulate reading, and promote thinking critically. It is on a mission to rethink education in ways that take into account technology advancements while yet honouring humanistic principles. Ultimately, incorporating software into humanities teaching is about more than just being current. Enriching the learning experience, making information accessible to everyone, and equipping learners to understand and influence a complex world with creativity, integrity, and insight are the main goals. Although educational practices are evolving, the goal of the humanities, which is to comprehend the human condition, has not changed. Software, when used with caution, imagination, and teamwork, may open up new and powerful avenues for us to achieve this objective.

GPSR Compliance

The European Union's (EU) General Product Safety Regulation (GPSR) is a set of rules that requires consumer products to be safe and our obligations to ensure this.

If you have any concerns about our products, you can contact us on ProductSafety@springernature.com

In case Publisher is established outside the EU, the EU authorized representative is:

Springer Nature Customer Service Center GmbH
Europaplatz 3
69115 Heidelberg, Germany

Batch number: 10110085

Printed by Printforce, the Netherlands